NEW BUSINESS VENTURES AND THE ENTREPRENEUR

FIFTH EDITION

NEW BUSINESS VENTURES AND THE ENTREPRENEUR

Howard H. Stevenson

Sarofim–Rock Professor of Business Administration
Harvard University Graduate School of Business Administration

Michael J. Roberts

Lecturer, Executive Director Entrepreneurial Studies
Harvard University Graduate School of Business Administration

H. Irving Grousbeck

Class of 1980 Consulting Professor of Management
Stanford University Graduate School of Business Administration

Amar V. Bhidé

Associate Professor of Business Administration
Harvard University Graduate School of Business Administration

Irwin
McGraw-Hill

Boston   Burr Ridge, IL   Dubuque, IA   Madison, WI   New York   San Francisco   St. Louis
Bangkok   Bogotá   Caracas   Lisbon   London   Madrid
Mexico City   Milan   New Delhi   Seoul   Singapore   Sydney   Taipei   Toronto

Irwin/McGraw-Hill

*A Division of The **McGraw-Hill** Companies*

NEW BUSINESS VENTURES AND THE ENTREPRENEUR

This book is printed on acid-free paper.

1 2 3 4 5 6 7 8 9 0 QPF/QPF 9 3 2 1 0 9 8

ISBN 0-256-20477-2

Vice president and editorial director: *Michael W. Junior*
Publisher: *Craig S. Beytien*
Sponsoring editor: *Karen M. Mellon*
Marketing manager: *Kenyetta Giles*
Project manager: *Jim Labeots*
Production supervisor: *Lori Koetters*
Freelance design coordinator: *JoAnne Schopler*
Supplement coordinator: *Rose Hepburn*
Compositor: *GAC Shepard Poorman Communications*
Typeface: *10/12 Times Roman*
Printer: *Quebecor Printing Book Group/ Fairfield*

Library of Congress Cataloging-in-Publication Data

Stevenson, Howard H.
    New business ventures and the entrepreneur / Howard H. Stevenson
. . . [et al.]. -- 5th ed.
      p. cm.
    Rev. ed. of: New business ventures and the entrepreneur / Howard
H. Stevenson. 4th ed. 1994.
    Includes bibliographical references (p. 000) and indexes.
    ISBN 0-256-20477-2
    1. New business enterprises. 2. New business enterprises--United
States. I. Stevenson, Howard H. New business ventures and the
entrepreneur. II. Title.
HD62.5.S75   1999
658.1'--dc21   98-8255

http://www.mhhe.com

to
Patrick Rooney Liles
(1937–1983)

Teacher
Scholar of Entrepreneurship
Business Leader
Athlete
Friend

INTRODUCTION

We have several objectives in writing this book. We believe that the topic of entrepreneurship is an exciting and important one. For those students of management who have decided to pursue a career as an entrepreneur, we think this book will provide some of the knowledge and skills required. For those who may be undecided, or perhaps committed to a more "traditional" career, many of the ideas in this book have value for those in more structured business settings. Executives are often called upon to deal with, and even to manage, entrepreneurs. Friends and colleagues may contemplate starting new ventures and want the advice and/or financial support of accountancies in management positions.

Most importantly, we believe that all students of management have a great deal to learn from the study of entrepreneurship. The process of identifying and pursuing opportunity in the face of limited resources, the hallmark of the entrepreneur, has become increasingly important to restoring and maintaining the competitive position of many U.S. industries in the international marketplace.

Organization and Contents

This book is organized in five parts:

Part I: Evaluating Opportunity and Developing the Business Concept. This first section of the book serves as an overview, and also looks at the first two steps in the process of starting a new venture. Its first two chapters provide a working definition of entrepreneurship, a framework for understanding the entrepreneurial process, and a method for analyzing new venture opportunities. Remaining chapters look at methods of valuing business opportunities, the process of preparing a business plan, and the various legal forms of business organization. The cases require evaluating business opportunities and formulating strategies to exploit opportunities.

Part II: Assessing and Acquiring Resources. This part looks at two of the entrepreneur's critical steps—assessing required resources and acquiring those resources. The chapters focus on understanding the techniques for acquiring both financial and nonfinancial resources. The cases cover a variety of issues, including deal structure, securities laws, venture capital, and intellectual property.

Part III: Acquiring an Existing Business. In this part of the book, we look at another avenue to an entrepreneurial career: purchasing an existing business. Chapters describe the search process, as well as some approaches to funding a search. The cases look at several examples of individuals who attempt to purchase an existing business.

Part IV: Managing the Growing Enterprise. Here we look at some of the unique challenges of managing an entrepreneurial firm. Chapters examine managing growth and the problem of bankruptcy. Cases focus on the operating issues faced by the managers of new ventures and the topic of managing growth in a rapidly expanding business.

Part V: Harvesting Value. This last part of the book examines the ways in which the entrepreneur and investors can harvest the value which the venture has created. The chapter focuses on the public offering of securities, and the cases examine various approaches to harvesting. Together these sections trace the entrepreneurial process from the initial idea through business operations to harvest.

Throughout the book, we have exhibited some of our own biases. One of which we are aware has to do with the material that has been included as exhibits. Whenever possible, we have included actual documents: business plans, prospectuses, leases, laws, and legal opinions. While some of this material is detailed and highly specific, it is well worth the effort. This is the stuff of which real business is made; better to discover some of the subtleties of the tax code or lease provisions now than when you're sitting down to form a real venture.

While this detail is included, please do not consider the technical notes, the exhibits, and the appendices as substitutes for detailed current investigation of law, regulation, markets, and practices. This is a rapidly evolving field. Although every effort has been made to be clear, current, and complete, you must consult good attorneys, accountants, and investment advisers before proceeding.

Acknowledgments

Patrick R. Liles taught the New Ventures course at Harvard Business School from 1969 to 1977. In a very real sense, his early work in the field, his first edition of this book, and his vision of the entrepreneur provided a strong foundation on which to build. We dedicate this book to Pat, both in recognition of his accomplishments and our respect for them, and out of our own sense of loss.

In addition to Pat's involvement with the course, many others participated in its teaching and development over the past 40 years. We are indebted to Myles Mace, Frank L. Tucker, Malcolm Salter, Thomas Raymond, Philip Thurston, Jim Morgan, Richard Reese, Richard Von Werssowetz, John Van Slyke, Matt Weisman, Joe Lassiter, Jay Light, and Myra Hart for building the course at Harvard and providing a solid foundation for our own work.

With this edition, our colleague Amar Bhidé becomes a co-author of this book. He has made an enormous contribution to the Entrepreneurial Management course at HBS, and you will see much of this work in this new edition.

Many other students and scholars of entrepreneurship not at Harvard have contributed helpful comments, including: Zenas Block, Neil Churchill, Ian MacMillan, Ken Morse, Jeffry Timmons, and Karl Vesper.

Thanks are also due:

- Peter Lombard and Ricardo Rodriquez for their help with ICEDELIGHTS.
- Richard Von Werssowetz for his help with Commercial Fixtures, Inc., and Steven B. Belkin.
- Richard E. Floor, of the law firm of Goodwin, Procter & Hoar, Boston, for his help with Viscotech, Inc., and the chapters on Securities Law and Private Financing and Securities Law and Public Offerings.
- Martha Gershun for Dragonfly Corporation and the chapter on bankruptcy.
- Jose-Carlos Jarillo Mossi for his help with R&R.
- E.J. Walton for his help with CVD vs. A.S. Markham Corp. and the chapter on the Business Plan.
- Deaver Brown for his help with the Deaver Brown and Cross River case.

- Professor Bill Sahlman and Research Associate Andrew S. Janower for the suggested readings.
- E.J. Walton, Lynn Radlauer, Ned Lubell, David Hull, Bryon Snider, Robert Stevenson, and Robert Winter for their help with Purchasing a Business: The Search Process.
- Susan Harmeling for her work on the Howard Head case.
- Joseph M. Welsh for Downtown Daycare and Heartport.
- Nick Mansour for David Dodson, Grand Junction, Eller Media, and Gordon Biersch Brewing Company.
- L.A. Snedeker for her help with Gordon Biersch Brewing Company.
- Val Rayzman and Chris Hackett for the DAG Group.
- Brian Mohan for help with Marcia Radosevich and Health Payment Review.
- Deborah Baker, John Corso, and Yosufi Tyebkan for the chapter on Early Career LBOs.

The case writing and research was sponsored by the HBS Division of Research; we are grateful to the Division as well as to the Associates of Harvard Business School, who provided much of the funding. Former HBS Dean John McArthur, and our current Dean, Kim Clark, have been supporters of our efforts in the entrepreneurship area. Without the support of many alumni this activity would not have been possible. Arthur Rock and Fayez Sarofim gave the first chair at Harvard to reestablish the focus on entrepreneurship. The depth of alumni interest and support has been most remarkable and rewarding as we have worked to build this area. Frank Batten, Arthur Rock, the Roy and Tibby Simmons family, and many others have provided substantial funds to further the research and teaching of entrepreneurship at Harvard Business School.

At Stanford, friends of the Graduate School of Business have been supportive of entrepreneurship in general and casewriting activities in particular. The class of 1990 Entrepreneurship Fund, Donald J. Douglas, John P. Morgridge, Robert Denzil

Alexander, and Frank Quattrone have been particularly generous.

The task of compiling this text was an arduous one. We wish to express our appreciation to Wendy Wilson, who kindly lent her energy and enthusiasm to the revision of this manuscript. Audrey Barrett was helpful in securing the permissions needed to complete the book.

We are indebted to the entrepreneurs who gave so willingly of their time, energy, and ideas so that we could collect this case material. They provide one of the most critical elements of entrepreneurial success: role models. Richard Reiss, Bob Donadio, Joe Connolly, Lesley Berglund, Jim Pottow, Greg Berglund, Rosemary Jordano, Dr. Wesley Sterman, David Dodson, Chris Hackett, Val Rayzman, Deaver Brown, Marcia Radosevich, Hira Thapliyal, Bob Goodman, Karl Eller, Lisa Mangano, Jennifer Runyeon, Chip Fichtner, Sidney Goodman, Steven Belkin, Heather Evans, Dan Gordon, Dean Biersch, and Howard Head are all real people who have shared their experiences with us; others have chosen to remain anonymous. To all we owe thanks for their cooperation. Ultimately, it is through the sharing of their experiences that we can learn.

Finally, each of us would like to make a more personal statement of thanks to our families:

- To my wife Fredi and to Willie, Charley, and Andy, thanks for the patience in helping me to pursue this passion; and to my late parents, Ralph and Dorothy Stevenson, and uncle and late aunt, Boyd and Zola Martin, thanks for helping me get a running start into this field.

  H.H.S.

- To my wife, Cynthia, for her love and support.

  M.J.R.

- To my wife Sukey for her love, laughter, adaptability, and constant encouragement.

  H.I.G.

- To my daughter Lila for infectious joy, my mother and sister for grown-up support, and my late father—an entrepreneur who never grew up.

  A.V.B.

FOREWORD

Obviously, the cases presented in this text can only scratch the surface of the possible industries, business models, and career options you might consider. Nonetheless, the cases are snapshots of interesting people in challenging junctures, and we've chosen their stories because we feel they harbor a more general truth.

What might you look for as you read these stories?

Inspirational Role Models. Conversations with our alumni suggest that the emotional and visceral aspects of an entrepreneurship course leave a profound and often more long-lived impression than many of the analytical aspects. Alumni well remember and will sometimes have derived inspiration from the entrepreneurs they encountered in their case studies and classes. The stories in this collection provide a wealth of role models that should resonate with a broad spectrum of readers. The protagonists featured come from a variety of demographic and socioeconomic backgrounds and

have different skills, temperaments, and goals. Contrary to the popular belief in the importance of conforming to a defined entrepreneurial "type," we see that many kinds of individuals—brash upstarts and mature veterans, introverts and extroverts, the broke and well-to-do, gamblers and cautious penny-pinchers—can all enjoy entrepreneurial success. We encounter different motivations—some entrepreneurs were congenitally unsuited to holding down a job whereas others were nudged by circumstance.

Hopefully, the stories will thus help rebut the facile notion that individuals have to be "born" entrepreneurs and instead encourage readers to reflect upon what kind of venture will best suit their individual personalities and aspirations. The stories should also reassure those who lack self-confidence in their creative abilities. Only a handful involve path-breaking inventions or visionary entrepreneurs. Most of the entrepreneurs built their ventures around incremental

Amar Bhidé prepared this note as the basis for classroom discussion rather than to illustrate either effective or ineffective handling of an administrative situation.

Copyright © 1998 by the President and Fellows of Harvard College.

Harvard Business School Note 9-898-204

innovations or took advantage of trends and changes that others had initiated.

Metrics for Success. The varying degrees to which the entrepreneurs here achieved fame and fortune, made sacrifices, or changed the world should also cause readers to ponder their attitudes toward success. What personal price is too high to make financial success unrewarding? Is success meaningful if it comes too easily? How important is fame and recognition?

Targets for Personal Development. The cases suggest that execution (doing things right) plays as much, and often more, of a role in a venture's success than does strategy (doing the right things). The protagonists, who often weren't the first or the only players in their markets, apparently outdid their rivals in clinching the vital sale, negotiating licenses, securing capital from skeptical investors, recruiting the most talented engineers, and so on. Limitations of space have precluded our fully describing how the case protagonists won through better execution or how they acquired the skills to do so. Perhaps this cannot be well described in a case of any length. Readers should, however, at least be able to find signposts to the sorts of skills they need to have or develop to succeed in the fields of their choice.

The Dynamics of New Ventures. The cases provide a guide for what an entrepreneur can expect in the course of nurturing a venture. We find very few examples of entrepreneurs moving smoothly from launch to harvest by executing their initial business plans. On both the business and emotional dimensions, the entrepreneurial journey usually appears to provide quite a wild ride. We find entrepreneurs in despair as they fight off the imminent liquidation of their businesses. At the same time, we also see entrepreneurs who started on a modest scale but achieved breakthrough successes by taking advantage of opportunities they had never expected to encounter. Apparently, long-term success usually depends more on the entrepreneurs' persistence and ability to adapt strategies and tactics to frequently changing circumstances than on the decisions taken at the time of launch.

Personal Theories and Rules of Thumb. The reader should not expect to find (here or elsewhere) a reliable set of formulae for success. Standard techniques for tree farming don't work in the entrepreneurial rain forest where each life form competes for its special niche in its own idiosyncratic way. Nevertheless, entrepreneurs cannot function without some generalizations and rules of thumb, however tentative and personal they may be. Entrepreneurs rarely make decisions by tossing coins. Even those choices supposedly made purely on instinct probably reflect an internalized rule or proposition derived from past experience, which the entrepreneur uses as a "working hypothesis" for new situations.

This collection of stories can help you develop or refine your theories. They suggest, for example, that successful ventures generally flower in fragmented or new markets where they avoid competing against incumbents with significant economies of scale and that taking advantage of industry changes is easier than initiating them. More importantly, the cases can help identify the circumstances under which certain approaches are likely to prove more effective than others. The answer, "It depends," begs the question, "On what?" The diversity of successful approaches described here may be exploited to develop points of view about issues such as:

- *The use of external capital.* Some ventures described here did exceptionally well without much initial capital. In other cases, severe cash shortages made the entrepreneurs wish they had raised much more capital up-front, even at the cost of diluting their equity stakes. What accounts for the difference?
- *Prior experience.* The stories include entrepreneurs with varying degrees of industry experience. Where and what kind of knowledge is it critical for the entrepreneur to have? How can individuals who are short on contacts and credibility compensate?
- *Strategic change.* Readers will encounter cases of ventures that, in the face of

adversity, stuck to their original concept, modified their original concepts, or did a complete U-turn. When should an entrepreneur choose persistence over flexibility?

- *Entrepreneurs' style and role.* We find here entrepreneurs who delegated extensively and built strong teams around them and others who called all the shots and made do with weak subordinates. What circumstances make the controlling "Theory X" type of leadership appropriate? When and what should the entrepreneur "let go"?

Models and Analogies. Entrepreneurs typically have to cope with limited information and great uncertainty: Often they lack money and time to do market research; even where they do, consumers don't know what they really want and would be willing to pay for; and the external turbulence that creates opportunities for entrepreneurs also makes the evolution of markets and technologies unpredictable. Therefore, in lieu of traditional planning and analytical techniques, entrepreneurs often reason by analogy, using models from other geographies, periods, or industries to make inductive leaps such as if espresso bars thrive in Italy, they should in Seattle as well. The stories presented here represent for the reader with imag-

ination a cornucopia of models potentially applicable to a variety of fields.

A word of advice. Do not read these cases passively. Challenge and critique the authors' and the protagonists' opinions and use the material to reexamine your own assumptions. This is a workbook, not a "how-to" book. It does not, for example, contain lists of the skills needed for different types of businesses—you will have to read between the lines and engage in a careful self-evaluation to determine the skills you choose to work on. You will not find consistent, well-articulated do's and don'ts either. In fact, you may puzzle over the contradictory advice offered in these pages by capable and accomplished entrepreneurs. You can, however, turn these contradictions to your advantage by figuring out the conditions that make the apparently conflicting claims more or less appropriate. Similarly, while we hope you will find all the stories interesting and entertaining, you will probably find some more inspirational than others. If you think deeply about why certain stories and entrepreneurs resonate more than others, you will probably be ahead of the game in making sound choices about your career path. What you get out of these cases will depend on what you put in.

Bon Voyage.

CONTENTS

PART

I

EVALUATING OPPORTUNITY AND DEVELOPING THE BUSINESS CONCEPT

In this first part of the book, we present in Chapter 1 a framework for defining entrepreneurship. Following this, we consider two fundamental issues the entrepreneur must address:

- Is this a good opportunity?
- What business strategy will most fully exploit the opportunity?

What Is An Opportunity?

One of the entrepreneur's most important tasks is to identify opportunities. The capacity to creatively seek out opportunity is the starting point of entrepreneurship for both the individual and the firm.

To qualify as a good opportunity, the situation must meet two conditions:

1. It must represent a future state that is desirable.
2. It must be achievable.

Obviously, this issue cannot be addressed in isolation. It is difficult to understand how attractive an opportunity is until one has developed an idea of what the business strategy will be, what resources will be required to pursue the opportunity, how much those resources will cost, and, finally, how much value will be left for the entrepreneur. Nonetheless, evaluating the opportunity is the starting point for this thought process.

In Chapter 2, we present a framework for considering some of the key issues entrepreneurs must address in actually starting-up a business.

Chapter 3, "Valuation Techniques," looks at some of the quantitative techniques for assessing the financial value of a business opportunity. It is important to remember, though, an opportunity may have significant nonfinancial value that these techniques cannot measure. Some opportunities, for example, may not be worth much but may open doors to other opportunities that have considerable value. For some entrepreneurs, the opportunity to work on an interesting idea, with good people, and to be one's own boss compensates for what may be only a mediocre opportunity in a financial sense.

Chapter 4, "The Business Plan," describes the uses of a business plan and how you can write one to meet your needs, as well of those of potential investors.

In Chapter 5, "The Legal Forms of Organization," we explore the various options for organizing a venture, and the tax and liability issues associated with each.

Finally, in Chapter 6, we offer a few guide posts for pursuing the path towards an entrepreneurial career. It is a road that more people travel than you might imagine.

Developing the Business Concept

Once an opportunity is identified, the entrepreneur must develop a business concept and strategy to exploit the opportunity. Often, this strategy will proximately determine the success or failure of a business, even if the entrepreneur has identified a wonderful opportunity. Federal Express, for instance, decided to serve the same market that Emery Air Freight was serving. But Federal Express chose a much different strategy: a high fixed-cost hub system that was critically dependent on volume. Federal Express's strategy has allowed it to operate at lower costs and thus to surpass Emery in the express delivery market.

To maximize the odds of its success, a new venture should offer products or services that can profitably meet the needs of the markets it attempts to serve. But a new venture has an important advantage over an existing business. It can be created specifically to respond to market needs. Too often existing firms spend enormous resources searching for a market for the products or services produced by their operating assets.

1

A PERSPECTIVE ON ENTREPRENEURSHIP

Entrepreneurship is a frequent topic in both the business and popular press. Many individuals aspire to be entrepreneurs, enjoying the freedom, independence, and wealth such a career seems to suggest. And larger corporations want to become more "entrepreneurial," their shorthand for the innovative and adaptive qualities they see in their smaller—and often more successful—competitors.

Our purpose in this chapter is to shed some light on the concept of entrepreneurship. We will define entrepreneurship as a management process and will discuss why we believe encouraging entrepreneurial behavior is critical to the long-term vitality of our economy. Finally, we will suggest that the practice of entrepreneurship is as important—if not more important—to established companies as it is to start-ups.

Increasing Interest in Entrepreneurship

It would be difficult to overstate the degree to which there has been an increase in the level of interest in entrepreneurship. A strong indicator of such interest is provided by the unprecedented rise in the rate of new business formation. The number of annual new business incorporations has doubled in the last 10 years, from annual rates of about 300,000 to over 600,000.

These trends are mirrored in the capital markets that fund these start-ups. The past decade has seen explosive growth in the amount of capital committed to

This chapter was prepared by Howard H. Stevenson.

Copyright © 1983 by the President and Fellows of Harvard College.

Harvard Business School Note 9-384-131.

venture capital firms in the United States. There was a concurrent dramatic increase in the amount of money raised in the public capital markets by young companies.

In addition to interest on the part of individuals who wish to become entrepreneurs and investors who wish to back them, there has been a wave of interest in what some refer to as *intrapreneurship,* or entrepreneurship in the context of the larger corporation. Building on the wealth of books and articles on the subject, some large firms seem to have recognized their shortcomings on certain critical dimensions of performance and have structured themselves in an attempt to be more innovative.

Indeed, we believe that the strengthening of entrepreneurship is a critically important goal of American society. The first 30 years of the postwar period in the United States were characterized by an abundance of opportunity, brought about by expanding markets, high investment in the national infrastructure, and mushrooming debt. In this environment, it was relatively easy to achieve business success, but this is no longer true. Access to international resources is not as easy as it once was; government regulation has brought a recognition of the full costs of doing business, many of which had previously been hidden; competition from overseas has put an end to American dominance in numerous industries; technological change has reduced product life in other industries; and so forth. In short, a successful firm is one that is either capable of rapid response to changes that are beyond its control or is so innovative that it contributes to change in the environment. Entrepreneurship is an approach to management that offers these benefits.

Defining Entrepreneurship

As we have discussed, there has been a striking increase in the level of attention paid to entrepreneurship. However, we've not yet defined what the term means.

As a starting point, it may be helpful to review some of the definitions scholars have historically applied to entrepreneurship. There are several schools of thought regarding entrepreneurship, which may roughly be divided into those that define the term as an economic function and those that identify entrepreneurship with individual traits.

The functional approach focuses on the role of entrepreneurship within the economy. In the 18th century, for instance, Richard Cantillon argued that entrepreneurship entailed bearing the risk of buying at certain prices and selling at uncertain prices. Jean Baptiste Say broadened the definition to include the concept of bringing together the factors of production. Schumpeter's work in 1911 added the concept of innovation to the definition of entrepreneurship. He allowed for many kinds of innovation including process innovation, market innovation, product innovation, factor innovation, and even organizational innovation. His seminal work emphasized the role of the entrepreneur in creating and responding to economic discontinuities.

While some analysts have focused on the economic function of entrepreneurship, still others have turned their attention to research on the personal characteristics of entrepreneurs. Considerable effort has gone into understanding the psychological and sociological sources of entrepreneurship—as Kent refers to it, "supply-side entrepreneurship." These studies have noted some common characteristics among entrepreneurs with respect to need for achievement, perceived locus of control, and risk-taking propensity. In addition, many have commented on the common—but not universal—thread of childhood deprivation and early adolescent experiences as typifying the entrepreneur. These studies—when taken as a whole—are inconclusive and often in conflict.

We believe, however, that neither of these approaches is sound. Consider, for example, the degree to which *entrepreneurship* is synonymous with *bearing risk, innovation,* or even *founding a company.* Each of these terms focuses on *some* aspect of *some* entrepreneurs. But, if one has to be the founder to be an entrepreneur, then neither Thomas Watson of IBM nor Ray Kroc of McDonald's will qualify; yet, few would seriously argue that both these individuals were not entrepreneurs. And, while risk bearing is an important element of entrepreneurial behavior, it is clear that many entrepreneurs bear risk grudgingly and only after they have made valiant attempts to get the capital sources and resource providers to bear the risk. As one extremely successful entrepreneur said, "My idea of risk and reward is for me to get the reward and others to take risks." With respect to the supply-side school of entrepreneurship, many questions can be raised. At the heart of the matter is whether the psychological and social traits are either necessary or sufficient for the development of entrepreneurship.

Finally, the search for a single psychological profile of the entrepreneur is bound to fail. For each of the traditional definitions of the entrepreneurial type, there are numerous counterexamples that disprove the theory. We simply are not dealing with one kind of individual or behavior pattern, as even a cursory review of well-known entrepreneurs will demonstrate. Nor has the search for a psychological model proven useful in teaching or encouraging entrepreneurship.

Entrepreneurship as a Behavioral Phenomenon

Thus, it does not seem useful to delimit the entrepreneur by defining those economic functions that are "entrepreneurial" and those that are not. Nor does it appear particularly helpful to describe the traits that seem to engender entrepreneurship in certain individuals. From our perspective, entrepreneurship is an approach to management that we define as follows: *the pursuit of opportunity without regard to resources currently controlled.*

This summary description of entrepreneurial behavior can be further refined by examining six critical dimensions of business practice. These six dimensions are the following: strategic orientation, the commitment to opportunity, the resource commitment process, the concept of control over resources, the concept of management, and compensation policy.

We shall define these dimensions by examining a range of behavior between two extremes. At one extreme is the "promoter" who feels confident of his or her ability to seize opportunity regardless of the resources under current control. At the opposite extreme is the "trustee" who emphasizes the efficient utilization of existing resources. While the promoter and trustee define the end points of this spectrum, there is a spectrum of managerial behavior that lies between these end points, and we define (overlapping) portions of this spectrum as entrepreneurial and administrative behavior. Thus, entrepreneurial management is not an extreme example, but rather a range of behavior that consistently falls at the end of the spectrum.

The remainder of this chapter defines these key business dimensions in more detail, discusses how entrepreneurial differs from administrative behavior, and describes the factors that pull individuals and firms toward particular types of behavior.

Strategic Orientation

Strategic orientation is the business dimension that describes the factors that drive the firm's formulation of strategy. A promoter is truly opportunity driven. His or her orientation is to say, "As I define a strategy, I am going to be driven only by my perception of the opportunities that exist in my environment, and I will not be constrained by the resources at hand." A trustee, on the other hand, is resource driven and tends to say, "How do I utilize the resources that I control?"

Within these two poles, the administrator's approach recognizes the need to examine the environment for opportunities but is still constrained by a trusteelike focus on resources: "I will prune my opportunity tree based on the resources I control. I will not try to leap very far beyond my current situation." An entrepreneurial orientation places the emphasis on opportunity: "I will search for opportunity, and my fundamental task is to acquire the resources to pursue that opportunity." These perspectives are represented in **Figure 1–1.**

It is this dimension that has led to one of the traditional definitions of the entrepreneur as opportunistic or—more favorably—creative and innovative. But the entrepreneur is not necessarily concerned with breaking new ground; opportunity can also be found in a new mix of old ideas or in the creative application of traditional approaches. We do observe, however, that firms tend to look for opportunities where their resources are. Even those firms that start as entrepreneurial by recognizing opportunities often become resources driven as more and more resources are acquired by the organization.

The pressures that pull a firm toward the entrepreneurial range of behavior include the following:

- Diminishing opportunity streams: Old opportunity streams have been largely played out. It is no longer possible to succeed merely by adding new options to old products.
- Rapid changes in:
  - Technology: Creates new opportunities at the same time it obsoletes old ones.
  - Consumer economics: Changes both ability and willingness to pay for new products and services.
  - Social values: Defines new styles and standards and standards of living.

FIGURE 1–1

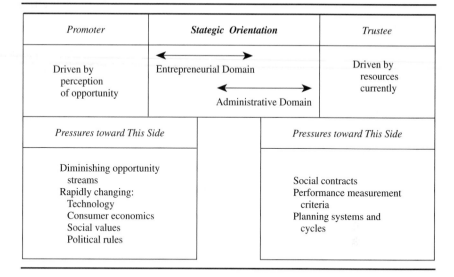

Promoter	***Stategic Orientation***		*Trustee*
Driven by perception of opportunity	Entrepreneurial Domain Administrative Domain		Driven by resources currently
Pressures toward This Side		*Pressures toward This Side*	
Diminishing opportunity streams Rapidly changing: Technology Consumer economics Social values Political rules		Social contracts Performance measurement criteria Planning systems and cycles	

     — Political roles: Affects competition through deregulation, product safety, and new standards.

Pressures that pull a firm to become more administrative than entrepreneurial include the following:

- The "social contract": The responsibility of managers to use and employ people, plant, technology, and financial resources once they have been acquired.
- Performance criteria: How many executives are fired for not pursuing an opportunity, compared with the number that are punished for not meeting return on investment targets? Capacity utilization and sales growth are the typical measures of business success.
- Planning systems and cycles: Opportunities do not arrive at the start of a planning cycle and last for the duration of a three- or five-year plan.

Commitment to Opportunity

As we move on to the second dimension, it becomes clear that the definition of the entrepreneur as creative or innovative is not sufficient. There are innovative thinkers who never get anything done; it is necessary to move beyond the identification of opportunity to its pursuit.

    The promoter is willing to act in a very short time frame and to chase an opportunity quickly. Promoters may be more or less effective, but they are able to engage in commitment in a rather revolutionary fashion. The duration of their commitment, not the ability to act, is all that is in doubt. Commitment for the

FIGURE 1–2

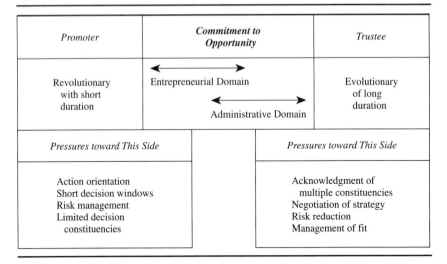

trustee is time consuming and, once made, of long duration. Trustees move so slowly that it sometimes appears they are stationary; once there, they seem frozen. This spectrum of behavior is shown in **Figure 1–2.**

It is the willingness to get in and out quickly that has led to the entrepreneur's reputation as a gambler. However, the simple act of taking a risk does not lead to success. More critical to the success of the entrepreneurs is knowledge of the territory they operate in. Because of familiarity with their chosen field, they have the ability to recognize patterns as they develop and the confidence to assume that the missing elements of the pattern will take shape as they foresee. This early recognition enables them to get a jump on others in commitment to action.

Pressures that pull a business toward this entrepreneurial end of the spectrum include:

- Action orientation: Enables a firm to make first claim to customers, employees, and financial resources.
- Short decision windows: Due to the high costs of late entry, including lack of competitive costs and technology.
- Risk management: Involves managing the firm's revenues in such a way that they can be rapidly committed to or withdrawn from new projects. As George Bernard Shaw put it, "Any fool can start a love affair, but it takes a genius to end one successfully."
- Limited decision constituencies: Requires a smaller number of responsibilities and permits greater flexibility.

In contrast, administrative behavior is a function of other pressures:

- Multiple decision constituencies: A great number of responsibilities, necessitating a more complex, lengthier decision process.

- Negotiation of strategy: Compromise in order to reach consensus and resultant evolutionary rather than revolutionary commitment.
- Risk reduction: Study and analysis to reduce risk slows the decision-making process.
- Management of fit: To assure the continuity and participation of existing players, only those projects that "fit" existing corporate resources are acceptable.

Commitment of Resources

Another characteristic we observe in good entrepreneurs is a multistaged commitment of resources with a minimum commitment at each stage or decision point. The promoters, those wonderful people with blue shoes and diamond pinky rings on their left hands, say, "I don't need any resources to commence the pursuit of a given opportunity. I will bootstrap it." The trustee says, "Since my object is to use my resources, once I finally commit I will go in very heavily at the front end."

The issue for the entrepreneur is this: What resources are necessary to pursue a given opportunity? There is a constant tension between the amount of resources committed and the potential return. The entrepreneur attempts to maximize value creation by minimizing the resource set and must, of course, accept more risk in the process. On the other hand, the trustee side deals with this challenge by careful analysis and large-scale commitment of resources after the decision to act. Entrepreneurial management requires that you learn to do a little more with a little less. **Figure 1–3** addresses this concept.

On this dimension we have the traditional stereotype of the entrepreneur as tentative, uncommitted, or temporarily dedicated—an image of unreliability. In times of rapid change, however, this characteristic of stepped, multistaged commitment of resources is a definite advantage in responding to changes in competition, the market, and technology.

The process of committing resources is pushed toward the entrepreneurial domain by several factors:

- Lack of predictable resource needs: Forces the entrepreneurs to commit less up front so that more will be available later on, if required.
- Lack of long-term control: Requires that commitment match exposure. If control over resources can be removed by environmental, political, or technological forces, resource exposure should also be reduced.
- Social needs: Multistaged commitment of resources brings us closer to the "small is beautiful" formulation of E. F. Shumacher by allowing for the appropriate level of resource intensity for the task.
- International demands: Pressures that we use no more than our fair share of the world's resources (e.g., not the 35 percent of the world's energy that the United States was using in the early 1970s).

The pressures within the large corporation, however, are in the other direction—toward resource intensity. This is due to the following:

FIGURE 1–3

Promoter	***Commitment of Resources***	*Trustee*
Multistaged with minimal exposure at each stage	Entrepreneurial Domain ⟵⟶ Administrative Domain ⟵⟶	Single-staged with complete commitment upon decision
Pressures toward This Side		*Pressures toward This Side*
Lack of predictable resource needs Lack of long-term control Social needs for more opportunity per resource unit International pressure for more efficient resource use		Personal risk reduction Incentive compensation Managerial turnover Capital allocation systems Formal planning systems

---

- Personal risk reduction: Any individual's risk is reduced by having excess resources available.
- Incentive compensation: Excess resources increase short-term returns and minimize the period of cash and profit drains—typically the objects of incentive compensation systems.
- Managerial turnover: Creates pressures for steady cash and profit gains, which encourages short-term, visible success.
- Capital allocation systems: Generally designed for one-time decision making, these techniques assume that a single decision point is appropriate.
- Formal planning systems: Once a project has begun, a request for additional resources returns the managers to the morass of analysis and bureaucratic delays; managers are inclined to avoid this by committing the maximum amount of resources up front.

Control of Resources

When it comes to the control of resources, the promoter mentality says, "All I need from a resource is the ability to use it." These are the people who describe the ideal business as the post office box to which people send money. For them, all additional overhead is a compromise of a basic value. On the other hand, we all know companies that believe they do not adequately control a resource unless they own it or have it on their permanent payroll.

Entrepreneurs learn to use other people's resources well; they learn to decide, over time, what resources they need to bring in-house. They view this as a time-

FIGURE 1–4

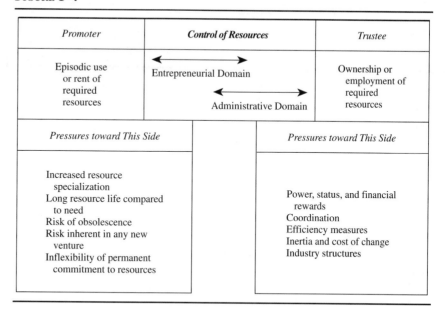

Promoter	***Control of Resources***	*Trustee*
Episodic use or rent of required resources	Entrepreneurial Domain Administrative Domain	Ownership or employment of required resources
Pressures toward This Side		*Pressures toward This Side*
Increased resource specialization Long resource life compared to need Risk of obsolescence Risk inherent in any new venture Inflexibility of permanent commitment to resources		Power, status, and financial rewards Coordination Efficiency measures Inertia and cost of change Industry structures

phased sequence of decisions. Good managers also learn that there are certain resources you should never own or employ. For instance, very few good real estate firms employ an architect. They may need the best, but they do not want to employ him or her, because the need for that resource, although critical to the success of the business, is temporary. The same is true of good lawyers. They are useful to have when you need them, but most firms cannot possibly afford to have the necessary depth of specialization of legal professionals constantly at their beck and call. **Figure 1–4** illustrates this dimension.

The stereotype of the entrepreneur as exploitative derives from this dimension: The entrepreneur is adept at using the skills, talents, and ideas of others. Viewed positively, this ability has become increasingly valuable in the changed business environment; it need not be parasitic in the context of a mutually satisfying relationship. Pressures toward this entrepreneurial side come from these:

- Increased resource specialization: An organization may have a need for a specialized resource like a VLSI design engineer, high-tech patent attorney, or state-of-the-art circuit test equipment, but only for a short time. By using, rather than owning, a firm reduces its risk and its fixed costs.
- Risk of obsolescence: Reduced by merely using, rather than owning, an expensive resource.
- Increased flexibility: The cost of exercising the option to quit is reduced by using, not owning, a resource.

Administrative practices are the product of pressures in the other direction, such as the following:

Figure 1-5

Promoter	Management Structure	Trustee
Flat with multiple informal networks	Entrepreneurial Domain ◄───► ◄───► Administrative Domain	Formalized hierarchy
Pressures toward This Side		*Pressures toward This Side*
Coordination of key noncontrolled resources Challenge to legitimacy of owner's control Employees' desire for independence		Need for clearly defined authority and responsibility Organizational culture Reward systems Management theory

- Power, status, and financial rewards: Determined by the extent of resource ownership and control in many corporations.
- Coordination: The speed of execution is increased because the executive has the right to request certain action without negotiation.
- Efficiency: Enables the firm to capture, at least in the short run, all of the profits associated with an operation.
- Inertia and cost of change: It is commonly believed that it is good management to isolate the technical core of production from external shocks. This requires buffer inventories, control of raw materials, and control of distribution channels. Ownership also creates familiarity and an identifiable chain of command, which becomes stabilized with time.
- Industry structures: Encourage ownership to prevent being preempted by the competition.

Management Structure

The promoter wants knowledge of his or her progress via direct contact with all of the principal actors. The trustee views relationships more formally, with specific rights and responsibilities assigned through the delegation of authority. The decision to use and rent resources and not to own or employ them will require the development of an informal information network. Only in systems where the relationship with resources is based on ownership or employment can resources be organized in a hierarchy. Informal networks arise when the critical success elements cannot be contained within the bounds of the formal organization. **Figure 1-5** illustrates this range of behavior.

Many people have attempted to distinguish between the entrepreneur and the administrator by suggesting that being a good entrepreneur precludes being a good manager. The entrepreneur is stereotyped as egocentric and idiosyncratic and thus unable to manage. However, although the managerial task is substantially different from the entrepreneur, management skill is nonetheless essential. The variation lies in the choice of appropriate tools.

More entrepreneurial management is a function of several pressures:

- Need for coordination of key noncontrolled resources: Results in need to communicate with, motivate, control, and plan for resources *outside* the firm.
- Flexibility: Maximized with a flat and informal organization.
- Challenge to owner's control: Classic questions about the rights of ownership as well as governmental, environmental, health, and safety restrictions undermine the legitimacy of control.
- Employees' desire for independence: Creates an environment where employees are unwilling to accept hierarchical authority in place of authority based on competence and persuasion.

On the other side of the spectrum, pressures that push the firm toward more administrative behavior include these:

- Need for clearly defined authority and responsibility: To perform the increasingly complex planning, organizing, coordinating, communicating, and controlling required in a business.
- Organizational culture: Often demands that events be routinized.
- Reward systems: Encourage and reward breadth and span of control.

Reward Philosophy

Finally, entrepreneurial firms differ from administratively managed organizations in their philosophy regarding reward and compensation. First, entrepreneurial firms are more explicitly focused on the creation and harvesting of value. In start-up situations, the financial backers of the organization—as well as the founders themselves—have invested cash and want cash out. As a corollary of this value-driven philosophy, entrepreneurial firms tend to base compensation on performance (where performance is closely related to value creation). Entrepreneurial firms are also more comfortable rewarding teams.

As a recent spate of takeovers suggests, more administratively managed firms are less often focused on maximizing and distributing value. They are more often guided in their decision making by the desire to protect their own positions and security. Compensation is often based on individual responsibility (assets or resources under control) and on performance relative to short-term profit targets. Reward in such firms is often heavily oriented toward promotion to increasing responsibility levels. **Figure 1–6** describes this dimension.

FIGURE 1-6

Promoter	Reward Philosophy	Trustee
Value-driven Performance-based Team-oriented	←———→ Entrepreneurial Domain ←———→ Administrative Domain	Security-driven Resource-based Promotion-oriented
Pressures toward This Side		*Pressures toward This Side*
Financial backers Individual expectations Competition		Societal norms Impacted information Demands of public shareholders

The pressures that pull firms toward the promoter end of the spectrum include the following:

- Individual expectations: Increasingly, individuals expect to be compensated in proportion to their contribution, rather than merely as a function of their performance relative to an arbitrary peer group. In addition, individuals seemingly have higher levels of aspiration for personal wealth.
- Investor demands: Financial backers invest cash and expect cash back, and the sooner the better. Increasingly, shareholders in publicly held firms are starting to press with a similar orientation.
- Competition: Increased competition for talented people creates pressure for firms to reward these individuals in proportion to their contributions.

On the other side, a variety of pressures pull firms toward more trusteelike behavior:

- Societal norms: We still value loyalty to the organization and find it difficult to openly discuss compensation.
- Impacted information: It is often difficult to judge the value of an individual's contributions, particularly within the frame of the annual compensation cycle performance review that most firms use.
- Demands of public shareholders: Many public shareholders are simply uncomfortable with compensation that is absolutely high, even if it is in proportion to contribution.

Summary

These characteristics have been gathered onto one summary chart (see **Figure 1–7**). In developing a behavioral theory of entrepreneurship, it becomes clear that entrepreneurship is defined by more than a set of individual traits and is different from an economic function. It is a cohesive pattern of managerial behavior.

This perspective on entrepreneurship highlights what we see as a false dichotomy: the distinction drawn between entrepreneurship and intrapreneurship. Entrepreneurship is an approach to management that can be applied in start-up situations as well as within more established businesses. As our definition suggests, the accumulation of resources that occurs as a firm grows is a powerful force that makes entrepreneurial behavior more difficult in a larger firm. But the fundamentals of the behavior required remain the same.

Still, our primary focus will be on the start-up. The situational factors that define a start-up situation do much to encourage entrepreneurship. As we look at the start-up process, however, it is worth keeping in mind that many of these lessons can be applied equally well in the large corporate setting.

FIGURE 1-7 *Summary*

Pressures toward This Side	Promoter	Key Business Dimension	Trustee	Pressures toward This Side
Diminishing opportunity streams Rapidly changing: Technology Consumer economics Social values	Driven by perception of opportunity	**Strategic Orientation** Entrepreneurial Domain ←→ Administrative Domain	Driven by resources currently contolled	Social contracts Performance measurement criteria Planning systems and cycle
Action orientation Short decisions windows Risk management Limited decision constituencies	Revolutionary with short duration	**Commitment to Opportunity** Entrepreneurial Domain ←→ Administrative Domain	Evolutionary of long duration	Acknowledgement of multiple constituencies Negotiation of strategy Risk reduction Management of fit
Lack of predictable resource needs Lack of long-term control Social needs for more opportunity per resource unit Interpersonal pressure for more efficient resource use	Multistaged with minimal exposure at each stage	**Commitment of Resources** Entrepreneurial Domain ←→ Administrative Domain	Single-staged with complete commitment upon decision	Personal risk reduction Incentive compensation Managerial turnover Capital allocation systems Formal planning systems

16

	Entrepreneurial Domain		Administrative Domain	
Increased resource specialization Long resource life compared to need Risk obsolescence Risk inherent in any new venture Inflexibility of permanent commitment to resources	Episodic use or rent of required resources	**Control of Resources** ↕ Entrepreneurial Domain ⟷ Administrative Domain	Ownership or employment of required resources	Power, status, and financial rewards Coordination Efficiency measures Inertia and cost of change Industry structures
Coordination of key noncontrolled resources Challenge to legitimacy of owner's control Employees' desire for independence	Flat with multiple informal networks	**Management Structure** ↕ Entrepreneurial Domain ⟷ Administrative Domain	Formalized hierarchy	Need for clearly defined authority and responsibility Organizational culture Reward systems Management theory
Individual expectations Competition Increased perception of personal wealth creation possibilities	Value-based Team-based Unlimited	**Compensation/Reward Policy** ↕ Entrepreneurial Domain ⟷ Administrative Domain	Resource-based Driven by short-term data Promotion Limited amount	Societal norms IRS regulations Impacted information Search for simple solutions for complex problems Demands of public shareholders

2

DEVELOPING START-UP STRATEGIES

Seize the day or look before you leap? Apparently, many entrepreneurs act before they analyze. Of the hundreds of thousands who "just do it" every year, only a few earn an attractive return. The great majority of start-ups fold or drag along in what one entrepreneur calls the land of the living dead. And although bad luck plays an important role, many failures are predestined and predictable. Then too, we find a great many individuals whose endless research precludes action: By the time they can fully investigate an opportunity, it no longer exists. Entrepreneurs may also lose their enthusiasm, as continued analysis engenders a corrosive pessimism.

Entrepreneurs don't need, however, a better manual for evaluating opportunities. The strategic and financial analytical frameworks used in large corporations require more time, money, and data than entrepreneurs can muster. Finding an effective middle ground between planning paralysis and none at all requires a more fluid, ad hoc approach. To minimize the time and effort spent, the astute entrepreneur screens out obvious losers quickly. Ideas that do pass the screen are analyzed parsimoniously, focusing on just those issues that matter. And action is so closely integrated with analysis that, on the surface, we may not even see any formal planning.

So Much to Do . . .

The decision to launch a new venture rests on an assessment of its *viability*—whether it can earn a profit—and its *attractiveness*, as compared to other opportunities that could be pursued.

Professor Amar Bhidé prepared this chapter.
Copyright © 1993 by the President and Fellows of Harvard College.
Harvard Business School Note 9-394-067.

Assessing viability requires analyzing a venture's ability to profitably compete for customers, capital, employees, and other resources. Entrepreneurs often focus on whether customers will buy their goods and services but not on why sales will lead to profits. Of course a start-up must attract customers; a viable enterprise must also enjoy higher prices or lower costs than its rivals so that its revenues exceed expenses.

Analyzing a start-up's competitive prospects, though, is daunting. A complete analysis must take a great many industry participants into account: As Porter and other strategy gurus have pointed out, a start-up faces competition not only from rivals offering the same goods but also potentially from substitutes, suppliers, buyers, and other new entrants. In bidding for employees and capital, a start-up even competes with firms totally outside its industry. Complementing the external analysis of competitors, internal core competencies and weaknesses should be probed. Entrepreneurs must analyze their costs and access to capital, technology, distribution channels, and so on.

Experts recommend dynamic analyses because the *when* of competitive advantage is as important as the *what*. The development of a new technology may be sufficient to overcome competitive barriers if it is completed by January, but worthless if delayed till December. And, the compleat strategist deals in hard numbers: What are the dollars-and-cents cost advantages of the incumbent's scale? What R&D expenditures are likely to be needed to invent around the incumbent's patents and the advertising costs required to gain a point of market share? If the industry suffers from excessive rivalry, how much higher must our margins have to rise to be profitable?

Well-reasoned, deeply footnoted tomes that document these tasks have found a goodly following in the corporate world. For start-ups, however, meticulous analyses are rarely feasible or particularly useful even. Entrepreneurs typically lack the time and money to interview a representative cross-section of potential customers, analyze substitutes, reconstruct competitors' cost structures, project alternative technology scenarios, and so on. The few individuals who do have the resources often lack the imagination and gumption to start a business. Opportunities are short-lived and, often, we find an inverse relationship between the data available to analyze an opportunity and its attractiveness. The more thoroughly the prospects of a start-up can be researched, the more intense the competition it is likely to face.

Not surprisingly, the evidence shows little relationship between planning and success. A National Federation of Independent Business study of 2,994 start-ups showed that founders who spent a long time in study, reflection, and planning were no more likely to survive their first three years than founders who seized opportunities that came by without much planning.[1] In corporations where systematic analysis is taken seriously, we often find a refined incapacity for seizing opportunities. The demand for hard data on market size and industry profitability

---

[1]*Inc.*, July 1992, p. 49.

delays entry until the business is proven, popular, and hence unprofitable. Or diligent analysis generates many obvious objections ("customers are tied to their existing suppliers") that are used to kill the idea.

Comparing the attractiveness of a venture to alternatives that could be pursued can also prove perplexing.

Many large corporations use the discounted cash flow (DCF) they expect from a project as the standard measure of its attractiveness. DCF apparently eliminates the biases inherent in other methods. Evaluating projects by their expected payback period, for example, will favor ventures that are expected to generate high but short-lived profits over those that promise sustainable profits after a long gestation period. DCF provides for a more reasonable trade-off between longevity and a quick return of capital.

Entrepreneurs, however, can't just use DCF. Cash flows from a new venture are highly unpredictable as compared to those from, say, expanding the capacity of an existing plant. Small changes in (largely unverifiable) assumptions lead to huge differences in projected value.[2] And, unlike a large corporation with relatively easy access to capital, entrepreneurs cannot back several projects simultaneously. Indeed, they can't count on obtaining resources at an acceptable price for a single venture. An unexpected need for cash (because, say, one large customer is unable to make timely payment or raw materials have to be bought to meet an unexpected surge of orders) may shut down a venture or force the entrepreneur to give away an unreasonably large share of the equity to the one investor who is willing to provide the funds.

Therefore, a wealth-constrained, one-venture-at-a-time entrepreneur must use multiple criteria, favoring ventures with:

- Low capital requirements—ventures that can be launched with little external capital and have the profit margins to sustain high growth with internally generated funds.

- High margin for error—ventures with simple operations and low fixed costs that are less likely to face a cash crunch because of technical delays, cost overruns, and slow buildup of sales.

- Significant payoffs—ventures whose rewards are substantial enough to compensate for the future opportunities the entrepreneur can't pursue because of a commitment to see this one through.

- Low exit costs—ventures that can be shut down without a significant loss of time, money, or reputation. Thus, for example, ventures whose failure is known quickly are better than projects that are not expected to make a profit for a long period and therefore cannot be reasonably abandoned in

---

[2]Some theorists may question whether the DCF of a new venture is at all meaningful. For example, Frank Knight in his 1921 classic *Risk, Uncertainty, and Profit* argued that entrepreneurs can expect a profit only to the extent that they bear unmeasurable and unquantifiable risk, which he called *uncertainty*; if the magnitude and volatility of a venture's cash flows can be reasonably estimated, it cannot be expected to yield a true profit.

the interim. Similarly, short payback periods have value because the entrepreneur's loss of self-esteem, reputation, and, of course, personal wealth due to the closing of a venture are lower if it has already returned the investment made in it.

- Options for cashing in—ventures that can be sold or taken public. An entrepreneur locked into an illiquid business cannot easily pursue other more attractive opportunities and faces problems of fatigue and burnout. Therefore, entrepreneurs should prefer businesses with a sustainable competitive advantage, such as a proprietary technology or brand name, that others would be willing to buy.

Evaluating the attractiveness of a start-up by these many criteria is much harder than applying a corporate rule of backing all projects with positive DCFs. Several criteria, for instance the opportunities for cashing in or the costs of exit, cannot be quantified. And ventures that shine by one measure are often questionable on another. For example, businesses with sustainable advantages that can be sold easily may entail more investment and complexity than ventures with quick payback.

Inevitably, therefore, assessing an opportunity and developing a strategy to exploit it requires a number of judgments; entrepreneurs cannot rely on a mechanistic flow chart or template. The entrepreneur has to judge which issues need careful analysis and what should be taken for granted. Judgment is required to determine whether the start-up can overcome critical obstacles. Can the capabilities of the established competitors' direct sales force be topped by a creative plan to use distributors? Can customers' loyalty to their current suppliers be overcome with a new ergonomic product design? There is no common unit of measurement to weigh the pros against the inevitable cons; equally experienced and astute entrepreneurs can easily disagree. The entrepreneur must make subjective assessments of attractiveness—whether, for instance, a quick payback provides adequate compensation for low sustainability.

Armchair Reflection: Screening Out Losers

The first issue an individual with an idea for a business confronts is whether the venture is worth researching. Timely judgments about the viability and attractiveness of a venture can save a great deal of wasted effort. Successful entrepreneurs, too, have many crazy ideas, but they discard or reformulate them quickly before drawing up financial projections, consulting experts, or interviewing potential customers.

What quick check for viability can an entrepreneur apply? A start-up's ability to compete depends on the *creativity* of the underlying concept and the entrepreneur's *capacity* to execute. (See **Figure 2–1**.) Creativity involves innovation or special foresight. Innovations change the existing order; entrepreneurs who would make waves in a mature industry must invent a new product or

Figure 2–1

How Start-Ups Overcome Competitive Barriers

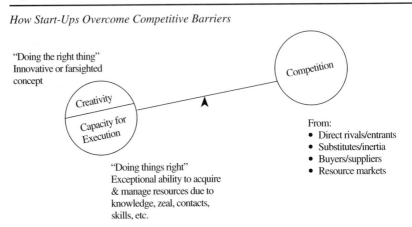

process to wrest business from established competitors. Foresight leverages external change. Entrepreneurs who want to ride a new wave must have a special insight about the direction, longevity, or consequences of the changes they expect to capitalize on. The gold rush made paupers of the thousands caught in the frenzy; however, Levi Strauss started a legend by recognizing the opportunity to supply rugged jeans to the prospectors.

But entrepreneurs can't just rely on inventing a new product or anticipating a trend; entrepreneurs must also have the capacity to execute well. Through their zeal, knowledge, contacts, personal commitment, and skill, entrepreneurs must persuade customers, investors, employees, and suppliers to support an uncertain enterprise and then manage competently what resources they can rustle up. Execution is especially critical when concepts can be easily copied. For example, if an innovation cannot be patented or kept secret, entrepreneurs must acquire and manage the resources needed to build a brand name or other barrier that will deter imitators. Superior execution can also compensate for a me-too concept in emerging or rapidly growing industries where doing it quickly and doing it right is more important than a brilliant strategy.

Many ventures obviously lack an innovative or far-sighted concept as well as any special capacity to execute. These can be discarded quickly, without much research or data collection. The entrepreneur should already be familiar with the basic facts about competitors' channels, customer behavior, technologies, and so on needed to judge whether a venture has prima facia merit. Lack of such knowledge constitutes a red flag. My research suggests that good ideas generally arise out of prior experience. Successful ventures solve problems their founders have personally grappled with as customers, employees, or bankers. Ventures like Federal Express, which reputedly grew out of founder Fred Smith's senior thesis in college, are rare.

Start-ups need not, however, possess an edge on every front. The creativity of successful entrepreneurs varies considerably. Some implement a radical idea, some modify, and some show no originality. Their capacity for execution varies as well. Selling an industrial niche product doesn't call for the charisma required to pitch trinkets through infomercials. There is no ideal entrepreneurial profile: Successful individuals may be gregarious or taciturn; analytical or intuitive; good or terrible with details; risk-averse or thrill seeking; delegators or control freaks; pillars of the community or outsiders and outcasts.

The necessary creativity and capacity to execute depends on what the entrepreneur hopes to accomplish and how. For example, ventures that seek to effect a *revolution* demand great creativity and an exceptional capacity to execute. Launching a Xerox or Federal Express requires a blockbuster new product or service rather than a marginal tinkering with carbon paper or existing delivery services. Revolutionary offerings usually require new processes or manufacturing techniques; competitive markets rarely fail to provide valuable products or services unless there are serious technological problems involved in providing them. For example, Federal Express founder Fred Smith may not have been the first to think of the need for reliable overnight package delivery, but he did pioneer the hub-and-spoke logistics needed to get the job done.[3]

Requirements for execution are also stiff. Revolutionary ventures consume vast resources. They require, for example, significant capital to develop new technology; build new facilities (Federal Express, for example, had to acquire its own fleet of aircraft); market a totally new product; and sustain losses during a long ramp-up period. Entrepreneurs therefore require exceptional charisma and evangelical ability to attract and retain the support of investors, customers, employees, and suppliers for a seemingly outlandish vision.

Entrepreneurs require unusual competence in managing resources. Often forced to make rather than buy, the entrepreneur must have the organizational and leadership skills to build a large, complex firm quickly. In addition, the entrepreneur may require considerable technical skills in deal making, strategic planning, managing overhead, and so on. The revolutionary entrepreneur, in other words, would appear to require almost superhuman qualities: Ordinary mortals need not apply.

Entrepreneurs who seek to build a *niche* business require less radical concepts. They do require some ingenuity to design a product that will draw customers away from more mainstream offerings and overcome the cost penalty of serving a small market, but, too-novel features can be a hindrance. A niche market will rarely justify the investment required to educate customers and distributors of the benefits of a radically new product. Similarly, a niche venture cannot support too much production or distribution innovation; unlike

---

[3]Revolutionary concepts do not, however, involve much foresight regarding external change. The revolutionary start-up generally throws a stagnant, mature industry into tumult instead of riding external changes. In fact, with great external uncertainty, customers and investors may be hesitant to back a radical product and technology until the environment settles down.

Federal Express, the specialty food manufacturer cannot afford its own fleet of trucks.

Moreover, a creative view of changing markets or technologies can compensate for the lack of independent innovation. For example, the personal computer revolution created opportunities to provide a variety of complementary goods and services such as add-on boards, math coprocessors, and software training videos and books. Entrepreneurs who recognized these opportunities quickly could build profitable businesses without an original technological breakthrough.

Entrepreneurs do not require exceptional ability to raise funds because the investment that can be justified by a niche market is limited. Nor do they require the revolutionary's ability to build and lead complex organizations. Rather the entrepreneur must have the capacity to make do with less—for example, to negotiate favorable terms with suppliers or use guerrilla marketing and word of mouth instead of national advertising to build brand awareness.

Creative concepts play an even smaller role in the success of *propagators* of an emerging technology or product who race to dominate a new market. For example, a new generation of microprocessors can spark a race in new downstream products, such as personal computers. Or a new downstream market, such as laptop computers, creates a race to produce new components, such as long-lived batteries. Successful ventures in these hot markets don't rely on an innovative concept; target customers and their needs are common industry knowledge. Choices about components, technologies, and distribution channels are limited, and the advantages and disadvantages of the alternatives are well known. Adopting an unconventional approach—for example, by departing from industry standards—can actually scare off investors and potential customers.

Success depends mainly on superior execution: the ability to design and produce a quality product on time and on budget and then sell it effectively. Losers usually fold because they lack a product that works, not because they have pursued a poor strategy. Investment requirements, though substantial, merely represent the entry fee for the race; more money rarely provides a competitive advantage. Correspondingly, entrepreneurs need superior skills in managing engineering, production, and marketing experts, and adequate competence in fund-raising and deal making.

Ventures based on *"hustle"*[4] in fragmented service businesses such as investment management, investment banking, head-hunting, or consulting also rely mainly on execution. Innovative strategies count for little in fields where imitation is easy and the perceived quality of the service provided is more critical than a unique technology, installed base, or captive distribution channel. The nature of superior execution is, however, different: Engineering, production, industrial marketing, and fund-raising are of little import. Rather, the entrepreneurs' personal selling skills, network of contacts, reputation for expertise, and ability to convince clients of the value of services rendered are crucial. A capacity for institution

---

[4]For a detailed discussion, see Amar Bhidé, "Hustle as Strategy," *Harvard Business Review*, September–October 1986.

building—recruiting and motivating stellar professionals, articulating and rein-forcing firm values, and so on—is also invaluable. With few natural economics of scale, the entrepreneur cannot create a going concern out of a one-man band or ad hoc ensemble without excellence in organization development.

Entrepreneurs who *speculate* in, for example, oil and gas properties when the energy market has collapsed or in office buildings in a real estate slump require foresight about the out-of-favor asset. The entrepreneur merely anticipates that the confusion or panic will pass; the concept does not entail significant innovation.

To execute, entrepreneurs must have the ability to raise funds for a contrarian bet; the entrepreneur's willingness to risk personal capital, connections with investors, and deal-making skills can be crucial. Successful execution does not however require exceptional managerial capacity. Organizational development, engineering, or marketing abilities add little value when an entrepreneur buys assets at a low price, expecting to sell them at a high price.

Gauging Attractiveness

Entrepreneurs should also reflect on the attractiveness of their ventures from a personal point of view—does the venture fit what they want to do as well as what they can do? Surviving the inevitable disappointments and near disasters requires passion for the enterprise; ability and desire are inseparable. Projects that enthuse one individual may well leave another cold, depending on their personalities, age, wealth, and so on.

Therefore, entrepreneurs should know what they're looking for and the sacri-fices they're willing to make. Do I want to make a fortune, or will a small profit suffice? Do I seek public recognition? The stimulation of working with exciting technologies, customers, and colleagues? Am I prepared to devote my life to a venture, or do I want to cash out quickly? Can I tolerate working in an industry with questionable ethical standards? High uncertainty? What financial and career risks am I prepared to take and for how long?

These deeply personal preferences determine the type of ventures that will enthuse and fortify an entrepreneur. For example, *revolutionary* ventures fit entrepreneurs who want to win or lose on a grand scale. Success can create dynastic fortunes and turn the entrepreneur into a near cult figure. But the risks also are substantial. Revolutions may fail for any number of reasons: The product is flawed, cannot be made or distributed cost effectively, serves no compelling need, or requires customers to incur unacceptable switching cost. Worse, the failure may not be apparent for several years, locking the entrepreneur into an extended period of frustrating endeavor. Even revolutions that are successful may not be financially rewarding for their founders, especially if they encounter delays en route. Investors may dump the visionary founders or demand a high share of the equity for additional financing.

The founder of a revolutionary venture must therefore anticipate recurring disappointments and a high probability that years of toil may come to naught. Unless entrepreneurs have a burning desire to change the world, they should not undertake revolutions.

Niche ventures often hold greater financial promise. Although, compared to a successful revolutionary venture, the niche venture may create less total wealth, the entrepreneur can often keep a higher share. Niche ventures require less capital and can achieve financial self-sufficiency faster; therefore, the entrepreneur's equity interest is less likely to be diluted through multiple rounds of financings. However, entrepreneurs must be willing to prosper in a backwater; dominating an obscure niche can be more profitable than intellectually stimulating or glamorous. Niche enterprises can also enter the "land of the living dead" because their market is too small for the business to thrive, but the entrepreneur has invested too much effort to be willing to quit.

Ventures that *propagate* a new technology can provide considerable thrill from racing against determined rivals in a hot field. The entrepreneur's downside is cushioned by the sometimes irrational willingness of investors to bear most of the risk. And, ventures that don't work out get put out of their misery quickly, freeing the entrepreneur to move on. The odds of winning big, however, are also low. Controlling investors may oust the founder in a panic. Competition is fierce and the winner of the current race may be overtaken when a new upstream component or downstream product sparks a fresh contest. Exit options are subject to the vagaries of the IPO (initial public offering) market: When the venture is hot, the IPO market might not be.

Hustle ventures also provide the satisfaction of working with talented colleagues in a fast-moving market. Capital requirements are low and investments can be staged as the business grows. Entrepreneurs can therefore avoid significant personal risk and meddling by outside investors. Although a hustle business can provide attractive current income, great wealth is elusive: Hustle businesses, which lack a sustainable franchise, cannot be easily sold or taken public at a high multiple of earnings. The entrepreneur must therefore savor the venture enough to make a long-term career of it rather than enjoy the fruits of its quick harvest.

The *speculators'* enjoyment lies in outwitting the market rather than building a firm or introducing an innovation to the world. The financial risks and returns depend on "the terms of the deal"—the capital the entrepreneur puts at risk, the conditions and amount of borrowing, and, of course, the price of the asset acquired. Risks are generally not staged—the entrepreneur is fully exposed when the asset is acquired. Liquidity or exit options often turn on the success of the speculation: If, as expected, prices rise, the speculator can expect many buyers for the asset owned, but if prices decline or stay depressed, market liquidity for the asset will be generally poor. All told, such ventures appeal most to entrepreneurs who enjoy deal-making and rolling the dice.

Pitfalls Avoided

Timely reflection should force entrepreneurs to confront a basic flaw in many start-ups: the lack of any special idea or capacity to execute that could provide a competitive edge. In their enthusiasm many entrepreneurs dilute the much-better-than-your-rivals imperative to an as-good-as standard. Perhaps they have been conditioned to believe that failure is the consequence of a pathological hubris or ineptitude. Just as we expect every healthy newborn to survive infancy, entrepreneurs assume that their ventures will naturally succeed. But, in fact, competition makes the demise of start-ups normal, to-be-expected events; expectations of profitable survival must be predicated on a superior idea or capacity for execution.

Entrepreneurs may also find a poor fit between what they have and what a particular venture takes. Common problems thus flagged include:

- Relying on hustle or a minor idea against entrenched competitors. High levels of operational excellence won't sustain a new hamburger chain against competition from rivals who enjoy national purchasing economies, brand names and high-traffic locations. Good management—listening to customers, maintaining quality, and paying attention to costs—which can improve the profits of a going business, can't propel a start-up over "structural" barriers. A creative new process or product is a must.

- Launching revolutionary products in niche markets. Steve Jobs introduced truly user-friendly personal computing through the Lisa in 1983. Positioned as a high-end $10,000 product, it couldn't attract the critical mass of software writers, value-added resellers, distribution channels, and users it needed to survive. When the same technology was reintroduced for a broader market as the Macintosh, however, the product was a smash hit.

Entrepreneurs should, however, use the initial screen to drop only truly dead-ended projects, not to kill all ideas by identifying their every shortcoming. And, with the right attitude, reflecting on entrepreneur-venture fit can, in fact, give courage to the waverers. Except perhaps in revolutionary ventures, success does *not* usually require extraordinary ideas, résumés, or talent, as the following examples illustrate:

- The advent of a new distribution option (such as home shopping channels) or a new regime (as in Eastern Europe) creates great opportunities for the determined novice. Entrepreneurs who are willing to act quickly can create profitable niche or hustle businesses with just a little ingenuity because they don't face entrenched competitors and customers tolerate imperfections and inexperience. Even buttoned-down IBM turned to a college drop-out, Bill Gates, to source the operating system for their first personal computer.

- In some service businesses dominated by fly-by-night or unreliable operators, modest professionalism can provide a meaningful edge. For instance, superior execution in providing transportation services for rock bands may simply require showing up on time.

- In a new technology race, native talent can prevail over qualifications and experience. In the work-station market, for example, Sun Microsystems beat over a dozen start-ups including Apollo, a text-book venture launched

by industry stars. Sun's four 27-year-old founders, who had virtually
no business or industry experience, simply out-engineered and outsold
their rivals.[5]

Parsimonious Planning and Analysis

To conserve time and money, entrepreneurs must minimize the resources they
devote to researching the ideas that pass their initial screen. Unlike the corporate
world, where foil-mastery and completed staff work can make a career, the
entrepreneur only does as much planning and analysis as seems necessary and
useful.

How much effort should an entrepreneur devote? The appropriate analytical
"budget" that a start-up merits depends on several factors: Ventures that require
significant capital have to be better researched and documented than ventures that
can be self-financed. Professional investors usually require a written business plan
because it provides clues about the entrepreneur's seriousness of purpose, concern
for investors, and competence, and it can be conveniently evaluated on airplanes.
Entrepreneurs must cobble together a plausible book, even if they are skeptical
about its relationship to subsequent outcomes. The degree of innovation attempted
also affects the utility of analysis. For example, focus groups and surveys have
little value in predicting demand for products that closely resemble existing
offerings or products that are so novel that customers can't express a useful
opinion. Market research helps most with intermediate levels of innovation.

Businesses with more complex operations or development tasks require more
analysis and planning. Complexity increases the costs of poor coordination or
timing; besides, the process of jointly thrashing out a plan can help build cohesion
in the multifunctional teams that such ventures require.

Changing technologies, customer preferences, regulations and so on militate
against extensive analysis. Entrepreneurs cannot rely on research conducted under
conditions of such turbulence; and besides, if they expect to take advantage of the
external changes, they can't spend time dotting i's and crossing t's. This is not to
imply, however, that start-ups in a stable environment merit leisurely investigation. Entrepreneurs can't allow the availability of time and other resources to
stimulate more analysis. With spreadsheet software, for example, it's easy to
churn out detailed but not particularly insightful analyses of a project's break-even
point, capital requirements, payback period, or DCF.

Given a limited budget, how should entrepreneurs set their analytical priorities? The entrepreneur may be tempted to touch lightly all of the innumerable
issues that might be analyzed or to spend a lot of effort in areas where data is most
readily available. Parsimonious analysis, however, entails a triage: With issues
where the impossibility of obtaining data precludes analysis, entrepreneurs simply

---

[5]See "Vinod Khosla and Sun Microsystems," HBS case no. 9-390-049.

have to take their chances. Other issues deserve only passing attention, because although lots of data can be collected, the analyses can't be acted on. Entrepreneurs should concentrate on issues that they can reasonably expect to resolve *and* that determine whether and how they will proceed. Resolving a few big questions—understanding what *must* go right and anticipating the venture-destroying pitfalls, for instance—is more important than investigating many nice-to-know matters.

An entrepreneur cannot use a standard checklist or a one-size-fits-all approach to analysis; issues most worthy of analysis will depend on the type of venture undertaken.[6] To illustrate consider that in *revolutionary* ventures, market size and growth is notoriously difficult to predict. At best, entrepreneurs may satisfy themselves that their novel product or service delivers considerably greater value than current offerings; how quickly it catches on is a blind guess. Leverage may be obtained, however, from analyzing how customers might buy and use the product or service. Understanding the purchase process can help identify the right decision makers for the new offering—in the case of Federal Express, for instance, it was important to go beyond the mailroom managers who traditionally bought delivery services. Similarly, understanding how products are used can reveal obstacles that must be overcome before customers can realize the benefit from the revolutionary offering.

Another important issue for revolutionaries lies in the appropriability of returns from their innovation. Many concepts are difficult to prove, but once proven, easy to imitate. Unless the pioneer is protected by sustainable barriers to entry, the benefits of the hard-fought revolution become a public good rather than the source of entrepreneurial profit. Given the magnitude of the organizational building task in a revolutionary venture, entrepreneurs may also address issues such as the values members of the firm will uphold, how they will communicate with each other and how they will resolve disputes. Resolving these corporate culture issues early can protect the organization from the subsequent stress of rapid growth.

Niche start-ups often fail because the costs of serving a specialized niche exceed the benefits to customers. Entrepreneurs should therefore analyze carefully the incremental costs of serving a niche, taking into account their lack of scale and the difficulty of marketing to a small diffused segment. Especially if the cost disadvantage is significant, entrepreneurs should determine whether their offering provides a significant price or performance benefit. Established companies may vie for share through line extensions or marginal tailoring of their products and

---

[6]The types of ventures I have described are not intended to be mutually exclusive or collectively exhaustive. Nor do I suggest that entrepreneurs should maintain purity of style and avoid hybrids. For example, there is nothing intrinsically flawed about a venture to establish a network that provides a revolutionary service to participants. I offer the typology merely as an aid to pruning the analytical task efficiently. If a venture straddles two types, entrepreneurs should construct an analytical approach that combines the relevant features of both or think of another analogy that is more appropriate. What should be avoided is a laundry-list approach, in which all possible issues are half-heartedly analyzed as well as a blind just-do-it attitude.

services; the start-up must really wow its target customers. A marginally tastier cereal won't knock Kellogg's corn flakes off supermarket shelves.

Another significant risk with niche ventures is that their payoffs are too small. For example, a niche venture that can't support a direct sales force may not generate enough commissions to attract an independent broker or manufacturers' rep. Entrepreneurs too will eventually lose interest if the rewards aren't commensurate with their efforts. Therefore, the entrepreneur should verify that everyone who contributes may reasonably expect a high, quick, or sustainable return even if the total profits of the venture are small.

The most critical issue for the *propagators* of a new technology—their ability to outpace rivals—cannot be easily analyzed. Who could have forecast, for example, that the inexperienced founders of Sun Microsystems would beat out Apollo's veterans? Entering a race basically requires faith in one's ability to finish ahead of the pack. Analyzing whether the rewards for winning are commensurate with the risks, however, can be more feasible and worthwhile. In some technology races, success is predictably short-lived. In the disk drive industry, for example, firms that succeed with one generation of products are often leap-frogged when the next generation arrives. In engineering work-stations however, Sun was able to realize relatively long-term gains from its early success because it established a durable "architectural" standard.

Operational analysis and planning usually deserves more attention than strategic planning, because getting a product that works out quickly is crucial. For example, Sun's business plan, one founder recalls, was mainly an operating plan, containing specific timetables for product development, opening sales and service offices, hiring engineers, and so on.

In ventures based on *hustle*, a detailed analysis of competitors and industry structure is rarely of much value. The ability to seize short-lived opportunities and execute them brilliantly is of far more importance than a long-term competitive strategy. Analysis of specific clients and relationships dominates general market surveys. Partnership agreements, terms for offering equity to later employees, performance measurement criteria, and bonus plans are important determinants of firm success and are best thought through before launch rather than hastily improvised later on. Although projections of long-term cash flows are not meaningful, back-of-the-envelope, short-term cash forecasts and analyses of break-evens can keep the entrepreneur out of trouble. Overall, though, the analytical preparation required for such ventures is modest.

With *speculative* ventures, two sets of analysis are crucial. One relates to the market dynamics for the asset being acquired, or, more specifically, why the prices of the asset may be expected to rise. Entrepreneurs should try to determine whether prices are temporarily low (due to, say, an irrational panic or a temporary surge in supply), in secular decline because of permanent changes in supply or demand, or merely correcting after an irrational prior surge. The other analysis is of the entrepreneurs' ability to hold or carry the asset till it can be sold at a profit, because it is difficult to predict when temporarily depressed prices will return to normal. Carrying capacity depends on the extent of borrowing used to purchase the asset, the conditions under which financing may be revoked, and the income produced by the asset. Rental properties or a producing well that provides ongoing income, for example, can be carried more easily than raw land or drilling rights. For certain kinds of assets—for example, mines and urban rental properties—the entrepreneur should also consider the risks of expropriation and windfall taxation.

Integrating Action and Analysis

Standard operating procedure in large corporations usually entails a clear distinction between analysis and execution. In contemplating a new venture, established firms face issues about its "fit" with ongoing activities: Does the proposed venture leverage corporate strengths? Will the resources and attention it requires reduce our ability to build customer loyalty and improve quality in our core markets? These concerns dictate a deliberate, "trustee"[7] approach: Before they can launch a venture, managers must investigate an opportunity extensively, seek the counsel of higher-ups, submit a formal plan, respond to criticisms by bosses and corporate staff, and secure a head count and capital allocation.

Entrepreneurs who start with a clean slate, however, don't have to obtain all the answers before they act. In fact, they often can't easily separate action and analysis. The attractiveness of a new restaurant, for example, may depend on the terms of the lease—low rents can turn the venture from a mediocre proposition to a money machine. But an entrepreneur's ability to negotiate a good lease cannot easily be determined from a general prior analysis; he or she must enter into a serious negotiation with a specific landlord for a specific property. Performing a lot of other analyses without first testing the ability to get a good lease can be a serious waste of time and money.

Acting before an opportunity is fully analyzed has other benefits. Doing something concrete builds confidence in oneself and in others. Key employees and investors will often follow the individual who has committed to action by, for instance, quitting a job, incorporating, or signing a lease. By taking a personal risk, the entrepreneur convinces others that the venture *will* proceed and, if they don't sign up, they could be left behind.

Early action can generate more robust, better informed strategies. Extensive surveys and focus group research about a concept can produce misleading evidence: Slippage can arise between research and reality because the potential customers interviewed are not representative of the market, their enthusiasm for the concept wanes when they see the actual product, or they may lack the authority to sign purchase orders. More robust strategies may be developed by first building a working prototype and asking customers to use it before conducting extensive market research.

---

[7]See Howard Stevenson and David Gumpert, "The Heart of Entrepreneurship," *Harvard Business Review,* March–April 1985.

The entrepreneurs' ability to undertake execution quickly will naturally vary. Trial and error is less feasible with large-scale capital-intensive ventures like Federal Express than with a consulting firm start-up. Nevertheless, we can find some common characteristics of an approach that integrates action and analysis, such as staging analytical tasks, plugging holes quickly, evangelical investigation, and flexible perseverance.

Staging Analytical Tasks

Given the uncertainties of a new venture, the returns from more fact gathering, interviews, or cash flow projections diminish rapidly. Therefore, rather than resolve all issues at once, the entrepreneur does only enough research to justify the next action or investment. For example, an individual who has developed a new medical technology may first obtain crude estimates of market demand to determine whether it is worth seeing a patent lawyer. If the crude estimates and lawyer are encouraging, the individual may do some more analysis to establish the wisdom of spending the money to obtain a patent. Several more iterations of analysis and action will follow before a formal business plan is prepared and circulated to venture capitalists.

Plugging Holes Quickly

As soon as analysis reveals problems and risks, the entrepreneur moves to find solutions. For example, suppose that an entrepreneur finds that it will be difficult to raise capital for a venture. Rather than kill the idea, the entrepreneur thinks creatively about solving the problem. Perhaps the investment in a fixed plant can be reduced by modifying the technology to use more standard equipment that can be rented. Or, under the right terms, a customer might underwrite the risk by providing a large initial order. Expectations and goals for growth might be scaled down, and a niche market could be tackled first. Except with obviously unviable ideas that can be easily ruled out through elementary logic, the purpose of analysis is not to find fault with new ventures or find reason for abandoning them. Analysis should be considered as an exercise in what to do next more than what not to do.

Evangelical Investigation

Entrepreneurs often blur the line between research and selling. As one individual recalls: "My market research consisted of taking a prototype to a trade show and see if I could write orders." "Beta-sites" in the software industry provide another example of simultaneous research and selling; customers actually pay to help the vendor test early versions of software and will often place larger orders if they are satisfied.

From the beginning, entrepreneurs don't just seek opinions and information, they also seek to gain others' commitment. Entrepreneurs treat everyone they talk to as a potential customer, investor, employee, or supplier or at least as a potential source of leads. Even if they don't actually ask for the order, they take the time to build enough interest and rapport so that they can come back later. This simultaneous listening and selling approach may not produce truly objective market research and statistically significant results, but the resource-constrained entrepreneur doesn't have much choice. Besides, in the initial stages, the deep knowledge and support of a few is often more valuable than broad, impersonal data.

Flexible Perseverance

Entrepreneurs who act on sketchy information and back-of-the-envelope plans must stand ready to change their strategies as events unfold. Successful ventures don't always proceed in the direction that they initially set out along. A significant proportion develop entirely new markets and products and sources of competitive advantage. Therefore, although perseverance and tenacity represent valuable entrepreneurial traits, they must be complemented with flexibility and willingness to learn. If customers who should be placing orders don't, the entrepreneur should consider reworking the concept. Similarly, the entrepreneur should also be prepared to exploit opportunities that didn't figure in the initial plan.

The apparently sketchy planning and haphazard evolution of many successful ventures doesn't mean that entrepreneurs should follow a ready-fire-aim approach. In spite of appearances, astute entrepreneurs do analyze and strategize extensively. They realize, however, that businesses cannot be launched like space shuttles, with every detail of the mission planned in advance. In fact, to paraphrase Cardinal Newman, the quest for the perfect start-up plan is often the enemy of the good. Initial analyses only provide plausible hypotheses, which must be tested and modified. Entrepreneurs should play with and explore ideas, letting their strategies evolve through a seamless process of guesswork, analysis, and action.

3

Valuation Techniques

One of the entrepreneur's critical tasks is assessing and determining value. This is important not only for the individual about to purchase a company, but also for the entrepreneur who is starting a firm and is attempting to estimate the value the business may have in the future. Finally, understanding value is a key step for the entrepreneur about to harvest a venture, either through sale or taking the business public.

Financial theorists have developed many techniques that can be used to evaluate a going concern. Of course, for a large public company, one could simply take the market value of the equity. For a going concern with a long history of audited financials, earnings and cash flow projections are possible. But the valuation of a small, privately held business is difficult and uncertain at best.

This note will briefly outline some of the more widely used valuation approaches, including:

- Asset valuations.
- Earnings valuations.
- Cash flow valuations.

Asset Valuations

One approach to valuation is to look at the underlying worth of the assets of the business. Asset valuation is one measure of the investor's exposure to risk. If

This chapter was prepared by Michael J. Roberts under the direction of Howard H. Stevenson.
Copyright © 1984 by the President and Fellows of Harvard College.
Harvard Business School Note 9-384-185.

within the company there are assets whose market value approximates the price of the company plus its liabilities, the immediate downside risk is low. In some instances, an increase in the value of the assets of a company may represent a major portion of the investor's anticipated return. The various approaches to asset valuation are discussed below.

Book Value

The most obvious asset value that a prospective purchaser can examine is the book value. In a situation with many variables and unknowns, it provides a tangible starting point. However, it must be remembered that it is only a starting point. The accounting practices of the company as well as other things can have a significant effect on the firm's book value. For example, if the reserve for losses on accounts receivable is too low for the business, it will inflate book value and vice versa. Similarly, treatment of asset accounts such as research and development costs, patents, and organization expense can vary widely. Nevertheless, the book value of a firm provides a point of departure when considering asset valuation.

Adjusted Book Value

An obvious refinement of stated book value is to adjust for large discrepancies between the stated book and actual market value of tangible assets, such as buildings and equipment that have been depreciated far below their market value, or land that has substantially appreciated above its book value that stands at the original cost. An adjustment would probably also reduce the book value of intangible assets to zero unless they, like the tangible assets, also have a market value. The figure resulting from these adjustments should more accurately represent the value of the company's assets.

Liquidation Value

One step beyond adjusted book value is to consider the net cash amount that could be realized if the assets of the company were disposed of in a "quick sale" and all liabilities of the company were paid off or otherwise settled. This value would take into account that many assets, especially inventory and real estate, would not realize as much as they would were the company to continue as a going concern or were the sale made more deliberately. Also, calculation of a liquidation value would make allowances for the various costs of carrying out a liquidation sale.

The liquidation value, it should be noted, is only an indication of what might be realized if the firm were liquidated immediately. Should the company continue its operations and encounter difficulties, most likely a subsequent liquidation would yield significantly less than the liquidation value calculated for the company in its current condition.

The liquidation value of a company is not usually of importance to a buyer who is interested in the maintenance of a going concern. One would assume, however, that the liquidation value would represent some kind of a floor below which the seller would be unwilling to sell because he should be able to liquidate the company himself.

Replacement Value

The current cost of reproducing the tangible assets of a business can at times be significant in that starting a new company may be an alternative means of getting into the business. It sometimes happens that the market value for existing facilities is considerably less than the cost of building a plant and purchasing equivalent equipment from other sources. In most instances, however, this calculation is used more as a reference point than as a seriously considered possibility.

Earnings Valuations

A second common approach to an investor's valuation of a company is to capitalize earnings. This involves multiplying an earnings figure by a capitalization factor or price-earnings ratio. Of course, this raises two questions: (1) Which earnings? and (2) What factor?

Earnings Figure

One can use three basic kinds of earnings:

• *Historical earnings.* The logic behind looking at historical earnings is that they can be used to reflect the company's future performance; there is no logic in evaluating a company on the basis of what it has earned in the past. As will be discussed below, however, historical earnings should be given careful consideration in their use as a guide to the future. They should provide concrete realism to what otherwise would be just a best guess.

Historical earnings per se can rarely be used directly, and an extrapolation of these figures to obtain a picture of the future must be considered a rough, and frequently a poor, approximation. To gain the benefit from the information in a company's financial history of past operations, it is necessary to study each of the cost and income elements, their interrelationships, and their trends.

In pursuit of this study, it is essential that random and nonrecurring items be factored out. Expenses should be reviewed to determine that they are normal and do not contain extraordinary expenses or omit some of the unusual expenses of operations. For example, inordinately low maintenance and repair charges over a period of years may mean that extraordinary expenses will be incurred in the future for deferred maintenance. Similarly, nonrecurring "windfall" sales will distort the normal picture.

In a small, closely held company, particular attention should be given to the salaries of owner-managers and members of their families. If these salaries have been unreasonably high or low in light of the nature and size of the business and the duties performed, adjustment of the earnings is required. An assessment should also be made of the depreciation rates to determine their validity and to estimate the need for any earnings adjustments for the future. The amount of federal and state income taxes paid in the past may influence future earnings because of carryover and carryback provisions in the tax laws.

• *Future earnings under present ownership.* How much and in what ways income and costs are calculated for future operations depends to a large degree on the operating policies and strategies of management. The existing or future owners' approach will be influenced by a host of factors: management ability, economic and noneconomic objectives, and so on. In calculating future earnings for a company, these kinds of things must be considered and weighed.

A calculation of value based on the future earnings of the company should provide an indication of the current economic value of the company to the current owner. To an investor, including the present owner as an investor, this figure should provide an economic basis for that individual's continued activity and investment in the company. (As we shall discuss later, there is usually more to a potential seller's position than just an economic analysis of his or her own future as an investor.) To an investor who anticipates a change in management with his investment, a calculation of value based on earnings from the current owner's continuing with the company is *not* a meaningful assessment of the value of the company to the investor.

• *Future earnings under new ownership.* These are the earnings figures that are relevant to the investor who is investing in the turnaround of a dying company or in the reinvigoration of a stagnant one. The basis for the figures—the assumptions, relationships between costs and income, and so on—will probably show significant variance from the company's past performance. Plans may be to change substantially the nature of the business. The evaluation and investment decision may also involve large capital investments in addition to the purchase price of the company.

It is the future earnings of the new operation of the business that are helpful in determining the value of the company to the entrepreneur as these are the earnings that will influence the economic return. Most likely these kinds of projections will have large elements of uncertainty, and one may find it helpful to consider the high, low, and most likely outcomes for financial performance.

In addition to deciding on an earnings period on which to focus, there is also the issue of "what earnings?" That is, profit before tax, profit after tax, operating income, or earnings before interest and taxes (EBIT). Most valuations look at earnings after tax (but before extraordinary items). Of course, the most important rule is to be consistent: Don't base a multiple on earnings after tax, and then apply that multiple to EBIT. Beyond this, the most important factor to consider is precisely what you are trying to measure in your valuation. A strong argument can be made for using EBIT. This measures the earning power and value of the basic, underlying business, *without the effects of financing*. This is a particularly valuable approach if the entrepreneur is contemplating using a different financial structure for the business in the future.

Price-Earnings Multiple

Next, we have the issue of what multiple to use. Assuming that the investor's primary return is anticipated to result from sale of the stock at some future date, the investor should then ask the question: Given the anticipated pattern of earnings of this company, the nature of the industry, the likely state of the stock market, and so on, what will the public or some acquisitive conglomerate be willing to pay me for my holdings? In terms of some multiple of earnings, what prices are paid for stock with similar records and histories? To estimate with any degree of confidence the future multiple of a small company is indeed a difficult task. In many instances, working with a range of values might be more helpful. This great uncertainty for a potential investor in estimating both a small company's future earnings *and* future market conditions for the stock of that company in part explains why his or her return on investment requirements for a new venture investment are so high.

Again, it is important to remember to be consistent: Always derive the multiple as a function of the same base you wish to apply it to—profit after tax, EBIT, or whatever.

Up until this point, we have been discussing methods of arriving at a value for the business as a whole. While the entrepreneur is naturally concerned with this issue, he or she is also concerned with the valuation of his or her piece of the business.

Residual pricing is a technique that addresses this issue. Essentially, residual pricing involves:

- Determining the future value of a company in year *n* through one of the methods described above.
- Applying a target rate of return to the amount of money raised via the initial sale of equity.
- Using this information to develop a point of view on how much equity the entrepreneur must give up in order to get the equity financing required.
- The "residual," or remaining equity, can be retained by the entrepreneur as his or her return.

For example, if a company is projected to have earnings of $100,000 in year 5, and if (after some analysis) it seems that the appropriate P/E for the company is 10, then we can assume that the company will be worth $1 million in year 5. Now if we know that the entrepreneur needs to raise $50,000 from a venture capital firm (in equity) to start the business, and if the venture firm requires a 50 percent annual return on that money, then that $50,000 needs to be worth $50,000 $\times$ $(1 + 50 \text{ percent})^5 = \$380,000$. So in theory at least, the entrepreneur would have to give 38 percent of the equity to the venture firm in order to raise this money.

Cash Flow Valuations

Traditional approaches to evaluating a company have placed the principal emphasis on *earnings*. Assuming that the company will continue in operation, the earnings method posits that a company is worth what it can be expected to earn.

But this approach is only partially useful for the individual entrepreneur who is trying to decide whether or not to invest in a business. Again, the entrepreneur must distinguish between the value of the business as a whole and the portion of that value that can be appropriated for himself or herself. The entrepreneur must address the need to acquire resources from others and must understand that he or she will have to give up a portion of the value of the business in order to attract these resources. In addition to personal or subjective reasons for buying a business, the entrepreneur's chief criterion for appraisal will be return on investment. Because an entrepreneur's dollar investment is sometimes very small, it may be useful to think of return more as a return on his or her *time,* than a return on his or her dollar investment. To calculate the latter return, the entrepreneur must calculate his or her *individual* prospective cash flow from the business. It is the entrepreneur's return *from* the business, rather than the return inherent in the business itself, which is important. As we shall see, there are several different types of cash flow that can accrue to the entrepreneur.

Operating Cash Flows

Cash or value that flows out of the business during its operations include:

- *Perquisites.* Perquisites are not literally cash at all, but can be considered cash equivalents in terms of their direct benefits. Business-related expenses charged to the company (e.g., company car) are received by the individual and are *not taxed* at either the corporate or personal level. Their disadvantage is that they are limited in absolute dollar terms.
- *Return of capital via debt repayment.* This class of cash flow is a *tax-free* event at both the corporate and personal level. An additional advantage to this type of flow is that it can occur while enabling the entrepreneur still to maintain a continuous equity interest in the company. Its disadvantage is, of course, that it requires him or her to make the original investment.
- *Interest and salary.* Both of these items constitute personal income and are taxed as such at the personal level. However, no tax is imposed at the corporate level.
- *Dividends.* As a means of getting cash from a venture, dividends are the least desirable as the resulting cash flow is forced to undergo the greatest net shrinkage. Dividends incur taxes first at the corporate level (at the 15 percent to 34 percent rate as income accrues to the corporation) and then again at the personal level (at the personal income tax rate as the dividend payment accrues to the individual). At the maximum corporate income tax rate of 34 percent and the typical personal income tax rate of 30 to 35 percent, we can see that this double taxation can easily reduce $1 of pretax corporate profit to only $0.44 aftertax cash flow to the individual.

Terminal Value

Another source of cash flow is the money the entrepreneur pulls out of the business when the venture is harvested. Again, there are several elements to this aspect of return.

• *Return of capital via sale:* If the owner/manager sells all or part of the business, the amount he or she receives up to the amount of his or her cost basis is a *tax-free* event at both the corporate and personal level. Since a sale of his or her interest is involved, however, it is evident that unlike a return of capital via debt repayment, the owner/manager does not maintain his or her continuous equity interest in the concern. Also, like a cash flow based on debt retirement, an original investment is necessary.

• *Capital gain via sale:* When capital gains are realized in addition to the return of capital on the sale of stock, no tax is imposed at the corporate level; a sale of assets typically generates personal *and* corporate taxes.

Tax Benefits

While not precisely cash flow, tax benefits can enhance cash flow from other sources. For example, if a start-up has operating losses for several years, and if these losses can be passed through to the individual, then they create value by sheltering other income. Because entrepreneurs are often in a low-income phase when starting a business, these tax benefits may be of limited value to them. However, if properly structured, these tax benefits can provide substantial value to investors who can use them. In a situation where the structure and form of the organization (i.e., a corporation), does not permit the losses to flow through to the individual, these losses can be used to offset income of the corporation in prior or future years.

The entrepreneur must also take into account his negative cash flows. Three types of negative cash flows are particularly important:

• Cash portion of the purchase price.
• Forgone salary.
• Additional equity capital.

Frequently, the most critical aspect of the cash portion of the purchase price is that it must be small enough for the entrepreneur to be able to pay in the first place. In this kind of situation, the seller finances the purchase of his or her company by taking part of the purchase price in the form of a note. The seller then receives cash later on from future earnings of the company or from its assets. Of course, the less cash he or she is required to put up, the more cash the entrepreneur has available for other uses and the greater the opportunity he or she has to produce a high ROI. On the other hand, too much initial debt may hamstring a company from the start, thereby hurting the venture's subsequent financial performance and the entrepreneur's principal source of return—be it the cash withdrawn from the company or the funds received from eventual sale of the company.

The significance to the entrepreneur of a negative cash flow based on a deficient salary is clear—a lower income for personal use than could be obtained elsewhere. In addition, there is the effect that these early negative flows may have on the entrepreneur: Faced with an immediate equity requirement for working capital or fixed assets, the owner/manager may be forced to seek outside investors, thereby diluting his or her future value in the business and also introducing the possibility of divergent goals in the financial and other aspects of the company's operations.

At this point in our analysis, it will appear obvious to some that the next step for the entrepreneur is to find the present value of the cash flow he or she predicts for the venture—in other words, discounting the value of future cash flows to arrive at a value of the venture in terms of cash today. We shall see, however, that in many respects this approach raises more questions than it answers, and therefore its usefulness to the analysis is questionable at best.

The essence of the problem is that present value is basically an investment concept utilizing ROI to determine the allocation of a limited supply of funds among alternatives, whereas the entrepreneur is faced basically with a personal situation where return on both investment and *time* are key. In addition, the entrepreneur may have made a considerable investment in generating the particular option, and it is difficult to weigh this tangible opportunity against unknown options. Because the entrepreneur does not have a portfolio of well-defined opportunities to choose from, he or she needs to define some standard of comparison. This is typically the salary that could be obtained by working.

In an investment analysis utilizing present value, the discount rate is selected to reflect uncertainty associated with cash flows; the higher the uncertainty, the higher the discount rate and, consequently, the lower the present value of the cash flows. In the corporate context, there is usually a minimal ROI criterion for non-critical investments to keep the ROI greater than the firm's cost of capital.

For the individual entrepreneur, however, the decision to buy or to start a company is fundamentally a subjective one. Return on investment and time for this kind of decision is measured not only in terms of dollars, but also in terms of what he or she will be doing, who his or her associates will be, how much time and energy will have to be expended, and what lifestyle will result. Different kinds of ventures present *different kinds of return* on time. As cash to the entrepreneur is an important enabling factor for *some* of the things the entrepreneur is seeking, it is important that he or she calculate what these cash flows might be and when they can be expected. However, because decisions affecting cash flow also affect the other returns to the entrepreneur and because these other returns may be at least as important as the financial returns, a present value calculation often is not the most important measure.

In thinking about the attractiveness of a particular opportunity, an entrepreneur rarely has easily comparable alternatives. More than likely the decision is either to go ahead with a venture or to stay where he or she is until something else comes along. Perhaps the most useful way to think of this position is to imagine an individual looking down a corridor that will provide a range of opportunities—opportunities to achieve different levels of financial and other rewards with their accompanying risks and sacrifices. Financial theorists, for instance, have recently begun to study investments in terms of their ability to generate a future stream of growth opportunities.

Summary

The previous discussion has outlined a variety of different approaches to the valuation of a firm. It is important to remember that no single approach will ever give the "right" answer. To a large extent, the appropriateness of any method of evaluation depends on the perspective of the evaluator. However, both in this course and in "real life" one must come to some point of view on the worth of a firm, no matter how scant the data. This is very important, even if the value is only a preliminary one, because it permits the individual to delve further into the issues at hand.

Nonetheless, the true purpose of the analysis is not to arrive at "the answer" but to:

- Identify critical assumptions.
- Evaluate the interrelationships among elements of the situation to determine which aspects are crucial.
- Develop *realistic* scenarios, not a best-case/worst-case analysis.
- Surface and understand potential outcomes and consequences, both good and bad.
- Examine the manner in which the value of the business is being carved up to satisfy the needs of prospective suppliers of resources.

No single valuation captures the true value of any firm. Rather, its value is a function of the individual's perception of opportunity, risk, the nature of financial resources available to the purchaser, the prospective strategy for operation, the time horizon for analysis, alternatives available given the time and money invested, and prospective methods of harvesting. Price and value are not equivalent. If the entrepreneur pays what the business is worth, he has not appropriated any value for himself. The difference is determined by information, market behavior, pressures forcing either purchase or sale, and negotiating skills.

THE BUSINESS PLAN

A business plan is a document that articulates the critical aspects, basic assumptions, and financial projections regarding a business venture. It is also the basic document used to interest and attract support—financial and otherwise—for a new business concept. The process of writing a business plan is an invaluable experience, for it will force the entrepreneur to think through his or her business concept in a systematic way.

This chapter will raise and address issues that most entrepreneurs encounter as they prepare their business plans. One of the factors that makes crafting a good plan so difficult is the fact that it has a multitude of purposes. As described, the plan is a blueprint for the company itself and, as such, is intended to help the firm's management. The plan is also typically used to attract potential investors. Finally, the plan may serve as the legal document with which funds are raised. These several uses highlight a constant conflict: To the extent that the plan is a "marketing document" for the company, it is likely to be a more optimistic, one-sided presentation than a critical business analysis. For the purposes of legally raising funds, however, the document needs to contain a full disclosure of risks and legal "boilerplate" (see Chapter 18, "Securities Law and Public Offerings"). Many a prospectus, for instance, contains the phrase—in big bold letters—"This investment is highly speculative and is suitable only for individuals who can afford a total loss of their investment." Thus, it becomes extremely critical to understand exactly what purpose the "plan" is serving and what audience such a purpose implies. Even if the document is clearly written to appeal to potential investors, it is important to know exactly what kind of investor. A busy venture capitalist or other professional investor will be more demanding than a private

This chapter was prepared by Michael J. Roberts.
Copyright © 1988 by the President and Fellows of Harvard College.
Harvard Business School Note 9-389-020.

individual, who rarely invests in new enterprises. Similarly, a commercial banker reading the same document would have a different set of questions. Thus, the first rule is to keep in mind *who* the reader is and make sure the document addresses his or her particular concerns.

The bulk of this chapter will focus on preparing a business plan for the professional investor—venture capitalist or otherwise. A plan that meets the needs of this most demanding investor can be scaled down or used for other private individuals, who may well have professional financial advisors review the document anyway. This plan for investors may well include portions of an internal plan that includes far more detailed operating and contingency plans that would be suitable for investors.

To be clear, however, when we say a business plan, we do *not* mean a legal document for *actually* raising funds, although many entrepreneurs do think of these two documents as identical. First, a prospectus (or "offering memorandum," "investment memorandum," or "offering circular") needs to contain so much legal language and protective boilerplate as to be an ineffective marketing document. Second, we do not recommend proposing a "deal" (exact type and price of the security) in the business plan. Professional investors simply have far more expertise in crafting the security, and pricing is typically a matter of negotiation. Nonetheless, it is important to be clear on how much money you are seeking to raise and how it will be paid back. If money is being sought from less experienced private investors, the situation is more complicated. Not to propose a deal implies negotiating with many separate individuals who may have very different ideas about the type of security they are interested in and how it should be priced.

One approach that can be used to resolve these issues raised by the multiple objectives of the business plan is to follow the distribution of the plan with a more formal offering memorandum. In this way, only those investors who seem genuinely interested are actually solicited. And this second offering memorandum can be used to meet the more rigorous legal requirements of a fund-raising document.

The Plan

The following sections of this chapter will describe the various sections of a standard business plan. Overall, it is important that the plan be relatively short (40 or so pages is appropriate) and clearly written. Do not assume that the reader will be an expert in the technology or market you are interested in. Finally, think of the plan as an argument, for every point you make—the attractiveness of the market, the price you can charge for the product, its competitive advantages—offers evidence to support your claims.

To achieve this level of end product, it is often helpful to get others to read drafts of the plan. Certainly, members of the management team should prepare their section of the plan and read all of the others. Financial advisors or accountants can also play a valuable role. It is also a good idea to review other entrepreneurs' business plans to get a feel for how others have approached the task. If you can, talk to some of these individuals about their experiences writing the plan and raising funds. Finally, if you can speak with lawyers, accountants, and even some investors (whom you won't be targeting), you're bound to learn from them as well.

It is also a good idea to have a plan read by a legal advisor—presumably the same person who will help you incorporate and draft the other legal documents necessary for financing and starting the business. The securities laws are quite complicated, and you'll need expert advice to assure that you're not running afoul of them. (See Chapter 18, "Securities Law and Public Offerings".) Counsel will want to assure that you are not making any claims that could later pose problems (i.e., "Investors are guaranteed an attractive financial return"). In addition, there is some standard boilerplate that will help protect you from possible securities laws violations. Copies of the plans should all be individually numbered and a log kept detailing who received them.

The Executive Summary

These few pages are the *most* critical piece of any business plan. Investors will turn immediately to this section in order to get their first impression of the venture. To ensure that this section encompasses all that it should, it should be written last.

The executive summary must clearly but briefly explain:

- The company's status and its management.
- The company's products or services and the benefits they provide to users.
- The market and competition for the product.
- A summary of the company's financial prospects.
- The amount of money needed, and how it will be used.

The Company

This section should describe the company's origins, objectives, and management. The plan should describe how the company will be organized, who will fill these roles, and what their responsibilities will be. Some background on the founders should be given and their more extensive résumés referenced in an appendix. The "story" of how the company came into being should be briefly told so that potential investors get some sense of its history. The section should describe the current status of the company: number of employees, sales and profits (if any), products, facilities, and so forth. Finally, this section should paint a picture of where the company hopes to go and how it envisions getting there—its strategy.

The Product or Service

Having introduced the product in the previous section, the plan should describe it in more detail here. What needs does the product meet, especially compared to competitor's products. If the product exists and is in use, some detailed descriptions of that usage, the results, and some customer testimonials will prove valuable. If the product has yet to be manufactured, a description of how you intend to make it—and what the key milestones in the process are—is also important. If a patent or proprietary technology is employed, it should be explained here (although the proprietary aspects, of course, should not be divulged).

The Market

A common mistake is to deal with the marketing portion of the business plan in a cursory manner. Investors want evidence that the founders of a company have studied the market, understood it, and indeed are driven by their desire to satisfy its needs. To convey this, the plan should address:

- The size, rate of growth, and purchasing characteristics of the target market. Investors will be interested in—and will want to assure that the entrepreneurs are interested in and understand—market segments, the buying process, and how purchase decisions are made.
- The company's perspective on the market. Investors will be curious about the entrepreneur's perspective on the market. Why do you think the company is bringing something new to the market? What trends in the market does the company see, and what changes does the company anticipate in the future?
- The reaction the company expects from the market. What hurdles does the company expect in introducing its product? How will it overcome them? What features and benefits does the company expect will be particularly popular?

Competition

No business plan is complete without a section that describes the competitive firms and products. Again, investors want to be assured that the entrepreneurs understand whom they will be competing against. Information on competitors' products, prices, and marketing approaches should be included.

Sales and Marketing

This section of the plan should explain the manner in which the product will be sold. The plan should describe how target customers will be identified and how awareness will be built through advertising, promotion, or direct mail. The plan should also detail what distribution channel will be utilized, and how the product will be sold—by a direct sales force, reps, direct mail, and so forth. This section should also address how the company will introduce its product to the marketplace. This might include public relations, advertisement, special promotions, or targeted growth.

Operations

In this section, entrepreneurs should explain how the product will be manufactured: the facilities required, the use of subcontractors, and what equipment will be needed to actually produce the product. In general, investors would prefer to see a firm purchase or subcontract much of its manufacturing needs, at least initially. In addition, it is often desirable to lease facilities. The other aspects of operations, including distribution, should also be touched on.

Financials

In this section, investors expect to see realistic financial projections, typically for a five-year time horizon. The following information should be included: an income statement, balance sheet, cash flow forecast, and break-even analysis. While the five-year forecasts should be relatively detailed, it is also important to highlight the key dimensions of the firm's financial performance—sales, earnings, and cash surplus (or deficit)—in some summary form.

It is critical that the financials be driven by *thoroughly documented assumptions.* For instance, don't just develop a sales forecast. Present detailed assumptions about unit volume and price. The same is true for expenses. This not only gives the investor the data he or she needs to evaluate your plan, it also speaks volumes about your careful thinking. The financials should also clearly state the amount of money being sought and to what uses it will be put.

Investors will also be interested in how the venture plans on turning their cash investment back into cash. That is, what is the anticipated exit route for the investor: a public offering, a sale of the company, or a repurchase of shares by the firm? In the financial section, try to give potential investors some idea of how they can cash out.

While it's impossible to know what's going to happen in the future, investors will familiarize themselves with other firms in the industry in order to develop a sense of the appropriateness of the numbers forecasts. Once they are satisfied that the projections are realistic, investors will use these financials to help them value the firm and calculate a potential price for their investment.

Finally, some would-be entrepreneurs make use of public accounting firms to prepare their financials. They feel that the opportunity to present their projections on a prestigious accounting firm's stationery lends credibility to the numbers, and they may well be right. Some entrepreneurs are also anxious to use this approach to gain access to the network of wealthy private investors with which these accounting firms are well connected. While you may consider this approach on its merits, one point is clear. To use an accounting firm in such a manner is no substitute for having these critical financial skills as part of the venture's start-up team. Someone who is part of the team *must* have the ability to develop income statement and cash flow forecasts and budgets.

Appendix

The résumés of all key personnel and their responsibilities should be included in this section. In preparing the résumés, entrepreneurs should make sure that they portray themselves as a well-balanced team. In addition, any sample product literature, letters from customers or suppliers, and so forth can be included in the appendix.

After the Plan Is Written

When the plan is finished, it's time to distribute it to potential investors. It is wise to avoid simply sending the plan to all the venture capitalists you can find. Investors generally avoid plans that come in "over the transom" and far prefer to look at a plan that has been recommended by a financial advisor, lawyer, or company founder that they know and whose judgment they trust.

There are a number of different sources of capital available to entrepreneurs. They run the gamut from friends and family members, with limited or no experience providing capital, to professional investors, who manage a portfolio of investments in young firms. Each of these sources is attractive for different reasons, and it's up to the entrepreneur to understand the advantages and disadvantages of each. Within each category, *who* you raise money from is vitally important. The ability to attract successful, professional investors will lend credibility to your venture idea and will introduce you to a wide range of helpful contacts. Finally, many of these people are successful because they provide excellent guidance, and it will be to your benefit to avail yourself of it.

Because venture capital is such a visible portion of this spectrum of potential sources, it's worth knowing a bit about it. The venture capital industry is a highly fragmented network of individuals and small firms that accounts for $15 to $20 billion of capital. Other potential investors include Small Business Investment Corporations (SBICs) and the venture capital aims of larger corporations. Firms in the venture capital industry can be distinguished along four basic dimensions:

- The size of the investment pool. As with any industry, venture capital firms differ in the amount of money under management. Large firms might manage 10 to 20 times more capital than smaller firms.
- The stage(s) at which they prefer to invest. Venture capitalists (VCs) tend to specialize in certain phases. Some prefer to invest in the seed and development stage so that they can own a larger part of the venture. Other VCs balk at the risks of this strategy and instead prefer to invest in later-stage companies. Venture capitalists typically divide the investment process into four distinct rounds or stages.
  - Seed: This stage is the highest-risk stage of investment because the company is usually newly organized and lacks an operational track record. In many situations, the company is little more than an idea.
  - Development: This stage is also characterized by high risk. Companies in this stage are usually building a prototype product and exploratory marketing.
  - Revenue: Investments made in this stage are characterized by less risk than those made in the seed and development stages. This is true because more information is available for venture capitalists to consider. Companies seeking funds in this stage usually have completed a prototype and have begun to market it to their customers.

— Profitable: Investments made in this stage are characterized by the least amount of risk. Venture capitalists prefer companies in this round because they are usually seeking capital to expand and grow.

- The minimum and maximum amount allocated in each investment. These amounts range anywhere from $150,000 to $5 million or more. Firms syndicate deals among many different companies to meet investment requests, which may be larger than the maximum amount considered.

- Preferred industries for investment. Venture firms may specialize by industry, believing that their ability to select attractive investments and add value is related to their degree of industry knowledge and expertise. Traditionally, high-technology industries such as microcomputers, telecommunications, and biotechnology have been popular with venture capitalists. More recently, low-tech and service sector businesses have become increasingly popular.

With these differences in mind, it's helpful to understand how venture capitalists tend to evaluate deals. They are quite busy and will rarely spend more than 5 to 10 minutes on an initial review of a plan. During this brief time, they will read the executive summary to get an understanding of the company's status and goals.

Plans that do not meet their criteria are rejected. Plans that seem to present an interesting investment opportunity are reviewed further. During this phase, venture capitalists try to understand and evaluate the key fundamentals of the business. These include:

- The management team. Professional investors are attracted by individuals with proven industry expertise and management ability, and some start-up experience is even better.

- The product/market. Venture capitalists like products that exist (in real life, not just in someone's mind), can be manufactured, and that have some evidence of acceptance into the market.

- The financials. Providers of capital like to see that their investment is likely to turn into value for them, typically within a three- to seven-year time horizon.

For all of these reasons, it is worth devoting some time and energy to a strategy to "get in the door." A 50-pound document and a form letter addressed to "To Whom It May Concern" is clearly a bad strategy. An introduction from a lawyer, another venture capitalist, or an entrepreneur whom the firm has backed are all superior options. Learn about the venture firm, its past investments, its strategy, and its people, and try to position your proposal in a way that fits with these elements.

Still, the process of evaluating a business plan is an imprecise art, not a science. Venture capitalists—who specialize in judging the potential of a business—make many investments that fail to live up to their expectations. Thus, many investors will use their "intuition" about a market, a business, and the entrepreneur to help make their decision.

Summary

Essentially, the plan serves as a vehicle to get you in the door to talk to investors. They will probe you about the plan and also about your career and management experiences, and those of any other members of the team. A professional investor will present a good many potential problems. After all, the road to starting and managing a new venture is littered with unanticipated problems and difficult challenges. By gauging how you respond to the issues inherent in the fund-raising process, the investor will be able to judge your diligence and business sense as well as the "fire in your belly"—sure to be as critical a factor in your success as a well-crafted plan.

5

THE LEGAL FORMS OF ORGANIZATION

One of the key issues an entrepreneur must resolve at the outset of a new venture concerns the legal form of organization the enterprise should adopt. This decision is driven chiefly by the objectives of the entrepreneur and the firm's investors, in terms of tax status, exposure to legal liabilities, and flexibility in the operation and financing of the business. The choices are made difficult by the inherent tradeoffs in the law. In order to get the most favorable tax treatment, one must often give up some protection from liability exposure, flexibility, or both.

This chapter will describe the various alternative forms of organization, and the advantages and disadvantages of each. This chapter will only cover the most fundamental elements of the various forms; a competent accountant or attorney should be consulted if such a decision presents itself.

Overview

The most prevalent legal forms of organization include:

- The sole proprietorship
- The partnership
  - general partnership
  - limited partnership

Professor Michael J. Roberts prepared this chapter as the basis for class discussion rather than to illustrate either effective or ineffective handling of an administrative situation.

– The corporation
  • the "regular" C corporation
  • the S corporation (formerly Subchapter S)
  • the limited liability company

The two most basic differences between these various legal forms of organization are the tax status each is afforded, and the protection from liabilities each form offers to the owners. This can be seen most easily by briefly examining the C corporation and the sole proprietorship as legal forms.

Sole Proprietorship

The sole proprietorship is the oldest and simplest form of organization: a person who undertakes a business without any of the formalities associated with other forms of organization; the individual and the business are one and the same for tax and legal liability purposes.

The proprietorship does not pay taxes as a separate entity. The individual reports all income and deductible expenses for the business on schedule C of the personal income tax return. Note that these earnings of the business are taxed at the individual level whether or not they are actually distributed in cash. There is no vehicle for sheltering income.

For liability purposes, the individual and the business are also one and the same. Thus, legal claimants can pursue the personal property of the proprietor, not simply the assets which are utilized in the business.

The C Corporation

The "C" corporation is the most common form of large business organization for several reasons.

First, in contrast to the point made above regarding the sole proprietorship, the firm's owners are personally protected from liability. Thus, in the case of the Exxon Valdez, for instance, even if the damages against Exxon had bankrupted the company, the courts could not have pursued the individual shareholders for further damages—liability is limited to the extent of investment in the firm. There is a corporate shell or "veil" which can only be "pierced" in the event of fraud.

In exchange for this status, the C corporation is considered a taxpaying entity. Because the firm does not get any deduction for dividends paid, the earnings of a corporation are thus taxed twice. The current maximum rate on corporate income is 35 percent; the maximum rate on individual income is likely to be approximately 40 percent when federal and state taxes are considered. Thus, $1.00 of pretax corporate income becomes $0.39 when it is distributed as dividends and taxed at the personal level. This double taxation creates powerful incentives for those enterprises that anticipate distributing earnings to utilize a tax-advantaged form. Conversely, the maximum corporate rate is lower than the maximum personal rate, creating an incentive for those entities that do not anticipate distributing earnings to utilize a corporate form. Indeed, if the firm is to be sold, the sale of shares may be eligible for taxation at the even lower capital gains rate.

Other forms of organization can best be understood in relation to these two forms. After discussing the tax status and liability protection afforded by each of the other forms, we will return to discuss a series of other factors that distinguish these forms, and which should be considered when selecting a legal form under which to operate a business.

Partnerships

Partnerships are business entities that consist of two or more owners.

The General Partnership

A partnership is defined as "a voluntary association of two or more persons to carry on as co-owners of a business for profit." A partnership is more complicated than merely a collection of individuals. The partners must resolve, and should set down in writing, their agreement on a number of issues:

- The amount and nature of their respective capital contributions. One partner might contribute cash, another a patent, and a third property and cash.
- The allocation of the business' profits and losses.
- Salaries and drawings against profits.
- Management responsibilities.
- Consequences of withdrawal, retirement, disability, or death of a partner.
- Means of dissolution and liquidation of the partnership.

A partnership is treated like a proprietorship for tax and liability purposes. Earnings are distributed according to the partnership agreement, and taxes paid at the personal level on the partner's share. For liability purposes, each of the partners is jointly and severally liable. Thus, a damaged party may pursue either or both of the partners for any amount—the claim may not be proportional to invested capital or the distribution of earnings.

The Limited Partnership

Limited partnerships are a hybrid form of organization. A limited partnership is a partnership which has *both* limited and general partners.

- The general partner assumes the management responsibility *and* unlimited liability for the business and must have at least a 1 percent interest in profits and losses.
- The limited partner has no voice in management and is legally liable only for the amount of capital contribution plus any other debt specifically accepted.

In a limited partnership, the general partner may be a corporation (a corporate general partner). In situations where a corporation is the sole general partner, in order to ensure that there are sufficient assets to cover the unlimited liability which the general partner must assume, the corporate general partner must have a net worth of at least $250,000 or 10 percent of the total capitalization of the partnership, whichever is less.

Note that in a limited partnership, profits and losses may be allocated differently from each other. That is, even if profits are allocated 20 percent to the general partner and 80 percent to the limiteds, the limiteds may get 99 percent of the losses. However, losses are deductible only up to the amount of capital at risk. Note that the distribution of profits is subject to all sorts of creative structuring, such as that which is often observed in certain venture capital and real estate partnerships: The limiteds get 99 percent of the profits until they have gotten their capital back, and then the general partner gets 20 percent and the limiteds only 80 percent. This flexibility is an important advantage of the partnership form.

The S Corporation and the Limited Liability Company

The S corporation is a creature of the law which is afforded the tax status of a partnership, but the protection from legal liability of a corporation. And, a limited liability company is a new creature designed to afford the same benefits. By this point, you will have concluded that there is no free lunch, and that this advantageous treatment must come at some cost—the IRS being unlikely to give up its ability to tax corporate entities out of the goodness of its heart. And, indeed there are such limitations.

In order to qualify for S corporation status, the organization must meet a number of rather restrictive conditions:

- have only one class of stock, although differences in voting rights are allowed.
- be a domestic corporation, owned wholly by U.S. citizens, and derive no more than 80 percent of its revenues from non-U.S. sources.
- have 75 or fewer stockholders.
- derive no more than 25 percent of revenues from passive sources, i.e., interest, dividends, rents, and royalties.
- have only individuals, estates and certain trusts as shareholders, i.e., no corporations or partnerships.

The election of S corporation tax status requires the unanimous, timely consent of all shareholders. This status may be terminated by unanimous election, or if one of the above mentioned conditions is broken.

The limited liability company (LLC) is similar to an S corporation in that it enjoys the tax advantages of a partnership and the liability protections of a corporation. While state laws differ somewhat, an LLC is like an S corporation, with none of the restrictions on number or type of shareholders. The LLC is similar to a partnership in that the LLC's operating agreement (the equivalent of a partnership agreement) may distribute profits and losses in a variety of ways, not necessarily in proportion to capital contributions.

How to Decide

There are a number of criteria which can be used to help choose a legal form of organization.

Who will the investors and owners be? If the investors and owners will be a small group of individuals, a partnership of some form is clearly a possibility, as is an S corp. or LLC. If, however, it is anticipated that the business will require venture capital or other types of professional investors, a corporation may be more suitable. This is because venture capital firms cannot be shareholders in S corps (because the VC firms are usually partnerships, which can not hold shares in an S corp.). In addition, the potential tax liability of a flow-through entity makes VCs and their limited partners nervous. For this reason, VCs do not typically invest in LLCs. Finally, a corporation offers the most flexibility in incentive stock option plans, as well as various types of preferred securities, all of which may be important in a venture-backed, high potential venture. Finally, a public offering will most likely require a C corporation.

What are the capital requirements and cash flow characteristics of the business likely to be? If the venture is projected to create large losses in the early years, then there may be some benefit to passing those losses through to investors, if the investors are in a position to use them to offset income and thus reduce taxes. This would favor the partnership or LLC. Similarly, if the business intends to generate substantial cash flow and return it to investors as the primary means of creating value for investors, then a flow-through entity is attractive. If, however, the business will require cash investment over the long term, and value is intended to be harvested through a sale or public offering, then a C corp. is probably most attractive.

What is the time frame for the life of the business? Partnerships dissolve upon the death or retirement of any one of the partners. Corporations, on the other hand, have a continuity of life that goes beyond that of any of the management or investors.

Other Tax Issues

As you have no doubt gathered, tax implications are an important factor in the choice of an entity. Indeed, the incentives of the tax code give rise to certain tactics which can be risky. For instance, the fact that distributed earnings of the corporation are doubly taxed gives rise to an incentive for the owners to pay themselves all of those profits as compensation, which is deductible as an expense to the corporation (unlike dividends) and is thus, not taxed twice. The IRS has certain rules on "reasonable" compensation designed to protect against just such behavior.

Note that the tax on individuals in "flow-through entities" like partnerships and LLCs is on the share of income *earned*, not cash *distributed*:

- The income of the partnership is taxed at the personal level of the individual whether or not any cash is actually distributed.
- The distribution of cash out of income or retained earnings is not itself a taxable event. The only time when cash distributions are a taxable event is when the cash distribution exceeds the partners' basis in the partnership.
- The basis is equal to the amount of capital originally contributed, plus the amount of income on which tax is paid, less any cash distributions. (Example: An individual invests $100 in a partnership, and his share of income in one year equals $30. He must pay tax on this $30 at the personal rate. His basis is now $130. If he receives a $20 cash distribution, his basis drops to $110.)

Summary

Of course, a business may move through many forms in its lifetime. A sole proprietorship may become a partnership and finally a C corporation. A limited partnership may become an LLC and then a C corporation. Rest assured that each of these changes will require considerable legal work and administrative burden for the current management and owners of the firm. The advantages of the right form of organization at each particular stage certainly may warrant this series of changes. On the other hand, high-potential ventures on a fast-track do not want to lose time and focus by getting tied up jumping through these hoops in the last moments before a financing. Entrepreneurs would do well to consider the likely evolution of their business before selecting a form of organization, and should certainly consult with a qualified tax attorney or accountant before making this important choice.

6

THE ROAD WELL TRAVELED

While the cases in this text present a fair spectrum of experiences, they still constitute a relatively small sample. Our students regularly want to anchor their own aspirations to a broader sample of experience. Who starts a business and becomes an entrepreneur? When and how do they do so? Are they glad they did? What makes an entrepreneur successful?

With these questions in mind, we have conducted a broader based survey of the entrepreneurial experience (see "The Road Well Traveled," by Amar Bhidé, HBS note 9-396-277 for a fuller report of the findings). This survey included two samples of HBS entrepreneurs, as well as a survey of 100 entrepreneurs from the "*Inc.* 500" companies. This chapter will relate some of the broad conclusions from that work.

Almost Everyone Can

It doesn't take an exceptional MBA graduate to start his or her own business. This survey reveals that many MBAs have been doing so for a great many years. The trend clearly predates the current popularity of the entrepreneurial folk heroes. The entrepreneurs surveyed don't appear obviously less capable of holding down a job than the rest of their classmates. They do work for several years for someone else; they don't switch jobs particularly frequently; and they don't start their businesses because they had a disagreement or have been fired by their employers.

Amar Bhidé prepared this chapter as the basis for classroom discussion rather than to illustrate effective or ineffective handling of an administrative situation.

Harvard Business School Note 9-898-205.

The self-employed do regard themselves as being greater risk takers than their classmates, but this may simply be an ex post facto assessment: Because they are more on their own, they suppose that they must have taken more risk.

Many individuals in the population at large may lack the basic drive to start a business, but such individuals are unlikely to apply to business school or secure admission if they do. Moreover, the wide range of potential opportunities that entrepreneurs can pursue allows many different types of individuals to succeed. For instance, the person who would flop as film producer may have just the right personality to start a money management firm for conservative clients. Given a baseline of ambition and business skills, therefore, becoming an entrepreneur is more a matter of finding the right fit between the individual and the opportunity than it is of conforming to an idealized entrepreneurial type.

The "*Inc.* 500" interviews and this survey should also reassure those who lack self-confidence in their creative abilities and prescience. Entrepreneurs seldom invent and market unique products; rather, they build their ventures around incremental innovations and modifications. They usually take advantage of industry changes that others initiate rather than lead or force change themselves. They don't even appear to get an especially early start in capitalizing on new trends—they tend to enter industries in their growth phase, not in their infancy.

The Rewards Appear Worthwhile

Albeit at the cost of somewhat greater stress, almost all entrepreneurs appear to find fulfillment in their work. Many also report significant financial rewards, turning modest initial net worth into millions a decade or so after graduation. Of course, not everyone did so, but starting their own businesses put the entrepreneurs in a position where a combination of luck and talent could lead to great wealth in a relatively short period of time. Few jobs in established firms offer as much potential, except for very senior executives.

And What's the Alternative?

Working in a large corporation is unlikely to offer enough long-term security or opportunity for advancement to compensate for the more limited financial opportunities. The data suggest that large companies, with their numerous entry-level positions, are a magnet for graduating MBAs. As the years pass, however, the typically ambitious and hard-driving MBAs find that the supply of the positions they seek is small compared to the demand. Let's assume (generously) that each of the 500 largest companies in the United States has 10 positions that an MBA would be satisfied with, 20 years after graduation. If the net retirement rate in these positions is of the order of 10 percent annually, then there are only 500 positions that the tens of thousands of MBAs who graduate every year can compete for.

Before large corporations got lean and mean, folklore held that managers who didn't climb to the top of the corporate ladder could rest on middle management rungs. Much data, however, suggests that even in the bygone era of corporate benevolence, "up-or-out" was the norm for many MBAs. Those in large companies who weren't promoted either left or were pushed out to make way for younger, cheaper, and hungrier replacements. This migratory process is likely to accelerate in the future for several reasons:

- The huge growth in the supply of MBAs (more than 60,000 degrees are now granted in the United States every year).
- The thinning of middle management ranks.
- The adoption of up-or-out, which has long been the de facto reality in many large firms, as an explicit general rule.

Don't Rush—or Wait Forever

Only a handful of MBA graduates start their businesses right out of school. The peak period for starting a business appears to be 5 to 10 years after graduation for alumni starting "traditional" ventures and somewhat longer for professional service entrepreneurs. The advantages of waiting seem to include:

- Exposure to opportunities. The data suggest that most entrepreneurs exploit opportunities they perceive in the course of their jobs rather than through top-down research. Besides, the passage of time increases the number of ideas that prospective entrepreneurs encounter (or that are brought to their attention) and therefore the likelihood of finding a good one.
- Time to accumulate personal capital to seed the venture.
- Building of credibility and relationships with potential clients, especially for professional service entrepreneurs.

At the same time, waiting too long may not be optimal. There is little evidence that very deep experience matters, except perhaps in starting professional service firms. This survey also suggests that the longer graduates put off self-employment, the more likely they are to start personal consulting practices rather than launch larger-scale traditional ventures. Although some individuals may want to operate solo, casual observation suggests that many are forced into independent consulting because they lost their jobs, don't have the idea or the energy to start any other kind of business, and need to generate income quickly. Therefore, while it is inadvisable to jump on the first opportunity that comes by, it probably helps to start looking early, begin thinking about start-up ideas, and cultivate the networks that might provide leads, rather than have to scramble in the face of an involuntary job transition.

Know Where the Fish Are

Entrepreneurially inclined individuals will tend to generate lots of ideas for a business, but they will have limited time to evaluate them, especially while holding down a full-time job. Evaluating potential opportunities is also challenging because reliable information can be difficult to obtain in the turbulent markets that often hold the most potential. The aspiring entrepreneur therefore needs to develop the capacity to weed out the obviously unusable ideas quickly and focus on the opportunities that are more likely to work. The experienced entrepreneurs surveyed suggest several rules of thumb for evaluating opportunities rapidly. For example, the typical entrepreneur who starts off without a proprietary, blockbuster idea should look for:

- Markets in flux rather than stable or mature markets. Entrepreneurs should ask themselves "Why wouldn't this concept have worked five years ago?" and be suspicious of situations where there has been no recent external change that has created the opportunity.
- Industries with low capital requirements and flat or declining returns to scale so that the start-up does not confront large incumbents.
- Markets where customers will pay a significant premium for customization and personalized service.
- Products or services where the unit sale is large enough to support a direct sales effort.

Prepare to Travel Steerage Class

Business school graduates enjoy some advantages in raising capital but can raise significant amounts only if they have a powerful concept for establishing sustainable advantages in a large market. Entrepreneurs usually do not often have this kind of compelling vision and must therefore rely on personal resources or relatively small amounts of capital raised from others. This lack of initial capital also forces entrepreneurs to operate in quite a different mode than they may have been used to as employees of established companies. For instance, they have to do without administrative support and infrastructures and perform many mundane or menial tasks themselves. They can't afford to advertise widely or implement the marketing approaches that are routine in large companies. They may have to live with marginal or unqualified employees and the lack of stimulation and feedback that talented colleagues can provide. Because they lack standby lines of credit and trained financial staff, cash flow is a constant concern.

Besides setting the appropriate expectations, the aspiring entrepreneur can prepare for the transition from employee to business owner by observing how others successfully make do with less. One suggestion is to build a "play book" of ways to generate free publicity, project a big company image, find employees who are "diamonds in the rough" and make the most of them, collect receivables early and stretch the payables, negotiate bank loans, and so on.

Maintain Low Personal Overhead

After having lived on student budgets, MBAs naturally feel the urge to enjoy a better lifestyle after they graduate. But high personal spending patterns can impair your chances of succeeding in an entrepreneurial career. As we have seen, the majority of MBA graduates cannot rely on starting businesses with other people's money and need personal savings to finance their ventures. Even those few who do have a venture that others are willing to fund can enhance their credibility and negotiating position if they commit personal funds to get the enterprise rolling. Moreover, whether or not a venture is self-funded, the entrepreneur can more easily nurture it through its start-up phase if he or she has low personal overhead and does not need to draw down funds to support a luxurious lifestyle.

Learn to Sell

The data suggest that face-to-face selling is a crucial skill: For most ventures to have any chance of success, the entrepreneur has to be able to call on a customer and secure an order for a product or service that usually performs the same functions as rival offerings. Such selling skills are often not well developed among MBAs. Although they all "sell" themselves to colleges, graduate schools, and employers and some may even have worked in a sales function, they will rarely have faced the special sales challenges confronted by entrepreneurs. These challenges include:

- The lack of a name or track record. Entrepreneurs don't have the entree that graduating MBAs have with recruiters or that IBM sales representatives have with MIS departments. Also, when they do get through a prospect's door, they are likely to face the "How do we know you are going to be around?" question.
- Extreme asymmetry of power. Graduating MBAs and IBM sales representatives have some leverage with recruiters and computer buyers who are predisposed to see the talent or product offered as necessary, valuable, and distinctive. Entrepreneurs, we have seen, are generally in a much weaker position—their products or services often represent a discretionary purchase, and their offerings lack inherent distinctiveness.
- The real-time integration of selling with marketing and strategy formulation. The data suggest that entrepreneurs often differentiate their offering by customizing features or ancillary services. And, to the extent that access to prospects is limited, the entrepreneurs have to make on-the-spot decisions about what features to offer, what to charge, and so on—which may have long-term implications for a firm's marketing and other strategies. The IBM salesperson, in contrast, operates off product and pricing policies that others have previously made and generally does not have to formulate strategy on the fly.

Developing the appropriate selling skills therefore requires work not only on the basics (such as eliciting information, objection handling, and closing) but also on attitudes. Entrepreneurs must learn, my interviews with the "*Inc.* 500" founders suggest, to utterly subjugate their egos. They have to deal with frequent rejection, suppress the desire to show how smart they are by scoring debating points, be willing to capitulate to unreasonable demands, and sometimes, as one founder put it, to beg for the order. These are typically not the reflexes MBAs develop in classrooms or in large companies.

Expect Major Course Changes

Only a few entrepreneurial voyages resemble those of spaceships launched with all the fuel they need to attain stable orbit after liftoff. Most begin, we have seen, with ideas and resources that cannot take them very far. They have little cash and weak personnel. Their profits derive more from the entrepreneur's hustle or temporary market dislocations than from durable competitive advantages. Moreover, approaches that help an entrepreneur get started with minimal resources often do not lead to a self-sustaining enterprise. The personal drive and attention that win over early customers, for instance, are not enough to sustain a durable franchise. If an entrepreneur wishes to build a business for the long haul, he or she has to consider making major changes. The personnel may have to be upgraded and new controls and systems introduced. Similarly, an underlying business concept may have to be restructured to establish sustainable advantages and realize economies of scale and scope.

Know What You Want

But why should an entrepreneur want a durable enterprise in the first place? There are some obvious trade-offs: Building a self-sustaining enterprise frees entrepreneurs from the constant effort of keeping their ventures going and gives them the option of harvesting the fruits of their past labors. At the same time, building such an enterprise often entails making long-term bets. That is, it involves risk. Unlike a solo consulting practice, which generates cash from the start but cannot outlive the entrepreneur, the venture needs continued investment in working capital to build sustainable advantages. And many years may pass before the entrepreneur sees any payoff.

This survey of entrepreneurs shows that individuals find attractive financial and psychological rewards from both large and small ventures, those that rely on the entrepreneur's personal capabilities as well as those with independent structural advantages. Apparently, decisions about what business to start and whether and how to grow it, are to a considerable degree matters of personal preference. Possibly the greatest luxury an entrepreneurial career affords lies in the freedom it gives the entrepreneur to pursue his or her own goals—provided, of course, that those goals have been well thought out in the first place. You have to know what you want.

R&R

During the summer of 1983, Bob Reiss observed with interest the success in the Canadian market of a new board game called *Trivial Pursuit.*® His years of experience selling games in the United States had taught him a rough rule of thumb: The sales of a game in the United States tended to be approximately 10 times those of sales in Canada. Since Trivial Pursuit had sold 100,000 copies north of the border, Reiss thought that trivia games might soon boom in the United States and that this might represent a profitable opportunity for him.

Reiss's Background

After his graduation from Harvard Business School in 1956, Reiss began working for a company that made stationery products. His main responsibility was to build a personalized pencil division, and he suggested that he be paid a low salary and a high sales commission. He was able to gain an excellent understanding of that market and by 1959 could start on his own as an independent manufacturer's representative in the same industry. His direct contact with stores that sold stationery products revealed that many of them were beginning to sell adult games. He decided to specialize in those products.

In 1973, Reiss sold his representative business to a small American Stock Exchange company in the needlecraft business in exchange for shares. He then set up a game manufacturing division and ran it for that company, building sales to $12 million in three years.

This case was prepared by Jose-Carlos Jarillo Mossi under the direction of Howard H. Stevenson.

Reiss decided to go into business for himself again in 1979 and left the company. He incorporated under the name of R&R and worked with the help of a secretary from a rented office in New York; Reiss promised himself that he would keep overhead very low, even in good years, and never own or be responsible for a factory. In addition to being a traditional manufacturer's representative, he did some consulting for toy manufacturers, using his extensive knowledge of the market.

The Toy and Game Industry

One of the main characteristics of the toy industry was that products generally had very short life cycles, frequently of no more than two years. Fads extended to whole categories of items: One class of toys would sell well for a couple of years and then fade away. Products that were part of categories tended to ride with the fate of that category, regardless to some extent of their intrinsic merit. Many new products were introduced every year, which made the fight for shelf space aggressive.

Promotional plans for a new product were a key factor in buy or no-buy decisions of the major retailers. At the same time, fewer and fewer retailers were dominating more of the market every year. The largest one, Toys "Я" Us, for example, had 14 percent of the entire market in 1984. The success of a product was often based on less than a dozen retailers.

A few large manufacturers were also becoming dominant in the industry, because they could afford the expensive TV promotional campaigns that retailers demanded of the products they purchased. Billing terms to retailers were extremely generous compared to other industries, thus increasing the need for financial strength. Financing terms ran from a low of 90 days to 9 to 12 months. In general, major retailers were reluctant to buy from new vendors with narrow product lines unless they felt that the volume potential was enormous. On the other hand, the large manufacturers tended to require a long lead time for introducing new products, typically on the order of 18 to 24 months.

The industry was also highly seasonal. Most final sales to the public were made in the four weeks prior to Christmas. Retailers decided what to carry for the Christmas season during the preceding January through March. There was a growing tendency among them, however, not to accept delivery until the goods were needed, in effect using the manufacturer as their warehouse.

The Trivia Game Opportunity

Trivial Pursuit was developed in Canada and introduced there in 1980. Its 1983 sales were exceptionally strong, especially for a product that had been promoted primarily via word of mouth. The game was introduced in the United States at the Toy Fair in February 1983 by Selchow & Righter, makers of Scrabble, under license from Horn & Abbot in Canada. Earlier, the game had been turned down by Parker Bros. and Bradley, the two largest game manufacturers in the United States.

Trivial Pursuit in the United States had a $19 wholesale price, with a retail price varying from $29.95 to $39.95, about 200 percent to 300 percent more expensive than comparable board games. Selchow was not known as a strong marketer and had no TV advertising or public relations budget for the game. The initial reaction at the Toy Fair in February had been poor. Yet by August the game had started moving at retail.

Reiss thought that if the success of Trivial Pursuit in Canada spilled over to the United States, the large game companies would eventually produce and market their own similar products. This would generate popular interest in trivia games in general and constitute a window of opportunity for him. The only trivia game in the market as of September 1983 was Trivial Pursuit. Two small firms had announced their entries and were taking orders for the next season. Bob Reiss decided to design and market his own trivia game.

Developing the Concept

Reiss's first task was to find an interesting theme, one that would appeal to as broad an audience as possible. On one hand, he wanted to capitalize on the new "trivia" category that Trivial Pursuit would create; on the other, he wanted to be different, and therefore could not use a topic already covered by that game, such as movies or sports. Further, his game would have its own rules, yet be playable on the Trivial Pursuit board.

As was his custom, Reiss discussed these ideas with some of his closest friends in the manufacturer's representative business. Over the years, he had found them a source of good ideas. One of the reps suggested television as a topic. Reiss saw immediately that this had great potential: Not only did it have a broad appeal (the average American family watches over seven hours of TV per day), it offered a great PR opportunity. A strong PR campaign would be needed since Reiss knew clearly that he was not going to be able to even approach the advertising budgets of the large manufacturers, which would probably surpass $1 million just for their own trivia games.

Because licensing was common in the toy industry and was a way to obtain both an easily recognizable name and a partner who could help promote the product, Reiss realized he could add strength and interest to his project if he could team up with the publishers of *TV Guide*. This magazine had the highest diffusion in the United States, approaching 18 million copies sold each week. It reached more homes than any other publication and could be called a household name.

On October 17, 1983, Reiss sent a letter, printed below, to Mr. Eric Larson, publisher of *TV Guide*.

Mr. Eric Larson, Publisher   October 17, 1983
TV Guide
P.O. Box 500
Radnor, PA 19088

Dear Mr. Larson:

I am a consultant in the game industry and former owner of a game company.

Briefly, I would like to talk to you about creating a game and marketing plan for a *TV GUIDE* TRIVIA GAME.

In 1984, trivia games will be a major classification of the toy industry. I'm enclosing copy of a forthcoming ad that will introduce a game based on the 60 years of *Time* magazine. I am the marketer of this game and have received a tremendous response to the game, both in orders and future publicity.

This project can benefit both of us, and I would like to explore the opportunities.

Sincerely,
Robert S. Reiss

In a follow-up phone conversation, Mr. Bill Deitch, assistant to the publisher of the magazine, asked Reiss for some detailed explanation on the idea. Reiss sent the following proposal:

Mr. Bill Deitch   November 14, 1983
TV GUIDE
P.O. Box 500
Radnor, PA 19088

Dear Mr. Deitch:

In response to our phone conversation, I will attempt to briefly outline a proposal to do a TV Trivia Game by *TV Guide.*

WHY A TV GAME? It is a natural follow-up to the emerging craze of trivia games that is sweeping the country. This category should be one of the "hot" categories in the toy/game industry in 1984. This type of game got its start in Canada three years ago with the introduction of Trivial Pursuit. It continues to be the rage in Canada and was licensed in the United States this year. It is currently the top selling nonelectronic game. It retails from $29.95 to $39.95 and is projected to sell 1 million units. It is not TV promoted. The *Time* Game, with 8,000 questions covering six general subject areas, only began to ship two weeks ago and had an unprecedented initial trade buy, particularly with no finished sample available for prior inspection.

WILL TV GUIDE BE JUST ANOTHER TRIVIA GAME? No. The next step is to do specialty subjects. Trivial Pursuit has just done a Motion Picture Game with excellent success. Our research tells us that a TV-oriented game would have the broadest national appeal.

THE MARKETS. This type of game has wide appeal in that it is nonsexual and is of interest to adults and children. We feel we can place it in over 10,000 retail outlets ranging from upscale retailers like Bloomingdale's and Macy's to mass merchants like Toys " Я " Us, Sears, Penney, Kmart, Target, etc. There is also a good mail-order market. The market is particularly receptive to good playing, social interactive games at this time. Video games are in a state of decline as their novelty has worn off. (To say nothing about profits.)

WHO WILL DEVELOP THE GAME? Alan Charles, a professional game developer who did the *Time* Game, is free at this moment to do work on the project. He has satisfied the strict standards Time, Inc. has set for putting its name on a product and mine for play value and product graphics in a highly competitive market. . . . No easy task.

WHO WILL PRODUCE AND MARKET THE GAME? There are two options for producing the game.

1. Give it to an established game company who would assume all financial risk as well as production and distribution responsibilities. Under this set-up, *TV Guide* would get a royalty on all goods sold.

2. *TV Guide* assumes all financial responsibilities for game. Production and shipping would be handled by a contract manufacturer. Bob Reiss would be responsible for hiring and supervising a national sales force to sell the game. This is not an unusual option, and I do have experience in this. All sales are on a commission basis. This way, *TV Guide* gets the major share of the profits.

   Attached exhibit explores some rough profit numbers for *TV Guide,* via both options.

POSITIONING OF GAME. We see the game as noncompetitive to Trivial Pursuit and *Time* Magazine Game. It can be developed to retail at $14.95, as opposed to $39.95 for Trivial Pursuit and $29.95 for *Time.* (Mass merchants generally discount from these list prices.) The TV Game should be able to be played by owners of both games as well as on its own. The name *TV Guide* is important to the credibility of the product. Sales of licensed products have been growing at geometric rates in the last decade. Consumers are more comfortable buying a product with a good name behind it.

PROMOTION OF GAME. Pricing of the product will have an ad allowance built into it. This will allow the retailers to advertise in their own catalog, tabloids and/or newspaper ads. An important part of promotion should be ads in *TV Guide.* Ads can be handled two ways: one, with mail-order coupon and profits accruing to *TV Guide;* the other, with listing of retailers carrying the item. As you have so many regional splits, the listing could be rather extensive. Financially, you would probably opt for the first option on a royalty arrangement and the second if you owned the product.

This product lends itself perfectly to an extensive public relations program. This is an excellent product for radio stations to promote. This should be pursued vigorously.

BENEFITS TO TV GUIDE

- Profits from royalties or manufacturing.
- Extensive publicity through wide distribution on U.S. retail counter, including the prestigious retailers as well as the volume ones. This is the unique type of product that can bridge this gap.
- Good premium for your clients. Can be excellent premium for TV stations. Can be used as a circulation builder. In projecting profits, I have not included premiums. The numbers can be big, but they are difficult to count on.

TIMING. To effectively do business in 1984, all contracts must be done and a prototype developed for the American Toy Fair, which takes place in early February 1984. Shipments need not be made until late spring.

WHO IS BOB REISS? He is a graduate of Columbia College and Harvard Business School who started his own national rep firm in 1959, specializing in adult games when it became a distinct category in 1968. He sold his company in 1973 to an American Stock Exchange company. He remained there for five years and built Reiss Games to a dominant position in the adult-game field. For the last three years, he has been consulting in the game/toy industry and recently acted as broker in the sale of one of his clients, Pente Games, to Parker Bros.

I am enclosing some articles that have a bearing on the subject matter. I think what is needed, as soon as possible, is a face-to-face meeting, where we can discuss in greater detail all aspects of this proposal as well as responsibilities for all parties.

Sincerely,

Robert S. Reiss

RSR/ck

encl.

Rough Profit Potentials to TV Guide

Assumptions

1. Average wholesale cost of $7.15 after all allowances. (This would allow department stores and mail order to sell at $15. Discounters would sell at $9.95 to $11.95.)
2. Cost to manufacture, $3 each.
3. Royalty rate of 10 percent. (Range is 6 percent to 10 percent, depending on licensor support and name. Assuming 10 percent, based on fact you would run No Cost ads in *TV Guide*.)
4. Mail-order retail in *TV Guide* is $14.95, and you would pay $4 for goods. Postage and handling would be a wash with small fee charged to customer.

Option I: Royalty Basis
Projected retail sales: 500,000 units.
*Royalty to *TV Guide* of $357,500.
Mail-order sales: 34,000 units. (.002 pull on 17 million
circulation.) Based on full-page ad with coupon. It is extremely
difficult to project mail-order sales without testing—too many
variables. However, this is a product that is ideal for your
audience.
*Profit to *TV Guide* of $372,300.

Option II: You Own Goods
Costs: (rough estimate)

Manufacture	$	3.00
Royalties to inventor		.36
Fulfillment		.30
Sales costs		1.43
Amortization of start-up costs		.10
Total cost	$	5.19
Profit per unit	$	1.96
Profit on 500,000 units		$980,000.00

(Does not include cost of money.)

Another phone conversation followed in which *TV Guide* showed a clear interest in pursuing the subject. Reiss answered with a new letter on December 12, 1983, that outlined clearly the steps that had to be followed by both parties should they want to go ahead with the venture. Reiss had to send still another letter with a long list of personal references that *TV Guide* could contact. *TV Guide* finally opted to be a licensor, not a manufacturer. They would give Bob Reiss a contract for him to manufacture the game or farm it out to an established manufacturer, provided he stayed involved with the project. *TV Guide* would receive a royalty that would escalate with volume. Royalties were normally paid quarterly, over shipments; Reiss, however, proposed to pay over money collected, which *TV Guide* accepted. As part of the final deal, *TV Guide* would insert, at no cost, five ads in the magazine worth $85,000 each. These would be "cooperative ads"; that is, the names of the stores selling the game in the area of each edition would also be displayed. Reiss thought that including the names of the stores at no cost to them would be a good sales argument and would help ensure a wide placement of the product.

Developing the *TV Guide* Trivia Game

The actual game was designed by a professional inventor, whom Reiss knew, in exchange for a royalty of 5 percent—decreasing to 3 percent with volume—per game sold. No upfront monies were paid or royalties guaranteed. Although the inventor delivered the package design in just a few weeks, the questions to be asked were not yet formulated, and Reiss realized he could not do this alone. *TV*

Guide's management insisted that their employees should develop them. Reiss would pay per question for each of the 6,000 questions he needed; employees could moonlight on nights and weekends. Reiss felt it was important to put questions and answers in books rather than cards like Trivial Pursuit. The cost would be considerably lower, and the most serious bottleneck in manufacturing—collating the cards—would be eliminated. Overall, the presentation of the game tried to capitalize on the well-known *TV Guide* name. The game also lent itself well to this approach, as the question books imitated the appearance of *TV Guide* magazine.

Initially, Reiss had not wanted to include a board with the game; he wanted people to use Trivial Pursuit's board and had made sure that the rules of the new game would take this into account. However, *TV Guide* wanted a complete game of its own, not just supplementary questions to be played on someone else's game. Another advantage of including a board, Reiss realized, was that a higher price could be charged.

Since *TV Guide* had opted for being merely a licensor, it was Reiss's responsibility to set up all the operations needed to take the game to market in time for the 1984 season, and there were only two months left until the February Toy Fair, where the game had to be introduced.

His first consideration was financial. He estimated that the fixed cost of developing the product would be between $30,000 and $50,000, but some $300,000 would be needed to finance the first production run. Those funds would be needed until the initial payments from sales arrived a few months later.

Reiss seriously considered raising the required money from the strongest among his manufacturer's representatives in the toy business, thinking they would push hard to sell the game to every account. Eventually, he decided against this approach: Not only would it not contribute that much to the venture, reps could be motivated to sell in other ways. Perhaps more important, Reiss feared the prospects of perhaps 20 partners who "would be every day on the phone asking how things are going."

Another option that passed through his mind, which he dismissed promptly, was venture capital. He realized that he would have to give up too much and, even worse, that venture capitalists would not understand this kind of deal—one that had very attractive short-term profits but few long-term prospects.

Trivia Incorporated

With the agreement with *TV Guide* in hand, Reiss called Sam Kaplan—a longtime friend who lived in Chicago. Kaplan, 65 years old, had a sizable personal net worth, yet kept working at his small but successful advertising agency (25 employees) "for the fun of it," as he liked to say. Reiss thought that teaming up could be an important help, and Kaplan was indeed enthusiastic about the idea.

Reiss proposed to establish a company, Trivia Inc., that would develop the project. The equity would be split evenly among the two partners. Kaplan, besides lending his line of credit to purchase supplies for the initial run, would use his office to handle day-to-day details. (In fact, Trivia Inc. ended up having only one full-time employee.) Also, because of his vast knowledge of printing and his contacts, Kaplan could secure press time and paper supplies on short notice, and he would supervise the product's manufacturing. This was especially important, since the special paper stock on which the game was printed was then in short supply, and long lead times were generally needed to obtain it. Kaplan would also produce all the ads and the catalog sheets. Reiss would take responsibility for sales and marketing of the product and would pay all reps and coordinate the publicity and the relations with *TV Guide*. An important part of the agreement was that R&R (Reiss's company) would have the exclusive rights to market the game and would receive a commission of 20 percent of the wholesale price from which it would pay the commissions to the reps.

Production, Shipping, and Billing

From the beginning, Reiss's intention was not to be a manufacturer. Through Kaplan's connections, they found not only good suppliers for the question books, the board, and the boxes, but they also even got lower costs than expected. But they still had to tackle the problem of assembly and shipping. Kaplan was a longtime consultant to Swiss Colony, a manufacturer of cheese based in Madison, Wisconsin. This company specialized in mail sales and had developed a strong capability to process mail orders. As a result, Swiss Colony's management had decided several years earlier to offer that fulfillment capability to other companies. They took the orders, shipped the product, and billed to the retailer.

In the deal ultimately reached, Trivia Inc. would have the components sent by the different suppliers to Madison on a "just-in-time" basis, and Swiss Colony would put the boards, dice, and questions in the boxes, package, and ship them. Swiss Colony would charge $.25 per box, including billing for the games, and would send complete daily information on sales to Trivia Inc. Trivia Inc. would pay $2,500 for a customized computer program. With all these measures, Reiss and Kaplan were able to lower their estimated costs by 30 percent and attained the flexibility they wanted. The final cost of manufacturing, assembling, and shipping was about $3.10, not including the royalties paid to the inventor and to *TV Guide*.

A final point was financing the accounts receivable, once the sales started rolling in, and collecting the debts. Reiss was somewhat afraid that the bills of some of the smaller stores carrying the game would be very difficult to collect, since R&R did not have the resources to follow up closely on its collections; moreover, Trivia Inc. needed the leverage of a factor in order to collect from the larger retailers on time. He and Kaplan decided to use Heller Factoring to check credit, guarantee payment, collect the money, and pay Trivia Inc., all for a fee of 1 percent over sales. Trivia Inc. would not need any financing for operations: After 45 days of shipping, Trivia Inc. would always be in a positive cash flow.

Thanks to Heller and Swiss Colony, Trivia Inc. had practically no administrative work left to itself.

Selling the Game

Selling was the most important issue for Reiss. He knew that placing the goods in the stores and selling them to the public (selling through) were two distinct, many times unrelated, problems. In any case, however, he thought that the game needed to be priced below Trivial Pursuit to make up for both the lack of a complete national advertising campaign that major manufacturers would launch, and the lack of the kind of brand recognition that Trivial Pursuit was achieving. Accordingly, the wholesale price was set at $12.50, with a retail list price of $25.

Reiss distinguished carefully between two different channels: the mass merchandisers and the department/gift stores. An important part of the overall strategy was to sell quickly to upscale retailers who would establish a full retail markup (50 percent). These were mainly department stores, such as Bloomingdale's or Marshall Field's, and mail order gift catalogs and specialty gift stores. This, it was hoped, would help sell mass merchandisers and give them a price from which to discount. Such a two-tiered approach was not common in the industry. On long-life products, many times only the full-margin retailers got the product the first year. But Reiss felt that this could not be done with his product, because it could well be only a one-year product. Mass merchandisers, however, had to be reached, since they accounted for at least 70 percent of the market. (**Exhibit 1** shows some of the stores Reiss thought had to be reached.)

Two different sets of reps were employed for the two different channels; on average, they received a 7 percent commission on sales. Reiss's personal knowledge of buyers for the major chains proved invaluable. He was able to obtain quick access to the important decision makers at the major chains. They also followed, when possible, the distribution pattern of *TV Guide* magazine. It was soon apparent that the statistics on demographics reached by *TV Guide,* which Reiss made sure all buyers saw (**Exhibit 2),** had a major impact. As Reiss said, "It appeared that every outlet's customers read *TV Guide.*" The cooperative ads in the magazine, with the possibility of including the store's name, were also a powerful attraction for different buyers, as Reiss had expected: The name of their stores would be displayed in far more homes than it would with a conventional advertising campaign in national magazines. The stores would not be charged to have their name in the ads, but minimum purchase orders would be requested. Many large customers, such as Kmart and Sears, placed large orders before the product was even finished. (**Exhibit 3** shows a cover letter that was sent to supermarket buyers.)

Promotion

In order to promote the game to the public, Trivia Inc. had a four-part plan, beginning with the five ads in *TV Guide*. The first ad broke in mid-September 1984 and was strictly for upscale retailers, with $25 as the price of the game. *TV*

Guide had eight regional issues, and different stores were listed in each area with a total of about 120, including Bloomingdale's, Marshall Field's, Jordan Marsh, and J. C. Penney. They all had to place minimum orders. The second ad, shown on October 6, was just for Sears. The third, on November 10, was devoted to mass merchandisers and did not include a retail price. The fourth, two weeks later, listed four of the most important toy chains: Toys "Я" Us, Child World, Lionel Leisure, and Kay Bee. The appeal to the public, then, was not just the ad: Reiss knew that showing well-known upscale stores carrying the game initially was the best way to obtain instant credibility for the product. Finally, Kmart, the largest U.S. chain, gave Trivia Inc. an opening order to all its 2,100 stores, even before the game went into production, in exchange for the exclusivity in the fifth ad to be run in *TV Guide* on December 8, 1984. In that ad, Kmart offered a three-day sale at $16.97.

The second part of the plan also tried to give credibility to the game. Trivia Inc. offered the department stores a 5 percent ad allowance (a 5 percent discount from wholesale price) if they put the product in newspaper ads, tabloids, or catalogs. For similar reasons, Reiss wanted to have the game placed in mail order gift catalogs. Their sales in the toy-game business were only moderate, but catalogs gave a lot of product exposure because of their large circulation figures.

The final part of the plan was to obtain free media publicity. The publisher of *TV Guide* magazine wrote a letter to be sent to the producers of such shows as "Good Morning, America," "CBS Morning News," "The Tonight Show," and to 25 top TV personalities, together with a sample of the game. Through *TV Guide*'s PR agency and the joint efforts of *TV Guide* and Trivia Inc., many newspapers, radio, and TV stations were reached. In all, more than 900 press kits were sent to media organizations. As a result, the game was mentioned on many talk shows (TV and radio), and news of it was published in many newspapers. The cost of this campaign was split between Trivia Inc. and *TV Guide*.

The Results

By October 1983, Selchow, manufacturer of Trivial Pursuit, started falling behind trying to meet the demand. By Christmas, when sales exploded, there was no hope of keeping up—and one of the most serious manufacturing problems was the bottleneck of collating the cards. By the February 1984 Toy Fair, most of the major manufacturers offered trivia games, which was projected to be the hottest category for the year.

R&R sold 580,000 units of the *TV Guide* Game in 1984 at the full wholesale price of $12.50. There were few reorders after mid-October, as the market became saturated with trivia games (over 80 varieties) and Trivial Pursuit flooded the market. By Christmas 1984, all trivia games became heavily discounted; many retailers ran sales on Trivial Pursuit at $14.95, having paid $19.00.

Bad debts for Trivia Inc. were about $30,000 on approximately $7 million billings, with hope of recovering $15,000. Losses from final inventory disposal (it was decided to close out the game) were less than $100,000.

TV Guide was extremely pleased with the royalty collected from the venture. Kaplan, through his 50 percent ownership in Trivia Inc., made over $1 million net. The total cost of designing and launching the product had been $50,000.

Commenting on the whole deal, Reiss said:

> I think the critical aspects of success in being a contract manufacturer are to take care of your suppliers and to take care of your sales representatives. We want our suppliers to charge us full markup, so that we are a good customer to them, and we try hard to give them enough lead time to deliver. We pay on time always, no matter what happens. In exchange, we demand perfect work from them. They understand and like this relationship. We need their cooperation, because we are completely dependent on them.
>
> The other aspect is how to deal with your customers, which for us are the manufacturer's representatives and the buyers of major chains. The manufacturer's reps are used to the fact that when sales really do pick up in any product and they can make a lot of money, many manufacturers try to "shave" their commissions, perhaps feeling that the reps are making too much money. I never do that: I am happy if they make millions, and they know it. I also pay on time always. With this, I have developed a loyal and experienced work force and have no fixed or upfront sales cost.
>
> All of these factors allowed us to move quickly. My contacts enabled me to print and manufacture the game for the same cost as a big company. But a Parker Bros. or Milton Bradley would have incurred fixed costs of roughly $250,000 just for design and development and would then have committed to an advertising and promotion budget of at least $1 million.

The Future

According to Reiss, the big question at the end of 1984 was, "Do we add on a new version of the *TV Guide* Game, do a new trivia game, or go onto something new in spite of the great market penetration and success of our game?"

He had been doing some planning for a new game to be called WHOOZIT? and, instead of questions, it would show photographs of famous people that the players would have to recognize. He had a preliminary royalty deal with Bettman Archives, who had the exclusive marketing rights to all the photographs of the news service UPI, in addition to its own extensive archives. But he was unsure about what the best follow-up for the success of 1984 could be.

The market, however, did not seem to be in the best condition. The 1984 Christmas season had ended with large unsold inventories of Trivial Pursuit and other trivia games. Some major companies, like Parker Bros., Lakeside, and Ideal, had closed out their games at low prices, further flooding the market. Many buyers were saying that trivia games, as a category, were over, although they seemed to accept Selchow's estimate of 7 million units of Trivial Pursuit sold in 1985. That figure was well below the 20 million units sold in 1984 but was still an exceptionally high figure compared with other board games. Selchow had also announced a plan to spend $5 million to promote the game in 1985. Some upscale retailers, however, had announced their intention to abandon Trivial Pursuit and other trivia games, mostly because of the heavy discounting.

Reiss thought that one of the reasons why the public seemed to have lost interest in trivia games is that they were hard to play: Too often, none of the players knew the answers. In retrospect, he thought that the *TV Guide* Game had had the same problem. But that would be different with WHOOZIT? He was thinking of making easier questions and giving several chances to each player, and he really expected the new game to be enjoyable.

In addition to improving the intrinsic playability of the game, Reiss wanted to have more flexibility selling it. He planned to offer three different price points, one of the versions having only the questions so it could be played on the Trivial Pursuit board. In spite of all these improvements, however, he was not sure whether he should try to replicate the success obtained with the *TV Guide* Game and wondered what his best strategy for a follow up could be.

EXHIBIT 1   Stores to Be Reached

	Number of Outlets
Sears	879
Penney	450
Federated	451
Dayton Hudson	1,149
R. H. Macy	96
Allied Stores	596
Carter Hawley Hale	268
Associated Dry Goods	332
Mercantile	79
Kmart	2,174
Woolworth	N/A
Wal-Mart	751
T.G.&Y.	754
Zayre	848
Bradlees	132
Murphy	386
Rose's	195
Kay Bee	500
Spencer Gifts	450
Hook's Drug	120
Toys "Я" Us	200

Bob Reiss thought that some 5,000 independent stores would be suitable targets, too.

EXHIBIT 2   **Data on *TV Guide*'s Audience**

February 3, 1984

Mr. Robert Reiss
President
R&R
230 Fifth Avenue
New York, New York 10001

Dear Bob:

I had our Research Department pull together some statistics about
TV Guide that should be useful in discussing the audience
dimensions of our magazine with major department stores and
mass merchandisers.

First off, *TV Guide*'s circulation averages over 17 million copies
each week.

Included in *TV Guide*'s average issue audience are:

1. 37,838,000 adult readers age 18 and over.
2. 8,829,000 teenage readers 12–17.
3. 46,667,000 total readers age 12 and over.
4. 19,273,000 readers 18–34.
5. 28,085,000 readers 18–49.
6. 10,312,000 adult readers in homes with one or more children
   10–17 years of age.
7. 16,334,000 adult readers in homes with $25,000+ household
   income.
8. 11,815,000 adult readers with one or more years of college.
9. 4,344,000 adult readers who bought games or toys for children
   12–17 in the past year.
10. 3,688,000 adult readers who bought games or toys for adults
    18+ in the past year.

EXHIBIT 3   Letter to Supermarket Buyers

TRIVIA
INCORPORATED
Exclusive Marketing Agent
R&R
230 Fifth Avenue, New York, NY 10001
1-212-686-6003 Telex 238131-RR UR

June 29, 1984

Mr. Lamar Williams
General Mdse. Buyer
JITNEY JUNGLE STORES of AMERICA
P.O. Box 3409
453 N. Mill St.
Jackson, MI 39207

Dear Mr. Williams:

Once every decade a product comes along that is just right!
We think we have that product for you. It has two key elements:

1. It is licensed by *TV Guide.* I'm sure we don't have to tell you
   about the sales strength of *TV Guide* with its 17 million-plus
   weekly circulation, 46 million readers, etc. If your supermarket
   is typical, *TV Guide* is one of your best sellers and has earned
   its exalted position next to the cash registers.

2. The trivia game explosion has taken America by storm and
   duplicated its Canadian heritage, where trivia games have
   reigned for four years.

We have put these two elements together and, with *TV Guide*'s
help, developed a *TV Guide* Trivia Game with over 6,000 questions
and answers. The enclosed catalog sheet gives full description and
pricing. All our sales are final. We will advertise the game in five
full page color ads in *TV Guide* this fall and will reach your
customers.

We feel this game is ideally suited to be sold in your stores. We
would be happy to send you a sample and/or answer any questions
you may have.

We look forward to the opportunity of working with you.

Sincerely,

Robert S. Reiss

Robert S. Reiss

RSR/ck

encl.

1–2

ICEDELIGHTS

On March 10, 1995, Paul Rogers, Mark Daniels, and Eric Garfield walked out of their final negotiating session with ICEDELIGHTS. The three were negotiating for the Florida franchise rights to ICEDELIGHTS, a European-style cafe/ice cream shop selling a variety of beverages and frozen desserts.

The session had gone fairly well, and they felt as though they had gotten most of the concessions that they wanted. Yet, mixed with this air of excitement was a sense of trepidation. There was a great deal of work that remained to be done on the deal, not the least of which was the securing of additional financing. In addition, other issues remained: Did the Florida market offer good potential for an ice cream business? Did the deal make good business sense? Was it right for them personally at this point in their careers? Did they have the skills and resources to make the business work, assuming that the deal came off? Did the same factors that made them good friends make them good business partners?

Background

Paul Rogers, Mark Daniels, and Eric Garfield were three second-year students at the Harvard Business School (HBS) who had all been classmates in their first year. (See resumes, **Exhibit 1**.) The idea of starting, or buying, their business arose during the week just prior to the start of second-year classes. The three had rented a house on Cape Cod for a week. Fresh from their summer jobs, they

---

Lecturer Michael J. Roberts prepared this case as the basis for class discussion rather than to illustrate either effective or ineffective handling of an administrative situation.

Copyright © 1998 by the President and Fellows of Harvard College.

Harvard Business School Case 9-898-196.

naturally shared their views of what their summer experiences had been like, and what impact these experiences would have on their career choices.

- Paul, 26, had spent two and a half years with State Street Bank in Boston. He had worked for the summer as an associate with the New York investment bank of Bear Stearns, and had enjoyed the experience. Paul, however, was excited by the challenge and rewards of creating and managing an enterprise of his own at an early stage in his career.
- Mark, 25, had spent two years with McKinsey & Co. and had also turned to investment banking for the summer. While he had enjoyed this experience, Mark felt a genuine desire for the independence and satisfaction of owning and managing his own business. He was unsure how additional work in either consulting or investment banking would bring him closer to this goal.
- Eric, 30, had spent five years with Celanese in the international finance area. After pursuing positions with investment banks and consulting firms, Eric accepted a position with McKinsey's Atlanta office. Although he enjoyed the experience a great deal, Eric also felt drawn towards owning his own business. The independence, financial rewards, and opportunity to manage and truly create an organization seemed unequaled in any other career.

During that week on Cape Cod they spent a great deal of time on the beach and in the local bars discussing their experiences, and speculating on what lay ahead. They talked about what they were looking for in a career: Each of them wanted a job he would truly enjoy, independence, and great financial rewards. In addition, there was something incredibly appealing about building and managing an organization—really creating a business—being an entrepreneur. Moreover, it was clear that none of the "traditional" opportunities offered this. The idea of "having our own business" took hold.

Each of them had, at different times, thought that running his own business might be fun. During that week, they realized that this opportunity was the only option that would truly satisfy their objectives. Slowly, the focus of their thoughts turned to "How do we get there?"

Their discussion surfaced two fundamentally different approaches:

- The first approach, the "conservative" one, had two possibilities:
- They could pick an industry, really try to learn a business, develop their management skills, and keep an eye out for opportunities; they were bound to learn a great deal, and they would be making their mistakes on someone else's money. In four or five years, they were bound to spot an opportunity and could then obtain the financing. Everyone says, "the money's there if you have a good idea."
- Or, they could get into the deal flow; go to work for a venture capital firm or the M&A area of an investment bank. They would learn how to

evaluate deals and make contacts with people that could provide financing. Then they would buy something for themselves and run it!

- The second approach was, "Why wait?" They argued that they had the skills and abilities to run a business. Not a high tech or sophisticated manufacturing firm, but surely there were some businesses that they had the collective talent to manage—all they had to do was find one. Further, in four or five years, it would be much harder to do. One would be used to the financial security and life-style of corporate life; it wouldn't be easy to go back to $25,000 or $30,000 and 80-hour weeks. Finally, with a spouse, family, car payments, a mortgage and a summer home or ski house on the way, the risks associated with failure would be far greater down the road.

As school began, they decided that it was certainly worth trying to find a business to buy.

The Search

The three began talking with professors at the Business School, lawyers, and business contacts. They asked for advice, and mentioned that they were in the market to buy a company. It soon became clear that they needed some concrete specifications regarding the businesses they were interested in, both as a guide to potential sources of information and to show a minimum level of commitment to the project. A brief specifications sheet was pulled together **(Exhibit 2)** which described the businesses they would be interested in, and included their resumes.

The process proceeded through October and November with little in the way of results. People were generally helpful and encouraging, but it was very tough to get specific leads.

In late November, Paul's father, Mr. Rogers, mentioned that some friends of the family had recently purchased the ICEDELIGHTS franchise for Oregon and California; he had heard that Florida might be available. The three were excited about the possibility even though retailing had not been one of the industries targeted in their specifications sheet. The skills required to run a food franchise seemed within their range of abilities. It sounded like a fun business, and the potential financial rewards seemed to be great.

ICEDELIGHTS

ICEDELIGHTS was a Boston-based chain of food outlets selling a variety of beverages, pastries, and frozen desserts. There were currently nine stores in the New England area (primarily Boston), with several more scheduled to be opened during 1995. ICEDELIGHTS had sold its first franchise rights (Oregon and California) in June 1994, and the first of these stores was scheduled to open in the summer of 1995.

The four of them met with ICEDELIGHTS on December 10. Bob Andrews, the chairman, revealed that they had received dozens of franchise requests for Florida. He mentioned seven individuals in particular, each with extensive experience in either the fast-food industry or Florida real estate and who clearly had the financial resources required. Yet he felt that, at this time, ICEDELIGHTS was stretched to its capacity. They had grown slowly and carefully, and were committed to maintaining a quality operation. Managing their existing locations and their own expansion, as well as providing a high level of assistance to the California franchise, would consume their available resources for the near future.

ICEDELIGHTS' conservative approach was due in large part to problems the company had had in its early years. Bob Andrews purchased ICEDELIGHTS when it had two locations. Early expansion resulted in financial problems when the company did not have the necessary organization and control systems in place.

Following this meeting, they met with the president of ICEDELIGHTS—Herb Gross. As the chief operating officer, he provided the group with a more detailed description of the ICEDELIGHTS operation. He, too, stressed ICEDELIGHTS' commitment to slow, *quality* growth. He felt, however, that there was some possibility that a deal could be worked out. Paul, Mark, and Eric expressed their enthusiasm for the business, and their desire to really get involved in the day-to-day, hands-on operations of ICEDELIGHTS. They left impressed with the quality of ICEDELIGHTS' management and its potential for growth.

During this conversation, Paul, Mark, and Eric gained a better understanding of how ICEDELIGHTS worked. The heart of the concept revolved around several factors: first, ICEDELIGHTS sold an Italian "gelati" type ice cream, which was extremely rich and "homemade" looking and tasting. Yet, through a great deal of effort, ICEDELIGHTS had been able to perfect the process of freezing this homemade ice cream. This enabled ICEDELIGHTS to manufacture each of the products centrally, freeze them, and then sell on the premises of each store location. Most shops with a high-quality ice cream made the product on the premises. Moreover, ICEDELIGHTS had built and developed a very impressive organization. Their ongoing standardization of production, training, accounting, and control systems, store management and store design and construction convinced Paul, Mark, and Eric that they would receive a great deal of support as a franchise. Finally, by marketing the concept as a cafe, this chain was able to derive sales throughout the day from coffee, pastries, and light snacks as well as ice cream in the afternoon and evening.

At this point, Paul, Mark, and Eric felt that a real opportunity was finally within their grasp. They realized that a great deal of work lay ahead if they were to have any chance of pulling the deal off. The opportunity to do a field study in the New Ventures area seemed to be an excellent vehicle to both accomplish this effort and get some advice from a knowledgeable advisor. They put together a proposal (**Exhibit 3**), which was accepted.

The group met briefly with ICEDELIGHTS again in early January. Bob Andrews and Herb Gross indicated that they were interested in pursuing the Florida franchise further. They were very impressed with Paul's, Mark's, and

Eric's abilities and willingness to get involved in the day-to-day operations of the franchise. The other groups had all been interested in purchasing the franchise as an investment. They viewed the desire to be involved in the operations as crucial to maintaining the quality of the operation. A dinner was scheduled for January 11 to discuss how to proceed.

The Deal

On January 11, Paul, Mark, Eric, and Mr. Rogers met Bob and Herb at a restaurant in Boston. ICEDELIGHTS indicated that they did want to go ahead with the Florida franchise, but because they were so stretched, they did not want to be legally bound to proceed. Nonetheless, they recognized that, because of their job search situation, Paul, Mark, and Eric did need some security that the deal would come off. So ICEDELIGHTS proposed the following terms:

The franchisees (Paul, Mark, Eric, and Mr. Rogers) would:

- Pay $200,000 up front.
- $100,000 development fees for the state of Florida; and,
- $100,000 in 5 prepaid franchise fees of $20,000 each. This was prepayment for the first five stores.
- Pay $20,000 per store opened (after the first five, which were prepaid as above).
- Pay a 5% royalty on sales.

In exchange, ICEDELIGHTS would allow them to use the ICEDELIGHTS name, sell them products for roughly 32% of suggested retail price, train them and one manager per store opened, and would provide them with assistance in finding real estate, selecting locations, and constructing stores. In effect, ICEDELIGHTS would provide them with the first few locations as "turnkey" operations.

Because ICEDELIGHTS did not wish to be legally obligated to proceed if they felt that their operation was still stretched to capacity, these terms would be subject to an option. The parties would sign an option which specified the terms of the franchise agreement (as above):

- The franchisee (Paul, Mark, Eric, and Mr. Rogers) would make a deposit of $75,000. If ICEDELIGHTS did not agree to proceed within nine months, the group would get back its $75,000 plus interest.
- If ICEDELIGHTS did agree to proceed, the franchisee would pay the remainder of the up-front fee ($125,000) and proceed.
- If the franchisees did not agree to pay the remaining fee and proceed, they would forfeit the $75,000 deposit.

ICEDELIGHTS stressed that they were personally committed to going ahead with the Florida franchise as soon as California was running smoothly. They said that it was in everyone's best interest that they not be obligated to proceed if they did not feel that they could provide the franchisees with the level of support required. They further felt that by locking in the terms of the franchise, they were bringing something to the deal.

Another dinner was scheduled for January 25, two weeks hence, when Paul, Mark, Eric, and Mr. Rogers would deliver their decision to ICEDELIGHTS.

Paul, Mark, and Eric had two weeks to make a decision. The main issue now seemed to be financing. As the former president of a Boston-area bank, Mr. Rogers had a great many friends and associates who were potential sources of financing. Mr. Rogers began approaching them in hopes of finding one or two individuals to back the entire deal.

In the meantime, Paul, Mark, and Eric met with ICEDELIGHTS to get some financial data which would allow them to generate pro forma financials and estimate both the financing required and the attractiveness of the operation.

First, they compared the terms of the ICEDELIGHTS franchise with those of other leading franchises (**Exhibit 4**). On one hand, ICEDELIGHTS seemed expensive for a new and unproven franchise. Yet, it appeared to offer excellent profit potential, and they were obtaining the rights to the entire state of Florida.

They did try to get some idea of the market potential that Florida offered, and pulled together the data shown in **Exhibit 5.**

Next, they looked at the store-level income statement (**Exhibit 6**). The operation appeared to be incredibly profitable, particularly in light of the investment required. At $160,000 investment per store, they estimated that they would require $750,000 in financing, as follows:

Up-front fee	$200,000
First 3 stores	480,000
Working capital	70,000
	$750,000

Next, they had to think about how to structure the deal and how much equity to keep: Could they keep enough to make it financially rewarding to them and attractive enough for investors? Would the operation require continued infusions of cash for growth?

They knew that the more debt they could put in the capital structure the better, due to the deductibility of interest payments, and the nondeductibility of dividends. Further, debt and fixed interest payments would both restrict their growth and increase the riskiness of the venture.

After running some preliminary pro formas (**Exhibit 7**), they decided on a first cut at the deal capital structure. It seemed as though they could give 25% of their company away, and still give investors an attractive return.

Mr. Rogers' contacts had said they were enthusiastic about the concept, but in the two-week period, they were unable to get any firm commitments. Mr. Rogers himself, however, had agreed to invest $75,000 in the venture.

On further reflection, Paul, Mark, and Eric decided that the deal was attractive to them even if they had to give up a good deal more than the 25 percent which they had projected. The enthusiasm which Mr. Rogers' contacts had expressed convinced them they would be able to raise the money. They decided to proceed.

On January 25, they met with ICEDELIGHTS and indicated that the terms were acceptable, and that they wanted to go ahead with the deal. They agreed that their lawyers would be in touch to draw up the papers.

Financing

The following weekend, Paul, Mark, and Eric raced to produce a prospectus. The document, excerpted in **Exhibit 8**, presented the concept for the business, and the proposed financing and capital structure. During the next three weeks, they spoke to friends and associates of Mr. Rogers', presenting their business plan. At the end of three weeks, they had informal "commitments" for 15 units, or $375,000. With Mr. Rogers' $75,000, they had $480,000, and were only $270,000 shy.

During this time, it became clear that they would have to give up more than the original 25% they had planned. Not surprisingly perhaps, potential investors were somewhat put off by the 75/25 split in the deal. Paul, Mark, and Eric decided that as long as they were giving up more of the company they could raise a bit more money, and revised the deal as shown in **Exhibit 9.**

In the process of determining the original deal structure, the three thought that investors would primarily be concerned with their overall return—ROI, IRR, NPV. But, in fact, their requirements were more complex:

- Short-term repayment of original investment, with significant control during this phase.
- Long-term capital gain with reduction in investor control once original investment repaid.

There were also significant differences in the level of sophistication of potential investors. Some liked the concept, and that was sufficient. For others, a detailed analysis of investors' versus founders' risk and reward was required. In addition, there were several other issues which remained to be settled, including:

- Form of organization. They had made a preliminary decision to use a straight corporation, but it was possible that a Sub-S, Limited Partnership, or LLC made more sense.
- Legal counsel. They had decided to use Ernest Brooke, an acquaintance of Mr. Rogers' who had indicated an interest in investing. Yet, a few weeks had gone by and he now seemed more hesitant. Further, he did not have any particular expertise in securities or corporate law, and had not been particularly helpful.

- The market. Was Florida really a good spot for this business? Throughout, they had attempted to obtain market information on Florida without spending the time and expense on a lengthy trip. The data they had obtained seemed inconclusive.

Throughout this period, the second-year recruiting season was in full swing. Because they were emotionally committed to the idea, and because it was consuming so much of their time, none of the three was actively pursuing other opportunities. Each of them had the opportunity to return to the firm where they had worked for the summer, as well as one or two other possibilities.

The Decision

It was now February 22, and they had gotten a preliminary set of documents to review. The time when they would actually have to sign papers and put down their $75,000 seemed to be drawing near. A meeting was set for March 10 to put the finishing touches on the agreement.

At this point, Mark began having some strong doubts about the advisability of proceeding. He expressed them this way:

> I started getting these funny feelings in the pit of my stomach. I guess it was fear. It seemed to me that we had all gotten very caught up in the enthusiasm of the project, and had not been as hard-nosed about the business decisions as we should have been.
>
> First, we had not even been to Florida. Eric lived there and was home at Christmas, but we never thoroughly investigated the market. We didn't know if there was competition there, and if there *were* other ice cream shops/cafes, how were they doing? Who knew if the Florida market would be attracted to the rich and different style of ice cream we offered? Finally, this was a "mall-based" retail economy. Who knew how we would do in malls?
>
> Second was the nature of our agreement and relationship with ICEDELIGHTS. It seemed to me that we were absolutely, critically dependent on them for real estate and product. We didn't have the credibility, contacts, or track record to get the prime real estate that we needed. We were dependent on Bob Andrews for that. Similarly, one of our real competitive advantages was the cost and quality of our product. They were under no legal obligation to supply us, and we had no right to build our own production facility. What happened if they decided to expand their own operation, and couldn't supply us? Gelati is not like a hamburger bun—you can't just pick it up anywhere. I thought that our agreements should recognize this dependency and that ICEDELIGHTS should take 25% of our company instead of the $200,000 up front. This would give them a real financial incentive to act in our best interests.
>
> Finally, there was my relationship with Paul and Eric. There had been some tension lately. It was obvious that I was more conservative, more risk-averse than they. I was worried about how this might affect our working relationship. I was uncomfortable with the notion that I could be outvoted on a decision and committed to a course of action that I wasn't comfortable with.

At this time, Mr. Rogers was in Florida and reported that there were a small number of ice cream shops/cafes serving gelati. Further, one of these shops was not doing too well. Obviously, there were a great many of the typical ice cream shops, including Haagen-Dazs, Baskin-Robbins, and several local chains. Still, he felt that there were ample locations to provide for a fast-growing business. They also learned that there were two other operations with a similar focus on gelati—Gelateria Italia and Gelato Classico—which were centered in California, but had recently started to franchise.

In preparation for their March 10 meeting, they decided that they would:

- Go to Florida over spring break to thoroughly investigate the market.
- Press ICEDELIGHTS to provide further assurances that they would be able to deliver the real estate support and product that they needed.

The issue relative to their attorney was still dragging on. Mark had mentioned his concerns about Ernest Brooke to a friend, John Stors, who was an attorney with a prominent local law firm. John had offered to check with other lawyers in his firm to see if anyone had ever dealt with Brooke. Sure enough, a half-dozen or so lawyers in the office knew Brooke and had dealt with him on tax, real estate, divorce, and estate issues. One mentioned that he had won a case in court over Brooke, a case that Brooke should not have lost. And, most damaging of all was the revelation that Brooke was known to be a very close, personal friend of Bob Andrews, ICEDELIGHTS chairman.

Based on this, they decided to use Evan Post and risk alienating Brooke, who seemed willing to invest $30,000 maximum. Post had a reputation as an excellent counsel for small start-ups, as well as good contacts with potential investors. They spoke with Brooke, who was quite accommodating, and who agreed that the lure of potential investors was attractive, and a legitimate reason for including Evan Post.

Finally, they had exhausted all of Mr. Rogers' contacts and were still about $400,000 short; some investors' "commitments" had evaporated over the past month. They had a meeting with a newly formed group of "angels" just prior to their March meeting. This group indicated that they were extremely interested, but they would require more ownership in the company for their investment. The group was a particularly attractive partner because its principals had extensive experience running a Kentucky Fried Chicken franchise.

At the March 10 meeting, ICEDELIGHTS responded to their concerns. First, they agreed that the franchisee wouldn't have to pay the remaining $125,000 until ICEDELIGHTS had furnished them with one suitable location and the lease had been signed. Further, ICEDELIGHTS agreed that the franchisee would have the right to build a production facility if ICEDELIGHTS became unable to supply them with product. The closing date for the deal was set for March 25; in two weeks they would have to put up their $75,000 and sign the franchise and option agreements. During this time, they had to decide whether to proceed or not:

- Was there real potential for this business in the Florida market?

- Did the option and franchise agreement make good business sense?
- Did the returns justify the risks?

If they did decide to proceed, they had to resolve the remaining financial issues:

- How much of the company could they give up and have the deal still be attractive to them? They had revised the deal as shown in **Exhibit 9**, but knew that they might have to give up even more of the company.
- Should they go ahead and commit $75,000 under the option agreement before they had the full $825,000 of financing secured, hoping to obtain the remainder before the option was exercised?
- Should they go with less than $825,000 and plan a second offering after the first store was up and running?

Finally, they each had their own personal feelings about the deal:

Mark

ICEDELIGHTS' concessions did reassure me to a certain extent, but I still have some very uncomfortable feelings.

First, the prospects for the business in Florida are still unclear to me; we haven't been to Florida yet, but I have the sense that we will find *some* attractive locations. But in order to meet our projections and investors' expectations, we have to grow extraordinarily quickly.

Second, even if the business does well, we are still critically dependent on ICEDELIGHTS. I think that real estate and product are our two key factors for success, and we really can't control them—they are in ICEDELIGHTS' hands. And if they don't perform, our only remedy is to sue. It really scares me to think that we will have the responsibility for $825,000 of other people's money, but can't control the two most important elements of the business.

Finally, I do question whether we have the skills to really make this work. I think that we have been pretty naive so far, and very much caught up in the excitement of actually doing a deal. Fortunately, it hasn't cost any money and we've learned a lot.

Paul

The concessions that we won from ICEDELIGHTS reassured me of their continuing commitment to the Florida franchise. We would have preferred giving ICEDELIGHTS a small equity stake in the company, but they were not interested in this proposition.

Like Mark, I was concerned about the market; I did want more than just a "gut feel" that the market is there. This issue was particularly pressing because the closing date of March 25 would come before we had a chance to get to Florida over spring break. We needed some concrete research before that.

Money was also still a problem. We have "informal commitments" for about $300,000 of the $825,000 needed; experience had taught us that these were often more "informal" than they were commitments. A venture capital firm had expressed very strong interest in a $400,000 to $500,000 investment, but we'd grown skeptical of verbal commitments, and were still looking for other investors.

Both Eric and I had picked up on Mark's concerns and felt that we were dealing with them. I started to get the impression, though, that Mark was veiling a lot of his more personal concerns about the venture in terms of business risk.

As far as I was concerned, we'd been lucky so far—things had gone very smoothly. Now it was time to start running fast, tying up all the loose ends. I was exhilarated by the prospect of this, and the thought that we were really right on the verge of finally having our own company.

Eric

I feel that we really have a great opportunity here. I'm really excited by the idea of creating and managing our own organization. It is a fairly simple business and ICEDELIGHTS has done a great deal to build and standardize the organization. With their systems and support, I am very confident that we can be successful.

I spent Christmas break in Florida, and I believe that the market prospects are very good. The population base is an Eastern, upscale, sophisticated one. The economies of the business are such that we can be profitable even with a small volume. Finally, all of our investors believe that Florida is an attractive market.

I think that ICEDELIGHTS' concessions assured us of the product supply and real estate support that we needed. After we get a few stores up and running, we will have developed a name for ourselves, and won't need their real estate assistance anyway.

I understand Mark's concerns, but there are always going to be risks. In this case, they are manageable, and the return justifies them. There is little to be gained by waiting to start our own business; in a few years the risks will seem even greater. Now we have very little to lose.

I really don't feel that any additional assurances will satisfy Mark's doubts. In fact, I think that Mark would be uncomfortable with *any* deal. His lack of commitment is a real problem at this point, and needs to be cleared up before it becomes a personal and business problem for all of us.

EXHIBIT 1   **Resumes**

PAUL ROGERS

education
1993–1995

HARVARD BUSINESS SCHOOL	**BOSTON, MA**

Candidate for the degree of Master in Business Administration in June 1995.

1986–1990

HARVARD COLLEGE	**CAMBRIDGE, MA**

Bachelor of Arts degree in June 1990. Majored in modern European history. Vice president of the Delphic Club; presently serves as graduate treasurer.

work experience
summer 1994

BEAR, STEARNS	**NEW YORK, NY**

Corporate Finance. Summer associate. Worked on the initial public offering of a manufacturer of computer memory devices. Assisted in the preparation of the prospectus, due diligence investigations, and marketing of this successful offering. In addition, performed preliminary debt rating analysis and lease-versus-buy analysis for prospective clients.

summer 1993

NEWBURY, ROSEN & CO., INC.	**BOSTON, MA**

Corporate Finance. Wrote the prospectus for a $600,000 private placement for a start-up venture in the electronic test equipment rental industry. Performed industry, competitive, and market analyses.

1990–1993
1993

STATE STREET BANK AND TRUST COMPANY, INC.	**BOSTON, MA**

Corporate Finance Department. Senior analyst. Worked with three-person team in structuring private placements and assembling prospectuses. Co-authored prospectus for $10 million private placement to regional retailing chain. Participated in presentations of services to a large high-technology firm.

1992–1993

Corporate Services Department. Senior analyst. Assisted vice president of department in establishing a Eurodollar loan syndication portfolio, in which State Street acted as lead manager and agent. Marketed this service to prospective clients. Made both individual and joint presentations to foreign banks interested in joining syndicates. Managed negotiations among the client, legal counsel, and the banking syndicate for a $10 million revolving loan syndication to a major toy manufacturer. Helped bring to a closing two additional term loan syndications totaling $14 million.

1990–1992

Commercial Credit Training Program. Trainee. Completed the training program in eighteen instead of the stipulated twenty-four months.

1987–1990

HASTY PUDDING THEATRICALS	**CAMBRIDGE, MA**

Producer of this Broadway-like musical comedy show. Selected script, hired professional director, set designer, music arranger, and costume designer, and coordinated an eighty-person company. Improved financial controls and initiated a fund drive.

personal background

Raised in Boston. Have lived and traveled extensively abroad. Flexible on relocation. Fluent in French.

references

Personal references available upon request.

EXHIBIT 1   *(continued)*

MARK DANIELS

education
1993–1995   HARVARD BUSINESS SCHOOL   BOSTON, MASSACHUSETTS
Candidate for the degree of Master in Business Administration in June 1995.
General management curriculum. Awarded First-Year Honors.

1987–1991   HARVARD COLLEGE   CAMBRIDGE, MASSACHUSETTS
Awarded Bachelor of Arts, *cum laude*, in Economics, June 1991. Wrote Senior
Honors Thesis on strategic implications of cost and market structure in the
publishing industry. Served as Editor-in-Chief, Harvard Yearbook Publications;
Treasurer, D.U. Club; Class Representative, 1991 Class Committee; Executive
Committee member, Harvard Fund. Elected Trustee of Yearbook.

business
experience
summer 1994   MORGAN STANLEY & CO.   NEW YORK, NEW YORK
Worked as a summer associate in corporate finance and mergers and acquisitions
areas. Assisted in the development and implementation of a strategy for divesting a
client's shipping subsidiary. Assisted in the defense of an oil services client
engaged in a hostile takeover.

1991–1993   McKINSEY & COMPANY   NEW YORK & TOKYO
Functioned as a consultant to top management of McKinsey's clients in the
telecommunications, computer, and office products industries. Assessed the
competitive cost position of a major international manufacturer of telecommunications products. Managed internal research project on Japanese
competition in high-technology industries. Transferred to McKinsey's Tokyo office
to develop a strategy for a British client seeking to enter the Japanese office
products market. Wrote and presented report to Board of Directors in London.

current
activities   Kirkland House (an undergraduate residence), and working as an admissions
counselor at the Harvard Business School. Specific responsibilities include:

- Tutor, Harvard College Economics Department, teaching "Managerial
  Economics and Decision Theory."
- Teaching Assistant, Harvard College General Education Department, teaching
  "Business in American Life."
- Nonresident Business Tutor, Kirkland House, advising undergraduates on careers
  and graduate education.
- Counselor, Harvard Business School Admissions Office, interviewing
  prospective students.

personal
background   Enjoy sailing, racquet sports, travel, and photography.

references   Personal references available upon request.

EXHIBIT 1   *(concluded)*

ERIC GARFIELD

education
1993–1995   **HARVARD BUSINESS SCHOOL**   **BOSTON, MA**
Candidate for the degree of Master in Business Administration in June 1995.
Pursuing a general management curriculum with emphasis on finance. Awarded
COGME Fellowship.

1982–1986   **UNIVERSITY OF FLORIDA**   **GAINESVILLE, FLORIDA**
Earned a Bachelor of Science degree in Accounting with additional concentration
in Economics. Awarded membership in Beta Alpha Psi and Phi Eta Sigma, two
honorary scholastic fraternities.

business
experience
summer 1994   **McKINSEY & COMPANY, INC**   **ATLANTA, GEORGIA**
Associate. Analyzed financial performance and product-line profitability, as part of
strategic plans and operating budgets. Prepared financial analysis for potential
foreign acquisitions and divestitures. Collaborated in cost reduction project
resulting in annual savings of $5 million.

1988–1993   **CELANESE CORPORATION**   **NEW YORK, NEW YORK**

1991–1993   *International Finance Manager.*
Supervised the preparation and analysis of strategic plans and operating budgets.
Prepared financial analysis for potential foreign acquisitions and divestitures.
Collaborated in cost reduction project resulting in annual savings of $5 million.

1990–1991   *Financial Analyst.*
Prepared financial analysis for capital expenditure projects and for actual monthly
results versus budget.

1988–1990   *International Auditor.*
Supervised audit team in performing operational audits. Developed audit programs
for foreign installations.

1987–1988   **MINNESOTA MINING AND**   **CARACAS, VENEZUELA**
                  MANUFACTURING (3M)

Senior Cost Analyst. Prepared product analysis required by the Venezuelan
government for the introduction of new products. Analysis included marketing,
production, and financial data.

1986–1987   **PRICE WATERHOUSE & CO.**   **MIAMI, FLORIDA**
Staff Auditor. Performed financial audits of manufacturing and service
organizations.

personal   Fluent in English and Spanish. Enjoy participative sports, reading historical novels
background   and international travel.

references   Personal references available upon request.

EXHIBIT 2   Specifications Sheet

Dear

We are currently second-year students at the Harvard Business School and are interested in acquiring a company. We have the skills and abilities necessary to successfully manage a going concern and to create value for our backers and ourselves.

As explained in the attached specification sheet, we seek to acquire a medium-size firm. We feel our skills are applicable to a broad range of industries—from general industrial to consumer goods.

As the accompanying resumes indicate, the three of us have varied and complementary skills. We have backgrounds in planning, finance, control, operations, and general management. We believe that our abilities, combined with hard work and intense commitment, will enable us to succeed in such a venture.

We would greatly appreciate the opportunity to discuss our ideas with you and would be grateful for any suggestions you might have.

Sincerely,

SPECIFICATIONS

General   Established manufacturing firms engaged in the production of Industrial and/or Consumer Goods

Sales Volume $5,000,000–$10,000,000

Location   Preferably, but not exclusively, Northeast

Product   Basic product with established market

Examples   Include, but are not limited to the following:
        Industrial Equipment
        Food Packaging and Processing
        Control Systems and Equipment
        Electronic Equipment
        Plastic Molding
        Construction Equipment
        Oil Field Machinery
        Sporting and Athletic Goods
        Precision Instruments

EXHIBIT 3   Field Study Proposal

OUTLINE OF PROPOSED FIELD STUDY

Step I   Understand Existing Operations in New England, including: products, manufacturing, distribution, retail location strategy, advertising/merchandising strategy, cost structure, customer profile, management structure and systems, and personnel requirements.

Step II   Evaluate Implications for Franchise, including: potential profitability and growth, competition, cost impact, tailoring of concept, relations with franchisor, key risks, and financial requirements.

Step III   Evaluate and Structure Deal, including: management structure and responsibilities, form of organization, and legal/tax aspects.

Step IV   Prepare Business Plan, including: introduction, company description, risk factors, products, market, competition, marketing program, management, manufacturing, facilities, capital required and use of proceeds, and financial data and financial forecasts.

EXHIBIT 4   Food Franchises—Terms

	Franchise Fee per Location ($000)	*Royalty (% of Sales)*
ICEDELIGHTS	20	5
Gelateria Italia	15	0
Gelato Classico	30	0
Baskin-Robbins	0	0
Carvel	20	Varies
Swensen's	20	5.5
Haagen-Dazs	20	$0.60/gallon
Long John Silver Seafood	10	4
H. Salt Fish & Chips	10	Varies
Kentucky Fried Chicken	10	4
Church's Fried Chicken	15	4
McDonald's	12.5	11.5
Wendy's	15	4
Burger King	40	3.5
Burger Chef	10	4
Taco Bell	45	5
Domino's Pizza	10	5.5
Pizza Inn	15	4
Shakey's Pizza	15	4.5
Orange Julius	18	6

EXHIBIT 5   Population Growth and Income Levels in Florida

	1/1/94 Population (000)	1988–1994 Growth (%)	1993 Median Per Capita Income
Boston[a]	3,255	0.8%	$18,354
Jacksonville	995	9.7	15,561
Miami	2,040	5.3	13,758
Tampa	2,200	6.4	15,500
Ft. Lauderdale	1,421	13.1	16,873
Orlando	1,417	15.7	15,979
Gainesville	199	9.4	13,703
Sarasota	537	9.7	17,788
Ocala	230	17.9	12,361
Daytona	449	12.4	13,978
Naples	188	23.6	22,490
Punta Gorda	130	17.2	14,675

[a]For reference only.
Source: Commercial Atlas and Marketing Guide, Rand McNally, 1995 ed.

EXHIBIT 6   Financials

PROFORMA INCOME STATEMENT: STORE LEVEL

Sales			$550,000
Fixed costs:	Rent (1000 to 1200 square feet)	$ 25,000	
	Management salaries	30,000	
Variable costs:	Cost of product	192,500	
	Payroll	52,500	
	Royalty	27,500	
	Shipping	16,500	
	Advertising	5,500	
	Other	11,000	
	Rent override[a]	13,500	
	Total costs		374,000
	Pretax store contribution		$176,000

CAPITAL REQUIREMENTS PER STORE

Construction, leasehold improvements	$ 60,000
Equipment costs	85,000
Fees & miscellaneous expenses, capitalized	15,000
	$160,000

[a]A "percent-of-sales" bonus to the landlord after a base sales level is reached.

EXHIBIT 7   Preliminary Proforma Cash Flow Statement ($000)

Year	1	2	3	4	5	6	7	8	9	10
Number of stores, total	2	6	10	15	20	20	20	20	20	20
New stores	2	4	4	5	5	—	—	—	—	—
Existing stores	0	2	6	10	15	20	20	20	20	20
Sales	800	2,600	4,600	7,000	9,500	10,000	10,000	10,000	10,000	10,000
Operating income	130	470	390	1,375	1,900	2,100	2,100	2,100	2,100	2,100
Store opening expenses	100	200	200	250	250	—	—	—	—	—
Franchise fees	40	80	80	95	75	—	—	—	—	—
Corporation overhead	115	205	425	575	725	800	800	800	800	800
Income	(125)	(15)	185	455	850	1,300	1,300	1,300	1,300	1,300
Tax	(60)	(7)	35	200	380	580	580	580	580	580
After-tax income	(65)	(8)	150	255	470	720	720	720	720	720
− Store investment	250	500	500	625	—	—	—	—	—	—
− Corporate investment	10	20	50	50	50	—	—	—	—	—
+ Depreciation	40	120	200	300	400	400	400	400	400	400
+ Franchise fees (prepaid)	40	80	80	—	—	—	—	—	—	—
Case + or −	(180)	(320)	(270)	(375)	(175)	400	400	400	400	400
Total cash + or −	(305)	(335)	(120)	(120)	295	1,120	1,120	1,120	1,120	1,120
Cumulative cash + or −	(305)	(640)	(760)	(880)	(585)	535	1,655	2,775	3,895	5,015

EXHIBIT 8   Excerpts from Prospectus

THE OFFERING

Terms of the Offering

The Company is offering 25 Investment Units. Each Unit consists of 100 shares of its Class A Common Stock (zero par value), offered for $2,000 and $25,000 of the Company's Debentures.

	Per Unit	*Total*
Equity	$ 2,000	$ 50,000
Debentures	25,000	625,000
Total	$27,000	$675,000

All subscriptions shall be for at least one full unit. The Company currently plans to call for each subscription according to the following schedule:

Approximate Timing	*Amount per Unit*	*Description*
Immediately	**$ 2,000**	**Equity**
July 1–September 1, 1995	15,000	Debentures
January 1–March 1, 1996	10,000	Debentures

The Company reserves the right to accelerate or delay the timing of these contributions as its business requires, and will give investors thirty (30) days' written notice of such requirements. Investors who are unable to meet subsequent contribution requirements will forfeit their contributions to date unless a suitable substitute can be found by the investor.

THE SECURITIES OFFERED HEREBY ARE NOT REGISTERED UNDER THE SECURITIES ACT OF 1933, AS AMENDED AND MAY NOT BE SOLD, TRANSFERRED, HYPOTHECATED OR OTHERWISE DISPOSED OF BY AN INVESTOR UNLESS SO REGISTERED OR, IN THE OPINION OF COUNSEL FOR THE COMPANY, REGISTRATION IS NOT REQUIRED UNDER SAID ACT.

Capitalization

The capitalization of the Company as of the conclusion of the Offering, assuming all units are sold, will be as follows:

Debt	$675,000
Equity	$ 75,000

This capital consists of the $675,000 raised from the Offering *plus* $75,000 contributed by the Founders.

The Founders will purchase 7,500 shares of the Company's Class B Common Stock for $25,000, and will also contribute $50,000 in debt.

EXHIBIT 8   *(continued)*

The resulting capitalization is detailed below:

Debt		
Investors	$625,000	
Founders	50,000	
		$675,000
Equity		
Investors	$ 50,000	
Founder	25,000	
		$ 75,000
Total Capital		$750,000

Description of Shares and Debentures

The investment units each consist of 100 shares of the Company's Class A Common Stock (zero par value) representing 1% of the total outstanding Common Shares of the Company. In total, the Class A stockholders will have representation on the Board of Directors equal to 50% of the total number of directors. When the Debentures have been repaid in full, the Class A board representation will be reduced to a pro rata share.

The Founders' Class B stock will be restricted as to dividends until the Debentures have been repaid in full.

The Debentures will be issued with a face value of $5,000 each, and will pay interest at 15% per annum, cumulative with the first payment deferred until the end of Year Two. Interest payments will be made annually. The Debentures will have a maturity of five (5) years, and will be callable.

Use of Proceeds

The amount to be received by the Company from the sale of the Investment Units offered herein is $675,000. The Company intends to use these funds, in addition to the $75,000 contributed by the Founders, for the following purposes:

Development rights for the State of Florida	$100,000
Prepaid franchise rights for the first five stores	$100,000
Capital for three ICEDELIGHTS stores	$480,000
Working capital	$ 70,000
	$750,000

Dividends

The Company plans to pay no dividends for a period of five (5) years, and until such time as the Debentures have been paid in full. Following this five-year period, the Company does have the intention of distributing dividends to its investors. No assurance can be made, however, that the Company will, in fact, be able to pay such dividends. Such payment is a matter to be determined from time to time by the Board of Directors and, of necessity, will be based upon the then existing earnings and cash position of the Company, as well as other related matters.

EXHIBIT 8   *(continued)*

Reports to Stockholders

The Company will furnish its shareholders audited financial statements on an annual basis as well as unaudited quarterly reports of operations and financial condition.

Financial Projections

Following a period of identifying suitable real estate, negotiating loans, and equipping locations, the Company anticipates commencing retail operations no later than early 1996. Ten-year financial projections (attached) are based on the following assumptions.

Store Openings

The Company anticipates opening stores according to the following schedule:[1]

					Year					
	1	2	3	4	5	6	7	8	9	10
Number of stores opened	3	4	5	5	5	2	2	2	1	1
Cumulative number of stores in operation	3	7	12	17	22	24	26	28	29	30

Sales Level and Growth

Based on its knowledge of sales volumes in existing ICEDELIGHTS locations, and its knowledge of the Florida market, the Company estimates $550,000 in base-level sales. This base level for new stores inflates at the rate of 5% per year. Store-level sales grow as follows:

Year	Total Rate of Growth	Real Growth	Inflation
1	5%	10%	5%
2–10	13	8	5

Capital Requirements

Based on its knowledge of existing ICEDELIGHTS locations, the Company estimates a cost per store of $160,000. This breaks down as follows:

Construction costs	$ 60,000
Equipment costs	85,000
Fees and miscellaneous expenses	15,000
Total Capital Costs	$160,000

[1]The decline in the rate of openings after Year Five reflects the Company's desire to show ten-year financial projections, and does not serve to indicate the Company's estimate of the total potential of the Florida market.

EXHIBIT 8   *(continued)*

The capital costs are depreciated or expensed as follows:

- Construction costs over ten years, the assumed life of a lease.
- Equipment costs over five years.
- Architectural fees and other expenses are expensed in the year incurred.

The Company estimates store level operating expenses as follows (as a percentage of sales):

	(%)
• Cost of product (including packaging)	35
• Payroll	15
• Rent (1,000 to 1,200 square feet required)	7
• Royalty	5
• Shipping	3
• Advertising	1
• Other (telephone, cleaning, etc.)	2
Total expenses	68%

Amortization

The $100,000 development rights are amortized over the twenty-year life of the agreement.

THE ATTACHED PROJECTIONS REPRESENT OUR ASSESSMENT OF THE POTENTIAL FOR THE FLORIDA MARKET. THESE ESTIMATES ARE BASED ON DISCUSSIONS WITH MANAGEMENT AND OUR OWN INVESTIGATION OF THE EXISTING OPERATION. WE BELIEVE THAT THESE FIGURES ARE REPRESENTATIVE OF CURRENT OPERATIONS AND DO FAIRLY REFLECT THE LEVEL OF OPERATIONS ANTICIPATED IN FLORIDA. NONETHELESS, THEY ARE ONLY PROJECTIONS, AND MUST BE VIEWED AS SUCH.

EXHIBIT 8   *(continued)*

Projected Income Statement ($000)

	Year									
	1	*2*	*3*	*4*	*5*	*6*	*7*	*8*	*9*	*10*
Net sales	962	3,340	6,617	10,815	15,719	20,392	24,580	29,386	34,482	39,839
Store level expenses:										
Variables	654	2,271	4,500	7,354	10,689	13,867	16,714	19,982	23,448	27,091
Fixed	53	174	330	521	730	900	1,025	1,160	1,784	1,398
Depreciation	69	165	295	430	575	585	574	545	480	415
Operating income	186	730	1,492	2,510	3,725	5,040	6,267	7,699	8,770	10,935
Start-up expenses	103	140	180	173	162	67	69	71	36	37
Corporate overhead	105	215	415	580	680	810	906	1,017	1,110	1,203
Amortization	5	5	5	5	5	5	5	5	5	5
Earnings before interest & taxes	(27)	370	892	1,752	2,878	4,158	5,287	6,606	7,619	9,690
Interest expense:										
Investor	0	216	101	101	75	0	0	0	0	0
Bank		15	15	15	0	0	0	0	0	0
Profit before taxes	(27)	139	776	1,636	2,803	4,158	5,287	6,606	7,619	9,690
Taxes	0	52	357	753	1,289	1,913	2,432	3,039	3,505	4,457
Net income	(27)	87	419	883	1,514	2,245	2,855	3,567	4,114	5,233

Projected Balance Sheet ($000)

	Year									
	1	*2*	*3*	*4*	*5*	*6*	*7*	*8*	*9*	*10*
Assets										
Cash	320	105	24	225	936	3,400	6,445	10,153	14,537	19,964
Prepaid fee	40	0	0	0	0	0	0	0	0	0
Development agreement	95	90	85	80	75	70	65	60	55	50
Net fixed assets	268	715	1,220	1,632	1,940	1,726	1,541	1,405	1,140	951
Total assets	723	910	1,329	1,937	2,951	5,196	8,051	11,618	15,732	20,965
Liabilities										
Bank debt	0	100	100	0	0	0	0	0	0	0
Investor debt	675	675	675	500	0	0	0	0	0	0
Total liabilities	675	775	775	500	0	0	0	0	0	0
Equity										
Paid-in capital	75	75	75	75	75	75	75	75	75	75
Retained earnings	(27)	60	479	1,362	2,876	5,121	7,976	11,543	15,657	20,890
Total equity	48	135	554	1,437	2,951	5,196	8,051	11,618	15,732	20,965
Total liabilities and equity	723	910	1,329	1,937	2,951	5,196	8,051	11,618	15,732	20,965

EXHIBIT 8   *(concluded)*

Projected Cash Flow ($000)

					Year					
	1	*2*	*3*	*4*	*5*	*6*	*7*	*8*	*9*	*10*
Net income	(27)	87	419	883	1,514	2,245	2,855	3,567	4,114	5,233
Depreciation	69	165	295	430	575	585	575	545	480	415
Amortization	5	5	5	5	5	5	5	5	5	5
Prepaid expense	60	40	0	0	0	0	0	0	0	0
Cash from operations	107	297	719	1,318	2,094	2,835	3,434	4,117	4,599	5,653
Capital expenditures										
Development agreement	100	—	—	—	—	—	—	—	—	—
Prepaid fees	100	—	—	—	—	—	—	—	—	—
Store construction and equipment	337	612	800	842	883	371	389	409	215	226
Cash generated										
Surplus/(deficit)	(430)	(315)	(81)	476	1,211	2,464	3,045	3,708	4,384	5,427
Financing:										
Equity	75	0	0	0	0	0	0	0	0	0
Debentures	675	0	0	(175)	(500)	0	0	0	0	0
Bank debt	0	100	0	(100)	0	0	0	0	0	0
Net cash flow	320	(215)	(81)	201	711	2,464	3,045	3,708	4,384	5,427
Beginning cash	0	320	105	24	225	936	3,400	6,445	10,153	14,537
Ending cash	320	105	24	225	936	3,400	6,445	10,153	14,537	19,964

Cash Flow and Internal Rate of Return to One Unit Shareholder ($000)

						Year					
	0	*1*	*2*	*3*	*4*	*5*	*6*	*7*	*8*	*9*	*10*
Investment	27	—	—	—	—	—	—	—	—	—	—
Interest	—	—	8	4	4	3	—	—	—	—	—
Return of Principal	—	—	—	—	4	21	—	—	—	—	—
Share of Cash Flow (1%)	—	—	—	—	—	—	25	30	37	44	54
Share of Estimated Market Value at 10 Times Earnings[a]	—	—	—	—	—	—	—	—	—	—	523
Net Cash Flow to Investor	(27)	—	8	4	8	24	25	30	37	44	577

Annualized Internal Rate of Return = 49%.
[a]For illustrative purposes only.

EXHIBIT 9 Summary of Changes to the Offering

The Offering

The Company is offering 25 investment units. Each unit consists of 150 shares of its Class A Common Stock (no par value), offered for $5,000 and $25,000 of the Company's 10% debentures.

	Per Unit	Total
Equity	$ 5,000	$125,000
Debentures	25,000	625,000
Total	$30,000	$750,000

All subscriptions shall be for at least one full unit. The Company currently plans to call for each subscription according to the following schedule:

Approximate Timing	Amount Per Unit	Description
Immediately	2,500	Equity
July 1–September 1, 1995	17,500	Equity and 3 Debentures
January 1–March 1, 1996	10,000	2 Debentures

The Company reserves the right to accelerate or delay the timing of these contributions as its business requires, and will give investors thirty (30) days' written notice of such requirements. Investors who are unable to meet subsequent contribution requirements will forfeit their contributions to date, unless a suitable substitute can be found by the investor.

The securities offered herein are not registered under the Securities Act of 1933, as amended and may not be sold, transferred, hypothecated or otherwise disposed of by an investor unless so registered or, in the opinion of counsel for the Company, registration is not required under said Act.

Capitalization

The capitalization of the Company, as of the conclusion of the offering, assuming all units are sold, will be as follows:

Debt	$675,000
Equity	150,000
Total	$825,000

The capital consists of $750,000 raised by the offering plus $75,000 contributed by the founders.

The founders will purchase 6,250 shares of the Company's Class B Common Stock for $25,000 and will also contribute $50,000 in debt.

EXHIBIT 9   *(concluded)*

| | Cash Flow and Internal Rate of Return to One Unit Shareholder ($000) | | | | | | | | | | |
| | Year | | | | | | | | | | |
	0	*1*	*2*	*3*	*4*	*5*	*6*	*7*	*8*	*9*	*10*
Investment	30	—	—	—	—	—	—	—	—	—	—
Interest	—	—	5	3	3	3	—	—	—	—	—
Return of Principal	—	—	—	—	5	20	—	—	—	—	—
Share of Cash Flow (1-1/2%)	—	—	—	—	—	—	37	46	56	66	82
Share of Estimated Market Value at 10 Times Earnings[a]	—	—	—	—	—	—	—	—	—	—	785
Net Cash Flow to Investor	(30)	—	5	3	8	23	37	46	56	66	867

Annualized Internal Rate of Return = 52%.

[a]For illustrative purposes only.

COMMERCIAL FIXTURES, INC.

It would take only a few quick strokes of his pen to fill out the bid form and but an instant to seal the envelope. Gordon Whitlock caught himself in momentary wonder that this simple form would have such a dramatic effect on the next few years of his life. Tomorrow, February 23, 1998, at 12:00 o'clock noon, the envelopes from Gordon and his partner, Albert Evans, would be opened to determine which of them would buy out the other and own Commercial Fixtures Inc., the company built by their fathers. After working together for over 25 years, the two partners had decided that this was the best way to resolve differences of opinion that had arisen over how to manage the company.

Company Description

Commercial Fixtures Inc. (CFI) manufactured custom-engineered fluorescent lighting fixtures used for commercial and institutional applications. Sales in 1997 were $4,400,000 with profits of $115,000.

Most sales were standard items within the nine major lines of products designed and offered by the company. Ten percent of sales were completely custom-designed or custom-built fixtures, and 15% of orders were for slightly modified versions of a standard product. In 1997, CFI shipped 66,000 fixtures. Although individual orders ranged from one unit to over 2,000 units, the average order size had been fairly consistently 15–20 fixtures. Modified and custom-

Lecturers Richard O. von Werssowetz and H. I. Grousbeck prepared this case as the basis for class discussion rather than to illustrate either effective or ineffective handling of an administrative situation. Professor Michael J. Roberts updated this case.

designed fixtures averaged about 25 per order. Gordon Whitlock, CFI president, described their market position:

> Our product marketing strategy is to try to solve lighting problems for architects and engineers. We design products that are architecturally styled for specific types of building constructions. If an architect has an unusual lighting problem, we design a special fixture to fit his needs. Or if he designs a lighting fixture, we build it to his specifications. We try to find products that satisfy particular lighting needs that are not filled by the giant fixture manufacturers. We look for niches in the marketplace.
>
> Having the right product to fit the architect's particular needs is the most important thing to our customer. Second is the relationship that the architect, the consulting engineer, or the lighting designer has with the people who are representing us. The construction business is such that the architect, engineer, contractor, distributor, and manufacturer all have to work as a team together on a specific project to ensure its successful completion. The architect makes a lot of mistakes in every building he designs, unless he just designs the same one over and over. Consequently, there's a lot of trading that goes on during the construction of a building, and everybody's got to give and take a little to get the job done. Then the owner usually gets a satisfactory job and the contractors and manufacturers make a fair profit. It requires a cooperative effort.
>
> Most of our bids for orders are probably compared with bids from half a dozen other firms across the country. Since a higher percentage of our orders are for premium-priced products, we are not as price sensitive as producers of more commonplace lighting fixtures. It is difficult for a small firm to compete in that market. As many as 30 companies might bid on one standard fixture job.

CFI owned its own modern manufacturing facility located outside Denver, Colorado. Production consisted of stamping, cutting, and forming sheet metal, painting, and assembly of the fixture with the electrical components which were purchased from outside suppliers. The company employed a total of 104 workers, with 34 in sales, engineering, and administration and another 70 in production and assembly.

The company sold nationwide through regional distributors to contractors and architects for new buildings and renovations. Prior to 1995, CFI sold primarily to a regional market. At that time, marketing activities were broadened geographically. This was the primary reason that sales had been increasing over the last few years. (See **Exhibit 1** for historical sales, earnings, unit sales, and employment.)

Background

Commercial Fixtures Inc. was formed in Golden, Colorado, in 1955 by Jonathan Whitlock and Julius Lacy. Each owned one-half of the company. Whitlock was responsible for finance and engineering and Lacy for sales and design. They subcontracted all manufacturing for the lighting systems they sold.

After several years, differences in personal work habits led Whitlock to buy out Lacy's interest. Jonathan Whitlock then brought in Paul Evans as his new partner. Evans had been one of his sheet metal subcontractors. Paul Evans became president and Whitlock the treasurer. Ownership was split so that Whitlock retained a few shares more than half because of his experience with Lacy.

In 1959, CFI began manufacturing and moved its operations to a multifloor 50,000-square-foot plant also located in Golden. The company grew and was quite profitable during the boom in construction of the 1960s. Whitlock and Evans were quite satisfied with the earnings they had amassed during this period and were content to let the company remain at a steady level of about $1,000,000 in sales and about $15,000 in profit after taxes.

Jonathan Whitlock's son, Gordon, joined CFI as a salesperson in 1975 after graduating from MIT and then Colorado Business School. Paul Evans's son Albert, who was a graduate of Trinity College, became a CFI salesperson in 1976. The two sons were acquaintances from occasional gatherings as they were growing up, but had not been close friends.

In 1978, Jonathan Whitlock had a heart attack and withdrew from the management of the business. Although he remained an interested observer and sometime advisor to his son, Jonathan was inactive in company affairs after this time. Paul Evans assumed complete management overview of the company.

Gordon Whitlock moved inside to learn about other parts of the company in 1979. His first work assignments were in manufacturing and sales service. Albert Evans joined his father in the manufacturing area a year later. Gordon became sales manager, Albert became manufacturing manager, and at Paul Evans's suggestion, another person was added as financial manager. These three formed a middle management triumvirate that worked well together, but major decisions were still reserved for Paul Evans, who spent less and less time in the office.

As the new group began revitalizing the company, a number of employees who had not been productive and were not responding to change were retired early or asked to leave. When the man who had been Paul Evans's chief aide could not work with the three younger managers, they ultimately decided he had to be discharged. Paul Evans became so angry that he rarely entered the plant again.

For several years the three managers guided the company as a team. However, there were some spirited discussions over the basic strategic view of the company. As sales manager, Gordon Whitlock pressed for responding to special customer needs. This, he felt, would be their strongest market niche. Albert Evans argued for smooth production flows and less disruption. He felt they could compete well in the "semistandard" market.

In 1981, the fathers moved to restructure the company's ownership to reflect the de facto changes in management. The fathers converted their ownership to nonvoting Class A stock. Each of them transferred 44% of their nonvoting stock to their sons. Jonathan Whitlock decided to relinquish his voting control at this time in an effort to help things work as the new generation took over. Accordingly, Gordon and Albert were each issued 50% of the Class B voting shares.

In that same year, Gordon Whitlock began to work with an individual in forming a company in the computer field that rented extra space from CFI. CFI provided management and administrative support, helping the new company with bidding and keeping track of contracts. Although Albert Evans was not active in this company, Gordon split his partial ownership in this new company with Albert because they were partners and because Gordon was spending time away from CFI with the computer company.

With the heavy demands of the start-up over the next three years, this new effort began to weaken the relationship between Gordon and Albert. At the same time, Albert and the financial manager began to have strong disagreements. These seemed to arise primarily from forays in cost analysis which led the financial manager to question some of Albert's decisions. There were also differences of opinion over relations with the work force and consistency of policy. Albert preferred to control the manufacturing operation in his own way. Gordon felt Albert could be more consistent, less arbitrary, and more supportive of the work force. When the computer company was sold in 1981, the financial manager joined it as treasurer and resigned from CFI.

Growing Conflict

The departure of the financial manager led to a worsening of the relationship between Gordon and Albert. Gordon had been made company president in 1982. Gordon recalled the decision:

> Paul Evans had resigned as president and the three of us were sitting around talking about who should be president. Albert Evans finally said, "I think you should be it." And I said, "OK."

Yet even with this change, the three managers had really operated together as a team for major decisions. Now, Gordon was upset that they had lost an excellent financial manager, someone critical to the operation (due, in his opinion, partially to the disagreements with Albert). There was also no longer a third opinion to help resolve conflicts. Although the financial manager was replaced with an old classmate of Albert's, the new manager became one of several middle-level managers who had been hired as the company grew.

The pressures of growth created more strains between Gordon and Albert. Sales had reached $1,800,000 and had begun to tax CFI's manufacturing capacity. Gordon felt that some of the problems could be alleviated if Albert would change methods that had been acceptable during slacker periods but hindered intense production efforts. Albert had different views. Both agreed to look for additional space.

The transition to a new factory outside Denver, Colorado, in 1989 eased the stresses between the partners. A major corporation had purchased an indirect competitor to obtain its product lines and sold CFI the 135,000-square-foot plant. CFI also entered into an agreement to manufacture some of the other company's light fixtures as a subcontractor. The plant was in poor condition and Albert Evans took over the project of renovating it and continuing production of the other company's lines. Gordon Whitlock remained in Golden running the CFI operation alone until it became possible to consolidate the entire operation in Denver. Gordon described this interlude:

> The next year was a sort of cooling-off period. Albert was immersed in his operation and I was geared into the continuing operation. Albert had always enjoyed projects of this sort and was quite satisfied with this arrangement.
>
> Then in 1991 we hired a plant manager to run the Denver plant and Albert came back to work in Golden. By that time, of course, a lot of things had changed. All of Golden had been reporting to me. I had somewhat reshaped the operation and the people had gotten used to my management style which was different than Albert's.
>
> Albert's reaction was to work with the design and engineering people, but he really wasn't involved very much with the daily manufacturing anymore. He developed a lot of outside interests, business and recreation, that took up much of his time.
>
> I was very happy with that arrangement because it lessened the conflict. But when he did come back, the disagreements would be worse. I guess I resented his attempts to change things when he only spent a small amount of time in the company.
>
> Then in 1992 we made the decision to sell the Golden plant and put the whole company in Denver. We were both involved in that. Most of our key people went with us. Albert and I were very active in pulling together the two groups, in integrating the operations.
>
> That began a fairly good time. I was spending my time with the sales manager trying to change the company from a regional company to a national one and was helping to find new representatives all over the country. Evans spent his time in the engineering, design, and manufacturing areas. There was plenty of extra capacity in the new plant, so things went quite smoothly. In particular, Albert did an excellent job in upgrading the quality standards of the production force we acquired with the plant. This was critical for our line of products and our quality reputation.
>
> This move really absorbed us for almost three years. It just took us a long time to get people working together, to produce at the quality level and rate we wanted. We had purchased the plant for an excellent price with a lot of new equipment and had started deleting marginal product lines as we expanded nationally. The company became much more profitable.

As the company expanded, a group of six people formed the operating team. Albert Evans concentrated on applications engineering for custom fixtures and new product design. In addition, there were a sales manager, financial manager, engineering manager, the plant manufacturing manager, and Gordon. Disagreements began again. Gordon recounted the problems:

> Our operating group would meet on a weekly or bi-weekly basis, whatever was necessary. Then we would have monthly executive committee meetings for broader planning issues. These became a disaster. Albert had reached the point where he didn't like much of anything that was going on in the company and was becoming very critical. I disagreed with him as did the other managers on most occasions. Tempers often flared and Albert became more and more isolated.
>
> He and I also began to disagree over which topics we should discuss with the group. I felt that some areas were best discussed between the two of us, particularly matters concerning personnel, and that other matters should be held for stockholders' meetings. The committee meetings were becoming real battles.

In 1996 Paul Evans died. Although he had remained chairman of the board, he had been generally inactive since 1980. Jonathan and Gordon Whitlock and Albert Evans became the only directors.

Search for a Solution

Gordon Whitlock was discouraged by the continuing conflicts with his partner and had sought advice on how to remedy the situation from friends and associates as early as 1988. In 1990, Gordon was beginning to believe that he and Albert had just grown too far apart to continue together. However, Gordon had to find a mutually agreeable way to accomplish a separation. One partner could buy the other out, but they would have to agree on this and find an acceptable method. Albert seemed to have no interest in such an arrangement.

During 1996, the differences between the partners grew. The vacillations in leadership were disruptive to the operation and made other employees very uncomfortable.

By early 1997, the situation was growing unbearable. Gordon recalled the executive committee's annual planning meeting in January:

> It was a total disaster. There were loud arguments and violent disagreements. It was so bad that no one wanted ever to participate in another meeting. We were all miserable.
>
> What was so difficult was that each of us truly thought he was right. On various occasions other people in the company would support each of our positions. These were normally honest differences of opinion, but politics also started to enter in.

When Gordon returned from a summer vacation in August, he was greeted by a string of complaints from several of CFI's sales agents and also from some managers. Gordon decided that the problems had to be resolved. Gordon sought an intermediary:

> I knew that Albert and I weren't communicating and that I had to find a mediator Albert trusted. I had discussed this before with Peter Dowling, our attorney. Peter was a boyhood friend who had grown up with Albert. I felt he had very high integrity and was very smart. Albert trusted him totally, and Peter was probably one of Albert's major advisors about things.
>
> When I first talked to Dowling in March, he basically said, "Well, you have problems in a marriage and you make it work. Go make it work, Gordon." He wasn't going to listen much.
>
> Then in early September I went back to say that it wasn't going to work anymore. I asked him for his help. Peter said that Albert had also seen him to complain about the problems, so Peter knew that the situation had become intolerable.

Dowling prepared a memorandum describing the various options of changing management and/or ownership that were available to partners who were having disagreements. Gordon decided to encourage one of Dowling's options, which called for each partner to name a price for the business. Previously, some of Gordon's own advisors had suggested this same outlet.

Both directly and through Dowling, Gordon pressed Albert to agree to such an arrangement. Although Albert, too, was unhappy with their conflicts, he was hesitant to accede.

Gordon felt that there were several principal reasons for Albert's reluctance. One was the fact that Albert's only work experience was with CFI. This was limited primarily to managing manufacturing operations he had known for years. Second, Gordon thought Albert was very uncertain as to how to value the company since he had little formal training in financial analysis and had not been directly involved in the financial operations. Gordon felt that this made Albert's task of setting a bid price more difficult than his own. Finally, there was the emotional tie to the company and the avoidance of such a momentous decision.

As discussions began to result in the formulation of a buy-sell agreement, Albert's reluctance waxed and waned. Just before Christmas, Evans called Whitlock who was sick at home and said he had decided to fire the financial manager and become the treasurer of the company. He could look at the figures for a year or so and then make a better decision. Gordon felt the financial manager was essential and could not be discharged. He thought this was really more of an attempt to buy time.

After two more months of give and take in developing a formula and bid conditions, Whitlock and Evans finally signed a mutual buyout agreement on February 17, 1998. It called for sealed bids in a specific format with the partner offering the higher price buying out the other (**Exhibit 2**). The bids would be submitted in one week. Gordon credited Peter Dowling with convincing Albert to sign:

> I think Peter got him to sign it by sheer force of personality. By saying this situation is just not right, it's screwing up the company, you're not happy. You won't be happy until it's solved. This is a reasonable way to solve it and you damn well ought to take the chance. Because later, if you pass this up, it's just going to get worse.

Valuing the Company

Before preparing his bid, Gordon reviewed the thinking he had done since first considering the idea of buying or selling the company. He began with the company's current position. With the serious discussions going on about the buyout agreement, preparation of the financial statements for 1997 had been accelerated and they were already completed. (These are shown together with the results for 1996 and 1995 as **Exhibit 3**.)

Gordon had also begun developing the bank support he might need to fund a buyout. The company's banker indicated that he would loan Gordon funds secured by his other personal assets if Gordon was the buyer, but that since he had not worked with Albert, the bank would decline to finance an acquisition with Albert as the buyer. In addition, the bank would continue the company's existing line of credit which was secured by CFI's cash and accounts receivable. The maximum that could be borrowed with this line was an amount equal to 100% of cash plus

75% of receivables. Both types of borrowing would be at 1% over the prime rate (then about 9%).

Gordon had worked with the banker to begin financial projections he could use in establishing his bid. These projections set out pro forma operating results *before* taking the bid conditions into consideration. By structuring the financial projections in this manner, the results of *operating* assumptions could be separated from *bid* structures. Various combinations of bid conditions could be easily tested based on this set of business operating results. Long-term debts that would be assumed with the business were included within the operating projections. Other bank financing requirements would be influenced by the bid terms and were left separate. The banker completed one sample projection using the minimum $500,000 bid and token $10,000 per year noncompete payments (**Exhibit 4**).

To be conservative, Gordon had made the sales projections about 10% lower each year than he really thought they would achieve. Because fixed costs would not rise appreciably with modest increases in sales, any improvements in sales volume would be particularly advantageous to profits. The asset and liability assumptions were based on company experience, but there could be fluctuations in items such as lengths of receivables and inventory turns. He felt he should consider how these various changes would impact his financing requirements and his price assessment.

Gordon also had sought out common valuation techniques. By looking through business periodicals and talking to friends, he found these methods were not necessarily precise. Private manufacturing companies were then most often valued at between 5 and 10 times after-tax earnings. Book net asset value also helped establish business worth, but was often adjusted to reflect differences between the market values of assets and the depreciated values shown on balance sheets. For CFI, this was true because they had obtained their new plant at an excellent price. Gordon felt it alone was probably worth $200,000 more than stated book.

To Gordon, the variations in worth suggested by these different methods not only reflected the uncertainty of financial valuation techniques but also showed that a business had different values to different people. His bid would have to incorporate other more personal and subjective elements.

One important consideration was what amount of personal resources he could and should put at risk. Both he and Albert were financially very conservative. Neither of them had ever had any personal long-term debt—even for a house. Gordon could gather a maximum of $650,000 of assets outside of CFI that could be pledged to secure borrowing. His bank had already confirmed that he could borrow against those assets. However, for him to put his entire worth at risk, he would want to be very comfortable that the price was a reasonable one. Gordon described his feelings:

> You get very protective about what you have outside the company. The problem you always have with a small company is that most of your worth is tied up in it and you may have very little to fall back on if something goes sour. We both have never been big leverage buyers or anything like that.

Besides the element of increased financial risk, there were several other considerations that tempered Gordon's willingness to pay a very high price. Since they had moved to the plant in Denver, the one-hour commute to work had been a bit burdensome. It would be nice not to have that drive. Gordon also felt he had good experience in the complete general management of a business, and his engineering undergraduate degree and MBA gave him a certain flexibility in the job market. This was important because, for both financial and personal reasons, he felt he would still have to work should he lose the bid.

On the other hand, some factors encouraged Gordon to be aggressive. His father cautioned him to be reasonable, but Gordon knew his father would be very disappointed if Gordon lost the company. And Gordon himself had strong emotional ties to CFI. Gordon also developed a point of view that in some ways he was buying the entire company rather than half:

> I'm sitting here with a company that I have no control over because of our disagreements. If I buy the other half share, I'm buying the whole company—I'm buying peace of mind, I could do what I want, I wouldn't have to argue. So I'd buy a "whole peace of mind" if I bought the other half of the company.

Gordon felt that differences in personal values had been the major reasons two friends had suggested two very different bids. Both had been business school friends and had been very successful entrepreneurs. However, one suggested a bid value for the other half of the company of $850,000 and the other suggested $1,100,000. Gordon commented:

> Philip, who suggested the lower bid, was much more similar to me in lifestyle. He was involved with his family and a number of other activities. Mark, who suggested the higher bid, was unmarried and intensely involved in his company. The company was his life. However, all of the many friends I consulted cautioned me that I would be better off financially if I bought the company and urged me not to "get cute" and undervalue it.

Finally, Gordon considered his competitive position with that of Albert. Although Albert had not accumulated the personal resources that Gordon had, he did have a relative with a private company that Gordon knew had an accumulated earnings problem and thus had the ability to match Gordon's resources. This relative would also be giving Albert financial advice in setting a value for the company. Albert also probably had fewer job prospects if he sold out. His undergraduate study was in liberal arts and his entire experience was within CFI. Gordon also thought Albert might have some doubts about his ability to manage the company on his own.

The Bid

The bid structure was a very simple one. The minimum bid was $500,000 in cash. Additional amounts could be added either to the cash portion and/or to a five-year noncompetition agreement. The bids would be evaluated on a present-value basis using an 8% discount rate. That rate was selected as equivalent to the current rate of return on corporate bonds. Both Gordon Whitlock and Albert Evans were satisfied that was fair. The minimum cash payment had been established to protect the interests of the seller and to reduce possible future uncertainty and unpleasantness if the company's position should change substantially. The noncompetition payments would be obligations of CFI but also would be personally guaranteed by the buyer.

Now it was time to decide on a price and then try to get some sleep. Gordon put the form down and walked around the room. He sat down once again, uncapped his pen, and began to enter his bid.

EXHIBIT 1   Historical Performance

Year	Net Sales	Profit After Tax	# Fixtures Shipped	Total Employees	Hourly Employees
1997	$4,412,191	$115,209	66,000	104	70
1996	3,573,579	101,013	58,000	94	58
1995	2,973,780	106,528	52,000	82	52
1994	2,935,721	63,416	54,000	82	50

EXHIBIT 2   Buy/Sell Agreement

AGREEMENT made on this 17th day of February, 1998 between Albert W. Evans of Denver, Colorado (hereinafter called "Evans") and Gordon M. Whitlock of Denver, Colorado (hereinafter called "Whitlock").

WHEREAS, Evans and Whitlock each own shares of the voting and nonvoting capital stock of Commercial Fixtures Inc. ("CFI") and desire to arrange for the purchase by one (or the purchase by CFI) of all shares of capital stock of CFI owned by the other;

NOW, THEREFORE, in consideration of the foregoing and of the mutual agreements contained herein, Evans and Whitlock agree as follows:

1. Evans and Whitlock will each submit to David Austin, the named senior partner of CFI's accounting firm, by noon on February 23, 1998 (the "Bid Date") a proposal to purchase (or to have CFI purchase some or all of) the other's shares of capital stock of CFI (such proposal to be on the Bid Form attached hereto as Attachment A):
   (a) such proposal shall include all of the stock owned by the other and shall specify the number of shares to be purchased by him, and by CFI and the purchase price, which price shall be not less than $500,000 in the aggregate and shall be paid in full at the Closing hereinafter specified, except as the parties shall otherwise agree;
   (b) such proposal shall specify the amount of the equal annual payments to be made by CFI over the five-year period from 1998 through 2002 in consideration of a noncompetition agreement for such period covering the United States to be executed by the seller in the form attached hereto as Attachment B [not included in case exhibit], such annual payments made in equal installments at the end of each calendar quarter commencing March 31, 1998.
2. If either Evans or Whitlock fails to submit such a proposal by the Bid Date (except for causes beyond his reasonable control in which event a new Bid Date will be established by Austin) the party so failing shall sell his capital stock to CFI upon the terms specified in the other's proposal. If neither party submits such a proposal by the Bid Date this agreement shall terminate.
3. With respect to each proposal, Austin shall add the amount of the purchase price submitted under Section 1(a) and the amount of the annual payment to be made under Section 1(b) above (discounted to present value as at January 1, 1998 as to all payments to be made on or after January 1, 1998 at the rate of 8% per annum), and thereby determine which of the submitted proposals is the highest price (the determination to be made as set forth in the Bid Form Computation attached hereto as Attachment C). The party submitting the highest proposal shall be the buyer (which term shall include CFI to the extent such proposal provides that it shall purchase shares). If both offers are determined by Austin to be equal, the buyer shall be determined by an auction as follows:
   (a) the parties with such others as they choose to bring shall meet at Austin's offices at a time and a date specified by Austin;
   (b) commencing with Evans (unless he declines to raise his bid in which case commencing with Whitlock) the parties shall submit successive bids of not less than $5,000 in excess of the last bid submitted by the other party;
   (c) a party shall have 15 minutes after the bid of the other party in which to submit his own bid and if he fails to submit a bid at least $5,000 higher than other party's last bid, then the last highest bid will be the buyer, except that if neither party raises his original bid then Austin shall determine the buyer by a flip of the coin;
   (d) if a party fails to attend such meeting, the other party shall be the buyer, unless such failure was for causes beyond the reasonable control of the party in which case Austin shall set a time and date for another meeting.

All determinations of Austin under this and the preceding Section, which shall include the question of whether causes beyond the reasonable control of a party prevented the party from acting, shall be final and binding on the parties. Compliance with this agreement shall be determined by Austin and his determination thereof shall also be final and binding on the parties.

4. If Whitlock is the seller, Evans shall cause CFI at the Closing either (a) to redeem for $75,107.50 all shares of capital stock of CFI owned of record or beneficially by Jonathan Whitlock upon tender of certificates for the same endorsed to CFI or (b) to continue to pay a $10,000 annual pension to Jonathan Whitlock and to pay the premiums on the $75,000 life insurance policy held by CFI on Jonathan Whitlock's life and to place such insurance policy in a separate trust which trust shall be the beneficiary under such policy, all in such a manner as to place such policy and proceeds beyond the reach of CFI's creditors, and promptly upon receipt the proceeds of such policy shall be paid by the trust to Jonathan Whitlock's estate in consideration of the endorsement to CFI of the certificate for the shares of capital stock of CFI held by the estate. The bills of Peter Dowling to CFI, including those for arrangements leading to this Agreement, shall be the responsibility of CFI regardless of which party is the buyer.

<u>**EXHIBIT 2**</u>   *(concluded)*

---

5. Austin shall notify the parties in writing promptly upon any determination that a party has failed to satisfy Section 2 hereof and promptly upon any determination made under Section 3 above. The closing date on which the buyer shall make his payment under Section 1(a) and the seller shall endorse his shares of capital stock of CFI to the buyer, shall be April 15, 1998 or such earlier date as the buyer shall designate. If the buyer shall fail to make the Section 1(a) payment at the Closing, the other party will become the seller upon the lower terms of the original seller's proposal and Austin shall reschedule the Closing on a date within 90 days. If at the new Closing the new buyer fails to make the Section payment, this agreement shall terminate. Payment of amounts owed by CFI under Section 1(b) above (and under Section 4 if Whitlock is the seller) shall be personally guaranteed by Evans or Whitlock, as the case may be, in the form attached hereto as Attachment D [not included in case exhibit], and overdue payments of such amounts shall bear interest at the rate of 15% from the date due. There shall be credited against payment to be made under Section 1(b) with respect to 1998 commencing March 31, 1998, the amount of salary received by the seller for 1998. At the Closing the seller shall execute an agreement not to compete with CFI for five years in the United States. The seller's employment, salary, Blue Cross/Blue Shield, group insurance and all other payments and benefits, except those provided herein, shall terminate at the Closing. The seller may retain the CFI automobile now used by him and ownership thereof will be transferred to the seller by CFI.

WITNESS our hands and seals on the date first set forth above.

_____

Albert W. Evans

_____

Gordon M. Whitlock

ATTACHMENT A—BID FORM

PURCHASE PRICE (SECTION 1-a)	$_____
NONCOMPETITION AGREEMENT (SECTION 1-b)	
AMOUNT PER YEAR	$_____
TOTAL AMOUNT (5 YEARS) (TO BE PAID IN EQUAL QUARTERLY PAYMENTS)	$_____

_____

Date

_____

Signature

ATTACHMENT C—BID COMPUTATION FORM

	Evans	Whitlock
PURCHASE PRICE (1a)	$_____	$_____
NONCOMPETITION AGREEMENT (1b):		
• YEARLY AMOUNT FOR FIVE YEARS	$_____ $_____	
• DISCOUNTED VALUE (DV)	$_____	$_____
TOTAL ADJUSTED PURCHASE PRICE	$_____	$_____

The discounted value shall be the present value of the yearly amount paid quarterly for 20 quarters discounted at an interest rate of 2% per quarter.

This shall be computed as follows:

$$DV = \frac{\text{Yearly Amount}}{4} \times 16.3514 = \text{Yearly Amount} \times 4.08786$$

EXHIBIT 3   Financial Statements

Balance Sheets

	December 31,		
	1997	*1996*	*1995*
ASSETS			
Current Assets			
Cash..	$ 51,248	$ 3,778	$ 70,520
Accounts receivable			
Customers	600,361	430,750	318,356
Refundable income taxes.........................	23,001	—	—
Other	—	2,276	5,289
	623,362	433,026	323,645
Less allowance for doubtful receivables..................	3,500	3,500	3,500
	619,862	429,526	320,145
Inventories			
Raw materials	291,790	259,550	277,072
Work in process..................................	534,438	483,357	316,113
	826,228	742,907	593,185
Prepaid insurance and other	14,028	20,134	26,070
Total current assets	1,511,366	1,196,345	1,009,920
Property, Plant, and Equipment			
Buildings and improvements........................	341,426	325,686	295,130
Machinery and equipment..........................	210,493	173,073	135,419
Motor vehicles...................................	32,578	32,578	29,421
Office equipment.................................	42,866	43,905	36,949
	627,363	575,242	496,919
Less accumulated depreciation	273,284	233,444	185,215
	354,079	341,798	311,704
Land...	11,101	11,101	11,101
	365,180	352,899	322,805
Other Assets			
Cash surrender value of life insurance policies (less loans of $19,748 in 1997, $19,590 in 1996, and $19,432 in 1995).	81,978	77,215	72,569
Total assets......................................	$1,958,524	$1,626,459	$1,405,294

EXHIBIT 3   (*continued*)

	December 31,		
	1997	*1996*	*1995*
LIABILITIES			
Current Liabilities			
Current maturities of long-term debt....................	$ 12,184	$ 10,558	$ 9,000
Note payable—bank[a].............................	325,000	200,000	—
Note payable—officer.............................	—	30,000	39,000
Accounts payable			
Trade	389,582	295,208	313,203
Employees' withholdings	4,875	3,197	3,070
Amount due for purchase of treasury stock.............	—	—	75,000
Accrued liabilities			
Salaries and wages.............................	93,713	57,534	48,413
Commissions...................................	41,474	26,010	12,878
Sundry	14,528	11,357	4,796
Income taxes	—	18,036	19,800
	149,715	112,937	85,887
Total current liabilities........................	881,356	651,900	525,160
Long-term debt	176,522	189,122	195,710
Stockholders' Equity			
Contributed capital 6%			
Cumulative preferred stock—authorized 10,000 shares			
of $10 par value; issued 2,000 shares	20,000	20,000	20,000
Common stock			
Class A (nonvoting) Authorized 15,000 shares of $10			
par value issued $8,305 shares	83,050	83,050	83,050
Class B (voting) Authorized 5,000 shares of $10			
par value; issued and outstanding 20 shares	200	200	200
	103,250	103,250	103,250
Retained earnings	892,396	77,187	676,174
	995,646	880,437	779,424
Less shares reacquired and held in treasury—at cost			
2,000 shares 6% cumulative preferred stock...........	20,000	20,000	20,000
2,308 shares Class A common stock	75,000	75,000	75,000
	95,000	95,000	95,000
Total stockholders' equity	900,646	785,437	684,424
Total liabilities.....................................	$1,958,524	$1,626,459	$1,405,294

[a]Converted to long-term debt in balance sheet projections in **Exhibit 4**.

EXHIBIT 3   *(continued)*

Statements of Earnings

	Year Ended December 31,		
	1997	*1996*	*1995*
Net sales	$4,412,191	$3,573,579	$2,973,780
Cost of goods sold			
Inventories at beginning of year	742,907	593,185	416,512
Purchases	1,599,426	1,275,665	1,109,781
Freight in	19,520	26,595	20,966
Direct labor	430,154	360,568	328,487
Manufacturing expenses	977,299	802,172	673,643
	3,769,236	3,058,185	2,549,389
Inventories at end of year	826,228	742,907	593,185
	2,943,008	2,315,278	1,956,204
Gross profit	1,469,183	1,258,301	1,017,576
Product development expenses	131,746	128,809	102,299
Selling and administrative expenses	1,112,542	915,140	740,801
	1,244,288	1,043,949	843,100
Operating income	224,895	214,352	174,476
Other deductions or (income)			
Interest expense	56,259	37,790	32,416
Payments to retired employee	10,000	10,000	20,000
Miscellaneous	(923)	(1,551)	(6,193)
	65,336	46,239	46,223
Earnings before income taxes	159,559	168,113	128,253
Provision for income taxes	44,350	67,100	49,000
Earnings before extraordinary income	115,209	101,013	79,253
Extraordinary income—life insurance proceeds in excess of cash			
surrender value	—	—	27,275
Net earnings	$ 115,209	$ 101,013	$ 106,528
Earnings per share of common stock	$ 19.15	$ 16.79	$ 13.10

EXHIBIT 3   *(concluded)*

Statements of Changes in Financial Position

	Year Ended December 31,		
	1997	*1996*	*1995*
Working capital provided from operations			
Earnings before extraordinary income	$ 115,209	$ 101,013	$ 79,253
Add item not requiring outlay of working capital			
Depreciation	55,978	50,658	44,267
Working capital provided from operations	171,187	151,671	123,520
Extraordinary income from life insurance proceeds	—	—	27,275
Capitalized equipment lease obligation	—	5,295	—
Proceeds from cash surrender value of life insurance			
policies	—	—	51,877
Total working capital provided	171,187	156,966	202,672
Working capital applied			
Additions to property, plant, and equipment	68,259	80,752	47,107
Increase in cash surrender value of life insurance policies—			
net of loans	4,763	4,646	5,954
Reduction of long-term debt	12,600	11,883	8,996
Purchase of 2,308 shares of nonvoting Class A stock	—	—	75,000
Total working capital applied	85,622	97,281	137,057
Increase in working capital	$ 85,565	$ 59,685	$ 65,615
Net change in working capital consists of			
increase (decrease) in current assets			
Cash	$ 47,470	$(66,742)	$ 64,854
Accounts receivable—net	190,336	109,381	(3,548)
Inventories	83,321	149,722	176,673
Prepaid expenses	(6,106)	(5,936)	(4,980)
	315,021	186,425	232,999
Increase (decrease) in current liabilities			
Current portion of long-term debt	1,626	1,558	500
Notes payable to bank	125,000	200,000	—
Note payable officer	(30,000)	(9,000)	—
Accounts payable	96,052	(17,868)	107,153
Amount due for purchase of treasury stock	—	(75,000)	75,000
Contribution to profit-sharing trust	—	—	(20,000)
Accrued liabilities	54,814	28,814	(7,619)
Income taxes	(18,036)	(1,764)	12,350
	229,456	126,740	167,384
Increase in working capital	85,565	59,685	65,615
Working capital at beginning of year	544,445	484,760	419,145
Working capital at end of year	$ 630,010	$ 544,445	$ 484,760

EXHIBIT 4   **Proforma Financial Statements**

Income Statement for Projections

Historical Percentage			Projected Percentage				(Thousands of Dollars)		
1995	*1996*	*1997*	*1998*	*1999*	*2000*		*1998*	*1999*	*2000*
100.00	100.00	100.00	100.00	100.00	100.00	Net sales	4,800	5,100	5,400
65.78	64.79	66.70	67.00	67.00	67.00	Cost of goods sold	3,216	3,417	3,618
34.22	35.21	33.30	33.00	33.00	33.00	Gross income	1,584	1,683	1,782
28.61[a]	29.28	28.25	28.00	28.00	28.00	Operating general & administrative[b] . . .	1,344	1,428	1,512
5.61[b]	5.93	5.05	5.00	5.00	5.00	Profit before taxes and purchase financing.	240	255	270
						Noncompete payments	10	10	10
						Interest for "Other Bank Debt"[d]	74	70	63
						Profit before taxes	156	175	197
38.02[c]	39.09	27.08	39.00	39.00	39.00	Taxes.	61	68	77
						Net earnings	95	107	120

[a]Historical and projected percentages include interest for long-term debt **only,** as well as a $25,000 cost reduction for the reduced salary requirements of a replacement for Evans.
[b]Profit after adjustments to operating G&A.
[c]Effective tax rate.
[d]Interest for "Other Bank Debt" is assumed to be 10% times "Other Bank Debt" outstanding at the end of the prior year.

Projected Beginning Equity Position

Total equity, December 31, 1997	$900,646
Less cash payment of purchase price	500,000
Beginning equity, January 1, 1998	$400,646

EXHIBIT 4   *(continued)*

Balance Sheet Accounts for Projections

(Thousands of Dollars)

	Historical			Projected				At Closing 1998	Dec 31,		
	1995	1996	1997	1998	1999	2000			1998	1999	2000
(Days)	39.3	43.9	51.3	52.0	52.0	52.0	Assets:				
(Turns)	3.3	3.1	3.6	3.8	4.0	4.1	Cash.	50	50	50	50
							Accounts receivable	620	684	727	769
							Inventories.	826	846	854	882
							Prepaids.	14	15	15	15
							Total current assets	1,510	1,595	1,646	1,716
							Net fixed assets	365	370	370	370
							(Assumed policies cashed in)	0	0	0	0
							Total assets.	1,875	1,965	2,016	2,086
							Liabilities and Equity:				
(Days)	59.0	47.0	48.9	50.0	50.0	50.0	Operating accounts payable.	394	441	468	496
($000)	205	200	189				Accrued expenses and taxes	150[a]	150	150	150
							Total existing long-term debt.	189	176	163	148
							Liabilities from ongoing operations. . .	733	767	781	794
							Other bank debt	741	702	632	569
							Total liabilities.	1,474	1,469	1,413	1,363
							Equity at beginning of year[b]	401	401	496	603
							Net earnings for year.	NA	95	107	120
							Total equity	401	496	603	723
							Total liabilities and equity.	1,875	1,965	2,016	2,086

[a]In a purchase by an **outside** buyer, this is often zero at closing. These liabilities are paid off rather than transferred, and new accruals are gradually rebuilt in the normal course of business.
[b]See calculations of beginning equity elsewhere in exhibit.

EXHIBIT 4   *(concluded)*

Sources and Uses of Funds
(thousands of dollars)

	1998	1999	2000
Net earnings.............................	95	107	120
Plus depreciation	56	56	56
Funds provided by operations	151	163	176
Increase in accounts payable	47	27	28
Increase in accrual expenses and taxes	0	0	0
Increase in other bank debt	—	—	—
Total sources	198	190	204
Uses			
Increase in accounts receivables	64	43	42
Increase in inventories.....................	20	8	28
Increase in prepaids	1	0	0
Increase in fixed assets[a]	61	56	56
Decrease in long-term debt	13	13	15
Decrease in other bank debt.................	39	70	63
Total uses.............................	198	190	204

Note: Total Sources must equal Total Uses.

[a]Reinvestment in plant and equipment is assumed to equal depreciation after the first year.

DOWNTOWN DAYCARE

Rosemary Norwood, the President of Downtown Daycare, was in a quandary. She had established the viability of backup daycare centers, and her company had earned a reputation as the best in the business. However, she needed to raise more money to fund the opening of additional centers. While she had had some positive feedback from her first round of meetings with potential investors, she was also receiving mixed signals, and was uncertain what actions should be taken next.

Background

The oldest of three children, Rosemary Norwood was raised in Albany, New York. After graduating from Wellesley with a BA in Economics and Psychology in 1984, she took a job as an analyst with the Wall Street firm of Merrill Lynch. Rosemary explained her thinking:

> It seemed challenging, and I fully expected to work there for two years and then attend business school. However, it was an odd experience. First, I learned that I had little aptitude for, and no interest in, finance. Second, I was working directly with a Managing Director, which might sound good, but I never worked on any standard deals. Everything was one-of-a-kind. It was frustrating.

This case was prepared by Joseph M. Welsh under the supervision of H. Irving Grousbeck, Lecturer in Management, Stanford University Graduate School of Business, as the basis for class discussion rather than to illustrate either effective or ineffective handling of an administrative situation.

This case was made possible by the generous support of Donald J. Douglass.

Stanford Business School Case S-SB-166.

123

Fortunately, Rosemary had applied for a Rotary Scholarship during her senior year at Wellesley, and toward the end of her first year at Merrill Lynch received word that she had won. In 1985, she began a two-year program at Oxford University in England, where she received a Masters degree in Developmental Psychology in 1987.

After completing her program at Oxford, Rosemary decided to pursue a career other than academics. Having large student loans from both Wellesley and Oxford, she contacted her previous employer, Merrill Lynch, and was offered a job working in corporate finance at Merrill's Los Angeles office.

Still intent on attending business school, Rosemary had applied to all the top schools toward the end of her studies at Oxford. After a few months at Merrill Lynch, she was accepted to Stanford's Graduate School of Business, where she began her studies toward an MBA in the fall of 1987.

Child Care

Her first year at business school was difficult. Rosemary was constantly flying back to Albany to visit her ailing mother. During that time, she was able to think about career alternatives, and decided that child care would be her calling. Rosemary described the situation:

> At Oxford, I had concentrated on child development. After going back into investment banking, I realized just how much passion I had towards children's issues, and how little acumen I had for corporate finance. I got a summer job in Boston with Daytime Solutions, a day care company, and loved it! When I came back to Stanford for my second year, I knew exactly what I wanted to do—I wanted to run a child care company. I took every small business and entrepreneurial class I could during my second year. I even met with a professor who specialized in starting businesses. When I told him of my desire to run a child care company, he said, "Child care is a social service, not a business." Nonetheless, I had my heart set on the industry.

After graduation in June of 1989, Rosemary accepted an offer to return to Daytime Solutions.

Daytime Solutions was a small company, run by two women, that had a single day care center located in an office park near Boston. Rosemary joined with a verbal promise from the President, Maggie Sullivan, that she would receive equity in the company as it grew.

The Concept of Backup Child Care

Soon after Rosemary joined Daytime Solutions full time, Garner & Toyle, a large Boston law firm, contacted the company to discuss an idea—backup child care. Garner & Toyle had many lawyers who were raising families, and they discovered that these lawyers would often need to take a day off when their normal child care broke down. The law firm thought it might be beneficial to provide employees with a temporary solution, near the office, that would still allow the lawyer to come to work. Rosemary was given full responsibility for this project, and commented on the opportunity:

> I thought it was a good idea. The law firm covered all the costs of developing this center for its employees, the employees could use it for a few days at a time, as needed, and our company would manage the center for a fee.

The Garner & Toyle backup center was opened in early 1990 and was an instant success. Absenteeism went down at the law firm, and employees loved the service. Rosemary started marketing the idea to other large employers in both Boston and New York City, and by the end of 1992 had commitments for three additional centers in Boston. In addition, two major investment banks had expressed interest in funding the development of several centers in New York.

A Broken Promise

It had now been over three years since Rosemary joined Daytime Solutions, and she felt it was time to get some equity. After all, she felt she had made significant contributions to the company by developing the backup care business on her own. She explained the problem:

> Unfortunately, I didn't have anything in writing. When I reminded Maggie of her promise, she said she never made any such offer. I was crushed—I didn't know what to do. I told Maggie that I might resign from the company.

Rosemary called a good friend who was an attorney. She related that the president of Daytime Solutions wanted her to sign a non-compete agreement if she quit, and that she had no employment contract in place. The attorney advised Rosemary to resign and set up her own backup care company. The attorney also felt that Rosemary could contact both the current and prospective clients of Daytime Solutions. Since Rosemary was the key element in the relationships, the attorney reasoned, the clients would all come over to her new company. Rosemary described her actions:

> I was never so anxious in my whole life! I really trusted this lawyer, so I decided to do what he said. I resigned in October of 1992, started my own company called Downtown Daycare, and invited a couple of key people from Daytime Solutions to join me. Everything went perfectly. Though Maggie threatened to sue me, she never did. Garner & Toyle gave me the contract to manage their center, and the two investment banks came along with me. Three other key people left Daytime Solutions, since they were sick of the treatment they had received from Maggie, and joined me at Downtown Daycare.

Initial Investor Discussions and Company Valuation—January 1993

The Garner & Toyle contract provided for an annual fee of $20,000 to be paid up-front. Also, the first of the investment banking clients, which had committed to a center, remitted its annual fee in quarterly installments of $8,750. Both companies also paid in advance, every three months, the estimated operating expenses for their centers, which were about $350,000 per center per year. However, Rosemary did not receive any salary. Payroll consisted of the people working at the child care centers and the three corporate employees. Further, the company would need some working capital of its own in the not-too-distant future. Rosemary decided to do something about financing the company, and explained her first step:

> A friend of mine knew a partner in the Merchant Banking group of a major investment bank. I wrote a business plan for the company (see **Exhibit 1** for selected segments), and had my friend give it to this partner and ask him to value the company. He came back a few days later and told me that the partner thought the company was worth $1 million as is.

With this valuation in hand, Rosemary contacted an old friend from Merrill, Brian Rose. While she knew she needed money shortly, Rosemary wanted to be certain that the business was going to work before she took any outside capital. Rosemary rounded up two other people, Mark Stewart (an LBO banker) and Mark's father-in-law, Larry Quinn, a lawyer. In February of 1993 this team of three promised Rosemary that they would invest $200,000 collectively when she needed it. They left the details of the investment (% equity, terms) undetermined.

In July of 1993, Rosemary did need some money, and Brian invested $50,000 on a handshake, with no documentation at all.

By the middle of 1993 Downtown Daycare Incorporated (DDI) had five corporate employees in the company, and was about to open its fourth center. The first three centers, Garner & Toyle (16 children—Boston), Investment Bank #1 (20 children—New York), and Banking Harborside (11 children—New York), were run on a management fee basis and were for the exclusive use of the sponsoring clients. The fourth center, Bankers Plaza, established a new practice for DDI: consortium centers. With the experience of the first three centers, DDI had determined that the optimal ratio of spaces to employees was one space per 250. This struck a good balance between having the center well utilized, yet limiting the number of desired users who were turned away due to a full center. Rosemary explained the consortium concept further:

> The first three centers were small, with a capacity of 11 to 20 children. The Bankers Plaza location only had 1000 employees, and it did not make sense to build a center with only four spaces. Our client wanted other companies to share the buildout costs. While they were extremely happy with the results of the Harborside center, they had a hard time committing that much capital to a project that was controlled by someone outside of their company. We decided to seek out other firms, sell them on the concept, and combine their needs with those of our initial client.

DDI was able to sell the backup care concept to some top-tier neighbors of its initial client, thereby adding the names of four investment banking firms to its customer list. The fourth center was opened in November of 1993.

All of the first four centers were operated on a management fee basis. DDI would select the site, negotiate the lease, plan and facilitate the leasehold improvements, hire the child care personnel, and manage the center. The client would pay for the leasehold improvements, typically $400–500K for a 40 space center. The client would also pay the rent, which ranged from $25 to $40 per square foot in a 2,500 to 3,000 square foot facility, and the operating expenses, which ranged from $400,000 to $700,000 per year. DDI would receive a management fee of $20,000 to $50,000 per year. Rosemary described the rationale behind the fee:

> When we signed the contracts for the first few centers, we had no idea how much to charge. We asked for $20,000, which was far too low, and I think our client knew that. We kept raising the price for subsequent centers, and settled on about $50,000 per year per center.

Raising Another $150K in Equity

By June of 1994, DDI had opened its fifth center, also located in New York. While prospects looked good, the cash situation was getting dire. (See **Exhibit 2** for DDI Financial Statements.) Rosemary decided to contact the three potential investors and ask them to invest the remaining $150,000 of their year-old commitment. She shared the rationale behind the investment:

> Brian, Mark, and Larry made good on their promise to invest. They each put up one third, with Brian investing only $16,667 now, since he had given us $50,000 last spring. We used the initial valuation from January 1993, and they each received 6.67% of the company for their $66,667. I owned the remaining 80%. I thought the valuation was too low, but it was a battle I did not want to fight.

Competitive Pressure

DDI had now gained experience in opening and operating five centers. But there were two competitors who were starting aggressively to pursue DDI's business.

Bright Horizons was an operator of full-time day care centers, with over 80 centers in operation throughout the northeast United States. While they had little experience in the backup day care area, they had come in to Garner & Toyle at the last minute and offered to develop their center for no fee—Bright Horizons would pay all up-front costs and charge a usage fee. Fortunately for DDI, Garner & Toyle was comfortable with the relationship it had developed with Rosemary and her team, and declined the offer.

McNeil, Inc., was a small, well-funded company run by Donna McNeil, who had previously been an executive at Toddlercenters, the largest operator of full-time day care centers in the United States, with over 1000 centers in operation. Donna's husband was the managing partner of a large law firm, and through her husband Donna had access to vast amounts of capital. McNeil had a backup care center in Washington, DC, and was beginning to engage in some ruthless practices to win business from DDI. For example, she hired Maggie Sullivan from Daytime Solutions as a consultant to help McNeil pitch her services against DDI's, and Maggie took great liberty in presenting Rosemary and her team as less than professional people who stole the backup care idea from her. McNeil also questioned the practice of having companies fund the costs of developing centers: "Why should *you* be in the child care business?" they would ask. McNeil pointed out the liability problems if something happened to a child in the center, and ended its pitch by offering to cover all development costs themselves—the client would need only to purchase a space in the center for $16,000 a year per space, plus a $35 fee for each usage.

Rosemary needed to respond to this competitive threat, and explained her situation:

> Our concept was working—every customer loved the service, their employees were happy, absenteeism was down, and we had not lost a single client. However, McNeil and her husband were scaring our customers by telling them that they could suffer large punitive damages if a child was ever injured in a center, and questioning their need to fund the development costs of the centers. We really had no choice but to raise more money and transition our business model toward company-owned centers.

Another mitigating factor was national expansion; many of DDI's clients were expressing a desire to have centers in other cities, such as Chicago, Los Angeles, and San Francisco. If DDI did not raise equity quickly, it risked losing out in these new markets to a competitor like McNeil.

Raising More Money

Company-owned centers required significant amounts of up-front investment. The only way to raise this sort of capital, Rosemary reasoned, was by selling additional equity. Since it had been almost two years since the original business plan was written, she decided it would be a good idea to generate another plan, this time featuring company-owned centers. However, she had little time to work on this herself.

In November of 1994, Rosemary met with her three investors and expressed a desire to raise more money. After some discussion, they agreed that it made sense and introduced Rosemary to Sharon Vickers, a business consultant in Boston who had many years of experience working in venture capital. Sharon was a graduate of Harvard Business School and had a number of contacts within the venture community in Boston. Rosemary gave Sharon a draft of a business plan, some rough numbers, and agreed to pay her $100/hour while Sharon completed the business plan. Rosemary described the process:

My investors recommended Sharon, so I decided to hire her. It did not go well. She ran up lots of hours and never produced a document. In January, things became even more complicated. Brian Rose lost his job, and he came to me and offered to manage the fundraising effort himself as my CFO. I was uncomfortable with Brian doing the fundraising because I was not sure our interests were aligned. After all, he and the other original investors said they would like 25% of the next offering, and I still felt uneasy about the terms of their original investment.

By July of 1995, Rosemary did not have a final document from Sharon, and Brian was continuing to express his interest in being the CFO of Downtown Daycare. Rosemary decided that she needed to dedicate herself to the fundraising effort. She terminated her relationship with Sharon, paying her over $10,000 for her services. Rosemary also met with Brian and, in a difficult meeting, informed him that she did not want him as either a full-time fundraiser or as CFO of the company.

With some assistance from her present investors, Rosemary finally completed the document in September of 1995 (see **Exhibit 3** for selected segments). On the advice of her investors, she did not include any detailed financial information or center-level projections. She shared the reasoning behind this decision:

> We thought it would be too risky to have all the numbers go out in the first mailing. We decided to mail the overview document, and if people were interested, we would ask them to sign a confidentiality agreement; we would then mail them the projections.

In early September, 1995, Rosemary mailed the overview document to the following individuals:

Ron Harberg: A retired venture capitalist in Boston who was an acquaintance of Mark. Ron was in his mid-to-late 60s, and used to run the Arthur Rosen fund.

Hudson Partners: A small, two-person venture firm in Boston that had cold-called Rosemary a month earlier.

Professor Silver: A professor of Rosemary's while in business school. Professor Silver passed the document on to William Eagle, a friend who ran a venture fund in Boston.

Charlie Werstein: A classmate from business school, Charlie was a close friend of an individual who invested in many start-up companies.

Andy Maxwell: Another classmate, Andy worked at a New York investment bank, and promised Rosemary that he would show the document to some experienced investors.

George Morgan: A partner in one of the most prestigious leveraged buyout firms in the country, George was a well-known name to everyone in the financial community. Larry Quinn had done legal work with George's firm and was confident that George would be interested in investing for his own personal account.

Ten days later, Rosemary contacted each of the people who had received the documents. Hudson Partners declined any interest, stating that it did not want to invest in any deal associated with real estate. The other parties all wanted more information. Rosemary was perplexed:

> My current investors did not want me to send out the information without obtaining a confidentiality agreement. When I talked to William Eagle, he said there was no way he would sign any such agreement. After lots of bickering, I convinced my investors that we should proceed with the distribution anyway (see **Exhibit 4**).

Rosemary contacted the recipients a week later, and was able to schedule face-to-face meetings with several of them. The sessions took place during October and early November of 1995. The results were as follows:

Ron Harberg: Ron wanted to represent DDI in its negotiations with other venture firms. He alluded to being able to raise at least $1 million for a fee of 5% of the money raised, and thought DDI was worth around $5 million pre-money.

William Eagle: He was interested, but was not willing to offer a price or an amount. William asked Rosemary what she thought was a fair price, and Rosemary did not offer a number.

Andy Maxwell: Rosemary had accepted Andy's offer to present the documents to a partner at his firm who managed many private equity placements. The partner advised that, hypothetically, he would want 0.75% of the equity for a $100,000 investment.

George Morgan: Rosemary, Mark, and Larry Quinn flew to California to meet with George in his office. At the last minute, George had to cancel, but two of his associates attended. These associates grilled Rosemary for over an hour about various financial projections, and then left the room. Larry was then asked to meet privately with the senior associate while Rosemary and Mark waited in the conference room. The senior associate then walked all three of them to their car, and wished them luck. Distraught by the finality of his send-off, Rosemary turned to Larry, who was sitting in the back seat. "Guess what," said Larry. "They would be willing to invest $1 million for 20% of the company.

Rosemary needed to determine what to do next with each of these investors.

Time Challenges—December 1995

Rosemary felt that she was under extreme time pressure, and could never find enough hours in the day to complete essential tasks. She continued to be directly involved in every aspect of the business. The organization chart had more holes than filled positions (see **Exhibit 5**). She knew it was time to bring more expertise into the company, but she was concerned about how to prioritize her job openings. DDI now had over 70 employees, of which ten worked in corporate and the remainder worked at each of the centers. Rosemary explained her concerns:

I needed to determine which of my top management positions were most important, develop a plan to find the right people and get them to join the company. I was starting to go crazy! I was in the middle of everything—sales, lease negotiations, marketing, raising money, hiring—you name it. I loved what I was doing, but I was starting to worry that I was in over my head.

She knew it was time to make some big decisions that would affect the future of her company. The question was, where should she begin?

EXHIBIT 1   Selected Segments from Original DDI Business Plan—January 1993

EXECUTIVE SUMMARY

Company:

Downtown Daycare ("DDI" or "the Company") was incorporated October 30, 1992 in Massachusetts and is located at Sixty State Street, Boston, Massachusetts 02109. DDI designs, implements and operates backup child care centers and is dedicated exclusively to working with corporations, real estate owners and developers to bring backup child care to the worksite.

DDI was founded by Rosemary Norwood previously the Vice-President of Daytime Solutions where she oversaw the development and operation of backup child care centers.

Product:

Backup child care centers are child care alternatives used when families' regular child care arrangements break down or are unavailable. These break-downs in care may occur when a regular caregiver (e.g., spouse, baby-sitter, nanny) is ill, on vacation or just unavailable or when a regular child care center is closed. These centers are also used during holidays, weekends and school vacations. Some of the more innovative uses for these centers include when an employee returns from maternity leave, works a flexible schedule or relocates to a new office. Unlike regular child care centers which serve only preschool children, these centers serve children from six weeks through 12 years of age.

Concept:

Backup child care centers enable employees to work on days that they would otherwise call in sick or take as vacation. Indeed, the average working parent misses between five and seven work days per year due solely to break downs in child care arrangements. Backup child care centers also serve families with school-age children which traditionally have very few options during Monday holidays, school snow days and school vacation periods. It should be noted that by the year 2000, it is expected that more than 70% of the women in the workforce will have children between the ages of five and twelve years. Thus, backup centers are and will continue to be an ideal means of helping employees balance work and family during school vacations. For corporations, these centers serve hundreds of different families each year, reduce absenteeism, assist in recruiting and retaining employees, enhance morale and bring positive publicity. Indeed, the value to firms in industries such as law, accounting and consulting is easily calculable because employee utilization may be translated into "save billable hours." Similarly, for real estate owners and developers, these centers are a fabulous, low cost amenity which assist in attracting and retaining tenant companies.

Note: Actual document, with exhibits, was 49 pages.

EXHIBIT 1 *(continued)*

DDI works with a company to design, implement and operate these centers which are funded in their entirety by participating firms. DDI has no capital investment at risk in the buildout or in the on-going operation of each center. DDI receives Consulting Fees for the design and development of the centers and annual Management Fees for the operation of the centers. DDI works to enter into long-term management contracts with a company or a group of companies. These contracts vary in length from one to five years and represent a recurring revenue stream.

Management:

Rosemary Norwood, President and Founder

Ms. Norwood graduated from Stanford University's Graduate School of Business in June 1989 and earned her master's degree in Developmental Psychology from Oxford University in 1986. Prior to founding DDI she was Vice-President of Daytime Solutions ("DS") where she was responsible for operating the company. In 18 months, DS had completed the marketing and development of four (4) backup centers and oversaw the management of these centers. Ms. Norwood also worked as Director of Sales & Marketing for Daytime Solutions where her responsibilities included overseeing the development and operations of traditional child care centers. Additionally, Ms. Norwood has worked as a Financial Analyst in Investment Banking with Merrill Lynch Capital Markets. She received her bachelor's degree in Economics and Psychology from Wellesley College.

Andrea Golden, Marketing Coordinator and Project Manager

Ms. Golden coordinates marketing efforts and oversees the management of projects currently under development. Previously, Ms. Golden worked at Marketing to Women, researching and writing articles for the monthly newsletter and consulting with clients in developing marketing strategies. Ms. Golden also has experience working in television and radio production with WHDH in Boston and WBBM in Chicago. Ms. Golden graduated from Wellesley College.

Brenda Marsh, Director of Operations

Ms. Marsh assists in the startup of new programs, the licensing of facilities and oversees the on-going daily operational issues for DDI and the centers. Ms. Marsh is also responsible for monthly financial reporting for both DDI and the centers in operation. Prior to joining DDI, Ms. Marsh was Director of Operations with Daytime Solutions Inc. overseeing the operations of four centers. Ms. Marsh has worked in child care and special needs settings providing speech services to children and adults. She is a graduate of Bridgewater State College.

Ann O'Malley, Administrative Assistant

Ms. O'Malley assists Downtown Daycare in project support and marketing. Previously, Ms. O'Malley worked at Associated Day Care Services in Boston researching parent needs for and satisfaction with child care arrangements. Ms. O'Malley also has direct experience working at an on-site child care center in Mobile, Alabama. She received a bachelor's degree in Sociology from Holy Cross College and a master's degree in Social Work from Boston University.

Additional resources are drawn from Directors of existing centers. The Directors assist in environmental design, hiring and training of staff and ongoing program evaluation. Although employees of DDI, the Directors are funded by an individual center's budget and paid an additional stipend for consultation on specific DDI projects.

EXHIBIT 1   *(continued)*

Educational
Consultants:

Nancy McDonald, Director of The Children's Place at Garner & Toyle
Ms. McDonald consults to DDI on Environmental Design and Program
Development. She has been Director of The Children's Place at Garner &
Toyle since its opening in July of 1990. Ms. McDonald worked as a Child
Development Advisor for ABCD Head Start and as a consultant in the area of
social and behavioral difficulties for the city of Cambridge, Massachusetts. Ms.
McDonald holds a master's degree from Wheelock College and a bachelor's
degree from Boston College.

Tracy Ross, Director of The Children's Center at Bankers Harborside Ms.
Ross brings over 20 years experience in designing, administering and
teaching early childhood programs. Ms. Ross holds an Ed.M. from Columbia
Teachers College in the area of Instructional Practices with Families and
Infants with Disabilities. She also holds an M.A. in Education and a
bachelor's degree in Audiology and Speech Pathology. She recently received
a Training Fellowship to work at Columbia's Center for Infants and Parents
and is currently working on her Doctorate at Columbia Teachers College. Ms.
Ross will assist DDI in Infant/Toddler Curriculum Development and Parent
Outreach Initiatives.

Arlene Ulrich, Director of The Children's Center for Investment Bank #1
Ms. Ulrich brings 20 years experience in the field of early childhood
education to DDI. She holds two master's degrees, one in Early Childhood
Education from Bank Street College and the other in Special Education from
Yeshiva University. She is the recipient of two fellowships for which she
trained teachers to work with developmentally disabled children. Ms. Ulrich
will assist DDI in the coordination of on-going training and development of
center staff.

DDI also relies upon renowned educational consultants, such as Dr. Joan
Black, in the development of educational curriculum and programming. Dr.
Black is a professor at Wheelock College specializing in Infant and Toddler
Behavior. She consults internationally on a broad range of early childhood
issues including environmental design. Dr. Black is also the President of The
Activities Club, an innovative program designed to introduce school-age
children to a broad range of fun and exciting topics such as sea life,
photography and the universe. The Activities Club is the foundation of the
school-age curriculum for DDI.

Financing:

In order to continue to expand in the development of new centers, DDI is
seeking $125,000 to fund marketing costs, to increase personnel for both
marketing and operations management and to provide working capital. DDI
anticipates thereafter that it will generate sufficient cash flow to fund any
further growth. The Company desires to secure financing through the sale of
debt, equity, or some mutually acceptable combination of both.

The enclosed proformas are provided on an annual basis. Break even status on
an operational basis is expected in year two. By the end of the fifth year of
operation, it is projected that DDI will have recurring operating revenues of
approximately $1,000,000.

EXHIBIT 1   *(continued)*

PROFORMA BALANCE SHEETS
Original DDI Business Plan—January 1993
(All figures are projected, not actual)

	1993	1994	1995	1996	1997
ASSETS					
Cash	10,000	10,000	80,742	390,645	894,577
Other Current	1,000	1,000	1,000	1,000	1,000
Total Current Assets	11,000	11,000	81,742	391,645	895,577
Fixtures & Equipment	8,200	14,200	20,200	26,200	32,200
TOTAL ASSETS	19,200	25,200	101,942	417,845	927,777
LIABILITIES AND EQUITY					
Short-Term Debt	121,553	62,662	0	0	0
EQUITY					
Common Stock	1,000	1,000	1,000	1,000	1,000
Retained Earnings	(103,353)	(38,462)	100,942	416,845	926,777
TOTAL	(102,353)	(37,462)	101,942	417,845	927,777
TOTAL LIABILITIES AND EQUITY	19,200	25,200	101,942	417,845	927,777

EXHIBIT 1   *(concluded)*

PROFORMA INCOME STATEMENTS
Original DDI Business Plan—January 1993
(All figures are projected, not actual)

	By December 31				
	1993	*1994*	*1995*	*1996*	*1997*
# of centers in operation	6	10	14	18	22
Sales					
Consulting Fees (1)	125,000	140,000	140,000	140,000	140,000
Management Fees (2)	102,500	320,000	504,250	704,675	925,143
Center Startup Fees (3)	1,500,000	2,000,000	2,000,000	2,000,000	2,000,000
Center Operating Fees (4)	2,916,000	5,292,000	7,884,000	10,476,000	13,068,000
Total Sales	4,643,500	7,752,000	10,528,250	13,320,675	16,133,143
Center Expenses	4,416,000	7,292,000	9,884,000	12,476,000	15,068,000
Contibution to Overhead	227,500	460,000	644,250	844,675	1,065,143
General & Administrative					
Corporate Salaries &					
Benefits (5)	139,240	170,982	227,531	238,908	250,853
Center Salaries & Benefits (5)	102,857	124,520	178,745	187,683	197,067
Other Expenses	88,600	92,682	97,316	102,182	107,291
Total	330,697	388,184	503,592	528,773	555,211
EBITDA	(103,197)	71,816	140,658	315,902	509,932
Interest Expense	5,356	6,926	1,253	0	0
Net Income (Loss)	(108,553)	64,890	139,405	315,902	509,932
Retained Earnings Begin	5,200	(103,353)	(38,463)	100,942	416,844
Retained Earnings End	(103,353)	(38,463)	100,942	416,844	926,776

PROFORMA CASH FLOW SCHEDULE

Net Income (Loss)	(108,553)	64,890	139,405	315,902	509,932
Purchases of Fixt. & Equip.	(6,000)	(6,000)	(6,000)	(6,000)	(6,000)
Borrow/(Repay) of Debt	121,553	(58,891)	(62,662)	0	0
Cash Begin	3,000	10,000	9,999	80,742	390,644
Cash End	10,000	9,999	80,742	390,644	894,576

NOTES:

(1) Assumes $140,000 of consulting fees each year.

(2) Management fees increase by 10% each year.

(3) Costs of opening new centers—all paid by sponsoring clients.

(4) Ongoing operating expenses of centers—all paid by sponsoring clients.

(5) G&A includes the portion of salaries and benefits associated with new business development.

(6) All expenses are projected to increase by 5% annually.

EXHIBIT 2   **Selected DDI Financial Information**

DOWNTOWN DAYCARE
Balance Sheets
Year Ending December 31
(in $ thousands)

	1993	1994
ASSETS		
Cash	345.6	161.8
Accounts Receivable	0.1	118.4
Prepaid Expenses	31.4	61.7
Total Current	377.1	341.9
Equipment and fixtures	12.2	20.1
Less accumulated depreciation	1.7	4.9
TOTAL ASSETS	387.6	357.1
LIABILITIES AND STOCKHOLDERS' EQUITY		
Note Payable—Bank	35.0	20.0
Note Payable—Shareholder	55.0	0.0
Accounts Payable	297.6	107.7
Client Advances	29.9	174.6
Due to stockholder	37.4	30.5
Deferred Revenue	6.3	164.9
Other	45.5	61.6
Total Current Liabilities	506.7	559.3
Common stock, $1 par value	1.0	1.2
Additional Paid-In Capital	0.0	199.8
Accum. Deficit—Prior Years	(120.1)	(120.1)
Accum. Deficit—Current Year		(283.1)
Total Stockholders' Equity	(119.1)	(202.2)
TOTAL LIABILITIES/EQUITY	387.6	357.1

EXHIBIT 2   *(concluded)*

DOWNTOWN DAYCARE
Yearly Income Statements
Year Ending December 31
(in $ thousands)

	1993	*1994*
Revenue	1,082.9	2,164.6
Center Operating Expense	885.1	1,783.4
Center Operating Income	197.8	381.2
CFI Corporate Expenses		
G&A	126.4	409.9
Marketing & Sales	189.6	255.1
Total Corporate Expense	316.0	665.0
Total Operating Expense	1,201.1	2,448.4
EBITDA	(118.2)	(283.8)
Interest Expense	2.7	3.0
Interest Income	(0.9)	(8.2)
Provision for taxes	0.0	1.3
Depreciation	0.1	3.2
Net Income (Loss)	(120.1)	(283.1)

**EXHIBIT 3   Overview Information on DDI which Was Sent to
Potential Investors**

EXECUTIVE SUMMARY

Downtown Daycare Inc. ("DDI") is the largest provider of backup child care services to corporate clients in the United States. The Company, headquartered in Boston, Massachusetts, was incorporated on October 30, 1992, and is developing a nationwide presence, with seven backup centers currently in operation in New York, New Jersey and Boston and three centers under development in Chicago, San Francisco and Los Angeles. These centers serve over 50 corporate clients with many clients contracting with DDI at several locations across the country.

The Service

DDI specializes in the design, development and operation of corporate backup child care centers. Backup child care centers are child care facilities which provide short-term child care for a company's employees when regular care arrangements are unavailable. The Company works exclusively with corporations and landlords to create centers at or close to the worksite, and serves children that range in age from six weeks through thirteen years. Centers are developed either for the exclusive use of a single company, or for use by a consortium of companies. DDI enters into contracts with these companies, which vary in length from one to three years, to provide backup child care for their employees at or near the workplace.

Investment Highlights

- The market for backup child care at the corporate worksite is expanding rapidly, and is estimated to have a potential size exceeding $500 million per year.
- DDI has established itself as the leader in corporate backup child care with seven centers opened to date and a commanding presence in the lucrative New York market. In response to existing client requests, DDI is well on its way to establishing a national presence with its current expansion into Chicago, Los Angeles and San Francisco. In this new child care niche, experience and quality of operations are the most important factors in selling the concept of backup care to potential clients.
- DDI has a blue-chip list of over 50 companies in a range of industries, including investment banking, accounting, law, consumer products, and entertainment.
- Backup child care is attractive to corporations not only because it is a highly visible benefit which aids in recruiting and retaining employees, but also because it is easily cost justifiable. According to U.S. Bureau of Labor Statistics, nearly two-thirds of today's work force is comprised of two wage-earner families and according to recent studies cited in a Pittsburgh Business Times and Journal article the average parent misses eight days per year solely due to breakdowns in child care. These missed days have been valued on average at over $4,000 a year per employee. In comparison, the average cost of providing backup child care, $0.32 per day, is relatively insignificant.
- The company's center-level staff are all highly qualified early childhood professionals with at least a bachelors degree in early childhood education. Directors and Assistant Directors are required to have masters degrees. Currently 68% of all staff have masters degrees. Turnover has been an extremely low 3% annually versus an annual average of 45% in the child care field.
- DDI will achieve sales of approximately $3.8 million in 1995 and is expecting a compound annual growth rate in revenues exceeding 65% over the next five years. Except for the marketing overhead expenses required to achieve this growth, the Company would have net income today. As is, the Company expects to break even in 1996.

Market Opportunity

Although the market is just emerging, DDI estimates that the demand for backup child care could exceed $500 million per year. This estimate is arrived at by identifying the number of companies in

---

EXHIBIT 3   *(continued)*

---

the top 200 cities in the U.S. which have greater than 500 employees at any given site. It is then assumed that each of these companies contracts for two spaces at DDI's average revenue per owned center of $22,000 per space. While DDI realized that some corporations already provide day care, a 1994 Families and Work Institute report estimates that currently only 0.1% of U.S. employers provide any form of child care for employees.

The Company actually believes that this market size estimate is conservative because employers with as few as 50 employees can economically justify participating in a backup child care center. Further, this estimate includes only the U.S. while DDI has already been asked to consider providing backup child care for clients with offices internationally. Finally, large corporate sites and office parks not situated in one of the largest 200 cities in the U.S. would also be likely candidates for backup care services.

According to the U.S. Bureau of the Census, the current estimate of the number of children under the age of five years is 20.2 million and is expected to remain in the 19 to 20 million range through the year 2010. This number of children, combined with the fact that labor force participation rates for mothers has increased from 44.4% in 1975 to 59.4% in 1993, supports the continued need for child care assistance for working families. Additionally, according to the Office for Children, by the year 2000 70% of all preschool children and 80% of all school-age children will have mothers in the work force.

Corporations have begun to realize they can easily cost justify backup child care through decreased absenteeism and increased employee productivity of both professions and their support staff. This is supported by The Boston Foundation which estimates the cost of lost productivity due to child care problems to be $3 billion annually. In addition, providing backup child care has enabled DDI's clients to realize further benefit by assisting in recruiting and retaining employees. The Employee Benefit Research Institute and the Gallop Organization conducted a survey in 1994 and found that 69% of Americans think employers should play a role in providing child care. In fact, 46% valued this so highly that they would take a reduction in current wages or other benefits.

Marketing Strategy

The Company's strategy is to be the "first-in" to a city, selling not only the concept of backup child care, but also the DDI model thereby establishing the standards of quality for those target corporations most likely to recognize the financial value of backup child care. To date, DDI has cautiously pursued entrance into new markets to allow for low cost, low risk expansion.

However, existing clients have, in fact, encouraged DDI to expand nationally to provide the same high quality service in other locations. These clients serve as anchor clients and references for additional centers in new cities. The high level of quality if particularly essential when selling to corporations, even more so than when selling to a parent. Client companies must have unequivocal certainty of the quality of staff, standards of operating procedures, and proactive risk management to minimize concern regarding liability.

By selecting new cities with existing clients in mind, DDI is able to accelerate the marketing process and, therefore, profitability of each center and prevent competitors from obtaining a strong foothold in any one market. Through this strategy, DDI will be the first in the industry to provide a national network of backup centers in metropolitan areas.

Organization

Rosemary Norwood, President, founder and 80% owner of DDI, was one of the first in the country to develop and to implement the backup child care concept. She is supported by an experienced management team highly qualified in backup child care, and well-trained teaching staff at each center who provide the day-to-day service. Currently DDI has a staff of 60, which will increase to over 100 by the end of 1995 with the addition of the new centers. A significant percentage of the staff exists to support the growth of DDI.

Exhibit 3   *(concluded)*

Financials

The financial summary to follow later in this section details the actual and projected revenue for the company through fiscal 1999. Up to now, DDI designed, developed and operated centers owned by clients in return for a management fee, which escalates over time. Due to the initial capital constraints of the Company, DDI relied on client companies to fund the capital costs necessary for the center buildouts. Although all capital and operating expenses were budgeted and managed by DDI, the Company was reimbursed by the corporate clients for these costs.

However, as DDI became more confident with the financial dynamics of operating a center and the potential profit, it became desirable to open wholly-owned centers. It is this model which DDI will follow as it expands. In these centers, clients purchase backup spaces at the beginning of a year for a specific fee per space. Once enough spaces are sold, DDI is able to realize significant operating leverage and therefore profits for each center in excess of that generated solely by a management fee.

FINANCIAL SUMMARY
Fiscal Year Ending December 31st
(in millions)

	Audited		Projected				
	1993	*1994*	*1995*	*1996*	*1997*	*1998*	*1999*
Revenue	1.083	2.165	3.843	8.164	14.086	21.683	30.650
EBITDA	(.118)	(.284)	(.560)	.354	2.520	5.309	8.707
Net Profit	(.120)	(.283)	(.611)	(.014)	1.386	2.375	4.010
Capital Expenditures	—	—	1.726	2.522	3.598	3.743	4.486
Number of Centers	4	6	10	15	21	28	36

Funds Required

In order to expand nationally, to gain the "first-in" position in new markets, and to take advantage of the profitability of company-owned centers, DDI requires $1,500,000 to fund expenses and to provide the capital necessary to construct centers in Chicago, Los Angeles and San Francisco. Current investors have committed to 25% of the offering, and 75% or $1.125 million remains available for new investors. DDI anticipated raising such funds through the sale of preferred stock.

Exhibit 4   Detailed Proforma Financials for DDI—July 1995

FINANCIAL PROJECTION SUMMARY, BY CENTER TYPE

	1995	1996	1997	1998	1999
Old-Style Centers (1)					
# centers	7	7	7	7	7
Revenue	3,451,967	4,141,157	4,431,447	4,653,019	4,885,670
Expense	2,991,351	3,486,349	3,691,560	3,887,860	4,073,372
EBITDA	460,616	654,808	739,887	765,159	812,298
New-Style Centers (2)					
# centers	3	8	14	21	29
Revenue	363,000	4,014,000	9,645,300	17,020,395	25,754,841
Expense	381,275	3,082,590	6,389,389	10,883,874	16,015,266
EBITDA	(18,275)	931,410	3,255,911	6,136,521	9,739,575
CFI G&A (3)					
Revenue	28,000	8,400	8,820	9,261	9,724
Expense	1,030,456	1,240,271	1,484,378	1,612,402	1,854,629
EBITDA	(1,002,456)	(1,231,871)	(1,475,558)	(1,603,141)	(1,844,905)
Total					
# centers	10	15	21	28	36
Revenue	3,842,967	8,163,557	14,085,567	21,682,675	30,650,235
Expense	4,403,082	7,809,210	11,565,327	16,384,136	21,943,267
EBITDA	(560,115)	354,347	2,520,240	5,298,539	8,706,968

Notes:
(1) Reflects five management contract centers and two percentage rent centers.
(2) New centers where DDI does the buildout and operates centers for a profit.
(3) Corporate overhead for development and operations of centers.

COMPARATIVE COMPANY ANALYSIS (ALL FIGURES IN MILLIONS)

Company	Market Valuation	Last Twelve Months EBITDA	Sales
Children's Discovery	$ 98.1	$ 6.8	$ 55.4
Kindercare	$423.4	$79.9	$510.1
Educational Dynamics	$ 39.0	$ 4.1	$ 33.1

Exhibit 5   DDI Organization Chart—July 1995

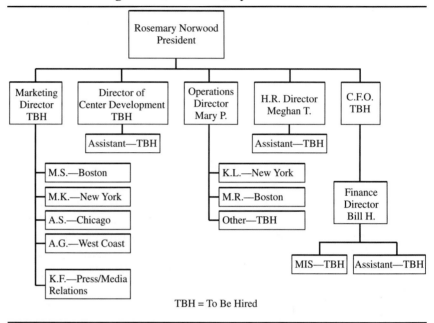

TBH = To Be Hired

THE DAG GROUP

As they began their drive from Washington to Boston on a cold January day in 1991, Chris Hackett and Val Rayzman felt that time was running out.

It had been a year since they'd begun trying to build a chain of upscale drycleaners. They had become industry experts—the next day they were to give a presentation to a drycleaning convention. But hadn't yet bought a single store and were running out of money. They had to do something soon: start or buy a store, or abandon their drycleaning pursuit altogether.

Background

Chris and Val were classmates in the MBA program at Harvard Business School. Val had spent four years as an investment banker in New York, and Chris had sold capital equipment in Cincinnati for his family's company. The two friends described how they came to be interested in the drycleaning industry.

> We were determined not to go back to our former careers, and the on-campus recruiting choices seemed unsatisfactory. We both wanted to run our own business, but neither of us had any idea what to do after graduation.
>
> One fall evening, while batting around different business ideas, Val brought up drycleaning. "Look Chris, here is an industry that is fragmented, undifferentiated, has low entry barriers, and is something that people use all the time. Why can't we do what others did to supermarkets, pizza parlors, and office supply stores?" The thought of transforming a sleepy industry with unappealing stores and poor service was

Valery Rayzman, MBA '90, and Christopher J. Hackett, MBA '90, prepared this case under the supervision of Professor Amar Bhide as the basis for class discussion.

Copyright © 1992 by the President and Fellows of Harvard College.

Harvard Business School Case 9-392-077.

exciting. As a first step, we arranged to do a field study in service management [a student research project] in the spring term with the goal of developing a plan to build a chain of drycleaning stores. We also formed a partnership—the DAG Group, a loose acronym for Drycleaning Acquisition Group.

The DAG Field Study

We worked closely with two large, professionally managed chains in the Boston area. In addition to interviews and plant observations, one of the cleaners also shared the computer data on customers, which we analyzed for retention rates, buying habits, that sort of thing. We traveled the Eastern seaboard visiting drycleaning plants, industry shows, associations, suppliers, brokers, etc. Finally, we conducted several focus groups with business school students and their partners.

The Industry

Drycleaning stores, we found, are either "plant" stores or "dry" stores. Plant stores have their own drycleaning and shirt laundry facilities (**see Exhibits 1 and 2 and Appendix**) or sometimes only drycleaning facilities. Dry stores may be part of a chain serviced by a central plant or independently owned and operated, contracting to have their cleaning done. There are about 18,000 plant stores and 10,000 to 20,000 dry stores in the United States.

About 95 percent of all outlets are single stores owned by a proprietor. Some owners of plant stores have opened dry stores in order to fill plant capacity, and then there are a few large chains. The largest chain belongs to the Johnson Group, a publicly traded British company, which operates 360 stores under 10 different trade names. The Johnson group bought DryClean USA, a franchising company with 184 stores, 82 of which are company owned. The next largest is Concord Custom Cleaners, which was purchased by a large drugstore chain and owns 180 stores from Illinois to Florida.

Real spending remained constant throughout the 1980s. The International Fabricate Institute, the industry association, estimated the total U.S. drycleaning revenue in 1990 to be approximately $4 billion. And the number of establishments increased sharply in the 1980s; in some parts of the country, long-established cleaners found themselves surrounded by three or four new stores.

Price competition is intense and the use of coupons is widespread because many owners, who don't have reliable cost data, believe their costs are fixed. Prices vary by region, depending on the local labor rates; drycleaning averages about $3.50 for a typical one-pound piece and regular laundry $1 for the typical half-pound piece. Per capita spending is about $16 per year, but it is not evenly distributed.

The quality of cleaning and service has deteriorated. Many cleaners feel they cannot afford to upgrade their plants, hire better employees, or settle customer claims generously. In many cities, drycleaners routinely make the Better Business Bureau's "Top 10" list of customer complaints. Customers often switch cleaners; a 35 percent to 40 percent turnover of high-volume customers is typical for a store.

Suppliers and Inputs

Space requirements range from 1,300 to 2,000 square feet for plant stores down to as little as 500 square feet for a dry store. Many stores are located next to grocery stores and can expect to pay $18 to $30 per square foot for that kind of location, compared with the grocery store itself, which may negotiate space for $10 per square foot. Drycleaning stores are also found in strip malls—almost every mall developer tries to include one.

Most large cities have three or four distributors who sell drycleaning and laundry equipment. Another set of distributors provides cleaners with supplies such as hangers, poly-bags, and supplies. Since plants generate hazardous waste, they also have to contract with disposal companies such as SafetyKleen. The solvent used in the drycleaning process is classified as a *possible* carcinogen by the EPA, and there is pressure to reclassify it as a *probable* carcinogen. Rules about emissions of solvent vapors are expected to be tightened, which will force many drycleaners to upgrade their equipment.

Some equipment distributors (and others) have started selling "turnkey" operations. They lease space in a shopping mall, put in the required equipment, counters, conveyors, etc., operate it for six months or a year, and then sell the complete store. Stores are usually priced at a multiple of sales rather than profits, because few cleaners keep good financial records. Typically, multiples range from 0.75 to 1.25 times sales, with the best locations commanding up to 1.5 times sales. Newly arrived immigrants often buy turnkey stores, and, we are told, exaggerated claims and various "hard sell" techniques are common. (See **Exhibit 3** for typical plant economics.)

Customer Segments

Our customer interviews, focus groups, and analysis of computer records led us to believe that drycleaning customers can be segmented into three categories:

- *Heavy users* need drycleaning for their everyday wear. Although a minority, heavy users represent the bulk of drycleaners' revenues. They launder shirts often and dryclean more expensive clothes. Heavy users value convenience and location—time is essential, since most of them are career-focused, affluent professionals. While a few heavy users care a great deal about how their clothes are cleaned, most only notice obvious problems such as missing buttons or shrinkage. And despite complaining about drycleaning costs, very few of them know just how much they pay. They are not really price sensitive.
- *Light users* dryclean their clothes regularly, but they do not need the store services for their daily attire. Although they do care about convenience and quality, they are much more likely than heavy users to use promotional offers and switch cleaners.
- *Occasional users* use drycleaners less than once a month, and some only seasonally. Price is usually their primary consideration, and loyalty is minimal.

Key Success Factors

We noticed that the most profitable cleaners were often surrounded by competitors who offered cheaper prices or better quality. Cleaners seemed to prosper in spite of tough competition when they:

1. Offered the most consistent (if not always the best) quality in their area—the buttons were attached, there were no stains, etc. Quality inspection was often done by the manager after all work was finished.

2. Were run by owners who thought of themselves as businesspeople, not just drycleaners. They understood their costs, analyzed and monitored operations closely, and attached importance to hiring, keeping, and developing good employees. The successful chains hired professional managers to run their stores.

3. Provided the best customer service of all cleaners in the area: long hours, quick turnaround, prompt settlement of claims, knowledgeable and pleasant counter clerks, etc.

4. Operated stores with outstanding location and appearance. They were located on busy streets, usually in freestanding buildings with good parking and easy access. The buildings looked nice, and the customer areas were brightly lit and pleasant.

Strategy for DAG

We concluded that the main driver of a drycleaner's profitability, just as in most service businesses, is its customer-retention rate. Therefore, we decided our strategy would be to:

1. Build large plant "superstores" capable of supporting about $750,000 in sales. Our interviews suggested that the "average" store revenues of $250,000 per year could be doubled without a proportionate increase in fixed labor, equipment, or real estate costs. Beyond $500,000, net margins would not increase significantly, although total profits would.

2. Locate the stores in affluent, dense areas where there are many heavy users. All our stores would be in freestanding buildings on busy streets with good visibility and ample parking.

3. Offer services that appeal to high-usage customers. These services would include long hours, being open on Sundays, same-day service, credit cards, and alterations. We would back these services with an unconditional money-back guarantee.

4. Price at a 10% to 15% premium to the area average.

Dynasty Cleaners

Chris and Val ranked major metropolitan areas on such factors as average age, average income, and density. Based on these rankings, they decided to build their chain in Washington, DC. First, however, they investigated an opportunity to buy Dynasty Cleaners (see **Exhibits 4 and 5** for financial statements), a large chain in Indianapolis:

In the course of our study, we had met an HBS alumnus, Michael Boulder, who was now a venture capitalist at Rainier & Co. in New York. Michael too had investigated drycleaners in a second-year field study, and his team had come close to purchasing Dynasty Cleaners. The deal had fallen apart after several months of discussions because one of the two brothers who owned Dynasty was reluctant to sell.

We met Michael and a partner from Rainier. The meeting went very well, and at the end Michael told us: "Work on your study, and look for deals at the same time. If you are serious about drycleaning, we'll finance your deal either through Rainier or privately."

We maintained contact with Michael, who seemed genuinely interested in financing a drycleaning deal. When we finished our study, he called the owners of Dynasty and found that the chain was struggling and both brothers now wanted to sell. Michael arranged for all of us to meet, and shortly after graduation, we drove to Indianapolis.

We spent the next three days with Michael performing due diligence. Dynasty had 4 plant stores and 26 dry stores. Most of the stores were in strip malls and were in poor condition. Most of the plants were old, the equipment was poorly maintained, and safety rules appeared to be disregarded, raising a possibility of future liability.

Dynasty was one of the oldest cleaners in the United States, and well known in Indianapolis. Apparently, it competed on price; its windows were painted with various price specials, and it distributed many coupons. We called people in the area at random, pretending to do a telephone survey. When we asked them what they thought of Dynasty, we heard comments like:

- "Of course I know Dynasty."
- "Their quality is bad. I'd never use them."
- "I take my inexpensive clothes to them because they have good deals, but I take my good clothes somewhere else."
- "I used to be their customer, but they always lose my stuff."

We looked at Dynasty's leases and found that many of the company's stores had short leases and their rents could be increased. And payroll records showed that employee turnover exceeded 300% annually, which meant that an average employee remained with the company less than four months. The situation was even worse among counter clerks, who were paid minimum wage. The average-sales-per-store figure of $115,000 seemed discouragingly low.

During our 17-hour ride to Indianapolis, Val had remarked "Here we are, barely graduated and we can buy a $3.5 million company. What could be better than to own something and to turn it around?" Now, although the thought of running a large business was still tempting, we decided that Dynasty was too risky and it would be wiser to look for better deals in Washington, DC.

Mr. Hackett and Mr. Rayzman Go to Washington

We loaded our belongings on a truck and set out for Washington. Through a college friend of Val's, we found a house under construction where we could stay one month for free. On the Delaware Turnpike, a special report came on the radio: Iraq had just invaded Kuwait. "Not a good omen," we thought.

Chris took a job at a local drycleaner to better understand the business. He did not mention his education beyond high school; his pay was $6 per hour. A month later, Val joined another cleaner, also at $6 per hour. Chris left his cleaner after 10 weeks and went to the industry association's 3-week General Drycleaning course. Meanwhile, using the Yellow Pages and a Dun and Bradstreet list (under SIC codes 7215 and 7216), Val put together a list of all drycleaners in the area.

We saw as many cleaners as we could. We also talked to suppliers, business brokers, and drycleaners to determine which businesses might be for sale. Based on criteria developed during our field study, we looked at all major drycleaning plants in the Northern Virginia and Montgomery County areas. We eliminated Washington, DC proper, because we wanted to be where people drove rather than walked to their cleaners. We believed that drivers would be more willing to go a few extra blocks than those who walked. Finally, we wanted to find an acquisition that was in good shape (no large losses, broken equipment, etc.) and able to support an increased volume of business.

At the same time, we looked into starting a drycleaning store from the ground up. This involved looking for things like a suitable site, proper equipment, and financing.

Superb Cleaners

In August, we presented our field-study findings to a group of the largest drycleaners in the United States. This meeting was sponsored by a chemical supplier. After the presentation, the president of the company introduced us to a friend who was considering selling his Northern Virginia cleaner, Superb Cleaners.

Superb was located in a freestanding building on a busy street. Its owner had a number of drycleaners and other business interests; he did not take an active part in day-to-day management. The man who had managed Superb died of a sudden heart attack, and the business had declined. Superb, nevertheless, did quality work and had a neat appearance. The on-site plant was spacious and had enough capacity to sustain volume far greater than excess of its current $386,000.

On the other hand, at least $40,000 would be needed for a computer system and washing machines—Superb's plant did drycleaning but not laundry. Some investment would also be necessary to bring the customer area up to our standards.

The location was not ideal. The building was on the "going home" side of a divided street, so that people driving to work could not make the left turn to enter the parking lot. Industry experts say that it is better to be located on the "going to work" side of the street. The business also appeared to be overstaffed given its volume. Finally, the owner seemed uneasy about allowing detailed due diligence to be performed on site.

The owner was asking $450,000 for Superb with some participation in the future upside, and he didn't seem very flexible on price. The owner gave us a P&L of Superb, but it was muddied by charges for his other businesses. From our general observation of the operations—we weren't allowed detailed due diligence on site—we constructed an approximate income statement for Superb. Based on these numbers, we decided to look at other deals first. (See **Exhibits 6 and 7** for financial statements.)

Situation in January 1991

A few months after looking at Superb, Chris and Val took stock of where they stood:

We have spent six months in the area and have found very few cleaners that meet our criteria. Most stores are located in strip malls and do not have room for capacity expansion. This was especially true of cleaners in desirable neighborhoods. Quite apart from the crucial issue of price, there are fewer than 10 cleaners we would even consider buying.

Starting our own store is also a challenge. We have very little personal capital or houses to borrow against. We would have to get a large portion of our capital from Michael Boulder and Rainier, and we may not be able to give them the 25% to 50% return they seek. Washington rents are high, and the economics of a store don't appear to be great. (See **Exhibits 8 and 9** for projected financials.)

A going business with customers, goodwill, and an existing work force can be improved incrementally and is less risky than a start-up. More important, an existing cleaner can be purchased with little equity. Sellers will usually take back a note for one-half to two-thirds of purchase price, typically for seven years with 10% interest.

Our personal finances are deteriorating rapidly. The Superb deal has a lot of problems, but it is the best cleaner we have found for sale so far. We have invested over a year of our lives in this project; we don't want to give up now.

Appendix: Plant Operations and Process

Drycleaning traces its roots back to nineteenth century France, when garments were disassembled and cleaned in turpentine. Now fabrics are cleaned with a detergent dissolved in a solvent (typically percloroethylene or *perc*). Fabrics typically drycleaned include wool, silk, and linen. Drycleaning machines are like very large home washing machines using solvents instead of water. The solvent is recycled into the machine after it is filtered through paper cartridges (or diotomacious earth). The cartridges constitute hazardous waste and must be handled and disposed using established procedures. In addition, the solvent is distilled periodically to remove the dirt and chemicals that have dissolved in it. There have been no significant technological innovations in this basic process in the last 20 years.

Regular laundry is done the same way it is at home but with a bigger washing machine. This process is usually reserved for cottons and some synthetic materials. Most of a typical cleaner's laundry consists of dress shirts worn with suits.

A clerk receives garments from customers at the store counter and makes an initial inspection, looking for stains or obvious damage. The customer is then given a receipt and the counter clerk makes a preliminary sort between garments that are to be drycleaned and those to be laundered. At this point, large orders may be divided into smaller lots (most cleaners limit any order size to six pieces of laundry or three pieces of drycleaning).

The garments are moved to the mark-in station, where they are further inspected and tagged. Each piece receives a color-coded tag that contains a series of numbers that identifies who the customer is, what lot the garment will be cleaned with, and when it is due to be completed. The garment inspection at this point involves looking for buttons that are broken or may break, finding rips and tears, removing items left in pockets, etc. The garments are then divided into lots to be cleaned. A lot is the number of pieces that may be processed by the plant in a given amount of time. The clothes are further divided into groups that can be cleaned together. For drycleaning, this classification is usually done by color (light or dark) and weight. For laundry, classification is done by color and whether or not the shirts are to receive starch.

The clothes are moved to the processing part of the store where they are inspected for spots. Any spots are then manually removed by applying cleaning agents to the clothes. The garments are then weighed and loaded into the drycleaning or washing machine. A typical drycleaning machine can handle 50 lbs. of garments per load.

The drycleaned garments go through a cleaning, extracting, and drying cycle (the whole cycle takes about 45 minutes). After the garments are dry, they are removed from the machine and put on hangers. The garments are inspected for spots and, if spots are found, returned to the spotter for further attention. Otherwise, the garments are pressed. Laundered items follow a similar course except that they are removed from the washing machine wet; drying occurs during the subsequent pressing. All clothes are then inspected and put on hangers.

After the garments are pressed and hung, they are moved to the order-assembly area, where they are put with the other garments on the same order, bagged, and filed on a conveyor to wait for customer pickup.

EXHIBIT 1   Drycleaning Establishments in Selected Cities

City	Total Number of Stores	Number of Stores in Largest Chain
Atlanta	450	17
Boston	480	14
Cincinnati	210	30
Chicago	1,000	10
Minneapolis	230	20
San Francisco	350	5
St. Louis	350	19
Washington, DC	300	7

Source: Yellow Pages.

EXHIBIT 2   Drycleaning versus Other Consumer Services

	Drycleaning	Auto Repair	Fast Food
Industry size ($millions)	$3,998	$28,664	$139,282
Sales per store ($thousands)	$ 188	$ 250	$ 419
Payroll	37%	27%	26%

Source: 1987 Census.

EXHIBIT 3   Cost Structure of Typical Drycleaning and Laundry Plant

---

(Approximately $250,000 per year)	100.0%
Expenses:	
Labor	30.0%
Management expense	10.0
Rent	10.0
Supplies	7.5
Utilities	5.0
Payroll taxes	4.0
Equipment depreciation	4.0
Interest expense	3.0
Legal, accounting, travel	3.0
Promotion	3.0
Insurance	2.5
Equipment maintenance	2.0
Other	10.0
Total Expenses	94.0%
Profit before Taxes	6.0%

Source: Industry interviews and cost surveys.

EXHIBIT 4   Dynasty Cleaners: 1990 Income Statement

Revenue	
Drycleaning	$2,413,300
Laundry	584,200
Other	507,650
Total Revenue	$3,505,150
Expenses	
Production labor & supplies	$1,225,000
Building & machinery	355,000
Selling & delivery	392,000
Store costs	1,230,000
General & administrative	367,100
Employee benefits	21,500
Total Expenses	$3,590,600
Profit (Loss)	($85,450)

EXHIBIT 5   **Dynasty Cleaners: Balance Sheet as of 12/31/90**

ASSETS
Current Assets

Cash	$ 56,200	
Accounts receivable	134,000	
Inventory	48,000	
Deposits	7,300	
Prepaid Expenses	5,000	
Total Current Assets		$ 250,500

Fixed Assets

Furniture & fixtures	$ 15,000	
Machinery & equipment	117,300	
Vehicles	31,900	
Capital lease equipment	99,000	
Leasehold improvements	106,000	
Total Fixed Assets		$ 369,200

Other Assets

Goodwill	$ 1,500	
Investment in subsidiary	13,500	
Officer's life insurance, cash	16,000	
Deposit—Workman's Compensation	1,000	
Intercompany transfers	(17,700)	
Total Other Assets		$ 14,300
Total Assets		$ 634,000

LIABILITIES & SHAREHOLDERS' EQUITY
Current Liabilities

Accounts payable	$ 237,000	
Accrued rent	40,000	
Accrued salary & wages	37,000	
Accrued payroll taxes	35,000	
Accrued expenses	1,400	
Accrued real estate tax	(4,500)	
Taxes withheld	49,500	
Misc. employee deductions	6,500	
Total Current Liabilities		$ 401,900

Long-Term Liabilities

Bank notes	$ 275,000	
Equipment loan	15,000	
Leases payable	113,000	
Total Long-Term Liabilities		$ 403,000
Total Liabilities		$ 804,900

Shareholders' Equity

Capital stock	$ 18,000	
Paid in capital	27,000	
Retained earnings	(340,400)	
Current earnings	124,500	
Total Shareholders' Equity		$(170,900)
Total Liabilities and Shareholders' Equity		$ 634,000

EXHIBIT 6   Superb Cleaners: 1990 Income Statement

Revenue	$386,600
Expenses	
Nonmanagement labor	$171,000
Cost of goods sold*	69,200
Management labor	35,000
Rent†	30,000
Utilities	23,200
Supplies	18,200
Promotion	8,000
Equipment maintenance	6,000
Claims	5,200
Miscellaneous	2,000
Interest expense	4,400
Depreciation	1,700
	$373,900
Profit (Loss)	$ 12,700

---

*COGS comprised primarily shirts that were cleaned off premises.
†The building was owned by Superb's proprietor. Market rent was estimated to be $70,000.

EXHIBIT 7   Capital Projects Estimated for Superb Cleaners

High Priority	
Computer system	$12,000
Shirt unit (used)	10,000
Washing machine (used)	5,000
Employee uniforms	2,000
Subtotal	$29,000
Lower Priority	
Customer area improvements	$15,000
Decorative awning for building	15,000
Sign	14,000
Subtotal	$44,000
Total	$73,000

EXHIBIT 8   Start-up Capital Expenditure Required for DAG Superstore
(Assuming $750,000+ Annual Volume)

	Quantity	Cost
Cleaning Equipment		
50 lb. Dry-to-dry cleaning machines	2	$ 45,000*
35 lb. Washer/extractor machines	2	7,500*
Utility tub	1	250
Commercial washing and drying machines	1	2,000
Spotting board	1	750*
Pressing Equipment		
Utility presses	2	5,000*
Hot head press	1	3,000*
Pants legger	1	3,000*
Pants topper	1	2,000*
Suzy body formers	3	4,500*
Puff irons	3	1,500*
Shirt pressing unit	1	20,000*
Button machine	2	1,500*
Commercial sewing machine	2	1,500*
Utility Equipment		
12 Horsepower boilers	2	10,000
10 Horsepower compressors	2	10,000
Vacuum system	1	3,000
Hot water tank	1	1,500
Cooling & ventilating system	1	15,000
Automatic conveyor systems	6	20,000
Management information system	1	15,000
Building Improvements		
Sliding doors for drive-through	1 set	2,000
Counters & call office improvements		36,000
Work stations & other facility improvements		15,000
Total Capital Cost		$225,000

*Used equipment; purchased for approximately 50% of original equipment cost.

EXHIBIT 9   Proforma Income Statements for DAG Superstore Start-up

	Year 1	Year 2	Year 3	
Revenue	$ 250,000	$500,000	$750,000	
Expenses				
Rent and other real estate costs	$ 75,000	$ 75,000	$ 75,000	10
Counter and marking labor	22,500	45,000	67,500	9
Drycleaning labor	22,500	45,000	67,500	9
Pressing labor	22,500	45,000	67,500	9
Management salaries and costs	40,000	50,000	60,000	8
Supplies	20,000	35,000	52,500	7
Utilities	20,000	25,000	37,500	5
Payroll taxes	12,500	25,000	37,500	5
Promotion	30,000	20,000	20,000	2.67
Insurance	15,000	20,000	20,000	2.67
Equipment maintenance	7,500	10,000	15,000	2
Government regulation compliance	12,500	12,500	15,000	2
Legal, accounting, travel	12,500	10,000	15,000	2
Compensation insurance	2,500	5,000	7,500	1
Office expenses	5,000	5,000	7,500	1
Claims	3,000	5,000	7,500	1
Miscellaneous expenses	12,000	17,500	26,250	3.5
Equipment depreciation	22,500	22,500	22,500	3
Interest expense*	17,500	17,500	17,500	2.33
Total Expenses	$ 375,000	$490,000	$638,750	85.2%
Income (Loss)	$(125,000)	$ 10,000	$111,250	14.8%

*Assumes a loan of $175,000 at a 10% interest rate.

ASSESSING AND ACQUIRING RESOURCES

This section addresses two of the most important issues faced by entrepreneurs as they start a new venture:

What resources are needed?

How are they to be acquired?

Assessing Required Resources

In order to translate the business concept into a reality, the entrepreneur needs first to assess the resources that the venture will require. Entrepreneurs are often required to do more with less. By definition, they are attempting to achieve goals that will require considerably more resources than they currently control.

One of the key skills lies in distinguishing between those resources that are absolutely essential and those that would be nice to have but are not crucial.

Another technique is to distinguish between resources that must be "owned" and those that may be rented, contracted for, or even borrowed. Perhaps professional advice can be obtained based on friendship or the promise of future business. Doing more with less requires buying only what is needed and using the rest without actually owning it.

Acquiring Necessary Resources

Having identified the required resources, it then becomes the entrepreneur's task to acquire them. This acquisition should be guided by a number of policies:

First, the entrepreneur must commit quickly, and sometimes fuller, in order to get to the next stage. This perhaps, is why entrepreneurs are perceived as risk takers.

Still, the entrepreneur must be flexible in these commitments, shifting resources once the desired end has been achieved.

Finally, the individual must approach the acquisition process with the intention of giving up as little as possible in order to attract the needed resources. The rest of the value created thus accrues to the entrepreneur.

Chapter 7, "Attracting Stakeholders," considers the task of acquiring resources in the broadest possible light.

Financial Resources

Clearly, financial resources—dollars—are the most frequently needed. Chapter 8, "Bootstrap Finance," describes how many businesses begin with relatively modest amounts of capital. Chapter 9 describes the spectrum of alternatives for obtaining financing. Chapter 10 looks at the technique of structuring a deal in order to obtain the required financial resources. Chapter 11 discusses the securities laws that affect the raising of funds and also describes the business plans and prospectuses that are typically used.

Nonfinancial Resources

The entrepreneur must also secure the nonfinancial resources that the venture needs—a building, plant or office space, technology, management, and other employees. Chapter 12, "The Legal Protection of Intellectual Property," describes the legal issues that surround ideas: patents, trademarks, trade secrets, confidentiality, and so forth. The entrepreneur must be aware of the serious repercussions that can result either from unfairly using someone else's idea or from failing to protect his or her own idea.

Finally, Chapter 13 examines the selling process—critical not only to selling the product or service upon which the business will rely, but also for recruiting suppliers of human and financial resources.

7

ATTRACTING STAKEHOLDERS

Acquiring resources—or to put it more broadly, attracting stakeholders—is a basic entrepreneurial task. While every enterprise needs employees, customers, suppliers, and financiers who are willing to risk their time and money, attracting these "stakeholders" to an entrepreneurial venture is a particularly difficult challenge. This chapter first describes the importance of the challenge and then the set of tasks the entrepreneur must work on in order to overcome it: Designing the enterprise to minimize the stakeholder investment needed, selecting the right stakeholders, and then convincing them to participate in the enterprise. We will use the example of a hypothetical entrepreneur (like Steve Jobs) who wishes to launch a revolutionary computer, but the principles we describe are generally applicable to any entrepreneurial venture.

The Challenge of Attracting Stakeholders

Many participants are at risk in any enterprise by virtue of the irreversible investment they make in it. The most obvious are the financial stakeholders—the venture capital firms, institutional and individual investors, bondholders, banks, or factors who provide our entrepreneur with the funds needed for R&D, machinery, new product promotion, and growth in inventory and receivables. Much of this investment is irreversible—if the enterprise fails, liquidation of its tangible and intangible assets will rarely make the financial

Professors Amar Bhidé and Howard Stevenson prepared this chapter.
Harvard Business School Note 9-389-139.

stakeholders whole, especially when their opportunity costs are properly taken into account.[1]

Employees, customers, and suppliers have an equally important, if less obvious, stake in the success of the enterprise they participate in as well. The individual who leaves IBM to head up marketing for our hypothetical entrepreneur's new computer project may be as much at risk as the venture capitalists who fund it. If the enterprise fails, the marketing manager is unlikely to be made whole for the time and effort she invested; IBM will not have her back in her old position and she may have to eat into her savings while looking for a new job.

Failure of the enterprise may similarly wipe out suppliers' and customers' investments. Suppliers may not recover the costs of designing and producing special components for the new computer or collect on their receivables. Similarly, customers may find they have invested time and money on hardware that cannot be easily serviced and upgraded.

Moreover, attracting the stakeholders needed to launch a new computer is much more of a challenge for an individual entrepreneur than it is for a large corporation like IBM. Since IBM's managers effectively control the corporation, they can mandate the investment of shareholder funds for a new product. In addition, since IBM has a well-established, profitable franchise in mainframe computers as well as a long-standing reputation for fair dealing, employers, suppliers, and customers have the confidence that they will not be left in the lurch if the new product fails.[2]

The individual entrepreneur who cannot inspire such confidence may therefore face employees, suppliers, customers, and financiers whose perception of their downside risk causes them to demand conditions of exchange that cannot be met if the enterprise is to be viable. In the extreme, they may not participate at all. Suppliers may refuse to dedicate a production run without a cash advance that a fledgling enterprise cannot provide; demands by venture capitalists and key employees for ownership stakes may exceed the total equity pie; and worst of all, conservative purchasing agents may not touch an innovative computer even if it does offer outstanding price/performance.

Minimizing Stakeholder Exposure

The extent to which stakeholders are at risk in a venture depends upon the irreversibility of their investment. While entrepreneurs cannot make the investment required by their ventures fully reversible, they can hold the required

---

[1]This is true, the record shows, even for the lenders whose investment is supposedly secured by assets.

[2]They may take heart from the example of the PC Jr. computer, which IBM kept alive for longer than might have been economically justified in order to protect the interests of the stakeholders. None of the employees who worked on the product were let go, as jobs were found for them elsewhere in the IBM organization.

"sunkenness" to a minimum and thus overcome stakeholders' reluctance to participate.

Reusable, Off-the-Shelf Inputs

Financiers', suppliers', and employees' risks may be reduced by using components, capital equipment, and other factors of production that can be easily put to alternative uses and, preferably, are available off the shelf. Then, financiers, suppliers, and employees do not have to commit substantial resources, and what resources they do commit can be easily recovered if the enterprise fails.

Using standard fungible inputs affects several strategic choices; for our computer start-up these might include:

- Hardware design that relies on off-the-shelf processors and subsystems.
- A product that is differentiated along easily comprehensible performance dimensions or on price. Then salespeople (or distributors) do not have to acquire special skills or knowledge in order to sell it.
- Software based on an industry standard operating system such as UNIX or MS-DOS.
- An assembly line restricted to elementary capital goods such as a conveyor belt and screwdrivers. Where required, general-purpose machine tools, ovens, and CAD-CAM tools can be used instead of special designs.
- A Silicon Valley, Route 128, or Research Triangle site so that key employees do not have to make an investment to relocate and can find alternative employment more easily.
- Modest volume or market share goals so that suppliers do not have to dedicate special production runs or build new capacity.
- A marketing plan that seeks product awareness through a few influential opinion makers in the industry rather than through advertising or missionary selling.

Even seemingly trivial decisions may matter. For example, using an industry standard accounting or word processing package reduces the training required for accounting and typing staff, enhances their marketability in the eyes of other employers, and thus reduces their risk in joining a new venture.

Customer Investment

Many of the product design decisions that help reduce other stakeholders' investment in an enterprise will often reduce customers' risks as well. For example, the use of industry standard components in a computer reduces the buyer's risk of being stuck without spare parts should the vendor go out of business. The adoption of an industry standard operating system likewise eliminates the investment a customer might otherwise have to make in adapting existing applications software to a new supplier's hardware. At the simplest level, products that can be easily purchased due to some simple cost or performance advantages do not require the customer to sink much time and money in the purchase decision and in employee education.

Other product decisions may be taken that directly reduce a customer's investment in learning, search, and adaptation. For example, a new computer may be designed to slot easily into customers' existing hardware networks. In the software arena, open system architecture, which allows the customer (or any other qualified firm) to easily modify or upgrade the product without the assistance of the original vendor may be adopted to reduce the customer's "stake" in the start-up.

Trade-Offs

Unfortunately, there is no free lunch. Securing the participation of stakeholders by reducing the "sunkenness" of their investment may reduce the profitability and long-run sustainability of the enterprise. For example, in the case of the computer start-up:

- Industry standard, off-the-shelf components may lead to higher variable costs and rapid knockoffs by competitors.
- Flexible capital equipment designed to have high salvage value may be more expensive.
- A Silicon Valley, Route 128, or Research Triangle location may entail high real estate and labor costs.
- A plug-compatible, me-too product with low switching costs for the customer may be vulnerable to competitors offering marginally better prices or features.

The entrepreneur may thus be squeezed between being unable to get the enterprise off the ground at all because the risks to stakeholders are too high or launching a marginally profitable, short-lived venture.

One key to resolving this dilemma lies in undertaking irreversible investment only where the greatest leverage is expected in terms of profitability or sustainability or where a stakeholder is most prepared to make the investment for idiosyncratic reasons. For example, a computer start-up may seek irreversible stakeholder investment in the one element, such as a proprietary microprocessor, unique architecture, a low-cost, out-of-the-way location, or new distribution channel, where stakeholder investment seems most readily available and/or where the investment will provide the greatest sustainable advantage. This same company will forcefully adhere to industry standards in all other areas. Asking the question: "Is this uniqueness really the key to a major competitive edge?" is often a good starting place.

Another resolution to the viability/sustainability dilemma can lie in phased investment. The enterprise may be launched with very low irreversible investment, gradually building to higher levels as stakeholder confidence is gained. Apple is a case in point. In its early years, its products were based on an industry standard operating system (CP/M), were promoted virtually without any advertising, and were manufactured in plants whose capital equipment consisted largely of conveyor belts and screwdrivers. As the company gained the confidence of stakeholders, however, its new products used a proprietary operating system, were assembled in highly automated state-of-the-art plants, and were launched with multimillion-dollar advertising budgets.

Selecting Stakeholders

Since irreversible investment required by an enterprise cannot be entirely eliminated, another entrepreneurial task is to select stakeholders who are the most willing to and capable of bearing the risk. All other things being equal, the most desirable stakeholders fit one or more of the following characteristics: They are diversified, experienced in the type of risks they are expected to bear, have excess capacity, and are risk seekers. Let us consider these in turn.

Diversification

Diversified stakeholders are more capable of bearing the risk of investing in an enterprise than these undiversified stakeholders. Thus, for a computer start-up:

- The venture capitalist with a large diversified portfolio of investments can be expected to be more capable of providing risk capital than an individual with no other start-up investments.
- The distributor who handles the products of a number of vendors will probably be less concerned about dedicating 10 percent of the time of 10 salespersons to the new machine than any one salesperson considering full-time employment with the start-up.[3]
- The buyer for a firm with an installed base of computers from a variety of manufacturers will likely be more comfortable trying out a new vendor than the buyer at a customer who has standardized on just one.

Experience and Specialization

The risk that a particular individual or firm sees in investing in an enterprise can depend as much upon the investor's past experience and knowledge as upon the objective dangers. Therefore, an entrepreneur should, when possible, seek the participation of stakeholders who are experienced in bearing the risks required of them. Our computer start-up may, for example, seek to establish relationships with:

- Customers who have bought (and preferably successfully used) computers from start-ups in the past rather than customers who have never strayed from "name" vendors.

---

[3]In general, we may note that employees in a single business start-up will not be able to diversify their risks to the same extent as "outside" subcontractors serving many businesses.

- Law and accounting firms that specialize in new ventures and recognize that an up-front investment in helping a start-up can pay off handily in the long term.
- Employees who have worked for a start-up that failed before and know that being laid off is a setback, not the end of the world. People who have been employed, for example, at IBM for their entire working lives may grossly overestimate the risks of not being able to find a new job.
- Lenders who have dealt with the industry and products often have a feeling of comfort about the downside and experience with the upside, which makes them more adventurous.

Experienced and specialized participants may not only be easier to sign on, but they can also help secure the participation of other stakeholders. Participants in a venture need reassurance about the competence and reliability of each other—the customer who orders a new computer has to be confident that the vendor's service staff is capable, and the key software engineer needs reassurance that the venture capitalists backing the project are solid. Targeting an experienced "team" of stakeholders can thus go a long way toward building this necessary mutual confidence.

"Bell cows"—individuals or organizations that have established reputations as leaders and as savvy precursors of the future—are especially valuable. If our entrepreneur can get Arthur Rock, the doyen of high-tech venture capitalists, or Steve Wozniak, designer of the first Apple, to sign on, a number of other investors, employees, suppliers, and customers will participate, too. If Rock or Wozniak are players, then the venture must be real!

Bell cows open doors and they often induce timely commitment for the entrepreneur. They are often the most important form of "reality check." Bell cows stand at the nexus of important networks. Entrepreneurs have two problems: finding them and convincing them.

Finding bell cows requires industry knowledge. The fledgling entrepreneur has to have it or access it. Having industry knowledge is a function of time, effort, and having knowledge to exchange. It helps to know who is doing what. It helps to read the industry trade papers, and it helps to have made friends.

Accessing industry knowledge beyond your own depends on building your team. Both insiders and service providers such as lawyers, accountants, advertising and P/R firms, and consultants are critical. Even more critical is the entrepreneur's reputation for reciprocity and follow-through.

Excess Capacity

The risks of participation are lower for stakeholders with excess capacity who are not required to make any "new" investment or incur significant opportunity costs and may even be under pressure to utilize existing resources. Therefore, our illustrative computer start-up may target:

- Customers with a well-staffed, technology evaluation department for whom the time required to assess a new product is "free" and who may also be under organizational pressure to make new product recommendations, rather than customers with a small, overworked purchasing department.

- Venture capitalists (or banks) with a large, unused "quota" of technology investments (or loans). Often newly raised venture funds or ones that have developed a bad reputation as being "slow off the mark" are likely targets.
- Writers of technical manuals and product literature who are not kept fully occupied by their employers or who may work part time for personal reasons.
- The young professionals in an accounting firm who are under pressure to "build a client base" in order to make partner.
- Distributors with a "hole" in their product line but good customer coverage.
- Board stuffers and other suppliers with unused capacity—especially note those who have recently undergone aggressive capacity expansion programs.

Obviously the stakeholders' unused capacity must be greater than the enterprise's needs for this criterion of selection to be useful; hence as mentioned in a previous section, staged growth and volume goals are a great help in attracting stakeholders. Capitalizing on "excess" capacity also requires the entrepreneur to carefully understand the cost structure and organizational dynamics of the target stakeholder.

Risk Seeking

Rather than target those stakeholders whose participation in an enterprise involves the least risk to them, the entrepreneur may instead cultivate risk seekers—individuals or firms who because of their temperament or circumstance take on projects that have a negative expected value. For example, the entrepreneur in our computer start-up might seek:

- "Leading edge" customers for whom the publicity and thrill of being the first user of a new technology far outweighs the economic downside.
- Cultist programmers who derive satisfaction from working for a "Mission Impossible"-type enterprise.
- Very wealthy individuals for whom an investment in the venture is like the casual purchase of a lottery ticket or a contribution made to support the local theater company.

There are, however, risks in seeking the participation of risk seekers. First, they may be fickle—the wealthy individual who invests with our entrepreneur on a lark may not be as prepared to invest in future rounds as a professional, level-headed venture capitalist. Second, the participation of risk seekers may scare away other more conservative players. The reputation of your stakeholders has potential for both a halo effect and a negative aura.

Convincing Stakeholders

Assume that our entrepreneur has formulated a plan that minimizes risk for stakeholders and has identified the most appropriate participants for the computer venture. The most formidable task—a challenging mix of analysis and action—remains. The project must be sold; expressions of interest and encouragement from the participants must be converted into firm commitments. This requires the entrepreneur to possess the necessary attitudes and reputation, go through a process of "ham and egging," and master basic closing techniques.

Entrepreneurial Attributes

A prerequisite for gaining stakeholder commitment is the entrepreneur's enthusiasm and belief in the project. The immediate payoff for stakeholders in an entrepreneurial project is almost always low—their decision to participate is based on expectations of substantial long-term reward. The entrepreneur cannot create this expectation without a strong inner conviction that the project can and will succeed.

Another requirement for the entrepreneur is a reputation for reliability. A track record for success is helpful—a Steve Jobs will have a tremendous edge in launching a new venture—but is not absolutely necessary. What participants will look for is evidence that in the past the entrepreneur has:

- Honored implicit as well as explicit promises and has fairly shared rewards with stakeholders.
- Has not abandoned ventures in midstream when things have gone badly.

Ham and Egging

Besides these attributes and reputation (which an entrepreneur either has or hasn't), there are a number of skills and techniques that can be adopted to secure commitment, one of the most important of which is "ham and egging."

The need for ham and egging arises from the desire of each participant to see the others commit first. Customers are reluctant to spend the time to evaluate, much less place an order for a new computer until the entrepreneur can actually deliver a product; employees are hesitant to sign on until the financing is in place; and investors are unwilling to step forward unless customers have shown a willingness to buy.

The ultimate ham and egging solution is for the entrepreneur to simultaneously convince each participant that everyone else is on board, or almost on board. Not all entrepreneurs have the ability to pull this off or can even feel comfortable trying to. The alternative is to ask for a small increment of commitment from a participant, parlay that commitment into another increment of commitment from the next participant, and repeat the cycle for as many times as is necessary.

Our computer entrepreneur may for example:

- Get customers to spend a little time talking about the general attributes they would like to see in a new machine.
- Use these customer reactions to raise money to build a prototype.
- Persuade an engineer to work part time on the prototype for payment in cash and equity.
- Go back to the customer with the prototype asking for more detailed feedback.

This sequential ham and egging process works particularly well if one or more of the participants is a "bell cow."

Basic Sales Closing Skills

Ham and egging is a process that is somewhat unique to launching new ventures. In addition, the entrepreneur needs to employ techniques that are basic to closing any kind of sale such as developing a schedule, knowing in depth what you are asking for, anticipating objections, managing advisors, and handling the problems after the close.

Developing a Schedule

Entrepreneurship is like driving fast on an icy road—it requires anticipation. Early in the selling process a schedule must be agreed upon so that the program can be checked and commitment tested. Intermediate points help you to know whether the stakeholder is stringing you along or is really going to participate. One of the greatest dangers in securing the commitment of stakeholders comes when one on whom you depend drops out. It destroys the ham and egging, it damages credibility, and leaves a critical resource gap. A schedule known to all induces social pressure and lets the entrepreneur maintain the appearance of control, since if others don't meet the schedule, the entrepreneur can initiate quickly a search for a replacement.

Knowing What You Need

It is always nice to have more. Successful entrepreneurs know what degree of commitment is required at any given moment and ask only for that degree. Knowing the bottom line for both time and commitment is a great aid to effective negotiation.

Anticipating Objections

Stakeholders have both real and imaginary concerns. Getting to closing on a commitment requires addressing both. Real objections need be met with both acknowledgment and contingency plans. A prospective employee wants to know that you are aware of the real risks that she is taking. Acknowledging that risk and discussing the window of foresight that will be available before problems become serious and even honestly discussing the "fume date" is often all the reassurance a prospective employee needs. A customer can be reassured about the risk of committing to your product by understanding how service could be handled even if your firm were gone.

Imaginary objections need be dealt with, too. Often, however, the important thing is to find out why the issue is being raised so that underlying uncertainty can be addressed with realistic answers and well-thought-through contingency plans.

Handling Advisors

Lawyers, accountants, and staff have different motives than principals. They often get no credit when things go right, but bear the brunt of blame when things go wrong. Agreed schedules, anticipation of objections, and a sense of being a valued team member are often critical to getting the job done. Your advisors and the stakeholders' advisors often are the roadblocks on the road to commitment. As an entrepreneur, you have to manage them closely and create an expectation and incentives for getting the deal done. Often this means getting them to see the closing of an agreement as the beginning and not the end of the relationship.

Following Up

Many deals have been broken after a commitment is secured. In spite of the hectic pace of the entrepreneurial life, one of the most critical skills is maintaining the commitment. New objections arise as customers see the problems in implementation. New alternatives arise for employees when their old employer sees their departure and recognizes the potential loss. The details of covenants, warranties, and representations become points of contention, then points of honor, then irreconcilable differences in the process of negotiation. The entrepreneurial task remains one of keeping the sale in place. That can only be done by constant attention and follow-up.

Summary

Securing stakeholders is the critical process for an entrepreneur who seeks to pursue opportunity beyond the resources that he or she currently controls. It requires understanding who will provide the needed resources, what resources will be needed, when they will be needed, and how the provider will benefit from his or her participation. The process is iteratively analytical and action oriented. It requires preparation and skill. It is, however, the key to leveraging an idea into opportunity and opportunity into a real business operation.

BOOTSTRAP FINANCE

Entrepreneurship is more celebrated, studied, and desirable than ever. Belief in a "big money" model of entrepreneurship often accompanies this enthusiasm. Books and courses on new ventures emphasize fund-raising: how to approach investors, negotiate deals, and design optimal capital structures. The media focuses on companies like Immulogic, which raised over $20 million in venture capital years before it expected to ship any products.

This big-money model has little in common with the traditional low-budget start-up. Raising big money requires careful market research, well thought-out business plans, top-notch founding teams, sagacious boards, quarterly performance reviews, and devilishly complex financial structures. It is an environment in which analytical, buttoned-down professionals can make a seamless transition from the corporate world to the world of entrepreneurship.

Without question, some start-ups powered by other people's money have rocketed to success. Mitch Kapor raised nearly $5 million of venture capital in 1982, enabling Lotus to launch 1-2-3 with the software industry's first serious advertising campaign. Significant initial capital is indeed a must in industries such as biotechnology or supercomputers where tens of millions of dollars have to be spent on R&D before any revenue is realized. But the fact is that the odds against raising big money are daunting. In 1987—a banner year—venture capitalists financed a grand total of 1,729 companies, of which 112 were seed financings and 232 were start-ups. In that same year, 631,000 new business incorporations were recorded.

Over the past two years, my associates and I interviewed the founders of 100 companies on the 1989 *Inc.* "500" list of the fastest growing private companies in

This chapter was prepared by Amar Bhidé.

the United States. These interviews attest to the value of bootstrapping: launching ventures with modest personal funds. From this perspective, Ross Perot, who started EDS with $1,000 and turned it into a multibillion-dollar enterprise (and a presidential campaign), remains the rule, not the exception. More than 80% of these companies were financed through the founders' personal savings, credit cards, second mortgages, and in one case, "a $50 check that bounced." The median start-up capital was about $10,000. Furthermore, fewer than one-fifth of the boot-strappers had raised equity for follow-on financing in the five or more years that they had been in business. They relied on debt or retained earnings to grow.

A Poor Fit

Many an entrepreneur's hopes are dashed when a venture capitalist rejects a promising business plan. But would-be founders should not interpret lack of interest from the investor community as a pronouncement that the business is doomed. Often entrepreneurs fail to qualify for venture capital not because their proposals are poor but because they do not meet the exacting criteria that venture capitalists must use.

Venture capitalists (and other investors in start-ups) are neither greedy nor shortsighted, as some disappointed entrepreneurs believe; they are simply inappropriate for most start-ups. Their criteria are understandably exacting: Venture capitalists incur significant costs in investigating, negotiating, and monitoring investments. They can back only a few of the many entrepreneurs who seek funding, and they must anticipate that several investments will yield disappointing returns. One study of venture capital portfolios by Venture Economics, Inc., indicates that about 7 percent of the investments account for more than 60 percent of the profits, while a full one-third result in a partial or total loss. Each project must therefore represent a potential home run.

Start-ups, however, typically lack all or most of the criteria investors use to identify big winners: scale, proprietary advantages, well-defined plans, and well-regarded founders.

Most start-ups begin by pursuing niche markets that are too small to interest large competitors—or venture capitalists. Venture capitalists are hesitant to pursue small opportunities where even high-percentage returns will not cover their investment overhead. They favor products or services that address hundred-million-dollar markets. Legendary investor Arthur Rock goes so far as to limit his investments to businesses that have "the potential to change the world."

Few entrepreneurs start with a truly original concept or a plan to achieve a sustainable competitive advantage through a proprietary technology or brand name. Instead, they tend to follow "me-too" strategies and, particularly in service businesses, to rely on superior execution and energy to generate profits. But it is hard for outside investors to evaluate an entrepreneur's ability to execute. Nor can they count on cashing in their investments in companies whose success cannot be sustained without the founders' capabilities.

Many entrepreneurs thrive in rapidly changing industries and niches where established companies are deterred by uncertain prospects. Their ability to roll with the punches is far more important than planning and foresight. Investors, on the other hand, prefer ventures with plausible, carefully thought-out plans to address well-defined markets. A solid plan reassures them about the competence of the entrepreneur and provides an objective yardstick for measuring progress and testing initial assumptions.

Finally, many entrepreneurs are long on energy and enthusiasm but short on credentials. Michael Dell was a freshman at the University of Texas when he started selling computer parts by mail order. Others are refugees from declining or oligopolistic industries, seeking new fields that offer more opportunity but where they lack personal experience.

Investors who see hundreds of business plans and entrepreneurs, however, cannot gauge or rely on the intangibles of personality. Thus Mitch Kapor was a good bet for investors because he already had a successful software product, Visiplot, under his belt before he launched Lotus. Bill Gates, on the other hand, a teenage college dropout when he launched Microsoft with his high school friend, Paul Allen, probably was not.

The Hidden Costs of Other People's Money

Entrepreneurs who try to get investors to bend their criteria or create the perception that they meet those criteria do so at their peril. Several entrepreneurs pointed to the pitfalls of rushing to raise external financing. Winning over investors too early, they said, can compromise your discipline and flexibility.

Bootstrapping in a start-up is like zero inventory in a just-in-time system: It reveals hidden problems and forces the company to solve them. "If we had had money," said Tom Davis of Modular Instruments, manufacturers of medical and research equipment, "we would have made more mistakes. This way, I wrote all the checks. I knew where the money was going."

There can also be problems with raising too much money. As one founder noted, "It is often easier to raise $5 million than $1 million because venture capitalists would rather not have to worry about a lot of tiny investments. But then you have $4 million you didn't need but spend anyhow."

George Brostoff, cofounder of Symplex Communications, which manufactures data communications equipment, agreed. "People in my industry think they need to be able to do x, y, and z at the outset. But the money gets burned up quickly, and it doesn't produce either profits or sales. Then they address the symptom—'we need more money'—instead of the underlying problems."

Diminished flexibility is often another consequence of premature funding. Start-ups entering new industries seldom get it right the first time. Success, especially in new and growing industries, follows many detours and unanticipated setbacks; strategies may have to be altered radically as events unfold. Failure to meet initial goals is a poor guide to future prospects.

Outside investors, however, can hinder entrepreneurs from following the try-it, fix-it approach required in the uncertain environments in which start-ups flourish. The prospect of a radical change in course presents outside investors with a quandary: Was the original concept wrong or was it poorly executed? The entrepreneur is sure the new strategy will work but was just as confident about the original plan. The investors wonder, Are we being fooled twice? Supporting the proposed new strategy rather than, say, changing management is an act of faith that requires investors to discard what seems like hard evidence of poor planning, bad judgment, or overselling.

For their part, entrepreneurs may develop the confidence to push back against investors once the business has taken shape. But in the early years, they tend to avoid direct challenges. Instead, they stick with their original plans even when they begin to lose faith in them because they fear that radical shifts will draw the wrong kind of scrutiny.

Conflicts between investors in a business and its day-to-day managers are a fact of life. They are less debilitating, however, after the entrepreneur has the credibility to be a true partner. Entrepreneurs who are unsure of their markets or who don't have the experience to deal with investor pressure are better off without other people's capital, even if they can somehow get investors to overlook sketchy plans and limited credentials.

Flying on Empty

Starting a business with limited funds requires a different strategy and approach than launching a well-capitalized venture. Compaq Computer, for example, was a venture capitalist's dream. Rod Canion, Jim Harris, and Bill Murto had all been senior managers at Texas Instruments, and they had a well-formulated plan to take on IBM with a technologically superior product. Seasoned investor Ben Rosen helped Canion raise $20 million in start-up capital—funds that allowed the new business to behave like a big company from the start. Canion could attract experienced managers by offering them generous salaries and participation in a stock option plan. Compaq also had a national dealer network established within a year of exhibiting its first prototype. Sales totaled more than $100 million in the first year.

Bootstrappers need a different mind-set and approach. Principles and practices imported from the corporate world will not serve them as well as the following axioms drawn from successful entrepreneurs.

1. Get operational quickly. Bootstrappers don't mind starting with a copycat idea targeted to a small market. Often that approach works well. Imitation saves the costs of market research, and the start-up entering a small market is unlikely to face competition from large, established companies.

Of course, entrepreneurs do not reap fame and fortune if their enterprises remain marginal. But once they are in the flow of business, opportunities often turn up that they would not have seen had they waited for the big idea.

Consider, for example, the evolution of Eaglebrook Plastics, now one of the largest high-density polyethylene recyclers in the United States. Eaglebrook was founded in 1983 by Andrew Stephens and Bob Thompson, who had been chemical engineering students at Purdue. At first, they bought plastic scrap, had it ground by someone else, then sold it, primarily to the pipe industry. One year later, they bought a used $700 grinder, which they operated at night so that they could sell during the day. Soon they moved up to a $25,000 grinder, but they only began to hire when they couldn't keep up with demand.

In 1985, the company developed an innovative process for purifying paper-contaminated plastic scrap—and began to make a name for itself in the industry. In 1987, with the profitability of scrap declining, the partners turned to recycling plastic bottles, a novel idea at the time. Next came plastic lumber made from recycled materials and then, most recently, a joint venture with the National Polyethylene Recycling Corporations to manage their styrofoam recycling operations. Few if any of these opportunities could have been foreseen at the outset.

2. Look for quick break-even, cash-generating projects. The rule in large companies and well-funded enterprises is to stick to the basic strategy. Not so with the bootstrapped start-up. Profit opportunities that might be regarded as distractions in a large company are immensely valuable to the entrepreneur. A business that is making money, elegantly or not, builds credibility in the eyes of suppliers, customers, and employees, as well as self-confidence in the entrepreneur.

For example, Raju Patel launched NAC with the ambitious goal of serving the Baby Bells created by the AT&T breakup. NAC's first offering, however, was a low-end auto-dialer targeted to the many start-ups that were reselling long-distance services from carriers like MCI. "We thought it would be appropriate to get a cash generator to make us known as a new entrant," Patel explained. Then at a conference, Patel happened to meet a reseller who mentioned his need for more accurate customer-billing capability. NAC stopped work on the auto-dialer and rapidly developed and shipped a billing system. The system was later phased out as the customers themselves began to fold. But its quick, albeit short-lived, success helped NAC attract the engineers it needed to grow because it enabled Patel to offer security as well as the excitement of a start-up. "We weren't seen as a revolving-door company. We were able to offer health plans and other benefits comparable to those of large companies." More ambitious products, aimed at the Bell companies, followed. Today NAC is well established as a small systems supplier to the Bell companies.

Robert Grosshandler's Softa group also used the cash flow from one business to develop another. "Our property management software was funded by selling hardware and peripherals to *Fortune* '500' companies. It was low-margin, but it had fast turnaround. Goods arrived in the morning and left in the evening. Our software, on the other hand, took nearly a year to develop."

Many entrepreneurs sustained themselves by part-time consulting. In the early days, says Robert Pemberton of Software 2000, which develops and distributes business applications software, consulting accounted for more than 50% of the revenue of the business.

3. Offer high-value products or services that can sustain direct personal selling. Getting a customer to give up a familiar product or service for that of a shaky start-up is arguably the most important challenge an entrepreneur faces. "When we first started selling," Modular's Davis recalled, "people would ask, 'When are you going to go out of business?' "

Many entrepreneurs underestimate the marketing costs entailed in overcoming customer inertia and conservatism, especially with respect to low-value or impulse goods. Launching a new packaged food product without substantial financial resources, for example, is an oft-undertaken and futile endeavor. Creating a serious business means persuading hundreds of thousands of customers to try out a new $5 mustard or jam in place of their usual brand. Without millions of dollars of market research, advertising, and promotion, this can be a hopeless task.

Therefore, successful entrepreneurs often pick high-ticket products and services where their personal passion, salesmanship, and willingness to go the extra mile can substitute for a big marketing budget. As John Mineck, cofounder of Practice Management Systems said, "People buy a salesperson. They bought me and I had no sales experience. But I truly believed our systems and software for automating doctors' offices would work—so the customers did too. Also, we did an awful lot for our first clients; if they wanted something, we'd deliver. We were providing service and support long before that became a cliché."

Like Mineck, three-quarters of the founders we interviewed were also their company's chief or only salesperson. They sold directly, usually to other businesses. Only 10 percent used brokers or distributors and only 14 percent offered consumer goods or services. The median unit sale was $5,000, an amount high enough to support direct personal selling and also, presumably, to get the attention of buyers. The few consumer items we encountered were also important purchases for buyers: a $20,000 recreational vehicle from Chariot Eagle or an SAT preparation course from the *Princeton Review*, rather than a $5 to $10 staple that consumers purchase without great thought.

Overcoming customer inertia is easier and cheaper if a product offers some tangible advantage over substitutes. Our successful entrepreneurs overcame reservations about their long-term viability by selling concrete performance characteristics—faster chips and fourth-generation language software, for instance—rather than intangible attributes like a tangier sauce or more evocative perfume. "We had no track record and no commercial office—I was running the company from my home," recalled Prabhu Goel, founder of Gateway Design Automation, which supplies CAE software tools. "So we went after the most sophisticated users who had a problem that needed to be solved. The risk of dealing with us was small compared with the risk of not solving the problem."

Concrete product attributes also contribute to important serendipitous sales. With just a prototype, Brostoff of Symplex got an order for 100 units from Mead Data, his first significant customer. "We didn't call them, they called us," Brostoff told us. "A high-level manager read an article about us that suggested our product could offer customers like Mead dramatic cost savings—as much as $55,000 annually on a one-time investment of $10,000 to $20,000. Mead had an on-line database product and was looking to cut costs."

Intangibles like responsiveness and attention do provide greater leverage for entrepreneurial selling in service and distribution businesses. Clay Teramo, founder of Computer Media Technology, a computer supplies distributor, described the way he used service—and the customer's perception of service—to make up for the fact that early on his competitors had far more resources. When someone called with a next-day order that Computer Media couldn't handle, Teramo would tell them that he didn't have the whole order in stock and ask if he could fill part of it the next day and part later on. If the customer agreed, he'd follow up personally to make sure everything had gone smoothly and to say thanks. As Teramo pointed out, his competitors could probably have filled the whole order at once. But the customer wouldn't think he had received any special service.

Carol Russell of Russell Personnel Services took a similar approach. "Our business is done on the cult of personality," she said. "You roll up your sleeves and say to the customer, 'Hi, I'm Carol Russell, and I'm going to work overtime to get you employed or employees.' In a people business, being a young company and visible is an advantage. In the large services, you won't meet the Mr. Olstens or the Mr. Kellys."

4. Forget about the crack team. It is not unusual for investor-backed start-ups to hire CFOs or marketing managers at $100,000 a year. Bootstrappers cannot afford this investment. Besides, if the entrepreneurs' credentials aren't strong enough to attract investors, they are even less likely to be able to attract a highly qualified team. Novices who are urged to recruit a well-rounded team rarely succeed. Steve Jobs had his pick of talent for NeXT; Apple, however, was built by youthful exuberance.

The start-ups that we studied attracted employees by providing them with opportunities to up-grade skills and build résumés, rather than by offering cash or options. Their challenge was to find and motivate diamonds in the rough.

"I never hired experienced people," said Bohdan Associates's founder Peter Zacharkiw, "and there are very few college graduates here. My vice president of sales was the best curb painter around—but that's the secret. He'll always be the best at what he does. Personality and common sense are the most important things that people here have."

John Greenwood's first employee at Micron Separations was a 62-year-old machine shop worker who had just been laid off. His production manager was a Worcester Polytechnic Institute graduate who had been working as an accountant in a company he hated and was looking for another job. "We never attempted to lure anybody away from another company," Greenwood told us. "One, we were cheap. Two, we had moral reasons—if we went under and it didn't work out for them, we wouldn't feel so bad. We never felt that we had an inadequate pool, though. I believe the people in the 'unemployment market' are just as good if not better than the people in the employment market. And we have no prejudice against people who've been fired. My partner and I started Micron after we were fired! In large companies, people tend to get fired for lack of political skills."

Not all entrepreneurs were so fortunate, however. Some had to cope with employees who had neither the formal qualifications nor the right temperament and attitude for their jobs. "Large companies can hire by credentials and screen people carefully," said Robert Rodriguez of National Communications Sales Promotion, a Miami-based company that helps customers manage their sales promotion campaigns. "We needed to have things happen quickly and took people on the basis of their initial presentation. But many didn't do what they said they could."

5. Keep growth in check. Start-ups that failed because they could not fund their growth are legion. Successful bootstrappers take special care to expand only at the rate they can afford and control. For example, they tend to invest in people or capacity only when there is no alternative, not in advance of needs. "Our first product was done before the company was founded," said Warren Anderson, founder of Anderson Soft-Teach. "I produced it, paid for it, took it to a trade show, and we started taking orders before we hired people. It was like brick-laying. We added one layer at a time. We didn't have a venture capitalist putting up money for us—just $30,000 of our own money—and we were selling our tapes for $200 each."

Keeping growth in check is not only financially prudent but it also helps the entrepreneur develop management skills and iron out problems under less pressure. Even entrepreneurs who don't have to make radical changes in strategy may have to make adjustments as they learn about the nuances of their chosen industry. Learning the nuts and bolts of running a business is particularly important for first-time entrepreneurs. Stephanie DiMarco and her partner encountered few major surprises when they started Advent Software. Nevertheless, in the early years, DiMarco noted, they felt constrained by their lack of knowledge and held back on their growth. "Instead of trying to create an organization, I wanted to prove myself first. It was important for me to learn the business before I hired someone else. I had never managed anyone before." After the partners learned how to run a business, Advent enjoyed explosive growth.

In their rush to grow, some entrepreneurs told us, they took on customers who nearly put them under. "When you are new and cold-calling customers," observed Fred Zak of Venture Graphics, "the business that comes your way is usually from customers who can't pay their bills or shop only on price—the worst kind of customer base. About 40% of our early work came from deadbeats. I soon determined that I would have to call on them personally, and I'd show up unannounced. It was nerve-racking, but they would pay us off so that they wouldn't have to see me again!"

Some will argue that controlled growth and reactive investments allow competitors to preempt the market. In fact, there are few businesses that entrepreneurs can realistically expect to start in which grabbing dominant market share first is crucial. In mature service industries such as temporary services, advertising, or public relations (where many of our entrepreneurs found their niches), dominance, early or late, is out of the question. But even in high-tech fields, first-mover advantages are often short-lived. Compaq's early start in the IBM clone market did not thwart later bootstrapped entrants like Dell Computer and AST Research. Similarly, WordPerfect, today's dominant player in word processing software, was not among the first half-dozen entrants.

Frequent changes in technology allow entrepreneurs who miss one wave while getting organized to ride the next. Several computer distributors we interviewed missed getting in on the first generation of PCs and so could not obtain the all-important "IBM Authorized Dealer" medallion. But the growth of Novell and local area networks created new opportunities, which the established, first-generation competitors, engrossed in traditional products, couldn't easily take advantage of.

6. Focus on cash, not on profits, market share, or anything else. A well-funded start-up can afford to pursue several strategic goals; bootstrappers usually cannot. For example, cash-constrained start-ups cannot "buy business." In venture capital-backed or intrapreneurial ventures, it may be feasible for a start-up to sell at a loss in anticipation of scale economies or learning curve advantages. But the bootstrapper must earn healthy margins, practically from day one, not only to cover the company's costs but also to finance growth. "I learned early that it is better to have a low-profile, positive cash-flow job than a high-ego, negative cash-flow job," said Keith Kakacek, founder of the commercial insurance group, SIR Lloyds. "If the market doesn't pay for your business—and you can't develop positive cash flow—you probably don't have a good enough concept."

Getting terms from suppliers and timely payments from customers are critical in managing cash. Ron Norris of Automotive Caliper Exchange told us he started with and maintained positive cash flow from operations in spite of rapid growth. Building on contacts developed over 20 years, he went to six suppliers and asked for 90- to 120-day terms for one time only on his first order. All but one agreed. Now established, Norris gives modest discounts to customers who pay quickly. But he won't tolerate any "gray" whatever. If a customer doesn't pay in 30 days—and hasn't called to explain why—the company won't sell to him any longer.

Equally important is knowing when to spend and when to economize. Successful bootstrappers are generally cheap, except in one or two crucial areas. "We began in a modest room," recalled Brian Cornish of Oscor Medical Corporation, which makes instruments for microsurgery. "We licked stamps instead of buying a Pitney Bowes machine. We never had plush offices or any of the other trappings of some start-ups. But we made sure we got the very best microscopes."

7. Cultivate banks before the business becomes creditworthy. It is common wisdom that bank loans can be a cheap alternative to external equity and crucial for financing additional inventory or larger receivables. But bank financing is often unavailable for start-ups, as many entrepreneurs we interviewed discovered. Winning bankers over requires preparation and careful timing.

Consider, for example, how Phil Bookman of Silton-Bookman went about managing his company's bank relationship. Bookman did not even try to borrow until his software company was creditworthy. But he made sure that the company kept good books, that its records were immaculate, and that its balance sheets were sound. In addition, he opened accounts with a big bank's local branch and from time to time asked the branch manager's advice to familiarize him with Silton-Bookman's business. Then when the company had been in business for the requisite three years, Bookman went to the banker with the company's business plan. "He looked over the numbers," Bookman explained, "and said, 'It looks like you need a $50,000 term loan.' We knew that all along, but it was important that he suggested it. We got the loan and paid it back, then used the same method the next year to get a line of credit."

Abandoning the Rules

Growth and change create difficult transitions for all entrepreneurial companies. The challenges faced by a charismatic founder in letting go and designing an organization in which authority and responsibility are appropriately distributed are well known. The bootstrapper's problem is particularly acute, however. To build a durable business—as opposed to a personal project or an alternative to employment—successful entrepreneurs not only have to modify their personal roles and organization, but they may also have to effect a U-turn and abandon the very policies that allowed them to get up and running with limited capital. As part of these changes, the start-up may have to:

• Emerge from its niche and compete with a large company. When *Princeton Review* was launched, it competed with private tutors of uneven quality in Manhattan. To become a nationally franchised operation, the company had to confront the well-established Stanley Kaplan chain.

• Offer more standard, less customized products. "We did a lot of things for our first clients that we wouldn't do today," said Practice Management Systems's Mineck. "The easiest thing for a salesperson to say is, 'we can do it,' and the hardest thing is, 'we can't do this for you.'"

• Bring critical services in-house. Automotive Caliper never hired an in-house controller because it didn't need the expertise. But it does have its own fleet of trucks. The smartly dressed drivers project the company's image, and they provide an important source of information because they can find out things the sales force cannot see.

• Change management's focus from cash flow to strategic goals. Phil Bookman, a self-confessed "cash management fanatic" in the early years, pointed out how important—and hard—it was to shift gears later on and remind people that they had to think more about the big picture and worry less about the little expenditures.

• Recruit higher priced talent, perhaps encouraging early employees to move on. Sometimes the need to turn over early employees and hire professionals in their place is an obvious business decision. At National Communications Sales Promotion, for example, all but two of Rodriguez's original employees left within a few years. A few had simply grown stale, but most were fired for unprofessional behavior or because their attitude was bad. To get people with the right attitude and experience, Rodriguez began to pay more and to look for different qualities: MBAs with family responsibilities replaced "swinging singles" who weren't above making side deals.

More often, however, replacing the start-up's early team presents the entrepreneur with one of the most difficult transitions he or she must confront. At Rizzo Associates, an engineering and environmental services company, four of the first seven employees had to leave because they could not grow with the company. "We promised employees substantial opportunities in terms of personal growth and sold them a future," William Rizzo recalled. "But we did not tell them that they had to live up to that future. In time, we had to bring people in over them, and they felt their future was sealed off. Eventually they said, 'The hell with you.' Today I would be more candid about the fact that our promises are contingent on their performance."

Changes in strategy or personnel at more "professionally" designed and launched start-ups may be less dramatic or personally wrenching. But hard as making these changes may be, they are unavoidable for the entrepreneur who succeeds enough to turn a start-up venture into an ongoing business.

ALTERNATIVE SOURCES OF FINANCING

One of the most common issues confronted by the entrepreneur revolves around securing financing for the venture. Questions of how and when to raise money and from whom are frequent topics of concern. This chapter will describe some common sources of capital and the conditions under which money is typically lent or invested. Chapter 10, "Deal Structure," discusses the specific terms and pricing of capital.

An Overview

As in most transactions, the owners of capital expect to get something in return for providing financing for the venture. In evaluating potential opportunities, the providers of funds will typically use some form of a risk/return model. That is, they will demand a higher return when they perceive a higher risk.

The entrepreneur's objective, of course, is to secure financing at the lowest possible cost. The art of successful financing, therefore, lies in obtaining funds in a manner that those providers of funds view as relatively less risky.

The entrepreneur can do several things to structure the financing so it will be perceived as "less risky":

- Pledge personal or corporate assets against a loan.
- Promise to pay the money back in a short period of time when the investors can judge the health of the business, rather than over the long term when its financial strength is less certain.

This chapter was prepared by Michael J. Roberts under the direction of Howard H. Stevenson.
Copyright © 1984 by the President and Fellows of Harvard College.
Harvard Business School Note 9-384-187.

• Give investors some measure of control over the business, through either loan covenants or participation in management (i.e., a seat on the board).

Note that these are only a few of the possible mechanisms.

The liabilities side of the balance sheet itself provides a good overview of the potential sources of financing. Because this side of the balance sheet is arranged in order of increasing risk, it follows that the lowest cost forms of financing will usually be available from the higher balance sheet items.

Start-Up Financing

Start-up financing provides the entrepreneur with a host of unique challenges. The highest risk capital (and therefore potentially highest return capital) is at the bottom of the balance sheet as equity. When a business is in the start-up phase, it is at its riskiest point. Therefore, equity capital is usually an appropriate source of financing during this period. That is not to say that debt capital is unattractive. It may even be available when secured by assets of the business, such as a building or equipment. However, some equity is usually required to get a business "off the ground." There is virtually no getting around the fact that the first investment in the business will be equity capital. This is required to demonstrate commitment on the part of the entrepreneur. Investors perceive, and rightly so, that the individual entrepreneur will be more committed to the venture if she or he has a substantial portion of personal assets invested in the venture. It is this fact that has led some to claim that: "You're better off trying to start a business with $5,000 than with $100,000 in personal resources. If you are relatively poor, you can demonstrate your commitment for a smaller sum." This statement presumes that you will be seeking capital from some *outside* source. If you were going to fund the venture all by yourself, you would naturally prefer to have $100,000 instead of $5,000.

There is another, more practical reason why this start-up phase will usually be financed with the entrepreneur's own funds. In order to raise money, you typically need more than an idea. The entrepreneur will have to invest some money in the idea, perhaps to build a prototype or do a market study, in order to convince potential providers of capital that the idea has potential.

This is not to say that these funds must be equity capital in the purest sense. That is, the money need only be equity from the point of view of potential investors in the business. The entrepreneur can obtain these "equity funds" by mortgaging personal assets like a house or car, borrowing from friends or relatives, even from a personal bank loan or credit card advances. The important fact is that when the money goes into the business, it does so as equity, not as debt to be repaid to the entrepreneur.

Some specialized firms provide "seed capital." Most venture capital firms require that a business move beyond the idea stage before they will consider financing it. Yet some businesses require a good deal of work (and money) to get from the concept phase to the point where they can obtain venture capital financing. Seed funds can provide this kind of capital.

Outside Equity Capital

Typically, the entrepreneur will exhaust his or her own funds before the business is a viable operation. At this point, it is usually still too early to obtain all of the required financing in the form of debt. The entrepreneur must approach outside sources for equity capital.

Private Investors

One popular source of equity capital is private investors, also known as *angels* or *wealthy individuals.* These investors may range from family and friends with a few extra dollars to extremely wealthy individuals who manage their own money. Many angels are successful entrepreneurs who wish to recycle their wealth by investing in new businesses. Wealthy individuals may be advised by their accountants, lawyers, or other professionals, and the entrepreneur must deal with these people as well.

In order to approach wealthy individuals, you will usually need at least a business plan. A formal offering memorandum has the advantage of providing more legal protection for the entrepreneur in the form of disclaimers and legal language. However, it suffers from appearing overly negative, being more costly to prepare (it usually requires legal counsel), and also being limited by the SEC laws in terms of its distribution. That is, some of the SEC rules permit only 35 "offerees." Some legal advisors believe that you can show the business plan to more individuals and then formally "offer" to only those individuals who have a real interest in investing.

One of the best ways to find wealthy investors is through a network of friends, acquaintances, and advisors. For instance, if you have used a local lawyer and accountant to help you prepare a business plan or offering document, these advisors may know of wealthy individuals who invest in ventures like yours.

At this point, it is worth reiterating the importance of following the securities laws and obtaining the advice of counsel. Because many of these wealthy individuals are "unsophisticated," they can (and often do, if the venture is unsuccessful) claim that they were misled by you, the conniving entrepreneur. A carefully drawn offering document is the key to legal protection in this instance.

Wealthy investors may be well suited to participation in equity financings that are too small for a venture capital firm to consider (e.g., under $500,000). Wealthy investors are also typically thought of as being a less expensive source of equity than venture capital firms. This may be true. It is also true that:

- Wealthy individuals do not often possess the expertise or time to advise the entrepreneur on the operations of the business.

- Wealthy investors are far less likely to come up with additional funds if required.
- These investors are more likely to be a source of "problems" or frustration, particularly if there is a large number of them. Phoning frequently or complaining when things are not going according to plan, they can create headaches for even the most well intentioned of entrepreneurs.

Venture Capital

Venture capital refers to a pool of equity capital that is professionally managed. Wealthy individuals invest in this fund as limited partners, and the general partners manage the pool in exchange for a fee and a percentage of the gain on investments.

In order to compensate for the riskiness of their investments, give their own investors a handsome return, and make a profit for themselves, venture firms seek a high rate of return on their investments. Target returns of 50 percent or 60 percent are not uncommon hurdles for firms to apply to prospective venture capital investments.

In exchange for this high return, venture firms will often provide advice to their portfolio companies. These people have been through many times what the entrepreneur is usually experiencing for the first time. They can often provide useful counsel on the problems a company may experience in the start-up phase.

Venture firms can differ along several dimensions. Some prefer investing in certain kinds of companies. "High-tech" is popular with most, although perceptions of what precisely this is will vary widely. Some firms have a reputation for being very involved with the day-to-day operations of the business; others exhibit a more hands-off policy.

In approaching venture capitalists, the entrepreneur needs a business plan to capture the firm's interest. Here the document serves a far different purpose than it would in the case of wealthy individuals. A venture capital firm will expend a good deal of effort investigating potential investments. Not only is this sound business practice on their part, but they also have legal obligations to their own investors.

Therefore, a business plan targeted to venture firms should be short, concise, and attempt to stimulate further interest, rather than present the business in exhaustive detail.

Most venture capitalists also report that it is only the naive entrepreneur who will propose the actual terms of the investment in the initial document. While the plan should certainly spell out how much financing the entrepreneur is seeking, to detail the terms (e.g., "for 28 percent of the stock . . .") is viewed as premature for an initial presentation.

One topic, which is frequently of concern to entrepreneurs, is confidentiality. On the one hand, it seems wise to tell potential investors about your good ideas to get them interested in the company; on the other, what if someone else takes them? In general, venture capitalists are a professional group and will not disclose confidential information. It is more difficult, however, to make this statement about private sources of capital, like wealthy individuals.

Whatever the target investor audience, it is generally *not* a good idea to put truly proprietary material in a business plan. These plans are frequently copied and could certainly be left accidentally on a plane or in an office. A business plan might, for example, describe the functions a new product would perform, but should probably not include circuit designs, engineering, drawings, and so on.

Venture firms may not invest via a pure equity security. Some may invest a package of debt and equity, convertible debt, or convertible preferred. Each of these has its advantages:

- A debt/equity package provides for the venture firm to get some of its funds back via interest, which is deductible to the company, and results in a tax savings. The investor can also recover tax-free cash based on repayment of loan principal.
- Convertible debt or preferred gives the venture firm a liquidation preference. If the venture should fail, the venture capitalist will have a priority claim on the assets of the business. Often too, the terms can force eventual repayment even if the firm never achieves "public" status.

Venture firms will usually "syndicate" a large investment. That is, they will attempt to interest other firms in taking a piece of the investment. This permits the firm to invest in a larger number of companies and thus spread its risk. This is particularly important on subsequent "rounds" or stages of financing. Other venture firms will want to see that the original firm(s) will continue their investment in the company. If the existing, more knowledgeable investors aren't interested in the company, why should a new venture firm be interested?

Public Equity Markets

Of course, the largest source of equity capital remains the public equity markets: the New York, American, and over-the-counter stock exchanges. Typically, however, a firm must have a history of successful operation before it can raise money in this way. In "hot" markets, some smaller, start-up companies have been able to raise public equity. The process is lengthy, detailed, and expensive. See Chapter 18, "Securities Law and Public Offerings" for a discussion of the public equity markets.

Whether the investment is made by wealthy individuals or a venture capital firm, terms will have to be negotiated. In exchange for their investment, the investor will receive a "security," which represents the terms of his or her investment in the company. In the case of a public offering, the investment bank negotiates the terms on behalf of its clients. Venture capital firms and investment banks, of course, tend to be more sophisticated than the average wealthy investor.

Debt Capital

The other large category of capital is debt. Debt is presumed to be lower risk capital because it is repaid according to a set schedule of principal and interest.

In order to have a reasonable expectation of being paid according to this schedule, creditors lend against:

- Assets: Firms can obtain asset-based financing for most hard assets that have a market value. A building, equipment, or soluble inventory are all assets that a company could borrow against.
- Cash flow: Lenders will allow firms to borrow against their expected ability to generate the cash to repay the loan. Creditors attempt to check this ability through such measures as interest coverage (EBIT ÷ Interest payments) or debt-equity ratio. Obviously, a healthy business with little debt and high cash flow will have an easier time borrowing money than a new venture.

Cash Flow Financing

Cash flow or unsecured financing is of several types and can come from different sources.

- Short-term debt: Short-term unsecured financing is frequently available to cover seasonal working capital needs for periods of less than one year, usually 30 to 40 days.
- Line-of-credit financing: A company can arrange for a line of credit, to be drawn upon as needed. Interest is paid on the outstanding principal, and a "commitment fee" is paid up front. Generally, a line of credit must be "paid-down" to an agreed-upon level at some point during the year.
- Long-term debt: Generally available to solid "creditworthy" companies, long-term debt may be available for up to 10 years. Long-term debt is usually repaid according to a fixed schedule of interest and principal.

Cash flow financing is most commonly available from commercial banks but can also be obtained from savings and loan institutions, finance companies, and other institutional lenders (e.g., insurance companies, pension funds). Because cash flow financing is generally riskier than asset-based financing, banks will frequently attempt to reduce their risk through the use of covenants. These covenants place certain restrictions on a business if it wishes to maintain its credit with the bank. Typical loan covenants concern:

- Limits on the company's debt-equity ratio.
- Minimum standards on interest coverage.
- Lower limits on working capital.
- Minimum cash balance.
- Restrictions on the company's ability to issue senior debt.

These, and other covenants, attempt to protect the lender from actions that would increase the likelihood of the lender not getting its money back.

Asset-Based Financing

Most assets in a business can be financed. Because cash flow financing usually requires an earnings history, far more new ventures are able to obtain asset-based financing. In an asset-based financing, the company pledges or gives the financier a first lien on the asset. In the event of a default on the financing payments, the lender can repossess the asset. The following types of financing are generally available:

- Accounts receivable: Up to 90 percent of the accounts receivable from creditworthy customers can usually be financed. The bank will conduct a thorough investigation to determine which accounts are eligible for this kind of financing. In some industries, such as the government business, accounts receivable are often "factored." A factor buys approved receivables for a discount from their face value, but collects from the accounts.

- Inventory: Inventory is often financed if it consists of merchandise that could be easily sold. Typically, 50 percent or so of finished goods inventory can be financed.

- Equipment: Equipment can usually be financed for a period of 3 to 10 years. One-half to 80 percent of the value of the equipment can be financed, depending on the salability or "liquidity" of the assets. Leasing is also a form of equipment financing where the company never takes ownership of the equipment, but rents it.

- Real estate: Mortgage financing is usually readily available to finance a company's plant or buildings; 75 to 85 percent of the value of the building is a typical figure.

- Personally secured loans: A business can obtain virtually any amount of financing if one of its principals (or someone else) is willing to pledge a sufficient amount of assets to guarantee the loan.

- Letter-of-credit financing: A letter of credit is a bank guarantee that a company can obtain to enable it to purchase goods. A letter of credit functions almost like a credit card, allowing businesses to make commitments and purchases in other parts of the world where the company does not have relationships with local banks.

- Government-secured loans: Certain government agencies will guarantee loans to allow businesses to obtain financing when they could not obtain it on their own. The Small Business Administration, the Farmers Home Administration, and other government agencies will guarantee bank loans.

Asset-based financing is available from commercial banks and other financial institutions. Insurance companies, pension funds, and commercial finance companies provide mortgages and other forms of asset-backed financing. Entrepreneurs themselves can also provide debt capital to a business once it has passed out of the risky start-up period.

Internally Generated Financing

A final category of financing is internally generated. This term describes:

- Credit from suppliers: Paying bills in a less timely fashion is one way to increase working capital. Sometimes, suppliers will charge you interest for this practice. In other instances, the costs may be more severe if a key supplier resource decides to stop serving you.
- Accounts receivable: Collecting bills more quickly will also generate financing.
- Reducing working capital: A business can generate internal financing by reducing other working capital items: inventory, cash, and so forth.
- Sale of assets: Perhaps a more drastic move, selling assets will also generate capital.

Each of these techniques represents an approach to generating funds internally, without the help of a financial partner. Although the purely financial costs are low, the entrepreneur must be wary of attempting to run the business "too lean."

Summary

We've attempted to describe the spectrum of financial sources that an entrepreneur can tap both during the start-up phase and as a going concern. **Figure 9–1** is a summary of these sources. Providers of capital try to manage the risk-reward ratio by (1) increasing reward by raising the cost of funds or (2) decreasing risk by asserting some measure of control over the business. Figure 9–1 shows in what ways capital providers try to raise the cost of funds or assert control over the business. This is not an exhaustive list, but an overview of the most popular sources. In every case, there is a high premium on understanding both your own needs and the specific needs of the financier.

FIGURE 9–1 Alternative Sources of Financing

	Cost							Control		
		Fixed Rate		Floating Rate						
Source	Zero	Short-term	Long-term	Short-term	Long-term	Percent of Profits	Equity	Covenants	Voting Rights	Guarantee of Debt
Self			X				X		X	X
Family and friends		X	X	X	X		X		X	X
Suppliers and trade credit	X	X		X		X				X
Commercial banks		X		X				X		X
Other commercial lenders		X	X		X			X		X
Asset-based lenders/lessors			X			X	X	X		
Specialized finance companies		X	X			X	X	X		
Institutions and insurance companies			X		X	X		X		
Pension funds			X			X	X	X		
Venture capital		X	X				X	X	X	X
Private equity placements							X	X	X	
Public equity offerings						X	X		X	
Government agencies (SBIC)			X		X	X				X
Other government programs			X					X		X

10

DEAL STRUCTURE

A critical aspect of the entrepreneur's attempt to obtain resources is the development of an actual "deal" with the owner of the resources. Typically, the entrepreneur needs a variety of resources, including dollars, people, and outside expertise. As in any situation, the individual who desires to own, or use, these resources must give up something. Because the entrepreneur typically has so little to start with, she or he will usually give up a claim on some future value in exchange for the ability to use these resources now.

Entrepreneurs can obtain funds in the form of trade credit, short- and long-term debt, and equity or risk capital. This chapter will focus on the structure and terms of the deal that may be used to obtain the required financial resources from investors. The chapter will also center on financial resources because raising capital is a common problem that virtually all entrepreneurs face.

What Is a Deal?

In general, a *deal* represents the terms of a transaction between two (or more) groups or individuals. Entrepreneurs want money to use in a (hopefully) productive venture, and individuals and institutions wish to earn a return on the cash that they have at risk.

The entrepreneur's key task is to make the whole equal to more than the sum of the parts. That is, to carve up the economic benefits of the venture into pieces that meet the needs of particular financial backers. The entrepreneur can

---

This chapter was prepared by Michael J. Roberts under the direction of Howard H. Stevenson.
Copyright © 1984 by the President and Fellows of Harvard College.
Harvard Business School Note 9-384-186.

maximize his or her own return by selling these pieces at the highest possible price, that is, to individuals who demand the lowest return. And the individuals who demand the lowest return will typically be those that perceive the lowest risk.

The Deal

In order to craft a deal that maximizes his or her own economic return, the entrepreneur must:

- Understand the fundamental economic nature of the business.
- Understand financiers' needs and perceptions of risk and reward.
- Understand his or her own needs and requirements.

Understanding the Business

The first thing the entrepreneur must do is assess the fundamental economic nature of the business itself. Most business plans project a set of economics that determine:

- The amount of the funds required.
  — The absolute amount.
  — The timing of these requirements.
- The riskiness of the venture.
  — The absolute level of risk.
  — The factors that determine risk.
- The timing and potential magnitude of returns.

It is important to remember that the venture itself does not necessarily have an inherent set of economics. The entrepreneur determines the fundamental economics when she or he makes critical decisions about the business. Still, there may be certain economic characteristics that are a function of the industry and environment and that the entrepreneur will generally be guided by.

For instance, a venture such as a genetics engineering firm has characteristics that differ greatly from those of a real estate deal. The genetics firm may require large investments over the first several years, followed by years with zero cash flow, followed by a huge potential return many years out. The real estate project, on the other hand, may require a one-time investment, generate immediate cash flow, and provide a means of exit only several years down the road.

One technique for understanding a venture's economic nature is to analyze the potential source of return. Let's take this example—a paint business with the following projected cash flows (in thousands):

	Year					
	0	*1*	*2*	*3*	*4*	*5*
Cash flow	($1,000)	$400	$400	$400	$400	$5,600

Now, we can break this cash flow down into its components:

- Investment: money required to fund the venture.
- Tax consequences: not precisely a cash flow, but nonetheless a cash benefit that may accrue if an investment has operating losses in the early years.
- Free cash flow: cash that the business throws off as a result of its operations before financing and distributions to providers of capital.
- Terminal value: the aftertax cash that the business returns as a result of its sale. Here, this is assumed to occur at the end of Year 5.

Let's assume that these flows are as follows (in thousands):

	Year					
Cash Flows	*0*	*1*	*2*	*3*	*4*	*5*
Original investment	($1,000)					
Tax consequences	—	$300	$300	0	($100)	($200)
Free cash flows	—	100	100	$400	(500	800)
Terminal value (after tax)	—	—	—	—	—	5,000
Total	(1,000)	400	400	400	400	5,600

Now, we can calculate the IRR of the total investment: 64.5 percent.

Next, we calculate the present value of each of the individual elements of the return *at that IRR,* and then the percent that each element contributes to the total return. Of course, the present value of the total return will be equal to the original investment.

Element	*Present Value @64.5% (000)*	*Element's Percent of Total*
Tax consequences	$ 263	26.3
Free cash flows	322	32.2
+ Terminal value	415	41.5
Total	$1,000	100.0%

This analysis illuminates the potential sources of return inherent in the business, as projected.

The task of the entrepreneur is now to carve up the cash flows and returns and sell them to the individuals/institutions that are willing to accept the lowest return. This will leave the biggest piece of the economic pie for the entrepreneur. To do so requires an understanding of the financiers' needs and perceptions.

Understanding Financiers

Providers of capital clearly desire a "good" return on their money, but their needs and priorities are far more complex. Figure 9–1 in Chapter 9 depicts some of the differences that exist among different financial sources. They vary along a number of dimensions, including:

- Magnitude of return desired.
- Magnitude and nature of risk that is acceptable.
- Perception of risk and reward.
- Magnitude of investment.
- Timing of return.
- Form of return.
- Degree of control.
- Mechanisms for control.

The priorities attached to the various elements may differ widely. For instance, institutions such as insurance companies and pension funds have legal standards, which determine the type of investment that they can undertake. For others, the time horizon for their return may be influenced by organizational or legal constraints.

Certain investors may want a high rate of return and be willing to wait a long period and bear a large amount of risk to get it. Still other investors may consider any type of investment, as long as there exists some mechanism for them to exert their own control over the venture. To the extent that the entrepreneur is able to break down the basic value of the business into components, which vary along each of these dimensions, and then find investors who want this specific package, the entrepreneurs will be able to structure a better transaction; a deal that creates more value for himself or herself.

If we return to our example of the paint business, which requires a $1 million investment, we can see how the entrepreneur can take advantage of these differences in investor characteristics.

- The tax benefits, for example, are well suited for sale to a risk-averse wealthy individual in a high marginal tax bracket. Because the benefits accrue as a result of operating losses, if the business does poorly, the tax benefits may be even greater. But let's assume that the wealthy individual believes that these forecasts are realistic and requires a 25 percent return. If we discount the tax benefits at this 25 percent required return, we arrive at a present value of $325,500. Therefore, this individual should be willing to invest $325,500 in order to purchase this portion of the cash flows. There must be economic substance to the transaction other than tax benefits. Care must be taken so that the investor can show prospect for economic gain. For this analysis, this tax-based requirement is ignored.

• The operating cash flows would, in total, be perceived as fairly risky. However, some portion of them should be viewed as a "safe bet" by a bank. Let's assume that the entrepreneur could convince a banker that no less than $60,000 would be available in any given year for interest expenses. Further, if the banker were willing to accept 12 percent interest and take all of the principal repayment at the end of Year 5 (when the business is sold), then she or he should be willing to provide $60,000 ÷ .12 = $500,000 in the form of a loan.

Now the entrepreneur has raised $825,500 and needs only $174,500 to get into business.

• The terminal value and the riskier portion of the operating cash flows remain to be sold. Let's assume that a venture investor would be willing to provide funds at a 50 percent rate of return.

First, we need to see precisely what cash flows remain (in thousands):

	Year				
	1	*2*	*3*	*4*	*5*
Total	$400	$400	$400	$ 400	$5,600
− Wealthy investor	300	300	0	(100)	(200)
− Bank	60	60	60	60	560
Remaining	$ 40	$ 40	$340	$ 440	$5,240

The remaining cash flows in Years 1 through 5 have a present value, at the venture firm's 50 percent discount rate, of $922,140. If we need $174,500, we need to give up $174,500 ÷ $922,140 = 18.9 percent of these flows in order to entice the venture investor to provide risk capital. These flows might well be sold to the tax-oriented investor in order to meet the requirements for economic substance. This leaves the entrepreneur with a significant portion of the above "remaining" flows. One can see how these differences in needs and perceived risk allow the entrepreneur to create value for himself or herself.

Understanding the Entrepreneur's Own Needs

The example we have just worked through was based on the assumption that the entrepreneur wants to obtain funds at the lowest possible cost. While this is generally true, there are often other factors that should affect the analysis.

The entrepreneur's needs and priorities do vary across a number of aspects including the time horizon for involvement in the venture, the nature of that involvement, degree of business risk, and so on. All of these variables will affect the entrepreneur's choice of a venture to pursue. However, once the entrepreneur has decided to embark on a particular business, his or her needs and priorities with respect to the *financing* of the venture will vary with respect to:

- Degree of control desired.
- Mechanisms of control desired.
- Amount of financing required.
- Magnitude of financial return desired.
- Degree of risk that is acceptable.

For instance, in the above example, the entrepreneur could have decided to obtain an additional $100,000 or $200,000 as a cushion to make the venture less risky. This would certainly have lowered the economic return, but might have made the entrepreneur more comfortable with the venture.

Similarly, the bank, which offered funds at 12 percent, or the venture investor might have imposed a series of very restrictive covenants. Rather than accept this loss of control, the entrepreneur might rather have given up more of the economic potential.

In addition, the entrepreneur may need more than just money. There are times when some investors' money is better than others. This occurs in situations where once an individual is tied into a venture financially, she or he has an incentive to help the entrepreneur in nonfinancial ways. For instance, an entrepreneur starting a business that depends on securing good retail locations would prefer to obtain financing from an individual with good real estate contacts than from someone without those contacts. Venture capital firms are frequently cited for providing advice and support in addition to financing.

Summary

Once the fundamental economics of a deal have been worked out, the entrepreneur must still structure the deal. This requires the use of a certain legal form of organization and a certain set of securities.

The vehicles through which the entrepreneur can raise capital include the general partnership, the limited partnership, the S corporation, and the corporation. While these forms of organization differ with respect to their tax consequences, they also differ substantially regarding the precision with which cash flows may be carved up and returned to various investors. In a limited partnership, for instance, virtually *any* distribution of profits and cash flow is feasible so long as it is spelled out clearly and in advance in the limited partnership agreement. (Losses, however, are usually distributed in proportion to capital provided.) In an S corporation, on the other hand, where only one class of stock is permitted, investors can get a return in the form of tax losses that can be passed through, but founder's stock is equivalent to investors' stock, and it is difficult to draw any distinctions in the returns that accrue to the two groups.

Securities can involve debt, warrants, straight or preferred equity, and a host of other legal arrangements. The structuring of securities requires the assistance of good legal counsel with expertise in securities and corporate law, as well as intimate knowledge of the tax code.

In the previous chapter, we looked at alternative sources of financing. Here, we've attempted to describe how the entrepreneur can structure a deal with these potential sources of capital. A well-structured deal will provide the financier with his or her desired return and still create substantial value for the entrepreneur.

11

SECURITIES LAW AND PRIVATE FINANCING

Many business financing transactions are regulated by state and federal securities laws. The Securities and Exchange Commission (SEC) administers federal securities laws, and state securities laws (Blue Sky laws) are enforced by the respective states.

Securities laws apply to private business transactions as well as to public offerings in the stock markets. This chapter will focus on private financing; see Chapter 18, "Securities Law and Public Offerings," for information on the public financing markets. Like tax laws, securities laws are complex and not always grounded in logic. The consequences of violation (even technical violation) can be vastly disproportionate to the harm inflicted and can include severe personal liabilities for management (including innocent management). In addition, a violation can preclude present and future business financings. Treatment and cure of violations, when possible, can be time consuming and expensive. To complicate matters, securities regulation has changed dramatically over the past dozen years—first in response to the speculative abuses of the late 60s and, more recently, in an attempt to modify regulations that would facilitate capital formation.

Statements contained in this chapter are of necessity general in nature and become outdated with the passage of time, and therefore they should not be relied on in formulating definitive business plans, but used rather as an indication of the nature and extent of securities regulation that may be applicable in various circumstances. In this regard, it should be borne in mind that in addition to the federal securities laws, there are securities laws in each of the 50 states—many of which vary substantially from state to state.

Michael J. Roberts prepared this chapter as the basis for class discussion. It is based, in part, on an earlier note written by Richard E. Floor of the law firm of Goodwin, Procter & Hoar LLP.

What Is a Security?

The securities laws are applicable only if a "security" is involved in the transaction. The statutory definition of *security* includes common and preferred stock, notes, bonds, debentures, voting-trust certificates, certificates of deposit, warrants, options subscription rights, and undivided oil or gas interests. In fact, the definition is broad enough to encompass just about any financing transaction, whether or not a certificate evidencing the investor's participation is issued, so long as the investor's participation in the business is passive or nearly so. Generally, a security is involved whenever one person supplies money or some item of value with the expectation that it will be used to generate profits or other monetary return for the investor primarily from the efforts of others. Thus, a limited partnership interest is a security. So is a cow, if purchased together with a maintenance contract whereby someone else will raise, feed, and sell the cow without the participation of the investor. Similarly, an orange grove is a security if coupled with an agreement to maintain, harvest, and sell the orange crop; a condominium unit is a security if coupled with an agreement to rent the unit to others when not occupied by the owner; and parcels of oil property may be securities if sold with the understanding that the promoter will drill a test well on adjoining land. A franchise may or may not be a security, depending on the extent of the participation of the investor. Generally, a transaction involves a security if there is an expectation of a "profit" or monetary return.

Despite the broadness of the above generalizations, there are some financing transactions that are deemed not to involve securities merely because they traditionally have not been considered to involve them. Thus, a note given in connection with a long-term bank loan is generally not considered a security although it falls squarely within the statutory definition. On the other hand, bank transactions only modestly removed from normal commercial practice may be deemed to involve securities. Active participation in the solicitation of a pledge of a third party's securities in connection with an outstanding loan to another party, for instance, would fit within the definition and thus be subject to the securities laws.

Business Financing Disclosures

The financing of a business frequently involves the investment of money or some other item of value by a person who is not a part of management or otherwise familiar with all of the material aspects of the business. In order for an outside investor to make an informed investment decision, he or she must be made aware of the material factors that bear upon the present condition and future prospects of the business and of the pertinent details regarding participation in the business and its profits. The securities laws thus impose an obligation upon a business and its management to disclose such information to a potential investor together with the factors that adversely affect the business or that may reasonably be foreseen to do so in the future. In addition to financings by a company, these laws impose similar disclosure requirements whenever a member of management or a principal equity owner sells his or her personal security holdings to an outsider.

In financings involving outsiders, it is common practice (whether required or not) for management to prepare a prospectus, offering circular, or memorandum describing the nature, condition, and prospects of the business and the nature and extent of the investor's participation in it. In this manner, the pertinent disclosures are set forth in a permanent written record so that there can be no argument as to whether or not the disclosures have been made or what they were. Such a document traditionally discloses the terms of the offering, the use of the proceeds, the capitalization of the business (before and after the financing), contingent liabilities (if any), the operations of the business, sources of supply, marketing techniques, competitors and market position, personnel, government regulation and litigation, management and management's remuneration, transactions between the company and management, the principal equity owners of the business, and balance sheets and earnings statements of the business. **Exhibit 11–1** provides an outline for such a document.

Historically, the SEC has discouraged the disclosure of forward-looking information such as projected earnings or dividends per share, and at one time implied that disclosure of such information might be inherently misleading. In late 1995, however, Congress enacted a statutory safe harbor for written and oral projections and other forward-looking statements. The safe harbor exempts projections from liability under the federal securities laws if the statements fits into one of the three categories. The most commonly used category covers projections made by a company, but only if the statement is identified as a forward-looking statement and is accompanied by "meaningful cautionary statements" identifying important factors that could cause actual results to differ materially from the projections. The safe harbor is subject to a variety of formal requirements and exceptions; for example, it does not cover projections in initial public offerings.

Despite the fact that disclosure documents are often prepared and reviewed by attorneys and accountants, the law imposes the primary obligation for complete and accurate disclosure upon the company, its management, and its principal equity owners.

It thus is essential that each member of management (including outside directors) and each principal equity owner be satisfied that the information in the disclosure document is accurate and complete based on his or her own personal knowledge of the company and its records. The financial statements, for instance, are generally deemed to be the company's disclosures rather than the accountant's, and the company itself remains principally responsible for their accuracy, even when an audit has been performed. In fact, the company has no "due diligence" defense at all in a federally registered offering and is absolutely liable if any material misstatements or omissions occur anywhere in the prospectus.

A disclosure document that satisfies these disclosure standards often appears negative in its presentation. Such a document need not be unduly so in order to

---

EXHIBIT 11–1   Outlines for a Business Plan and a Prospectus

BUSINESS PLAN

1. Introduction (or Executive Summary). Includes short description of:
   - Business objectives.
   - Product.
   - Technology and development program.
   - Market and customers.
   - Management team.
   - Financing requirements.
2. Company Description.
   - History and states.
   - Background and industry.
   - Company's objectives.
   - Company's strategies.
3. Risk Factors.
4. Products.
   - Product description and comparisons.
   - Innovative features (patent coverage).
   - Applications.
   - Technology.
   - Product development.
   - Product introduction schedule and major milestones.
5. Market.
   - Market summary and industry overview.
   - Market analysis and forecasts.
   - Industry trends.
   - Initial product(s).
6. Competition.
7. Marketing Program.
   - Objectives.
   - Marketing strategy.
   - Sales and distribution channels.
   - Customers.
   - Staffing.
8. Management.
   - Founders.
   - Stock ownership.
   - Organization and personnel.
   - Future key employees and staffing.
   - Incentives (employee stock purchase plan).
9. Manufacturing.
10. Service and Field Engineering.
11. Future Products (Product Evolution).
    - Engineering development program.
    - Future R&D.
12. Facilities.
13. Capital Requirements.
14. Financial Data and Financial Forecasts.
    - Assumptions used.
    - 3-year plan.
    - 5-year plan.
15. Appendixes.
    - Detailed management profiles.
    - References.
    - Product descriptions, sketches, photos.
    - Recent literature on product, market, etc.

PROSPECTUS

When the business plan is used as a legal prospectus, or offering memorandum, the following additions or changes should be made:

- Affix federal and state securities legends.
- Affix disclosures.
- Add a detailed "Use of Proceeds" section.
- Add a section that describes the securities offered, in detail.
- Expand the "Risk Factors" section to include dilution, nontransferability, and other risk factors that relate specifically to the securities being offered.

Remember: Obtain the counsel of a competent securities attorney.

Note: Use and dissemination should be restricted; document should be treated as confidential.

---

provide the necessary protection, and, in any event, what appears "negative" to management may not necessarily appear negative to the financial community, which is accustomed to reading disclosure documents of this type.

In order to alleviate this negative effect, some entrepreneurs will first prepare a business plan, which is *not* an offering/disclosure document. The purpose of this document will be to stimulate investor interest. Having screened investors, the entrepreneur will then circulate a more formal offering/disclosure document. This technique is often effective, but still imposes a duty on the entrepreneur not to make any misleading claims in the business plan. In a public offering such an approach (called *gun-jumping*) would clearly be illegal. See **Exhibit 1** for outlines of a business plan and a prospectus.

Private Offerings

Private offerings are distinct from public offerings in a number of ways. Public offerings typically involve larger sums of money and may be sold through brokers. Public offerings require that the company go through an expensive and lengthy registration process to register the securities with the SEC. This process is discussed more fully in Chapter 18.

Federal securities laws and many state securities laws have long reflected the view that some potential investors are sufficiently sophisticated in business investment matters to be as able to investigate a business and assemble relevant data as are management and regulatory authorities. More recently, Congress has recognized that small businesses wishing to attract capital may be unduly hampered by burdensome filing requirements. In either circumstance, preparation of an orderly and systematic discussion of the business in a formal prospectus and the review of this presentation by government agents is deemed unnecessary because the offerees are competent to assess the venture independently, or because the issuer seeks to raise very limited amounts of capital. Thus, registration is unnecessary, and the company and its management and principal equity owners may rely upon one of the so-called private offering exemptions. Local state securities laws in every state where a *purchaser* is residing should always be reviewed. (It may also be prudent to similarly review state securities laws where any offeree resides, since the offer itself may be a violation even if no sale is made.)

Historically, the principal criteria of the availability of the private offering exemption have been the business acumen or "sophistication" of the offerees, access to material information concerning the company, and the number of offerees *(not purchasers)*. All of these items were highly subjective, and the absence of guidelines often resulted in liability for issuers who mistakenly believed they came within the exemption. Beginning in the 1970s, however, for purposes of federal regulation, the SEC attempted to create more order by releasing a series of rules that provide safe harbors within the general ocean of uncertainty embodied in these three traditional criteria. Regulation D represents the commission's most recent attempt to foster coherence and certainty.

Regulation D: The Various Rules

Six administrative rules, three of which set forth general definitions and three of which provide safe harbors for certain private offerings, comprise Regulation D. The operative rules—504, 505, and 506—broaden the scope of the private offering exemption. Collectively, they are designed to simplify the existing rules and regulations, to eliminate unnecessary restrictions on small issuers' ability to raise capital, and to create regulatory uniformity at the federal and state levels. Each of the rules requires that a notice be filed with the SEC on Form D.

Rule 504

The first exemption, Rule 504, is especially useful to issuers seeking to raise relatively small amounts of capital from numerous investors. It permits an issuer to sell up to $1 million of its securities during any 12-month period. Rule 504 does not limit the number or sophistication of the investors or prescribe any specific form of disclosure. The effect of the rule, then, is to delegate substantial responsibility regulating small issuers to the state agencies. Because Rule 504 is designed to assist small businesses, moreover, it is unavailable to investment companies or to companies that do not have an existing business ("blank check" companies), which must use the separate (and more restrictive) Rule 504A. Companies required to file periodic reports under the Securities Exchange Act are also denied the use of Rule 504.

Rule 506

In contrast to Rule 504, Rule 506 permits an issuer to sell an unlimited amount of its securities, but only to certain investors. In this regard, the rule represents a continuation of the SEC's effort to codify some of the practices developed by lawyers and courts in applying the general private placement standards of sophistication, information, and numbers and permits issuers to raise potentially substantial amounts of capital without registration. Rule 506 is available for transactions that do not involve more than 35 purchasers. Sales to accredited investors (defined below), relatives of investors, or entities controlled by investors are excluded from this total. The issuer must determine that each nonexempt investor meets the sophistication test, either individually or through a knowledgeable "purchaser representative," but no longer need inquire as to the investor's ability to bear the financial risk of his or her investment. In determining sophistication, the issuer can insist that each purchaser or group of purchasers be represented by a person who would clearly meet any test of sophistication. Subject to certain exceptions, the representative cannot be an affiliate, director, officer, employee, or 10 percent beneficial owner of the company (although he or she can be paid by the company as long as this is disclosed) and must be accepted by the purchaser in writing as his or her representative.

Perhaps the most significant aspect of Rule 506 is the "accredited investor" concept. Such investors are presumed to be sophisticated and thus do not count against the 35-investor limitation. They include institutional investors such as banks, savings and loan associations, broker-dealers, insurance companies, investment companies, certain ERISA employee benefit plans, private business development companies, corporations, certain trusts, partnerships and tax-exempt organizations, the issuer's directors, executive officers, and general partners. In addition, individuals whose net worth exceeds $1 million at the time of the purchase, or individuals with incomes in excess of $200,000 (or joint income with spouse in excess of $300,000) in each of the last two years, are considered accredited investors.

When an issuer sells securities under Rule 506 to accredited investors only, it is not compelled to make disclosures of any sort. If the sale involves both accredited and nonaccredited investors, by contrast, the disclosure requirements are more complex. Nonreporting companies must disclose (1) the information contained in Part II of Form 1-A for offerings of up to $2 million of their securities (including an audited balance sheet), (2) the information contained in Part 1 of Form S-18 or available registration when offering up to $7.5 million of their securities (including two-year financials audited for the most recent year), and (3) the information contained in Part 1 of an available form of registration when offering more than $7.5 million of their securities. If obtaining audited financial statements requires "undue effort and expense" for an issuer other than a limited partnership (to which separate provisions apply), then only a balance sheet as of 120 days prior to the offering need be audited. Reporting companies, on the other hand, must furnish (1) their most recent Rule14a-3 annual report, definitive proxy statement, and Form 10-K if requested, *or* the information contained in their most recent Form S-1, Form 10, Form S-11, FormS-18, or Form 10-K; and (2) any other reports or documents required to be filed under the Securities Exchange Act subsequent to distribution or filing of special reports or registration statements together with information concerning the offering and material changes, regardless of the size of the offering. All companies selling securities to accredited and nonaccredited investors must also furnish nonaccredited investors a written description of any written information accredited purchasers receive, and must give all purchasers an opportunity to ask questions and receive answers and to obtain any additional information that the issuer possesses or can acquire without unreasonable effort or expense prior to the sale. Finally, no issuerutilizing Rule 506 may engage in general solicitation or advertising.

Rule 505

Rule 505 adds some flexibility to Rule 506 for certain issuers. It permits the sale of up to $5 million of unregistered securities over any 12-month period to any 35 investors in addition to an unlimited number of accredited investors. The primary advantage of Rule 505, therefore, is the elimination of the sophistication test for unaccredited investors entirely and with it the elimination of the need for a purchaser representative.

Investment companies and issuers disqualified under Regulation A are ineligible to use Rule 505. Like Rule 506, Rule 505 prohibits general advertising or solicitation through public media of any kind and imposes disclosure requirements identical to the Rule 506 requirements discussed above.

Section 4(6)

Section 4(6) of the Securities Act, enacted as part of the Small Business Investment Incentive Act of 1980 and not technically a part of Regulation D, permits companies to issue up to $5 million of their securities in any single offering without registration and restricts the class of purchasers in any such transaction to accredited investors. Issuers are not required to disclose any specific information and may not engage in any form of solicitation in connection with offers or sales. Given these requirements, any issuer who can meet the requirements of Section 4(6) can also qualify under Rules 505 or 506.

Regulation D: Other Information

In addition to these specific exemptions, Regulation D includes a number of broadly applicable provisions designed to streamline and simplify private offerings. For example, when calculating dollar limitations, issuers must integrate the proceeds from all offers and sales made more than six months before or after a Regulation D offering. The regulation also provides that any securities issued pursuant to one of its exempting provisions (other than securities issued under Rule 504) may not be resold without registration. In this regard, the company must exercise reasonable care to prevent further distribution and should accordingly place restrictive legends on its certificates, enter "stop-transfer" orders, advise purchasers of the restrictions on resale, and secure representations that the securities are purchased for the individual's own account and not with any intention to redistribute. The issuer in a Regulation D or Section 4(6) private offering must file five copies of Form D with the SEC not later than 15 days after the first sale.

The burden of proving the availability of an exemption is on the person asserting it. In order for the risk of nonavailability of the exemption to be reduced to an acceptable level, the issuer must complete positive and compelling documentary proof that each of the requirements for exemption has been met. This is particularly important if none of the safe-harbor rules applies. The sophistication of offerees should be thoroughly investigated *before* they are approached, and a memorandum setting forth their background and the reasons for their sophistication placed in the log. In making the initial presentation, use of a private placement memorandum should be made, each such memorandum being numbered and containing a legend that is not to be reproduced or disclosed to outsiders. The number of the memorandum and the date on which it is submitted to the offeree should be set forth in the log. If the offeree becomes an investor, the date on which the offeree or his or her representative reviews the books and the records of the company, the books and records so reviewed, and the date on which the offeree or his or her representative engaged in face-to-face negotiation should be recorded in the log. At the end of the offering, a memo should be placed in the log stating that no persons other than those set forth in the log were contacted or offered any of the securities, such memo reciting that *offer* is understood to mean nothing more than creating a situation that can be construed as seeking a commitment (even informal) to acquire a security to be issued by a described company at a given price. The log should be placed in the company's permanent files as evidence of the availability of the private offering exemption as to the financing.

Finally, and perhaps most important, an issuer must remember that all offerings, even if exempt from federal registration, remain subject to the antifraud and civil liability provisions of the federal securities laws and to the general requirements of state Blue Sky laws. Particular note should be taken of the fact that the safe-harbor exemptions provided under Regulation D are generally not available under state Blue Sky laws and that registration may be necessary in a given state for an offering that fully complies with Rules 504, 505, or 506.

Resale of Restricted Securities

Securities issued under one of the private offering exemptions (other than securities issued under rule 504) or held by a member of management or a principal equity owner of the company (no matter how acquired, and whether registered or not) are subject to restrictions on resale that severely limit their liquidity unless the securities are subsequently registered under the Securities Act of 1933. For this reason, it is common practice for venture capital firms, private placement investors, management, and such owners to obtain an agreement from the company to register the securities upon demand or to include them "piggyback" in any other SEC registration that the company might undertake.

If the securities are not registered or covered by Regulation A when they are resold, as a practical matter the resales must be made under SEC Rule 144, or one of the private offering exemptions (not including the Regulation D exemptions for this purpose). Absent such an exemption, the resales will constitute unregistered offerings and subject the issuer and seller to potential liability. In addition, if the securities are transferred without consideration—by gift or upon death, for example—the restrictions generally bind the recipient.

Restrictions upon subsequent resale must be disclosed to potential investors in a private placement or the financing will be deemed by the SEC to violate the antifraud provisions of federal securities laws. This disclosure is often recited as part of the "investment letter" signed by the investor.

Consequences of Violation

As a practical matter, in the past a vast majority of securities laws violations have not been investigated or litigated. However, the possibility of nonenforcement provides little comfort to potential defendants when commercial transactions of any size are involved. Moreover, transactions of today are potential lawsuits five years from now, when investors may be more aware of their rights under the securities laws and more inclined to enforce them.

The consequences of violation of the securities laws in connection with a company's prior financings are rarely serious so long as its operations continue to be successful and this success is reflected in the price of its securities. If public estimates of a company's success have been too conservative, however, an investor who has sold his securities too cheaply may complain. Investors and regulators tend to scrutinize company disclosures in minute detail when a business turns sour, with the hopes of discovering some technical or other securities law violation to use in unwinding a financing, or holding management responsible.

The most serious consequence of violation of the securities laws is potential civil liability that may be incurred by those persons deemed to have violated such laws or to have aided and abetted violations. When a corporation or other business entity is involved, management (i.e., officers and directors, general partners, etc.) and the company's principal equity owners may be held liable as controlling persons. In this regard, the corporate entity, which serves as an effective shield from liability in other situations, affords no protection from securities laws violations. The magnitude of the liabilities that may thus be incurred can be enormous. If a violation involves improper disclosure, the applicable statute of limitations does not begin until the person harmed discovers or reasonably should discover the improper disclosure. Furthermore, agreements to indemnify management and owners from liability for securities laws violations are of little use. Insurance from these liabilities is expensive and often difficult to obtain.

Suit under the securities laws by damaged investors or others is relatively easy to bring. Such suit may be brought in federal court in any jurisdiction in which any defendant is found or lives or transacts business, and service of process may be made anywhere in the world. A single plaintiff may bring a class action on behalf of all persons similarly situated, and courts award attorneys' fees liberally to successful or settling plaintiffs' attorneys as an inducement to bring such suits as private guardians of the public.

A company that makes an offer to an ineligible offeree in a nonregistered offering in which the private or intrastate offering exemption is relied on is thus subject to a contingent liability to all investors in the offering for the aggregate amount of their investment. Under past practice, this contingent liability was deemed by the SEC staff to be cured by a subsequent registered or Regulation A offer to the investors to repurchase the shares sold in violation of the registration provisions. Subsequent financings without either the offer to repurchase or a disclosure of the contingent liability violate the antifraud provisions of the securities laws. Under recent SEC staff interpretations, even a registered offer to repurchase may not remove the contingent liability, and the contingent liability must be disclosed in subsequent financings until the three-year statute of limitations has run, or else an antifraud violation will occur.

Uncorrected securities laws violations can preclude subsequent Regulation A or registered financings. The SEC may take administrative, civil, or criminal action, which can result in fine, imprisonment, court order requiring restoration of illegal gains, order suspending or barring activities with or as a broker-dealer, or other sanctions reflecting the nature and seriousness of the violation.

Summary

Like many areas of the law, securities regulation is complex territory, fraught with countless opportunities for the entrepreneur to stumble. In the case of securities laws, an error can be particularly costly, making it difficult for the individual or the company to raise funds. For this reason, competent legal counsel is vitally important.

12

THE LEGAL PROTECTION OF INTELLECTUAL PROPERTY

In recent years, the world's major economies have become considerably more knowledge-based. High value-added, knowledge-intensive industries such as software and information services businesses have grown at the expense of resource-based and commodity businesses. The rationale for this trend is clear: Such knowledge-intensive industries offer superior opportunities to create sustainable competitive advantage and superior economic returns.

As the U.S. economy has become more knowledge intensive, legal minds have grappled with the issue of intellectual property: Who owns an idea? How can valuable knowledge and information be protected?

This chapter will address the various categories of protection afforded by the law, describe the nature of what can be protected, and discuss how that protection is achieved.

Intellectual Property

The area of intellectual property has challenged the legal system for hundreds of years, and continues to do so. Common law has historically protected property rights of individuals and corporations. But the area of intellectual property presents challenges to the legal system. If someone stole a piece of physical property—like your wedding band—it would be fairly easy to prove: That individual would have the ring, and you would be without it.

This chapter was prepared by Professor Michael J. Roberts as the basis for class discussion.
Copyright © 1998 by the President and Fellows of Harvard College.
Harvard Business School Note 9-398-230.

Yet, how can you tell when someone has taken an idea or a concept? A copy of a software program does not diminish the physical attributes of the original, only the economic interests of the owner. Intellectual property issues are particularly complex in situations where an individual is working on some state-of-the-art process for his employer. During the course of developing the design, the employee has some "inspiration" which was outside the scope of the project's original bounds. Does this idea belong to the employer or the employee? Does it matter whether the inspiration occurred on the company's premises or while the employee was at home in the shower? Could the employee continue to work for the employer, but set up an independent business to exploit the idea?

A special system of patent law and patent court system was developed to deal specifically with these questions. Recently, however, intellectual property issues have arisen outside the bounds of traditional patent and trade secret law. The legal system is currently in the midst of grappling with these problems, and recent (1995) legislation has attempted to clarify certain issues.

Intellectual Property and the Law

Historically, it has been a specific goal of U.S. public policy to create the incentives required for the progress of technology. One of the means to this end has been through the system of patents and copyrights. These classes of intellectual property have arisen out of the statutes of the United States government, which are, quite literally, the laws of the United States as passed by Congress.

They include "titles" such as: Title 11-Bankruptcy; Title 23-Highways; Title 39-Postal Service; and Title 50-War and National Defense.

Each of the "Titles" lays down the law relating to the subject at hand, as well as the administrative systems the U.S. government will put in place to support each of the areas. There are two titles specifically relating to intellectual property: Title 17-Copyrights; and Title 35-Patents.

Patents and copyrights receive protection directly under this statutory framework, but the law in these areas is not governed exclusively by the language of the U.S. Code itself. Through their application and interpretation of the statutes in individual cases, judges define (and, indeed create) relevant legal standards. Such "common law," or judge-made law, adapts the patent and copyright laws to modern circumstances (short of constitutional amendments to the statutes themselves).

Out of common law principles have grown other areas of law which address intellectual property issues. These areas include trademarks, trade secrets, and confidential business information. Each of these topics will be explored in detail.

Patents

Patents are issued by the U.S. Patent and Trademark Office. There are three specific types of patents:

- Utility Patents: for new articles, processes, machines, etc.;
- Design Patents: for new and original ornamental designs for articles of manufacture; and
- Plant Patents: for new varieties of plant life.

It is important to understand the concept of a patent. A patent *does not* grant an individual exclusive rights to an invention. The inventor *already* has that exclusive right by dint of having invented the device in the first place; he/she can merely keep the invention a secret and enjoy its exclusive use. Rather, the government grants the inventor the "negative right" to exclude others from making or using the invention. This right is granted in exchange for placing the information in the public domain.[1]

For instance, let's assume that the electronic calculator was a patentable invention, and that Mr. Sharp was issued a patent on the device. Now, let us further assume that the idea of a checkbook holder with an electronic calculator was also patented, and that Mr. Chex was issued a patent on this invention. Mr. Chex would have the right to prevent others including Mr. Sharp from manufacturing this device. However, Mr. Chex *could not* produce his article without the consent of Mr. Sharp. In the event that patent infringement does occur, the patent holder can sue in civil court for damages. Should the patent holder become aware of potential infringement before the actual infringement occurs, he/she can sue for an injunction to prevent the infringement from actually occurring.

As mentioned, these kinds of legal battles occur in the civil courts. The purpose of the patent court system is to mediate patent claims. For example, when a patent claim is published in the *Patent Gazette,* others could come forward and challenge the patentability of the invention in the patent court system. One basis of challenge is for another inventor to claim that he/she was actually the first inventor. For this reason, it is recommended that inventors keep a daily record of their progress in a notebook. These notes should record the inventor's progress, and be signed and witnessed on a daily basis. In the event of a challenge, such a record will prove invaluable.

The three types of patents each cover different kinds of intellectual property, and are governed by different regulations.

Utility patents   A utility patent is issued to protect new, useful processes, devices, or inventions. Utility patents are issued for a term of 20 years from date of application. First, what constitutes a patentable "invention"? The invention must meet several requirements:[2]

- It must fall within one of the statutory categories of subject matter. There are four brand classes of subject matter: machines, manufacture, composition of matter, and processes.

---

[1]David A. Burge, *Patent and Trademark Tactics and Practice* (New York: John Wiley & Sons, 1980), p. 25.

[2]Illinois Institute for Continuing Legal Education, *Intellectual Property Law for the General Business Counselor* (Illinois: Illinois Bar Center, 1973), pp. 1-16 through 1-24.

- Only the actual, original inventor may apply for patent protection. In the case of corporations, for instance, the patent, when issued, is always granted to the individual and then *assigned* to the corporation.
- The invention must be new. That is, it will be considered novel if it is:
  - not known or used by others in the U.S.;
  - not patented or described by others in a printed publication in this or a foreign country;
  - not patented in this country;
  - not made in this country by another who had not abandoned, suppressed, or concealed it.
- The invention must be useful, even if only in some minimal way.
- The invention must be nonobvious. If the invention has been obvious to anyone skilled in the art, then it is not patentable.

Finally, even if an invention meets all of these requirements, a patent can be denied if the application was not filed in a timely fashion. Specifically, if you used sold, described in print, or attempted to secure a foreign patent application *more than one year prior* to your U.S. application, the patent will be denied.

The process of obtaining a patent is quite laborious. Patent attorneys, who specialize in the area, will draft the patent application which includes specific claims for the patentability of the invention. After several iterations of discussions with the patent office, some or all of the claims may be approved. This process frequently takes two years or longer.

Following acceptance of the patent by the Patent Office, a general description of the invention is published in the *Patent Gazette.* Interested parties may request the full patent from the Patent Office for a very nominal fee.

During the time between application for a patent and its issue, the invention has "patent pending" status. In some ways, this offers more protection than the actual patent. The invention will not be revealed by the government during this time, and others may be afraid to copy the invention for fear of infringing on the forthcoming patent.

Design patents   A design patent protects the nonfunctional features of useful objects. Design patents are issued for 14 years. In order to obtain a design patent, the following requirements must be met:[3]

- Ornamentality—the design must be aesthetically appealing and must not be dictated solely by functional or utilitarian considerations.
- Novelty—the design must be new. The same criteria used for a utility patent will be applied here.
- Nonobvious—the design must not be obvious to anyone skilled in the art. This is a difficult standard to apply to a design, and is quite subjective.

---

[3]Burge, pp. 137, 138.

    – Embodied in an article of manufacture—the design must be an inseparable part of a manufactured article.

    Plant patents   A plant patent is attainable on any new variety of plant which that individual is able to reproduce asexually. The new plant must be nonobvious. A plant patent is issued for a term of 20 years.

Copyrights

Copyright protection is afforded to artists and authors, giving them the sole right to print, copy, sell, and distribute the work. Books, musical and dramatic compositions, maps, paintings, sculptures, motion pictures, and sound recordings can all be copyrighted.

    To obtain copyright protection, the work must simply bear a copyright notice which includes the symbol © or the word "copyright," the date of first publication, and the name of the owner of the copyright.

    Copyrighted works are protected for a term of 50 years beyond the death of the author.

Trademarks, Service Marks, and Trade Dress

A trademark is any name, symbol, or configuration which an individual or organization uses to distinguish its products from others. A service mark is such a name which is used to distinguish a service, rather than a tangible product.

    Trademark law is *not* derived from statutes of the Constitution, but is an outgrowth of the common law and service dealing with unfair competition. Unfair competition is deemed to exist when the activities of a competitor result in confusion in the mind of the buying public.

    There are several regulations that govern the proper use and protection of trade- and service marks.[4] The scope of protection under the law is a function of the nature of the mark itself.

    – Coined marks—a newly coined, previously unknown mark is afforded the broadest protection, e.g., Xerox as a brand of copier, Charmin as a brand of toilet tissue.

    – Arbitrary marks—a name already in use, and applied to a certain product by a firm, but without suggesting any of the product's attributes, e.g., Apple Computer, Milky Way candy bars.

    – Suggestive marks—a name in use, but suggesting some desirable attribute of the product, e.g., Sweet-n-Low as a low-calorie sweetener, White-Out correction fluid.

---

[4]Burge, p. 114.

- Descriptive marks—a name which describes the purpose or function of the product. Descriptive marks cannot be registered until, over time, they have proven to be distinctive terms, e.g., "sticky" would probably not be approved as a trademarked brand name for glue.
- Unprotectable terms—generic names, which refer to the general class of product. Escalator, for instance, once a trade name, is now a generic term for moving staircases. One could not introduce a new brand of orange juice and call it "O.J."

In order to maintain a trademark, an owner must continue to use it and protect it. In this vein, some consumer product companies routinely produce and sell a few hundred items of several brand names that they have trademarked and wish to protect, but are not in normal production. Similarly, Coca-Cola has a crew of agents who routinely order "a coke" in establishments which do not serve Coca-Cola. If they are served a soda, they prosecute. In this way, they can maintain that they have attempted to keep their brand name from becoming a generic. Aspirin, Cellophane, Zipper, and Escalator are all names which have lost their trademark status due to failure of their owners to protect the usage of the term.

Until a trademark is registered with the Patents and Trademark Office, it is desirable to use the ™ symbol after the name of a product, ˢᴹ for services. After registration, the legend ® should be used.

Trade dress is a term that refers to the look and feel of a retail establishment. Just as the courts have sought to protect the value businesses have built up in a brand name, they have been asked to protect the distinctive "look and feel" of certain retail concepts. In a recent example, for instance, one Mexican restaurant chain successfully sued a "knock-off" of the concept, arguing that the imitator had copied the unique trade dress of the original concept, unfairly trading on the value created by the concept's originator.

Trade Secrets

A trade secret is typically defined as any formula, device, process, or information which gives a business an advantage over its competitors. To be classified as a trade secret, the information must not be generally known in the trade.

One cannot, by definition, patent a trade secret, because the patent laws require that the invention be fully disclosed.

One advantage of a trade secret is that the protection will not expire after the 20-year term of the patent. Coke, for instance, maintains its recipe as a trade secret rather than patent it. Yet, should the information become public knowledge, their advantage could disappear quickly, and the inventor would have no claim on the process because it had not been patented.

Finally, should a firm decide to maintain a patentable advantage as a trade secret, and should another firm independently discover and patent that invention, this "second" inventor will have the right to collect royalties or force the "first" inventor to cease patent infringement. For this reason, many corporations routinely "defensively patent" and publish inventions so that others cannot.

In order for a company to maintain trade secret status for advantageous information, the company must keep the information secret and take precautions to keep it secret. These precautions include:

- Having certain policies relating to secret information.
- Making employees sign confidentiality and noncompete agreements.
- Marking documents "confidential" or "secret."

Confidential Business Information

The courts have also seen fit to protect a class of information less "secret" than a trade secret, but which is nonetheless confidential. The key here is that the information is disclosed in confidence, with the clear understanding that the information was confidential. A contractual obligation is established in which the receiver of the information agrees to treat it as confidential, and to use it only in furtherance of the objectives deemed appropriate by the owner. Even if the information is in the public domain, if the recipient derives some value from the confidential disclosure, he/she can be held liable for claims of unjust enrichment. There are several cases, for instance, where an inventor disclosed an idea, the recipient searched out the idea in *existing* U.S. patents, found the idea was already the subject of a patent, and bought that patent from the holder. The courts held that he had to give the patent to the submitter of the disclosure because of the confidential nature of their relationship.[5] One class of information that is commonly treated in this way, for instance, is a company's customer list.

Employees' Rights

Much of the law has evolved in an attempt to protect the rights of the enterprise. This has always been balanced, however, by the employee's right to earn a livelihood in the *best* potential source of livelihood. For instance, as an atomic engineer, the courts would protect my right to make a living *as an atomic engineer*, not merely earn a wage as a waiter or a bartender.

When a relationship between an employee and employer is severed, it is often the content of the written documents that will govern who has rights to what. Employment contracts, confidentiality, nondisclosure, and noncompete agreements all come into play. For this reason, prospective employees are well advised to read these documents carefully, and negotiate, rather than merely sign all of the papers which are typically associated with the first day on the job.

An employee can bargain away some of his/her rights in this area by signing inventions agreements, noncompete contracts, or employment agreements.

---

[5]Illinois Institute for Continuing Legal Education, pp. 6–9, 10.

However, the courts will not let an employee bargain away his/her fundamental right to earn a living from the best potential source.

If an employee signed an agreement that the courts found to be overly restrictive, the entire agreement would be thrown out. It is this fact which gives rise to the lawyer's advice that "It is better to sign an unreasonable employment agreement than a reasonable one."

There are three dimensions to the reasonableness test that the courts apply to employment agreements:

- time horizon;
- geographic scope;
- nature of employment.

For instance, an employment contract which required an employee not to compete for six months, in the state of New York, as a designer of petroleum process facilities might be viewed as reasonable. While an agreement which specified a time horizon of one year and a geographic area of the United States would probably be viewed as unreasonable.

Summary

In summary, it is clear that the body of legal knowledge in the intellectual property area is evolving rapidly. Yet, the processes which the law prescribes remain vitally important; in this area in particular, dotting the "i's" and crossing the "t's" is key. Whether it be keeping notebooks and records, filing patent claims, or reading the fine print on an employment contract, it is hard to overemphasize the importance of understanding the detail.

In order to gain sufficient command of the relevant body of law, specialized legal counsel is called for. In an area that is changing so rapidly, one cannot rely on prior practices and "industry standard policies" for protection.

Bibliography

1. American Bar Association. *Sorting out the Ownership Rights in Intellectual Property: A Guide to Practical Counseling and Legal Representation.* American Bar Association, 1980.
2. Burge, David A. *Patent and Trademark Tactics and Practice.* John Wiley & Sons, 1980.
3. Gallafent, R.J., N.A. Eastway, and V.A.F. Dauppe. *Intellectual Property Law and Taxation.* Oyez Publishing Ltd., 1981.
4. Illinois Institute for Continuing Legal Education. *Intellectual Property Law for the General Business Counselor.* Illinois Bar Center, 1973.
5. Johnston, Donald F. *Copyright Handbook.* R.R. Bowker Company, 1978.
6. Lietman, Alan. *Howell's Copyright Law.* BNA Incorporated, 1962.
7. White, Herbert S. *The Copyright Dilemma.* American Library Association, 1977.

13

SELLING AS A SYSTEMATIC PROCESS

This chapter summarizes some useful techniques for developing a thoughtful, systematic selling approach. Think of sales as a multistage process that cannot be completed in a single sales call. You need a strategy to progress through a series of intermediate objectives before you attain the ultimate goal of "getting the order." The purpose of this chapter is to describe a structure for organizing the process and some techniques for its execution. It does not represent the only systematic approach to selling; it is instead an approach that may provide you with a point of departure in developing your own tools and techniques.

First, it is useful to divide the selling process into a series of distinct phases, or steps:

- Generating attention and interest.
- Identifying requirements.
- Gaining conditional commitment.
- Developing the sale.
- Closing.

The amount of time and effort spent in each phase depends on the product, the customer's sophistication, and your overall strategy. For example, all the phases of selling a vacuum cleaner can be completed in a single sales call, whereas merely generating attention from a sophisticated buyer of jet engines

Michael Alter, Harvard Business School MBA 1994, prepared this chapter under the supervision of Professor Amar Bhidé as the basis for class discussion rather than to illustrate either effective or ineffective handling of an administrative situation.

may require a number of sales calls. Similarly, automobile dealers who follow a transactional strategy will seek to execute the selling phases in one customer visit, whereas those who believe in a relationship selling approach may encourage a number of customer visits. Regardless of the time and number of calls required, there are techniques that can improve the effectiveness of each phase.

Generating Attention and Interest

The purpose of this phase is to develop personal rapport and credibility and to create interest in the product.

To effectively establish rapport, you must get the customer to start talking. Sometimes, it is appropriate to do so by engaging the customer in personal discussions: for example, walking into an office and striking up a conversation about children or any other interests evident from the office decor. Such an approach may work best with customers who have a similar personal background. If you have little in common with your potential customer, then ask them open-ended questions, such as:

- Tell me about your company, your background, and your products?
- What is/are your strategy and your concerns?
- How did you get started in the business and decide on this firm?

Generally, customers will respond with detailed answers, particularly if your responses demonstrate attention and empathy. Occasionally, some customers may not be forthcoming in their responses. If further questioning is fruitless, it is best to move more quickly on to the second objective of this phase: creating interest in your product so that the customer has an incentive to continue talking with you.

The best method for generating interest is to cite how the product or service has been beneficial to other companies (especially their competitors). When references are not available, stress the competitive advantages your product provides. It is important to remember that customers will be interested in your product only if they perceive it as helping to meet their needs, which can be both those of the business *and* those of the persons buying the product for their company. To confirm success in generating interest, you can ask a closed-ended question,[1] such as:

- Do you think this benefit might be applicable to your business?
- Are you interested in discussing this benefit further?

---

[1]Closed-ended questions are an effective tool for re-establishing control of the conversation in order to gain closure or effect a transition in all phases of the selling process. In contrast, open-ended questions are an effective tool for getting your customer to disclose information or concerns.

Identifying Requirements

The purpose of this phase is to identify the needs that you must satisfy so that later in the process these needs can be mapped to specific product benefits. Open-ended questions can flush out the customer's requirements. Typical questions might include:

- Tell me about your concerns or major business issues.
- What would be the ideal solution to your problems?

Remember, open-ended questions must be asked with the customer's concerns and internal politics in mind. Some customers, for example, may not wish to discuss business problems because they would, in effect, be admitting to a past mistake or an inability to run their departments properly.

An alternative to open-ended questioning is the funneling methodology, which may help to overcome a reluctance to discuss business problems. The funneling process involves asking customers, in sequence, the following: their key goals, their quantitative objectives, their strategies, and their specific requirements.

FUNNELING METHODOLOGY

G   O   A   L   S
O b j e c t i v e s
S t r a t e g i e s
Requirements

The following is a (highly simplified) example of a salesperson's attempts to identify a customer's requirements by employing the funneling technique.

Salesperson:	What are your goals for this business unit over the next five years?
Customer:	My goal is to increase profitability.
Salesperson:	What objectives have you set for this goal?
Customer:	I want to increase sales by 5 percent in five years and decrease costs by 3 percent in the next two years.
Salesperson:	What strategy or plans do you have for increasing sales by 5 percent over the next five years?
Customer:	I plan to expand sales into China and to introduce a new product in our industrial division.
Salesperson:	What do you need to do to successfully expand your sales into China?
Customer:	I need to hire and train new salespeople with Asia experience, and I need to develop language skills among some of my existing salespeople. I need to develop

marketing and sales brochures for our products in China. Finally, I need to set up offices and distribution systems within China.

Determining which technique to employ depends on the kind of sale involved. For example, a simple product may lend itself best to the open-ended questioning technique, whereas a more involved product or service may require the funneling approach (although the funneling technique may be adapted for simpler selling environments as well).

Gaining Conditional Commitment

The purpose of gaining conditional commitment is to develop an understanding of the decision process and to establish an implicit contract.

You must confirm a true understanding of the customer's requirements and then ask the customer (in some form or other): If I can show you how my product or service meets your needs, as we discussed, will you—and do you have the authority to—buy the product?

Asking for conditional commitment prevents you from wasting time and effort selling to a person with no interest in purchasing your product. But even an interested party may lack the authority to make the ultimate decision. If so, you must gain conditional commitment on the terms under which the person would be willing to support your proposal with the actual decision maker.

Developing the Sale

The purpose of the fourth phase is to develop a product or solution and gain commitment from the key decision makers that it satisfies their needs. By this stage, you should already have confirmed that your product or service matches the customer's basic criteria. Now your challenge is to refine and tailor your offering. When selling a complex product or service, you may have greater scope to customize your proposal. But even with simple commodity items, you should think about modifying terms such as delivery times or payment schedules.

The next step is to gain commitment. The following process is often effective.

1. State the perceived customer need.
2. State the product benefit that satisfies the need.
3. Explain how the specific feature meets the customer's need.
4. Through a closed-ended question, obtain the customer's concurrence that the feature satisfies the need.

For example, suppose you are selling a computer system to a customer service department. Your prospect had stated a need to reduce the time necessary to solve each customer's problem. Therefore, you could use the following statements and questions.

1. You stated a need to reduce the time it takes to handle a customer request.
2. Our computer system has a 15-millisecond seek time.
3. A faster seek time means that you can retrieve your data faster and therefore reduce the time your customer spends waiting for a response.
4. Do you agree that this faster seek time would reduce the time it takes to handle a customer's request?

Usually, you will have to repeat this sequence until you have matched all of your product benefits to your customer's needs. Though it may appear very simplistic and somewhat time-consuming, it is a critical step in establishing a foundation for closing the sale. Be careful how you position your product benefits to ensure that the customer's past buying decisions do not appear to have been wrong.

Closing

This phase represents the culmination of the entire process—getting the order and establishing an action plan. Although quite obvious, explicitly asking for the order is extremely important. Inexperienced salespeople do not ask for the order, expecting the customer to state a desire to buy. This does not often occur. Following are several techniques that can be effective in asking for the order:

The straightforward or direct close: Summarize the benefits and ask for the order.

Subordinate question close: Ask a minor question that implies yes to a major question. (Example: What color would you like? or, Cash or charge?)

The window of opportunity close: Ask for the order based upon the benefits of having the product/service before a particular event. (Example: Do you want the product delivered before the end-of-the-quarter budget closes?)

Puppy dog close: Ask for a trial order over some time period, with no obligation.

Multiple choice close: Give the customer alternative choices, both of which imply commitment. (Example: Do you want the 20-inch or the 25-inch TV?)

Asking for the order often brings out customers' objections, even when you think they have agreed in the previous phase that the product or service will meet their needs. The ability to handle such objections is the hallmark of a good salesperson. A good approach is to take control of the conversation, using the previously established implied contract as leverage and employing questioning techniques such as: I don't understand . . . (or Help me understand, or What am I missing?), Didn't we already agree that you would buy if the product met your requirements, and you stated earlier that it did? This kind of questioning will surface concerns that you have not yet identified or properly addressed, or represent the customer's attempt to negotiate better terms. In either case, you should:

1. Listen and clarify to make sure you understand the real objection.
2. Empathize with the customer.
3. Address the objection, using the information and commitments you have gained in the previous phases. There are a number of ways to handle objections. For example, suppose your customer objects to the weight of your computer.

   Direct answer: Provide a direct answer to the objection. (It weighs less than any other computer on the market. Or, You stated a need for a computer weighing less than 5 pounds; this one weighs only 4 pounds.)

   Outweigh objection: Play down the importance of the objection as compared with other benefits. (For your needs, the ability to have a CD ROM player and a portable color screen far outweigh the half-pound of extra weight.)

   Minimize objection: Reduce the importance or restate the objection in more favorable terms. (This is a desktop computer, and, therefore, the weight is not really important.)

   Reverse objection: Turn the objection into a reason to buy. (We have found that thieves avoid heavier computers.)

4. Question to make sure the objection was handled.
5. Attempt to reclose. If this does not work, then, as a last resort, take responsibility for failing to close and ask for the customer's help. This may create an opportunity to reclose based on the customer's objections to the sale.

Final Suggestions

Never break a silence. After asking a clarifying or closing question, never break the silence, because, as uncomfortable as the silence is for you, it is worse for the customer. Many people lose orders or waste time because, after asking for the order, they break the silence by attempting to resummarize the benefits or continue selling.

Listen and key off of the customer. Adjust your approach and response to your customer. Listen to what they are saying and not what you want to hear.

Do not disparage or degrade the competition. Criticizing the competition only creates questions in the customer's mind about the benefits of your products and services. If your products really are better, you should be able to prove it by demonstrating their unique and superior value and not by degrading the competition's products or services.

Plan each sales call. You do not have to close every sale on the first call. Establish a strategy and objectives for each sales call based on where you are in the selling process. For example, in your first call, your objective might just be to get a second meeting.

Do not waste time once you have obtained your call objective. If your call is intended to close, for example, after getting the order, set an action plan and leave. It is a natural reaction to continue selling your product but once you have the order, you are done. Do not give your customer a reason to take away the order.

Finally, sales is about people and relationships. People are selling in most situations; it is just more subtle at some times than at others. Whether trying to convince somebody to buy a product, your boss for a raise, your classmates of the value of your comment, or your spouse where to go for dinner, you are selling! An understanding of the selling process and some key sales techniques can help you to be more effective. By adapting these techniques and processes to your personality, you can be successful at whatever you are selling, without losing or sacrificing your own personal flair or approach.

2–1

STEVEN B. BELKIN

Wake up, Steven! It must be some mistake, but American Express is calling and says it's important. It's something about your credit rating.

His wife's voice roused Steven Belkin from a fitful sleep. A cascade of problems swept through his mind as Joan handed him the telephone:

This must be about my $15,000 overdue credit card bill. Joan hasn't realized I'm in quite so deep . . . she's going to be a bit shaken by this. I can see I'd better reassure her when I get off the phone . . . but to tell the truth, if I don't find investors soon, I'm really in trouble.

It was 11:30 the night of December 5, 1973. Steven Belkin had charged many of his expenses while trying to set up a new group travel business. Finding investors was proving much more difficult than he had anticipated, and he had had to let his bill slip for a couple of months. Steven was going to have to find a new financing strategy fast to keep The Travel Group from being a one-way ticket to disaster.

Background

Steven Belkin, age 26, had lived in Grand Rapids, Michigan, as a youth. There he had his earliest business experiences. When he was 12, his grandfather had given him some salvaged automatic letter openers. Steven decided to set up a raffle with $1 tickets and the letter openers as the prize. He enjoyed selling the tickets and felt

This case was prepared by Richard O. von Werssowetz under the direction of Howard H. Stevenson.

Copyright © 1982 by the President and Fellows of Harvard College.

Harvard Business School Case 9-383-042.

wonderful telling the purchasers who had won. Another time he sold light bulbs door to door. Taking the idea from a school fund-raising project, he made it a summer job for his own profit. Steven's parents were of modest means, and financial pressures were a source of family discord. Steven resolved that his own excellence and success would provide family happiness.

Several people advised Steven that the way to success was to couple engineering with business school. After graduating from high school where he had been captain of his basketball and tennis teams, Steven received an industrial engineering degree from Cornell. He concentrated on obtaining good grades at Cornell and also was active in student government and other school activities to improve his chances for admittance to graduate school. After graduation in 1969, Steven entered the MBA program at Harvard. Steven recalled an interview he had set up:

> I tried to figure out how best to improve my odds to get in. I came down and had an interview and talked to different people. I don't know if it helped—they say it doesn't, but I don't know. I always took the attitude to absolutely give everything you have. Then if you don't make it, at least you have given all you've got.

Steven saw life as a series of plateaus. At Cornell, grades had been important to reach the next level. Having reached business school, Steven now wanted to concentrate on learning about different kinds of business and on getting to know his classmates. Steven recalled:

> I felt I needed to get there faster than the usual course. It wasn't OK for me to get there in the regular process, riding someone else's wave. I needed to get ready to jump on my own wave. In order to do that, to speed up the process, I needed to have more experience and contacts than my years. You get that extra knowledge from the experiences of others. And the families and friends of your classmates are a wealth of contacts.

Steven and another student obtained the résumé concession at Harvard Business School, which not only helped with expenses but also gave him a chance to meet all members of his class.

Innovative Management

During the summer between the first and second years of the MBA program, Steven decided he wanted to do consulting for small businesses. He asked friends and professors for leads, with little success. However, he did find that four graduating students were starting a new consulting company in that area that they would name Innovative Management (IM). Actually, one student had some possible business sources and had found a financial backer who would provide $50,000 for working capital. That student had asked the others to join for a salary and 5 percent portions of equity. Steven joined in the same fashion and the group quickly got underway. Steven described their start-up:

> We would go to bankers and individual venture capitalists who had made loans or investments in companies that weren't doing as well as they had hoped. We offered to

go in and analyze the situation and either suggest that they write off the situation or propose a plan to improve the company. Then we would actually go in and implement our suggestions.

The bankers and private investors we approached often didn't have the time or the ability to do this type of analysis. So they would go to the head of a company in trouble and point out that things weren't going very well, then suggest that the company employ us for the study as a condition of providing more funds. The companies would pay our fees, which usually were $4,000 to $5,000.

Initially, we would approach a new source of projects and offer to do the first job at no cost. After we showed what we could do, they would usually give us additional assignments.

Our customers were companies with annual sales from $2 million to $10 million. Most were fairly new entities. Usually we could provide a needed control system, a marketing strategy—an entire business plan. Although the owners usually were under considerable pressure to let us in, they often were very stimulated by what we did. They knew they had problems and they didn't have the luxury of our education. After we gave our report to the financial backer, we also gave it to the company. Often we could provide our recommendation in only three or four days.

By the end of the summer, we were so successful that we began hiring additional business school graduates. I continued to manage several others during my second year of school.

In addition to running the résumé service and continuing his consulting business, Steven did a survey of interest in small business among students in the top 10 business schools as his second-year project.

My purpose was to show that there was a strong interest among these students in new ventures and starting your own company even though most schools were not teaching that. The survey confirmed this, and I used the data to write some articles that we used to publicize our consulting firm. For example, we had stories in the *Boston Globe* and the SBANE [Small Business Association of New England] paper.

People are always fascinated about people who do surveys and who have statistics. It makes you an instant expert to have a survey! It bought us new contacts and more credibility.

Looking back, Steven commented that he had done too much during the second year:

I was incredibly busy. I cut a lot of classes. But the income was tempting, and I was just ready to get the second year over with. But you are always going to have work, yet you only have the second year of business school once. I missed an awful lot. I didn't realize then that the cases contained so much practical experience—I felt they were "text booky." I just didn't absorb that they really reflected day-to-day problems.

During the last half of the second year, Steven explored the job market, interviewing primarily with consulting firms. Although none of the firms caught his fancy, Steven thought the process was worthwhile:

It was a terrific educational experience to be able to talk to these high-caliber people in the different companies where they were trying to sell you and tell you all about their companies. But I guess I was a bit spoiled after already having my teeth in it, giving suggestions to people and seeing them implement them the next week. The big companies seemed a little academic—nothing, really, compared to what I was doing.

Steven remained with Innovative Management when he graduated in June 1971. A year later, however, the company was sold and Steven decided to leave. Steven explained:

We grew from 5 people to 22 in that first two years. Then one of the individual venture capitalists who had given us some work wanted to buy the company. The other four founders wanted to sell, but I thought that we would lose our objectivity as an affiliated consultant. I wasn't very happy about it, so I left the firm.

Group Touring Associates

Having decided to leave Innovative Management, Steven Belkin reviewed his situation. Financially, he had limited resources. Steven had been earning almost twice the $12,000 typical starting salary of his class. Joan, whom he had married just after graduation, worked as a teacher for a smaller salary. Steven had received $15,000 for his interest in the consulting company but also still owed several school loans that were not yet due for payment. Their net worth was about $10,000. Steven had no special ideas for starting a different business and was not attracted to seeking a job with a larger company. It appeared to him that he should continue small business consulting on his own.

The sale of IM took place at the end of the summer of 1972. Before Steven embarked on an independent course, however, he was approached by Frank Rodgers, the original investor in Innovative Management. Rodgers had been squeezed out of that investment when the company was sold. Rodgers said he would like Steven to work for him helping other companies in which Rodgers had investments, and Steven agreed.

Steven found he had a special attraction for a group travel company that was one of Rodgers' first assignments. This company, Group Touring Associates (GTA), developed tours that were sold to various groups by mail using their membership lists. GTA had been started by Robert Goode in 1966 with the backing of Rodgers and a few other private investors. Rodgers had invested $200,000 to date; the others, another $200,000.

Sales had grown to $1.8 million over the past year, but GTA had yet to make a profit. Losses had been increasing from $50,000 four years ago to over $250,000 last year. Robert Goode had convinced his investors to continue their backing by pointing to the rising sales. He contended that the front-end marketing costs of mailings and of setting up the trips would cause him to show losses as he grew. On the other hand, the unearned customer deposits made prior to the trips provided much of the cash needed for the growing operation. Rodgers agreed that some losses might have been necessary as the company got its start, but now was alarmed by the continuing deficits. Rodgers felt that the deposit cash flow was disguising more fundamental problems and wanted Steven to help the situation.

After a brief analysis of the business, Steven felt GTA had excellent potential and that it could be built profitably with better management. He accepted an offer to join the company and became GTA's executive vice president:

> Looking back at my other consulting clients, there wasn't one business that I wanted to do. I had done one project for another tour operator, but they marketed through travel agents and student groups. The combination of group travel with direct mail made this very fascinating to me—this was the business for me. OK, I needed solid experience in this one. This was a good opportunity, and I could earn a piece of the action.

A year later, Steven could point with pride to sales that had grown 50 percent and to a profit of over $150,000. Steven credited the turnaround to basic planning and well-managed execution:

> There was little organization when I came: no business plan, budgets, or anything like that. What I did was to clearly define our product and focus our operational and selling efforts. All within a budget and a plan. Before, the salespeople would try to find what trips various groups might be thinking about and come back and try to put one together. I introduced the strategy of defining the trips with the greatest general demand, then putting the trips together, and having the salespeople fill them up.
>
> This strategy let us buy better, put together better promotional material, and better control our costs. I was very sensitive to the fact that we were in the direct-mail business rather than just the group travel business. We had to provide better value for the travel dollar and promote it well by mail.

At the end of his first year as executive vice president, Steven reopened discussion about his future role in GTA with Robert Goode. He had initially accepted a salary of $22,000 with the understanding that they would renegotiate his position after Steven had proven himself. Now Steven felt he should receive a $30,000 salary and also be given 10 percent of the company. Robert would not agree. Steven recalled:

> Robert and I went back and forth quite a bit. GTA was finally making money, and I felt I deserved part ownership. Robert wouldn't go over $25,000 in salary and wanted to wait another year for the equity.
>
> As we reached an impasse, Frank Rodgers arranged several more meetings between us. However, now that the company was profitable, Goode no longer needed more equity, and Rodgers didn't have enough power to force Goode to agree to my demands. I think Robert also felt that he had run the company for six years and, now that I had gotten GTA over the hurdle, he wanted to be the boss again.
>
> I tried very hard to reach an agreement; I wanted to stay. I felt that if I could be earning the $30,000 and have 10 percent of a profitable, growing company, I would be on my way to being successful. I was really running the show; I felt I was going to make money; I was fulfilling my entrepreneurial goals.

Considering an Independent Course

As Robert Goode's position hardened, Steven began to consider leaving GTA to start his own group travel packager. Looking at the industry structure made him feel this segment was a good opportunity. Potential air travelers could arrange pleasure trips directly on their own, choose ground packages offered by "tour wholesalers" such as American Express, or select complete air/ground packages such as those organized by GTA using chartered airlines. Traits of these choices are shown in **Table 1.**

Although the group air charter industry had only developed over the last 10 years after the introduction of jet air service, this mode of touring had already become a popular travel alternative. Steven felt the key attractions were lower cost, professional tour management, and the comfort and peace of mind of the sponsoring organizations' endorsements.

The lower costs were the direct result of the use of chartered aircraft—the group tour organizer guaranteed to pay for all seats and took the risk of filling the flight. Many travelers were willing to accept the fixed schedules of charters to take advantage of the lower prices. The offer of complete tour packages with professional tour guides was convenient, especially for travelers unfamiliar with the desired destination. Also, each traveler was a member of a group that sponsored the tour and could feel that his or her own representative would make sure the tour was a good trip and that the group would receive everything for which they had paid. This was particularly important in 1973 because there had been some recent publicity about tours that had been stranded or given inferior accommodations or service.

Steven saw these advantages as clear distinctions between group charter companies and tour wholesalers that used scheduled air carriers. The tour wholesalers also marketed primarily through retail travel agents whereas charter tours were normally sold using direct mail.

Looking at competition, Steven knew there were 10 major group tour operators in the United States. GTA ranked about seventh in that list. Where GTA provided tours for about 8,000 people per year, the largest U.S. operators moved about 50,000 customers yearly. As he viewed the market, he felt there was certainly room for one more:

> In the United States, there were regulations that you had to belong to an organization to go on a group trip. These had been eliminated about six years ago in Europe. With that, some of the group tour operators did more business than some of the scheduled carriers. The largest European companies running group charters were moving over a million people per year each. These regulations were relaxing in the United States, so I felt there would be great opportunities.

Steven received encouragement from Alan Lewis, GTA's most productive salesman. During Steven's negotiations with Robert Goode, Steven had described his growing frustration to Lewis. When Steven mentioned that he would be happy for Alan to join him if he left, Alan suggested that Steven should go out on his

TABLE 1   Comparison of Pleasure Travel Options

	Direct Selection by Traveler	*Use of "Tour Wholesaler"*	*Charter Tours*
Air travel	Via scheduled airline	Via scheduled airline	Chartered airplane
Land arrangements	Individual plans and arranges directly with provider or through retail travel agents	Provided by tour wholesaler	Provided by group travel wholesaler
Flexibility	Complete	Travel timing flexible	Fixed departure and return schedules
		Only selected destinations and accommodations	Only selected destinations and accommodations
Usual cost	Highest price	Sold as service; cost often same as direct	30 percent to 40 percent lower
Sold by	Individual carriers, hotels, etc.; retail travel agents	Retail travel agents	Group-sponsored direct mail, some retail travel agents
Other limitations			Must be member of "affinity group"

own whether or not Goode agreed to his demands. Alan would like to join him and was anxious to get an ownership position himself.

Steven's discussions with Goode made no further progress, so Steven resigned and left in early September 1973. Alan Lewis also resigned, and the two of them began to develop The Travel Group, their own group travel business.

The Travel Group

Steven's idea for The Travel Group (TTG) was to duplicate the strategy that had been successful for Group Touring Associates. They would start with limited tour offerings to the most popular destinations, then expand as their reputation grew. They would use five sales representatives to call on groups across the United States to develop sponsors for direct-mail promotions. They would carefully control their customer service and tour operations to minimize costs and gain customer satisfaction.

The tours they would offer were complex logistical tasks with large financial commitments. Running a tour meant chartering an entire plane, which would accommodate up to 200 passengers. The company would also have to commit to blocks of hotel rooms and meals and provide ground transportation and other assorted support services. Once the package was planned, promotional material had to be written, printed, and distributed. Then inquiries had to be answered and reservations made.

To run the company, Steven would be president and major shareholder. He would be responsible for raising the capital they would need, for negotiating the trip arrangements, and for setting up the internal operations. Alan Lewis would be executive vice president. He would hire and manage the sales force, cover key clients personally, and work with sponsoring groups to fill the tours. Steven described their deal:

> I had planned to give five key salespeople 5 percent of the company each. Alan convinced me to give him the entire 25 percent, and he would give away whatever was necessary to hire the others. Thus, we became partners, but I would have a minimum of 51 percent ownership, Alan up to 25 percent, and the remainder would be for me or the investors. He ended up keeping all 25 percent after hiring four other excellent salespeople. Equity for our financial backers would come out of my share.

Steven and Alan immediately swung into action. Steven concentrated first on creating a business plan, while Alan began his search for salespeople and selling efforts for an initial tour he and Steven had outlined. By October 1, 1973, the business plan was finished, and Steven prepared to raise $250,000:

> Developing the plan was fairly straightforward. We knew the basic charter travel destinations and seasons. We planned to run one airplane a week in season during the first year, two planes a week the second, and build each year. It was important to run "back to back" tours as much as possible so that the chartered plane could take one tour and return with the prior week's group. I added cost projections and made cash flow assumptions to give an overall financial plan.
>
> The plan showed an accumulated deficit of $155,000 for the five months before our first tour. Then I expected profits and tour deposits to provide cash for growth. I felt I should raise $250,000 for a safe cushion to fund that deficit with room for unexpected costs, delays, or errors.

The business plan for The Travel Group is shown in **Exhibit 1.** Steven intended this document to be a simple, easy to follow business plan rather than a formal investment memorandum. He explained his reasoning:

> Most people make business plans so complicated that people understand nothing and get scared by them. If you repeat things two or three times, then they say, "Oh, yes. I understand that." They think they understand what they are investing in. If you keep giving them more and more inputs and ideas, they just can't absorb it.
>
> When people finish reading my verbal description, they understand what I have said. That does not mean they understand the business. But they have understood what I said, so therefore they think they understand the business.

Financing Strategy

Steven and Alan had direct experience in the operational tasks confronting them. Finding the needed financing was less familiar. However, several of Steven's earlier IM consulting assignments had involved raising money for smaller companies. Steven described IM's role:

> Some situations we investigated needed more equity along with the strategic and management changes we might suggest. If asked to implement our plan, we would agree to raise the money along with providing an executive vice president to bolster man-

agement and increase the company's credibility to investors. In return, we would receive part of the equity.

We tried to keep this from being threatening to the president. Rather, we worked to convince the president that we'd be adding some new skills and helping to make the company valuable. Not like we were after the president's job.

We'd approach individual venture capitalists for investments of $25,000 to $50,000 each. Our total needs were usually $100,000 to $200,000. The Rodgers family was very well connected, and we had developed other contacts in the course of our projects.

Pricing was rather arbitrary. The company probably didn't have earnings, and we were selling the future. There was no scientific approach. We tried to show that the investors would double their money in a three-year period, then double it again to a value four times their original investment by the end of year five.

Structurally, these investments sometimes ended up as a combination of debt and equity. This might be a loan with stock warrants. If all went well, they'd get most of their money back in a year or so and keep an equity ride with the warrants. The investors were very interested in not losing—not making mistakes, and less worried about how to get their equity out. That was less well structured—something down the road.

With this limited fund-raising experience, Steven developed a financing strategy. First, he assessed the situation from an investor's point of view. TTG had a large upside. Few start-ups could show the rapid sales growth Steven had projected. There were good margins that gave an excellent profit potential and unusually attractive cash flows. The management team had strong credentials. Steven's education was a plus, and both he and Alan had been successful running a similar company. They would also be using an experienced sales force. The group travel market in the United States had much less penetration than in Europe and should grow rapidly. Finally, there was little sophisticated competition in this industry, so their management skills would give them an extra advantage.

To demonstrate long-term potential, Steven could also show evidence that a group tour operator could be attractive as a public stock offering. One large U.S. tour operator had gone public in 1967 at a price of $10 per share. Within two years, the price had risen as high as $93 per share. The shares were currently trading for about $8, but this was primarily the result of that company's poor results in diversifying into restaurants, cruise ships, and hotels.

Steven decided that this set of characteristics made TTG a good deal for institutional venture capital groups. He would attempt to raise the $250,000 in five units of $50,000. He hoped that two or three investors would subscribe to the entire total. Steven felt this was a better alternative than going to wealthy individual investors for smaller units:

I thought the larger shots would be easier. I had the right background and credentials and a good business plan. I was sophisticated enough to present it to institutional investors. I felt this was a good package to offer, that they would buy me and would buy the business plan.

As insurance, Steven would also present the plan to a few individual investors, but his main thrust would be the institutional groups.

For leads, Steven turned to the "hit" list he had been developing since he had been in business school:

> I kept a notebook of people I met who might be good contacts. I'd put in notes on meetings and phone calls, addresses, correspondence. Some were filed in various institutional categories—others were just alphabetical.
>
> I put the people I would approach in priority by relationships. I wasn't going to ask people directly to invest. Rather, I would ask for their help: "What should I do to raise money?" I didn't want to put them on the defensive—once you ask them if they'd invest they have to protect themselves. This way, they could talk to me totally straight and really give me advice. If they *were* interested, then they would say they'd like to look at my plan further. Either way, they'd often recommend someone else to see.

Prospects, 5: Investors, 0

Steven had contacts with five well-known institutional venture capital companies. He approached each, describing his idea and asking advice. Out of these five, two were interested enough to ask to consider his plan. After being initially encouraged by this interest, Steven soon began to feel that none of these firms was likely to invest. He described the problem areas he encountered:

> First, I was confronted with the developing fuel crisis. There were headlines in the newspapers saying airlines were canceling charter flights. Only needed scheduled flights would be flying. There I was telling people I was starting a new charter company just as TWA was grounding all of its charters!
>
> I had to explain that I could buy space on regular flights if necessary, but that the *charter airlines* would continue to run. The charter airlines were separate airlines encouraged by the government so that additional aircraft would be available in a national emergency. They only flew charters and were not canceling their flights. I also argued that if flights were rationed, my old relationships with the airlines and the professionalism we would be bringing in would give us preference in charter assignments.
>
> I felt I was making some of the venture capital companies comfortable about the fuel problem, but I also found them reluctant to invest because there were no hard assets to "lend" against. They'd say, "There's nothing there! You aren't buying any machinery; all the money's going for working capital. There's no product line, no proprietary technology."
>
> I believe they were thinking that if it didn't work, with hard assets they could still minimize their losses somehow and get something out of it. I got the feeling they were just more liberal bankers, which was different from my earlier concept of venture capitalists.

Approaching Wealthy Individuals

Scheduling appointments and follow-up visits with the venture capital companies took most of October with some discussions continuing into November. At the same time, Steven also was calling on wealthy acquaintances in a more casual way:

I'd say, "You know I'm raising money on Wall Street, but this might be something you'd be interested in. I'd like to get your input. Do you have any suggestions?" I'd mostly ask for advice and references to other venture capitalists or investment bankers.

As it became evident that the venture capital companies were not showing great enthusiasm, Steven more seriously pursued wealthy individuals:

I primarily approached other successful business executives who either still ran their own businesses or had sold their businesses in the last few years. I thought that a $50,000 investment would be easy for them. It was a lot tougher than I thought.

By November, I was letting everyone know I was trying to start this company. I was using every contact I could to get referrals to wealthy investors.

Out of all of his contacts, Steven developed two serious leads. One investor who was also a friend indicated he might provide $20,000. The other wanted Steven to come back when he had raised most of the remainder of the offering. Steven had expected wealthy individuals to be excited by the opportunity he saw in TTG. Now he found that wealthy individuals were going to be more difficult to attract as investors than he had anticipated.

Offer of a Bank Loan

Steven's discussions with the wealthy individual who knew him did lead to an unexpected offer of debt financing. Steven explained:

I didn't think any part of my deal was bankable at all. I clearly felt that all equity money would be required. Yet the one wealthy individual who was my friend said he did think the idea had merit and that he would introduce me to his bank. He gave me a very strong personal endorsement and to my surprise, his banker said he would match every dollar of equity I raised with one dollar of debt!

Once this bank opened my eyes, I approached several downtown banks to see what they would do. They wouldn't have any part of a loan—there were no assets to lend against.

The bank willing to give me a credit line was located outside of the main metropolitan area. They were more aggressive to compete, but they also saw TTG as a good cash flow generator and needed the deposits.

The loan offer opened welcome new possibilities to Steven. Now if he could raise as little as $125,000 in equity, the total of $250,000 would be available to him. However, the use of the debt line would greatly increase his own exposure because the bank would be lending against his personal guarantee. He was not anxious to do this himself, and the idea was frightening to Joan:

I was signing a $125,000 note, but my net worth was less than $10,000. Sure. I decided it didn't make any difference—if things went bad, I couldn't pay it anyway, so why worry about it? I would be more concerned about signing a $25,000 note because I conceivably could pay that.

But they also required Joan to sign it, and this was very, very stressful for her. It was overwhelming and very upsetting. We talked about it, and I said it was the same way for me too. But if it's $125,000 or it's a million, it doesn't make any difference right now.

The note Steven and Joan Belkin signed was a contingent line of credit at 2 percent over the prime lending rate. The credit line would equal the amount of TTG's equity up to a maximum of $125,000. Steven could draw on the line at his discretion. However, both he and Joan were very anxious not to use this credit so that they would not actually incur the personal liability of their guarantee.

Growing Pressures

Signing the credit line agreement and the slow progress in raising the needed equity were not the only sources of the pressures Steven felt building. There was also the hectic pace of beginning TTG operations.

If TTG was to run its first tour during the late winter season, the package must be put together and ready for sale by the beginning of January. To do this, Steven and Alan had been continually working to develop their first trip and get their sales effort underway since October. By October 15, they had hired a secretary who had worked with them at GTA and set up operations in Steven's apartment. By the end of October, they had added another secretary and the first additional salesman. Steven described what it was like:

> We just assumed we would get the money and that we had to make it work. So we had to get the sales.
>
> Joan was teaching, so she went off to work at seven o'clock and came home about 3:30. She had been very, very helpful in putting together the business plan, but she's a very organized person and had her own work to do. When all the people were in the apartment, that started getting to her. Not only would there be no privacy and no quiet to plan her classes and grade her papers, but sometimes we'd raid the refrigerator for lunch, and she'd find that what she had planned for supper had disappeared. We would often work past seven o'clock talking to the West Coast. She could go into a bedroom by herself, but in that small two bedroom apartment, it was more of a prison than a refuge.
>
> On November 15, we rented a 10-foot by 20-foot office that had been the rental office in my apartment building so things were a bit better, but we still used my apartment. We were sharing desks and had no place to have meetings with potential backers or sales contacts. I always met people at the airport, said I was just leaving on a flight, then waited until they had gone before going back to our office.

Steve Belkin and Alan Lewis were funding the office expenses and salaries for the other employees from their own pockets. So far they had invested almost $10,000 in cash. In addition, each of them was charging every possible expense on their personal American Express credit cards. Since both of them were traveling around the United States and Europe to talk to group sales prospects, interview sales representative candidates, and set up the first tour, they had accumulated outstanding charges of about $15,000 each. They had both been heavy users of their credit cards before, which gave them high credit limits. They had made no payments since September and were starting to get overdue reminder letters, which emphasized they were about to lose their hard-earned credit.

As business paused for the Thanksgiving holiday, Steven wasn't quite sure how much he should be thankful. There was little progress finding equity investors, and Steven's bills and responsibilities grew.

He felt he had to provide others emotional support just when he was the least sure of what he might have done to his own position:

> I was having to play Mr. Completely-in-Control: "Everything is great. We're going to get our money." The only one who was really starting to worry was Alan. He was the only one I really talked to. He hadn't had much exposure to raising money. I was starting to let him know I was getting nervous, and he didn't know how to read that. "What does it mean when Steve's nervous?"

> I'd also gone far enough that everyone knew I was doing this. It's not like I could have a quiet failure. I'd gone to close friends and family for contacts—the ones I'd worked so hard to impress. I'd always been Mr. Successful: "Here's Steve. He went to Harvard, was captain of his tennis team and basketball team, and always got good grades. He had his own consulting firm." Now Mr. Successful was starting his own company, and Mr. Successful was in trouble.

What Now?

By the first week of December, Steven knew he had only a few weeks left before TTG would start to unravel. Finding money was the key:

> I felt I really had to switch gears here. I had to scrape it together. Initially I wanted to do it the business school way. Now, I had to become a street fighter. I might have to go out and beg, and it would be very difficult for me to go to people and say, "I need your help."

> I only had a little time. Should I put more emphasis on the venture capital route and really try to close one of those? Should I continue with the wealthy investors? Or should I go to friends and relatives and try to piece it together in fives and tens? Because I had so little time left, I really felt the main options I should consider were to find one venture capitalist for $250,000 or to go to friends for small amounts.

In deciding on his last-ditch strategy, Steven also contemplated whether he should change his offering to be more attractive. Pricing had never been explicitly discussed with the institutional venture firms. When talking to wealthy individuals, Steven was offering to sell 250,000 shares at $1 per share. He and Alan would be issued 750,000. What ways of repricing or restructuring the deal would help him to raise his equity fast?

"This is not exactly how I thought it would be," Steven thought to himself as he struggled to find a creative solution that December evening. "This is a good opportunity. Why haven't I been successful raising the money yet? I wonder if it was a mistake to resign so quickly? Well, here I am. Maybe I'll think of something tomorrow." It seemed that he had just drifted away, when the phone rang.

EXHIBIT 1   TTG Business Plan—October 1, 1973

[The entire narrative of the business plan is reproduced below. Title pages have been removed and the layout has been condensed. Only selected financial exhibits are included.]

I. THE INTRODUCTION

The Travel Group is being formed to meet the tremendous need for low cost group travel. People now have more leisure time than ever before, and they are becoming aware that group vacations are available at prices almost everyone can afford. A week in Europe or the Caribbean for $199 per person is an affordable price for most people.

The group travel industry is less than 10 years old. The market penetration for this new industry has barely begun. There are unlimited groups available. Alumni organizations, professional associations, religious groups, fraternal organizations, employee associations, unions, corporations, women's clubs, etc. The Travel Group will be concentrating on "prime groups." These are organizations that are known to be extremely responsive to group travel (e.g., Shriners, medical associations, bar associations, teacher associations).

The Travel Group will provide "deluxe" group tours. The attitude of management is to send "prime groups" during "prime season." Hotel accommodations will be at deluxe hotels (e.g., Hilton, Sheraton, Hyatt), and air transportation will be via scheduled carriers (e.g., United, Braniff, American) when possible.

The Travel Group will be classified as a "back-to-back wholesaler" in the travel industry. The corporation will market its group tours to travel agents throughout the United States. This should comprise less than 10 percent of the sales during the first two years, but eventually should produce 25 percent of the sales volume.

The primary source of sales for The Travel Group will be through direct sales. The corporation will have its own sales force, and each salesman will be assigned a different territory.

During the first year of operations, The Travel Group projects the movement of only 6,861 passengers. The four salesmen that management will offer positions currently move more than 18,000 passengers per year. Thus, the first year projection of less than 7,000 passengers is quite conservative. Management has also allowed six months before the departure of the first flight. This will provide the sales force with more than sufficient time to sell the first back-to-back charters to Hawaii.

Sales of $2,766,397 are projected during this first year and a profit of $169,223.

The second year of operations, 1975, should produce sales of $8,059,589 with a profit before tax of $832,636. In five years, 1978, The Travel Group should achieve a sales volume of $18,241,542 and a before tax profit of $2,150,121.

There is a tremendous positive cash flow in the group charter business. This allows for rapid expansion without additional financing. The potential of The Travel Group is open-ended, but management will expand cautiously.

II. THE INDUSTRY

The back-to-back group charter business is in the early stages of growth. The industry is less than 10 years old. The management in the industry is quite unsophisticated. Financial and management controls are lacking. The market penetration of group charters has barely begun. Few companies have creative and organized marketing programs.

The main regulatory organization in the industry is the Civil Aeronautics Board (CAB). The trend in the past two years has been for more and more "low cost group travel." The CAB is oriented toward making travel available at a cost affordable for the mass public. This is very favorable for firms like The Travel Group, and, thus, governmental regulation should be beneficial to the company.

The United States is several years behind Europe in low cost vacations. In 1972 group vacation charters provided more revenue to the European airlines than the regularly scheduled flights.

In the United States, the same growth pattern is developing. In the past four years, charters on the North Atlantic have grown at the rate of 58 percent per year. In 1972 charter flights accounted for 30 percent of all passengers flown on the North Atlantic.

It is easy to understand this tremendous growth in the group charter business by simply looking at the money saved by a typical vacationer.

EXHIBIT 1   *(continued)*

Assume an individual would like to travel to Hawaii for one week. He departs on a weekend, flies coach class, and all accommodations are deluxe:

	Regular Rate	*Group Charter Rate*	*Savings*
Airfare	$510	$225	$ 285
Hotel	140	84	56
Dinners	56	40	16
Transfers	20	10	10
Tour operator's fee	0	113	−113
Total cost	$726	$472	+$ 254
	***	***	***

Thus, an individual can save 35 percent, or $254, during a one-week visit to Hawaii.

III. THE COMPANY

The Travel Group will be selling deluxe back-to-back group charters. *Back-to-back* means that, for a set period of time, groups will be sent *every* week to a particular destination. The aircraft, which takes one group to the destination, will pick up the group that is ending their vacation. This allows substantial savings on airfare. There is also tremendous buying power at the hotels because rooms are utilized every week.

These cost advantages will allow The Travel Group to sell vacations to destinations all over the world at savings of 35 percent or more (see Industry section).

The Travel Group will have salesmen assigned to different territories in certain sections of the country. These salesmen will call on prime traveling groups. They will be selling deluxe packages, principally during prime season. The "sell" is usually easy because the organization has nothing to lose and much to gain. The Travel Group will pay for the mailing of a brochure describing the vacation to all the members of the organization. For each reservation the group produces, the organization will be given about $15. Thus, if a group fills a 150-seat airplane, the organization will receive $2,250 (150 × $15) and will have provided vacations for its members at substantial savings.

Groups that will be approached by the sales force include Shriners, Masons, medical associations, bar associations, Elks, Moose, alumni associations, teacher associations, unions, employee groups, and Knights of Columbus. There is an unlimited number of groups. Management will develop a mailing list of all the prime groups in the country to provide additional direction for the sales force.

The cash flow in the business is very favorable. Deposits from passengers are often received more than 90 days in advance. Final payments from passengers are due 45 days before departure. Payments to the airlines occur 30 days before departure, and hotel bills are not paid until 30 days after departure. Thus, the majority of receipts are in-house 45 days in advance of departure while disbursements occur 15 to 90 days after the initial receipts are in.

IV. THE COMPETITION

The group travel industry is in its early stages of growth. The industry is less than 10 years old, and there is only a limited number of group tour operators. Sophisticated and experienced management is scarce in the industry. The few back-to-back group travel companies that do exist have had substantial sales growth in the past three years. In the last 18 months, there have been several new companies started that have been running back-to-back charters. One of these companies had sales of close to $8 million during its first year and before tax profits of over $500,000.

EXHIBIT 1   *(continued)*

Competition in the industry has not developed to the point of pricing of the same packages. Sales growth is achieved by contacting the proper groups and then appropriately following up these leads.

Back-to-back operators always concentrate on a few destinations. With the vast number of destinations, there is limited competition among tour operators in providing packages to the same place. For instance, one of the new tour operators is just specializing in running trips to Greece, while another has programs just to the Orient.

Currently the East Coast is the only section of the country that has become familiar, to some extent, with group charters. Amazingly, 60 percent of all charter flights are out of New York. The South, Midwest, and Central States have barely been touched.

Less than five back-to-back tour operators have a national sales force. The Travel Group's national sales force will be comprised of experienced travel salesmen who are currently working in different territories throughout the United States for other tour operators.

V. THE MANAGEMENT

There are two key departments in the group charter business. One is sales, and the other is operations. By providing a well-organized business plan and by making equity available, The Travel Group has attracted some of the most qualified people in the industry.

Mr. Steven B. Belkin will be president. He will be responsible for directing the operations of the company. Mr. Belkin is thoroughly familiar with the day-to-day operations as well as the overall business planning of a back-to-back tour operator.

He is a graduate of Cornell University and Harvard Business School. He was one of five founders of Innovative Management, a small business consulting firm in the Boston area. Some of his consulting projects included the development and implementation of a marketing program for a ski charter travel firm, running a chain of sporting goods stores with sales of over $6 million, and serving as president of a film school and production company. When Mr. Belkin left and sold his interest in this consulting firm, it had grown to 22 full-time consultants.

For more than a year, Mr. Belkin has been devoting full time to a travel group charter firm, which was in severe financial difficulties. With the development and implementation of a new business plan, creation of a national sales force, and tighter management and financial controls, this firm has now been turned around. The year before Mr. Belkin's involvement, the firm had sales of approximately $1 million with a loss of over $250,000. This year the company has already reported a respectable profit for the first six months and has more than doubled the previous year's sales.

The sales force that is available is comprised of some of the best salesmen in the industry. Each man has thorough familiarity and personal contacts with the prime groups in the different sections of the country.

The sales team will have a minimum of six months before the first back-to-back charter will start. This should provide more than sufficient time to sell the program. During the first year of operations, the sales force needs to move only 6,861 passengers. This year the four salesmen being considered moved more than 18,000 passengers. Thus, the first-year programs should be sold fairly easily, and this will allow the sales team to start concentrating on the second-year programs well in advance.

VI. THE FINANCIALS

[Some exhibits omitted.]

A. TRIP COST ANALYSIS
 Exhibit I Hawaii
 Exhibit II San Juan
 Exhibit III Ad hoc
 Exhibit IV Acapulco
 Exhibit V Spain

B. PROFIT AND LOSS STATEMENTS 1974 and 1975
 Exhibit VI Pro Forma Profit and Loss Statement (1974 and 1975)
 Exhibit VII Plane and Passenger Projections (First Year 1974)
 Exhibit VIII Monthly Pro Forma Profit and Loss Statement (First Year 1974)
 Exhibit IX General and Administrative Expenses
 Exhibit X Plane and Passenger Projections (Second Year 1975)
 Exhibit XI Monthly Pro Forma Profit and Loss Statement (Second Year 1975)

EXHIBIT 1   *(continued)*

C. CASH FLOW ANALYSIS

Exhibit XII Cash Flow Assumptions
Exhibit XIII Monthly Cash Flow Projections (First Year 1974)
Exhibit XIV Monthly Cash Flow Projections (Second Year 1975)

D. FIVE-YEAR PROJECTIONS

Exhibit XV Pro Forma Profit and Loss Statements (1974–1978)

A great deal of time and effort has been devoted to the preparation of the following financial exhibits. Management will use them for budgeting as well as for projections.

The Trip Cost Analysis section clearly outlines the revenues and expenses associated with each trip on both a per passenger and per airplane basis. The airfare, hotel, meals, transfers, mailing, giveaways, and load factor are all expenses that have been determined by historical statistics and actual experience.

The Profit and Loss Statements for the first two years have been prepared on a month-to-month basis. Management has determined the number of planes and passengers that can be accommodated each month to a particular destination. During the first year of operation, no passengers are projected to be moved until June. There is a good possibility that ad hoc programs will be sold before this time, so sales and profit could be greater than projected.

The Cash Flows have been prepared for the first two years on a month-to-month basis. The cash flow assumptions are very important, and management feels the assumptions made are conservative.

The five-year, pro forma profit and loss statement illustrates the potential of this new and growing business. The Travel Group hopes to have sales of over $18 million within five years and profits before tax of over $2 million.

EXHIBIT 1
COST ANALYSIS PER PASSENGER
HAWAII

Selling price	$429	+ 10% =	$ 471.90
Direct costs: Air	$225		
Hotel	84		
Meals	40		
Transfers	10		−359.00
Gross profit before acquisition costs			$ 112.90
Acquisition costs:			
Mailing cost 10¢ brochure			
+ Nonprofit mailer			
(.50% return rate)	$ 20.00		
Giveaways ($20/reservation)	20.00		
Load factor (90%)	20.00		−60.00
Gross profit:			$ 52.90
			*******

****

EXHIBIT 1   *(continued)*

<u>Hawaii Trip Analysis per Plane</u>

Total sales	= $471.90 × 135 passengers	= $63,706
Cost of sales	= $419.00 × 135 passengers	= $56,565
Total profit	= $ 52.90 × 135 passengers	= $ 7,141

Options: $10 net/passenger = $1,350/plane
(Options include additional profit on such items as bus tours, which are arranged through the charter operator.)

EXHIBIT VI
THE TRAVEL GROUP, INC.
PRO FORMA PROFIT AND LOSS STATEMENT (1974 AND 1975)

	1974	1975
SALES	$2,766,397	$8,059,589
Cost of sales	2,345,594	6,870,953
Gross profit	$ 420,803	$1,188,636
General and administrative	251,580	356,000
Profit (before tax)	$ 169,223	$ 832,636
	**********	**********
Earnings per share	$ .17	$ .83
Value/share (10 multiple)	$1.70	$8.33
Number of planes	44	128
Number of passengers	6,861	22,183

EXHIBIT 1 *(continued)*

EXHIBIT VII
THE TRAVEL GROUP, INC.
PLANE AND PASSENGER PROJECTIONS
FIRST YEAR OF OPERATION (1974)

	January	February	March	April	May	June	July	August	September	October	November	December	Total
HAWAII													
Passengers						750	600	750	600	600	750	600	4,650
Planes						5	4	5	4	4	5	4	31
SAN JUAN													
Passengers											895	716	1,611
Planes											5	4	9
AD HOC													
Passengers						150	150	150	150				600
Planes						1	1	1	1				4
TOTAL PASSENGERS	0	0	0	0	0	900	750	900	750	600	1,645	1,316	6,861
TOTAL PLANES	0	0	0	0	0	6	5	6	5	4	10	8	44

239

EXHIBIT 1 (continued)

EXHIBIT VIII
THE TRAVEL GROUP, INC.
PRO FORMA PROFIT AND LOSS STATEMENT
FIRST YEAR OF OPERATION (1974)

	January	February	March	April	May	June	July	August	September	October	November	December	Total
SALES													
Hawaii (150-seat plane)	(31 planes)	(4,650 passengers)				318,530	254,824	318,530	254,824	254,824	318,530	254,824	2,766,397
Hawaii options (net)						7,500	6,000	7,500	6,000	6,000	7,500	6,000	
San Juan (179-seat plane)	(9 planes)	(1,611 passengers)									263,120	210,496	
San Juan options (net)											4,475	3,580	
Ad hoc programs	(4 planes)	(600 passengers)				65,835	65,835	65,835	65,835				
TOTAL SALES	44 planes	6,861 passengers				391,865	326,659	391,865	326,659	260,824	593,625	474,900	2,766,397
COST OF SALES													
Hawaii						276,070	220,856	276,070	220,856	220,856	276,070	220,856	
San Juan										219,200	175,360		
Ad hoc programs						59,850	59,850	59,850	59,850				
TOTAL COST OF SALES						335,920	280,706	335,920	280,706	220,856	495,270	396,216	2,345,594
General and administrative costs	15,000	15,000	18,000	18,000	22,716	22,716	22,716	22,716	22,716	24,000	24,000	24,000	251,580
Net profit (before tax)													$ 169,223
													*********

EXHIBIT 1   *(continued)*

EXHIBIT XII
CASH FLOW ASSUMPTIONS

A. Receipts
1. Deposits and final payments are only received 15 days before the date of the trip (very conservative since final payments are due 45 days before departure, and deposits are often received 90 days in advance).
2. Net Operational Tour Receipts are received the week of the trip.

B. Disbursements
1. Airlines are paid 30 days in advance.
2. Hotels are paid 30 days after the trip (requires letter of credit and cash deposits).
3. Meals and transfers are paid 30 days after the trip.
4. Acquisition costs are paid 30 days in advance.
5. Ad hoc program payments require $10,000 deposit 30 days before departure and the balance paid the week before departure.
6. General and administrative expenses are assumed to be paid/disbursements during the month they are expensed. (Conservative since telephone and travel and entertainment expenses are usually not disbursed until a minimum of 30 days after being expensed. These two expense categories are approximately 20% of G + A expenses.)

EXHIBIT 1 *(continued)*

EXHIBIT XIII
THE TRAVEL GROUP, INC.
CASH FLOW PROJECTIONS
FIRST YEAR OF OPERATION (1974)

	January	February	March	April	May	June	July	August	September	October	November	December
RECEIPTS												
Hawaii					159,265	286,677	286,677	286,677	254,824	286,677	286,677	254,824
Hawaii options (net)						7,500	6,000	7,500	6,000	6,000	7,500	6,000
San Juan										131,560	236,808	210,496
San Juan options (net)											4,475	3,580
Ad hoc programs					32,918	65,835	65,835	65,835	32,918			118,504
TOTAL RECEIPTS	—	—	—	—	192,183	360,012	358,512	360,012	293,742	424,237	535,460	593,404
DISBURSEMENTS												
Hawaii					192,375	153,900	282,825	226,260	244,350	264,735	226,260	244,350
San Juan										100,000	80,000	199,200
Ad hoc					10,000	59,850	59,850	59,850	49,850			92,880
General + administrative	70,608	15,000	18,000	18,000	22,716	22,716	22,716	22,716	22,716	24,000	24,000	24,000
TOTAL DISBURSEMENTS	70,608	15,000	18,000	18,000	225,091	236,466	365,391	308,825	316,916	388,735	330,260	560,430
MONTHLY CASH SURPLUS (DEFICIT)	(70,608)	(15,000)	(18,000)	(18,000)	(32,908)	123,546	(6,879)	51,186	(23,174)	35,502	205,200	32,974
BEGINNING CASH BALANCE	—	−(70,608)	(85,608)	(103,608)	(121,608)	(154,516)	(30,970)	(37,849)	13,337	(9,837)	25,665	230,865
ENDING CASH BALANCE	(70,608)	(85,608)	(103,608)	(121,608)	(154,516)	(30,970)	(37,849)	13,337	(9,837)	25,665	230,865	263,839

EXHIBIT 1 *(continued)*

EXHIBIT XIV
THE TRAVEL GROUP, INC.
CASH FLOW PROJECTIONS
SECOND YEAR OF OPERATION (1975)

	January	February	March	April	May	June	July	August	September	October	November	December
RECEIPTS												
Hawaii	254,824	286,677	286,677	254,824	254,824	286,677	286,677	286,677	286,677	286,677	286,677	382,236
Hawaii options (net)	6,000	6,000	7,500	6,000	6,000	6,000	7,500	6,000	7,500	6,000	7,500	6,000
San Juan	210,496	236,808	236,808	157,872	52,624					105,248	210,496	315,744
San Juan options (net)	3,580	3,580	4,475	3,580	1,790						3,580	3,580
Acapulco	237,008	266,634	266,634	177,756	59,252					118,504	237,008	355,512
Acapulco options (net)	5,400	5,400	6,750	5,400	2,700						5,400	5,400
Spain					148,006	333,014	333,014	333,014	333,014	148,006		
Spain options (net)						4,500	5,625	4,500	5,625	4,500		
TOTAL RECEIPTS	717,308	805,099	808,844	605,432	525,196	630,191	632,816	630,191	632,816	668,935	750,661	1,068,472
DISBURSEMENTS												
Hawaii	226,260	264,735	226,260	244,350	226,260	264,735	226,260	282,825	226,260	282,825	226,260	398,250
San Juan	175,360	195,360	175,360	159,200	95,360	47,680				80,000	80,000	255,360
Acapulco	92,880	234,900	211,680	194,940	118,800	59,400				92,880	92,880	304,560
Spain					174,600	218,250	252,900	316,125	252,900	97,875	78,300	
General and administrative	28,000	28,000	28,000	28,000	28,000	30,000	30,000	30,000	30,000	32,000	32,000	32,000
TOTAL DISBURSEMENTS	522,500	722,995	641,300	626,490	643,020	620,065	509,160	628,950	509,160	585,580	509,440	990,170
MONTHLY CASH SURPLUS/ (DEFICIT)	194,808	82,104	167,544	(21,058)	(117,824)	10,126	123,656	1,241	123,656	83,355	241,221	78,302
BEGINNING CASH BALANCE	263,839	458,647	540,751	708,295	687,237	569,413	579,539	703,195	704,436	828,092	911,447	1,152,668
ENDING CASH BALANCE	458,647	540,751	708,295	687,237	569,413	579,539	703,195	704,436	828,092	911,447	1,152,668	1,230,970

EXHIBIT 1   *(concluded)*

EXHIBIT XV
THE TRAVEL GROUP, INC.
PRO FORMA PROFIT AND LOSS (1974–1978)

	1974	*1975*	*1976*	*1977*	*1978*
SALES	$2,766,397	$8,059,589	$12,029,894	$15,124,878	$18,241,542
Cost of sales	$2,345,594	$6,870,953	$10,305,490	$12,910,496	$15,481,421
Gross profit	420,803	1,188,636	1,724,404	2,214,382	2,760,121
General and administrative	251,580	356,000	480,000	540,000	610,000
Profit (before tax)	$ 169,223	$ 832,636	$ 1,244,404	$ 1,674,382	$ 2,150,121
Earnings per share	$.17	$.83	$1.24	$1.67	$2.15
Value/share (10 price/earnings)	$1.70	$8.33	$12.44	$16.74	$21.50
Number of planes	44	128	192	240	288
Number of passengers	6,861	22,183	33,275	41,595	49,915

HEATHER EVANS

It was May 10, 1983, and Heather Evans's graduation from Harvard Business School was less than a month away. Although she had just taken the last of her final exams that morning, Heather's thoughts could not have been further from school as she boarded the Eastern Shuttle and headed back to New York. The trip was a familiar one, for Heather had been commuting between school and Manhattan in an attempt to get her dress company off the ground.

Many of the elements of the business were falling into place, but the securing of $250,000 in financing remained elusive. Her business plan had been in the hands of potential investors for over a month now, and her financing group was simply not coming together. Her contact at Arden & Co., a New York investment firm and hoped-for lead investor, was not even returning her phone calls. A number of small, private investors had been stringing along for some weeks, but whenever Heather tried to go that next step and negotiate specific financing terms with any one of them, the rest of the group seemed to move further away. Heather expressed her frustration:

> I was really counting on Arden & Co. to be my lead investor; this would lend both credibility to the deal and give me *one* party to negotiate terms with. Then I could go to these private investors, point to the deal I'd struck with Arden and say, "These are the terms—make a decision."
>
> Now, if I give each of these investors what they want, I'll end up giving the company away. But I do need the money, and fast. In order to get out a holiday (winter) line, I need to start placing orders for fabric in the next month. All this, in addition to the rent and salaries I'm committed to.

This case was prepared by Michael J. Roberts under the direction of Howard H. Stevenson.
Copyright © 1983 by the President and Fellows of Harvard College.
Harvard Business School Case 9-384-079.

I don't know whether I should stick with the private investors I have and somehow try to hammer out a deal; or really work on getting a venture firm as a lead investor—maybe there is still a chance of bringing Arden & Co. around. Maybe I should try to get less money, or move back my timetable and wait for spring to introduce a line.

Heather Evans

Heather Evans graduated from Harvard College in 1979, having earned her bachelor's degree in philosophy in three years. A Phi Beta Kappa graduate, Heather had been a working model throughout her college career, appearing in such publications as *Mademoiselle, Seventeen,* and *GQ.*

Heather applied to the Harvard Business School during her senior year and was accepted with a two-year deferred admit to the class entering in 1981. She accepted a position with Morgan Stanley as a financial analyst. Heather explained the origin of her interest in a business career:

> My father is an attorney with a Wall Street firm, and many of my parents' friends were "deal-makers" who had gone to the Business School. I thought that I would like that kind of work and the lifestyle that went along with it. In addition, my career as a model gave me a taste of running my own business—the independence, the travel, the people—and I loved it. I knew, though, that I would need a good solid background to gain the skills and credibility necessary for success.
>
> I thought that working for an investment bank like Morgan Stanley would give me the technical and financial training that I would need during my career.

Heather left Morgan Stanley and began her two years at HBS with her basic orientation unchanged:

> I was still focused primarily on a deal-making, venture-capital type of career. I had always been interested in the fashion business and thought that I might, at some point, financially back a designer. I decided to work on Seventh Avenue for the summer and got a job as the assistant to Jackie Hayman, president of a woman's clothing company.

Heather saw the business and financial side of the business as well as the design and marketing aspects:

> I was convinced and confident that I could run a business like this. That summer was actually the first time I believed that business school education had much value at all. I was able to understand the business very well, and my education and experience allowed me to grasp the fundamental issues quickly.

Heather returned to HBS in September, committed to starting her own venture in the garment industry.

The Evolution of Heather Evans Incorporated

Heather began by defining the concept of the company and its product line. Based on her experience in investment banking and at business school, Heather was convinced that the current mode of business dress for women—primarily suits—was, in fact, ill-suited to the demands and desires of businesswomen. Heather conceived a line of dresses in natural and wear-worthy fabrics that would better meet these women's needs (see business plan for full description).

In September, she began working with Robert Vin, an assistant designer in New York, in an attempt to transfer her concepts to finished design sketches and patterns. By November, it was clear to Heather that this arrangement was not going to work out; she decided that she would be both the chief designer and operating manager of her firm. Although it was an extremely untraditional approach to a start-up in the garment business, Heather reasoned that it would make more sense for her:

> First, I didn't get along that well with Robert on a personal level. More important, though, I found myself doubting both his design sense and my own ability to judge someone else's design sense. Fundamentally, I had more trust in myself and my abilities as a designer.

Thus was Heather Evans Incorporated born.

Heather spent November and December flying between Boston and New York and developing, in further detail, her concept of the business. By December, Heather had put together a plan of action, which she submitted for approval as a field study (see **Exhibit 1**). After her first-semester exams ended, Heather moved to New York. She scheduled all of her classes on Monday and Tuesday and planned to spend the rest of her time in New York getting the key elements of her business in place.

Staff

Heather decided that the first person she needed was an assistant designer. "I wanted someone who had the technical training and experience in design that I lacked. I needed someone who knew more about design than I did, but who didn't mind working for me as an assistant."

Heather interviewed several individuals and in early February offered the position to Belinda Hughes, who had served as an assistant designer with two major firms. Heather began paying Belinda (out of her own pocket) to do freelance work based on detailed discussions with Heather about the content of the line, with the promise that full-time employment would begin in April or May.

Heather also began looking for a pattern-maker: someone who could transform a sample dress into specifications and a design for production.

Heather asked several industry acquaintances, and a vice president at Marjori (a major fashion manufacturer) recommended Barbara Tarpe. Heather called Barbara and the two hit it off. During their meeting, Barbara indicated that she would like an equity position in the company. Heather thought that Barbara could make a significant contribution and that her request was reasonable. Heather genuinely liked Barbara and thought that she would make a good partner.

One week later, before proceeding further, Heather decided to call another friend in the industry who might know Barbara.

> Martin is an old friend, and I trust his judgment; he told me that Barbara was a terrible liar and had no real talent. I looked back at my original notes after our meeting: "Very good rapport with Barbara. She seems *HONEST*. Feel she can run entire inside of business." I didn't hire Barbara and was shocked at how wrong I could be about someone. I had always felt comfortable trusting my own judgment.

Office and Showroom Space

Heather spent countless afternoons scouring New York's garment district (around Seventh Avenue from 42nd to 34th Streets) for potential showroom, office, and working space. Showroom space is very important, because store buyers visit here during the buying season to make their decisions.

> I decided that I needed about 1,500 square feet of space for an office, sample and pattern-making space, and a showroom. For $7 or $8 per square foot, I could get space in buildings which were somewhat off the main center of the district and which housed other relatively "unknown" designers. For $20–$25 per foot, I could be in a building that was more centrally located and that housed better-known firms.

By late February, Heather had decided to lease 1,500 square feet of space in a building at $10 per foot, or $15,000 per year.

Although the building was in a less desirable location and would get less traffic from buyers than more expensive buildings, Heather reasoned that she should attempt to conserve as much cash as possible. Heather sent a deposit on this space and would begin paying rent May 1.

A month later, an acquaintance in the garment business called and offered Heather space in 550 Seventh Avenue—the most prestigious building in the garment center, housing such designers as Ralph Lauren, Oscar de la Renta, and many other famous names. Heather would have her own office space and would share the showroom space with another designer (who sold a line of clothing that would not compete directly with Heather's). Heather accepted his offer on the spot, even though she would have to start paying rent as of March 15, and the rent was $2,000, substantially more than the other building, and there was less space.

Financing

In the fall, Heather had begun talking informally with potential investors—friends at school and former colleagues in the investment banking and garment industry. She was hesitant, however, to do more than this until she had a business plan and a proposed deal.

Then in February, a friend and recent Business School graduate called to suggest that the two get together for a drink.

> Anne Snelling and I had both worked for Morgan Stanley and then gone on to the Business School. She had graduated one year earlier than I and gone to work for

Arden & Co. (a private investment bank). I assumed that our meeting would be social, but Anne was soon putting on the hard-sell for Arden, convincing me that they should do the whole deal. I was quite surprised and pleased. Arden had an excellent reputation, and their financing would be a "stamp of approval" on the deal.

Heather and Anne met once or twice during January and February, and Anne asked Heather to accompany her to Vail for a week of skiing over spring break the first week in March. Heather reasoned that it would be a wise move to go.

I didn't really feel comfortable taking off for a week—I had an incredible amount to do. Yet I was anxious for Arden's participation, so off to Vail I went. I was unsure whether Anne intended our week to be business or pleasure, but I brought along all of my papers and was prepared to negotiate a deal.
   Once we got there, Anne said she wanted to talk about the deal, but was constantly on the phone pursuing other business. I came back to New York feeling pretty discouraged; we had never had a chance to really discuss my business.

Heather called Anne that next week and voiced her concern: time was running out, and Heather still had no clear idea where Arden or Anne stood on the issue.

Anne suggested that we get together for dinner that evening and tie things up—I was relieved. But when I walked into the restaurant, Anne was sitting there with her sister, Susan, and Susan's fiance. She apologized—they had just flown into the city, and Anne had asked them to join us. I was livid.

At this point, Heather realized that the financing was not going to come as easily as she had hoped, and she began pushing some of her other potential investors to get a sense of their interest. She raced to finish the business plan (see **Exhibit 2**) and sent this out to Arden & Co. and 15 individual investors during the first week in April.

Down to the Wire

During the month of April, the pace of Heather's efforts accelerated and the business began eating up more cash. Belinda's part-time salary was now running about $1,000 per month; rent was running $2,000 per month. Finally, Heather had begun shopping the fabric market and would soon have to order and pay for $3,000 worth of sample fabric.

Heather had already invested about $10,000 of her own funds in the business, and her remaining resources were dwindling quickly. Because of the timing of the cycles in the garment industry (see **Exhibit 3**) Heather would have a great many more expenses before any cash came back into the business; most significantly, she would have to pay for the fabric for the entire holiday line—about $40,000 worth.

Yet Heather was having a difficult time bringing the investor group together. Anne Snelling was not returning her phone calls, and the private investors were interested, but had made no firm commitments. Heather's major problem was trying to negotiate with all of these potential investors individually; without a lead investor, there was no one party to negotiate the terms of a deal with.

The process of raising funds was hampered by Heather's extremely busy schedule. Besides talking to retailers, working on designs, and getting settled in her new office space, Heather was still going to school during this time, and exams were coming up. Heather commented on the strain:

> The spring semester was a rough one; trying to get my company started really took its toll. I had always considered myself a responsible student. I prepared about a half-dozen cases the entire semester and only made it to half my classes. I felt bad about it, but I knew I had to do it to get my business going.

Financing Options

Heather had several options available, but knew that she did not have sufficient time to pursue them all.

Arden & Co.   Heather held out some hope that Arden was still interested in the deal. Perhaps if she really pushed for a commitment, Arden would come through.

Venture Capital Firms.   Heather had spoken with one or two firms that had indicated some interest. She knew that starting fresh with people who were unfamiliar with the company, as well as dealing with the bureaucratic decision-making process, would take a great deal of time. In addition, Heather suspected that they might drive a harder bargain than private investors, but at this point she welcomed the opportunity to negotiate with anyone just to get an idea of what valuation to put on the company.

Helen Neil Fashions, Inc.   Heather had approached another small venture capital firm that had Helen Neil Fashions, Inc., in its portfolio of companies. Helen Neil herself was a proven designer, and the company had established a base of relationships with manufacturers and retailers. The company, however, lacked any real operating management. This venture firm had indicated an interest in financing Heather if she would ally herself with Helen Neil and essentially embark on a joint venture. This idea had not yet been broached with Helen Neil, however, and Heather knew that any deal was dependent on the approval of Helen and her company's management.

Private Investors.   Heather had a pool of 20 or so private individuals who seemed interested in investing in the company. The problem here was the amount of time it took to negotiate with each of these people individually, and their diverse desires for the terms of the investment. Heather was unsure how to structure the deal to satisfy the divergent interests of these individuals whom she was fairly sure would invest under any reasonable set of terms. She had spoken to a small sample of these investors (see **Exhibit 4**) to get their point of view, but was hesitant to speak to any more investors before she could present them with a deal.

Heather's Requirements

Heather had given some thought to the different aspects of the deal and had decided that the following terms were important to her:

- Control of the company: Heather felt that she should be able to control over 50 percent of the equity, as well as have a majority of the voting control of the company.
- License of the name *Heather Evans:* Heather felt that she had already expended considerable effort in building up her own name, and that if she left the company, she should have the right to use it.
- Ability to remain private: Heather did not want to be in a position where her investors could force her to become a public company. Liz Claiborne, a successful women's clothing company, had recently gone public, and potential investors were naturally excited by the returns inherent in a public offering. (See **Exhibit 5** for excerpts from the Liz Claiborne prospectus.) Heather knew that she had to offer her investors some means of exit and getting a return on their investment.

With exams finally over, Heather could concentrate her full energies on pulling together her financial backing and getting the business off the ground.

EXHIBIT 1   Field Study Plan

The purpose of this project is to develop a business plan and a strategy for approaching investors for a women's designer clothing manufacturing company, which I will form upon graduation from HBS. This company will offer high price, high quality dress and jacket combinations to executive women, ages 27 to 45.

The business plan will include:

    I. A marketing plan, including an analysis of the relevant market, how I will position my product (in terms of price and image), and a retailing and promotion strategy.

    II. A description of the organization, including people and physical plant.

    III. Pro forma financial statements, based on sales projections from I, and operating costs from II.

    IV. A financing proposal.

The attached time schedule outlines the process of putting together this plan. You will note that I have allotted substantial time to drafting and redrafting the plan, relative to research. This is because I have already spent a lot of time gathering information and find that I now need to organize that information in order to see what is missing. I will, however, spend the first half of January meeting with department store buyers to refine my retailing strategy, which I recognize is weak.

The final product for my Independent Research Report (IRR) will be the business plan actually presented to investors and a broader strategic document describing how the plan fits into my investor strategy.

Field Study Project Schedule Week of:

December 13, 1982	• Settle issue of advisor for IRR.
	• Gather examples of business plans.
December 20	• Complete survey of existing market research and financial information on comparable companies. (Sources: Fairchild Publications' library; 10-Ks ordered from companies.)
December 27	• Vacation.
January 3, 1983	• Prepare preliminary outline of plan.
	• Review outline with advisor.
	• Set up meetings with buyers from Filene's, Nieman's, Macy's, Bergdorf, Saks, Bloomingdales, Nordstrom, and others.
January 10 and 17	• Prepare first draft of plan Parts I and II.
	• Meet with buyers.
January 24 and 31	• Talk with various industry contacts to fill information "holes," especially regarding Part II of plan (e.g., salary levels for various employees, equipment needs and costs, and optimal showroom and design studio locations).
February 7	• Prepare second draft of plan, including detailed pro formas (Part III).
	• Begin interviewing candidates for design assistant, sales/PR director, and business manager positions. (These individuals should be named in the plan.)
February 14	• Review second draft with advisor.
	• Present plan to CPA for review.
	• Prepare list of potential investors and consider order of approach.
	• Select law firm.
February 21 and 28	• Select and recruit key employees.
	• Revise plan, Parts I–III.
	• Present revised plan to lawyer.
	• Explore financial structure alternatives with lawyer, advisor, and others.
March 7	• Draft Part IV of plan.
	• Determine preferred investor group profile and strategy for approaching investors.
	• Select factor and discuss terms, to the extent appropriate at that point.
March 14, 21, 28	• Vacation.
April 4 and 11	• Meet informally with key investors.
	• Finalize plan.
April 18	• Distribute plan to potential investors.

EXHIBIT 2   Heather Evans Incorporated Business Plan, April 7, 1983 *(Confidential)*

TABLE OF CONTENTS

HEATHER EVANS INCORPORATED BUSINESS PLAN
I. SUMMARY

COMPANY
HEATHER EVANS INCORPORATED, incorporated in New York on March 9, 1983, and located in New York City.

BUSINESS
The Company will design, contract for the manufacture of, and market a line of clothing for professional women.

MANAGEMENT
Heather H. Evans, President and Designer
Ms. Evans will graduate from Harvard Business School in June 1983. She has worked as assistant to the president of Catherine Hipp, a designer clothing firm; as a financial analyst at Morgan Stanley, an investment bank; and as a photographic model, with Ford Models.

Belinda Hughes, Assistant Designer
Most recently, Ms. Hughes was head designer at Creations by Aria. For two years before that, after her graduation from Parsons School of Design, she worked as Mr. Kasper's assistant at Kasper for J.L. Sports.

CONCEPT
The Company will offer a "designer" line to fit the lifestyle of professional women. Based on her experience in investment banking and at business school, Ms. Evans has conceived a style of clothing, based primarily on dresses, which better fits the lifestyle and demands of businesswomen than the suits and other looks currently offered to them by existing clothing manufacturers.

STATUS
The Company has already begun designing its holiday line, obtained showroom and studio space in a prestigious designer building, reserved production capacity in a high-quality factory, and arranged for credit with an apparel industry factor.

In order to present its first line for the Holiday 1983 season, the Company must be assured financing prior to May 1983. The Company is seeking $250,000, to cover start-up expenses, to fund development of its first line, and to provide initial working capital. Thereafter, the Company anticipates that it will generate sufficient cash from operations, which, together with normal industry factoring, will fund growth internally.

Legal Counsel: Kaye, Scholer, Fierman, Hays & Handler
Accountants: Rashba & Pokart
Bank: Citibank

II. CONCEPT

HEATHER EVANS INCORPORATED aims to become a substantial apparel company. Its success formula is a combination of powerful elements:

- a new look,
- for an unmet and quickly growing market,
- promoted and sold by a unique individual, Heather H. Evans,
- within a professionally managed and controlled organization.

Ms. Evans recognized the need for a *new look* for professional women when she shopped for clothes to wear to her job at an investment bank. She found few clothes that fit the functional demands of her work, while having some "style." Since then, she has spoken with hundreds of professional women who voice the same complaint. They work in an environment that strictly defines what is considered appropriate; "Seventh Avenue" does not understand these women.

EXHIBIT 2   *(continued)*

The HEATHER EVANS "look" will be based on dresses, worn with untailored or softly tailored jackets, with:

- A clean and elegant silhouette.
- Distinctiveness through cut and line, without frills, excessive detail, or sexual suggestiveness.
- Undistracting colors, in solids or subtle patterns (e.g., Glen plaid or pinstripe).
- Comfortable fit.
- Travel-worthy fabrics in all-natural fibers, such as silk-wool blends.
- Quality construction.

Dresses and jackets will be priced and sold separately, along with coordinated skirts and tops, as a *complete* line:

- To permit the customer to coordinate an entire workplace wardrobe from the line.
- To position the line in "sportswear" departments of department stores, which are more updated and better displayed than "dress" departments.
- To avoid resistance to the high price tag of a combined outfit, from a customer who usually buys sportswear pieces.

Each collection will include 30 to 70 pieces, depending on the season, which is comparable to other complete designer sportswear lines. The Company will sell five collections: for the holiday, early spring, spring, transition, and fall seasons. These are the regular "sportswear" market periods.

Unlike most designer collections, which include many kinds of clothes for different activities and different times of day, the HEATHER EVANS collection will include only clothes appropriate for the conservative workplace. This focus is critical in establishing the confidence of upper-strata professional women in the "look" for officewear. Later, the Company can introduce other lines (e.g., leisurewear) under the HEATHER EVANS name, in order to benefit from its reputation and customer franchise.

HEATHER EVANS clothes will be sold through better department and specialty stores. The line will be marketed as "designer" clothing, but will be priced at the upper end of the "bridge" category, which is the next lower price category. The bridge category was born and grew dramatically with such lines as Liz Claiborne and Evan Picone, which targeted the flood of women into the workplace over the past decade; HEATHER EVANS will capitalize on the second stage of this demographic trend, as women become accepted in large numbers in better-paid, professional and managerial roles. Positioning the line at the top of the bridge category:

- Will place the line in stores next to other lines currently bought by the target customer (e.g., Tahari, Harve Bernard, Nipon Collectibles).
- Responds to growing price resistance among customers, *but*
- Permits the Company to create a quality garment.
- Develops the HEATHER EVANS label for future licensing potential.

Heather H. Evans:

Ms. Evans is uniquely qualified to develop and sell a new style of clothing for conservative businesswomen. As a former investment banker and a graduate of Harvard Business School,

- She has lived the lifestyle of these women, and knows their needs.
- She understands the limits of appropriateness within a formal office environment, which Seventh Avenue designers, who have tried to capture this customer, clearly do not.
- She can gain the confidence of the target customer through identification of her own background with their own lives.

Moreover, as a former model, Ms. Evans has experience at projecting herself through the media and can attract publicity as a designer/personality. She will actively seek to publicize the Company in business media, as well as fashion media, to reach the target customer. She is currently working on stories about the Company with writers from *Vogue* and *Savvy*. (Ms. Evans's résumé is included as Appendix A.)

III. MARKET

HEATHER EVANS will initially position its products as designer clothing for the "formal" professional woman to wear to the office. Later, the Company can serve a virtually unlimited number of markets based on its reputation for quality and taste, as established through its original line of clothing.

EXHIBIT 2   *(continued)*

PROFESSIONAL WOMEN'S CLOTHING

Target Market:

HEATHER EVANS will target the upper end of a subsegment of the working women's clothing market, identified as "formal professional" women in a 1980 market study by Celanese.

These women are an extremely attractive market because they are:

- a large, fast-growing group,
- with high disposable incomes,
- who are concentrated in metropolitan areas,
- where they buy at a select group of better department and specialty stores,
- with relative insensitivity to price,
- attention to quality,
- apparel brand loyalty,
- and *still-developing tastes and preferences in professional clothing.*

Celanese found the formal professional segment to be a well-defined purchasing group: it "includes accountants, lawyers, sales managers, executives, and administrators who work in highly structured and formal environments. They can be characterized by a strict dress code and overriding concern with presenting a professional image. Members of this group wish to convey occupational status at work and in nonwork activities and can be considered investment dressers."

- 4.3 million women fall within this group.
- They spend $5 billion per year on clothes.
- They represent the fastest growing segment of the working women's clothing market, with real growth forecast at 8–10 percent per year.

HEATHER EVANS will target the upper end of this group, whose concerns about quality and appropriateness are highest, commensurate with their level of income and responsibility.

The following statistics suggest that the upper end of the market is growing even faster than the formal professional market as a whole:

- In 1980, 793,000 women made over $25,000 per year.
- 147,000 women made over *$50,000* per year, up *22 percent* from the previous year.

Thus, HEATHER EVANS will target the new ranks of established executive and professional women. Whereas Liz Claiborne and others capitalized on the initial entry of women into the work force in the 70s, HEATHER EVANS will capitalize on their acceptance in positions of responsibility in the 80s.

Style Trends:

Formal professional women are a ripe market for a well-conceived new clothing label because their tastes and habits in officewear are evolving, but they have few options among existing clothes.

Women in the upper end of the market, HEATHER EVANS's target, are still wearing mostly classic or modified tailored suits, with a blouse and neck ornament. The lower end shows movement toward softer looks and, particularly, dresses. Ms. Evans believes that this trend toward more varied looks will also be seen in the upper end of the market. However, the existing untailored bridge lines, dress lines, and designer sportswear lines are inappropriately styled for that segment.

Manufacturers have recently seen the demand for suits flatten, as interest in dresses has renewed. Responding to this trend, Liz Claiborne and Albert Nipon both opened dress divisions aimed at executive women, priced in the "better" range. The president of Liz Claiborne Dresses voiced the expectations of many in the industry when she told *Women's Wear Daily* that, unlike the 70s when working women wore mostly tailored sportswear for fear of standing out, "in the 80s I think they're going to be a lot more adventuresome in what they wear." As evidence, the dress division of Liz Claiborne hit around $10 million in wholesale sales in less than a year, approximately 10 percent of the entire company's sales.

These examples illustrate the receptivity of the working women's market to new styles and designers. However, the offerings of these companies and others are inappropriate for the more conservative elements. HEATHER EVANS intends to fill this gap.

EXHIBIT 2   *(continued)*

Competition:

The "designer" fashion market is a relatively easy one to enter, because

- *Competition is fragmented.* For example, although there are no comprehensive trade statistics available, it is worth noting that Liz Claiborne, which is one of the two largest companies in the market, can claim less than 3 percent of the market, with $155 million in latest 12 months sales.
- *Channels welcome new products.* Department store buyers are responsible for identifying and promoting new, promising lines, so that customers perceive the buyer's store as a fashion leader. In particular, major department store chains are seeking new lines in the bridge price range, in which HEATHER EVANS will position its products. They foresee this price category becoming increasingly important.

Retailers are encountering consumer price resistance, which suggests that the designer-priced sportswear market has matured: the continual "trading-up" by customers in the 70s has ended. In response, manufacturers are generally lowering prices, both within existing lines and by introducing new lines in lower price categories. Many designer companies will target the bridge market, where customers are value-conscious, but have disposable income. The Company anticipates that the opportunities created by renewed interest in this area will favor the Company's strategy and outweigh the threat of other new entrants and competition.

DESIGNER PRODUCTS MARKET

Once it has established a franchise in the expensive businesswear market, HEATHER EVANS can expand into any of several immediately related markets:

- Accessories (e.g., belts, shoes, scarves) in a similar price category to coordinate with the original clothing line.
- Leisure clothing in the same price range for the same customer as the original line.
- Lower-priced office-wear for a different, wider customer group (i.e., the rest of the 4.3 million formal professional women).

Finally, numerous tertiary markets exist for a well-managed designer name. For example, Bill Blass has licensed his name for chocolates, while Ralph Lauren has licensed his for a full line of home furnishings.

In the past, these designers have developed their names in the couture or designer sportswear levels; however, the extraordinary success of Norma Kamali, whose clothes retail for $30 to $100, demonstrates that a "designer" name can be made in any price range.

Thus, the Company can serve a virtually unlimited number of markets based on its reputation for taste and quality, as established through its original line of clothing. In Calvin Klein's case, his name is used on products with combined retail sales of $1 billion.

Licensing:

Designers profit enormously from licensing agreements, through which they attach their names to products in return for a 5–10 percent royalty. These products are manufactured and marketed—and often designed—by the licensee. For example,

- Pierre Cardin reaps over $50 million a year in royalties on $1 billion of wholesale sales on 540 licenses, with minimal related expenses.
- The top 10 designers collect over $200 million in royalties between them each year.

Long-Run View:

The designer label has replaced the better department store label as the arbiter of taste and quality for the American consumer. After some designers (most notably Cardin) licensed their names indiscriminately in the name-craze of the mid-70s, consumers became more evaluative about the value of a given designer's name, but they continue to purchase according to that name.

This shift has been disastrous for department stores, which have lost their business to discounters, which carry the same designer names for less with comparable service, and to specialty stores, which offer superior service at comparable prices. Although this shake-up in the retail industry will have repercussions for designers, it is unlikely to reverse a now well-entrenched phenomenon.

EXHIBIT 2   *(continued)*

IV. MANAGEMENT AND OPERATIONS

ORGANIZATION AND PEOPLE

Design:

The design group is the core of the Company: it creates five new product lines each year, on which the eventual success of the Company will depend. It is important to recognize that sales of the line will depend as much on existing specifications of fit, construction, fabrics, and coordination of pieces within the line as on the design sketches themselves; these are all parts of the design function.

The design process for each line takes approximately nine months, so that several lines are being worked on in various stages at any time. For each line, the design function is to—

- Plan the line; determine the number of styles, colors, and fabric groups, on the basis of overall line balance, ranges of buyer climates and tastes, and other marketing factors.
- Define the theme and tone of the line.
- Choose and order specific fabrics and other supplies, after surveying the market for these products.
- Create and select sketches.
- Cut, drape, and sew samples. Perfect fit of samples.
- Select final samples for the collection.
- Prepare patterns for production and communicate with normal industry contract manufacturers.

Ms. Evans will spend 40 percent of her time on design and production functions. She will oversee the entire process, with emphasis on *planning* and defining the theme of each line, and *selecting* fabrics, sketches, and final samples.

Ms. Hughes and Ms. Evans will work as a team on all design-related tasks. Ms. Hughes has significant expertise in the creative and technical aspects of fashion design. She is experienced in creating specific styles from a general concept for a line. Her vocabulary of stylistic detail, production feasibility, and textile characteristics complement Ms. Evans's market-driven design direction. (Ms. Hughes's background is described in Appendix B.)

Ms. Hughes has already been retained by Ms. Evans on a free-lance basis and is designing a Holiday line. It is expected that Ms. Hughes will join the company on a full-time basis shortly after funding is received.

The Company plans to hire a design assistant in June. The design assistant will make sample patterns, cut the samples, and oversee the sample makers. She will work with an outside pattern maker on production patterns and with the factory to assure that the final product meets the specifications of the sample garments.

The Company plans to hire one sample maker in June and another in September 1983.

Production:

The production function manages the process from the sample through the shipment of the final garment to the stores. The concerns of the production staff are quality, timely delivery, and cost. During the first two years, Ms. Evans and the design assistant will oversee production as part of their design responsibilities.

Following normal industry practice, the Company will subcontract all manufacturing, including the grading and marketing of its patterns, cutting of its piece goods, and sewing of its garments, to independent suppliers. Initially, all its suppliers will be located in New York City and other locations in the northeastern United States. There is capacity available in suitable shops in this area, where management can carefully monitor the quality and timing of production. As production volume increases, the Company may consider manufacturing in Hong Kong, Taiwan, or elsewhere, where manufacturing costs for quality workmanship may be lower.

Malcolm Wong, a contractor located at 226 West 37th Street, has agreed to reserve time to produce production patterns and sew the Company's entire first collection. Mr. Wong's factory is a high-quality, nonunion shop, with 20 operators. Ms. Evans may use other contractors for all or part of the line, if these contractors offer a more favorable price.

The Company has arranged for its shipping to be done through Fernando Sanchez, as part of its rental arrangement with that firm (see Facilities and Equipment). Fernando Sanchez will provide space, shipping personnel, and shipping supplies. After July 1984, the Company expects to add one shipping employee of its own.

Sales and Promotion:

Sales are made during "market weeks," which last approximately three weeks for each of the five seasons, spread through the year. Store buyers write orders based on the sample line, which they view in the Company's showroom or in one of several regional marketplaces. The Company plans to join the New York Fashion Council, Inc., and has tentatively arranged through this group to reserve space in the key regional market shows.

EXHIBIT 2   *(continued)*

Ms. Evans will spend 40 percent of her time in sales and promotion.

Initially, Ms. Evans will handle all department store sales and some specialty store sales, in the showroom and in "trunk shows" to the Dallas and L.A. markets. Ms. Evans's personal attention is important in this stage to communicate the philosophy of the line, to use her Harvard Business School contacts in department store managements, and to save money.

The Company plans to retain an established, independent representative to sell the line to specialty stores in the Northeast (except New York City). Ms. Evans is currently negotiating with a well-known representative for several designer lines, with whom she has worked previously. The representative will show the line to his customers in the Company's showroom.

Once critical customer relationships have become established and sales volume warrants, Ms. Evans will hire full-time, experienced showroom personnel and, possibly, retain additional independent sales representatives. Ms. Evans will then direct her efforts to more promotional activities and to managing the sales personnel.

Ms. Evans will also carry out an active campaign of nonsales promotion. She will communicate with customer fashion directors, concerning use of samples in cooperative advertising and scheduling personal in-store appearances, and with newspaper and magazine editors to encourage editorial coverage. She will also oversee production of promotional materials to announce the opening of each collection.

Control:

Financial and production control will occupy 20 percent of Ms. Evans's time. These functions are critical to, but often neglected in, apparel manufacturing companies. In particular, fabric purchasing and production decisions must be made so as to maximize sales, yet minimize inventory at the end of the season when it becomes obsolete. Ms. Evans's experience in financial analysis and her business school training are valuable assets in the control function.

The Company plans to hire a part-time bookkeeper during its first months of operation. In July 1984 or thereafter, the Company will retain a full-time office manager.

FACILITIES AND EQUIPMENT

The Company has arranged for showroom and design studio space in the 550 Seventh Avenue building. This is one of the most prestigious buildings in the garment district, with such other tenants as Bill Blass, Halston, Ralph Lauren, and Oscar de la Renta.

HEATHER EVANS's showroom will be within the showroom of Fernando Sanchez, a new and successful high-priced, designer line. Ms. Evans feels that the exposure of the HEATHER EVANS line alongside the Sanchez line and within the 550 Seventh Avenue building will be very beneficial for the Company. The Company's line does not compete with the Sanchez line and will often be bought by different buyers from a given store.

The Company's design studio and office space will be adjacent to the Fernando Sanchez showroom, with its own entrance. The Company will be provided with shipping space at another location, 226 West 37 Street, as part of its arrangement with Fernando Sanchez. These facilities should be adequate for the first two years of operation.

V. FINANCIALS

The Company anticipates raising $250,000 in equity capital. This level of capitalization is adequate, together with normal industry factoring, to develop and to grow a substantial apparel company, without additional equity financing. This is a business plan and is not intended, of itself, to be an offering of stock or debt.

Industry Financial Characteristics:

High fashion apparel manufacturing offers high returns on capital within a short time frame to those companies whose clothing becomes "*fashion.*"

- Margins run 40 to 60 percent.
- Operating costs after cost of goods sold and sales commissions (approximately 10 percent of sales) are relatively fixed. Basically, the cost of designing a line is the same at $1 million in sales as at $20 million.
- Investment in working capital is low: with 60-day terms from fabric suppliers and receivables factoring, cash received from shipment of finished goods can be applied to the cost of those same goods.
- Investment in fixed assets is limited to equipping and remodeling showroom, studio, and shipping space. All manufacturing is subcontracted.
- After an initial introductory period of one to two years, acceptance of a line may proceed extremely rapidly, with annual sales growth rates of 100 to 500 percent not unusual.

EXHIBIT 2   *(continued)*

Whether a line does become "fashion" and to what extent depends on a number of variables that cannot be tested or foreseen until the clothing is presented to the fashion press and the consumers. These variables include the appeal of the specific styles and fit of the line, general fashion trends and specific competitive styles offered at the time the line is presented, and media interest in the line. Thus, investors are rewarded for putting at risk the cost of developing, producing, and marketing a line of clothing during an initial introductory period.

Sales Projections:

The Company has prepared sales projections for the first two years of operation, as presented in Exhibit I. These projections are based on typical order sizes for new lines in the Company's price range and reasonable rates of trial by stores, taking into account supplier credit limits.

For reasons mentioned above, having to do with the nature of fashion, the Company cannot meaningfully forecast sales growth beyond the introductory period.

Financial Statements:

Projected financial statements for the company's first and second years of operation are included as Exhibits II and III, respectively. These forecast net income of $167,173 on sales of $1,712,500 in the second year.

A detailed list of assumptions for the forecasted financial statements is included as Exhibit IV. These estimates were developed by Ms. Evans, based on the experience of comparable companies, and discussed in detail with Rashba & Pokart, certified public accountants, who have extensive experience with apparel industry clients.

EXHIBIT 2 *(continued)*

HEATHER EVANS INCORPORATED

Sales Projections

EXHIBIT I

	Season	Market Period	Shipping Period	Specialty Store			Department Store			Total ($000)
				Number of Orders	Avg. Order Size ($000)	Sales Volume ($000)	Number of Orders	Avg. Order Size ($000)	Sales Volume ($000)	
Year 1	Holiday	August	October–November	38	$2	$ 75	9	$ 8	$ 75	$ 150
	Early spring	September	December–January	50	1	50	12	4	50	100
	Spring	October	February–April	50	3	150	12	12	150	300
	Transition	February	May–June	58	1	57.5	14	4	57.5	165
	Total									$ 715
Year 2	Fall	March	July–September	62	3.5	217.5	15	14	217.5	435
	Holiday	August	October–November	60	2	120	15	8	120	240
	Early spring	September	December–January	75	1	75	19	4	75	150
	Spring	October	February–April	94	4	375	23	16	375	750
	Transition	February	May–June	80	1	80	20	4	80	160
	Total									$1,735

EXHIBIT 2 (continued)

HEATHER EVANS INCORPORATED

Projected Statement of Income
Year Ended May 31, 1984

EXHIBIT II

	Total	June	July	Aug.	Sept.	Oct.	Nov.	Dec.	Jan.	Feb.	Mar.	April	May
Total Sales	607,500	0	0	0	0	75,000	75,000	50,000	50,000	100,000	100,000	100,000	57,500
Less: Discounts	48,600	0	0	0	0	6,000	6,000	4,000	4,000	8,000	8,000	8,000	4,600
Net Sales	558,900	0	0	0	0	69,000	69,000	46,000	46,000	92,000	92,000	92,000	52,900
Cost of Goods Sold													
Inventory—Beginning Piece Goods	0	0	0	0	24,375	61,875	53,750	41,250	57,500	82,500	82,500	68,688	48,750
& Trimmings	257,438	0	0	24,375	24,375	16,250	16,250	32,500	32,500	32,500	18,688	20,000	40,000
Contracting Costs	116,313	0	0	0	13,125	13,125	8,750	8,750	17,500	17,500	17,500	10,063	10,000
Total	373,750	0	0	24,375	61,875	91,250	78,750	82,500	107,500	132,500	118,688	98,750	98,750
Less: Inventory—Ending	70,000	0	0	24,375	61,875	53,750	41,250	57,500	82,500	82,500	68,688	48,750	70,000
Cost of Goods Sold	303,750	0	0	0	0	37,500	37,500	25,000	25,000	50,000	50,000	50,000	28,750
Gross Profit	255,150	0	0	0	0	31,500	31,500	21,000	21,000	42,000	42,000	42,000	24,150
Operating Expenses:													
Production	149,100	11,300	11,300	11,300	12,800	12,800	12,800	12,800	12,800	12,800	12,800	12,800	12,800
Selling and Shipping	53,513	1,000	1,000	1,700	1,000	8,825	5,125	3,750	3,750	6,500	10,200	6,500	4,163
General and Administrative	120,369	9,727	9,727	9,727	10,132	10,132	10,132	10,132	10,132	10,132	10,132	10,132	10,132
Factor's Charges	24,300	0	0	0	0	3,000	3,000	2,000	2,000	4,000	4,000	4,000	2,300
Total Operating Expenses	347,282	22,027	22,027	22,727	23,932	34,757	31,057	28,682	28,682	33,432	37,132	33,432	29,395
Net Income (—Loss)	−92,132	−22,027	−22,027	−22,727	−23,932	−3,257	443	−7,682	−7,682	8,568	4,868	8,568	−5,245

See accompanying Summary of Significant Projection Assumptions and Summary of Significant Accounting Policies.

Preliminary Draft
For discussion purposes only; all exhibits are tentative and subject to change.

EXHIBIT 2 (continued)

HEATHER EVANS INCORPORATED

Projected Schedule of Operating Expenses

Year Ended May 31, 1984

EXHIBIT II

	Total	June	July	Aug.	Sept.	Oct.	Nov.	Dec.	Jan.	Feb.	Mar.	April	May
Production Expenses:													
Designer's Salary	30,000	2,500	2,500	2,500	2,500	2,500	2,500	2,500	2,500	2,500	2,500	2,500	2,500
Assistant Designer and Samplehand's Salaries	55,500	3,500	3,500	3,500	5,000	5,000	5,000	5,000	5,000	5,000	5,000	5,000	5,000
Pattern Maker Salary	39,600	3,300	3,300	3,300	3,300	3,300	3,300	3,300	3,300	3,300	3,300	3,300	3,300
Design Room Supplies	24,000	2,000	2,000	2,000	2,000	2,000	2,000	2,000	2,000	2,000	2,000	2,000	2,000
Total	149,100	11,300	11,300	11,300	12,800	12,800	12,800	12,800	12,800	12,800	12,800	12,800	12,800
Selling and Shipping:													
Salesmen's Commissions	30,375	0	0	0	0	3,750	3,750	2,500	2,500	5,000	5,000	5,000	2,875
Travel and Entertainment	20,100	1,000	1,000	1,700	1,000	4,700	1,000	1,000	1,000	1,000	4,700	1,000	1,000
Freight Out	3,038	0	0	0	0	375	375	250	250	500	500	500	288
Total	53,513	1,000	1,000	1,700	1,000	8,825	5,125	3,750	3,750	6,500	10,200	6,500	4,163
General and Administrative:													
Rent	24,000	2,000	2,000	2,000	2,000	2,000	2,000	2,000	2,000	2,000	2,000	2,000	2,000
Office Salary	9,600	800	800	800	800	800	800	800	800	800	800	800	800
Telephone	8,400	700	700	700	700	700	700	700	700	700	700	700	700
Stationery and Office	12,000	1,000	1,000	1,000	1,000	1,000	1,000	1,000	1,000	1,000	1,000	1,000	1,000
Legal and Audit	12,000	1,000	1,000	1,000	1,000	1,000	1,000	1,000	1,000	1,000	1,000	1,000	1,000
Dues and Subscriptions	3,600	300	300	300	300	300	300	300	300	300	300	300	300
Depreciation and Amortization	2,700	225	225	225	225	225	225	225	225	225	225	225	225
Insurance	7,200	600	600	600	600	600	600	600	600	600	600	600	600
Business and Payroll Taxes	13,470	1,010	1,010	1,010	1,160	1,160	1,160	1,160	1,160	1,160	1,160	1,160	1,160
Utilities	4,500	375	375	375	375	375	375	375	375	375	375	375	375
Employee Benefits	22,899	1,717	1,717	1,717	1,972	1,972	1,972	1,972	1,972	1,972	1,972	1,972	1,972
Total	120,369	9,727	9,727	9,727	10,132	10,132	10,132	10,132	10,132	10,132	10,132	10,132	10,132

See accompanying Summary of Significant Projection Assumptions and Summary of Significant Accounting Policies.

Preliminary Draft

For discussion purposes only; all exhibits are tentative and subject to change.

EXHIBIT 2 *(continued)*

HEATHER EVANS INCORPORATED

EXHIBIT II

Forecasted Balance Sheets
June 1983 through May 1984

Assets	June	July	Aug.	Sept.	Oct.	Nov.	Dec.	Jan.	Feb.	Mar.	April	May
Current Assets:												
Cash and Due From Factor	203,398	181,596	159,094	122,262	119,230	124,273	116,816	100,609	109,402	114,495	130,726	125,769
Merchandise Inventories	0	0	24,375	61,875	53,750	41,250	57,500	82,500	82,500	68,688	48,750	70,000
Total Current Assets	203,398	181,596	183,469	184,137	172,980	165,523	174,316	183,109	191,902	183,183	179,476	195,769
Fixed Assets—Net	17,775	17,550	17,325	17,100	16,875	16,650	16,425	16,200	15,975	15,750	15,525	15,300
Other Assets	6,800	6,800	6,800	6,800	6,800	6,800	6,800	6,800	6,800	6,800	6,800	6,800
Total Assets	227,973	205,946	207,594	208,037	196,655	188,973	197,541	206,109	214,677	205,733	201,801	217,869
Current Liabilities:												
Accounts Payable	0	0	24,375	48,750	40,625	32,500	48,750	65,000	65,000	51,188	38,688	60,000
Stockholders' Equity	227,973	205,946	183,219	159,287	156,030	156,473	148,791	141,109	149,677	154,545	163,113	157,869
Total Liabilities and Stockholders' Equity	227,973	205,946	207,594	208,037	196,655	188,973	197,541	206,109	214,677	205,733	201,801	217,869

See accompanying Summary of Significant Projection Assumptions and Summary of Significant Accounting Policies.
Preliminary Draft
For discussion purposes only; all exhibits are tentative and subject to change.

EXHIBIT 2 *(continued)*

HEATHER EVANS INCORPORATED

Projected Statements of Cash Flow
Year Ended May 31, 1984

EXHIBIT II

	Total	June	July	Aug.	Sept.	Oct.	Nov.	Dec.	Jan.	Feb.	Mar.	April	May
Cash and Due From Factor—Beginning	0	0	203,398	181,596	159,094	122,262	119,230	124,273	116,816	100,609	109,402	114,495	130,726
Receipts:													
Initial Capitalization	250,000	250,000	0	0	0	0	0	0	0	0	0	0	0
Net Sales	558,900	0	0	0	0	69,000	69,000	46,000	46,000	92,000	92,000	92,000	52,900
Total	808,900	250,000	203,398	181,596	159,094	191,262	188,230	170,273	162,816	192,609	201,402	206,495	183,626
Cash Disbursements:													
Accounts Payable—													
Piece Goods & Trimmings	197,438	0	0	0	0	24,375	24,375	16,250	16,250	32,500	32,500	32,500	18,688
Contractors Payable	116,313	0	0	0	13,125	13,125	8,750	8,750	17,500	17,500	17,500	10,063	10,000
Operating Expenses—Net	344,582	21,802	21,802	22,502	23,707	34,532	30,832	28,457	28,457	33,207	36,907	33,207	29,170
Security Deposits	6,800	6,800	0	0	0	0	0	0	0	0	0	0	0
Purchase of Fixed Assets	18,000	18,000	0	0	0	0	0	0	0	0	0	0	0
Total	683,132	46,602	21,802	22,502	36,832	72,032	63,957	53,457	62,207	83,207	86,907	75,770	57,857
Cash and Due From Factor—Ending	125,769	203,398	181,596	159,904	122,262	119,230	124,273	116,816	100,609	109,402	114,495	130,726	125,769

See accompanying Summary of Significant Projection Assumptions and Summary of Significant Accounting Policies.

Preliminary Draft

For discussion purposes only; all exhibits are tentative and subject to change.

EXHIBIT 2 *(continued)*

HEATHER EVANS INCORPORATED
Projected Statement of Income
Year Ended May 31, 1985

EXHIBIT III

	Total	June	July	Aug.	Sept.	Oct.	Nov.	Dec.	Jan.	Feb.	Mar.	April	May
Total Sales	1,171,250	57,500	145,000	145,000	145,000	120,000	120,000	75,000	75,000	250,000	250,000	250,000	80,000
Less: Discounts	137,000	4,600	11,600	11,600	11,600	9,600	9,600	6,000	6,000	20,000	20,000	20,000	6,400
Net Sales	1,575,500	52,900	133,400	133,400	133,400	110,400	110,400	69,000	69,000	230,000	230,000	230,000	73,600
Cost of Goods Sold:													
Inventory—Beginning	70,000	70,000	113,750	113,750	105,625	93,125	78,500	56,000	112,875	200,375	200,375	145,125	81,250
Piece Goods & Trimmings	585,000	47,125	47,125	39,000	39,000	24,375	24,375	81,250	81,250	81,250	26,000	47,125	47,125
Contracting Costs	299,625	25,375	25,375	25,375	21,000	21,000	13,125	13,125	43,750	43,750	43,750	14,000	10,000
Total	954,625	142,500	186,250	178,125	165,625	138,500	116,000	150,375	237,875	325,375	270,125	206,250	138,375
Less: Inventory—Ending	98,375	113,750	113,750	105,625	93,125	78,500	56,000	112,875	200,375	200,375	145,125	81,250	98,375
Cost of Goods Sold	856,250	28,750	72,500	72,500	72,500	60,000	60,000	37,500	37,500	125,000	125,000	125,000	40,000
Gross Profit	719,250	24,150	60,900	60,900	60,900	50,400	50,400	31,500	31,500	105,000	105,000	105,000	33,600
Operating Expenses:													
Production	153,600	12,800	12,800	12,800	12,800	12,800	12,800	12,800	12,800	12,800	12,800	12,800	12,800
Selling and Shipping	114,288	4,163	8,975	9,675	8,975	11,300	7,600	5,125	5,125	14,750	18,450	14,750	5,400
General and Administrative	149,524	10,132	12,672	12,672	12,672	12,672	12,672	12,672	12,672	12,672	12,672	12,672	12,672
Factor's Charges	63,020	2,116	5,336	5,336	5,336	4,416	4,416	2,760	2,760	9,200	9,200	9,200	2,944
Total Operating Expenses	480,432	29,211	39,783	40,483	39,783	41,188	37,488	33,357	33,357	49,422	53,122	49,422	33,816
Income Before Provision for Income Taxes	238,819	−5,061	21,117	20,417	21,117	9,212	12,912	−1,857	−1,857	55,578	51,878	55,578	−216
Provision for Income Taxes	71,646	−1,518	6,335	6,125	6,335	2,764	3,874	−557	−557	16,673	15,563	16,673	−65
Net Income (−Loss)	167,163	−3,542	14,782	14,292	14,782	6,448	9,038	−1,300	−1,300	38,905	36,315	38,905	−151

See accompanying Summary of Significant Projection Assumptions and Summary of Significant Accounting Policies.

Preliminary Draft
For discussion purposes only; all exhibits are tentative and subject to change.

EXHIBIT 2 (continued)

HEATHER EVANS INCORPORATED

Projected Schedule of Operating Expenses
Year Ended May 31, 1985

EXHIBIT III

	Total	June	July	Aug.	Sept.	Oct.	Nov.	Dec.	Jan.	Feb.	Mar.	April	May
Production Expenses:													
Designer's Salary	30,000	2,500	2,500	2,500	2,500	2,500	2,500	2,500	2,500	2,500	2,500	2,500	2,500
Assistant Designer and Samplehand's Salaries	60,000	5,000	5,000	5,000	5,000	5,000	5,000	5,000	5,000	5,000	5,000	5,000	5,000
Pattern Maker Salary	39,600	3,300	3,300	3,300	3,300	3,300	3,300	3,300	3,300	3,300	3,300	3,300	3,300
Design Room Supplies	24,000	2,000	2,000	2,000	2,000	2,000	2,000	2,000	2,000	2,000	2,000	2,000	2,000
Total	153,600	12,800	12,800	12,800	12,800	12,800	12,800	12,800	12,800	12,800	12,800	12,800	12,800
Selling and Shipping:													
Salesmen's Commissions	85,625	2,875	7,250	7,250	7,250	6,000	6,000	3,750	3,750	12,500	12,500	12,500	4,000
Travel and Entertainment	20,100	1,000	1,000	1,700	1,000	4,700	1,000	1,000	1,000	1,000	4,700	1,000	1,000
Freight Out	8,563	288	725	725	725	600	600	375	375	1,250	1,250	1,250	400
Total	114,288	4,163	8,975	9,675	8,975	11,300	7,600	5,125	5,125	14,750	18,450	14,750	5,400
General and Administrative:													
Rent	24,000	2,000	2,000	2,000	2,000	2,000	2,000	2,000	2,000	2,000	2,000	2,000	2,000
Office Salary	31,600	800	2,800	2,800	2,800	2,800	2,800	2,800	2,800	2,800	2,800	2,800	2,800
Telephone	8,400	700	700	700	700	700	700	700	700	700	700	700	700
Stationery and Office	12,000	1,000	1,000	1,000	1,000	1,000	1,000	1,000	1,000	1,000	1,000	1,000	1,000
Legal and Audit	12,000	1,000	1,000	1,000	1,000	1,000	1,000	1,000	1,000	1,000	1,000	1,000	1,000
Dues and Subscriptions	3,600	300	300	300	300	300	300	300	300	300	300	300	300
Depreciation and Amortization	2,700	225	225	225	225	225	225	225	225	225	225	225	225
Insurance	7,200	600	600	600	600	600	600	600	600	600	600	600	600
Business and Payroll Taxes	16,120	1,160	1,360	1,360	1,360	1,360	1,360	1,360	1,360	1,360	1,360	1,360	1,360
Utilities	4,500	375	375	375	375	375	375	375	375	375	375	375	375
Employee Benefits	27,404	1,972	2,312	2,312	2,312	2,312	2,312	2,312	2,312	2,312	2,312	2,312	2,312
Total	149,524	10,132	12,672	12,672	12,672	12,672	12,672	12,672	12,672	12,672	12,672	12,672	12,672

See accompanying Summary of Significant Projection Assumptions and Summary of Significant Accounting Policies.

Preliminary Draft
For discussion purposes only; all exhibits are tentative and subject to change.

EXHIBIT 2 (continued)

HEATHER EVANS INCORPORATED

Forecasted Balance Sheets
June 1984 through May 1985

EXHIBIT III

	1984							1985				
	June	July	Aug.	Sept.	Oct.	Nov.	Dec.	Jan.	Feb.	Mar.	April	May
Assets												
Current Assets:												
Cash and Due From Factor	104,309	132,776	153,418	179,135	188,572	209,584	207,952	175,695	231,498	283,601	369,154	373,163
Merchandise Inventories	113,750	113,750	105,625	93,125	78,500	56,000	112,875	200,375	200,375	145,125	81,250	98,375
Total Current Assets	218,059	246,526	259,043	272,260	267,072	265,584	320,827	376,070	431,873	428,726	450,404	471,538
Fixed Assets—Net	15,075	14,850	14,625	14,400	14,175	13,950	13,725	13,500	13,275	13,050	12,825	12,600
Other Assets	6,800	6,800	6,800	6,800	6,800	6,800	6,800	6,800	6,800	6,800	6,800	6,800
Total Assets	239,934	268,176	280,468	293,460	288,047	286,334	341,352	396,370	451,948	448,576	470,029	490,938
Liabilities and Stockholders' Equity												
Current Liabilities:												
Accounts Payable	87,125	94,250	86,125	78,000	63,375	48,750	105,625	162,500	162,500	107,250	73,125	94,250
Income Taxes Payable	–1,518	4,817	10,942	17,277	20,041	23,914	23,357	22,800	39,474	53,037	71,710	71,646
Total Current Liabilities	85,607	99,067	97,067	95,277	83,416	72,664	128,982	185,300	201,974	162,287	144,835	165,896
Stockholders' Equity	154,327	169,109	183,400	198,182	204,631	213,669	212,369	211,069	249,974	286,289	325,193	325,042
Total Liabilities and Stockholders' Equity	239,934	268,176	280,468	293,460	288,047	286,334	341,352	396,370	451,948	448,576	470,029	490,938

See accompanying Summary of Significant Projection Assumptions and Summary of Significant Accounting Policies.
Preliminary Draft
For discussion purposes only; all exhibits are tentative and subject to change.

EXHIBIT 2 *(continued)*

HEATHER EVANS INCORPORATED

Projected Statements of Cash Flow
Year Ended May 31, 1985

EXHIBIT III

	Total	June	July	Aug.	Sept.	Oct.	Nov.	Dec.	Jan.	Feb.	Mar.	April	May
Cash and Due From Factor—Beginning	125,769	125,769	104,309	132,776	153,418	179,135	188,572	209,584	207,952	175,695	231,498	283,601	369,154
Receipts:													
Net Sales	1,575,500	52,900	133,400	133,400	133,400	110,400	110,400	69,000	69,000	230,000	230,000	230,000	73,600
Total	1,701,269	178,669	237,709	266,176	286,818	289,535	298,972	278,584	276,952	405,695	461,498	513,601	442,754
Cash Disbursements:													
Accounts Payable—													
Piece Goods & Trimmings	550,750	20,000	40,000	47,125	47,125	39,000	39,000	24,375	24,375	81,250	81,250	81,250	26,000
Contractors Payable	299,625	25,375	25,375	25,375	21,000	21,000	13,125	13,125	43,750	43,750	43,750	14,000	10,000
Operating Expenses—Net	477,732	28,986	39,558	40,258	39,558	40,963	37,263	33,132	33,132	49,197	52,897	49,197	33,591
Total	1,328,107	74,361	104,933	112,758	107,683	100,963	89,388	70,632	101,257	174,197	177,897	144,447	69,591
Cash and Due From Factor—Ending	373,163	104,309	132,776	153,418	179,135	188,572	209,584	207,952	175,695	231,498	283,601	369,154	373,163

See accompanying Summary of Significant Projection Assumptions and Summary of Significant Accounting Policies.
Preliminary Draft
For discussion purposes only; all exhibits are tentative and subject to change.

Exhibit 2 *(continued)*

EXHIBIT IV

ASSUMPTIONS FOR PROFORMA FINANCIAL STATEMENTS

Income Statement
1. Sales: See Exhibit I, Sales Projections
2. Discount: 8 percent (assume discount taken on all sales)
3. Cost of goods sold:
   - Inventory—see Balance Sheet below
   - Piece goods and trimmings—65 percent of COGS
   - Contracting costs—35 percent of COGS
4. Gross profit: 50 percent of gross sales (42 percent of net sales)
5. Operating expenses—see below
6. Factor's charge—4 percent net of sales (actual charges will be commission equal to a fixed percentage of sales plus interest charge for advances against uncollected receivables)

Operating Expenses
1. Production expenses:
   - Salaries
     Designer—$2,500 per month, starting June 1983
     Assistant designer—$2,000 per month, starting June 1983
     Samplehands—$1,000 each per month, starting June 1983, another starting September 1983
     Pattern maker—$3,300 per month, starting June 1983
2. Selling and shipping:
   - Salesmen's commission—10 percent on all specialty store sales, based on standard independent representative commission rate
   - Travel and entertainment—
     General travel and entertainment—$1,000 per month
     Announcements—$700 each holiday, spring, and fall market period
     Trunk shows—$3,000 each spring and fall market period
   - Freight out—0.5 percent of sales
3. General and administrative:
   - Rent—$2,000 per month
   - Office salary—
     Part-time bookkeeper—2 days per week, at $100 per day, starting June 1983
     Office manager—$2,000 per month
   - Telephone—$700 per month
   - Stationery and office—$1,000 per month
   - Legal and audit—$1,000 per month
   - Dues and subscriptions—$300 per month
   - Depreciation and amortization—$225 per month, based on $18,000 investment in equipment, furniture, and lease improvements, depreciated on a straight-line basis over an average life of 7 years.
   - Insurance—$600 per month
   - Business and payroll taxes—10 percent of full-time payroll
   - Employee benefits—18 percent of full-time payroll

EXHIBIT 2   *(continued)*

EXHIBIT IV

ASSUMPTIONS FOR PROFORMA FINANCIAL STATEMENTS

<u>Balance Sheets</u>
1. Cash and due from factor—includes 100 percent of invoices for goods shipped in each month
2. Merchandise inventories—includes piece goods and trim received 60 days in advance of sale; finished goods shipped within month
3. Fixed assets—net—depreciated straight-line over 7-year average life, from $18,000 base, as follows:

Sample room equipment	$ 7,000
Office and showroom furnishing	6,000
Remodeling	5,000
	$18,000

4. Other assets—includes lease deposit of $6,000 (3 months) and telephone deposit of $800
5. Accounts payable—includes piece goods and trimming payable within 60 days; contractors paid within 30 days; all other expenses assumed paid within month
6. Stockholders' equity—$250,000 initial capital

EXHIBIT 2   *(continued)*

APPENDIXES

Résumé of
HEATHER H. EVANS

Education

1981–1983

HARVARD GRADUATE SCHOOL OF BUSINESS ADMINISTRATION

Candidate for the degree of Master of Business Administration in June 1983. Awarded First Year Honors (top 15 percent of class). Resident Business Tutor, South House, Harvard College: supervised pre-business program and oversaw student activities in residential unit of 350 undergraduate students. Instructor, Economics Department, Harvard College: designed and taught full-credit undergraduate course in managerial economics and decision analysis.

1976–1979

HARVARD COLLEGE

Bachelor of Arts degree, *cum laude*. Philosophy major. Phi Beta Kappa. Dean's list all semesters. Completed undergraduate course requirements in three years.

Publisher and Executive Committee member, *The Harvard Advocate* magazine. Vice Chairman, South House Committee.

Work Experience

Summer 1982

JACKIE HAYMAN, INC.

Assistant to President. Aided president of young firm that manufactures designer clothing under Catherine Hipp label. Involved in all areas of business, including sales, public relations, working capital management, credit, design, production, and shipping.

1979–1981

MORGAN STANLEY & CO. INCORPORATED

Financial Analyst.

Mergers and Acquisitions: Identified possible acquisition targets, recommended prices for those companies, and formulated strategies to locate buyers. Analyzed financial and market data to determine the target's long-range earning potential and the effect of the acquisition on the buyer.

Corporate Finance: Supervised preparation of debt financings for 10 clients. Negotiated terms of security documents and coordinated the activities of teams inside and outside Morgan Stanley.

1975–1979

FASHION MODEL

Managed own career as a fashion model. Represented by Ford Models, Inc., New York, N.Y.; The Model's Group, Boston, Mass.; and L'Agence Pauline, Paris, France. Credits include: *Mademoiselle, Seventeen, GQ, LeMonde, Boston*, and *The Boston Globe*.

Summer 1978

RESOURCE PLANNING ASSOCIATES

Research Associate. Planned and executed study that led RPA to add antitrust economic support work to its services. Worked on projects in oil price forecasting and U.S. mineral reliance.

Personal Background

Attended The Spence School, New York, N.Y., and Lycée Montaigne, Paris, France. Speaks fluent French and conversational Greek.

EXHIBIT 2 *(concluded)*

Background of
Belinda Hughes

Belinda Hughes received her Bachelor of Fine Arts Degree in fashion design from Parsons School of Design in May 1981. After graduation, she worked as Assistant Designer to Kasper at Kasper for J. L. Sports. She designed pants, blouses, and jackets for the Kasper line and prepared sketches and maintained records of fabrication and styles for the company's Japanese licensee. In May 1982, Ms. Hughes became head designer for Creations by Aria, a moderate-price dress house. She covered layout of the dressy dress line, from selection of fabrics to preparation of dresses, and oversaw the sample room staff. Recently, Ms. Hughes has been working as a free-lance designer for several lines, including Choo-Chee, Elan Shoe Corp., Roslyn Harte, and College Town, for which she has designed collections ranging from shoes to loungewear.

Ms. Hughes's design talent has been recognized by many academic and industry awards, including: Recognition in Design Citation from Levis (1979), scholarship award from St. John's University (1979), scholarship award from the Switzer Foundation (1980), ILGWU Design Merit Award (1980), ILGWU Design Creativity Award (1981).

EXHIBIT 3   Timing of Cycles in the Garment Industry

	March	April May	June July	August	September	October
Holiday line	Order sample fabrics	Sketch and design line	Make samples and order production quantities of fabric	Market weeks— take orders	Contract out cutting and sewing	Deliver garments to stores
Early spring line			Early spring line cycle begins			
Spring line			Spring cycle begins			
Transition line					Transition line begins	
Fall line		Fall line finishes up				

EXHIBIT 4   Heather Evans's Notes on Preliminary Discussions with Potential Private Investors

---

1. <u>David Ellis,</u> attorney, family friend (excerpt from April 28, 1983, letter):

   From an investor's point of view, one would expect at least a 50 percent equity share, and probably substantially more although in nonvoting stock. The investors' stock would be convertible into voting (and indeed, control) stock in case certain minimum standards of solvency and cash flow and performance weren't met. Additional stock would be made available to management if certain performance goals were exceeded. Thus management might start with 25 percent, plus an option on a second 25 percent if the company proves to be a world-beater.

   That of course may sound too complicated; but if it's to be an arm's-length <u>minimally</u> attractive proposal, I think you have to offer investors at least 50 percent or 60 percent, albeit in nonvoting shares.

   If it were a proposal such as that, I would be thinking in terms of a $20,000 or $25,000 participation for myself (i.e., an investment).

   But if you can get 70 percent for yourself, with only 30 percent to investors—<u>take it!</u> If that's the way it goes, I would want to make a gesture of support and encouragement—thus a $5,000 unit.

2. <u>Paul Hood,</u> classmate, HBS:
   - Says he is interested in investing for three reasons:
     —Heather Evans: trusts intelligence, dedication, design sense, and business judgment.
     —Concept: gut feel that there is a market need, has spoken with women in business about idea.
     —Upside: mentioned Liz Claiborne deal.
   - Key needs in a deal:
     —<u>No</u> limit to upside via forced call on equity.
     —Wants company to own "Heather Evans" name rather than licensing; if Heather Evans can walk after business established, this limits upside.
   - Willing to invest $25,000 to $40,000.

3. <u>Herbert Greene,</u> president, Greene Textiles:
   - I felt that Greene was a good contact with potential fabric, textile suppliers.
   - Name (especially if on board) adds credibility on Seventh Avenue/Garment Business.
   - Was in on Liz Claiborne deal, made *very* big dollars.
   - Wants in deal terms:
     —Right to force registration/issue in public market in five to seven years.
     —Low limit on my salary with incentive compensation.
     —Investors get board control until minimum performance criteria met.
   - Willing to invest $35,000–$55,000.

4. <u>John Merrill,</u> old friend, HBS classmate:
   - Wants company to own name: says if company does very well, main value created will be in name, company should own this.
   - Liquidation protection (i.e., if company goes bust, investors get what's left before I get anything).
   - Three- to five-year employment contract with three-year noncompete clause at termination of employment contract.
   - Right to sell equity, pro rata, on same terms as Heather Evans in any offering.

EXHIBIT 5   Liz Claiborne Prospectus—Excerpts

liz claiborne, inc.
Common Stock
(Par Value $1 Per Share)\

Of the shares of Common Stock offered hereby, 345,000 shares are being sold by the Company and 805,000 shares are being sold by certain stockholders. The Company will not receive any proceeds from the sale of shares by the Selling Stockholders. See "Principal and Selling Stockholders."

Prior to this offering there has been no public market for the Company's Common Stock. See "Underwriting" for information relating to the method of determining the initial public offering price.

THESE SECURITIES HAVE NOT BEEN APPROVED OR DISAPPROVED BY THE SECURITIES AND EXCHANGE COMMISSION NOR HAS THE COMMISSION PASSED UPON THE ACCURACY OR ADEQUACY OF THIS PROSPECTUS. ANY REPRESENTATION TO THE CONTRARY IS A CRIMINAL OFFENSE.

	Price to Public	Underwriting Discounts (1)	Proceeds to the Company (2)	Proceeds to the Selling Stockholders (2) (3)
Per Share	$19.00	$1.28	$17.72	$17.72
Total	$21,850,000	$1,472,000	$6,113,400	$14,264,600

(1) See "Underwriting" for a description of indemnification and insurance arrangements among the Underwriters, the Company and the Selling Stockholders.

(2) Before deducting expenses estimated at $356,201 payable by the Company and $168,369 payable by the Selling Stockholders.

(3) The Selling Stockholders have granted the Underwriters an option to purchase up to an additional 115,000 shares to cover over-allotments. If all such shares are purchased, the total Price to Public, Underwriting Discounts and Proceeds to the Selling Stockholders will be increased by $2,185,000, $147,200 and $2,037,800, respectively.

The Common Stock is being offered subject to prior sale, when, as and if delivered to and accepted by the several Underwriters and subject to approval of certain legal matters by counsel and to certain other conditions. It is expected that certificates for the shares of Common Stock offered hereby will be available on or about June 16, 1981. The Underwriters reserve the right to withdraw, cancel or modify such offer and to reject orders in whole or in part.

Merrill Lynch White Weld Capital Markets Group
Merrill Lynch, Pierce, Fenner & Smith Incorporated

June 9, 1981

EXHIBIT 5   *(continued)*

PROSPECTUS SUMMARY

The following information is qualified in its entirety by reference to the detailed information and financial statements (including the Notes thereto) appearing elsewhere in the Prospectus.

Liz Claiborne, Inc.

Liz Claiborne, Inc. (the "Company") designs, contracts for the manufacture of and markets an extensive range of women's clothing under the LIZ CLAIBORNE and LIZ trademarks. Since the Company's founding in 1976, it has concentrated on identifying and furnishing the wardrobe requirements of the business and professional woman. Although the Company's products are conceived and marketed as "designer" apparel, they are priced to sell in the "better sportswear" range. The Company's products are sold to over 900 customers operating over 3,000 department and specialty stores throughout the United States. Products are manufactured pursuant to the Company's specifications by independent suppliers in the United States and abroad. See "Business."

The Offering

Common Stock to be sold by:	
Company...	345,000 shares
Selling Stockholders..................................	805,000 shares (1)
Common Stock to be outstanding after the offering................	3,479,560 shares
Estimated net proceeds to the Company........................	$5,757,199
Use of net proceeds by the Company	To reduce indebtedness and for certain capital expenditures. See "Use of Proceeds."
Dividends	None. See "Dividend Policy."
Proposed NASDAQ Symbol..................................	LIZC

(1) Assumes the Underwriters' 115,000 share over-allotment option is not exercised.

SELECTED CONSOLIDATED FINANCIAL DATA
(in thousands of dollars except per share amounts)

	Jan. 19, 1976 (Inc.) through Dec. 31, 1976	Fiscal Year Ended				Three Months Ended	
		Dec. 31, 1977	Dec. 31, 1978	Dec. 29, 1979	Dec. 27, 1980	March 29, 1980	March 28, 1981
							(unaudited)
Net sales	$2,060	$7,396	$23,279	$47,630	$79,492	$20,747	$26,523
Net income	50	342	1,189	3,497	6,220	1,953	2,687
Earnings per common share (1)	$.02	$.12	$.38	$1.12	$1.98	$.62	$.86

Exhibit 5   *(continued)*

	March 28, 1981 (unaudited)	
	Actual	*As Adjusted (2)*
Working capital	$11,854	$16,307
Total assets	27,918	32,613
Long-term debt, including current portion	63	—
Short-term debt	3,884	2,884
Stockholders' equity	13,589	19,346

(1) Adjusted to reflect the issuance of 65 shares of the Company's Common Stock for each share of its predecessor company's common stock pursuant to a merger effected on April 21, 1981. See Notes 1 and 5 of Notes to Consolidated Financial Statements.

(2) Adjusted to reflect the sale of the shares offered by the Company hereby and the anticipated use of the net proceeds therefrom as well as the repayment of long-term debt in April, 1981. See "Use of Proceeds" and "Capitalization."

See "Dilution" and "Shares Eligible for Future Sale" with respect to the availability of shares for sale after this offering and the immediate dilution in net tangible book value per share to be incurred by the public investors.

IN CONNECTION WITH THIS OFFERING, THE UNDERWRITERS MAY OVER-ALLOT OR EFFECT TRANSACTIONS WHICH STABILIZE OR MAINTAIN THE MARKET PRICE OF THE COMMON STOCK OF THE COMPANY AT A LEVEL ABOVE THAT WHICH MIGHT OTHERWISE PREVAIL IN THE OPEN MARKET. SUCH STABILIZING, IF COMMENCED, MAY BE DISCONTINUED AT ANY TIME.

SELECTED FINANCIAL DATA

The following tables set forth information regarding the Company's operating results and financial position and are qualified in their entirety by the more detailed Consolidated Financial Statements included elsewhere in the Prospectus.

EXHIBIT 5   *(continued)*

SELECTED INCOME STATEMENT DATA

	Jan. 19, 1976 (inc.) through Dec. 31, 1976	Dec. 1, 1977 (unaudited)	Fiscal Year Ended			Three Months Ended	
			Dec. 31, 1978	Dec. 29, 1979	Dec. 27, 1980	March 29, 1980	March 28, 1981
Net sales	$2,060,118	$7,395,898	$23,279,304	$47,630,227	$79,492,035	$20,747,500	$26,523,023
Net income	49,862	342,489	1,188,857	3,496,575	6,219,592	1,952,998	2,686,670
Earnings per common share (1)	$.02	$.12	$.38	$1.12	$1.98	$.62	$.86
Dividends declared per common share (1) (2)	—	$.007	$.023	$.046	$.077	—	—

SELECTED BALANCE SHEET DATA

	Dec. 31, 1976	Dec. 31, 1977	Dec. 31, 1978	Dec. 29, 1979	Dec. 27, 1980	March 28, 1981 (unaudited)
Working capital	$246,471	$454,196	$1,179,071	$4,456,954	$9,302,745	$11,854,311
Total assets	674,806	1,901,492	5,144,142	10,786,982	19,281,718	27,918,402
Long-term debt, including current portion (3)	170,000	173,333	173,333	134,815	77,037	62,593
Short-term debt (4)	—	—	—	—	—	3,883,676
Advances from factor (4)	330,696	666,077	2,782,863	—	3,546,098	—
Stockholders' equity	135,029	455,128	1,571,649	4,923,551	10,902,023	13,588,693

(1) Adjusted to reflect the issuance of 65 shares of the Company's Common Stock for each share of its predecessor company's common stock pursuant to a merger effected on April 21, 1981. See Notes 1 and 5 of Notes to Consolidated Financial Statements.

(2) The Company has no present plan to continue to pay dividends. See "Dividend Policy."

(3) The Company repaid its long-term debt in April 1981.

(4) Factoring advances were replaced by a line of credit in March 1981. See Notes 2 and 10 of Notes to Consolidated Financial Statements.

<u>**EXHIBIT 5**</u>   *(continued)*

BUSINESS

Introduction and Background

The Company designs, contracts for the manufacture of and markets an extensive range of women's clothing under the LIZ CLAIBORNE and LIZ trademarks. Organized in 1976 by its present management, the Company has concentrated primarily on identifying and furnishing the wardrobe requirements of the working woman, providing apparel appropriate in a business or professional environment as well as apparel suitable for leisure wear. The Company offers its customers a broad selection of related separates (referred to in the apparel industry as *sportswear*) consisting of blouses, skirts, jackets, sweaters, and tailored pants, as well as more casual apparel such as jeans, knit tops, and shirts. The Company believes that the increasing number of business and professional women has contributed both to the Company's own growth and to the growth of the market for women's sportswear in general.

LIZ CLAIBORNE products are conceived and marketed as designer apparel, employing a consistent approach to design and quality, which is intended to develop and maintain consumer recognition and loyalty across product lines and from season to season. The Company defines its clothing as "updated," combining traditional or classic design with contemporary fashion influences. While the Company maintains a "designer" image, its products are priced in the better sportswear range, which is generally less expensive than many designer lines. Although no comprehensive trade statistics are available, the Company believes, based on its knowledge of the market and such trade information as is available, that measured by sales of women's better sportswear, it is the second largest producer of such merchandise in the United States.

In 1980, LIZ CLAIBORNE products were sold to over 900 customers operating over 3,000 department and specialty stores throughout the United States. Measured by their purchases of LIZ CLAIBORNE apparel, the Company's largest customers during 1980 included Saks Fifth Avenue, Lord & Taylor, Bamberger's, J. L. Hudson, Bloomingdale's and Macy's—New York. A great many retail outlets that carry the Company's products maintain separate LIZ CLAIBORNE areas in which a range of the Company's products are sold. Approximately 25 percent of the Company's 1980 sales was made to the Company's 10 largest customers; approximately 71 percent of 1980 sales was made to the Company's 100 largest customers. Certain of these customers are under common ownership. For example, 16 different department store customers owned by Federated Department Stores, Inc. (which include Bloomingdale's, Abraham & Straus, and Burdine's) accounted for approximately 12 percent of the Company's 1980 sales. The Company believes that each of these department store customers makes its own decisions regarding purchases of the Company's products.

Exhibit 5   *(continued)*

Although the Company expects that sales to its 100 largest customers will continue to account for a majority of its sales, increasing emphasis is being placed on sales to local specialty stores and direct-mail catalog companies. The Company began licensing its trademarks in 1978 and presently receives royalties under arrangements with three licensees that sell various products under the LIZ CLAIBORNE and LIZ trademarks.

The Company's products are designed by its own staff and are manufactured in accordance with its specifications by independent suppliers in the United States and abroad. Domestically produced merchandise accounted for approximately 55 percent of the Company's sales during 1980; the remaining approximately 45 percent consisted of merchandise produced abroad, almost entirely in the Far East. Company personnel in the United States and abroad regularly monitor production at facilities that manufacture its products.

PRINCIPAL AND SELLING STOCKHOLDERS

The following table sets forth certain information, as of March 28, 1981, with respect to the number of shares of Common Stock owned, to be offered for sale, and to be beneficially owned after this offering, by all persons who were known by the Company to own beneficially more than 5 percent of the then outstanding Common Stock, all Selling Stockholders, each of the Directors of the Company, and the Company's officers and Directors, as a group:

	Ownership of Common Stock prior to Offering (1)			Ownership of Common Stock after Offering (1)(2)	
Name and Address	*Number of Shares*	*Percent*	*Shares to be Sold (2)*	*Number of Shares*	*Percent*
Elisabeth Claiborne Ortenberg (3) 1441 Broadway New York, NY	523,640	16.71	134,478	389,162	11.18
Arthur Ortenberg (3) 1441 Broadway New York, NY	523,640	16.71	134,478	389,162	11.18
Leonard Boxer 4 Emerson Lane Secaucus, NJ	523,640	16.71	134,478	389,162	11.18
Jerome A. Chazen 1441 Broadway New York, NY	523,640	16.71	134,478	389,162	11.18
J. James Gordon 1101 Park Ave. New York, NY	65,000	2.07	16,693	48,307	1.39

(1) All shares listed are owned of record and, to the Company's knowledge, beneficially.

(2) Assumes the Underwriters' 115,000 share over-allotment option is not exercised. Percentage is based on total shares to be outstanding after this offering.

(3) Arthur Ortenberg and Elisabeth Claiborne Ortenberg are husband and wife; each disclaims beneficial ownership of all shares owned by the other.

EXHIBIT 5   *(concluded)*

Name and Address	Ownership of Common Stock prior to Offering (1)		Shares to be Sold (2)	Ownership of Common Stock after Offering (1)(2)	
	Number of Shares	*Percent*		*Number of Shares*	*Percent*
Joseph Gaumont 200 E. 57th Street New York, NY	227,500	7.26	58,425	169,075	4.86
Charness Family Investments Ltd. 2 St. Clair Avenue, East Toronto, Canada	162,500	5.18	41,733	120,767	3.47
Catway Investments Ltd.	97,500	3.11	25,040	72,460	2.08
Albert Fink Milton	97,500	3.11	25,040	72,460	2.08
Elizabeth Fenner Milton	65,000	2.07	16,693	48,307	1.39
Albert Fenner Milton, Custodian, F/B/O Elizabeth Hunt Milton under the Uniform Gifts to Minors Act	9,750	0.31	8,346	1,404	0.04
Jerome Gold	65,000	2.07	16,693	48,307	1.39
Martin J. Tandler	65,000	2.07	16,693	48,307	1.39
Jacob Rosenbaum	40,625	1.30	10,433	30,192	0.87
Belle Rosenbaum	40,625	1.30	10,433	30,192	0.87
Theodore Brodie	40,625	1.30	10,433	30,192	0.87
Simmi Brodie	40,625	1.30	10,433	30,192	0.87
All officers and directors as a group (7 persons)	2,159,560	68.90	554,605	1,604,955	46.13

ONSET VENTURES

Terry Opdendyk scooped a stack of files off his desk and loaded them into his briefcase. As he did so, he was careful to include materials he would need to think through several significant issues that faced ONSET Ventures, the venture capital firm of which he was a founding partner. It was a Friday afternoon in July of 1997, and ONSET was in the midst of raising an $80 million fund—its fourth and largest to date. Terry was proud of what ONSET had achieved over the past 13 years, since its initial $5 million fund. The firm had become known as a top-tier seed investor in the major leagues of Silicon Valley Venture Capital (VC) firms. It had an enviable deal flow, and its limited partners had "re-upped" for the new fund in only nine days. Indeed, they had made commitments for $140 million, significantly more than the partners wanted to raise.

ONSET had been founded on a well-thought-out analysis of the VC industry and operated according to strict principles that its partners had articulated and refined over the years. But, the VC business was changing, and Terry wanted to be sure ONSET's strategy evolved in an intelligent manner along with the industry. Thus, one of the issues he and his partners had to resolve related to whether the fund should raise more money than they had originally decided upon.

Finally ONSET's partners faced an additional issue related to investing some of the funds that remained in ONSET II, the previous fund. ONSET had been "incubating" an interesting investment opportunity: A team of entrepreneurs had been working to develop a new software for managing sales force compensation. This company—TallyUp—had been in incubation for about a year, under the

Senior Researcher Nicole Tempest and Lecturer Michael J. Roberts prepared this case at the HBS California Research Center as the basis for class discussion rather than to illustrate either effective or ineffective handling of an administrative situation.

sponsorship of ONSET partner Darlene Mann. The team and business model had come together during this time, but the Company had not achieved all of the objectives ONSET had set when the original seed financing of $1 million had been provided in December 1996. Specifically, TallyUp had not yet developed a "beta" version of the software product. Thus, the partners at ONSET needed to decide whether to invest an additional $1 million round of seed-level financing in TallyUp or to bring the company—in its current state of development—to more traditional VCs for follow-on first round funding.

Opdendyk waved to Mann as he walked through ONSET's offices and headed home for the weekend. "See you Monday," he said, looking forward to the partners' meeting where they would discuss both how much money they should accept for ONSET's latest fund, and what financing approach they should advocate for TallyUp.

Background

ONSET was founded in 1984 as a seed stage venture fund. The first fund—simply called ONSET—had been raised by Opdendyk and David Kelley in 1984. This was a $5 million "feeder" fund that had been financed by three later-stage capital firms and 31 CEOs and entrepreneurs. The purpose of the "feeder" fund was to make seed stage investments that would move up the "food chain" to the three later-stage VC firms for follow-on financing. From 1984 through 1989, Terry, David Kelley, and later, Rob Kuhling, honed the seed stage strategies that were to become the basis for later funds.

Following this first fund, a $30 million fund—ONSET—was raised in 1989. ONSET II, a $67 million fund, was raised in 1994. By mid-1997, two-thirds of that capital had been invested in seed and follow-on investments, and the principals were reserving the remainder of the funds in ONSET II for follow-on investments in businesses already funded. Thus, ONSET was seeking to raise its fourth fund—and its largest fund to date. The partners had decided to seek a minimum of $80 million of capital and a maximum of $95 million.

(See **Exhibit 1** for excerpts from ONSET III offering memorandum that describe the investment history and performance of ONSET I and II, as well as a more detailed description of ONSET III.)

ONSET Ventures: Strategic Foundation

Opdendyk had a master's degree in computer science, and had joined Hewlett-Packard as a software engineer in 1970. Three years later he left to join Intel, and after seven years there, he became president of Visicorp, one of the early successes in the personal software industry (e.g., "Visicalc," one of the first spreadsheet programs). Upon leaving Visicorp in 1984, Opdendyk was intrigued with the process of starting and growing a new business. Thus, he decided to undertake a systematic study of how this process worked, at least as practiced by venture capitalists.

> We knew that only 1 percent of the businesses that sought VC funding actually obtained it. And, of those companies that did get funded, less than 25 percent succeeded in the first financing. We wanted to see if we could figure out if there were any principles that explained which companies were successful.

Opdendyk and his partners interested several large and successful VC firms in an investigation of these issues. These firms opened their records for a confidential study of 300 separate investments that were included in their portfolios. Opdendyk explained the principles that were distilled from the analysis:

> First, if you had a full-time mentor who was not part of the company's management team, and who had actually run both a start-up *and* a larger business, the success rate increased from less than 25 percent to over 80 percent. Genentech, Compaq, Lotus, all fit this model. Certain venture capitalists had this skill set, and were willing to invest the time to add this level of value. It was clear that if VC partners defined their relationship with a company as a personal commitment rather than simply as a portfolio investment they simply did not let most failures happen.
>
> The second principle related to whether or not the business continued operating on its initial business model. It turned out that this was a good way to fail. The successful companies always *changed* their business model as they progressed; a business plan is great, but only the market will tell you if you have a business model that really works. You need to be sensitive to what the market is telling you, and adapt. And you have to do this continuously.
>
> Third, it makes sense to wait until the business model is validated before hiring the CEO. If the CEO is hired before the business model is refined, you will get the business model that the individual used in their last job. If you wait until you have refined the business model through several iterations you have a much better shot at choosing a person who can really execute that model.
>
> Fourth, you spend money *only* to add value as perceived by those individuals providing the next round of investment capital. Once you get to cash flow positive, you have the luxury of focusing solely on the operating tasks of the business—those activities that generate revenues and profits, But, until you get there, you are dependent upon the next set of investors to survive. So, also you need to focus as well on what will add value in *their* eyes.
>
> Fifth, there has to be a want, not just a need, for the product. The company needs to have a unique reason to succeed. During the early years of a business, it is very difficult to change the way that potential customers think. You need to find an immediate source of pain that people will pay to eliminate. For example, when Lotus 123 came out, it was a more sophisticated product than Visicalc—it integrated database, graphic, and spreadsheet tools. But the reason it was successful was that the product had variable column widths. Financial analysts were screaming for variable column width, and Lotus had it; they made the pain disappear.
>
> Finally, only special people make a special business. You simply cannot compete successfully with larger, established companies if you have ordinary people.

ONSET in 1997

Based on these ideas, ONSET was founded in 1984. The firm evolved over the next dozen years, and refined the principles articulated above. As of mid-1997, ONSET had offices in both Silicon Valley and Austin, Texas. It had 4 partners, and had invested in 47 companies. Given the importance of experienced mentors in the ONSET model, the firm had no junior-level personnel (see **Exhibit 1, Appendix C** for ONSET partners' resumes). Opdendyk observed: "When you look at what we are doing during the incubation process, we are often serving as the CEO. You need people who have actually run a business to do this effectively and credibly."

The process of refining ONSET's business principles had led to the development of the firm's incubation process. This was a series of steps through which business ideas were developed, refined, and ultimately pursued; or alternatively, rejected. There were two distinct phases to the incubation process: "pre-seed," which referred to the stage prior to a funding commitment, and "seed," after a financing.

The Incubation Process: Pre-Seed Phase

The pre-seed stage referred to the stage during which a partner from ONSET worked with an entrepreneur or team, trying to decide if their business concept could be the basis of an attractive investment. During this phase, ONSET attempted to discern the assumptions that lay behind the business proposition, as well as the analysis that could be done to determine the merit of those assumptions. The issue was whether ONSET could spend a "reasonable" amount of money—approximately $1 million—to substantially reduce the risk. As Rob Kuhling, an ONSET partner described it:

> The basic principle of what we do is to take as much risk out of the equation for as little money as possible in as short a period of time as we can. This means something different each time, depending on the business model and the industry. In medical devices, the early risk reduction points are proving that the technology works in animals, proving it works in humans, and then demonstrating that it can obtain FDA approval.

Another dimension of the pre-seed analysis concerned the people involved: Were the entrepreneur and the team up to the task? Opdendyk described how ONSET addressed this issue:

> We work with the founders, trying to gauge their skills and temperament. One of the key hurdles is the "would you rather be rich, or would you rather be king?" test. When we start working with an entrepreneur, they are in the selling mode. But, usually, after a few meetings, they get more comfortable talking about the problems they see, rather than simply trying to convince us to invest. This is a key step. They have to demonstrate that they are willing to learn and adapt, not just take our money and charge ahead with their original business plan.

We also assume that we may need a new CEO. Fifteen years ago, we took for granted the ability to find the person we wanted. Now, talent is so scarce in the Valley that we need to be more confident of getting the right person. Now, before we are willing to go into the seed stage, we need to have some sense of who the individual is, and also that we will be able to get a headhunter to sign up for the job.

You might ask, "What about the entrepreneur who comes through the door with the business idea—isn't he or she the CEO?" Well, we have learned that they are often not the right person. We are up-front with everyone who comes to us about the process. Most people think that they will be the exception to the rule, and there *are* exceptions. What usually happens is that we ask the founding team to do some piece of analysis to help refine the business model—to pull apart the value chain and see what elements of the business are really crucial. Well, the team comes back a few days later and asks for help; they haven't made much progress. So, we help them do it. And then, there is another assignment, and they ask for more help. And after a few iterations, they ask, "Can you get someone full-time to help us—this is just what we need." And we say, "That person would be a CEO." And they get the idea. Often, we will push them to wait beyond that point, because we want the business model better defined; this helps us articulate exactly the kind of CEO we need. And this is a luxury we can afford because of the role that we are willing to play in the process. The key to playing this role credibly is to add value in every single meeting we have with the entrepreneurs. Sometimes, we get part way down this path, and it is clear that it is not working. And we have to be willing to walk away.

In addition to the work described above, ONSET also talked to both potential customers and other venture capitalists during this phase. In discussions with customers, ONSET was trying to get a feel for whether "the dogs will eat the dog food." And, meetings with VCs were aimed at discerning what would be required to add value in the eyes of those who would be providing the next round of financing, assuming ONSET decided to fund the seed stage. The output of a successful pre-seed analysis was an incubation plan that described the analysis that would be undertaken during the seed stage, as well as the milestones the team would meet.

The Incubation Process: Seed Phase

Opdendyk described how the process unfolded once ONSET made a financing commitment:

Once we write the check—usually about $1 million—we are in the seed stage. We start to work on the incubation plan that was the output of the pre-seed process. We attack the issues where the business model seems most vulnerable.

We have developed a process to ensure that we are adding real value during this process called "projection and reflection." We go to the venture funds whom we think would make good first or second round investors and tell them what we plan on accomplishing during incubation. We ask them what the business would be worth in a financing if we actually reach those objectives, and then we do the math. Simply put, we know what kind of step-up in value we need to make our internal hurdle rates. On a classic seed stage investment it is 2.5x. So if the VCs will value it at $5 million pre-money at our milestone, and if it will take $1 million of capital to get there, then we know how much we can pay in the seed stage. Almost every time we do this with a potential investment, the initial answer is that you can't get there from here. We need to reengineer the model, either make it worth more, or get there with less money.

As an example of what can go wrong when we do not think carefully about this, we had a seed stage company whose plan included spending $500,000 to get an ASIC (chip design) done. Well, all the potential VC investors believed that this was an easily accomplished task—they never saw any risk in it. So the fact that we did it did not raise the value of the company in their eyes.

By going to other VCs early, we quickly validate what the most significant risk is. It's usually one of five issues: the technical risk (will the technology work?); market risk (are there enough customers?); operating risk (can we actually build it for the required cost?); distribution & pricing (is there a distribution channel that will get the product to the customer cost effectively?); and, finally, the team (can they execute?).

Rob Kuhling described the lessons he'd gleaned from years of going through ONSET's incubation process:

Initially, when I started looking at venture investments, I thought that a solid "business strategy" was the most important determinant of success. Maybe this isn't surprising, given my background at BCG. Later, I thought the key was proprietary technology, because it gave you time to make the inevitable mistakes, and fix the strategy that was often off the mark. Now, I think it is the people. The skills and energy of the entrepreneur can make even a mediocre idea a success, but average people will ruin even a good idea. If a team walks through the door, and it is populated with second-rate people, I have learned that it is just too much work to drag them up the hill. My time has a significant opportunity cost, given the number of deals we can do. Unless the idea is so big and so powerful that it could be an absolutely huge hit, it just isn't worth the sacrifice of committing the time and energy to a mediocre team.

The Venture Capital Industry in 1997

In July of 1997, as ONSET was raising the capital for ONSET III, the venture capital industry was in the midst of an extraordinary year. High returns on VC investments had caused limited partners to put more and more money into venture capital and private equity investments. Venture capital firms with reputations for high returns were in the best position to compete for these funds, and the economics of the business provided a significant incentive to create larger and larger funds. Thus, by mid-1997, the size of the average VC fund had increased 40 percent: from $50 million in 1996 to $71 million. (Source: *Venture Capital Journal,* February 1997.) There were several consequences to this infusion of money. The VC firms were forced to bring new employees into the business to do some of the work. In 1997, for instance, 72 graduating MBAs from HBS—8 percent of the graduating class—found jobs at VC/private equity firms. (For other summary statistics on the venture capital industry, see **Exhibit 2.**)

The active state of the IPO market from 1995 to 1997 was a further boost to the VC market, as investments became liquid more quickly and at high multiples, improving returns to investors. Thus, by many measures the timing of ONSET's entry into the market for ONSET III could hardly have been better.

Economics of ONSET's Business

Over time, ONSET refined its incubation process in order to build on practices that were most likely to generate the high returns (IRR) that would attract investors for future rounds, as well as reward the ONSET partners themselves. Opdendyk described some of the key economic dimensions of the business:

> Our bare minimum target rate of return—at the fund level—is a 30 percent IRR over a 12-year cycle. This translates into higher numbers for individual investments, in order to cover fees, expenses, and the General Partners' carried interest. Given standard investment liquidity cycle times, this implies a 2.5x step-up in the seed to first round, a 2.0x step up from the first to second round, and a 1.5x step-up in the second to third round. We assume about a year between these "steps." If you look at our last fund, we invested in 18 companies. We have four partners, and the "investing" life of a fund is about four years. So, we are basically incubating one company per year per partner. With the kind of intensive work we do with a company, it is hard to do more. On average, we put in about $4.5 million per company: $1 million in the seed round, $1.5 in the second, $2 million in the third. Even though we are putting in more money per round, valuation is going up by a sufficient amount that we are not staying even with our original ownership position. Interestingly, people have looked hard at the numbers in terms of what you need to do to get the full benefits of "diversification" in a portfolio. It turns out that once you get to 10 companies, you have almost all of the diversification you can get. Any more, and you really have very little benefit to show for it.
>
> When you look at the economics, you will understand a fatal flaw of our fist fund. We teamed up with three of the premier VC firms in the Valley. We had a $5 million fund, and we did the seed round, and they had the right to do the future rounds. They had no obligation to let us put any money in on anything but the seed round. At their option, we could invest in follow-on rounds. But we only got this opportunity when they didn't fully subscribe for the company's financing. Well, they did 100% of the A and B level deals, and we only got to do the C & D level deals. This skewed our returns badly, and we gave up on that strategy and went out on our own.
>
> Now, the fact that we control deal flow is a huge plus for us. We usually do 100% of the seed stage for any company we back. This is a hard round to share. We like to say, "It's tough having more than one chef in the kitchen when you don't know what the recipe is yet." Once you know the recipe, you get some leverage from multiple chefs, but before that all you get is confusion.
>
> Yet, because we are so dependent on the seed round—and because of our philosophy—we are vulnerable to local "irrationality" in deal pricing. We believe that each round has to stand on its own. You can't do a bad deal in the seed round and hope to fix the problem in later rounds. If a big venture fund decides that they don't have the deal flow they want, they can decide to pay what we think of as an "uneconomic price" in the seed round, and hope to make it up in later stages. This is one of the reasons why we opened an office in Austin. We decided that having a presence in multiple markets would diversify the risk of pricing abnormalities in a single market.

ONSET had developed some "rules of thumb" which the partners believed would help the firm meet its return targets. Opdendyk explained:

- We will not lead a start-up in an industry where we don't have the ability to reinvent a business model. If we haven't led a deal in a segment before, we won't try to learn that segment by leading a start-up.

- We will only invest in a deal where we have a local presence. We've learned that if we are not in close touch with the company, it is much harder to add value.

- In general, if a company needs more than $30 million of private capital then it is not an opportunity for us. We will simply suffer too much dilution at the back end to make it worth our while.

- We will not invest in a deal that is "under the spotlights." There are certain industry segments that everyone is chasing, where—we believe—other investors are likely to make irrational decisions about valuations and financing size. We'd rather play off to the side a bit, and give ourselves a chance to make a few mistakes.

ONSET's returns were, of course, influenced by its strategy of focusing on seed stage investments. The exhibit below describes private equity returns by type of investment.

Limited Partner Returns by Stage of VC Investment

Year	Seed	Early	Balanced	Later	All Venture
1981	5.60%	33.70%	16.40%	17.40%	19.00%
1982	−18.70	57.00	27.40	25.50	32.20
1983	20.50	61.40	35.30	37.50	40.00
1984	−9.50	−6.20	−2.70	−3.50	−3.40
1985	−9.10	−5.60	2.50	2.00	1.20
1986	5.10	5.20	8.90	1.70	8.00
1987	4.30	8.80	6.20	15.70	7.20
1988	−1.00	−2.00	3.10	4.10	2.60
1989	7.10	−0.30	6.10	7.80	5.40
1990	6.60	5.90	0.00	5.80	1.20
1991	15.70	29.70	17.10	47.10	22.10
1992	8.10	5.30	12.80	19.40	12.70
1993	17.30	12.20	17.60	43.90	18.90
1994	14.70	13.10	13.50	12.40	14.60
1995	46.30	62.60	43.70	51.00	49.50
1996	46.70	43.60	41.00	33.70	42.10

Note: Returns are calculated on a year-by-year basis using year-end appraisals of investment values. Returns are net of fees, expenses, and carried interest. These are not fund IRRs or "class year" IRRs. Source: Venture Economics.

ONSET III: Deciding How Much Money to Raise

As ONSET II entered its third year of existence, approximately $22 million of capital remained in the fund, which the principals anticipated using primarily for later round investments in companies already in the portfolio. Thus, thoughts turned to raising a new fund— ONSET III. Opdendyk described the thought process:

As we thought about ONSET III, we naturally did some calculations. We have four partners, and we do one seed stage deal per partner per year. The average number of dollars per deal has increased over the past several years. In ONSET I it was $2.5 million, in ONSET II it was $3.5 to $4 million, and in ONSET III we anticipate $4.5 to $5 million. In part, this is due to the fact that it costs a little more just to get into business, so the seed stage investment is somewhat larger. This has also been a result of our getting more disciplined in our own approach, and doing the seed round increasingly on our own. But, for ONSET I and II, we have gone back and analyzed the data, and found that we under-invest in our winners. Our returns would have increased if we had put more money in the follow-on rounds of all of our deals. So, we anticipate that the average company in ONSET III will take a little more capital than in the past—say $5 million. If you look at the time cycle of the fund, it is 10 to 12 years. Because we are a seed fund, it takes—on average—six years from initial investment to liquidity. (Lately, due to the cycle we are in, it has taken only four years to get from seed to liquidity, but it would be unwise to count on this going forward.) Thus, if we want to shoot to close out the fund in ten years, we can make our last seed investment in year four. So, four partners times one deal per partner times $5 million per deal times four years is $80 million. If you add $10 to $15 million in expenses and fees, you get to $95 million or so. This was the upper end of the target for the amount of money we set out to raise.

When we bring new VCs in during follow-on financings, we want to add top-tier players to the deal. To do this, we have to be willing to let them invest the amount of money that makes their economics work. So, if we are doing a $5 million round, we might like to split it equally with a large venture fund. But they need to put more money in simply because their funds are so big. Some of these funds, for example, are trying to put out over $400 million per year.

When we called on our limited partners to make our pitch for $80 million for ONSET III (see excerpts, **Exhibit 1**), it only took two weeks before we had commitments for $140 million. So, now we have a decision to make. If you look around, you can certainly conclude that times are unusually good—that we should take the money because you can't be sure it will be there in four years when we go out to raise another fund. But, that raises the question of what we actually do with the money. We have thought hard about the business model we have built, and how it fits into the basic economics of the venture business. We like the niche we have staked out, and we are doing well in it. We don't want to be just another "diversified balanced" venture fund. And, it is clear that our limited partners behave like rational institutions—they all want to put their money in "top quartile" funds.

Rob Kuhling offered his perspective on the decision confronting the partners:

Seed stage is where we want to play. While there are periods during a business cycle where seed stage investments perform less well than other stages, generally, over time, seed stage provides a better return. The other round that historically does well is the round closest to the liquidity event, and this is driven more by the short time horizon to liquidity as it is by the multiple you are getting on your investment. But, it is very tough to play in *just* this round—you usually need to be in the deal earlier to have the opportunity to invest in this round.

ONSET III: The TallyUp Decision

In addition to deciding how much capital to raise in ONSET III, the partners at ONSET needed to make a decision about one of the companies that had been seeded in ONSET II—TallyUp. Darlene Mann, a partner at ONSET, had been working closely with TallyUp since August, 1996. She described the issues that ONSET and the TallyUp management team faced:

> TallyUp is developing a new software product for use in managing complex compensation systems, like those used for a commissioned sales force. Our original incubation plan called for them to hit a number of key milestones, and then go out and raise a first round of traditional VC money. Well, we've spent the seed round capital and hit many of the key milestones, but we still do not have a product in the beta stage yet. The issue we face is whether ONSET should invest an additional $1,000,000 to enable TallyUp to develop its beta product, and hold off on raising the first round of venture funding from traditional VCs until the product is ready in mid-1998, or go out to the market now to raise $3-$4 million and use the money for both product development and sales and marketing. And, if we do proceed now with a round of outside financing, what is the appropriate valuation for TallyUp?

TallyUp Company Background

Andy Swett, the co-founder of TallyUp, was introduced to Mann, a partner at ONSET, through a mutual friend in August 1996. Mann reflected on their early meetings:

> When Andy first came to ONSET, he described his business idea as a billing system for service and content providers on the Internet. With the rapid growth of small companies doing business over the Internet he believed there was a real need for an inexpensive billing system since the existing systems in the market cost on the order of $500,000. Based on my experience in the software industry I didn't think there was a sufficient market for the product, but I was very impressed by Andy's technical background, determined entrepreneurial personality, and his willingness to accept help. I felt that even if this was not a great product, Andy was an entrepreneur who possessed all the traits necessary for success. I suggested that Andy work with a consultant, Scott Kitayama—who later joined Andy as co-founder of TallyUp—to validate his business idea, using a loan from ONSET to pay the consulting fees. This study quickly concluded that there was not yet a sufficient market for an Internet billing system. However, I was still very intrigued by the settlements technology which was at the core of Andy's product and we brainstormed about the various business opportunities which could leverage this technology.

Swett reflected on this period:

> I though ONSET was going to bail out after the Internet billing system idea didn't work out. That's what I expected from a venture capital firm. But, ONSET was different—they stuck with us through this period while we came up with the next idea.

Mann continued:

> Based on these brainstorming sessions, Andy came up with the idea for a sales force compensation system. Having previously been a VP of Sales, I knew there was a real need for a product like this. However, to better understand the level of market demand, we interviewed over 25 companies to determine what systems they were cur-

rently using and what issues they were facing. We found that these companies were spending $100,000 to $200,000 per year on managing the administration of sales force compensation, and would be willing to pay hundreds of thousands of dollars for a sales force compensation system without blinking. We were very encouraged and decided to move ahead with the idea.

Collectively, Andy, Scott, and I sat down to determine what questions needed to be answered and what issues needed to be addressed before ONSET would invest the seed capital required to get started. Two critical issues quickly surfaced.

First, we needed an expert in the compensation field to work with us on product design, to set-up and lead discussions with potential users, and to give TallyUp credibility with customers. However, we were not prepared to bring someone on full time at this stage, so the person had to be willing to serve in a consulting role. We interviewed about 30 people and identified one, Jim Finkelstein, who would be an excellent fit for the company. Jim had been the director of compensation at PepsiCola and a compensation consultant at Towers Perrin before starting his own compensation consulting practice. The fact that he had his own practice worked well for us because he could work with us on a part-time basis and with his own clients the rest of the time. We negotiated a deal with Jim where he would be paid partly in cash and partly with both participation-based and milestone-driven equity. ONSET's role in the interviewing process was critical since we lent credibility to the team and the business model.

The second question we had to answer was whether we could design a sales force compensation system that could be an off-the-shelf product. Many of the potential customers we interviewed expressed the view that compensation plans were too complex and varied too widely between companies to be supported by a standardized product. However, as we dug deeper, we learned that in reality there were only so many different compensation methods with the real variability revolving around the percentage commission, the number and type of distribution channels used, the complexity of products offered, and overall size of the sales force. So, using the latest rules-based technology we could capture this in an off-the-shelf product.

Incubating TallyUp

By December 1996, the team had developed an operating plan (see **Exhibit 3** for excerpts from the operating plan) and ONSET invested $750,000 to purchase preferred shares (at $1 each), in return for 31.5 percent of the company, based on a $2,375,000 post-money valuation. The agreement was structured so that ONSET would later invest an additional $250,000—at the same $1 per share price—to further help the company accomplish its key milestones, if needed. The company elected a board of directors, which included Mann, Swett, and Terry Opdendyk, with the agreement that Terry would turn over his board seat to the new CEO when he or she was hired. In addition, ONSET also required that they play a role in all substantive decisions, such as hiring senior staff and purchasing capital equipment. However, on a day-to-day basis, ONSET's involvement primarily focused on the team's work plan.

Once ONSET invested, the real incubation process began. Mann acted in a day-to-day CEO role for TallyUp working to achieve the five goals that she and the management team had established:

- Validate, size, and segment the market;
- Bring the product to the beta stage;
- Develop the business plan;
- Hire a top-flight CEO; and
- Bring in 2 to 3 development partners who would put in money in return for early access to a sales force compensation system designed with their requirements in mind.

Mann reflected on how the plan helped them minimize risk:

> In every new business there's technical risk and market risk. We did not feel that the technical risk centered on *whether* the product could be built, but rather *what* product was built—what customer needs it addressed. We felt the technical risk was really on the execution side. In terms of market risk, our biggest concern was whether the market was large enough. In order to minimize both of these risks, we invested significant time and resources into market research. As we interviewed companies to gain a better understanding of the market and their specific needs, we also marketed our product idea in hopes of attracting at least two corporate partners with whom we could develop a product. We were successful in attracting two paying development partners. This reduced the risk for us; not only were they putting their own capital at risk, but serious, paying customers helped us attract the attention of the venture capital community.

Kitayama, now serving as vice president of marketing, reflected on ONSET's role in the process:

> ONSET kept putting manageable hurdles in front of us—these took the form of questions we needed to answer before proceeding. It made it tough at times, but it also gave us a clear roadmap for what we needed to focus on. For example, ONSET believed that either you develop a $500 product and sell hundreds of thousands of them through the retail channel or you develop a $100,000 product that you sell through a direct sales force. Anything in the middle is purgatory. So we had to prove that our product could be priced at, or above, $100,000.

The team worked on several of the goals in parallel: Kitayama and Mann focused on developing a detailed understanding of the market, while Swett pushed forward on product design. Early on, it became clear that to tackle both these issues they needed to get access to potential customers to understand their needs in detail. They set up 31 one-on-one interviews with potential customers to determine how the sales force compensation function was currently being handled and what a technical solution could possibly look like. Mann reflected on their findings:

> We talked with CFOs, directors of compensation, and sales managers and the answer came back the same—the administration of compensation plans is a real headache. It's a highly time-consuming and unproductive process. Most companies have one administrative person per 50 sales people and that person spends most of his or her time pouring over spreadsheets trying to understand the discrepancies between what the salespeople had been paid and what they thought they should have been paid. Furthermore, many of these companies would rebuild their system each year as the compensation plans changed. There was clearly a need for a system that streamlined

this whole process. We discovered that the early adopters would be companies in the high-tech and financial services industries since their distribution capabilities created complicated sales environments.

Mann also sounded out four venture capital firms as part of ONSET's projection and reflection process to determine the risks that they perceived. Mann found that the venture capital firms were most concerned with who the CEO would be and whether the market was large enough to justify an investment. Since the market size issue came up several times during their discussions, the TallyUp team dedicated a significant amount of time to studying the market in order to develop a fact-based estimate of its size. The team estimated the market for replacing existing dedicated sales force compensation systems to be around $400 million. However, when the market was expanded to include all variable-based incentive plans, the team estimated the size of this larger market at $1.5 to $2.0 billion.

In 1996, 7.6 percent of all exempt employees in the United States were paid based on variable compensation plans and the trend was accelerating: Incentive compensation was becoming popular at more companies and at lower levels of these organizations.[1] This large and growing market had naturally attracted the attention of several major software firms, including Oracle, SAP, and Peoplesoft. Some of these firms were developing applications targeted towards the same market as TallyUp's product. The TallyUp team believed that its product was superior, and that they had a lead in developing an offering for the market which they needed to protect by moving quickly.

Hiring a CEO

In keeping with ONSET's key principles, Mann and TallyUp held off on hiring a CEO until they had completed their extensive market research to validate the attractiveness of the market and understand the nature of the business opportunity. As was frequently the case with start-ups, it was clear early on that TallyUp would need to bring in a CEO from the outside. Mann described how ONSET dealt with this issue:

> We always have conversations with the founders up front about their positions in the company. We don't invest if the founders don't understand that they may not have their current positions in the future. In fact, the more successful the company is, the less likely it is that they'll keep the role they began with.

Swett reflected on ONSET's role in the recruiting process:

> At the time we were looking for a CEO, there were 300 CEO searches going on in the valley and only 150 of those got the attention of an executive recruiter. ONSET's relationship with an executive recruiter, who they keep on a retainer basis, was a tremendous advantage to us since finding the right CEO was a make-or-break decision for us.

---

[1]*Compensation and Benefits Review,* September/October 1996.

The team's investment in market research and in the development of a compelling business concept enabled them to successfully attract an experienced software executive to be the CEO of TallyUp. Mann considered this to be a major victory given the shortage of senior leadership talent in Silicon Valley. TallyUp's new CEO—Reed Taussig—came to the company after having served as the SVP of Worldwide Operations for Unify Corporation and SVP of Sales and Marketing for Gupta, both database tools companies, and most recently had founded an Internet company, named inquiry.com. Taussig reflected on his decision to join TallyUp:

> I was looking for an opportunity with a company with a very clear value proposition. Software companies were spending 10 percent to 12 percent of revenue on the administration of compensation plans and those dollars were mostly going towards developing and maintaining complex Excel spreadsheets. That was a very compelling value proposition for me.

Once Taussig was hired, ONSET invested the additional $250,000 they had planned to put in, raising TallyUp's (post-money) valuation to $2,625,000.

Decisions Ahead

Conducting market research and hiring a CEO had taken almost nine months. This was longer than the team had planned. It had also cost TallyUp most of the $1,000,000 in capital they had raised from ONSET. Mann reflected on the decision to spend the money on developing a solid understanding of the market versus building the product:

> It's an interesting question: Do you spend the initial money on building the product or developing the business model? A lot of venture firms and entrepreneurs will build the product first, then refine the business model. However, at ONSET, if we are fairly confident that a product can be built, which is generally the case for software these days, then we'll focus our efforts on reducing the market and execution risk. The way we like to work is to spend $1,000,000 or less to understand the business and determine *how* to build the product. The question really comes down to whether you prefer market risk or technical risk—is your bias toward how the business model is formulated or how the product is developed? In this case, we were more worried about the market and the business model.

Thus, in November of 1997, ONSET and TallyUp needed to decide whether ONSET should invest an additional $1,000,000 into TallyUp to develop a beta version of the product, or whether TallyUp should go out to the venture capital community at the current stage—without a product—to raise $3 to $4 million for product development and product launch.

Mann explained why $1 million was needed to complete the beta product, when this figure was equal to the amount of TallyUp's entire initial funding:

> Given the growth in the organization and the need to support both existing development partners and sales to new customers, the company would require an additional $1 million to get to the beta stage while supporting baseline marketing and sales capabilities.

Mann knew that either option would raise difficult choices:

A beta product would certainly raise TallyUp's valuation by at least the $1,000,000 it would cost to develop the product. If we go this route, ONSET would likely be the sole investor and we'd get tangled in a discussion with management over the valuation in this interim round. On the other hand, securing first-round VC financing would be a lengthy and all-consuming process for the management team, and I worried about the impact this would have on the momentum the team had generated coming out of their intensive market research process. I'd also be concerned that Taussig—with so little experience at the company—might have a tough time selling the concept, without a product, to the venture capital community.

Mann was optimistic that—if TallyUp went to market for $3 to $4 million of VC now, without a beta product—the venture capital firms would be very interested. She based this view partly on the sense that the VC market was "hot"—who knew if the money would be available in six months? Finally, there was the issue of time. Given the looming presence of some of the larger software companies in this segment, Mann was eager to get to market as soon as possible. Was she better off recommending the company raise the money now and getting this phase behind them, so that the team could concentrate on getting a product to market without interruption?

Mann knew there were many criteria to consider in determining the valuation for TallyUp if they went forward with the outside financing now. First, TallyUp had decided to set aside a portion of shares to be used as stock options for new employees hired. The value of these options would likely be $750,000 (750,000 shares at $1 per share), which would increase TallyUp's valuation by the same amount. Second, she knew that ONSET's business model called for a 2 to 3 times step-up in valuation from the seed stage (from a base which now included the value of the stock option pool). Third, she knew that in a first round financing of this nature, venture firms would want a 15 percent to 20 percent ownership stake (post their investment). Finally, she knew that ideally, ONSET wanted to invest 50 percent of the $3 to $4 million raised.

"Have a good weekend Terry," Mann called out to Opdendyk as he headed out the door. She turned her attention to the stack of files on her own desk. Mann wondered whether she should advocate outside VC financing for Tally-Up, and if so, on what terms? How much of this financing should she recommend ONSET itself provide?

EXHIBIT 1   Excerpts from ONSET III Investment Memorandum

Table of Contents

Summary of Terms

Overview

Offering Description

Appendices

*Included.

Overview

Investment Focus

Like its predecessor funds, ONSET III will distinguish itself from other venture capital funds by its investment focus. First, ONSET III will focus on initial and follow-on investments in seed stage projects, because excellent returns are possible from such investments. Second, ONSET III will increase seed stage company success rates by investing the partners' time, skills, and resources using the Partnership's proven value-added incubation and development methodology. Third, ONSET III will primarily invest in technology-based companies that match the partners' experience and ability to add value. Fourth, ONSET III will locate most of its companies in Northern California and Austin, Texas, to facilitate the ability of the partners to work closely with the companies as they develop.

Seed-Stage Investments

ONSET III will target seed stage projects because the returns from successful seed stage investments can be several times higher than later-stage investments. Even though the potential for higher returns is generally recognized, relatively few venture capital funds focus primarily on such investments, mostly because successfully managing the risks of seed stage investments demands more from the investment management team than the traditional monitoring approach used for later-stage investments. Selecting the targets requires greater care and investment discipline, and implementing the supportive incubation process requires more experience and hands-on, day-to-day involvement. This underserved investment segment creates an opportunity for ONSET II, a venture fund focused on and capable of developing seed stage companies.

Selecting seed stage projects requires great skill. All ventures will be evaluated on not only the merits of technology, but also on how well the incubation process can offset the risks. For example, ONSET III will seek projects that it can develop into companies that:

- have excellent personnel,
- can be the leaders in their markets,
- are in emerging growth markets,
- have proprietary product technology with compelling competitive advantages,
- have clear return on investment leverage,
- can be financed easily after a successful seed financing,
- require moderate amounts of capital, and
- have the types of risks that can be mitigated during the incubation stage.

However, at the point ONSET III will make its initial investment decision, a project may be little more than an intriguing idea, an exciting technology, or a capable entrepreneur. Such projects generally lack one or more key elements that traditional venture investors look for and that are necessary for eventual success. For example, a seed project will often have one or more of the following characteristics:

- an unproven technology,
- incomplete marketing and distribution plans,
- inadequate business and operational plans, and
- an incomplete or inadequate management team.

ONSET III is structured through its proven incubation process to provide the expertise and attention necessary to assist its seed projects in overcoming these inadequacies.

The Incubation Process

The incubation process to be employed by ONSET III was developed by its predecessor funds and the general partner organization. The ONSET Ventures' incubation process and its importance to ONSET III's investment strategy have already been described briefly. But how does it really operate?

The incubation process will often begin prior to ONSET III making an investment commitment. When an idea, technology, or entrepreneur shows promise, the first step is to explore fully the opportunity. To do so, ONSET III often will locate the entrepreneur in its Menlo Park or Austin facility. The exploration process may last months and will involve the equivalent of one full-time partner. In some cases, small amounts of capital may be used to finance particular exploration goals prior to a formal seed financing, further ensuring the viability of the business and reducing investment risk. ONSET III will make its seed stage financing commitment only after both the entrepreneurial team and ONSET III are convinced of the project's potential and appropriateness for the ONSET ventures' incubation process.

The second step is to articulate clearly and agree on what should be accomplished during the incubation. Once the goals are articulated, ONSET III's partners (generally acting as interim officers of the company), the company's management, and other professionals work together as a team to accomplish the goals.

Typically, the incubation process takes 6 to 12 months. The process ends when the company is sound enough to succeed without the support structure provided by ONSET Ventures and is able to attract traditional venture capital financing. By the end of the process, most companies will have:

- proven the technology,
- demonstrated the project concept and design,

- positioned the product (and the company) in the marketplace,
- developed strategic and operational plans to reflect a viable business model, and
- completed its management team.

The final step in the incubation process is to provide for future funding of the successful seed company. The Partnership will organize a syndicate of other venture capital funds to participate with ONSET III in funding the next stage, usually known as first-round financing. This downstream financing syndication is a critical element in the success of seed stage investing. ONSET III will typically introduce projects in their earliest stages to other major venture firms (including the more than 40 firms that have co-invested with earlier ONSET Ventures' funds) to facilitate first-round investment. Upon completion of the financing, the company will have successfully emerged from the incubation phase and established a more conventional venture capital relationship with ONSET III.

ONSET Ventures' Incubation Process

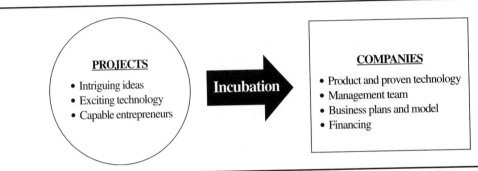

Value-added Approach

As a company transitions from the incubation phase to independent operation, the ONSET Ventures' partners will remain active on the company's board and will continue to be involved throughout the company's development. The principals of ONSET Ventures couple their past experiences as operating executives in both small and large businesses with a personal commitment to achieving success in each portfolio company.

Technology-based Industries

ONSET III will target seed investments in high-technology industries (particularly computer software and hardware, communications products and services, pharmaceuticals delivery, and medical devices and instrumentation) for several reasons. First, companies based on an advanced technology usually have significant early risks that ONSET Ventures and the project team can reduce during the incubation process, substantially increasing the companies' chances of success and value. Second, companies in technology-based industries often have many of the desired investment characteristics described above in "Seed-Stage Investments." Finally, the partners have extensive investment and managerial experience in technology businesses in these areas.

Northern California and Texas Focus

Most of ONSET IIIs projects will be in Northern California or Texas, often initially located in ONSET Ventures' facilities in Menlo Park or Austin. The incubation process requires that the project team and the general partners work together closely on a frequent basis. Locating the process in or near ONSET Ventures' offices facilitates this interaction.

Key Success Factors

To be successful, a seed stage venture capital fund must:

- be exposed to a flow of high-quality investment opportunities,
- be selective in its investments,

- provide focus, guidance, and managerial assistance to its seed projects,
- have access to capital for follow-on company financings, and
- provide ongoing company monitoring and guidance.

ONSET III has the expertise, commitment, and structure to address these requirements.

Exposure to Investment Opportunities

ONSET III will have several advantages in exposure to high-quality investment opportunities:

- The partners of the General Partner have developed relationships with entrepreneurs and executives throughout Silicon Valley through their association with existing and prior portfolio companies, other venture capital funds and prior employment at leading high-technology companies. In addition, the partners have established strong deal flow over the past three years in Austin, Texas, and are well positioned to take advantage of this burgeoning new center of entrepreneurial activity.
- Investment opportunities are frequently referred by Paul Gomory, a premier executive recruiter that maintains extensive contracts with entrepreneurial companies and the best executive talent.
- David Kelley, as president of IDEO, a prominent product design firm, and as a professor at Stanford University, has a broad network of entrepreneurial contacts that offer investment opportunities.
- ONSET Ventures' location in Silicon Valley, where more venture-backed companies are formed each year than in any other region, results in high exposure to entrepreneurial activity.
- ONSET Ventures' unique position as the first Silicon Valley venture firm to establish an office in Austin, Texas, positions the firm to be a leader in an environment with strong high-technology job formation and entrepreneurship, and limited early-stage capital availability.
- Fewer venture firms compete for the seed stage investments on which ONSET III will focus.

Careful Selection of Investments

Selecting which companies to invest in may seem an obvious critical factor in the success of seed stage venture capital funds. However, it requires looking beyond the conspicuous flaws and defects of seed stage projects to understand their potential, given adequate development, for becoming successful companies. This potential is resident in relatively few opportunities. ONSET I and ONSET II both invested in less than one percent of the potential opportunities presented to them—a model of selectivity that ONSET intends to continue.

Because uncertainties surround early-stage investments, ONSET III will often follow an incremental investment policy. That is, when a project shows promise, the Partnership will often move the project team into ONSET Ventures' incubation facility without a seed-financing commitment. The partners will then work closely with the entrepreneurs exploring the dimensions of the opportunity. When both the entrepreneurs and ONSET III are satisfied with the definition of the opportunity and have a clear understanding of what needs to be accomplished during the incubation process, the Partnership will commit to seed-round financing. Often this commitment will involve incremental funding contingent upon accomplishing agreed upon milestones.

Focus, Guidance, and Managerial Assistance

Successful entrepreneurs generally have an overriding sense of optimism, self-confidence, drive, and creativity. They are rarely individuals of broad general-managerial background. They are frequently technically oriented, possessing a particular insight. They infrequently appreciate marketing and other functional specialties necessary for company success. This is particularly true in seed stage situations.

To increase a seed stage company's chance of success, it is necessary to provide constructive counsel and value-added support during the early months of a new company's development. Typically, the Partnership will devote the equivalent of one full-time partner to working with each company. This intensive commitment limits the number of investments ONSET III will make each year but increases the likelihood that each investment will succeed.

Access to Capital for Follow-on Company Financings

Seed-stage companies often fail because they lack the ability to attract first-round financing after the seed investment. ONSET III's incubation approach in itself lessens this risk, but beyond this, ONSET Ventures also offers transitional support.

ONSET III will introduce its projects to other venture capital firms at an early stage, often before making its own investment commitment. This facilitates first-round financing by creating an understanding of the needs and desires of the later-stage investors and recognition of the need to adjust the incubation plan accordingly. The partners' knowledge of the characteristics of attractive first-round investments and the partners' contacts in the venture community lay the groundwork for a smooth transition to later financings. In fact, more than 40 different venture capital organizations have invested in the later-stage financings of ONSET Ventures-led seed stage companies.

Ongoing Company Monitoring and Guidance

Beyond the seed stage, companies still face developmental hurdles: sales ramp-up, quality manufacturing, subsequent product research and development, team building, reaching profitability, and evaluating additional financing options. ONSET III is committed to building strong boards of directors for its companies, thereby increasing the developing companies' chances of success.

ONSET III intends to maintain a significant ownership position in its companies and to contribute to their later-stage development through active participation on the boards of directors. The partners have participated in the financing and later-stage guidance and monitoring of nearly 50 companies over the last 50 years.

Prior Funds

ONSET I

ONSET I is a $30 million fund formed in late 1989 for the purpose of investing in high technology companies with a special focus on incubating seed stage investments. The general partner, ONSET Management, L.P., is managed by Rob Kuhling, Terry Opdendyk, and NEA as general partners. David Kelley is a special limited partner of the general partner. The investors of ONSET I include institutions and successful entrepreneurs and other individuals. (A list of the institutional investors can be found in **Appendix D.**)

As of March 31, 1997, ONSET I had invested $22,467,635 in 20 companies. Of these companies, eight are medical technology related, primarily drug delivery and medical devices, 12 are in information technology with a software focus.

ONSET I is over seven years old and the portfolio is mature, with distributions of $60,200,000 and a fund IRR of 26% at year end 1996. To date, eight companies are public, six have been acquired and several others are prospects for 1997–1998 acquisitions or IPOs.

The following table summarizes ONSET I's IRR performance since inception in 1989:

ONSET I Annualized Cumulative Internal Rate of Return

	1989	*1990*	*1991*	*1992*	*1993*	*1994*	*1995*	*1996*
Fund	−38.12%	−23.67%	−12.77%	1.05%	5.10%	19.11%	26.62%	26.30%
Limited partner	−38.12%	−23.67%	−12.77%	0.70%	3.87%	15.10%	22.26%	21.72%

ONSET II

ONSET II is a $67 million fund formed in late 1994 for the purpose of investing in high technology companies with a special focus on incubating seed stage investments. The general partner, ONSET II Management, L.P., is managed by Rob Kuhling, Terry Opdendyk, and Tom Winter as general partners. David Kelley, Alexis Lakes, Darlene Mann, and NEA are special limited partners of the general partner. The investors of ONSET II include institutions and successful entrepreneurs and other individuals. (A list of the institutional investors can be found in **Appendix D.**)

As of May 9, 1997, ONSET II had invested or reserved for investment $43,214,765 in 19 companies. Of these companies, seven are medical technology related, primarily medical devices and drug delivery, and twelve are in information technology with a focus on software, services, and communications. ONSET II was the initial venture investor in eight of the companies; fourteen of these were at the seed/start-up stage when ONSET Ventures made its first investment. Fourteen of the companies are located in California, mostly in the San Francisco Bay Area.

The following table summarizes ONSET II IRR performance since inception in 1994. (Given the early stage of development reflected by the majority of companies represented in the ONSET II portfolio, these numbers should be viewed as highly variable and not necessarily indicative of the long-term performance of the fund.)

ONSET II Annualized Cumulative Internal Rate of Return

	1994	1995	1996
Fund	−14.26%	−36.32%	15.49%
Limited partner	−14.26%	−36.32%	11.69%

ONSET I vs. ONSET II Comparison

The following graph compares the annualized cumulative Internal Rate of Return (IRR) of ONSET I vs. ONSET II for the same period within each fund. Note that the ONSET II IRR was substantially greater than was the ONSET I IRR at the same point (Year 2) of the fund's life.

ONSET, a California Limited Partnership ("OLP")

OLP, a company incubator, was founded in 1984 with $3 million from three venture-fund limited partners and $2 million from 31 individual investors. OLP was structured to serve as a "feeder" fund to provide later-stage financing opportunities to the venture-fund limited partners and tax advantages to the individual investors.

While OLP was not a traditional venture fund, its focus was to establish the ONSET Ventures investment approach of creating and investing in seed stage, high-technology companies lacking the completeness necessary to attract capital from traditional venture investors. It was in OLP that the ONSET Ventures' incubation process was developed and refined (see "The Incubation Process"). At this time, the fund is inactive, with one final security awaiting liquidity.

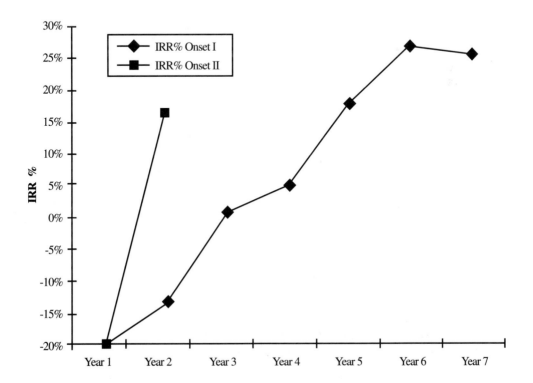

Offering Description

The Offering

ONSET III expects to raise $80 million through investment in limited partnership interests by selected investors who are capable of assuming the substantial financial risks and illiquidity of venture capital investing. The initial closing may be held when at least $60 million of committed capital has been raised. ONSET III may elect to continue this offering on the same terms and conditions for up to 12 months after the initial closing. The General Partner may increase the amount of this offering to a maximum of $95 million of Limited Partner interest.

The General Partner will contribute an amount equal to 1% of the total capital of the Partnership on the same draw-down schedule as the Limited Partners. The General Partner's capital contributions may be made either in cash or by an interest-bearing full recourse promissory note.

Allocation of Income, Gains, and Losses

Generally, all income, gains, and losses will be allocated 75% to all Partners based on the respective amounts of their capital commitments and 25% to the General Partner. However, if the Partnership has cumulative net realized losses, all income, gains, and losses will be allocated to the Partners based on the respective amounts of their capital commitments. Distributions of securities to the Partners will be treated as sales for the purpose of calculating realized gains and losses.

Investor Committee

The Partnership will have an Investor Committee consisting of at least three members chosen by the General Partner from among the Limited Partners, which will serve at the discretion of the General Partner.

The functions of the Investor Committee will be to confer with the General Partner as to the conduct of the business generally, without advising as to the merits of Partnership Investments, and to: (1) review the annual operating budget of the General Partner; (2) review certain changes in the fee paid to the General Partner and approve changes in the percentages of such fees allocated among the ONSET Ventures' partnerships; (3) review certain distributions authorized by the General Partner; (4) approve certain guarantees for the Partnership on behalf of its portfolio companies; (5) approve the values established by the General Partner for portfolio assets and liabilities; and (6) resolve questions relating to certain potential conflicts of interest between the Partnership and the General Partner or between the Partnership and ONSET I or ONSET II, including an investment by the Partnership in a portfolio company of ONSET I or ONSET II. All actions taken by the Investor Committee must be authorized by a majority of the Committee members.

APPENDIX C   Resumes

Robert F. Kuhling, Jr.

Work Experience

1987–Present
ONSET Ventures, Menlo Park, CA

General Partner, ONSET III (in formation)
General Partner, ONSET II
General Partner, ONSET I
General Partner, ONSET, a California Limited Partnership
Special Partner, New Enterprise Associates V, VI & VII
Special Partner, Chemicals and Materials Enterprise Associates, L.P.

1985–1987
SUN MICROSYSTEMS, Mountain View, CA

Director, Design Automation Marketing Group. Started up and managed Sun's entry into the design engineering markets. Responsible for marketing, technical support and sales development.

1983–1985
CALMA COMPANY (a General Electric subsidiary), Milpitas, CA

Vice-President, Electronic Design Automation Products & Marketing. Responsible for Calma's $100 million electronic CAE and CAD/CAM business including Product Development (R&D), Marketing and Sales Development.

Director, Microelectronics Marketing.

Director, Business Development.

1980–1983
THE BOSTON CONSULTING GROUP, Boston, MA and Menlo Park, CA
Case Team Leader. Managed teams of consultants developing business strategies for U.S. and international corporations. Specialized in high-technology assignments.

1972–1978
THE CHARTER COMPANY, Jacksonville, FL and Houston, TX

Assistant Vice President. Worked in several Charter divisions, including real estate finance, commercial banking and petroleum exploration but primarily in commercial real estate development.

Education

1980
HARVARD BUSINESS SCHOOL

Master of Business Administration, with Distinction

1971
HAMILTON COLLEGE

A.B. with Honors, Economics

APPENDIX C   *(continued)*

Darlene K. Mann

Work Experience

1996–Present

ONSET Ventures, Menlo Park, CA

Venture Partner, ONSET III (in formation)
Venture Partner, ONSET II

1995–1996

AVANTOS PERFORMANCE SYSTEMS, Emeryville, CA

Vice President, Marketing and Sales. Managed all sales, marketing, and technical support functions for start-up software company in the Human Resources and Electronic Performance Support Systems market.

1993–1995

BROADVISION, INC., Los Altos, CA

Vice President, Marketing and co-founder. Responsible for all marketing activities for next-generation electronic commerce systems provider.

1993

PARAMOUNT COMMUNICATIONS, Sunnyvale, CA

Director, Product Marketing. Managed marketing staff and business planning functions for multimedia educational product representing $80M in revenue.

1989–1993

VERITY, INC., Sunnyvale, CA

Director, Product Marketing. Managed product management, marketing and sales development activities during growth of business from start-up through $20mm in revenue for recognized market leader in text retrieval applications.

1986–1989

LOTUS DEVELOPMENT CORPORATION, Cambridge, MA

Product Planning Manager, Lotus Notes. Responsible for product management and market research teams for first product in the "Groupware" category.

Manager, Inside Sales and Customer Support, Information Services Division. Developed and managed inside sales and customer support organizations to support lead generation and leverage performance of direct sales force.

1984–1986

DATA TRANSLATION, INC., Marlborough, MA

Senior Technical Sales Representative. Managed major accounts and OEM sales at leading vendor of analog to digital conversion and image processing products.

Education

1982

UNIVERSITY OF CALIFORNIA AT SAN DIEGO, REVELLE COLLEGE

Bachelor of Arts with Honors, Psychology

APPENDIX C   (*continued*)

Terry L. Opdendyk

Work Experience

1984–Present   ONSET Ventures, Menlo Park, CA

General Partner, ONSET III (in formation)
General Partner, ONSET II
General Partner, ONSET I
General Partner, ONSET, a California Limited Partnership
Special Partner, New Enterprise Associates V, VI & VII
Special Partner, Chemicals and Materials Enterprise Associates. L.P.

1980–1984   VISICORP, San Jose, CA

President, Chief Operating Officer. Responsible for all company activities, organization and P&L during the growth of the business from a start-up to a $40 million leader in the personal computer software industry.

1973–1980   INTEL CORPORATION, Santa Clara, CA

Several responsibilities including:

Co-Manager of the Development Systems Business Segment. Responsible for the P&L, marketing, manufacturing and R&D of microcomputer system products.

Manager, Computer Systems Engineering. Responsible for microprocessor architecture and hardware and software systems R&D in California, Oregon, Arizona and Israel.

Manager of the Corporate Human Resources Business Segment.

1970–1973   HEWLETT-PACKARD, INC., Cupertino, CA

Project Manager/Member of Technical Staff. Responsible for design and development of systems software products. Also responsible for corporate software strategy and methodology for software management.

Education

1972   STANFORD UNIVERSITY

Master of Science, Computer Science

1970   MICHIGAN STATE UNIVERSITY, The Honors College

Bachelor of Science with High Honors, Computer Science

APPENDIX C   *(continued)*

Thomas E. Winter

Work Experience

1993–Present	ONSET Ventures, Menlo Park, CA

General Partner, ONSET III (in formation)
General Partner, ONSET II
Consultant, ONSET I
Special Partner, New Enterprise Associates VII

1991–1993	BIRD MEDICAL TECHNOLOGIES, INC., Palm Springs, CA

President, Chief Executive Officer and Director. Returned company to profitability, positive cash flow, re-structured bank debt and re-staffed senior management team during turnaround of this $50 million manufacturer of respiratory care equipment and disposables.

1983–1991	BURR EGAN DELEAGE & COMPANY, San Francisco & Costa Mesa, CA

General Partner of the general partner, of partnerships managed by Burr Egan Deleage & Co investing in early stage high technology enterprises within the information science and biomedical products fields, including Alta III, L.P., Alta IV, L.P., Alta Subordinated Debt, L.P., and Alta Subordinated Debt II.

1981–1993	BURROUGHS CORPORATION, Detroit, MI

Executive Vice President Finance and Director. Responsible for all financial and administrative activities.

1966–1981	XEROX CORPORATION, Rochester, NY and Stamford, CT

Numerous assignments combining staff and operating responsibility including:

Vice President Operations/Information Products Group
Corporate Controller
Vice President Finance/Information Systems Group
Director Distribution/Information Systems Group
Controller & Director Planning/Research & Engineering Division
Director Pricing & Strategy Analysis

1963–1966	AEROJET GENERAL CORPORATION, Sacramento, CA

Various engineering positions in test and project management.

Education

GEORGIA INSTITUTE OF TECHNOLOGY

1963	Master of Science, Industrial Management
1959	Bachelor of Science, Aeronautical Engineering

APPENDIX D

INSTITUTIONAL LIMITED PARTNERS OF ONSET I

Ameritech Pension Trust
Computrol Limited, BVI
Crossroads Providence Limited Partnership
Delaware State Employees Retirement Fund
The Ford Family
Henry J. Kaiser Family Foundation
Hughes Aircraft Retirement Plans
The James Irvine Foundation
Kansas Public Employees Retirement System
Metropolitan Life Insurance Company
Meyer Memorial Trust
NED Delaware Co, Ltd.
Oberlin College
St. Paul Fire and Marine Insurance Company
Technology Funding Venture Partners IV
T. Rowe Price Associates

INSTITUTIONAL LIMITED PARTNERS OF ONSET II

The Casey Family Program
Computrol Limited, BVI
Delaware State Employees Retirement Fund
The Ford Foundation
Hitachi Chemical Research
Hughes Aircraft Retirement Plans
The James Irvine Foundation
Henry J. Kaiser Family Foundation
Ewing Marion Kauffmann Foundation
Meyer Memorial Trust
Nippon Enterprise Development Corp.
Oberlin College
Pratt Street Ventures IX, LLC
Prime New Ventures Management, L.P.
Scinet Development & Holdings, Inc.
St. Paul Fire and Marine Insurance Company
United States–Japan Foundation
Ziff Investors Partnership, L.P. II

EXHIBIT 2   Summary Statistics on Venture Capital Industry—Mid 1997
Most Active Venture Firms (Ranked by Number of 1996 Investments)

Venture Firm	1995	1996	1st Half 1997
1. New Enterprise Associates	108	105	41
2. Robertson, Stephens & Company, L.P.	35	63	32
3. Norwest Venture Capital	62	58	NA
4. Oak Investment Partners	NA	52	39
5. Hambrecht & Quist Venture Partners	52	51	40
6. Sprout Group	29	51	NA
7. Accel Partners	32	49	NA
8. Sequoia Capital	NA	46	NA
9. U.S. Venture Partners	46	46	32
10. Mayfield Fund	44	45	NA
11. St. Paul Venture Capital Inc.	33	45	31
12. Institutional Venture Partners	NA	44	NA
13. Burr, Egan, Deleage & Company	58	43	NA
14. Enterprise Partners	NA	42	NA
15. Greylock Management Corporation	NA	42	NA
16. Kleiner Perkins Caufield & Byers	66	39	NA
17. Bessemer Venture Partners	30	37	29
18. Crosspoint Venture Partners	25	37	NA
19. OneLiberty Ventures	39	37	NA
20.[a] Advent International Corporation	NA	36	39
20.[a] Dominion Ventures	NA	36	NA

[a]In a tie for 20th place, both Advent and Dominion had 36 investments in 1996.
Source: *The Private Equity Analyst,* February 1997.

EXHIBIT 2   (*continued*)
Venture Capital Activity 1995 thru 6/30/97

		Investment[a] ($ billions)	Number of Deals	Average Per Deal ($ millions)	Median Pre-Money Valuation ($ millions)
1995	Q1	1.1	276	4.0	NA
	Q2	1.8	436	4.1	NA
	Q3	1.6	407	3.9	NA
	Q4	2.1	424	5.0	NA
Total		6.6	1,543	4.3	
1996	Q1	2.3	489	4.7	12.2
	Q2	3.0	584	5.1	14.1
	Q3	2.3	519	4.4	10.9
	Q4	2.5	571	4.4	12.9
Total		10.1	2,163	4.7	
1997	Q1	2.4	586	4.1	12.0
	Q2	3.2	684	4.7	14.9
Total	1st Half	5.6	1,270	4.4	

[a] VC investment into portfolio companies.
Source: *Private Equity Analyst,* August 1997 and *Venture Edge 3Q,* 1977.

EXHIBIT 3   **TallyUp Operating Plan—Excerpts**

SEED ROUND OPERATING PLANS

Responsibility/Task	*Deadline*
A) Office of the President	
Achieve Objectives for First-round Financing	**Q4 97**

Objectives for first-round financing, planned in October of 1997, include:

- Hire key employees to achieve seed plan
- Bring product to "trial" stage
- Sign 3-5 "development partners" with expectation of installing two paying partners in target markets
- Significant progress towards signing one key marketing partner
- Develop and validate business model, including market size, pricing, and sales and distribution
- Develop business plan and presentation for first-round financing

Develop and Validate Business Model	**Jun. 97**
Develop Critical HR Policies & Guidelines	**Feb. 97**
Recruit Core Team	**Ongoing**
Establish Product Advisory Board	**Q3 97**
B) Engineering	
Deliver Sales Prototype	**Apr. 97**
Complete Product Design and Roadmap	**Apr. 97**
Deliver Development Partner Release	**Oct. 97**
C) Marketing	
Prove a Viable Attainable Market	**Jun. 97**
Complete Corporate Identity	**Jan. 97**
Complete Sales Collateral	**Jan., Apr., Nov. 97**
Assist Development with Product Direction	**Mar. 97**
Deliver Marketing Requirements Document	**May 97**
D) Sales and Business Development	
Sign 2 Development Partners in Key Markets	**Jun. 97**
Prove Sales and Distribution Model	**Jun. 97**
Progress Towards Signing Strategic Marketing Partner	**Sep. 97**
Sign 2 Strategic Marketing Partners	**Q4 97**
Develop Lead Tracking System	**Feb. 97**
Hire VP of Sales	**Q4 97**
E) Finances and Operations	
Establish Financial and Board Reporting Systems	**Jan. 97**
Retain Payroll, Benefit, and Audit Services	**Feb. 97**
Secure Office Space and Office Equipment	**Mar. 97**
F) Staffing	
Hire According to Plan	**Ongoing**

CVD INCORPORATED VERSUS A.S. MARKHAM CORPORATION (A)

It was 2:00 a.m. on April 10, 1997, and Bob Donadio and Joe Connolly sat in a small Boston coffee house thinking about their trial against A. S. Markham Corporation, a billion-dollar defense contractor. The two founders of CVD Inc. had sued their former employer—Markham—for relief from what they believed to be an onerous licensing contract. Markham, in turn, had sued them and their small company for a series of alleged infractions including breach of employment contracts, misappropriation of trade secrets, and misuse of confidential information.

The testimony in the trial had ended earlier that afternoon and the two men had spent five hours preparing their side's closing arguments with their lawyer. They would make those arguments tomorrow, the trial would end, and the jury would begin its deliberations—a process that was expected to take several days.

As Donadio and Connolly sat in the coffee house, they knew that if they lost the trial, the judgment against them would likely bankrupt the company. On the other hand, if they won, Markham could appeal the decision to a higher court and prolong the dispute even further. Perhaps, they wondered, they should try to settle the case with Markham before the jury returned with its verdict.

Background

Bob Donadio and Joe Connolly met in 1985, when Donadio recruited Connolly to work for Markham's Advanced Materials Department (AMD). In the seven years

Research Associate Ennis J. Walton prepared this case under the supervision of Professor Michael J. Roberts as the basis for class discussion rather than to illustrate either effective or ineffective handling of an administrative situation. Certain facts have been disguised, and some information has been narrowed for teaching purposes.

that followed, they both had satisfying careers working on Markham's research and development projects sponsored by various agencies of the United States government (see **Exhibit 1**).

Despite their good feelings about Markham, however, by 1992 both Donadio and Connolly wanted to explore new options. Thinking back, Donadio recalled:

> It wasn't an easy decision to leave Markham. I had put in twenty damn good years with them and I had obtained all the perks that a person with my seniority could expect to receive. I also had a family to think about: With a wife and three children, two of whom were of college age, I couldn't just leave the company without thinking about the possible impact my decision would have on the rest of my family. In time, I discussed things with my family and they supported my desire. They weren't completely thrilled at first, but they eventually agreed with me.

Donadio's basic idea for CVD Inc. was to use his knowledge of the chemical vapor deposition (cvd) manufacturing process to become a supplier of infrared materials. Explaining the core technology, Donadio said:

> The cvd process is an extremely useful way to combine different chemical compounds. First, gases or vapors of the compounds are brought together in a specially designed furnace. While in the furnace, the gases will react with one another to form a solid metal-like material which collects on a substrate and then hardens as it cools. There are many different ways to form these vapors—the simplest is to heat blocks of material in the furnace.
>
> Following this, the solid is polished until it resembles a glass-like material capable of transmitting infrared light and high energy lasers. Once the material reaches this glass-like state, it must be subjected to a battery of tests in order to verify its purity—if it isn't pure, it won't transmit infrared light or lasers properly.
>
> In most cases, materials manufactured by this process have properties that make them better than the same materials produced by another manufacturing process. This is particularly true for zinc selenide (ZnSe/cvd) and zinc sulfide (ZnS/cvd)—the two materials most frequently manufactured in this manner.

Donadio's original plan for the new company was to supply ZnSe/cvd to optical fabricators that used it to make output windows for commercial high energy laser (HEL) applications such as automobile body welding, steel plate cutting, and "bloodless" surgery. "We had suggested these commercial applications to Markham," said Donadio, "but they seemed uninterested." As the company grew, Donadio also expected to manufacture both ZnSe/cvd and ZnS/cvd to create infrared optical lenses used for thermal imaging in military applications which required night vision and thermal sensing in weapons.

Recalling his reasons for joining Donadio, Connolly said:

> Bob first mentioned his idea for a new company to me one day after work in Markham's parking lot. This came as a welcome surprise to me since I was quietly looking around for a new job anyway. I really didn't have much to lose—I knew I could work well with Bob, so I decided to join him instead of joining a different company.

A few days after Donadio and Connolly decided to leave Markham, Donadio advised his supervisor, Dr. Smith, of their decision. During the meeting, Dr. Smith told Donadio that he and Connolly would have to appear before Markham's lawyers if they were serious about starting a cvd processing company. Reflecting on the meeting, Donadio said:

> At the time, talking to Smith seemed like the right thing to do. I had consulted with him on many issues before—including this one. At one time, we even entertained the idea of combining our vast knowledge of cvd processes to form the new company. It only seemed right to let him know first.
>
> During that meeting, however, Smith seemed to forget about all that. Instead, he told me that I would have to go before Markham's legal staff if I was serious about leaving to start a cvd processing company. A few hours later, he called Joe in his office to say the same thing.

Connolly added his perspective on being called into Markham's legal department for questioning:

> For a scientist like me, it was quite bizarre to get summoned by Markham's lawyers. The entire atmosphere was different from everything that I knew about the company. Unlike the lab where I worked, the law department seemed cold and impersonal.

After the meeting with Markham's lawyers, it was obvious to Donadio and Connolly that they needed to hire a lawyer to protect their rights. As Donadio recalled:

> We hadn't done anything wrong, but Markham didn't see it that way. Instead, they claimed that we were planning to steal and use its "proprietary information."
>
> We tried to point out that because Markham's cvd research was funded under government contract, it was part of the public domain. I knew this because I'd spent the better part of my career preparing reports for the government that illustrated the cvd process.
>
> From our perspective, Markham didn't have any "proprietary" information regarding the chemical vapor deposition process. They certainly didn't have any patents on the process. Moreover, Joe and I had enough expertise with the cvd processes to start a company that purposefully avoided everything that Markham considered "proprietary" or a "trade secret." Had they told us exactly what they considered to be trade secrets, we could have worked around them. But they just kept claiming that the entire process was "proprietary."
>
> After the meetings with Dr. Smith and the lawyers, I worked at Markham for about another month. During that time I was restricted to my desk and no one bothered to talk to me—for a researcher, that's like professional death. In our business, you live off the flow of information between your colleagues. I'm not naive and I'm certainly not a romantic, but I don't understand how stable personal and professional friendships could be lost in one day. I cannot understand why my friends and colleagues decided to ostracize me. Maybe they were under pressure to follow the company line—I don't know.

Initial Negotiations

Taking Markham's threats seriously, Donadio and Connolly hired Jerry Cohen, an attorney specializing in intellectual property issues, to serve as their lawyer. As their attorney, Cohen maintained a spirited debate with Markham's legal counsel, Len Davis, in an attempt to clarify Markham's case.

On one occasion, Cohen, Donadio, and Connolly met with Len Davis to discuss the alleged proprietary information. In that meeting Cohen provided evidence from publicly available government documents to dispute Markham's proprietary claims. However, despite that information, the two sides were unable to reach a mutually acceptable agreement. Instead, Markham threatened to sue Donadio and Connolly for breaching their employment contracts (see excerpts, **Exhibit 2**) if they formed a new firm that used any of Markham's alleged "proprietary" information or trade secrets without a license from the company.

In January 1993, Donadio and Connolly formed CVD Incorporated. Without the benefit of salaries and with the threat of a long and costly lawsuit, Donadio and Connolly worked out of their homes during the first few months until they could design the company's manufacturing facility, finish their business plan, and raise capital.

In writing their business plan, Donadio used his knowledge to list eighteen different domestic and international commercial companies that might purchase CVD's products. CVD's business plan also included a list of thirty-five government agencies that might purchase ZnSe/cvd and ZnS/cvd within the next five years. In all, CVD's business plan estimated that its company would generate before tax profits of approximately $310,000 on sales of $1,400,000 during its third year of manufacturing operations. After that time, the company estimated that its overall sales would increase at an annual rate of 20%.

Despite a completed engineering design and optimistic figures, the process of attracting money for their venture was more difficult than they had initially expected. CVD's attempts were mired from the beginning by investors' fears that the company would be caught in an acrimonious and protracted legal fight. Prospective investors were also concerned that Markham would lower its prices and use its established position to maintain its hold on the market.

The License

Thus, after many frustrated attempts to raise capital in the spring of 1980, Donadio and Connolly, with advice from Jerry Cohen, decided to sign a licensing agreement with Markham (see **Exhibit 3**). The terms of the license called for CVD to pay Markham 15% and 8% on the net selling price for ZnSe/cvd and ZnS/cvd, respectively, for a ten-year period. Once under license, Donadio and Connolly lowered their business plan's projections to reflect the terms of the Markham license.

The license quieted investors' fears, and Donadio and Connolly were successful in raising the funds. The two men received $450,000 by mid-June 1993 from the following sources: $300,000 from a loan from the Small Business Administration; $80,000 from a prospective customer; and the remainder from the men's family and friends.

Beginning Operations

Donadio and Connolly put the firm's money to work immediately, purchasing equipment and signing a lease for a 4,500 square foot facility in Woburn. By February 1994, the firm had made significant progress: Net sales had reached $751,000. Despite this progress, Donadio and Connolly still worried about the firm's $109,000 licensing fee, which when added to the company's costs and expenses produced a net earnings before taxes of negative $99,000. Remembering his thoughts, Donadio said:

> Our revenues and costs were in good shape for a start-up, but it was clear that CVD couldn't survive with the original terms of the license—it was like having a tax on our gross revenues.

Based on an important clause in its license with Markham (see **Exhibit 3**), CVD informed Markham that it wanted to exercise its right to renegotiate the terms of the license. Markham, however, refused to alter the terms of the contract. In all, the company tried and failed to renegotiate on three separate occasions. Finally, Donadio and Connolly decided not to pay Markham until the company honored CVD's right to renegotiate the terms of the license.

In June 1994, Markham informed CVD that it was in default. Markham also advised CVD that if all obligations were not immediately paid in full, it would cancel the agreement and seek legal action. CVD responded to Markham's notices by seeking new counsel. With little time, Donadio and Connolly, aided by Jerry Cohen, identified Blair L. Perry—a high-technology and antitrust specialist—as a good attorney to handle their case.

The Suit

After a short period of negotiations, Perry agreed to handle the case. In exchange, CVD agreed to pay Perry's firm $6,000 as a monthly retainer for its legal representation.

In August 1994, CVD filed a complaint against Markham in federal court, arguing that the license was invalid because it represented a violation of the Sherman Antitrust Act which restricts illegal attempts to maintain a monopoly and restrain competition.

Blair Perry recalled his strategy:

We filed an antitrust claim for several reasons. First, we wanted to claim the high ground by being the plaintiff. Second, an antitrust violation was the only means of getting the case heard in the federal court system. Here, you can get to trial in two years instead of the five it takes in the state courts. The federal judges are also more used to dealing with the sort of complex issues this case presents.

A few days later, Markham responded with a counter-claim, arguing that the license was valid and enforceable. Markham also claimed that Donadio, Connolly and CVD Inc. had engaged in unfair and deceptive business practices to obtain Markham's proprietary information. As a result, Markham claimed monetary losses in excess of $4 million as well as other damages. The basis of the dispute was as follows:

CVD argued that the license was invalid because:

- Markham did not have any trade secrets related to the production of ZnSe/cvd and ZnS/cvd;
- Markham acted in bad faith when it compelled CVD to sign the license because it knew that it didn't have any trade secrets;
- The license was signed under duress; and
- The license was counter to public policy objectives in that it restrained competition and helped sustain Markham's monopoly in this market.

Markham disputed CVD's claims, arguing instead that the license was valid and enforceable because:

- Markham had trade secrets and confidential business information related to the production of ZnSe/cvd and ZnS/cvd;
- Donadio and Connolly had learned Markham's trade secrets and confidential business information while employed by Markham;
- Donadio and Connolly had signed employment contracts that prevented any employee from using or disclosing any of Markham's proprietary information unless expressly authorized by Markham;
- The license agreement was a valid legal document—irrespective of whether or not Markham actually had trade secrets or proprietary information—which granted CVD the right to use Markham's knowledge related to the production of ZnSe/cvd and ZnS/cvd;
- Donadio and Connolly signed the license willingly and with a competent attorney protecting their legal rights;
- Donadio and Connolly had breached contracts and duties of good faith outlined in their employment contracts;
- Donadio, Connolly and CVD had misappropriated Markham's proprietary information relating to the production of ZnSe/cvd and ZnS/cvd; and
- CVD had breached fiduciary duties mandated by the license.

Pretrial Actions

After reviewing the claims of each party, the court urged CVD Inc. and Markham to attempt to settle the matter out of court. In extensive pretrial settlement discussions CVD offered to pay approximately $450,000 to Markham in return for freedom from the royalty obligations and from trade secret claims. Markham refused that offer and in exchange proposed that it would end its legal claims if CVD paid $3,000,000 to Markham. Unable to compromise beyond this point, both sides began the lengthy pretrial preparation process. Recalling some of the reasons why it took so long to make it to court, Blair Perry said:

> The most difficult part of the pretrial process started when we tried to demystify Markham's "trade secret" claims. No matter what we did, we couldn't get a comprehensive list of what they were claiming as "trade secrets." We eventually had to prepare our own list of possible trade secrets in order to be ready for trial—a process that was very time consuming and full of frustrations.
>
> For example, Markham told us that its "trade secrets" could be found in some of its engineering drawings that we were going to inspect. When I got to Markham's offices, they took me to a room and showed me a stack of about 2,000 drawings. I was simply amazed!
>
> After a cursory look at the evidence, I tried to get the court to force Markham to be more specific. To my dismay, however, the court ruled in Markham's favor, and so I spent a number of days sorting through all those drawings trying to determine which ones were really relevant.

After two years of preparations, the opposing attorneys entered court to empanel a jury. This process was important because each side expected the case to turn on the testimony of the witnesses. In the end, a twelve-person jury was selected that featured a chemical engineer as the foreman.

The Trial

On March 5, 1997, the case of CVD Inc. versus Markham went to trial before Justice Stevenson of the United States District Court, District of Massachusetts. Sparing no expense, Markham appeared in court with five lawyers while Blair Perry alone represented CVD.

After hearing each side's opening statements, Justice Stevenson made two important decisions that affected the way the issues were argued. First, he ruled that Markham could not use the term "proprietary" because it was unclear and not well grounded in legal precedent. The court also ruled that in order for CVD to obtain relief from the license, it had to show by "clear and convincing" evidence that Markham knew it didn't have trade secrets when it enacted the licensing agreement with CVD.

The information presented during the trial focused on the following topics:

I. The CVD Process: Witness called by Markham offered the following testimony regarding the cvd process:

- The Advanced Materials Division, where Donadio and Connolly were employed, had engaged in the development of unique and sophisticated methods and equipment used to produce ZnSe/cvd and ZnS/cvd since 1959.
- An expert witness testified that there was an art or skill required to produce ZnSe/cvd and ZnS/cvd that could only be obtained through years of skilled experience.
- When asked what he would need to design, build, and operate a cvd furnace to make ZnSe/cvd and ZnS/cvd, an expert witness claimed that he would need "an experienced staff."
- Markham claimed that in 1993, it was the only company with an experienced staff (seven people) capable of producing ZnSe/cvd and ZnS/cvd.
- Markham asserted that Donadio and Connolly had acquired their knowledge of the specific processes, equipment, and methods used by Markham during their employment with Markham.
- Markham argued that no detailed information about the cvd process had been disclosed in public documents and it claimed that CVD had misappropriated the following trade secrets:

    (a) Passivation Gas Mixture—This gaseous mixture was used by Markham to scrub out the discharge lines from the cvd furnace before it was opened to prevent fires or explosions when fine zinc dust mixed with normal air. Markham's officials testified that the company had had three fires and two explosions before it discovered that a mixture of 97% nitrogen and 3% oxygen would stabilize the zinc dust and prevent fires and explosions.

    One expert witness testified that during the jury's visit to CVD's facilities, he had noticed that CVD had tried to hide its own passivation gas tank (by covering it with brown paper) to prevent Markham and the court from knowing that it used the same passivation gas mixture that Markham employed.

    (b) Alumina Insert Hydrogen Sulfide Injector—This was an insert that was placed over the tip of the hydrogen sulfide injector to prevent the corrosion of the stainless steel mixing chamber where gases were mixed. By using this, Markham was able to prevent hydrogen sulfide gas from reacting with and corroding the injector tip.

    One of Markham's expert witnesses testified that the composition and exact positioning of the alumina insert was critical because corrosion would make it impossible to complete the long furnace phase of the cvd process (usually one to two days) necessary to produce high-quality materials. He also testified that there were other ceramic materials that could be used instead of alumina.

(c) Hexagonal Graphite Nut—This piece fit inside Markham's sulfide injector assembly to allow argon gas to be distributed uniformly, thereby making it possible for the company to manufacture high-quality zinc sulfide.

- Markham asserted that it always denied public access to its furnace facilities to protect its trade secrets.

The following points regarding the cvd process were made by CVD during the trial:

- The cvd process was well known to scientists in general and chemical engineers in particular.
- The cvd process was taught throughout the educational system from grade school to college chemistry courses.
- Donadio and Connolly testified that they acquired knowledge about the process before, after, and during their employment with Markham.
- Donadio and Connolly testified that they returned all documents belonging to Markham at the end of their employment with the company; and, they stressed that their employment contracts did not contain non-compete clauses.
- CVD produced evidence that a U.S. patent on certain aspects of the cvd process had been issued to another individual in 1964 (see **Exhibit 4**).
- Markham's patent attorney testified (under cross examination) that he had learned of this patent when Markham tried to patent ZnSe/cvd and ZnS/cvd, and therefore, he had stopped the patent process. He explained that Markham had stopped the patent process because Markham believed that there were no commercial applications of the process. Because the government was the only likely customer, and because it already held a royalty-free license on the process, it didn't make sense to proceed with the patent. Moreover, he admitted that he had informed both Donadio and Dr. Smith in a memo that Markham would not seek a patent on these products.
- Markham's patent attorney admitted that Markham had a computer system which listed all information that the company officially protected as trade secrets, and CVD produced evidence which showed that neither the cvd process, nor ZnSe/cvd and ZnS/cvd had been listed by this system.
- Markham's patent attorney testified that Markham had a company policy which required all protected engineering drawings to be marked or stamped secret and placed in a special drawer. Connolly testified that he had made hundreds of detailed engineering drawings and he had never been told to mark them "secret."
- CVD provided evidence that Markham had disclosed elements of the cvd process in government reports, lectures and films. These disclosures included information about Markham's hexagonal graphite nut.

- One of Markham's expert witnesses testified (under cross examination) that a "competent" engineer could construct Markham's manufacturing process from the information disclosed in the government reports.

- One of Markham's witnesses admitted that many of Markham's alleged trade secrets were known in the industry. For example, the expert witness admitted (under cross examination) that it was well known in the industry that zinc dust would ignite if exposed to oxygen. He also acknowledged that any undergraduate engineer would recognize that a passivation gas containing less oxygen than normal air would slow the rate of oxidation which caused fires and explosions.

- Another one of Markham's expert witnesses admitted (under cross examination) that it would be obvious to any engineer that a corrosion-resistant material would be needed to prevent the corrosion of the stainless steel injector tip. He further admitted that it made logical sense to use an alumina insert over the stainless steel injector tip because alumina was inert and had a high melting point.

II. The Products: CVD made the following points regarding the ZnSe/cvd and ZnS/cvd products:

- Due to their unique light transmission properties, ZnSe/cvd and ZnS/cvd were extremely popular among military and commercial customers, and these customers used the products, rather than other infrared materials made by different manufacturing processes.

- Markham's ZnSe/cvd and ZnS/cvd had outstripped Eastman Kodak's ZnSe and ZnS made by the "hot pressing process"; Kodak had discontinued its ZnSe production.

- Before 1980, Markham produced and sold 65% and 98% of the ZnSe/cvd and ZnS/cvd, respectively.

- Markham had imposed a "price squeeze" by reducing its prices in situations where it knew it was in direct competition with CVD. Markham knew CVD could not reduce its prices, pay exorbitant royalties, and still operate on a profitable basis.

- Markham reduced its prices 20% on January 21, 1993 with the intent of preventing CVD from competing.

- Markham had maintained its prices at the January 21, 1993 rate despite inflation and increasing production costs.

- Markham had falsely represented to various potential customers that CVD was in violation of its contract obligations and was thus an unsuitable supplier.

Markham disputed CVD's claims, arguing:

- ZnSe and ZnS, irrespective of the manufacturing process, along with 40 other materials can be used for their optical, infrared, and electrical properties.

- Markham only has a 9% market share of all 42 infrared materials sold in the United States.
- Donadio admitted that before leaving Markham, he had participated in the formation of the company's prices which became effective on January 21, 1993.
- Markham claimed that its prices never fell below the average costs necessary to produce ZnSe/cvd and ZnS/cvd.

III. The License: CVD made the following claims about the license:

- Donadio and Connolly testified that Markham threatened to sue them unless they signed a license; this action, they claimed, left them with no other viable alternatives.
- Markham had never listed its "trade secrets" in its negotiations with CVD; therefore no specific information had been granted by the license.
- Jerry Cohen testified that he had tried and failed to get Markham to limit the terms of license.
- Markham's lawyer, Len Davis, acknowledged that he had implied to Donadio, Connolly, and Cohen that the terms of the licensing agreement were less than equitable before they signed the agreement.

Markham took exception to CVD's argument:

- Markham claimed that the processes, methods and techniques that were used by Markham represented trade secret and confidential business information.
- Donadio and Connolly testified that they had been offered new jobs inside Markham, but they turned them down to start CVD.
- Markham claimed that Donadio and Connolly voluntarily, with aid of a lawyer of their own selection, executed an agreement which recognized the authenticity of Markham's trade secrets and confidential business information.

IV. The Employment Contract: Markham argued that Donadio and Connolly had broken their employment contracts:

- Markham provided evidence that Donadio and Connolly, along with all other Markham employees, had signed employment contracts that prohibited them from using or disclosing any of the information that they had learned or practiced while they were Markham's employees for their own benefit at any time unless they were specifically authorized by Markham.
- Markham provided evidence, described earlier, that Donadio and Connolly had indeed misappropriated proprietary information and were therefore in violation of their employment contracts.

CVD presented evidence, discussed earlier, that the information which Markham claimed to be proprietary was, in fact, well-known in the industry.

After twenty-six days of testimony, each side was permitted to submit to the judge its own "Suggested Instructions to the Jury." These suggested instructions would be "boiled down" by the judge into a single set of instructions, which the jury could then use to help guide its deliberations. Both CVD's and Markham's suggested instructions are reproduced (see **Exhibits 5** and **6**) as a means of understanding the particular arguments which each felt were important to its case.

Conclusion

As the two men reviewed the past month of testimony, they were optimistic about the outcome. Yet, they also knew that with a jury, anything could happen. Blair Perry felt good about the way the case was going, but he too had urged caution. As Donadio and Connolly contemplated the future, it was the consequences of this uncertainty that loomed before them. Donadio commented:

> I feel confident, but if we lose, we're out of business. Even if we win, Markham can keep us in court on appeal for years. Perhaps the testimony has convinced Markham that their chances of winning are not very good. Maybe, they'd be willing to settle for a reasonable amount, or even renegotiate the license.

While the possibility of resolving this uncertainty was attractive, the two men were also cognizant of the fact that they had spent tremendous time and nearly a quarter of a million dollars in legal fees ($156,000 of which they had yet to pay). While they felt they could afford some settlement (see **Exhibit 7** for financials), to back down now seemed not only wrong, but also an admission of guilt that neither man truly felt.

EXHIBIT 1   The Plaintiffs

Name: Robert Donadio

Title: President, CVD Inc.

Education: B.S. and M.S. degrees in Mechanical Engineering from Northeastern University 1971 and 1976, respectively.

Work Experience: Served as Principal Scientist for Markham's Advanced Materials Department (AMD); Managed Markham's domestic and international infrared materials marketing programs.

Special Recognition: Invented Markham's CVD Zinc Selenide and Zinc Sulfo-Selenide with Dr. Smith, B. Henderson, and W. Jung in 1986 (patent was not pursued by Markham). Known as an international expert in the area of chemical vapor deposition.

Personal: Married with three children whose ages range from 15 to 21.

Name: Joseph Connolly

Title: Vice President, Operations, CVD Inc.

Education: A.E. degree in Mechanical Engineering from Wentworth Institute in 1982; B.S. and M.S. degrees in Mechanical Engineering from Northeastern University in 1985 and 1989, respectively.

Work Experience: Joined Markham's Advanced Materials Department in 1985. Eventually served as senior scientist for Markham's AMD and lead engineer on the production of infrared windows for a number of government and commercial contracts.

Personal: Separated with three children whose ages range from 3 to 15.

EXHIBIT 2   The Employment Contract Signed by Donadio and Connolly

In consideration of the employment of _____ by the employer, Markham Corporation (Markham), in the course of which employment is contemplated that the Employee may make create products and/or compose subject inventions and/or proprietary information, and the trust and confidence responded in the Employee by Markham with respect thereto, it is agreed as follows:

1. "Subject Invention" means any invention, improvement, or discovery of the Employee, whether or not patentable, other than those identified below, which during the period of his employment by Markham is (a) conceived by the employer, or (b) first actually reduced to practice by or for Markham, and which arises out of or is related to any of the business activities of Markham or any other company which is owned or controlled by Markham.

2. "Information" means secret or private information concerning Markham's design, manufacture, use, purchase or sale of its products or materials, such as may be contained in but not limited to, Markham's manufacturing methods, processes or techniques, treatment or chemical composition of material, and plant layout or tooling, all to the extent that (a) such information is not readily disclosed by inspection or analysis of the products or materials sold, leased or otherwise disposed of by Markham, and (b) Markham has protected such information from unrestricted use by others.

3. All Subject Inventions and Proprietary Information are and shall remain the sole and exclusive property of Markham, subject only to any prior encumbrances attaching thereto. The Employee agrees to disclose all Subject Inventions, and all Proprietary Information generated by the Employee, promptly, completely and in writing to Markham and such others and under such conditions as may be designated by Markham.

4. The Employee agrees (a) to execute all documents requested by Markham for vesting in Markham the entire right, title and interest in; and to (i) all Subject Inventions, (ii) all Proprietary Information generated by the Employee, and (iii) all patent applications filed and all patents issuing on such Subject Inventions; (b) to execute all documents requested by Markham for filing and prosecutions; such applications for patents as Markham may desire covering such Subject Inventions; and (c) to give to Markham all assistance it reasonably requires in order to process Markham's rights in its Subject Inventions and Proprietary Information.

5. The Employee agrees that his obligation to perform the acts specified in Paragraph 4 above shall not expire with termination of his Employment. However, the period during which Markham's rights to Subject Inventions, and Proprietary Information generated by the Employee are created shall not be extended by virtue of the previous sentence. Markham agrees to pay the Employee at a reasonable rate for any time that the Employee actually spends in the performance of the acts specified in Paragraph 4 above at Markham's written request after termination of the Employee's employment and to reimburse the Employee for expenses necessarily incurred by him in connection with such acts.

6. All documents, records, models, prototypes and other tangible evidence of Subject Inventions and Proprietary Information which shall at any time come into the possession of the Employee shall be the sole and exclusive property of Markham and shall be surrendered to Markham upon the termination of the Employee's employment by Markham, or upon request at any other time.

7. The Employee agrees that, unless duly authorized in writing by an Officer of Markham, he will not either during his employment by Markham, or thereafter as long as the Employee is unable reasonably to demonstrate that Markham Proprietary Information has passed into the public domain other than as a consequence of the Employee's own acts, divulge, or use for his own or another's benefit, any of said Proprietary Information.

8. The Employee represents and warrants that he has not entered and will not enter into any agreement inconsistent herewith.

EXHIBIT 3   Excerpts from License Agreement

The license signed between CVD Inc. and Markham had the following important clauses:

1. Markham's cvd process used to manufacture zinc selenide and zinc sulfide, trademarked "Martran," represents proprietary trade secrets.
2. Markham grants CVD Inc. the nonexclusive right to use its proprietary process for which CVD Inc. agrees to pay Markham royalties of 15% and 8% on the net selling prices of its ZnSe/cvd and ZnS/cvd products produced pursuant to this agreement.
3. Markham agrees to allow CVD Inc. to renegotiate the terms of this original agreement if they prove inequitable.
4. Markham retains the right to cancel the agreement at any time if CVD Inc. fails to pay the royalties.
5. No termination of the license shall release any party from the royalty obligations that have incurred.
6. This license shall be construed under the laws of the Commonwealth of Massachusetts.
7. This license is effective retroactively from January 1, 1993 until December 31, 2003.

EXHIBIT 4 **Vapor Phase Crystallization Patent, Dated February 11, 1964, Granted to H.J. Gould (Excerpts from U.S. Government Patent Filing)**

This invention has to do with the crystallization from the vapor phase of crystals at least one component of which is a metal that is solid at normal temperature.

The invention has to do, more particularly, with improved methods and apparatus for supplying to a furnace chamber the vapor of a metallic component that is solid at normal temperature.

This invention is particularly useful in, but is not limited to, the production of semiconductive crystals such, for example, as cadmium and zinc sulphide, selenide, and telluride and mixtures of such components. It is well known that crystals of that type can be produced in good purity by vapor phase crystallization.

In producing such illustrative crystals, the nonmetallic component is ordinarily supplied to the furnace as a continuous stream of gas, typically as hydrogen sulphide, selenide, or telluride. The rate of supply of such a gaseous component is accurately and conveniently controllable by known methods.

The metallic component is ordinarily supplied by inserting in the furnace in the gas stream a boat containing the metal in solid or liquid form. The metal then evaporates into the gas stream at a rate that is roughly controllable by variation of such factors as temperature, the rate of gas flow, and the area of the exposed metal surface.

Such control, however, is less accurate than is often desirable, and is unsatisfactory for many other reasons. Even rough control of the vaporizing temperature usually requires a special furnace zone for that purpose. The rate of gas flow that is most suitable for metal vaporization may be undesirable for other reasons. And the area of metal surface usually decreases in an uncontrollable way as the initial charge is exhausted. Moreover, the rate of evaporation from a given surface area is very sensitive to contamination of the surface, which typically increases as the metal charge is consumed.

The present invention avoids all of those difficulties in a remarkably economical and convenient manner. In accordance with one aspect of the invention, the metallic component is supplied in the form of a fine wire, and is fed to the furnace at a definite velocity. The described method has the further great advantage that under equilibrium conditions of operation, the rate of vapor supply is essentially or completely independent of virtually all other variable factors. Hence, those factors may be adjusted arbitrarily as required to meet other conditions.

In accordance with a further aspect of the invention, the metal wire is fed to the furnace chamber through a capillary passage formed of suitable inert material such as quartz, for example. The passage is so arranged that the advancing metal reaches vaporizing temperature at a point spaced from the exit mouth of the passage. Vaporization then occurs within the capillary passage, and the metal leaves the passage mouth as a continuous and uniform stream of vapor. A further advantage of that structure is that, by suitable form and placement of the passage, the metal vapor can be delivered accurately to any desired point of the furnace chamber.

A further aspect of the invention provides means for surface cleaning of the metal wire immediately prior to melting and vaporization. That may be accomplished by passing the wire through a reducing chamber which is continuously washed by a reducing gas, such as hydrogen, for example. The reducing chamber is preferably maintained at an elevated temperature, which may be only slightly less than the melting point of the metal.

A full understanding of the invention, and of its further objects and advantages, will be had from the following description of certain illustrative manners in which it may be carried out, of which description the accompanying drawings form a part. The particulars of that description are intended only as illustration, and not as a limitation upon the scope of the invention, which is defined in the appended claims.

[Drawings and explanations have been omitted for brevity.]

I Claim the Following as Patented:

1. The method of supplying vapor of a metal at a controlled rate to a furnace for production of a crystal by vapor crystallization, said method comprising providing a capillary passage communicating with the chamber, feeding a wire consisting essentially of the metal into the passage toward the chamber at such a temperature that the wire is vaporized within the passage.

2. The method of supplying vapor of a metal at a controlled rate to a furnace chamber for production of a crystal by vapor phase crystallization, said method comprising providing a capillary passage that opens into the chamber, maintaining in the passage at a point spaced from said opening a longitudinal temperature gradient that is steeper than the gradient in the chamber adjacent to the passage and that embraces the melting temperature and the vaporizing temperature of the metal, and feeding a wire consisting essentially of the metal into the passage toward the chamber at a controlled velocity.

Exhibit 4   *(concluded)*

---

3. The method of supplying vapor of a metal at a controlled rate to a furnace chamber for production of a crystal by vapor phase crystallization, said method comprising providing a passage communicating at one end with the chamber, feeding wire consisting essentially of the metal into the passage toward the chamber at a controlled velocity, maintaining the passage at such temperature that the wire is vaporized therein adjacent said passage end, and contacting the wire in the passage prior to said vaporization with a gas that is substantially inert with respect to the metal and that chemically reacts with impurities carried by the wire.

4. The method of producing a semiconductive crystal comprising a metallic component and containing a substantially uniform relative concentration comprising providing a solid wire which consists essentially of the metallic component and doping agent in said relative concentration, feeding the wire at a controlled velocity into a capillary tube, maintaining a temperature gradient along the tube to vaporize the wire, and crystallizing the resulting vapor to form said semiconductor crystal.

5. The method of producing a semiconductive crystal containing substantially uniformly distributed therein a minor proportion a doping agent, said method comprising providing a solid wire composed primarily of metal selected from the group consisting of cadmium and zinc and containing said doping agent in a concentration corresponding to said proportion, feeding the wire at controlled velocity into a capillary tube, maintaining a temperature gradient along the tube to vaporize the wire, combining the resulting vapors in substantially constant ratio with gas selected from the group consisting of hydrogen sulphide, hydrogen selenide, and hydrogen telluride, and crystallizing said semiconductive crystal from the resulting vapor phase.

EXHIBIT 5   Excerpts from CVD's Suggested Instructions to Jury

---

[Note: Included in these instructions were legal citations which mentioned specific cases where these points of law were made or reaffirmed. These citations have been omitted in the interest of brevity.]

Donadio and Connolly's Rights as Employees

1. An employee of a company has the right to quit his job and engage in a competing business unless he has a contract of employment which forbids him to do so. In this case there is no evidence that either Mr. Donadio or Mr. Connolly had such a contract with Markham.

2. Mr. Donadio and Mr. Connolly had the right to use the general knowledge, experience and skill they had acquired while working for Markham for the purpose of engaging in a competing business.

3. If a contract between an employer and an employee or former employee provides that the employee will not use his general knowledge, experience and skill for the benefit of a new employer, or for the benefit of himself, such a provision is contrary to public policy and is unenforceable.

4. Although an employee has the right to leave his employment and to use his general knowledge, skill and experience for the benefit of a new employer, he has an obligation not to use "trade secrets" of the old employer for the benefit of the new one.

No Trade Secrets

5. A "trade secret" may be any information which is used in a business and gives the company which uses it an advantage over competitors who do not know it. For example, a secret manufacturing process or a secret machine of unique design could be a trade secret.

6. However, information that is generally known in an industry cannot be a trade secret.

7. Information cannot qualify for protection as a trade secret unless it is information which gives to the company which knows it an advantage over competitors or potential competitors who do not have the information. Information which would be obvious to a competent engineer experienced in the particular field, or which easily could be determined by a competent engineer by means other than obtaining it from the company which has it, cannot be protected as a trade secret.

8. You must determine in this case whether the information which Markham claims as trade secrets in fact was secret and not generally known outside Markham.

9. A United States patent is a matter of public record and is available for inspection by any member of the public. Information which is disclosed in a United States patent cannot be a "trade secret" after that patent has been issued, even if it was a "trade secret" before the patent was issued.

10. If you find that information about the chemical vapor deposition process used by Markham was disclosed in reports made to government agencies and other companies, without restriction on the use of such information, then you should find that such information was not "trade secret" information.

11. An employer who wishes to preserve information as a trade secret must inform the employees who know the information that it is to be treated as secret, and must take all proper and reasonable precautions to keep the information secret. If the company fails to do so, it cannot later prevent use of the information on the theory that it is a trade secret.

12. You have heard testimony of Markham's lawyer, Mr. Davis, to the effect that he was unable to deliver a list of the items that Markham claimed to be its trade secrets to Mr. Cohen, the lawyer for the plaintiffs, because it was impossible to make a detailed and complete list of the claimed trade secrets. If you find that as of February 15, 1993 Markham was unable to identify what it claimed to be its trade secrets, then you would be justified in finding that Mr. Donadio and Mr. Connolly had not been put on notice while they were employees of Markham as to what it was that Markham claimed to be its trade secrets, and accordingly that Markham cannot now assert a right to trade secret protection for the information.

The License

13. In **some** circumstances a contract may be binding upon the parties **even if** it later is found that the contract was based on an invalid claim when the person who asserted the claim upon which the contract was based did so in good faith. However, in the case of a contract regarding the use of trade secrets, another principle of law must be considered. Some types of agreements are unenforceable because they are considered to be contrary to public policy, even if they are signed voluntarily by the parties.

EXHIBIT 5   *(concluded)*

---

14. A contract that is signed under what the law regards as unreasonable coercion or "duress" cannot be enforced by the party responsible for such coercion or duress. If you find that Markham threatened to sue Mr. Donadio and Mr. Connolly and their new company for alleged use of trade secrets, and that Markham made such threats in bad faith, knowing that it had no legitimate basis for the claims that it threatened to assert, and that the plaintiffs signed the license agreement because of such threats, then you should find that the license agreement was signed under what the law calls economic duress and is not enforceable. Also, threats to prevent a person from earning a living or engaging in a lawful business may constitute duress.

15. In deciding whether the license agreement was signed under duress, you may consider the following:
    a) the relative bargaining power of the parties;
    b) whether the license required CVD Incorporated to pay royalties at excessive or unreasonable rates;
    c) whether the plaintiffs could have obtained a judicial decision on the Markham trade secrets claims in time to save their proposed new business.

16. Under Section 1 of the Sherman Act, which is part of the antitrust laws of the United States, any contract that unreasonably restrains interstate commerce within the United States or foreign commerce of the United States is illegal.

17. It is also a violation of Section 2 of the Sherman Antitrust Act for a company to use illegal or unreasonable means to preserve or maintain "monopoly power" in a "relevant product market" for a "relevant geographical market," even if that "monopoly power" has been acquired by lawful and proper means or simply historical accident.

18. A company can have "monopoly power" without having 100% of a market, so long as it has the power either to exclude competition or to set its own prices without regard for competitive pricing.

19. A particular type of product may constitute a "relevant product market" for antitrust purposes if a major customer has specified that the particular material must be used for a particular purpose, and has selected its suppliers accordingly.

20. Even if two products have the same chemical composition, like a diamond and lead in a pencil, they are not the same "relevant product market" if one of them has physical characteristics and those characteristics lead customers to prefer one over the other for certain purposes.

21. If two companies compete in selling a product to customers located throughout the United States, then the entire country can be the "relevant geographical market."

22. You may find that the February 1993 license agreement was a contract that unreasonably restrained trade if you find **either** (1) that the license agreement required CVD Incorporated to pay royalties for the use of information which in fact was not trade secret information, **or** (2) that the license agreement required CVD Incorporated to pay royalties which were unreasonably high in amount and thus unreasonably restrained CVD Incorporated in its ability to compete with Markham.

EXHIBIT 6   Excerpts from Markham's Suggested Instructions to the Jury

[Note: Included in these instructions were legal citations which mentioned specific cases where these points of law were made or reaffirmed. These citations have been omitted in the interest of brevity.]

An Employer's Rights

1. The employee agreements signed by Donadio and Connolly with respect to Markham inventions and proprietary information are valid and binding. These agreements prevent Donadio and Connolly, upon termination of their employment, from using for their own advantage, confidential information gained by them during their employment.

2. An agreement not to use or disclose methods and procedures involved in manufacturing processes is binding on an employee and is a reasonable restraint.

3. Donadio and Connolly, who occupied positions of trust at Markham, owed a duty of loyalty to Markham, a duty which includes not using and disclosing Markham's trade secrets and confidential information even after the termination of employment.

4. The duty of loyalty owed to Markham by Donadio and Connolly preclude them from using, for their advantage, or that of a rival and to the harm of Markham, trade secrets or confidential information gained during the course of their employment at Markham.

5. The confidential information that Donadio and Connolly were under a duty to Markham not to disclose, including not only particular information that Markham told them constituted Markham trade secrets and confidential information, but also any information they knew Markham would not want revealed to others. Their duty of nonuse and nondisclosure applies to unique business information and methods of Markham, trade secrets, customer lists, and the like.

Trade Secrets

6. A trade secret may consist of any formula, pattern, device, or compilation of information which is used in one's business, and which gives him an opportunity to obtain an advantage over competitors who do not know or use it. It may be a formula for a chemical compound, a process of manufacturing, treating or preserving materials, a pattern for a machine or other device. . . . A trade secret is a process or device for use over time in the operation of the business.

7. Manufacturing processes specifically are entitled to protection as trade secrets.

8. Because it is the policy of the law to encourage and protect invention and commercial enterprise, the law protects processes of manufacture invented or discovered by an employer against employees who—in violation of their employment contracts and in breach of the duty of trust and confidence that the law also imposes—seek to apply such processes for their own use or to disclose them to third persons.

9. The fact that Markham's process of manufacturing and producing zinc sulfide and zinc selenide by chemical vapor deposition may to some extent be a combination and adaptation of known principles to new purposes does not prevent that process from being a trade secret, if you find that the process as distilled or parts of it accomplish a result which gives Markham a competitive advantage due to its efforts, ingenuity, research and development.

10. Even if you determine that general information regarding the technology of chemical vapor deposition and furnaces used in conjunction therewith may be known elsewhere, it does not follow that Markham's detailed engineering drawings, the configuration of its furnaces, apparatus and equipment, the precise materials, techniques and procedures—which Markham claims are trade secrets and confidential information—have been disclosed.

11. General descriptions or explanations of a process or manufacturing apparatus do not constitute disclosures of detailed manufacturing drawings and designs particularly if the equipment cannot be reproduced by others absent such detail.

12. Detailed manufacturing drawings are prima facie trade secrets.

13. Only reasonable steps are required to preserve the secrecy of the information embodied in the process, machinery, and manufacturing techniques for the production of zinc sulfide and zinc selenide by chemical vapor deposition. Although there is no general rule to determine whether the security precautions taken by the possessor of a trade secret are reasonable, the existence or absence of an express agreement restricting disclosure is an important reasonable step.

14. Markham did not have to stamp "confidential" or "proprietary" on its drawings; or tell Donadio and Connolly that any component of the furnaces were confidential and proprietary. Such specificity is not required to put employees on notice that their work involves access to trade secrets and confidential information.

Exhibit 6   *(continued)*

Confidential Business Information

15. Confidential information acquired by an employee in the course of his employment is the property of the employer, which the employee holds in trust for the employer and cannot use in violation of his trust.

16. Donadio and Connolly's contractual and fiduciary obligations to Markham also include their agreement and an obligation in law not to use confidential information regarding customer lists and sources of supply to Markham's detriment upon termination of their employment with Markham.

17. It does not matter that Donadio and Connolly could have obtained some knowledge of Markham's manufacturing processes and techniques from public treatises or documents. For if you find that they obtained their knowledge through their confidential relationship with Markham, they incurred a duty not to use that information to Markham's detriment.

The License

18. Agreements for the licensing of trade secrets are commonplace and enforceable by courts of law. Through a licensing agreement, a company may protect itself from the wrongful use or disclosure of trade secrets and the preservation of confidential information by reaching mutually acceptable terms for payment and confidentiality with a licensee.

19. Payment of royalties for the right to use other parties' trade secrets is consistent with the Massachusetts law of contracts and does not conflict with federal laws and the policy of the patent laws. All agreements, including a licensing agreement, in order to be enforceable must have consideration. That is, for example, a bargained for exchange of rights, promises or payments. In the license agreement at issue in this case, the defendant granted the plaintiffs a license to use its information to make ZnS/cvd and ZnSe/cvd in exchange for the payment of royalties.

20. In deciding whether the license agreement was premised upon sufficient consideration to be binding and enforceable, you must also consider that our law requires a duty of good faith and fair dealing in business transactions. If you find that Donadio and Connolly occupied positions of trust at Markham and that through their employment they became aware of trade secrets and confidential or proprietary information, then you must find that they had a continuing duty not to use and disclose these secrets and this information after they left the employ of the defendant. The protection of trade secret law is against breaches of trust.

21. In Massachusetts law, duress generally means that one party acted in such a way so as to have made the other party enter an agreement under such fear that would preclude the exercise of his free will and judgment. If the plaintiffs entered this agreement freely and voluntarily, you cannot find that there was duress.

22. In a business context such as the one presented in this case the elements necessary for you to find that the plaintiffs only entered the agreement under duress are that:
    (i)   the plaintiffs accepted the terms of the defendant involuntarily;
    (ii) the circumstances did not permit them any other alternative; and,
    (iii) those circumstances were the result of coercive acts of the defendant.

23. It is not duress sufficient to avoid a contract, for a party to threaten that it will exercise its legal rights, because the enforcement of legal rights by legal means is not evidence of duress.

24. In considering the circumstances that form the basis of the plaintiffs' claim of duress, you shall also consider whether there can be duress when the plaintiffs consulted with legal counsel throughout their negotiations and that their counsel who negotiated the terms was competent and experienced. You shall also consider the parties themselves and their knowledge and understanding of the terms of agreement and their obligations thereunder.

25. Section 2 of the Sherman Antitrust Act provides: Every person who shall monopolize, or attempt to monopolize, or combine or conspire with any other person or persons, to monopolize any part of the trade or commerce among the several states, or with foreign nations, shall be deemed guilty of a misdemeanor.

26. Monopolization violative of Section 2 of the Sherman Act has two elements: first, the "possession of monopoly power in the relevant market" and, second, the "acquisition or maintenance of the power" by other than such legitimate means as patents, "superior product, business acumen, or historical accident."

27. Monopoly power is the power to control prices or to exclude competition in the relevant market. Your first task, therefore, is to ascertain the relevant product market. The relevant product market is that area of goods in which the product or products offered by Markham effectively compete.

EXHIBIT 6   *(concluded)*

28. There are two related tests for determining whether two products are actually competitive with each other: (1) reasonable interchangeability of use and (2) cross-elasticity of demand. Thus, if the product and its substitutes are reasonably interchangeable by consumers for the same purposes, or if they have a high cross-elasticity of demand in the trade, they are to be included in the same market for the purpose of determining the existence of monopoly power.

29. The test of reasonable interchangeability emphasizes two factors. They are (1) use or uses, and (2) physical characteristics. If the substitutes have essentially the same end uses as the product, they are deemed to be interchangeable with each other and may, therefore, be included in the same product market. Similarly, if the physical characteristics of the substitutes are essentially the same as those of the product, so that customers may practically switch from one commodity to another, they are part of the same market.

30. Once you have ascertained the relevant product market you must decide whether Markham possesses monopoly power in that market—i.e., whether Markham has the power to control prices or exclude competition.

31. The antitrust laws do not prohibit monopoly in and of itself. Thus, it does not condemn one who merely by superior skill and intelligence got the whole business because nobody could do it as well.

32. If Markham's conduct was reasonable in light of its business needs and in accordance with ordinary business dealings and competition, it cannot be found to have used improper means in competing with CVD.

33. If you find that Markham's prices exceeded its total average cost of producing the goods, you must conclude that its pricing practices are lawful and do not constitute an act of monopolization in violation of Section 2. This is because the purpose of the Sherman Act is to encourage a competitive market price and lower prices to consumers.

34. Even if you find that Markham had monopoly power in the relevant market and even if you find that its prices fell below its total average cost, you must determine whether those price reductions by Markham, if any, were in response to price cuts made by CVD. If the prices charged by Markham were made in good faith to meet lower prices charged by CVD, then Markham's prices would be lawful under Section 13(b) of the antitrust laws. That Section provides for the so-called meeting the competition defense. To avail itself of the defense, Markham need not show that its prices were in fact equal to CVD's, but only that facts led Markham, as a reasonable and prudent person, to believe that the granting of the lower prices would meet the equally low prices of another.

EXHIBIT 7   CVD Incorporated, Income Statement ($ thousands), Year Ending February 28,

	1997	1996	1995	1994
Revenues:				
Net sales	$2,840	$2,387	$1,547	$751
Contract research	417	342	160	—
	$3,258	$2,729	$1,707	$751
Costs and expenses:				
Cost of goods sold and cost of contract research	$1,538	$1,451	$ 805	$460
Selling, general, and administrative	835	837	508	229
Research and development	193	52	—	—
Interest	75	89	88	51
Markham royalties (set aside)	—	—	86	109
	$2,642	$2,429	$1,487	$849
Earnings before income taxes and extraordinary items	616	300	220	(99)
Income taxes	252	37	42	—
Income (loss) before extraordinary items	364	264	178	(99)
Extraordinary items	—	—	27[a]	—
Net income (loss)	$ 364	$ 264	$ 205	($ 99)

[a]Utilization of net operating loss carry forward.
Note: Figures may not add due to rounding.

EXHIBIT 7   *(concluded)*

Balance Sheets

Assets	Feb. 28, 1997	Feb. 28, 1996
Current assets:		
Cash	$ 30,334	$ 154,407
Accounts receivable	548,463	379,307
Unbilled progress receivables on contract research	—	26,826
Notes receivable—officers	73,821	—
Inventories	710,189	506,922
Prepaid expenses and deposits	37,127	23,915
Deferred income taxes	—	112,000
Total current assets	$1,399,934	$1,203,377
Equipment and improvements—net	594,701	649,419
Other assets	—	3,119
	$1,994,635	$1,855,915

Liabilities and Stockholders' Equity	Feb. 28, 1997	Feb. 28, 1996
Current liabilities:		
Notes payable	$ 70,000	$ 80,000
Accounts payable	170,281	249,013
Accrued salaries and related expenses	48,275	48,601
Accrued expenses	159,874	139,719
Accrued royalties	—	194,825
Income taxes	47,761	24,187
Current maturities of long-term debt	111,804	111,804
Deferred revenues	221,100	—
Customers' advances	—	25,000
Total current liabilities	829,095	873,149
Deferred accounts payable	86,340	166,340
Deferred income taxes	199,200	43,500
Long-term debt, less current liabilities	182,482	314,286
Stockholders' equity	697,518	458,640
	$1,994,635	$1,855,915

VISCOTECH, INC.

Kenneth Jones, president of Viscotech, walked through the lobby of the Park Tower Building and headed toward a small restaurant near Chicago's business district. He needed some time away from the office, time to ponder the difficult situation in which he found himself. It was March 1998, and only seven months ago, Jones had left his position with a large pharmaceutical firm to become Viscotech's president. Stock, options, and a hefty salary increase had made the future seem bright. Now, all that seemed to be slipping away.

Jones had just come from a meeting with an attorney, Paul Benjamin, who had informed Jones that Viscotech might have committed violations of U.S. securities laws. Jones had to evaluate this information in light of the entire chain of events that had led up to that morning's meeting with Benjamin. As he considered his predicament, he realized that he needed to evaluate both Viscotech's and his own exposure to a potential SEC violation.

Viscotech

Viscotech was incorporated in 1991 by Dr. Samuel Evans, a surgeon and professor at the Midwestern Medical School; Louis Brown, a research scientist at the Chicago Institute of Technology; Dr. Harold Stein, a nutritional specialist at the Midwestern Medical School; and Melvin O'Connor, an accountant and attorney in the Chicago area.

This case was prepared by Professor Michael J. Roberts, Richard E. Floor of Goodwin, Procter & Hoar, Boston, and Professor Howard H. Stevenson. Professor Michael J. Roberts updated this case.

Copyright © 1993 by the President and Fellows of Harvard College.

Harvard Business School Case 9-393-117.

The company was founded in order to design, develop, and market a device that could measure the viscosity of saliva. It had long been known that this type of analysis of saliva could help physicians assess nutritional inadequacies in patients.

Between 1991 and 1996, the company had spent almost $500,000 pursuing its research agenda. These funds had been obtained from the company's founders in the form of debt and equity.

By late 1996, Viscotech had succeeded in obtaining several patents that covered the core technology used in the device. Viscotech had focused its efforts on developing its first product, the Doctor's Office Device. This device would be simple, easy to use, and would allow doctors to perform a comprehensive nutritional analysis in their offices. In addition, the technology had broader applications in the feeding and breeding of cattle and swine.

The announcement of the device had received a great deal of favorable attention in the medical press. By the end of 1996, Viscotech had developed a working prototype of the device, which was ready for more extensive clinical testing and subsequent submission to the Food and Drug Administration for approval.

1997—The Need for Capital

In early 1997, it became clear to Viscotech's principals that the company would require another infusion of cash in order to:

- Complete testing and receive FDA approval.
- Develop engineering and manufacturing specifications.
- Research new applications for the technology.

In April of 1997, a group of physicians who were friends of Viscotech's founders indicated that they were interested in investing in the venture. At about the same time, O'Connor had been in touch with the venture capital community seeking funds for Viscotech. At a meeting in late April, the four founders decided to pursue the raising of capital from other acquaintances in the medical community because the venture firms were offering too meager a price for an equity investment.

At this point, O'Connor agreed to proceed with the raising of funds in this manner. In order to protect the founders, he thought it prudent to raise money with a very carefully drawn offering circular. However, because his schedule was quite full with other business commitments, O'Connor knew that he would be unable to prepare such a document for several months.

The Medical Investment Fund Trust

Because of these constraints and the fact that Viscotech needed money quickly, O'Connor suggested that funds be raised through another vehicle—the Medical

Investment Fund Trust (MIFT). MIFT could then invest the money in Viscotech, and then Viscotech could spend these funds. Later that year, an offering circular would be presented, and each investor given the option to withdraw and receive his or her funds back. If investors chose to subscribe, they would agree to exchange their investment in MIFT for Viscotech shares.

O'Connor was confident that the trust offered a means of raising money on an interim basis, while avoiding the final commitment until the offering circular was issued. As such, the structure was similar to an arrangement O'Connor and Viscotech had used several years earlier to raise funds.

It was decided that investors who advanced funds through MIFT would receive a certificate representing shares in MIFT. MIFT, in turn, would be granted an option on shares of Viscotech. They would attempt to raise $2,000,000 in 250 units of $8,000 each. Each unit would represent a claim on 0.1 percent of Viscotech stock.

In June 1997, O'Connor drew up the trust instrument and a brief description of MIFT for potential investors (see **Exhibit 1**). This package contained information on Viscotech that had previously been made public. Prior to distributing the MIFT package, the company raised $100,000 from six relatives and friends of the principals to meet its needs during the interim.

Beginning in June, and continuing throughout the summer, acquaintances of Viscotech's principals advanced funds to MIFT. The funds were routinely forwarded to O'Connor's office and disbursed by him.

As part of the financing effort, Viscotech conducted a series of informational seminars for friends and acquaintances of the principals. These discussions centered around the technology, the history of the company, and potential markets for the company's devices. No formal offers were made at these seminars, nor were there any discussions of price. Many of the individuals who were present, however, did subsequently invest.

In August, O'Connor began to realize that his schedule was not going to be free for quite some time. Therefore, he contacted a friend of his, Leonard Atkins, an experienced attorney with the Chicago firm of Dewey & White. O'Connor informed Atkins of the MIFT arrangement and told Atkins that he wanted him to draw up an offering circular to close the MIFT financing. Atkins suggested that Viscotech undertake a private offering, but O'Connor said that he would prefer to have the SEC review any materials. Accordingly, they decided to attempt to raise funds through a Regulation A offering. This plan was approved at the annual shareholders' meeting in mid-August, and Atkins was given instructions to proceed.

Kenneth Jones

Later that August, Viscotech hired Ken Jones as its president. The original principals were able to spend only a portion of their time on Viscotech because of their medical and research responsibilities. In addition, as the product got closer to market, the principals felt the need for an individual with business experience.

Jones had graduated from the U.S. Naval Academy, and subsequent to his sea duty had attended the Midwest Business School. He had worked for a major international pharmaceutical firm as a product manager for four years before joining Viscotech. Jones was given 1,620 shares of Viscotech, options on further shares, and a salary of $65,000 per year.

Jones did not become heavily involved in the financing efforts because most of the potential investors were acquaintances of the founders. He did understand the MIFT arrangement, however, and understood from O'Connor that Atkins had cleared this vehicle for raising funds. Jones did attend and speak at several of the informational seminars, and he was briefed by Atkins on what to say. Specifically, Atkins told him to be wary of making statements that could be interpreted as "promises about Viscotech's future performance."

During the fall, Jones met with Atkins and O'Connor several times regarding the Regulation A offering. Jones edited several drafts of the offering circular. During this process, Atkins was supplied with Viscotech's financial statements prepared by O'Connor, which showed the liability for stock subscriptions through MIFT and detailed the expenditures of funds received. At one point, Jones asked Atkins how MIFT would be treated, and Atkins responded by saying, "We don't need to talk about MIFT."

By early December of 1997, $976,000 had been raised by MIFT from 34 investors. By February, the Regulation A offering circular was in draft form. Atkins had prepared the material for submission to the SEC. The principals decided to send the material off in early March.

The SEC Issue

The last weekend in February, Ken casually mentioned the financing plans to a friend at a neighborhood party. This friend, an attorney with the prestigious local firm of Cole & Eggers, thought that something sounded a bit odd. He suggested that Ken see one of his colleagues, Paul Benjamin, an expert on securities law. Ken made arrangements to see Benjamin during the first week of March and sent him a draft of the circular.

Jones explained the events of the past months to Benjamin, and they reviewed a copy of the circular. The attorney felt that the use of MIFT as a vehicle to insulate Viscotech was not effective, and that both Jones and Viscotech were exposed to SEC charges arising out of the manner in which MIFT had raised its funds. He recommended that Jones "come clean" and go to the SEC. Benjamin felt that this would show Jones's good faith and limit his own personal exposure to SEC charges. In addition, he advocated "freezing" all existing funds in MIFT as a further show of good faith. Viscotech could then raise its funds with a Rule 505 offering that required notifying the SEC but did not require SEC approval. Benjamin drafted a version of this offering, which appears as **Exhibit 2**, and which gives investors the option of withdrawing their investment. Benjamin also stated that the company would have to hire an individual to prepare the required two years of audited financial statements since O'Connor had had a financial interest in Viscotech while his firm was involved in the company's accounting.

What to Do

Jones's head was spinning when he left Benjamin's office. He wanted to do what was legal and ethically right. Yet, he also knew how desperately Viscotech needed funds to gear up for manufacturing and marketing of the Doctor's Office Device. Going to the SEC seemed to minimize his personal risk, but could implicate the rest of the company's principals and would surely harm the company's chances of raising money. Viscotech could go ahead with the Rule 505 offering, which merely required notifying the SEC. Benjamin said that there was a low probability that the SEC would request further documentation or the actual offering circular. However, in the event that the SEC did request the offering circular, Benjamin advised that it be very conservatively drafted, like the version excerpted in Exhibit 2. Ken felt, however, that this draft was *so* conservative that many investors would be likely to take recission (i.e., request the return of their investment) if they received this document.

Ken didn't know what to do. Any course that would successfully raise the funds Viscotech needed seemed to involve a good deal of risk.

EXHIBIT 1   MIFT Offering Circular

<u>Confidential Investment Memorandum</u>

Medical Investment Fund Trust

The Medical Investment Fund Trust (MIFT) has been formed as a vehicle to raise funds for Viscotech, Inc. Each $8,000 investment in MIFT will represent a claim on 200 (roughly 0.1 percent) of Viscotech's shares. MIFT seeks to raise $2,000,000 in this manner.

In the near future, Viscotech, Inc., will distribute an offering memorandum to those individuals who have invested in MIFT. At that time, any investor who desires to do so shall have the right to sell his/her MIFT shares back to the company for the amount of the original investment.

The Business

Viscotech was formed in 1991 by Dr. Samuel Evans, Midwestern Medical School; Louis Brown, Chicago Institute of Technology; Dr. Harold Stein, Midwestern Medical School; and Melvin O'Connor, Esq., O'Connor & O'Connor. The company has spent $500,000 of its founders' funds perfecting a technology that can assess nutritional inadequacies in patients through an analysis of saliva.

Patents

The company has filed and been granted 15 patents, which cover the core aspects of Viscotech's technology. In addition, the company has filed for 63 additional patents, which have yet to be ruled on. These patent applications have been made in 20 countries.

Products

Viscotech plans to produce the following devices:

- Doctor's Office Device: A complex instrument capable of analyzing deficiencies in a patient with respect to vitamins, minerals, blood sugar, amino acids, hormones, and trace elements.
- Home Device: A simpler instrument that will enable individuals to easily assess their own vitamin, mineral, and blood sugar levels.
- Farm Animal Device: A simple instrument that will allow breeders of cattle and swine to determine the optimal feed content for their animals.

With the tremendous increase in individuals' concern with their own nutritional well-being, the company is confident that these instruments will be extraordinarily successful. Imagine being able to take a simple test, using saliva, to determine the adequacy of vitamin and mineral intake, and to make dietary adjustments accordingly.

Markets

The markets for these products offer tremendous potential. In addition to lucrative U.S. markets, incredible potential exists in Third World markets where malnutrition is a problem. Individuals will now be able to test undernourished people to determine the precise therapeutic treatment. The government of India has indicated a strong interest in making a grant of $250,000 to Viscotech for the purpose of developing such an instrument for its use. The company currently plans to introduce the following devices:

The Doctor's Office Device: There is no other product available that performs these tests with the ease, accuracy, speed, and inexpensive price of the Viscotech instrument.

- Projected Potential Market: The potential market is projected to be doctors dealing regularly with patients with nutritional problems:

EXHIBIT 1   *(continued)*

	Nutritionists	*G.P.s*	*Total*
United States	14,000 of 24,000	6,000 of 56,000	20,000 of 80,000
Europe	10,000 of 20,000	5,000 of 70,000	15,000 of 90,000
Rest of world	4,000(est.)	1,000(est.)	5,000
Total potential market			40,000

- Average Instrument Usage
  - 6 tests per patient per month, or 75 tests per year.
  - 4 ongoing patients per doctor.
  - 75 × 4 = 300 tests per doctor per year.

- Sales Price
Instruments	$3,000.00 each
Disposables	$ 2.40 per test

Market introduction is projected for the third quarter of 1999 in both the United States and Europe. First-year projected sales of 250 instruments represents a less than 1 percent penetration of the potential market, with second-year sales of 400 instruments reaching a cumulative penetration of 1.9 percent.

Viscotech plans to initially distribute the doctor's instrument through regional dealers and manufacturers' reps in the major metropolitan areas where the primary market is concentrated. Given the large number of potential customers and the need to demonstrate the instrument to each of these potential customers, economics dictate that Viscotech make use of existing sales and distribution channels into these targeted doctors' offices. Viscotech will have a small, highly qualified in-house sales team to manage this distributor network. Viscotech will also handle all product services directly.

The Home Device: This device will allow individuals to safely and easily sample their own saliva to determine the levels of key nutritional variables: vitamins, minerals, and blood sugar levels.

Viscotech has developed working prototypes of the saliva collection device and the measuring device that comprise the Home Device System. Both components are significantly different from those used with the Doctor's Office Device.

At present the company is having a prototype mold constructed for the saliva collection device with a capability to produce 3,000–5,000 parts. Availability is scheduled for mid-September, after which we will begin the first in-use testing of the Home Device.

We estimate that design finalization will take 1–2 years and market introduction 2–3 years.

- Projected Potential Market: the potential market is projected to be men and women in the 15–45 age group that are currently using vitamins, dietary supplements, or have a nutritional problem. This represents an immediate worldwide market of about 100 million individuals:

United States	25 million
Europe	34 million
Japan	12 million
Rest of world	30 million
	101 million

- Average Instrument Usage: Minimum average of 5 tests per month or 70 tests per year.
- Sales Price
Instrument	$45.00
Disposables	$ .90
- Estimated Manufacturing Cost
Instrument	$10.00
Disposables	$ .20
- Total Potential Dollar Market
Annual disposable sales	7 billion tests	@ $ 0.90 = $6.3 billion
One time instruments sales	100 million	@ $45.00 = $4.5 billion

EXHIBIT 1   *(continued)*

- Sales Projections: Market introduction in the United States is projected for the second quarter of 2001. Projecting sales in such an enormous market is at best difficult. If a 1 percent share of the potential market were achieved during the first five years, end-user purchases of disposables would be $60 million annually, and instrument sales would average $9 million annually. The company feels that it is possible to achieve a 20 percent share of the potential market during the next 5–10 years.
- Marketing and Distribution: An arrangement with a very large multinational consumer marketing company appears to provide the most logical and reasonable path to the marketplace. Such a company could provide both the dollar investment and expertise required to successfully develop sales of the Home Device. Additionally it could provide indemnity for Viscotech against any product liability claims.

Discussions with International Pharmaceutical have taken place over the last six months and have developed to an advanced point. International has the broadest line of any company in the field and is part of a premier, highly successful company in the health care industry. International has made two offers in writing (June 8 and July 12), and Viscotech has made one counterproposal in writing (July 31).

The Farm Animal Device: The instrument system proposed for use by doctors in managing patients is, conceptually, equally applicable for increasing the productivity of food animals such as swine, dairy cattle, and beef cattle.

The objective is to develop an effective instrument system and verify its feasibility for improving the rate of weight addition in swine and cattle. This development process entails empirically modifying the doctor's instrument system to accommodate the saliva of swine and cattle.

Swine and cattle were chosen because they appeared to offer the greatest immediate commercial opportunity.
- Both are maintained and bred primarily in large confined herds, which facilitates management and recordkeeping.
- Both represent large potential markets in terms of numbers of annual breedings.
- Swine represent the largest per capita consumed meat in the world.

Dairy Cattle: Projected Potential Market: The potential market is projected to be only farms with over 50 milk cows, where the payback on an instrument system would be very high.

- Projected Potential Market: Farms with over 50 milk cows.
  United States—50,000 farms out of total 588,000 farms with milk cows.
  These farms have 4.8 million of the total 12.5 million milk cows in the United States. Our potential market in the United States is, therefore, 8.5 percent of total farms that have 38.5 percent of total milk cows.
  Europe—estimated 40,000 farms have 5 million of the over 50 million milk cows in Europe.
  Rest of world—conservative estimate 10,000 farms.
  Total market potential—100,000 farms.
- Average Instrument Usage
  - 11 tests per cow per year.
  - 144 cows per farm, which assumes 50 percent of sales will be to farms with 50–100 cows and 50 percent to farms with over 100 cows. This assumption results in penetration of market potential being greater for disposables than instruments.
  - $11 \times 144 = 1,584$ tests per farm per year.
- Sales Price
  Instrument $2,500 each
  Disposables $2 per test

Viscotech is currently funding a research program with dairy cattle at the University of the Midwest.

Market introduction is projected for the third quarter of 1999. First-year sales of 210 instruments represent a less than .5 percent penetration of the potential U.S. market. Second-year sales of 525 instruments brings the cumulative penetration to .7 percent of the total world market.

Distributor arrangements for sale to the dairy industry have not yet been set up.

EXHIBIT 1   *(concluded)*

<u>Swine: Projected Potential Market:</u> The potential market is projected to be only larger operations that average 250 sows. The animals are in a confined controlled environment, and the economic payback of an instrument system would be very high.

- Projected Potential Market

    United States—8,000 operations averaging 250 sows in confinement, which account for 40 percent of total 5 million sows in the United States.

    Europe—estimated 4,000 operations accounting for 25 percent of 4 million sows.

    Rest of world—estimated 2,000 operations accounting for 10 percent of 5 million sows.
- Average Instrument Usage
    1. 19 tests per sow.
    2. 250 sows per farm.
    3. $19 \times 250 = 4,750$ tests per farm per year.

Note: This averages 13 tests per day, meaning larger operations of 400–600 sows would definitely need two or three instruments for scheduling purposes. Instrument sales are projected conservatively at one per operation, but with replacement sales beginning after five years of heavy usage.

- Sales Price

    Instrument $2,500 each
    Disposables $1.25 per test

Note: Economics of sow breeding require lower cost per test to provide attractive payback. Competitively, lower disposables' price can be justified based on much higher volume of testing per farm as compared to dairy cattle. Gross margin will be reduced significantly, but still remain attractively above 40 percent.

Viscotech has recently signed a joint R&D/Distribution agreement with National Swine Breeders, Inc. This company is the largest producer of hybrid breeding stock in the United States.

Market introduction is projected for the second quarter of 1999. First-year sales of 100 units represents a 1.25 percent penetration of the potential U.S. market. Second-year sales of 200 instruments brings the cumulative penetration to 2.1 percent of the potential world market.

PROJECTED INCOME STATEMENTS ($000)

	2000	2001	2002
Sales	$2,726	$7,629	$23,400
Commissions (33%)	908	2,391	7,722
Cost of goods sold	661	1,974	5,850
Gross profit	1,157	3,264	9,828
Research and development	352	438	512
Sales and marketing	283	441	742
General and administrative	511	630	803
Interest	77	65	0
Depreciation	12	19	28
Profit before tax	(78)	1,668	7,743
Tax	—	—*	3,716
Profit after tax	(78)	1,668	4,027

*Due to prior losses and tax credits.

EXHIBIT 2   Viscotech Investment Memorandum

<u>Confidential Investment Memorandum and Recission Offer</u>

50,000 SHARES OF COMMON STOCK

This Confidential Investment Memorandum has been prepared in connection with the offering by Viscotech, Inc. (the "Company") of up to 50,000 shares of its Common Stock, $.10 par value, at $40 per share. The minimum subscription is 100 shares ($4,000).

This memorandum presents background information, has been prepared for the confidential use of private investors, and is not to be reproduced in whole or part. This offering is not made pursuant to any registration statement of Notification under Regulation A filed with the Securities and Exchange Commission, and the securities offered hereby are offered for investment only to qualifying recipients of this offering. The Company claims an exemption from the registration requirements of the Securities Act of 1933, as amended under Section 4(2) of that Act and Rule 505 thereunder.

Nothing set forth herein is intended to represent or in any manner imply that the stock offered hereby has been approved, recommended, or guaranteed by the Government of the United States or of any state, or by any of the agencies of either.

THE SECURITIES OFFERED HEREBY ARE HIGHLY SPECULATIVE AND INVOLVE A HIGH DEGREE OF RISK. PURCHASE OF THESE SECURITIES SHOULD BE CONSIDERED ONLY BY THOSE PERSONS WHO CAN AFFORD TO SUSTAIN A TOTAL LOSS OF THEIR INVESTMENT. SEE "RISK FACTORS."

THIS OFFERING INVOLVES IMMEDIATE SUBSTANTIAL DILUTION FROM THE OFFERING PRICE. FOR FURTHER INFORMATION CONCERNING THIS AND OTHER SPECIAL RISK FACTORS, SEE "RISK FACTORS" AND "DILUTION."

The offering price has been determined arbitrarily, and bears no relationship to the book value per share. Since all such shares must be acquired for investment only, no market for the shares offered hereby will arise, and no sales of such stock will be permitted in the future except pursuant to an effective registration statement or an exemption from registration under the Securities Act of 1933, as amended. Hence, the Company can offer no assurance that the stock will be salable at any time when the subscriber desires, or that the stock will be able to be resold at any time at or near the offering price.

The offering of the common stock is not underwritten. The Company plans to sell shares of common stock by personal solicitation or otherwise, through efforts of its distributors and officers. Such persons will receive no compensation other than reimbursement of out of pocket expenses incurred by them in connection with the sale. Such officers may be deemed "underwriters" as that term is defined in the Securities Act of 1933, as amended.

Unless 50 percent of the shares offered hereby are sold within 90 days from the date hereof, all subscribers' funds will be returned to them without interest or deduction.

EXHIBIT 2   *(continued)*

TABLE OF CONTENTS

Risk Factors

Viscotech, Inc. (the "Company") was incorporated under the laws of the State of Illinois on December 17, 1991, to do research on, and to develop, instruments and devices to measure precisely and accurately the amount of, and the variations in, elasticity and viscosity (known as viscoelasticity) of saliva in humans and other mammals. It has not yet marketed any such instruments or devices.

Prospective investors should be informed of the following risk factors involved in this offering:

(A) Insolvency:
1. To date, the Company has been engaged only in research and development, has generated no sales, and is, consequently, currently insolvent.
2. A substantial portion of this offering has already been raised and the funds have been used to pay current obligations. (See "Use of Proceeds.")
3. Even if the offering is fully subscribed, unless operations soon become profitable, or the Company raises additional funds elsewhere, investors will stand to lose their entire investment.

(B) Dilution:
In the event all the shares offered hereby are sold, those persons who purchase these shares will incur an immediate substantial dilution in the book value of $33.73 per share from the offering price of $40 per share while the book value of the presently outstanding shares will increase from a negative $3.91 per share to $6.37 per share solely by reason of the proceeds raised through the offering.

(C) No Operating History:
The Company has no operating history, and there is no assurance that it will operate profitably.

(D) No Present Product Market:
The Company has no contracts or commitments from potential users of its products and can give no assurance that the products will be marketed successfully.

EXHIBIT 2   *(continued)*

(E) <u>Limited Personnel:</u>

The Company has only three full-time employees, a Chief Executive Officer, and two Engineers. The development of the devices it intends to market has been, and will continue to be, of an indeterminate time, dependent upon part-time efforts of its founders, and of outside consultants.

(F) <u>Food and Drug Administration Approval:</u>

The Food and Drug Administration has not approved the Company's complete instrument system for sale, and no assurance can be given that it, or any other governmental agency with jurisdiction, will do so.

(G) <u>Use of Proceeds for Research and Development in Other Areas:</u>

A significant amount of the Company's funds will be used for further research and development in the fields of animal husbandry, consumer products, industrial products, and possibly other areas, and no assurance can be given that this research and development will be successful.

(H) <u>Need for Additional Funding:</u>

The Company believes that it will be necessary to secure funding in addition to that offered pursuant hereto in order to enable the Company to achieve its objectives. The Company will seek to raise such additional funds through any one or more of loans, grants, or additional equity. Should the Company seek to raise additional equity, it may be required to do so at a price per share less than that being offered pursuant hereto, in which case investors will suffer a dilution in the value of their shares. The Company can give no assurance that such additional funding will be available to it on any basis.

(I) <u>Competition:</u>

Many companies with resources far greater than those available to the Company are involved in the field of nutrition and may be able to compete with the Company.

(J) <u>Dividends:</u>

The Company has never paid dividends, and does not expect to do so in the foreseeable future.

(K) <u>No Cumulative Voting:</u>

The common stock of this Company does not have cumulative voting rights. Hence, the holders of more than 50 percent of the shares voting for the election of directors may elect all the directors if they so choose. Since the present management holds more than 50 percent of the shares to be outstanding, it will be in a position to reelect itself as directors.

<u>Business</u>

It has long been known that the viscoelasticity of saliva decreases in the event of nutritional deficiency. To date, however, to the knowledge of the Company, there is no instrument or method capable of accurately measuring this decrease at a reasonable cost and evaluating the extent and cause of nutritional inadequacy. Such measurements can be of significant aid to doctors in diagnosing the problems of overweight, obese, or anorexic individuals and to breeders of such animals as cattle and swine. The instruments that the Company has developed are, it believes, capable of making such measurements on minute quantities of saliva, which consists of a variety of nonhomogeneous materials, without homogenizing them or otherwise destroying their integrity. The instruments developed by the Company do not rely on hormonal, chemical, or other ingested material, nor on any implanted devices. Rather, a sample of saliva is extracted and placed on a grid in the instrument, which is capable of determining the exact amount of viscoelasticity present in the sample.

Food and Drug Administration approval is a necessary prerequisite to the marketing of the Company's products for human medical use in the United States. Approval has been granted for the Company's saliva aspirator. Application for approval of the Company's Doctor's Device (the first major product that the Company intends to market) will be submitted subsequent to the completion of clinical trials presently in progress. There can be no assurance that approval will be forthcoming. A delay in the grant of such approval, or the attachment thereto of conditions, or the denial thereof, might have a serious, adverse effect on the Company.

Although the Company has developed prototype machines and other products for use by doctors, clinics, and other medical personnel, such machines have not been distributed, and so their effectiveness in the field remains unproven. The Company has distributed a limited number of its products to users who are not associated with the Company, in order to secure from them reports as to results and other comments. The Company cannot guarantee that such reports or comments will be favorable.

In addition, the Company is planning to contract for the production of several hundred Doctor's Devices to be available for sale to doctors, clinics, and hospitals for delivery commencing in 1998. Although the Company has had negotiations with manufacturers, no commitments or contracts have been made. In consequence, no assurance can be given that the machines can be produced within the projected time and at a favorable price, or that if produced, a sufficient number can be sold to offset the investment.

EXHIBIT 2   *(continued)*

The Company is presently attempting to develop a device at a commercially reasonable price that would enable a person to sample his own saliva and determine his own nutritional levels. There can be no assurance that its efforts will be successful within a reasonable time and at reasonable cost, or that in any event, Food and Drug Administration approval will be granted, or that such a device would have the degree of consumer acceptance necessary for economic viability.

The Company also has research projects planned to measure bronchial secretions, synovial fluid, spinal fluid, serum, and meconium, any or all of which may be of importance in other branches of medicine. In addition, the Company is supporting research at a university agricultural school to experiment in the application of the Company's concepts in the field of swine production.

All of these activities will take considerable time to complete. No assurance can be given that any will be completed successfully, or within the resources of the company, or that if successfully completed, commercially salable products can be developed and marketed.

Patents

The Company has filed and been granted patents on certain applications of its basic concepts and has filed further patent applications which are presently pending. Patent applications corresponding to certain of the Company's U.S. patents have been filed in twenty or more countries. A schedule setting forth the patent status is included as Appendix A. The Company can offer no assurance that any pending patent application will be granted, that the grant of any patent ensures that the product covered thereby can be marketed successfully, that any patent is valid and enforceable, or that any of its patents cannot be circumvented or attacked by others. Nor can it assure that any of its present or future products will not infringe on patents of others.

Use of Proceeds

The net proceeds of this offering, assuming the sale of the 50,000 shares offered hereby, will be approximately $1,800,000 after deducting estimated expenses of $200,000. The Company will apply the net proceeds to satisfy its liability on Stock Subscriptions which as of the date hereof totals $976,000 (see Note 8 of Financial Statements), such liability having been created by the receipt by the Company of subscriptions to this offering prior to the issuance of this Confidential Investment Memorandum. The funds creating this liability have been used since June 1997, as follows:

- $300,000 to reduce bank indebtedness.*
- $250,000 to pay current indebtedness to creditors.
- $30,000 to process patent applications.
- $396,000 for working capital, including the salary of the Company's President, other employees, research and development, and other expenses of the Company.

The balance of the proceeds from the offering ($1,124,000) will be used to pay the estimated expenses of the offering (approximately $200,000), and the balance ($924,000) added to working capital.

Since there is no underwriting for the shares being offered, there is no assurance that all of the shares will be sold. As of the date of this offering, the Company has received subscriptions for the purchase of substantially all shares offered hereby, and has accepted funds for the purchase of 24,400 of the shares offered hereby. Such subscriptions cannot be accepted except pursuant hereto. Unless subscriptions pursuant hereto are received within 90 days from the effective date of this Memorandum for at least 30,000 shares offered hereby, all subscribers' money will be returned to them without interest or deductions. In any event, any subscriber who has sent money to the Company for the purchase of the securities offered hereby prior to the receipt of this Confidential Investment Memorandum, who so requests or who fails to complete and return the subscription form attached hereto within such 90-day period will be refunded his or her subscription money in full without interest or deduction.

---

*The remaining balance of $65,000 indebtedness to the bank is to be paid, by agreement, $5,000 per month, commencing April, 1998. The Company's original indebtedness of $365,000 to the bank was personally guaranteed by certain of the Company's directors. The proceeds of the loan were used in part to repay Company indebtedness to its directors.

EXHIBIT 2   *(continued)*

Certain Transactions

  Indebtedness to Affiliates

  As of February 28, 1998, the Company was indebted to certain of its officers and other related parties as follows:

Creditor	Amount Due	Date Due	Consideration
Louis J. Brown	$ 7,500	Sept. 1, 1999	Services rendered.
Harold J. Stein	$25,000	Sept. 1, 1999	Services and expenses.
Fredericks Communication	$63,562	$2,000/month commencing Oct. 1, 1998	Expenses; employees' services.
O'Connor & O'Connor	$23,000	Sept. 1, 1999	Expenses; employees' services.
Melvin I. O'Connor	$16,782	Sept. 1, 1999	Cash advanced.

All amounts due bear interest ranging from 8 percent to 12 percent per year.

Mr. Brown and Dr. Stein are consultants to the Company. The debt to Mr. Brown represents accrued consulting fees; and that to Dr. Stein represents approximately $11,000 in accrued consulting fees and approximately $14,000 advanced by him as salary to a nurse engaged to assist him in his research for the Company.

Fredericks Communication, and its subsidiaries, furnished services in fabricating parts, materials, and devices used by the Company, and also conceived, developed, and produced slide shows, display equipment, and audiovisual shows used by the Company at exhibits and medical meetings. The indebtedness to Fredericks consists of services of employees and out of pocket expenses.

The indebtedness to the Company's accountants is produced by services of employees and out of pocket expenses in recordkeeping, statement and tax return preparation, and clerical services.

Melvin I. O'Connor advanced funds at various times. The liability to him represents interest on various loans ($4,282) and the remaining balance on these cash loans to the company ($12,500).

The Company intends to continue its arrangements with Mr. Brown for consulting services at a cost to the Company of $1,500 per month, plus out of pocket expenses. In addition, the Company intends to use, as required, the services of Dr. Stein and the staff accounting services of the Company's accountants at the generally applicable rates of each for such services. If the Company deems it advisable it may utilize the services or facilities of other affiliates for compensation to be negotiated in each instance. The Company has negotiated an informal arrangement with Fredericks Communication Co., Inc., whereunder the latter has constructed an office and engineering laboratory in a building owned by Fredericks Communication Co., Inc., and has leased it to the Company on a tenant-at-will basis. Such arrangement has not been formalized by any written agreement.

Fredericks Communication Co., Inc.

Fredericks Communication Co., Inc. ("Fredericks"), originally known as Fredericks Recording Co., Inc., was contracted by the Company in 1995 to supply the Company with disposable grids, then contemplated to be plastic squares with uniform ridges. Thereafter, the Company and a subsidiary of Fredericks known as Fredericks Research & Development, Inc., entered into a joint venture to procure, manufacture, or have manufactured for it the grids required by the Company on an exclusive basis. On November 17, 1997, the Company acquired by merger Fredericks Research & Development, Inc., for 10,980 shares of the Company's stock (after giving effect to the August 1997 stock split). At that time Fredericks Research & Development, Inc.'s share of expenses (excluding fixed costs, overhead, and executive salaries) for research and development on Company products was $46,466.34.

The Company has used Fredericks to procure substantially all of the molds, dies, boxes, aspirators, machinery, extruders, and other equipment required by the Company. Fredericks also provided research and development for the grids and other items in connection with the Company's business, and rendered assistance to the Company in conceiving, designing, and producing film strips, slides, and other display material used by the Company in its presentations at trade and other shows. Fredericks principals, Messrs. Smith, Green, and Marvin, in September 1996, purchased 3,960 shares of the Company's stock, after giving effect to the August 1997 stock split, for $120,000 ($30.30 per share). Messrs. Smith, Green, and Marvin loaned the Company $50,000 cash, which was repaid in July 1992, and Mr. Green, along with other Company principals, endorsed a Company Note for $165,000 to a bank in July 1997. Mr. Smith has been at various times Clerk, Assistant Clerk, and Director of the Company, and both he and Mr. Green are currently Directors.

EXHIBIT 2   *(continued)*

Fredericks has charged the Company for these various services, for its actual costs of materials, services of its staff and special personnel other than executive personnel. The Company intends to continue its arrangements with Fredericks respecting procurement and the providing of other services, and to reimburse Fredericks in connection with these activities for Fredericks's expenses and services of its personnel other than executive personnel.

Capital Structure and Description of Common Stock

The capitalization of the Company as of the date of this Offering Circular, and as adjusted to give effect to the sale of the shares offered hereby, is as follows:

	Prior to Offering	Following Offering if All Shares Sold
Notes payable—bank	$365,000	$ 65,000
Notes payable—shareholders	135,844	135,844
Accounts payable	47,506	47,506
Stock subscriptions	976,000	-0-
Capital stock	14,412	19,412
Additional paid-in capital	462,028	2,257,028

The Company's Common Stock, of $.10 par value, is its only authorized class of capital stock. At all meetings of stockholders, holders of Common Stock are entitled to one vote for each share held. The holders of Common Stock have no preemptive or subscription rights. All the outstanding shares of Common Stock are fully paid and nonassessable and are entitled to dividends if and when declared by the Board of Directors.

The Common Stock of the Company does not have cumulative voting rights. Hence, the holders of more than 50 percent of the shares voting for the election of directors may elect all the directors if they so choose. Since the present management holds more than 50 percent of the shares to be outstanding, it will be in a position to reelect itself as directors.

Dividends

Holders of shares of the Company's Common Stock are entitled to receive dividends as may be declared by the Board of Directors out of funds legally available therefore and to share pro rata in any distribution to shareholders. The Company does not contemplate the payment of any dividends in the foreseeable future.

New Financing

The Company believes that it will be necessary to secure funding in addition to that offered pursuant hereto in order to enable the Company to achieve its objectives. By letter dated March 8, 1997, the Indian U.S. International Industrial Research & Development Foundation, a foundation sponsored and funded by the governments of the United States and India, advised the Company that its Board had approved a first-year grant of up to $250,000 to be expended on research and development of the Company's products, subject to various conditions and the negotiation of a formal contract. The Company believes that conditions to this grant will include (*a*) establishment of a joint program with an Indian company for research, development, preproduction, and premarketing of the Company's products, (*b*) expenditures by the Company and its Indian partners on the program during the first year of the grant of amounts equivalent to those received from the grant during the same time. The Company cannot give assurances that a final contract for the grant will be executed, or that if it is, the Company will be able to satisfy the conditions thereof.

Remuneration

Mr. Jones was engaged as Chief Executive Officer on September 1, 1997, at a salary of $65,000 per year. Mr. Brown is paid consulting fees of $1,500 per month. None of the other officers or directors are compensated. In November 1995, O'Connor & O'Connor, of which Mr. O'Connor is a partner, were issued 900 shares of stock (after giving effect to the 12 for 1 split) in satisfaction of $7,500 of liability to them for cash advances and staff services rendered. The shares were distributed to the partners of O'Connor & O'Connor, other than Mr. O'Connor, who disclaims any benefit therefrom or control thereover. Mr. Jones has devoted full time to his duties as president of the Company since September 1, 1997, and is currently in the process of moving his residence to Illinois.

EXHIBIT 2   *(continued)*

<u>Applicable Regulations</u>

As indicated above, the products contemplated by the Company for use by doctors and by individuals require approval of the Food and Drug Administration (FDA). There is no assurance that the Company will be able to comply with the FDA regulations or that the necessary approval of the Company's operations and all the products can be achieved. To date it has only received such approval for its aspirators. The Company is in the process of compiling clinical data with respect to the balance of its products, to be supplied to the FDA as required. The Company believes that these contemplated products, however, may be utilized in animal husbandry without FDA approval and, if manufactured abroad, may be utilized outside the United States without FDA approval, although they may require approval by appropriate regulatory agencies in each country. The Company also believes that no government regulations are applicable to any of the contemplated uses in industry, inasmuch as no hazardous procedures are associated with the utilization of the Company's proposed products.

<u>Litigation</u>

The Company is not involved in any litigation and knows of no threatened or contingent liabilities.

The Company, at the request of any subscriber or Advisor (as defined in the Subscription Agreement), will make available for inspection copies of these documents, will provide answers to questions concerning the terms and conditions of this Offering, and will provide such additional information that is necessary to verify the accuracy of the information contained herein or that may otherwise pertain to the Company or to this investment, to the extent the Company has such information or can acquire it without unreasonable effort or expense.

EXHIBIT 2   *(continued)*

Financial Statements

Consolidated Balance Sheet
(Unaudited)

	February 28, 1998	June 30, 1997	1996	1995	1994	1993	1992
ASSETS							
Current assets:							
Cash	$ 21,110	$ 1,104	$ 6,437	$ 4,745	$ 1,207	$ 10,331	$ 12,514
Inventories (Notes 1 and 2)	150,023	18,359	—	—	—	—	—
Subscriptions receivable (Note 3)	131,000	—	73,413	—	—	—	3,000
Prepaid items	1,000	—	—	—	—	—	—
Total current assets	303,133	19,463	79,850	4,745	1,207	10,331	15,514
Fixed assets (Notes 1 and 4)	31,274	26,775	2,074	—	—	—	—
Other assets:							
Patents and patent applications	325,753	183,753	115,467	59,595	33,942	17,637	—
Unamortized organization and other expenses	831	673	279	171	287	403	519
	326,584	184,426	115,746	59,766	34,229	18,040	519
Total assets	$ 660,991	$ 230,664	$ 197,670	$ 64,511	$ 35,436	$ 28,371	$ 16,033
LIABILITIES AND SHAREHOLDERS' EQUITY/(DEFICIT)							
Current liabilities:							
Medway advances (Note 5)	$ —	$ —	$ —	$ —	$ 43,850	$ 33,850	$ —
Current maturities of note payable—bank (Note 6)	50,000	—	—	—	—	—	—
Current maturities of amounts due to shareholders (Note 7)	10,000	269,000	2,500	9,000	—	16,000	16,000
Accounts payable and accruals	47,506	196,487	44,075	22,833	6,912	184	1,702
Total current liabilities	107,506	465,487	46,575	31,833	50,762	50,034	17,702
Long-term debt:							
Note payable—bank (Note 6)	15,000	—	—	—	—	—	—
Amounts due to shareholders (Note 7)	125,844	—	—	—	—	—	—
	140,844	—	—	—	—	—	—
Amounts received on stock subscriptions (Note 8)	976,000	20,000	—	—	—	—	—
Shareholders' equity/(deficit) (Note 9):							
Common stock, par value $.10 Authorized 300,000 shares Issued 144,120 shares	14,412	476,440	461,440	103,940	37,940	9,940	9,940
Additional paid-in capital	462,028	—	—	—	—	—	—
Accumulated deficit	(1,039,799)	(731,263)	(310,345)	(71,262)	(53,266)	(31,603)	(11,609)
	(563,359)	(254,823)	151,095	32,678	(15,326)	(21,663)	(1,669)
Total liabilities and shareholders equity/(deficit)	$ 660,991	$ 230,664	$ 197,670	$ 64,511	$ 35,436	$ 28,371	$ 16,033

The accompanying notes are an integral part of the consolidated financial statements.

EXHIBIT 2 *(continued)*

Consolidated Statement of Operations and Accumulated Deficit
(Unaudited)

	Feb. 28,	June 30,					
	1998	1997	1996	1995	1994	1993	1992
Sales	$ —	$ —	$ —	$ —	$ —	$ —	$ —
Expenses:							
Rent	1,888	—	—	—	—	—	—
Office and clerical expenses	11,385	10,853	17,975	6,575	27	130	118
Meetings expenses	7,741	3,266	5,305	2,959	1,340	681	—
Advertising, shows, public relations	9,482	46,355	26,524	5,499	—	—	—
Telephone	3,130	2,021	946	160	114	184	—
Taxes	2,276	1,520	948	116	116	116	—
Miscellaneous	1,086	106	142	—	—	—	—
Interest	12,385	8,750	—	—	—	—	—
Depreciation	819	—	—	—	—	—	—
Payroll and payroll expenses	33,909	—	—	—	—	—	—
Research and development (Note 11)	224,435	348,047	187,243	2,687	20,066	18,883	11,319
	308,536	420,918	239,083	17,996	21,663	19,994	11,609
Net loss	(308,536)	(420,918)	(239,083)	(17,996)	(21,663)	(19,994)	(11,609)
Accumulated deficit, beginning	(731,263)	(310,345)	(71,262)	(53,266)	(31,603)	(11,609)	—
Accumulated deficit, ending	($1,039,799)	($731,263)	($310,345)	($71,262)	($53,266)	($31,603)	($11,609)

The accompanying notes are an integral part of the consolidated financial statements.

EXHIBIT 2 *(continued)*

Consolidated Statement of Changes in Financial Position
(Unaudited)

	8 Mos. Ended Feb. 28, 1998	Years Ended June 30,					
		1997	1996	1995	1994	1993	1992
Resources provided:							
From operations:							
Net loss	($ 308,536)	($ 420,918)	($ 239,083)	($ 17,996)	($ 21,663)	($19,994)	($ 11,609)
Add items not affecting working capital:							
Depreciation and amortization	904	325	251	116	116	116	58
Working capital applied to operations	(307,632)	(420,593)	(238,832)	(17,880)	(21,547)	(19,878)	(11,551)
Amounts received on stock subscriptions	956,000	20,000					
Proceeds of bank note	15,000						
Amounts due shareholders	125,844						
Capital investment		15,000	357,500	66,000	28,000		9,940
	789,212	(385,593)	118,668	48,120	6,453	(19,878)	(1,611)
Resources applied:							
Purchase of fixed assets	5,403	25,026	2,325				
Other assets	158	394	108				
Patents and patent applications	142,000	68,286	55,872	25,653	16,305	17,637	577
	147,561	93,706	58,305	25,653	16,305	17,637	577
Increase/(decrease) in working capital	$ 641,651	($ 479,299)	$ 60,363	$ 22,467	($ 9,852)	($ 37,515)	($ 2,188)
Changes in the components of working capital:							
Increase/(decrease) in current assets:							
Cash	$ 20,006	($ 5,333)	$ 1,692	$ 3,538	($ 9,124)	($ 2,183)	$ 12,514
Inventories	131,664	18,359					
Subscriptions receivable	131,000	(73,413)	73,413			(3,000)	3,000
Prepaid items	1,000						
	283,670	(60,387)	75,105	3,538	(9,124)	(5,183)	15,514
Increase/(decrease) in current liabilities:							
Medway advances				(43,850)		33,850	
Current maturities of notes payable—bank	50,000				10,000		
Current maturities of amounts due to shareholders	(259,000)	266,500	(6,500)	9,000	(16,000)		16,000
Accounts payable and accruals	(148,981)	152,412	21,242	15,921	6,728	(1,518)	1,702
	(357,981)	418,912	14,742	(18,929)	728	32,332	17,702
Increase/(decrease) in working capital	$ 641,651	($ 479,299)	$ 60,363	$ 22,467	($ 9,852)	($ 37,515)	($ 2,188)

The accompanying notes are an integral part of the consolidated financial statements.

EXHIBIT 2 *(continued)*

NOTES TO CONSOLIDATED FINANCIAL STATEMENTS
February 28, 1998
(Unaudited)

Note 1—Summary of Significant Accounting Policies
    Principles of Consolidation
        The consolidated financial statements include the accounts of Viscotech, Inc., and its wholly owned inactive subsidiaries, Nutrico, Inc., and Animal Technology, Inc. All intercompany balances and transactions have been eliminated in consolidation.
        The Company was organized December 29, 1991; and the subsidiaries were organized in December 1994: Nutrico, Inc., for the exploitation of the Company's concepts related to industrial viscometry and Animal Technology, Inc., for the exploitation of the Company's concepts related to animal nutrition.

Inventories
    Inventories are valued at the lower of cost (first-in, first-out basis) or market.

Fixed Assets
    Fixed assets are carried at cost and depreciated on the straight-line method over estimated useful lives as follows:

Display equipment	Five (5) years
Molds and dies	Seven (7) years
Machinery	Ten (10) years
Office equipment	Ten (10) years

Note 2—Inventories
    Inventories consisted of the following:

	February 28, 1998	June 30, 1997
Machines completed awaiting modification	$116,500	$16,500
Machine parts	15,000	—
Aspirators—finished	8,138	500
Grids	3,961	—
Packing materials	5,799	1,121
Instruction booklets, tapes, calibrating fluids, etc.	625	238
	$150,023	$18,359

Note 3—Stock Subscriptions
    The Company has offered its shares through the Medical Investment Fund Trust. The Company has not yet received payment for all shares subscribed.

Note 4—Fixed Assets
    Fixed assets consisted of the following:

	February 28,	June 30,	
	1998	1997	1996
Display equipment	$2,183	$2,183	$2,183
Molds and dies	23,730	22,163	—
Machinery	5,367	2,758	—
Office furniture	1,141	—	—
	32,421	27,104	2,183
Less accumulated depreciation	1,147	329	109
	$31,274	$26,775	$2,074

EXHIBIT 2   *(continued)*

Note 5—Medway Advances

In fiscal years 1993 and 1994, the Company received nonrefundable advances from Medway, Inc., to finance research and patent applications. Medway, Inc., was given an exclusive marketing arrangement during this period. Medway's contract for exclusive marketing expired in December 1994.

Note 6—Note Payable—Bank

In July 1997, the Corporation borrowed $365,000 from a bank, unsecured but guaranteed by several shareholders. Of the proceeds, $255,000 was used to repay the shareholders who had loaned that amount to the Corporation. The note, which bears interest at the bank's prime rate plus 2 percent, originally matured in January 1998. At that time, $300,000 was paid. The remaining balance is to be paid in monthly installments of $5,000, commencing in April 1998.

Note 7—Due to Shareholders

In February 1993, several shareholders-creditors accepted term notes for amounts due them as follows:

Shareholder-Creditor	Amount	Interest	Payable	Nature of Debt
Louis Brown	$ 7,500	8%	Sept. 1, 1999	Services rendered
Harold J. Stein	25,000	Prime	Sept. 1, 1999	Research services, out of pocket expenses
Fredericks Communications	63,562	Prime	$2,000/month commencing Oct. 1, 1999	Out of pocket expenses, services of employees
O'Connor & O'Connor	23,000	8%	Sept. 1, 1999	Out of pocket expenses, services of employees
Melvin I. O'Connor	16,782	8%	Sept. 1, 1999	Cash advances
	$135,844			

Louis Brown and Harold J. Stein had been employed as consultants at $1,500 per month each. In addition, Dr. Stein advanced the salary and expenses of a nurse employed by the Company in his office.

Fredericks Communications and its subsidiaries furnished services in fabricating parts, materials, and devices used by the Company, and also conceived, developed, and produced slide shows, display equipment, and audiovisual shows used by the Company at exhibits and medical meetings. The indebtedness to Fredericks consists of services of employees and out of pocket expenses.

The indebtedness to O'Connor & O'Connor is produced by services of employees and out of pocket expenses in recordkeeping, statement and tax return preparation, and clerical services.

Melvin I. O'Connor advanced funds at various times. The liability to him represents interest on various loans ($4,282) and the remaining balance on these cash loans to the Company ($12,500).

Note 8—Amount Received on Stock Subscriptions

Funds have been received from subscribers to the stock of the Corporation. Issuance of the stock has been delayed pending approval of a registration under Regulation A of the Securities and Exchange Commission. The registration involves 50,000 shares of $.10 par value stock, to be issued at $40 per share. At June 30, 1997, 500 shares had been subscribed and paid for, and at February 28, 1998, a total of 24,650 shares had been subscribed.

Note 9—Common Stock

On August 31, 1998, the Corporation voted to change its authorized capital stock from 12,500 shares of no par value to 300,000 shares of $.10 par value and to exchange 12 shares of the newly authorized stock for each share of old stock then outstanding. This exchange of shares has been given effect in the accompanying financial statements by transferring from common stock to additional paid-in capital the amounts in excess of par as of February 28, 1998.

Note 10—Merger

On August 31, 1997, the shareholders voted to issue 915 shares of old no par stock (equivalent to 10,980 shares of new $.10 par stock) to Fredericks Research & Development Corporation in exchange for all the outstanding stock of that corporation and to merge Fredericks Research & Development Corporation into the Company. The assets acquired from Fredericks Research &

EXHIBIT 2   *(continued)*

Development Corporation were certain technical procedures in production and the right to limited participation with the Company in certain production profits. No value was recorded for the assets acquired from Fredericks; accordingly, common stock was credited and additional paid-in capital charged for the par value of the shares issued.

Note 11—Operations

The Corporation has used most of its resources since its inception in research and development of its concepts for measuring the viscoelasticity of oral mucus in humans and animals and developing instruments for commercial medical application. Expenditures to date are as follows:

Fiscal year June 30, 1992	$ 11,319	
June 30, 1993	18,833	
June 30, 1994	20,066	
June 30, 1995	2,687	($43,850 defrayed by others—Note 5)
June 30, 1996	187,243	
June 30, 1997	348,047	
July 1, 1997 to February 28, 1998	224,435	
	$812,630	

Note 12—Taxes on Income

The Company's net operating losses are available to offset future taxable income. Losses through 1994 may be carried forward five (5) years and subsequent losses, seven (7) years.

For tax purposes, the Company has capitalized research and development costs, as discussed in Note 11, which costs will be written off over sixty (60) months from commencement of significant sales.

APPENDIX: ACCREDITED INVESTOR QUESTIONNAIRE

THE INFORMATION IN THIS INVESTOR QUESTIONNAIRE IS BEING SOLICITED SOLELY TO DETERMINE THE STATUS OF THE UNDERSIGNED AS AN ACCREDITED INVESTOR AND THE SUITABILITY OF THE INVESTMENT IN THE _____ STOCK FOR THE UNDERSIGNED. THIS INFORMATION WILL BE KEPT STRICTLY CONFIDENTIAL AND WILL NOT BE USED FOR ANY OTHER PURPOSE.

Investor Questionnaire

In connection with the potential purchase by the undersigned investor (the "Investor") of shares of the _____ (the "Shares") of _____ Inc. (the "Company") contemplated by a certain Confidential Private Placement Memorandum regarding the Company dated _____, 19___ (the "Memorandum"), the Investor hereby represents, warrants and covenants to the Company as follows:

1. Investor Status. The Shares will only be offered for sale to persons and entities who either (i) qualify as "accredited investors" as defined in Rule 501 of Regulation D promulgated under the Securities Act of 1933, as amended (the "Act"), [or (ii) are presently holders of the Company's outstanding _____ stock with participation rights entitling them to invest in the Shares]. Answer the following questions yes or no to establish your status as an "accredited investor."

(a) The Investor, or the Investor and his or her spouse jointly, have a net worth in excess of U.S. $1,000,000. _____

(b) The Investor's income for each of the past two years has been in excess of U.S. $200,000 (or joint income with the Investor's spouse has been in excess of U.S. $300,000) and the Investor has a reasonable expectation (alone or with his or her spouse, as the case may be) of reaching the same level of income this year. _____

(c) The Investor is a bank as defined in Section 3(a)(2) of the Act or a savings and loan institution or other institution as defined in Section 3(a)(5)(A) of the Act whether acting in its individual or fiduciary capacity; a broker or dealer registered pursuant to Section 15 of the Securities Exchange Act of 1934; an insurance company as defined in Section 2(13) of the Act; an investment company registered under the Investment Company Act of 1940 or a business

EXHIBIT 2 *(continued)*

development company as defined in Section 2(a)(48) of that Act; a Small Business Investment Company licensed by the U.S. Small Business Administration under Section 301(c) or (d) of the Small Business Investment Act of 1958; a plan established and maintained by a state, its political subdivisions, or any agency or instrumentality of a state or its political subdivisions, for the benefit of its employees, if such plan has total assets in excess of $5,000,000; an employee benefit plan within the meaning of the Employee Retirement Income Security Act of 1974, if the investment decision is made by a plan fiduciary, as defined in Section 3(21) of such Act, which is either a bank, savings and loan association, insurance company, or registered investment adviser, or if the employee benefit plan has total assets in excess of $5,000,000, or, if a self-directed plan, with investment decisions made solely by persons that are accredited investors. _____

(d) The Investor is a private business development company as defined in Section 202(a)(22) of the Investment Advisers Act of 1940. _____

(e) The Investor is an organization described in Section 501(c)(3) of the Internal Revenue Code, a corporation, a Massachusetts or similar business trust, or a partnership, not formed for the specific purpose of acquiring the Shares, with total assets in excess of $5,000,000. _____

(f) The Investor is a director or an executive officer of the Company. _____

(g) The Investor is a trust with total assets in excess of $5,000,000, not formed for the specific purpose of acquiring the Shares, whose purchase is directed by a sophisticated person as described in Rule 506(b)(2)(ii) of Regulation D. _____

(h) The Investor is an entity in which all of the equity owners are accredited investors. _____

2. Investor Suitability. In addition to the requirement of Investor Status, Shares will only be offered for sale to qualified investors with respect to whom the Company has determined that their proposed investment in the Shares is suitable. All potential investors must answer the following questions yes or no to establish their suitability as an investor.

(a) The Investor has adequate means of providing for his or her current needs and personal contingencies, has no need for liquidity in connection with this investment and can afford the loss of his or her entire investment in the Shares. _____

(b) The Investor's overall commitment to investments which are not readily marketable is not disproportionate to the net worth of the Investor, and the Investor's investment in the Shares will not cause such overall commitment to become excessive. _____

(c) The Investor has evaluated the risks of investing in the Shares, has recognized that the Investor could sustain a total loss of the investment, and has determined that the Shares are a suitable investment for the Investor. _____

(d) Name of current business, business address and telephone number:
_____
Type of current business: _____
If applicable, position held in current business, responsibilities involved in position and number of years employed in position: _____

(e) Please provide either (i) the name of your accountant, attorney, broker or other person familiar with your finances who may be contacted to verify the financial information contained in Section 1 of this Investor Questionnaire or (ii) complete the financial information requested on Exhibit A attached hereto:
Name: _____ Relationship: _____

(f) Do any significant contingent liabilities exist for which you may be obligated?
Yes _____ No _____ If yes, please indicate type and amount: _____

(g) Are you involved in any significant litigation which, if determined adversely, would have a material adverse effect on your financial condition? Yes _____ No _____ If yes, please provide details. _____

(h) Please indicate the number and total dollar amount of investments you have made within the last three years in illiquid securities issued by start-up companies, such as the Shares.
Number _____   **Total Dollar Amount** _____

EXHIBIT 2   *(concluded)*

---

3. <u>General.</u>

(a) The Investor acknowledges that the Company will rely on the Investor's representations contained herein as a basis for the exemption from registration.

(b) The Investor received the Memorandum and first learned of this investment in the jurisdiction of his or her business or residential address set forth on the signature page hereto, and intends that the securities laws of only that jurisdiction shall govern this transaction.

(c) The Investor, if a resident of a foreign jurisdiction, has considered the effect of the securities laws of such jurisdiction on his or her potential purchase of the Shares and such laws do not in any way prohibit, otherwise conflict with, or impose any substantive or procedural limitations on, such potential purchase.

(d) The Investor, either alone or with his or her purchaser representative, has such knowledge and experience in financial and business matters as to be capable of evaluating the merits and risks of the prospective investment in the Shares.

EXHIBIT A

Please provide the following information as of the most recent practicable date, indicating such date below:

Month _____ Day _____ Year _____

<u>ASSETS</u>

Liquid Assets
  (cash, money market funds, publicly-traded stocks and bonds) $_____

Illiquid Securities
  (non-publicly traded securities, such as the Shares) $_____

Other Assets
  (real estate, personal property and other assets) $_____

Total Assets $_____

<u>LIABILITIES</u>

Current Liabilities
  (liabilities coming due within one year) $_____

Long-Term Liabilities
  (liabilities coming due in more than one year) $_____

Total Liabilities $_____

<u>NET WORTH</u>

Total Assets—Total Liabilities $_____

DEAVER BROWN AND CROSS RIVER INC.

Deaver Brown, co-founder and CEO of Cross River Inc., had finally connected with the buyers of K-Mart and Macy's. Deaver and his partner, Alex Goodwin, had started Cross River in 1970 to manufacture, market, and sell baby strollers. A year later, the company was selling approximately 2,000 units a month almost entirely through small stores. Deaver and Alex believed that Cross River now had to sell through higher volume channels such as discount stores and department store chains; otherwise, their company would struggle along going nowhere and eventually disappear. Therefore, Deaver felt, his presentation to the K-Mart and Macy's buyers could determine the future of their company.

Background

After graduating from Harvard Business School in 1968, Deaver had joined General Foods. A year later, he began investigating opportunities to start his own business. Deaver recalled:

> I had worked at General Foods on one highly advertised, differentiated brand, Cool Whip, and on one commodity oriented product line, Birds Eye Vegetables. I had found that the Vegetable business was more fun than Cool Whip because no one cared much about it. They left it to me; trusted me with the decisions; appreciated my successes and were not overly concerned with my failures. It seemed as if I was running my own little backwater business. It was fun and I learned a lot as I won a few and lost a few

Deaver Brown and Professor Amar Bhidé wrote this case as the basis for class discussion rather than to illustrate either effective or ineffective handling of an administrative situation.
Copyright © 1993 by the President and Fellows of Harvard College.
Harvard Business School Case 9-394-042.

battles along the way. The clear feedback was probably the most satisfying element of the job: successes were mine; failures were mine. No excuses were available!

This helped me define my thinking about a new business to pursue on my own. Essentially, I decided to pursue backwater businesses that had a steady customer stream in the consumer product area. After many investigations and false starts, I teamed up with an old friend, Alex Goodwin, to make an innovative baby stroller.

Alex had found a light weight folding stroller, invented by an Englishman. The inventor had tried to license the product but all of the American companies in the industry turned it down because the conventional wisdom said it was not heavy and durable enough for the American consumer. Alex had found the easy-to-carry stroller perfect for his mobile lifestyle and suggested that we get the license.

We checked out the market facts about strollers. We found that 1,400,000 baby strollers and 300,000 carriages were sold at wholesale in 1969. Total wholesale sales of baby strollers were $24,500,000 and total sales of carriages were $14,000,000. Despite the visibility of these products—one often sees strollers rolling down streets—the category was very small. The birth rate was in decline; parenting was out of favor. Only about 5% of the population at any time had a use for a baby stroller either for personal or family use or as a gift.

The market was divided among about 20 manufacturers. The primary methods of distribution were general mass merchants such as Sears, Wards, Penney; department stores such as Macy's; small juvenile furniture shops, especially in large cities such as New York; and emerging retail classifications such as discounters, mail order, and catalog showrooms.

I checked out the production facts and found the product that I dubbed the Umbroller, a contraction of the words **umb**rella and st**roller**, would cost approximately $8.00 to make in reasonable volumes and $6.50 in 100,000's of units. The assembly process would be reasonably complex with 42 rivets, a frame consisting of 12 pieces of tube, one seat, 12 steel brackets, and plastic handles. A lot of work!

The fragmentation of competition, among 20 plus companies, coupled with the fragmentation of distribution, meant that getting started would not be too difficult because no dominant players existed. The problem, however, was that though our company might get launched and even survive, the odds of becoming a large, dominant player were small. Distribution channels, for example, were extremely fragmented and no single success would have a large payback. In sum, a successful launch might not bring much return other than a company in what I called "The Land of the Living Dead."

The First Year

I left General Foods, and we invested about $30,000 from a combination of personal savings and a bank loan backed by personal guarantees to launch Cross River. We had expected to license the product after launch and we offered big money for the rights, but we were turned down. We decided to go ahead anyway; we had studied the patent and Alex thought we could beat it in court. We were subsequently sued, and the matter is now pending.

We made prototypes and tried a test market in Buffalo but no retailer would buy it. Nevertheless we took our product to a trade show to see if we could get orders.

Alex and I had sold various things together in high school. They ranged from products for teenagers to a niche Maine record called "Bert and I," with Maine humor, to record stores. We sold the records through hustle and salesmanship. Alex and I were back to hustle and salesmanship.

At the trade show, Alex and I were pretty good at button-holing small dealers, getting pencil to paper, and getting the orders. But dealing with salaried buyers from the big chains was like sinking in Jell-O. We got nowhere.

We did button-hole a buyer from Bradlees who bought our argument about a new and exciting product. He bought 600 of them—our first big order. Months later, we found out the buyer had left Bradlees to start his own business. We had not been good salesmen to this guy; we had been lucky. We had met someone like ourselves trying to get out of the big company world.

My MBA training and GF work experience coupled with Alex's flair for sales and marketing helped us put together a solid marketing foundation. We had the first four-color self-service carton; we advertised in the one niche periodical, *American Baby*, a small consistent ad; we advertised in two trade journals; we put together a solid sales literature package. We hired about 20 reps who worked for the company on a commission only basis.

Small business economics are very simple, though unforgiving. We needed to sell 2,000 strollers per month to break-even:

- We received $13.50 per unit from the retailers (who then sold it with a mark-up[1] for about $25).
- Our variable cost per unit was $9.35: $8.00 of product cost plus 5% commission of $.675 plus 5% miscellaneous variable expense of discounts, returns, and the like of $.675. So Cross River netted $4.15 per stroller.
- Our fixed costs ran at $8,300 per month. We paid ourselves $2,500 ($1,250 each). Our monthly ads in *American Baby, Small World*, and *Juvenile Merchandising* cost $1,935. The rest was spent on travel expenses, phones, promotional material, professional fees, and the like.

We had achieved break-even through November 1971 on a month to month basis. But we hadn't shipped product for the orders we had written in October 1970 until January 1971 and we ate up our capital during this period.

Landing a Major Account

We had to do more than break even. In facing up to our problems of mediocrity, we determined the problem was bagging a major account or two that could take us up to the level of 4,000 to 6,000 units per month and propel us to a higher level of success.

We eliminated the **mass merchants:** this was an old boy network; we were unlikely to crack it and a major effort would be required. **National discounters** were a more likely group. Compared to the established mass merchants, these were the Young Turks, more anxious to "do things" and "try things." We had already achieved

---

[1]Retailers generally referred to "mark-ups" as a percentage of the retail price.

some success with small, local discounters. However, the discounters were blue collar oriented. They wanted a lower price than we felt we could give them. We also saw an opportunity with **major department store chains** which were a major factor in hard-goods and liked new things. We had achieved some local successes with smaller department stores as well.

We've secured an appointment with a buyer at Macy's. Macy's is the most prestigious department store chain in the country with outlets in New York and several other large metropolitan areas. They carry a line of promotional strollers starting at a retail price of $19.99 and going up to $49.99. They have a middle price range of strollers ranging from $50.00 to $100.00, and a carriage line running from $100 to $300. Their markups are approximately 40% to 50%, with larger markups prevailing at the higher end of the line.

Although Macy's provides a wide variety of hardgoods and apparel products, appealing from the blue collar consumer all the way up to the highest income groups, it cultivates an image of an upscale department store. Macy's is a very big deal—and they know it! If we get the Macy's account it will give us great national credibility.

The Macy's buyer, who works in New York City, was willing to see us because he had seen our product at a few other department stores and had an ongoing relationship with our independent sales representative who secured the appointment for me.

I had met the buyer at a trade show once. He's a long term Macy's employee who has never risen above the buyer level in 30 years of work and seems to be waiting out his time until retirement. He's quite knowledgeable about the technical aspects of the products and the Macy's merchandising and buying system.

Our other hot prospect is the national K-Mart buyer in Troy, Michigan. K-Mart is the leading national discounter and is much better capitalized and has far greater buying power than its competitors. K-Mart typically buys five times the volume of its rival discounters. Unlike Macy's, K-Mart has no pretensions of being an upscale store. It targets blue collar workers.

K-Mart carries three baby strollers and no carriages. It has a promotional stroller at $9.99, a moderate priced unit at $19.99, and its highest priced model at $29.99. Its hardgoods markups are approximately 30% to 40%.

The K-Mart buyer is a seasoned buyer and department manager who does not want his world changed. He has become a millionaire through K-Mart stock options and, although loyal to his company, now just wants to go smoothly into the sunset.

I had tried, in the past, to make an appointment to meet with the buyer but had always been turned down. Next I tried to hire a sales representative to get an appointment and was told they only worked directly with the factory. Then, I resorted to calling the buyer from the New York Airport saying I was in the Detroit (Troy) area and could I stop by to see him. On this basis, he said yes once, I flew out to Detroit and made an acquaintance with him and his entourage of assistants.

This time I expect to arrange the same kind of trip.

With one firm appointment and virtual certainty of getting the other, I now have to figure out what I'm going to say at each meeting. I need to get the presentation done in 10 to 15 minutes; at that point, if I have the buyers' interest, we can wind down the meeting and arrange for future orders.

MARCIA RADOSEVICH AND HEALTH PAYMENT REVIEW: 1989 (A)

Marcia Radosevich, president of Health Payment Review (HPR), wondered what it would take to convert prospects into customers.

Marcia and several health care experts had launched HPR in 1987 to develop and market software that would review reimbursement claims submitted by doctors, hospitals, and laboratories. HPR management believed that reviewing claims for overcharges and inconsistencies could result in significant savings for providers of health plans such as HMOs, insurance companies, and corporations. Payments for surgical procedures, for example, could be reduced by 5% to 15%. And, using software would be far less costly than manually inspecting claims.

With $750,000 provided by the Caterpillar company, a leading manufacturer of earth-moving equipment, HPR had begun developing its first product, *CodeReview*. Two years later, in 1989, it had developed a prototype that ran on personal computers (PCs) and that it hoped to convert to a mainframe-based product. The company had nearly exhausted its cash, however, and Marcia decided to sell the PC version in order to fund development of the mainframe product. By March, her sales efforts had come to naught: many potential customers had shown great interest, but none had given HPR an order.

Background

Marcia, the third of six children, was born and raised in Iowa. Her father had died when she was 13. In 1974, after graduating with a sociology degree from Cornell

Professor Amar Bhidé and Brian Mohan, MBA '94, prepared this case as the basis for class discussion rather than to illustrate either effective or ineffective handling of an administrative situation.

College in Iowa, she worked as legal secretary and paralegal. After nine months, she decided against a legal career and entered graduate school at the University of Iowa. A Ph.D. in sociology in 1982 led her to faculty positions at Boston College and Yale, where she studied social deviance and white-collar crime. Marcia found her research enjoyable, but not her teaching assignments and, in 1984, decided on another career change. She ruled out law and government, where she feared the excessive bureaucracy and red tape, and although she felt that business was where "dumb people went," she enrolled in Wharton Business School's summer program. The program, which limited enrollment to 40 and compressed an academic year's worth of courses into a summer term, attracted many other "refugees from the world of academia."

Her certificate in Business Administration and fascination for quantitative analysis and research led Marcia to a job with a premier health care consulting firm. There she managed high-visibility projects with Chrysler, General Motors, and the UAW, developing expertise in analyzing health care costs as well as in compiling and interpreting clinical and statistical data.

Marcia left the consulting firm in 1986. She recalled:

> It was a tremendous organization with outstanding people. But I still felt stifled by the research. It was too academic and we didn't have the power to implement real change. I wanted to make things happen.

In her next job, as regional director for Managed Health Care Services (MHCS), Marcia developed and managed a preferred provider organization (PPO) for the Travelers Insurance Companies. She enjoyed her experience at MHCS:

> I used my skills to create something—putting together hospital and physician PPO deals. I could make things happen, even when others said it was impossible: I developed networks, which were among the fastest growing in the country, in markets that skeptics in the company said were saturated. And, I learned how to sell and negotiate from the two principals of the firm. They were the best teachers I've ever had.
>
> I had imagined salespeople to be slick, fast-talking, amusing persons. I had imagined negotiating was pounding your shoe on the table. These guys taught me that selling is about building a relationship. It's about getting in early, defining the playing ground and the rules of the game, creating a sense of urgency, and building toward a conclusion. It's about being nonthreatening: "Go ahead and think I'm some nice girl from Iowa, and I'm a Ph.D., and I would never be threatening to anyone." It's about patience, it's about controlling the timing.
>
> These guys never raised their voices. They were smart, unassuming, and their egos didn't get in the way. They let somebody else take credit for their ideas. They spent all the time they needed to—morning, noon, and night—being available. Clients would sometimes say to them, "Here's the language I want in the contract" and it would be totally unacceptable. They'd never say "No"; they'd say "let me understand what your concern is here. What's the problem you are trying to solve with this language?" Then they'd find out that you didn't really want their first-born child.

When a large company acquired MHCS, in 1988, Marcia prepared to take a six-month sabbatical and go scuba diving. Instead, the HPR opportunity came along.

Launching Health Payment Review

HPR began as a joint research project between Boston University (BU) and Caterpillar, Inc. headquartered in Peoria, Illinois. For many years, Dr. Robert Hertenstein, medical director of Group Insurance at Caterpillar, had reviewed reimbursement claims manually for accidental or intentional errors and saved the company about $500,000–$600,000 a year. For example, Hertenstein often found "unbundling" claim errors—billing separately for the components of a treatment instead of for a less expensive inclusive procedure. Thus he would look for doctors who submitted an "a la carte" bill of $4,500 for the components of a hysterectomy rather than the $2,400 bundled flat fee.

Concerned about its growing health care claims and its reliance on the skills of one individual, Caterpillar sought the help of BU's Health Policy Institute (HPI). The HPI team working on the Caterpillar project—Drs. Richard Egdahl, George Goldberg, and William Ryker—were well-known researchers in health care cost containment who also had extensive clinical experience. In the course of their study, the team concluded that an automated system to review claims would produce considerable savings for organizations such as Caterpillar. And, they decided to form a private, for-profit company to develop and sell such systems.

Marcia got involved with the HPI team as a result of her friendship with Goldberg, whom she had worked with in her previous consulting job. For about six months, before HPR was formally launched, she served as a consultant to the HPI doctors. In this capacity, she urged them to seek financing from Caterpillar and helped negotiate the terms. Then, in July 1988, the doctors appointed Marcia president.

> They needed a businessperson, and as far as they were concerned, I was a business genius! These men were brilliant researchers and academics, but they were completely without a clue on all aspects of the business. I had been out of academia for four years at the time, and they thought I was very experienced. I was immensely attracted to the concept. I liken the product to a paper clip or the Post-It note pads. I couldn't believe that no one else had developed software to review claims. It was such a simple and ho-hum idea—and yet an incredible amount of money could be made.

Although by June, Caterpillar had agreed, in principle, to provide $750,000 in return for a royalty on HPR's product, the parties had not signed a contract. Marcia recalled:

> When I walked in the door, it was through an academic BU appointment at HPI. There was no money in HPR, just these incomplete agreements, with brackets around paragraphs for the incomplete stuff. My first job was to try to do this deal. I was being paid an academic salary, with the proviso that as soon as I got the money from Caterpillar I could go back to a quasi-normal private-sector level. So I was highly motivated.
>
> I knew the negotiations could go on forever. They **had** been going on forever. Nobody knew what they were doing. The guy at Caterpillar who was trying to do it was the benefits manager, and the guy at HPI was a Ph.D. in Operations Research. They would talk on the phone, and then two weeks would go by before they had

another discussion. Every time somebody would change something, they would give it back to the lawyers to have them completely redraft the whole thing.

We had to create a sense of urgency. The first day I walked in, I called the guy at Caterpillar and said, "We have to get this done within 30 days, or else I'm going to shop it. I'm not getting paid, and there are other people interested in this. Just do it or not." He tried to tell me that Caterpillar goes on vacation in August. I said, "No, this has all got to be done by then."

We ended up signing in six weeks. I worked night and day. I was calling this guy at home. I was faxing things to him, I was courier-ing things to him at home. He never had this done to him before. He kept wanting to wait until next week. I said, "No." I was driving everybody crazy. He said, his lawyers couldn't turn documents around that fast. I asked him for the names of the lawyers. I would call them: "Please do this for me. I'm desperate, I'm not getting paid, we've got to get this done." I think that's one of the many areas where being a woman really helped me, because they perceived me as much less threatening. This was all I did—morning, noon, and night. I wrote stuff, and I would try to keep lawyers out of it as much as I could. I had this Ph.D. in operations research writing things. He said, "Marcia, I'm not a lawyer." I said, "It doesn't matter. Write it up, write it in English." Then we gave it to HPR's lawyer and I told him, "You have to write this up immediately." He was a BU patent attorney who said he wasn't a corporate lawyer. And I said, "William'd give me this . . . just write it up." He had a couple of percentage points of HPR because he had incorporated the company. I said, "You've got to earn your money here. Come on, I'm going to make you rich." So he worked late weekends, and he wrote this agreement up. It's far from being a perfect legal document, but it was legal; it was enough, and they signed it.

Caterpillar agreed to put up $750,000 in three equal installments. At the very beginning, they had said, "Rather than give you the money, we'll just develop the software ourselves." We asked, "How much would it cost you?" They said $750,000. We agreed to do it for them for $750,000, and we promised to throw in on-going maintenance and support for free. We knew that $750,000 wasn't enough, but it would get us through the first 6 to 12 months, and we could get a PC version done. We would need more money for a mainframe version, but we would cross that bridge when we got there.

The deal could have been structured in a variety of ways. The most obvious way was for Caterpillar to take a large equity position. That I badly did not want. I didn't want a big company as a partner. They would want to try to run everything. They wouldn't understand the business I was in: They build earth-moving equipment, they don't build software. I was hoping to grow the company and take it public; but big-company partners that don't need you to make a lot of money are less likely to let you do the kinds of things that you need to do in order to get rich. Big companies often use little companies as a think tank or an R&D extension.

We tried to figure out a deal that would give Caterpillar some upside potential, and then when I was still a consultant, we came up with the idea of a royalty stream. Then William Ryker wrote it up—he has to write up everything—and I reviewed and edited it. He then just wanted to send it to the Caterpillar guy, but I made William call first and read it over the phone and then follow up in writing. We went through many iterations, with William writing quite elaborate equations for the royalty, which amounted to about 5% of net and 1% of gross. I wonder if the Caterpillar people really understood William's equations—I don't think our chairman, Dick Egdahl, who is brilliant, understood. But, by the time I joined HPR full time, they had agreed to the formula.

William is very sincere, and we were able to show them how much money they would make, if we were successful, without all the hassles of equity.

Then the problem became that they wanted an open-ended royalty stream. But deals are good only if you can get out of them. I didn't want this ongoing obligation to Caterpillar; one of these days, we would go public, and I didn't want to write in my prospectus that I owed Caterpillar 1% of the gross revenues of my flagship product. At first, it seemed unfair, to them, but we eventually obtained an option to buy them out, according to a formula we negotiated. They didn't want us to be able to buy them out, but they understood, from a business perspective, why it made sense.

They began wanting to postpone final agreement on the buyout provision, and I wouldn't let them. I knew if we got the deal signed, if we got the money, and if they got their software, we were never going to agree on how I could buy them out early. So I told them to sign the entire deal, or I would shop it somewhere else. I told them Aetna would give me money. And I gave them all the reasons why I would not buy them out early, while I was getting them to tell me that I could. They finally just agreed. Part of it was creating the momentum and the sense of urgency. It had to be done by the end of August, or I would go elsewhere. I had to get paid. Part of it was forcing them to agree to all of it at once. And finally, we just outlasted them. They had been in negotiations at this point almost a year. They just wanted to get it over with and get on with doing the work.

We also gave a little bit of equity in HPR to BU's venture capital fund. Our chairman, Dick Egdahl, wanted to create a model whereby for-profit enterprises could be spun out of universities, where the university would not be a stone around the entrepreneur's neck, yet would have some recognition and upside. We didn't use any of BU's money; still, the fact is that the Caterpillar relationship came about as a result of the university. And by giving a little bit of equity, we got a lot of attention from the BU people. They felt great: they hadn't given us any money, and they got equity.

March 1989

With Caterpillar's money in hand, HPR began developing *CodeReview*, which belonged to the category of software known as expert systems. Expert-systems software helped users in fields such as oil exploration, process control, and medical diagnosis solve difficult problems by incorporating the rules of thumb of experienced practitioners. Similarly, HPR planned to draw upon the knowledge of more than 50 experienced physicians, surgeons, and subspecialists and include tens of thousands of clinical-decision rules in *CodeReview*. It would update this knowledge base annually, as procedures and their payment schedules changed.

The company planned to develop a PC-based prototype and then a version for mainframe computers. HPR programmers could develop the PC prototype relatively quickly using D-Base, a popular off-the-shelf database package. Caterpillar would use this version immediately, as a substitute for its manual reviews. The prototype would not, however, process large numbers of claims quickly. Moreover, because most organizations processed their medical claims on mainframes, they would have to enter data twice—on the PC for review and then for normal processing. Therefore, HPR planned to follow the PC-based prototype with a mainframe version. But developing the mainframe version would be more time consuming and difficult. HPR wanted a program that could easily be adapted to many types of mainframes and, unlike the PC version, could not build on an off-the-shelf package like D-base.

In accordance with its plan, in 1989, HPR delivered a PC product to Caterpillar on January 2. It covered, Marcia said, "Just the surgical section, but it was enough to call it a product, and it was all Caterpillar wanted at the time." Soon thereafter she decided to try to sell the PC prototype to other customers, before HPR had developed the mainframe version. Marcia recalled:

> Rule 101 in software development is: you never sell the prototype. But, we were running out of money, because William Ryker, who's brilliant, decided he wanted to be vice president for software development. He went to the BU bookstore, bought a book on expert systems, and decided how to build the system. And he's been giving much of the money we got from Caterpillar over to two computer consultants who aren't building anything useful. They live in Iowa so that they can meditate with the Maharishi Yogi there. I've been sweating bullets. It's like an hourglass; every drop of sand is another dollar. But, William is a founder of the company . . .
>
> We have monthly expenses of $85,000. We now have on staff three full-time employees and five full-time consultants—two programmers (the two in Iowa), two product developers—who generate the coding rules—and one salesperson who is an M.D.
>
> I thought, we're going to go bankrupt. I looked around for things to sell, and the only thing we can sell is the prototype. I thought, "Screw the rules, we've got to sell this PC thing, even if it wasn't built as a commercial system." We hired a consultant to do some technical writing and the documentation to make it look like a product, and we started trying to sell it. We drew up a licensing agreement—$100,000 for installation and $60,000 for annual maintenance and updates of the knowledge base.
>
> There are a lot of people in the industry who know me or Dick Egdahl, so it wasn't any problem getting an audience. Dick also lent us the services of Steve, a young M.D. at the Health Policy Institute who wanted to learn how to sell. Steve and I visited several dozen potential customers.
>
> We've really worked at building relationships with prospects. To build a relationship, you have to spend time with someone. You have to have face time, and you have to spend money on airfares to get it. And you send them little articles to keep your name visible: "I saw this article in the *Wall Street Journal*; you might be interested." Of course, the guy has seen the article, but you thought of him and talked it over with him. That helps a lot. So I've been working to get as much face time as I can, and I've been coaching Steve as well.
>
> Steve, who has a great personality, can play the doctor bit up to the hilt. He tells them war stories about working in the Emergency Room, and they feel that they were in there, too, and that maybe they are as smart as Steve. Dick Egdahl says that most people don't get five minutes with their doctor, and now here's Steve lavishing attention on them. And when benefits managers deal with doctors or Ph.D.s, it makes them more comfortable: **We** are not salespeople; we are not even businesspeople. We are intellectuals, right?
>
> But, we haven't made a sale yet. We've encountered great skepticism. *CodeReview* runs only on PCs, and many of the guys we've talked to run big mainframe shops and have severe mainframitis. Nobody has done anything like this before, and they're

afraid that doctors will react negatively to reviewing claims. The payers of health care still have a lot of doctor fear. It's OK for Caterpillar, they say, because they own Peoria. HPR is a brand-new company—what if they use it, make it an integral part of their operations, and then HPR sinks? They have a million reasons not to do it. I actually think a number of them are interested, but they're afraid to be the first ones.

And we have only a couple of weeks' worth of cash left. Beyond that, I suppose we could ask BU's venture capital fund for a short-term loan. Dick Egdahl also has some grants at the HPI, and we could put some more people on the Institute payroll and pay the Institute back when we get some revenues. But that can only be a stopgap. We have to make a sale.

EXHIBIT 1   Excerpts from License Agreement with Caterpillar Inc.

Background

HPR is a start-up company which intends to develop and market a computer software product which, in general, is useful in applying medical judgment to the evaluation of medical claims submitted by health care practitioners prior to payment of such claims.

CATERPILLAR desires to facilitate the development of such computer software product and to use the product at any of its facilities or the facilities of its subsidiaries, wherever located.

Section 2.1

HPR shall initially develop a microcomputer version of the SOFTWARE to run on IBM AT or PS/2, or compatible hardware, with 640k RAM and 10mb hard disk drive, and deliver the same to CATERPILLAR for acceptance testing.

Section 2.4

After completion of said microcomputer version above, HPR shall develop a version of the SOFTWARE that will interface with CATERPIILLAR's mainframe computer claims processing system in a language mutually agreed upon by the parties and deliver a prototype version of the same to CATERPILLAR within 6 months of the completion of said microcomputer version.

Section 2.5

To assist HPR in the development of the SOFTWARE and as additional consideration of the rights herein granted to CATERPILLAR, CATERPILLAR agrees to provide, at no charge, the services of Robert D. Hertenstein, M.D. to serve as a consultant to HPR.

Section 4.1

Upon acceptance as herein provided, HPR shall grant to CATERPILLAR a non-exclusive, non-transferable and perpetual CORPORATE LICENSE to use the OBJECT CODE of the SOFTWARE, as provided herein.

Section 5.1

For the rights to be granted to CATERPILLAR, CATERPILLAR shall pay HPR a total sum of Three Hundred Thousand Dollars ($300,000.00).

EXHIBIT 1   *(concluded)*

Section 11.1

For a period of twenty (20) years from the date of this Agreement, HPR shall provide MAINTENANCE SERVICE to CATERPILLAR . . . to the extent that it is made available to HPR's other customers. Such MAINTENANCE SERVICE shall include, but is not limited to:

One copy of each UPDATE to the SOFTWARE and SOURCE CODE at the time of its release.

Reasonable written or telephone consultations regarding use of or problems with the SOFTWARE.

EXCERPTS FROM LOAN AGREEMENT

Section 2.01

. . . to make a loan in the principal amount of Four Hundred Fifty Thousand Dollars ($450,000.00) (the "Loan") to the Borrower in three equal installments as follows:

1. One Hundred Fifty Thousand Dollars ($150,000.00) within 20 days after Lender's acceptance (as such term is used in the License Agreement) of the first prototype version.
2. One Hundred Fifty Thousand Dollars ($150,000.00) within 20 days after Lender's acceptance of the second prototype version.
3. One Hundred Fifty Thousand Dollars ($150,000.00) within 20 days after Lender's acceptance of the third prototype version.

Section 2.02

(a) REPAYMENT. Borrower shall repay said Four Hundred Fifty Thousand Dollars ($450,000.00) plus interest thereon by making the following two types of payments to Lender:

(1) Borrower shall pay Lender an amount equal to five percent (5%) of Borrower's gross sales from the date of this Agreement, until an amount equal to Seven Hundred Fifty Thousand Dollars ($750,000.00) has been paid to Lender. If, however, an amount equal to $750,000.00 has not been paid to Lender as of December 31, 1993, on that date Borrower shall pay that portion of said $750,000.00 which has not previously been paid.

(2) Immediately following the payment of the foregoing Seven Hundred Fifty Thousand Dollars ($750,000.00), Borrower shall pay Lender for a period of twenty years (measured from the date of the final installment on such $750,000.00 payment) less the number of years for which it takes Lender to repay said $750,000.00, the greater of 1% of gross sales for each fiscal year or 5% of net after-tax profit for each fiscal year.

(b) SALE OF STOCK. In the event that a majority of the issued stock of Borrower is, in a single transaction, either a) sold to a third party not presently a stockholder . . . In the event that a sale is made prior to full payment by the Borrower of the $750,000.00 due under Section 2.02 (a) (1), or, made after such payment but prior to two full calendar years of Section 2.02 (a) (2) payments, the amount to be paid to the Lender shall equal a) any remaining amount due under Section 2.02 (a) (1), plus b) the average of the amounts which were paid by the Borrower under Section 2.02 (a) (2), or would have been paid by Borrower under such Section had the amount in 2.02 (a) (1) previously been paid, for the two full calendar years preceding the sale, multiplied by the number of years remaining under the Section 2.02 (a) (2) payment obligation.

CHRIS MILLER

Chris Miller turned down the radio and began to concentrate on a pressing dilemma. Chris was 10 minutes away from the downtown office building where the second board meeting of the newly formed Boston Benefits Group (BBG) was about to be held. Chris was a member of the board and had advised the two founders—Linda Gibbons and Ellen Ravisson—on the start-up of their benefits consulting firm.

Linda and Ellen had met at a larger firm in the benefits consulting business where they both worked as benefits consultants, helping large firms purchase and provide benefit plans for their employees. The two had both quit when the management of this firm had demanded that everyone sign a noncompete agreement, forbidding them from going into the benefits consulting business on their own or from trying to woo any existing clients. While Linda and Ellen had no thoughts of doing so, they felt that the noncompete was overly restrictive. They refused to sign it and had been fired as a result. Thus, they decided that they would go into business on their own. The women had—with Chris's considerable help—developed a business plan that indicated that the business could be quite successful.

Chris had been involved in the venture because Linda was a close friend and because Chris's experience as a financial consultant was valued by the two founders. All had gone smoothly until two weeks ago, when—in a conversation about the business—Linda related that Ellen had just discovered that she was two months pregnant.

Over the past month, Chris had helped the two develop their business plan and projections and had negotiated the start-up financing they would need. At this

Professor Michael J. Roberts prepared this case.

Copyright © 1992 by the President and Fellows of Harvard College.

Harvard Business School Case 9-393-076.

afternoon's meeting, the closing would occur, and BBG would receive $80,000 in start-up financing from John Blackwell, a local and wealthy physician, who happened to be Drew Gibbons's partner in a cardiology practice. (Drew was Linda Gibbons's husband.) Linda and Ellen had decided that they did not want to tell Blackwell of Ellen's pregnancy:

> He's a male chauvinist, and he'll think that Ellen won't be able to be actively involved in the business. He'll back out of his financing commitment. Ellen will just take two months off, and while she's home, she'll work.

Indeed, Chris was inclined to agree with their assessment of Blackwell. At an early meeting to hammer out the details of the financing, Blackwell had flatly stated: "Be sure you girls get life insurance in case you get hit by a bus or get pregnant or something."

Yet, for all his blustering, Blackwell was giving the two women the money on extremely favorable terms. The $80,000 was essentially a loan that could be paid out of profits; Blackwell wasn't really participating in the business's upside. Chris was sure that Blackwell was being so generous on account of his relationship with Linda and her husband. Blackwell was also a member of the board, yet his involvement in the business seemed destined to be extremely passive.

Chris had asked Linda and Ellen to be available half an hour before the scheduled start of the board meeting so that the three could discuss the situation. Chris intended to offer the two strong advice to tell Blackwell of Ellen's condition, yet, as the hour approached, things seemed more and more confusing. Chris wondered what the right thing to do was, how strongly those views should be presented to Ellen and Linda, and also whether the board membership that Chris held imposed any additional obligations with respect to fellow board member Blackwell.

Chris guided the Volvo into the underground garage and immediately spotted Linda and Ellen exiting from their car. They waved expectantly, and Chris walked over to meet them.

PART

III

ACQUIRING AN EXISTING BUSINESS

In this part of the book, we examine an alternative approach to an entrepreneurial career: purchasing an existing business. This approach has allure for many would-be entrepreneurs who think they don't have a creative idea for a "better mousetrap," but who nonetheless would like to be in business for themselves.

Chapter 14 describes the search process for a company: potential sources of leads and how to assess, value, and finance the purchase. Unlike the start-up process—which is more or less in control of the entrepreneur—purchasing a business involves a critical relationship with the seller, and that relationship must be managed carefully. Chapter 15 describes a relatively new approach to actually funding a search for a business.

14

PURCHASING A BUSINESS: THE SEARCH PROCESS

Purchasing an existing business is an excellent alternative for individuals interested in running a small to medium-sized company. While not usually considered as "entrepreneurial" as developing the next generation of personal computers in a tiny garage, purchasing a company demands making many of the same difficult decisions required of a successful entrepreneur. In addition, it provides an opportunity for the purchaser to leverage his or her financial resources and concentrate sooner on "value adding" issues that are traditionally taught in business school management courses.

Buying a business is an informal process. No one has yet written a book that successfully defines the correct steps and best alternatives for every situation. Hence, there is no substitute for personal commitment, good business sense, and a cautiously optimistic exploration of every opportunity. Success in this process may occur randomly and can often depend on serendipity—being the right person in the right place at the right time. It is a mistake, however, to depend on good luck rather than good work.

This chapter will provide a framework that outlines many of the steps necessary to identify, evaluate, and negotiate a successful buyout. It is important to note, however, that this framework is not exhaustive. Rather, it provides a starting point that can be tailored to suit the particular nature of your search.

The areas discussed in this chapter are as follows:

- *Self-Assessment:* Understanding your motives, expectations, risk profile, and financial and professional resources, and determining the seriousness of your search process.

This chapter was prepared by Research Associate Ennis J. Walton under the direction of Professor Michael J. Roberts.

- *Deal Criteria:* Clarifying the dimensions of the project and characteristics that you find attractive.

- *Deal Sources:* Learning how to differentiate between the various deal sources in order to find a source that best fits your personal needs and established criteria.

- *Resources:* Evaluating and garnering the additional cash, credibility, personal and professional contacts, and information necessary to begin the deal process.

- *Deal Process:* Recognizing the sequential, often random, search process; establishing a deal timing schedule and work plan that allows you to evaluate deals that do not occur in parallel; understanding how to start the process, keep it moving, and establish initial contact with prospective sellers; and assessing the sellers' motives, weaknesses, strengths, and special nonfinancial requirements.

- *Evaluation Process:* Understanding the various analytical methods used by sellers, requesting or obtaining the key financial indicators, and analyzing the important financial dimensions of the deal.

- *Negotiating the Deal:* Identifying potential deal killers, learning from the collapsed deal, and pursuing attractive deals.

- *Adding Value:* Applying your managerial skills to add new value to the enterprise and understanding important harvesting options for the new enterprise.

Self-Assessment

The first step in buying an existing business is a personal assessment. This step is crucial because it will help you identify, articulate, and evaluate your hidden motives, expectations, risk profile, and ultimately, the seriousness of your search. Without a good sense of these personal values, the search process can become unfocused and unrewarding, causing you to waste time, resources, and energy.

The problems that could materialize in the absence of a thorough self-evaluation are intensified if you are attempting to purchase a company with another individual. In such cases, it is absolutely essential that all parties understand and agree on their motives and goals. Proceeding with a false sense of those aspirations will more than likely lead to problems—disagreements that impact on the efficiency and effectiveness of the group during the later stages of the process when clear vision and communication are important to make important decisions.

A good self-assessment will probably place you in one of three broad categories.

Serious

The serious and realistic search involves the following:

- A high level of commitment to the search.
- An ambitious set of expectations consistent with the degree of effort and commitment.
- A willingness to:
  — Risk at least some personal wealth/security.
  — Deeply research the target industry.
  — Be patient and wait for the "right" opportunity.
  — Move quickly and decisively as needed.
  — Pursue the search full time, if needed.

Casual

The casual and realistic search involves:

- A set of expectations that is consistent with this lessened degree of commitment and effort.
- Less willingness to move quickly or decisively on opportunities.
- No specified time horizon for search.
- Not being overly hungry to control one's own firm.

Unrealistic

The unrealistic search involves:

- Objectives that are inconsistent with level of commitment.
- Waiting for a "great deal" to fall in place.
- Looking for bargains and shortcuts.

While there is nothing wrong with either of the first two categories, the number and quality of opportunities discovered is proportional to the intensity of the search. This is not to say, however, that one cannot find excellent deals by "shopping" the market casually, but only that the process may take quite a while.

Another aspect of the self-assessment process that many people deal too lightly with is the listing of any and all business or personal relationships that can be called upon to add credibility or offer advice. Since the search process is lengthy and filled with important decision points, it is of great value to have others whose opinions you trust to call upon for advice.

The most important reason for the self-assessment, however, is tactical. Throughout the search process, you will have to deal with sellers or their intermediaries to get a sense of the deal. Because these individuals are often reluctant to invest their time with individuals unless they sense a degree of rational forethought and commitment, it's important to have a clear and convincing sense of what it is you're looking for. Thus, the better you have assessed yourself, the easier it will be to persuade others to take you seriously or work productively on your behalf.

Deal Criteria

A consistent and thorough screening method is essential for the successful completion of the acquisition process. Consistency is required so that analyses performed on one company are more readily comparable with those of other candidates. Thoroughness is required because all relevant aspects of a potential acquisition must be identified and analyzed. While thoroughness is critical, the screening method should have a clear focus and be kept fairly simple.

There are numerous ways to define the desired target company profile. At a minimum, one should think along such dimensions as:

- Size of deal (purchase price) desired.
- Preferred industry.
- Key factors for success (logistics, marketing, technology, etc.).
- Type of customer base (i.e., industrial versus consumer, national versus regional, etc.).
- Geographic preference.
- Profile of current ownership (i.e., how many, willingness to sell, reputation).

The mechanical dimensions highlighted above establish a preliminary framework for identifying deals that are appropriate for the particular search being undertaken. The screening process must then tackle the issue of distinguishing *good* deals from *bad* deals. Though there are several intangible and intuitive issues involved in this process, as a rule of thumb, an ideal buyout target should include:

- Potential for improving earnings and sales.
- Predictable cash flow.
- Minimum existing debt.
- An asset base to support substantial new borrowings.

When searching for a business, the buyout candidate will most likely not fit in a "nice, neat, little box," so flexibility is important. One must constantly rethink and reassess the criteria developed. Do they fit? Are they appropriate? Is this the best way to examine this company? Will the criteria help to achieve the objective in mind?

Deal Sources

Initiating and sustaining the deal flow is one of the most challenging tasks in buying a business. In general, expect to look at dozens of deals for every one that might appear worth pursuing; there are simply a lot of poor deals out there. A seemingly endless amount of groundwork is often necessary to initiate a deal, and a targeted effort is far more likely to result in a high percentage of attractive candidates. Thus, one of the first orders of business when starting out to locate a company is to know where to look.

Depending on what size deal is sought, there are a number of potential deal sources, and each has its own approach to acquisitions. The chart that follows is a subjective assessment of the various sources of deals and the territory they cover.

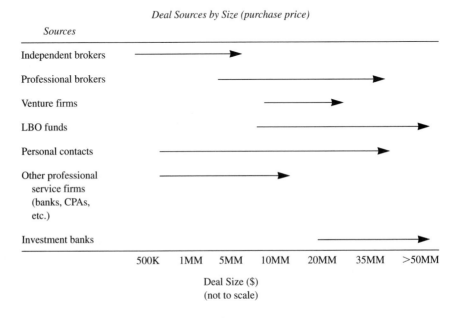

Deal Sources by Size (purchase price)

Sources							

Independent brokers

Professional brokers

Venture firms

LBO funds

Personal contacts

Other professional service firms (banks, CPAs, etc.)

Investment banks

| 500K | 1MM | 5MM | 10MM | 20MM | 35MM | >50MM |

Deal Size ($)
(not to scale)

The number of deals in the lower ranges—particularly in the $1 million to $5 million category—is on the rise. Mainstream investment banks, on the other hand, are rarely interested in any deal valued less than $10 to $20 million. Recognizing the particular niches these players inhabit will help to minimize lost time and unnecessary frustration chasing deals where they are not likely to be found. The paragraphs below will help identify sources according to the size of deal handled.

Business brokers—independent and professional alike—are the most readily available resource; they are listed individually in the Yellow Pages of most phone directories and advertise in the business sections of many newspapers. The broker's primary function is to work on behalf of sellers to find appropriate buyers for their clients' businesses, and he or she is compensated by the seller for closing a deal based on a percentage of the price basis. Occasionally, a broker will work for a buyer to search for a business in return for a retainer fee and/or a percentage of the ultimate purchase price. It should be emphasized, though, that the broker's motivation is to close each transaction; he or she should not necessarily be considered a business consultant in the search process.

Business brokers obtain listings through cold calls and advertising. Because these listings are actively marketed, it is safe to assume that you are probably not the first prospective buyer to see the business. More reputable brokers tend to regulate how "shopped" a business becomes in order to preserve its value and may not even list properties that the seller himself has already tried to market.

At your initial meeting with the broker, you should be prepared to describe your financial constraints and industry preference. It is also valuable to indicate that you have a well-defined time horizon for a search and some knowledge of the target industry. You might want to touch base occasionally with each broker whom you meet, but it is a safe bet that you will be notified if there is an interesting opportunity and if you are a qualified buyer.

Some attention should be focused on the role of independent brokers since they are often the first place people turn for deal flow. Independent brokers are almost entirely unregulated. Because no license is required, and anyone can claim to be one, it is essential to check references (should the broker not supply them) and reputation with other intermediaries and past clients. Fourteen states require brokers to have a real estate broker's license, but, for the most part, anyone with a telephone can call himself or herself a business broker. The largest network of independent brokers is VR Business Brokers, headquartered in Boston, Massachusetts. VR has 10 franchised brokerages operating offices in 500 cities. VR claims to close up to 7,500 deals per annum, 80 percent of which are companies with sales below $800,000. On the other end of the spectrum, one can find a seemingly endless supply of one-person brokerage services in most any city. As such, one must be exceedingly cautious when trying to land a deal via this route. First of all, the deals are going to be small, less than $500,000 in sales. Second, they are most likely to be owned by entrepreneurs who have an unrealistic impression of the value of their businesses, an impression often fueled by the brokers themselves.

As for professional brokers, a few prominent ones are worth noting here:

- Geneva Business Services in Costa Mesa, California.
- W. T. Grimm & Co. in Chicago, Illinois.

These organizations tend to operate on a far more professional basis than the independents, but keep track of the fact that they still represent the seller. Their interest is in getting the highest possible price for the company, thereby ensuring high commission fees (usually around 10 percent to 12 percent at closing). Also, note that deals coming via professional brokers are very likely to be highly "shopped." The deals' legitimacy are often prescreened, but count on paying a premium for businesses carried by professional brokers.

Venture capital firms will most likely be looking for liquidity on investments they made three to five years earlier. Venture-backed companies that have reached this stage are generally beyond many of the risks associated with start-ups and may pose a solid acquisition opportunity. Several points should be noted, however. First, venture capitalists are highly sophisticated investors and will likely extract the highest possible price for the company. Second, they want liquidity for their investment and will be less interested in earn-outs and other creative financing than a deal that is primarily financed with cash. Finally, existing management will likely be highly entrepreneurial and will be wary of the control issues introduced by new owners in the company.

Leveraged buyout (LBO) funds in some sense pose competition to the buyout effort. As a potential deal source, however, there may be opportunity to pick up on deals that are of no interest to the LBO fund. Such deals may still be attractive candidates if they were passed over simply because the deal did not match the particular focus of the LBO fund.

Personal contacts, although often overlooked, may be helpful. Self-initiated contacts with people who have successfully completed the search process for their own businesses may be a good source of both information and moral support. Depending on your specific situation and their area of expertise, they may be able to suggest specific contacts and strategies or allow you to tap their network. Additionally, you may be able to learn some of the common pitfalls they encountered and some rules of thumb they use. These resources may be located through your network or by tracking recently completed deals.

On occasion, combing prominent business periodicals will identify opportunities. Indications that a company will be spinning off subsidiary operations are frequently mentioned in articles in some level of detail. Nationally, *The Wall Street Journal* and publications such as *Inc.* and *Venture* routinely list business opportunities. On the local or regional level, there are business journals, franchise fairs, classified ads, and notices of bankruptcies and deaths. Newspapers and the offices of the county clerk and court clerks are good sources, as are computer data bases, available on a time-sharing basis that provide lists of prospective buyers and sellers of businesses. Academic and commercial institutions in some communities sponsor industry forums or trade association meetings. Industry and phone directories (Yellow Pages, Dun & Bradstreet, *Million Dollar Directory,* Thomas' *Register of American Manufacturers,* etc.) may be useful for a cold call or letter writing campaign and as a possible screen for industry, size, and location. You can run this process in reverse by placing your own advertisement in newspapers or journals stating your desire and criteria for purchasing a business.

Local banks represent a broad range of local businesses and have in-depth knowledge of their finances and managerial situations. Like business brokers, the M&A-type departments of banks are primarily interested in closing transactions. Their inventory of deals may include both banking clients that may be for sale or other firms that have engaged the bank to help them find a suitable buyer. A bank may also be amenable to helping you conduct a search on a success-fee basis. A good banker will also be instrumental in structuring the financial arrangements of the newly acquired business. As with lawyers and accountants, the bank may often expect to become the new firm's principal banker.

Trust departments of banks often are the executors of estate business. In cases where there is a need to dispose of such a business, a bank trust officer may serve the same role as an estate lawyer. However, the trust officer has a fiduciary responsibility to the beneficiaries of the estate and will seek the highest price for the business consistent with keeping the transaction clean, fast, and, to the greatest extent, in cash.

Bank work-out departments are another potential source of "bargain" opportunities. While the bank certainly has a strong interest in not disclosing credit problems, it may be a confidential go-between for a potential buyer and the owners of a deeply troubled client if a mutually satisfactory offer were presented. However, bankers indicate that because of pressures within the bank to reschedule the debt and the willingness of owners to personally collateralize additional loans, most troubled loans are in fact worked out.

Traditional, mainline investment banks pose both a problem and an opportunity for buyers seeking a midsized deal. The problem is that investment banks are rarely interested in deals below, say, $20 million. Attracting their attention can be troublesome and getting them to spend time moving on a relatively small deal requires patience and tenacity. The opportunity, for nearly the same grounds, exists because small deals carried by the investment banks are unlikely to have been widely shopped. Owners who rely exclusively on an investment bank to market their company will probably not receive extraordinary service. A buyer who works this route may find a fairly responsive seller on the other end of this inattentive deal pipeline.

No matter where the deal comes from, there will be a seller to contend with. Whether the seller is a single individual, a group of investors, or the shareholders of a small public company, one will have to evaluate their motivations. Issues of timing, types of financing, credibility, desire to remain with the company after acquisition, and the like, are all relevant points of thought when approaching the seller. Fairly early on, conversations should focus on the seller's motives for selling the business and his or her expectations as to the value and form of deal. A cautious investor will also use this opportunity to gauge the character and integrity of the seller, as such traits will likely have influenced how the business has been managed in the past.

Resources

Aside from tireless energy and a wealth of patience, resources critical to the buyout project are cash, credibility, and contacts. These three factors, more than anything else, govern the success of the effort. How much will be required is simply a question of deal size. Purchasing a $300,000 business certainly requires fewer resources than putting together a $20 million buyout. As deals get larger, one is competing with a more sophisticated group of potential buyers. Larger deals are more complex, and sellers of larger companies will demand of the potential buyer those credentials they believe are necessary to put the deal together. Lacking the resources necessary to pull off the deal, the potential buyer may not even be successful in establishing an initial meeting with the seller. To get farther than the first phone call with larger deals, one should be prepared to satisfactorily respond to such inquiries as:

- How much cash do you have available?
- Who are your backers?
- What other deals have you done?
- What kind of management talent do you bring?
- What do you plan to do with the company?

Sellers value their time as much as the prospective buyer does. Neither wants to spend fruitless energy on meetings where there is an obvious mismatch between what the buyer brings to the table and what the target company will require. No amount of debt leverage will compensate for a lack of the equity capital and demonstrated personal background needed to purchase and operate the target company. Take stock of the resources available for the buyout project, and then target deals that can be reasonably snared with the resources at hand.

If buyers plan to employ the resources of backers, they must realize the extent to which they are dependent upon the backers and gauge how committed the backers are to the project. All the backers' cash and contacts are absolutely useless if they are unwilling to spend the time and energy needed to pursue the deal. Evaluate the backers' incentives. How important is the project to them? How much time have they agreed to set aside? Do their timing considerations match those of the group? Some backers are quite willing to employ the free efforts of a buyout group simply hoping they will luck into a treasure chest. Be cautious of working like a neglected employee, rather than a respected partner. Such characteristics may prove difficult to evaluate, particularly early on when enthusiasm runs high for the project. Make a critical and even skeptical assessment of the backers' sincerity, interest, and ability to follow through on their part of the bargain before relying on them for the resources critical to the effort's success.

In addition, an experienced lawyer is absolutely essential to the prudent buyer. An attorney's principal role in the search process is usually to review documents with the aim of protecting the client with adequate contractual conditions and to ensure proper disclosure and legal and regulatory compliance. An attorney can also provide tax advice and may be able to identify potential risks and liabilities in a transaction. In many cases, more experienced lawyers turn out to be cheaper because they know the appropriate safeguards and can create good standard documents without extensive new research. In addition, as established members of the local professional community, attorneys may have access to a wider network of contacts than the buyer. For example, they sometimes sit on the boards of local businesses and may have a variety of contacts in the target industry. While tapping into this network might not generate a deal, it may provide you with opportunities to learn about the target industry and to gain credibility therein.

Occasionally, in larger law firms, there may also be an "inventory" of business acquisition opportunities. The buyer must usually compensate the lawyer for time and effort, and if the deal is successful, he or she generally expects to become the newly acquired firm's corporate counsel. As for selecting a business lawyer, there are issues to consider. For instance, you should determine whether or not the lawyer has a potential conflict of interest (e.g., if he is representing the seller). Although no reputable attorney would pursue an engagement while conflict exists without full disclosure, it is still up to you to determine the services she or he might provide. Another issue is the lawyer's reputation. It is wise to do some background or information checks of individual attorneys or their firms. Finally, your choice of lawyer should reflect your perceived legal and other professional needs at various stages of the search and deal process.[1]

The Deal Process

Once you have specified the characteristics that you are looking for in a company, understand the best ways to generate deal flow, and have garnered the resources necessary to successfully purchase an existing company, you should prepare to enter the deal market. At this phase, it is important to recognize and prepare for the random nature of the process.

There are two important timing issues to be concerned with when you enter the deal market. First, the sequential nature of the search process makes it difficult to compare deals in parallel. Rarely will you be able to view two deals within a time frame that allows you to evaluate them comparatively. Given that fact, it is important to realize that if you let one deal pass, you will probably encounter another one in the near future. An analytical framework to help you screen businesses (see Figure 14–1) will better equip you to track and compare various deals as you interface with sellers, deal sources, and other active parties at different points throughout the deal process (see also Chapter 2, "Developing Start-Up Strategies").

The second critical issue concerns the timing of the approach: before it hits the market, as soon as it hits the market, or after it has been "shopped." There are advantages and disadvantages to entering at each stage. In some cases, being the first person to see a deal (before it is on the market) may give you the inside track or first right to refuse. Yet, at this early stage, the seller will not have developed a realistic perspective on his or her demands (asking price, terms, inclination to provide desired information, willingness to actually part with the business, etc.). In such a case, discussions might be futile or you may end up paying a relatively high price. In a later stage, the seller may be more eager to sell, but you should be concerned about the health or the attractiveness of the business that has been on the market for a lengthy period.

Once you understand these basic timing issues and prepare a schedule and work plan, you should begin your search. Most of the search resources are amenable to a free introductory meeting even on the basis of a cold call. A persuasive presentation at this first meeting might include a demonstration of your industry research or experience, a well-thought-out preliminary business plan, a realistic assessment of your financial resources, and suitable dress and demeanor.

---

[1]For example, a lawyer with the technical knowledge to structure the deal from a tax perspective may not be the most skilled negotiator.

FIGURE 14–1   **Purchasing a Business: The Search Process**

Business Screening Analyses

1. General
   Company, business strategy, age and history, trends.
2. Product
   Description/technical specifications, function, volume, prices, value added/commodity, patents.
3. Management Team
   Key employees—names, positions, education, track record, skills.
   Organization chart.
   Is management team complete? Efforts/ability to hire new management?
   Willingness to remain after purchase?
   Characterization of management team (i.e., aggressive/passive, young/old, etc.).
4. Market Position
   Market size ($, units).
   Market growth and growth drivers.
   Segmentation of the market (geographic, functional).
   Who, how, and why does the buyer buy (identification of buyer)?
   Relationship with customers (number, loyalty, concentration).
   Distribution channels (types, support/training required, advertisement strategy).
   Market share of major players.
   Company's major differentiating factors (price, quality, service, features, brand identity).
5. Competition
   Barriers to entry/exit—economies of scale, proprietary technology, switching cost, capital requirements, access to distribution, cost advantages, government policy, expected retaliation, brand identity, exit cost.
   Competitive factors—number, strength, characterization, product differences, concentration, diversity, management, financial/ration analysis, industry capacity, competitive advantages, corporate stakes.
   Substitution threat—relative price/performance of substitutes, switching cost, buyer propensity to substitute.
   Suppliers' power—relationship, concentration, manufacturing/marketing process, presence of substitute inputs, importance of volume to supplier, switching cost of supplier, cost relative to total purchases, impact of inputs on cost or differentiation, threat of forward integration, supplier profitability.
   Buyers' power—bargaining leverage, buying patterns, concentration, volume, switching cost, ability to backward integrate, substitute products, price sensitivity, price/total purchases, product differences, brand identity, impact on quality/performance, buyer profitability, decision-making units' incentives and complexity.
   Trends—technology, economic, changes in tax law.
6. Operations
   Work force—size, union/nonunion, work rules, contract expiration, age and skill level, match with developing technology, attrition, attitude, manufacturing/engineering staff competence.
   Manufacturing flow and scheduling—job shop/batch continuous, systems, process flow, material handling, multiplant strategy/logistics, cost accounting, work discipline, work order tracking, percent dead time.
   Capacity—percent of total capacity, bottlenecks current and projected.
   Purchasing—opportunities for redesign, fewer parts, add/subtract vendors, larger discounts, incoming material sampling, out-sourcing policies.
   Quality control—attitude/priority, problem areas, methodology.
   Capital equipment—age/maintenance, sophistication, general versus special purpose, level of automation, trends.
   R&D—percent of sales compared to industry, type, technical strengths/weaknesses, organization, importance, trends.
   Information systems—importance, competitive advantage, level of sophistication, systems under development.
7. Financials
   Sales/profitability
   Income statement.
   Historical and two-, three-, five-year pro formas.
   Growth—sales, costs, profits, EPS, sustainable growth rates.

FIGURE 14–1 *(concluded)*

Quality of earnings—accounting, pension funding, depreciation, write-offs, earnings segments, earnings patterns, earnings sensitivity.

Ratio analysis—compared to competitors and industry averages, gross margins, ROS, ROE, P/E comparables.

Leverage and liquidity

Balance sheet.

Historical and pro formas.

Examination of equity and debt composition.

Ratio analysis—current and quick ratios, debt as percentage of total capitalization, assets/equity, days' receivable, days' payable, days' inventory.

Funds flow

Statement of changes.

Historical and pro formas.

Analysis of sources and uses of cash.

Assets

Composition and type, quality, bankability, book and market values, obsolescence, age.

8. Valuation

Terminal value—FCF perpetuity/annuity, book value, liquidation value, P/E value.

Components of value (i.e., investment tax credits, depreciation, energy cost savings, etc.).

Sensitivity analysis.

Expected returns analysis.

9. Risk/Reality Check

Industry.

Technology.

Financial.

Product/company liability.

Employee/supplier/customer response.

Seller's desire to do the deal.

Is value appropriate?

Prohibitive terms?

Value to be added.

Academic credentials help your chances of getting in the door, as does the referral of a mutual acquaintance. This meeting should not necessarily result in a commitment; in fact, you might consider meeting with many attorneys, CPAs and bankers, or others you deem helpful before committing to work with anyone in particular. You might also schedule some "warm-up" sessions with some of these professionals before meeting with your highest priority contacts.

The preliminary meeting should serve several purposes: Resources will be interested in qualifying you both as a realistic, potential buyer and as someone they will want to work with. You should attempt to determine their expertise and willingness to help, along with any conditions on your relationship with them. With regard to establishing fees, practice ranges from hourly fees to contingent fees; the arrangement of one lawyer may be substantially different from another. This is another reason to meet with many professionals before committing to work exclusively with any one in particular.

In most of these preliminary discussions, the issue of what to tell and what to hide arises. While this is a personal decision, a perspective on your financial resources, level of commitment, and objectives is probably best expressed frankly. You may want to be more vague if you are dealing with an intermediary who represents a potential seller or if you have reservations about the person with whom you are meeting. The fact that your backers may want their identities shielded will also push you to be somewhat guarded. Checking out the reputations of such individuals before divulging any of your private information is the only prudent course of action.

The average time required to find the right business runs about one year—significantly longer if your search is more casual or if your target is more elusive. Therefore, depending on your degree of commitment, your financial flexibility, and your time schedule, you may elect to manage your own search by calling on the search resources periodically, or you may choose to retain a search resource to conduct the search for you.

An attorney, for instance, could make cold calls and write letters to industry sources on your behalf. While his personal and professional contacts may unearth your dream business, much of the research you pay him for could be easily done yourself from industry directories, Yellow Pages, etc. Thus, if time permits or your budget requires and you are sophisticated enough about basic business and legal issues, you may choose to undertake many of the basic research tasks yourself. This also provides first-hand contact with the marketplace.

The industry-specific knowledge you pick up may be invaluable to you later on, when you need to demonstrate expertise or commitment to financing sources or to a seller. In some industries, acquisition opportunities rarely reach the marketplace because the industry is essentially closed. Therefore, if you are interested in entering such an area, you must "network" your way in. This might include meeting owners or executives of any firms in that industry whether or not they are interested in selling their own businesses. Industry association meetings or trade meetings can be good places to meet people and become more of an insider.

You might consider periodically touching base with some of the individuals in your new network to see if they have any ideas for you and to reiterate your degree of interest. But be sensitive to the demands you are making: A short phone call every three or four weeks is appropriate—more frequent contact may be annoying. You might also update them on your progress, especially because they may be able to help you more at different phases in your search. Keep in mind that they would more likely readily share information or leads with you if you exchange any ideas or intelligence with them.

Once underway, you may come across a potential acquisition candidate. An inexpensive way to obtain financial and operating information on the company and biographical background on the owners or officers is through a Dun & Bradstreet report or by other background checks. Note that the D&B report is based upon information provided by the subject company and is not independently verified.

In addition to doing some preliminary investigative research, it is important to meet the owner(s) and visit the business. An aspect of this evaluation is to understand the "seller's psychology," for it is critical to appreciate the seller's needs—financial and psychological. There are cases in which the owner has no emotional attachment to the business, and he or she would willingly sell to the highest bidder. More likely, especially in small operations, much of the seller's life is tied up in the business, resulting in a high degree of emotional involvement. There may be other significant psychological considerations, you could identify, such as the seller's age, marital situation, illness, or family situation. Usually, a deal structure will need to reflect these factors in the form and terms of the consideration. In these cases, you may need to "sell" the seller.

Selling the seller does not simply include a generous financial package (e.g., insurance, providing for his family), but may require demonstrating your commitment to preserve the character, quality, and spirit of the enterprise he worked long and hard to build. Occasionally, even when an owner indicates a willingness to sell, he or she may in fact be unwilling to part with the firm when it comes to closing the deal and transferring control. Reading the owner's psyche ahead of time may avoid such fruitless discussions or may provide insight into a more mutually satisfying deal structure.

In this respect, your professional resources may be able to provide a great deal of insight and advice because they may either know the seller or have dealt with similar situations previously. It also may be helpful to have your agent negotiate on your behalf for a variety of reasons: to preserve your rapport with the seller, to neutralize personality clashes, and to preserve and improve decision options.

The Evaluation Process

After preliminary research and introductory meetings with the prospective seller, you may decide to pursue the opportunity, which would involve reviewing confidential operating and financial statements and interviewing key employees and customers.

"Getting the numbers" can be more easily said than done. Generally, small-business owners are reluctant to share any operating and financial data with outsiders, often for tax and competitive reasons. Typically a buyer does not receive any meaningful financials until after signing a purchase agreement and putting down a deposit. Thus, a good understanding of the business and the industry may give you increased credibility and leverage with the seller. A seller with a distressed business may be more willing to provide numbers earlier in the process, and for bankrupt firms, the numbers may be part of the public domain. In most cases, confidentiality agreements must be signed before reviewing any financials.

While not necessary, you are well advised at this point to retain your own counsel to ensure that you are protected and are covering all bases, especially if you are signing any documents or agreements. An accountant might also be very useful depending on the complexity of the situation (financial reports, taxes, inventory, etc.). Other experts may help investigate leases and contracts. To the extent that these are people with whom you have already worked, you will be more comfortable dealing with them and trusting them.

It is often useful to collect a thumbnail sketch of the deal's financial attractiveness prior to performing any detailed analysis. As some preliminary checks, one can screen against company size, profitability, and attractiveness of the balance sheet. Some deals may be thrown out on this basis, while others will merit a more thorough examination of the numbers.

There are several ways to reasonably estimate the value of a company, and it is most often useful to employ more than one method when performing a valuation analysis. How much to pay, how much debt and from what source, and potential harvest values are going to be valued differently. Each plays an important role in the assessment of the opportunity at hand. Below are types of analysis that can prove useful in establishing an estimate of the deal's price (see Chapter 3, "Valuation Techniques"):

Method Used	*What the Results Indicate*
Discounted cash flow	Underlying operating value of the business and ability to service debt.
Asset valuation	Liquidation value and/or adjusted book value of assets.
Multiples	Multiples of cash flow, P/E, sales, or EBIT are useful to establish some sense for market value relative to other firms in the same industry and offer some indication of harvest potential. Each type of multiple has its own merit; what is critical is that one be consistent in applying them.

Both cash flow analysis and multiples analysis estimate the opportunity's value based upon future events, either operating results or market reaction to public offering. When trying to place a value on a business in this manner, there are a multitude of assumptions that must be made. Some of the most prominent include:

- Level of risk: How volatile are the company's cash flows?
- Competition: How fiercely contested is the market for the company's products?
- Industry: Is this a growing or declining industry, and what profitability trends exist?
- Organizational stability: How well established is this company in the intended line of business?
- Management: Is a competent and complete team in place?
- Company growth: Historically, has the company been growing or shrinking, and how fast?
- General desirability: To what degree does the marketplace find this line of business attractive?

A cautionary note on valuations: Many deal proposals are put together with "recast financial statements." In theory, such a practice is legitimate and endeavors to reflect true operating results possible in the business. In reality, assumptions implicit in the recast are not always reasonably attainable and can be downright misleading. Always ask whether or not the financials shown have been recast, and, if so, understand all adjustments that have been made to the statements. No assumption should be left unchallenged. This will be particularly true for smaller companies whose owners will often have previously operated with numerous adjustments to minimize their tax burden.

Once a general idea on price is established, the deal will have to be structured with attractive returns to one's equity investment. There are two fundamental considerations. First, is the overall financeability of the deal, which includes:

- Assets to secure bank financing.
- Cash flow to support further debt instruments (i.e., company-issued debentures).
- Personal collateral, if any.

Second, one must consider (possibly in conjunction with the above analysis) the actual structure of the financing. What is desired here is a structure that caters to the interest of all parties involved. The buyer might, for example, establish financing "strips" of debt and equity to provide both secured fixed income and participation in potential capital appreciation. Tax losses may be scrutinized and sold to investors who will find such items attractive (see Chapter 10, "Deal Structure").

Negotiating the Deal

When you discover a company whose purchase is financially feasible and meets your other criteria, it is important to recognize any situations that could prevent you from closing the deal successfully. The following represent a few important obstacles:

- Forcing the deal: One must be responsive to timing issues inherent in a less than perfect process. This may be the area of greatest difficulty due to the lack of control associated in timing the buying of a company. Patience and persistence go a long way toward managing one's expectations in this area. One's attitude plays a role here, as well. While the deal should not be forced, one must recognize there are always reasons *not* to do a deal. Buying a company is an emotional as well as intellectual process, and there are times when the cynical outlook should be tempered with a bit of positive thinking.
- Competition: One should expect to run into competition from other buyout firms or larger companies in the same industry, perhaps with greater resources. A professional buyout firm will typically have the

resources, capital, time, and sophistication to move quickly and expertly on a deal. In particular, with the great mergers and acquisitions activity of the mid- to late 1980s, many buyout firms who in the past would have sought relatively larger deals have begun searching for small and medium-sized deals ($10 to $20 million). Larger companies in the same industry may be willing to pay a higher premium due to operating synergies in common with the target acquisition candidate. This makes for a challenging search process and means that if deals can be found that have not been shopped around, then one's chances of success improve dramatically.

- Poor communication: This pertains to all parties involved—backer, target company, project team, and the many professionals required to complete a deal. There is plenty of opportunity for communications to either drag out or break down entirely. Demonstration of commitment is again prominent, as frequent and regular discussion will sustain each party's involvement and better move a deal to completion.

Such obstacles do not necessarily have to get in the way, but one should be prepared to meet them if they do appear. Indeed, you may have to walk away from your share of deals. While having to walk away from a business you wanted can be disappointing, you should learn several important lessons. For example, you should become a better judge of character and business situations. This is knowledge that will be invaluable to you as you continue the deal process. Also, the firsthand experience and knowledge you gain about the industry in the collapsed deal may result in greater credibility in the future with sellers or their intermediaries.

Adding Value

Before you purchase a company, you can begin to concentrate on ways to improve the firm's performance. Indeed, such plans are a vital component of understanding a business's potential and your willingness to pay. Adding value to a new firm can be accomplished in many ways:

- Making operational changes: You should give a good deal of thought up front as to what you plan to do with the company after the acquisition. You may recognize opportunity to broaden distribution, open new markets, and otherwise make operational changes that boost sales and/or margins. In evaluating such possibilities, be realistic. Chances are the easy things have already been tried, so exercise some creative thought in defining positive operating improvements. This also requires an assessment of the management team and personnel in place. In short, are they reliable, competent, honest, and are they the right people for the challenge that lies ahead for the business?
- Changing the financial structure of the business: In many small businesses, the very essence of the company can be improved if the underlying

financial structure is modified. For example, negotiating a longer payment schedule with your creditors, creating incentives for your customers to pay bills sooner, and obtaining lines of credit from commercial banks can help change the dynamics of the business and improve cash flow.

Conclusion

Searching for a small business to buy can be difficult; not only is there no established marketplace for these firms, but you are trying to purchase an entity created and cultivated by another individual, and you are attempting to meld it with your own style, character, and interests. This process can be extremely time consuming, expensive, and frustrating. And although available research indicates the good acquisition candidates are few and far between, sound search techniques and a realistic personal assessment can significantly improve your chances of success and allow you to achieve some measure of control over some of the more random elements of the process.

Finally, remember that this process is also an investment decision. Even a superb company is of little value to an investor if nobody is willing to pay for it. Identifying an appropriate "exit" strategy to make one's investment liquid will define the project's monetary returns. This can include running the company in perpetuity, getting out in a secondary public offering, liquidating the assets, or selling out to another organization.

15

LBOS USING THE "SEARCH FUND" MODEL

Over the past decade or so, a number of recent MBAs have pursued acquisitions using the search fund model. In this model, the MBAs raise a blind pool of capital to fund a search for an acquisition target. In exchange for putting up this money, the investor gets first call on the right to invest in the actual purchased business, assuming one is found. The MBA principal (or principals, if a team is involved) get enough money to pay the search expenses and compensate themselves at a minimal level.

This chapter describes the experiences of approximately 17 such search efforts. In 10 cases, they were carried out by individuals, in the other 7 cases by teams of two MBAs. In all cases, the MBAs were searching for leveraged buyout (LBO) candidates. That is, the MBAs were looking for businesses to buy where debt could be employed as one means of financing the purchase. Typically, this has implications for the type of business purchased, suggesting a business with leverageable hard assets and stable cash flow.

The average time to buy a business for the 12 search funds that succeeded in buying a business was 28 months (2 ceased their effort and 3 are still looking, as of the date of this writing):

- 3 months to raise the search fund.
- 19 months to search for (and find) the acquired company.
- 6 months to negotiate and close the deal.

The description of the process used is taken from interviews with 17 of these search fund principals. (See **Exhibit 15–1**.)

Deborah Baker, MBA '96, John L. Corso, MBA '96, and Yosufi M. Tyebkhan, MBA '96, prepared this chapter under the supervision of Professor Howard Stevenson as the basis for class discussion rather than to illustrate either effective or ineffective handling of an administrative situation.

Harvard Business School Note 9-897-092.

EXHIBIT 15–1   List of Principals with Financed Search Funds

Principal Number	Partner?	Close of Search Fund	Current Status	Size of Firm ($000)	Industry
1	Yes	January '94	Running firm	$ 7,950	Paint brush manufacturer
2	No	April '93	Running firm	16,800	Hinge manufacturer
3	No	September '88	Sold company	16,500	Alarm systems distributor
4	No	August '92	Running firm	15,100	Backplane manufacturer
5	No	February '93	Stopped	—	—
6	Yes	June '90	Running firm	14,600	Medical supplies distributor
7	No	February '95	Searching	—	—
8	No	September '91	Stopped	—	—
9	No	March '84	Sold company	43,000	Insurance form printing
10	No	November '91	Running firm	3,900	Cable company
11	Yes	March '94	Running firm	8,000	Emergency roadside assistance
12	Yes	August '85	Running firm	4,000	Technical school
13	No	January '92	Running firm	5,550	Medical products—prostheses
14	Yes	July '90	Running firm	NA	Beer distributor
15	Yes	January '88	Running firm	NA	Box manufacturer
16	Yes	June '94	Searching	—	—
17	No	June '95	Searching	—	—

The Seven-Step Search Fund LBO

The search fund model enables an individual (the principal) to search for and acquire a company through a seven-step process. The principal raises money in two stages. Initially, he or she raises a relatively small sum ($150,000 to $300,000) from 8 to 12 investors. These initial funds cover most of the search expenses and allow the principal to draw a modest salary while searching for a company to acquire. In return, individuals investing in the first stage obtain the right of first refusal on investing in the acquisition, effectively obtaining an option. Regardless of their participation in the second stage, they also receive some equity in the acquisition. This equity is generally stepped-up in value; that is, the dollar value of the equity received in the acquisition is greater than the dollars invested in the original search fund investment. Investors are chosen for both their ability to help with the search as well as for their ability to make a subsequent investment. This serves to mitigate the risks that arise from the principal's inexperience.

Two years are typically required to identify a suitable firm for acquisition. Ideally firms are chosen to compensate for the principal's operating and management inexperience. One experienced advisor to a number of search funds characterizes the process with the following anthology:

> Imagine a horse [the company] going around a track. The jockey [seller] is going to get off, and another [the principal] is going to get on, while the horse is in motion. The

new jockey learns to ride while the horse goes around a couple more times. It is at this point that the new jockey may start to make changes.

Having identified an acquisition target, the principal enters into concurrent negotiations with the seller of the company, the banks, and the search fund investors. If the seller agrees to sell, and bank financing is arranged, investors from the first round have the option to participate in a second round of financing to fund the equity portion of the LBO. Typically, the principal raises about $1 to $5 million from 8 to 12 investors. The search fund's two-stage financing reduces the risk to the investor much like a multistage investment in a start-up reduces the risk to a venture capitalist—each structure allows the investor to gain confidence in an opportunity prior to making a greater commitment.

Once the deal is closed, the principal typically assumes the role of CEO. He or she learns the business and grows it. Ultimately the principal creates a return for the investors by either selling the company or by buying them out. In the first case, the principal is rewarded through his carried interest—much like the principal of a venture capital fund. Otherwise, the principal can buy out his investors to own 100 percent of the company.

By way of summary, the search fund seven steps are diagrammed in **Exhibit 15–2**.

Deciding to Do It

Many students have only two to three years of work experience prior to business school and feel that they should work at an established firm upon graduation. This will provide them with a recognizable name on their résumé and a significant opportunity to learn. However, those involved in search funds argue that these funds pose little risk to a principal's reputation and offer an even greater learning opportunity. Bob Latta, a lawyer for several search funds, notes:

> In the space of one transaction, this process (search and acquisition of a company) is a complete experience. The principal learns everything that American Corporations can throw at them.

Another advisor adds: "The evidence points to the conclusion that you should do it right away" and explains:

> Maybe its because this is a natural break point in life. Later you're working with stimulating peers, doing well in your job, traveling first class. You get caught up in your life. You are too tired to do this on your own time. So it becomes a dream that you had when you were at business school.

Understanding the motivations and the characteristics of those who have participated in search funds may help individuals assess whether search funds are for them.

Motivations

The majority of principals share two motivations:

Exhibit 15–2 Steps in the Search Fund Process

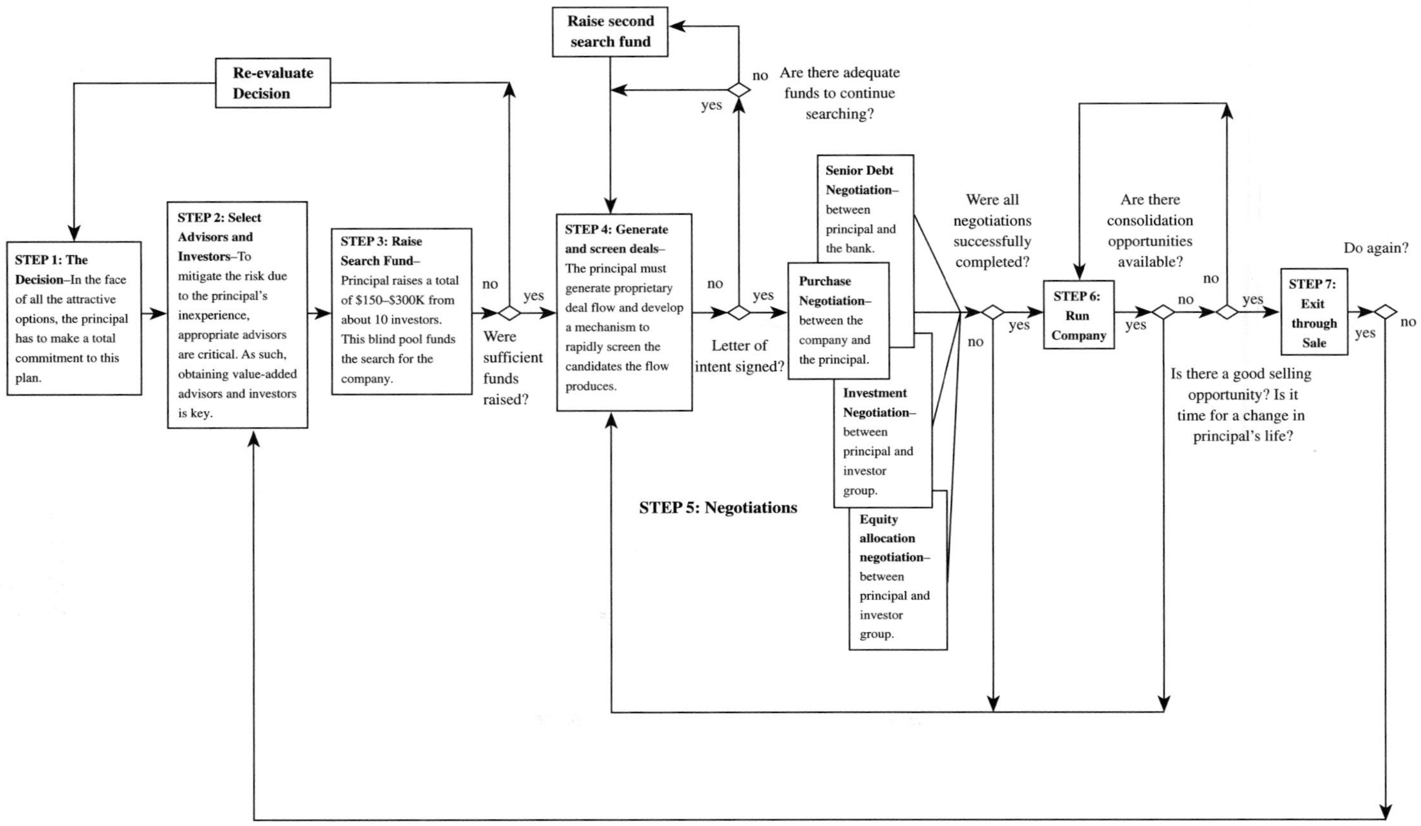

- **To be their own boss by running and building a business, not by starting one.** Principals share a strong desire to work for themselves. There are many reasons why principals want to be their own boss. While some come from entrepreneurial families, most are driven by a desire to have greater control over their career. For most of the principals, the difference between running a company and starting one is significant. Unlike a start-up, an LBO does not require a unique offering. As a result, it is a better fit for an individual who sees himself as an *improver or a builder, not an idea or start-up person.* Search funders are also more attracted to LBOs because they do not bear the "market acceptance risk" of start-ups.
- **To achieve high financial upside.** The financial payoff of a search fund differs from that of a traditional career path. Forgoing a high starting salary and in many cases a considerable signing bonus, the principal lives on a relatively low income through most of the process. The real payoff to the search fund principal, if it comes, occurs upon exit.

The principals share a belief that the search fund payoff outweighs most others. Indeed two principals have to date bought and sold companies and have realized an average return of $11.2 million. This translates to over $1 million per year for each year of their involvement. For those who have yet to exit, there is evidence of a substantial increase in their company's value and consequently their personal net worth.[1]

Characteristics

As with any entrepreneur, a successful search funder typically displays mental toughness, a strong will, and emotional fortitude. Since he is typically inexperienced, he must also be able to listen to and take the advice of those who are often older and more experienced investors. Because the principal depends on this advice, he must have the ability to get investors to truly believe in him and really want him to succeed. The principal has to have a willingness to work alone as much of the search process is done independently. Approximately one-half of the search fund principals mitigate this by enlisting a partner to work with them throughout the process.[2] Personal work style will often determine whether or not someone will choose a partner. Those working with partners commented that they simply work better in pairs. In addition, they feel that the potential diversification of skills and division of labor would be advantageous, allowing them to cover more ground and more quickly close a deal. However, partnerships do not seem to impact the speed of the search. Those that did not have a partner commented that they work better alone and that a partner would complicate the deal, potentially leading to conflict. A quicker burn rate of the search fund and not having to split financial upside were also cited as reasons to go at it alone.

---

[1]Based on principals who have owned their companies for more than four years. Present company value assumes a constant multiple of EBITDA.

[2]Of the 22 groups that have purchased, or are still searching for, a company, 10 are partnerships. Of these, only one to date has dissolved, with the remaining partner still running the company.

Choosing Advisors and Investors

Given the principal's inexperience, one of the most important aspects of a successful search fund is identifying and using good advisors. According to both principals and investors, the advisors played a vital role in the success of the funds. This view was echoed by one, who commented that "successful search funders surround themselves with successful people and listen to them." Advisors assist search funders in many ways. They:

- Provide a sounding board for ideas and are a source of advice (especially in areas where principals may lack specific knowledge and expertise).
- Provide personal support in good times and in bad.
- Furnish industry contacts to help generate deal flow.
- Provide leverage with lawyers, accountants, and bankers.

An advisor must provide more than professional assistance. The search fund process is long, tiring and at times discouraging. In the words of one investor, ". . . it is a very lonely vigil." As such, it is important to seek out advisors with whom one feels comfortable and who are approachable in good times and in bad. The best advisors are ones that have the interest, ability, and willingness to help the principal. Other than paid professionals such as lawyers and accountants, advisors can include other search fund principals, investors, business school professors, and friends.

Search Fund Principals

Principals currently involved in the process provide insight based on experience and can help new search funders not only avoid pitfalls but develop ways to anticipate them. Principals who have closed one or more deals can be very helpful postacquisition by providing insight on taking over and effectively running a business. While current and former search funders are very busy, they have proven incredibly willing to spend time with those wishing to start their own search fund.

Investors

The minimum investment requirements of a search fund limit investors to individuals with considerable net worth. Most investors view the search fund as an attractive investment in spite of its inherent risks. In one investor's view, "The deal structure is attractive—I prefer stable cash flow to a huge upside. It gives me an option on someone's mind. Really the only risk you have to look out for is bankruptcy." Even so, those who invest in search funds are typically looking for something more than financial return. The same investor adds, "I also get some sort of psychic pleasure out of seeing a young person succeed. It's a different feeling than giving money to some unknown person."

The structure of the search fund is such that a principal has the potential to earn extraordinary returns through his carried interest. Many investors are not comfortable participating in such an arrangement and therefore should not be approached. As one investor puts it, "If an investor is not willing to make other people rich or has not participated in ventures where people have gotten rich, you don't want him." This takes on special importance during the equity allocation negotiation. The investor warns, "These people are tough come allocation time."

Investors can help principals in many ways. They can be an excellent source of deal flow and, as advisors, offer valuable business insight. Principals can also leverage the investors' established relationships with professionals such as bankers and lawyers. One investor emphasizes these facts to aspiring principals. He comments: "The first piece of advice I give principals is make sure you're going to get more than money out of your investors."

Despite the benefits they bring, some investors are surprised at how infrequently principals seek out their advice. One investor comments: "I'm always amazed when I initiate the call to see how things are going." He, like many search fund investors, is willing to spend time with the principals in which he invests. He adds, "I've never found those calls to be wasted time and energy."

Business School Professors

Business school professors can help the principal in many ways. They can provide valuable industry and functional expertise as well as contacts for the principal's search. Moreover, they are generally willing to talk to former students.

Friends

In addition to professional relationships, principals often cite friends, former co-workers, and classmates as particularly helpful throughout the search fund process. In addition to providing some insight and perhaps access to information, they are extremely valuable to the search funder on a personal basis as he or she goes through what can be an extremely trying process.

Raising the Search Fund

Once the principal has committed to the process and identified his advisors and investors, he is ready to raise the search fund. In order to do so, he must prepare a formal proposal. In the process, he must be careful not to contravene federal or state securities laws that govern the raising of investment moneys. Indeed, the principal must remain conscious of these laws throughout the process.

The search proposal is much like a business plan. It describes the principal's background and lays out his needs and objectives. **Exhibit 15–3** gives a summary of a typical search fund proposal. Time and effort should be put into preparing this document. It is an initial point of contact with investors and, as such, will reflect the principal's level of commitment and professionalism.

Before starting this process, most principals felt that raising a search fund would be difficult. Yet, on average, the search fund took just over three months to raise. As one, a principal, comments, "Looking back, raising the search fund

---

EXHIBIT 15–3   Search Fund Proposal Sample Table of Contents

SEARCH FUND PROPOSAL

1. Executive summary: an overview of the goals of the fund and the amount of financing sought.
2. An introduction to the search fund process: for prospective investors who are not familiar with this type of acquisition strategy, a brief explanation is offered, often citing some previous examples.
3. Search criteria for the industry and company, or what type of business the entrepreneur is looking to buy: a list of the criteria that will be used to qualify and screen businesses seen as potential acquisition targets.
4. Timelines for the search process: a list of activities to be carried out and the expected time for each.
5. An explanation of the financing sought and structure of the search fund vehicle: includes a statement of the size and number of search fund units sought, an estimate of the follow on investment, and the structure of the fund (partnership or corporation).
6. Budget breakdown for the search phase: includes principal's salary, rent, office furniture and equipment purchases, travel and due diligence costs, and legal and accounting fees.
7. Future plans for the company/exit options: a description of potential improvement plans for the firm, and a viable exit option for the investors—e.g., buy back of shares, sale, IPO.
8. Personal background of the principals and allocation of future responsibilities: details of previous experience, and, if there is more than one principal, a description of how responsibilities will be shared in the search, acquisition, and operational phase of the process.

---

seemed quite an easy process." In fact, of the 26 attempts at raising a fund, 22 succeeded. Those close to the process cite the principals' lack of commitment and/or leadership skills as reasons for fund-raising failures.

One reason that the search fund is easy to raise is that ultimately it requires only 8 to 12 investors. According to one principal:

> You only need a small number to say yes. Even the ones who say no will usually tell you who else you should talk to. In fact 80 percent of our investors came from a reference of a reference—with 60 no's and 5 yes's, you still win.

In raising the fund, the principals must give considerable thought to how much money they will need and raise more than that amount. For the investor group, the difference between the level of investment in a "bare bones" fund and one with a level of safety is marginal. Says one principal, "Raise more than you think you'll need, the difference between $10,000 and $15,000 to these guys is nothing once they've decided to do it."

Identifying and Screening Potential Acquisitions

There are three steps in identifying target companies for acquisitions:

1. Generating deal flow—creating a stream of candidates.
2. Screening—determining a candidate's suitability for acquisition.
3. Assessing seller interest—determining a seller's commitment.

Generating Deal Flow

Given the principal's lack of experience and reputation, generating deal flow can be a daunting task. This is further compounded by the fact that principals lack committed funds and thus business brokers and other agents have little incentive to show search funders anything but the poorest deals. To find a company, it is necessary for search funders to be more creative in their approach.

As a first step, principals should decide to focus their search in one of two general ways: by geography or by industry. Geographic searches are generally conducted by principals who, for family or other reasons, wish to reside in a particular area. At the center of this approach is the belief that establishing regional networks will better allow the principal to generate deal flow and secure financing. According to one principal who is focusing his search in eastern Michigan, "geographic-based searches allow you to network with people so you will be on their short lists. Michigan is [a] tight [community]." He adds that geographic focus also allows for better response: "You want to be there when the founder says they want out."

Industry-based searches generally target one to three industries. Principals select industries that will accommodate their limited capital, experience, and risk profile. The benefit of an industry-based search is that it allows the search funder to rapidly become an expert in a few industries. This will allow him to:

- Understand industry drivers to better identify candidates, including those which may not appear attractive to others.
- Better screen suitable candidates by leveraging off previous due diligence.
- Gain credibility through a better understanding of the seller's industry.

According to another principal, an industry search is:

The right way to search for a company. By becoming an expert in an industry, you see the hidden treasures. Had I not understood the alarm industry, I would have never bought Smith Alarm.

The following is a list of some potential pitfalls of pursuing an industry-based search along with suggestions to avoid them:

Pitfall	*Recommendation*
Industry dynamics continuously change	Pursue several industries in parallel. Avoid becoming captive to one that is no longer attractive.
The search for the "perfect" industry	Avoid getting bogged down searching for the perfect industry. Many are close, but none exist.
Ignoring geographic preference	Be realistic with geographic criteria, it *will* impact the decision. Firms in areas where the principal will not live should not be pursued.

Of the 17 groups interviewed, 14 chose an industry-based search while only 3 chose a geographic-based one. The sample, however, does not provide conclusions on the relative effectiveness of one form of search over another.

Once the principal has identified his search focus, he switches his attention to generating proprietary deal flow.[3] As one principal says, "Deal flow is number one." To be effective, the principal should let everyone in the target geography or industry know that he is in the market. According to one investor, "The issue is how you get enough credibility to get a continuous stream of deals. You need to have some clear-cut parameters."

Methods of generating deal flow vary across principals but include the following:

- Attending industry trade shows.
- Conducting target mailings.
- Networking with industry insiders and experts.
- Networking with lawyers, accountants, and local bankers.

The data suggest that finding the right company is a "numbers game." The more companies the principal looks at, the higher the probability of success. To acquire *one* company, a search funder on average contacts 150 companies; visits and analyzes 25 of them; and makes five bids. However, the range is significant—in their respective searches, two principals contacted over 300 firms and another made 12 bids. One principal summarizes what it takes to be successful, "You must get efficient at rejecting opportunities and keep your energy up."

Screening

The search fund model encourages principals to search for companies that compensate for their lack of operating and management experience. Potential target companies should be simple businesses, with few locations and product lines, strong middle management, and, most importantly, stable cash flow. A sample list of the criteria used is given in **Exhibit 15–4**. One advisor cautions that the search process is such that there is a big risk of acquiring a company without growth potential, or what he calls "the living dead." To avoid this, the principal must target companies that are constrained in some way but are fundamentally healthy. These include firms with family succession issues or subsidiaries of large companies that no longer fit their parent companies' strategic imperatives.

In addition to the above requirements, the principal also suggested the following when acquiring a company:

- *Like the business that you are buying and be comfortable with role that you will play.* The search fund model dictates that the principal will run the business he acquires. In screening candidate companies, the principal must be cognizant of

---

[3]Proprietary deals are those that are originated by the principal. Often they are opportunities created where none exist.

his likes and dislikes. Having committed to a business for three to four years, he must be sure that it is one that he does not hate. More importantly, he must identify the key aspects of the role he will be expected to play and be comfortable with it. An investor cautions:

> You [the principal] are going to spend more than 60 hours a week for four years in a business. If you don't like sickness and are not willing to negotiate with government regulators, then don't get into the health-care business. Regardless of how attractive you think it is.

• *Buy the largest business that you can get financed.* As the search funder is rewarded by a carried interest in a deal, his return is directly tied to the size of the company he buys. Furthermore, the work required to originate and screen companies does not vary greatly with the size of the deal. Thus within the spectrum of companies that he can get financed, it is in the principal's interest to purchase the largest company he can find.

Assessing Seller Interest

A key element of the search phase is qualifying sellers. One investor says, "Finding ways to quickly qualify a seller as a prospect, rather than a suspect, is the most important thing, even ahead of the industry due diligence." Even if a company owner enters into a negotiation, he may not be truly interested in selling his firm. There are instances where unscrupulous owners used principals to value their business or to get free consulting work. Often, owners are just unable to part with the companies they built. This happened to one principal who said the biggest mistake he made in the search process was that he "spent too much time in negotiations with sellers who weren't emotionally ready to sell."

In order to be confident that a seller is serious, there need to be systematic reasons for him or her to want to sell. As one investor puts it:

> If he is 45, likes running his own business and has young kids, he is probably not serious. If he is 55, looks tired, has a sloppy operation, and has no successors, then he is probably a seller.

Principals use several methods to qualify seller interest. These include:

• Getting access to employees and line management within the company.
• Having the seller inform company employees of his intent to sell.
• Getting the seller to state his price.
• Obtaining a signed letter of intent.

One principal is firm in his belief in using price as a test of commitment. He asks for a price early in a negotiation and will stop negotiating if the price he is given does not make sense. As one investor summarized, "You need to ask for a commitment and get it."

EXHIBIT 15–4   Sample Criteria for Identifying Industries and Firms

---

Criteria	Rationale
Industry	
Fragmented	Many small firms increases likelihood of acquisition
No large players consolidating the industry	Principal able to acquire without entering an auction (which he will likely lose)
Low tech	Operations easy to understand
Recurring revenues (razor and blade model)	Revenues will continue while principal learns to manage the business, before beginning improvements
Company	
Operations:	
Few locations and product lines	Easier to supervise as less logistical/scheduling complexity
Strong middle management	Facilitate transition in ownership, learning, and subsequent running of the company
Marketing:	
Commercial users for products (as compared with consumers)	Easier market in which to sell
Direct customer base	Easier to target customers
Proprietary products	Limited competition
Finance:	
$5 to $20 million in revenue	Principal has limited access to capital
Generating free cash flow	Necessary to pay down the debt
Not a turnaround	Turnarounds are complex and require immediate attention. Thus they do not give the principal time to learn the business.
Conservative balance sheet, with high fixed asset base	Needs debt capacity to finance the acquisition. Bank will be more likely to agree to asset backed lending.

The Negotiation

Having identified a target company, the principal must enter four separate negotiations. These negotiations are grueling as they are interdependent and take place simultaneously with different parties. The following is a summary of the agreements that need to be negotiated and lists the parties involved:

1. Purchase (seller/principal).
2. Senior Debt (bank/principal).
3. Investment (investors/principal).
4. Equity Allocation (investors/principal).

Purchase Negotiation (Seller/Principal)

As in any negotiation, the search funder must work to establish trust. A well-established reputation for fair dealing can be an extraordinary asset. However, the lack of a track record means the search funder must work additionally hard to earn and sustain a seller's trust.

In many situations, the seller is the founder of the business being acquired and is usually emotionally attached to it. In order to sell, the founder often needs to feel that the new owners will continue to run the company and care for the employees as he did. For these reasons, some sellers have chosen search funders who offer a lower price than strategic buyers. This happened to one successful bidder who relates:

> The owner was a well-known figure in the local community and did not want a trade sale. Strategic buyers would shut the factory and move production elsewhere. The seller probably accepted a million less from us because we wanted to grow the business.

Part of any successful negotiation is managing seller expectations. Having grown the company, many sellers have an inflated view of their companies' worth.[4] While price is clearly an important issue, understanding a seller's needs can help a principal bridge a gap with a seller and close a deal. While sellers are usually looking for a particular dollar figure, they often have additional concerns such as maintaining health benefits or country club memberships. In order to achieve their number, sellers may also accept deferred payment through a seller note or earn out arrangement. The CEO of a Boston-based LBO firm reinforces this view, "Don't go in with a deal structure. Instead ask 'How can I satisfy the seller's needs without giving him the cash amount he says he wants?'."

Sellers often have unrealistic expectations of the time and effort it takes to close a deal. To manage this, the entrepreneurs are almost forced to set unrealistic commitments to get the seller roped in. Says one, "You tell them it will be about three months, then at the end of this say just another month, then a week, then next Tuesday . . . and then deliver Friday."

Many difficult issues come up in a negotiation. Because of a search funder's time constraints, difficult issues should generally be dealt with up front to avoid wasting time on dead ends. However, the search funder must use judgment. Some issues will become easier to resolve later in the negotiation, when trust with the seller has been established. Says one principal, "Some issues, had they come up right away, would have killed the deal."

During the negotiation, a balance between due diligence and closing the deal is difficult to strike. Detailed operational information and audited financial state-

---

[4]Search fund LBOs are traditionally priced off of cash flow, that is, a multiple of EBITDA. The stable nature of the cash flows are such that it is difficult for search fund LBOs to provide adequate returns at prices greater than six times EBITDA. Most search fund LBOs are completed at between four to six times EBITDA.

ments are often difficult to obtain. As a result, principals get bogged down. In the end, the principal will not have all the information he wants and must assess whether what he does have is sufficient. As one observer said, "The amount of due diligence you do is worth a multiple of the work done afterwards," but cautions "be careful not to fall into the analysis paralysis trap."

Senior Debt Negotiation (Bank/Principal)

Few financial institutions are familiar with the concept of a search fund or understand its workings. Consequently, banks must give search funds greater attention. This, in addition to a search fund's relatively small size and perceived high default risk, make it unattractive to many institutions. For those banks that do finance search funds, asset-backed financing is preferred. A principal must therefore be prepared to pay a premium and accept more restrictive terms to finance his acquisition. The specialized nature of a search fund loan may require the principal to make a "good faith deposit" to have his proposal reviewed. Once negotiations begin, it will likely take two months to secure financing. Given the complexity of the financial arrangements, principals must establish relationships with banks while still searching for acquisitions.

Bank relationships often come by way of a principal's investors who have credibility and leverage with a variety of lenders. While high-profile investors can help principals get in a bank's door, a deal must stand on its own merit to get financed. In the end, banks lend on the basis of the target company's fundamentals: simple operations, recurring cash flow, consistent profitability, and a solid balance sheet. As one investor put it: "To get leverage, you need to convince the bank that a monkey could run the company."

Prior to obtaining financing, the principal will be thoroughly questioned and his deal will be intensely scrutinized. This will serve as a reality check for the principal who, having worked long and hard to find the company, may have lost some of his objectivity. Having withstood the bank's review, the principal can gain some comfort on the quality of his acquisition.

Despite being extremely busy, the principal must be careful not to neglect any details when negotiating his debt financing. A principal warns, "We paid little attention to covenants in the negotiation and they killed us." Unable to meet what were, in hindsight, restrictive covenants, his company ended up on its bank's workout list. The company was later removed from the list, but only after considerable management time and energy was spent.

Investment Negotiation (Investors/Principal)

In their capacity as advisors, most investors are aware of potential deals before they are formally approached to invest in them. Thus, it is no surprise that slightly more than 85 percent of search fund investors follow up their initial investment with participation in an acquisition. According to one investor whose investment perspective is representative of others, "I will not do anything I do not have a competitive advantage in," adding, "if I don't understand the business, I don't want to do it." Investors look beyond financial projections in assessing the quality of an opportunity. One investor adds that he is skeptical if the projected returns to both the principal and investor seem too good to be true. In addition, investors may have other situation-specific reasons for not investing. If many investors refuse to participate, the principal would be wise to reevaluate the viability of his venture before seeking alternative investors.

Equity Allocation (Investors/Principal)

Principal participation in deals is structured in the form of carried interest in the common stock of the company that he will acquire. The amount of carry is subject to negotiation and is deal specific. However, this figure tends to hover around 25 percent to 30 percent.

While most carries are fixed for the deal, some include performance incentives. These incentives increase the principal's ownership when agreed-upon targets are achieved and can be powerful motivations. The danger is that financial issues can strain relationships and create conflicts of interest. This could be particularly detrimental in a search fund where investors are often a principal's most needed and trusted advisors. In one case, performance incentives were designed to ratchet the carried interest from 25 percent to 48 percent. When the ratchet triggered, the principal had difficulties with one of his investors: "Initially my investors were fine with the equity allocation but when the ratchet started to kick in, one investor complained that we had not adequately explained it to him."

The equity allocation negotiations are the first time the principal finds himself across the table from his investors. As previously discussed, equity appreciation is a prime motivation for doing a search fund. Thus, while important not to appear greedy, principals must be careful not to leave too much value on the table.

After successfully negotiating with all parties, the deal is closed. **Exhibit 15–5** provides a sample deal structure.

Running the Company

Having completed the acquisition, the search funder begins running the business. Not surprisingly, many are not quite sure what to do. Some do things that, in hindsight, would have been better left undone. One summarizes his initial experience: "I have got to believe that all the changes I made in the first 90 days were wrong. It is wiser (for the principal) to walk around and just learn for the first 90 days, especially if management is in place."

The principal's first challenge on taking over the operations of the company is to prove to the company's employees that he is a credible manager. He can begin to manage this issue by clearly communicating his vision and demon-

EXHIBIT 15–5   **Search Fund Hypothetical Deal Structure**

	Percent Total Financing	Percent Equity Ownership
Debt		
Bank		
Senior debt	50	
Revolving debt	10	
Seller (previous owner)		
Seller note	10	
Investors		
Subordinated debt	10	
	80	
Equity		
Investors		
Preferred stock	10	
Common stock	10	70
Principal		30
Common stock	0	
	20	
Total	**100**	**100**

Subordinated debt & preferred stock:	Often the investors get several types of securities including subordinated debt and preferred stock. This allows the investor to recoup some of their investment prior to the sale of the company, or stock repurchase.
Principal—common stock:	The entrepreneur has a carried interest, typically of 25% to 30% of the ownership of the company. (Many principals negotiate an ownership interest that increases as performance targets are met.)

strating his willingness to listen and learn from them. Indeed, most principals began their tenure with a companywide communications meeting.

Many principals take great pains to make sure the transition has little effect on employee turnover. "On day one, everyone is scared," says one principal. "You need to find the most important people and meet with them individually." In the case of this principal, he met individually with all his salespeople and addressed their concerns. "Remember," he adds, "your employees are the flag bearers of your company."

The previous owners and existing employees are the best resources from which the principal can learn a business. One principal continued to employ the previous owners and had them involved in the operations of the company— "I learned the business from them." Many new principals, however, don't have this option. Either the previous owners want to leave the business or it would be detrimental if they were to stay. In such cases, existing management and employees are critical. In Dodson's case, the previous owners left after the sale and he learned the business from the management team that was in place.

It is possible, however, that much of a company's underperformance is attributable to existing management. Thus as an owner/manager, one must balance the competing needs of learning and maintaining a business and causing change. Turnover can be extremely disruptive and can impede a company going forward. According to one principal, if turnover is required, "it's better to occur sooner rather than later." In his case, all top management left within his first year.

Much like a public company, a search fund company appoints a board of directors. However, the principal's lack of experience means the board plays a particularly critical role in the company's success. Usually comprised of four to seven investors and the principal, the board meets formally four to six times a year. An investor who sits on the board of a search fund–acquired company summarizes it best:

> It is like many other public boards, you have the same discussion: What has been accomplished? What are the challenges? Opportunities? What are the big discussions that need to take place? Ultimately, the manager has to make the decisions. You (as a board member) can be a good outside thought leader for the manager. You have experience. It's up to the entrepreneur to figure out how to use you.

The relationship between the board and the principal should be close and mutually beneficial. The principal gains from the experience of the board member, while investors can stay informed and remain more actively involved in their investment. One investor enjoys attending the board meetings and values his role as a "sounding board." Despite the closeness between board members and principals, the relationship remains very professional. Adds Peterson, "The meetings are very efficiently done with well prepared materials that come to the board members ahead of time." Boards also make their share of difficult decisions. In one case, the board forced one of its two principals out due to poor company sales performance.

Exiting the Business and Beyond

There is little precedent on how principals have exited search fund–generated LBOs. Out of the 17 principals profiled, to date only 2 have exited their acquisitions with a third currently pursuing a sale.

There are different views on the length of time a principal should hold a company before divesting it. One investor believes that a principal should view the investment as a long-term one, with a minimum three- to five-year time horizon. He attributes his view to the belief that acquisitions go through stages:

> If you have a clunker, you'll know within six months. But if things are going well (the fundamentals are good), it will take a year for the entrepreneur to get in control of

things. It will take another year to translate that into a strategic view of where you are going and a couple more years to execute on it. By this time, you (investors and principals) have the chance to think about liquidity paths and the principal is starting to think about what he would like to do next.

Another investor further emphasizes the long-term outlook. He says that he prefers to invest in principals with "a long-term vision" adding that he is "not particularly enthused about someone with a trading mentality."

Constantly competing with the company's growth and expansion plans are the investor's and principal's desires to realize returns. As a result, the principal is forced to constantly reassess the business he has acquired and at times may be pressured to exit. Consequently, a principal's career may include several acquisitions and divestitures.

Indeed, some principals believe that the primary goal of their first deal is to gain experience and funds to position them for a second larger and more lucrative deal. In fact, both principals who have sold their companies are proceeding with second search funds.

Conclusion

The search fund process has proven quite successful for the small number of principals who have used it to fulfill their goal of owning and managing a small business soon after business school. The model is structured such that individuals with little experience and even less capital can search for, acquire, and operate a company. Some 28 months after starting, principals find themselves running a several-million-dollar business.

Relatively few business school graduates pursue entrepreneurial opportunities immediately out of school. For the 22 groups who have raised search funds, the "path less traveled" has been difficult, lonely, and at times disheartening. Nonetheless, given the opportunity, those who have done a search fund would do it again. In fact, some have. The search fund process has enabled individuals to realize their dream of running their own business. In the process it has also allowed them to generate significant financial returns. With the wealth of opportunities available upon graduation, business school students have to determine whether raising a search fund is the one for them.

PAINT-PEN, INC.

On April 19, 1997, Warren G. Hamer received a telephone call from John M. Dublois, a business broker, about a company which was for sale, Paint-Pen, Inc. After being reassured by Hamer that he would receive a finder's fee of 5 percent of the purchase price, Dublois indicated that he would personally deliver the information to Hamer in the morning. Dublois apologized for not thinking of Mr. Hamer earlier in the auction process, but only five days were left to submit a bid.

Dublois appeared early the next morning at Hamer's office with the three pages of summary information contained in **Exhibits 1, 2, and 3**. Paint-Pen manufactured and distributed liquid paint in easy-to-use "ball point dispensers." This paint could be applied to all sorts of materials and was generally used by hobbyists and crafts people. Paint-Pen products were sold via the "home party plan" in which distributors recruited hosts to sponsor events in their homes, during which the products were sold.

There were certain aspects of the purchase which made Hamer apprehensive about the deal. First, the manner in which the company was being sold was very unusual, and the time period to evaluate the situation was very short. Second, no assurance could be given that the present management would stay on, and Hamer did not want to become actively involved in the management of a small company such as Paint-Pen. Finally, Hamer was worried about the restriction on contacting the company's distributors and the effect the company's sale might have upon their continued loyalty.

Lecturer Michael J. Roberts prepared this case as the basis for class discussion rather than to illustrate either effective or ineffective handling of an administrative situation.
Harvard Business School Case 9-898-156.

Not wanting to commit a significant amount of his assets to the venture if he decided to undertake it, Hamer contacted a former associate, Edmund Blake. Blake was a vice president at P.W. Brooks & Co., a medium-sized Wall Street investment banking firm that specialized in asset-based financings of companies in the utility and chemical industries.

On Friday, April 21, Mssrs. Hamer and Blake met with Mr. Henry L. Aaron, President of the E-I Mutual Association and with Mr. Joseph Reimann. The company's office was in one corner of a large, basement room in an old commercial section of the city. The entire production facility consisted of vats and tanks for mixing and filling the ball-point tubes and a shipping area for packaging the tubes after they were filled. The history of the company, as presented by Aaron and Reimann, is summarized in **Exhibit 4**.

Party Plan Selling

There are three basic methods of house-to-house direct selling in which a salesperson demonstrates and sells products in a prospective customer's home: cold canvassing, coupon advertising, and party plan selling. The differentiating characteristic between these forms of direct selling is the method of generating prospects.

In cold canvassing a salesperson, without first having made an appointment, systematically knocks on every home or apartment door of a street until she encounters an interest in her product. If invited into the home, she demonstrates the product and attempts to make a sale.

Coupon advertising generates potential customers by means of reader service coupons attached to advertisements and promotional materials. When a reader of an advertisement or promotional handout sends in a reader service coupon requesting more information about a product, a salesperson is sent to the reader's home to demonstrate and sell the product.

The party plan generates prospects by encouraging potential customers—usually women—to host a coffee for friends; the stated purpose of the party to the guests is the opportunity for the company salesperson to demonstrate and sell the company's products. The incentive for the host is the prospect of receiving a gift certificate from the company's gift catalogue, which usually includes both company and non-company products. The value of the host's gift is a function of the dollar sales resulting from the party, the number of people who attended, and the number of additional hosts recruited from the party.

For example, a Paint-Pen dealer might start developing a prospect-customer list by persuading a friend or relative to host a Paint-Pen Embroidery Party in return for a gift. At this party the dealer would exhibit the range of materials to which Paint-Pen could be applied, available predesigned patterns, and all the necessary accessories needed to accomplish Paint-Pen embroidery. The dealer would receive from this party (1) a commission from the sales that were made and (2) leads on additional hosts for future parties. Thus, the party process frequently tended to "snowball" because of the "friends have different friends" phenomenon, which could generate a constant supply of new prospects for the distributor as well as produce a customer list for potential repeat sales.

The major advantage of home selling to Paint-Pen is that it focuses the attention of potential buyers only on the company's product. This elimination of competing products tends to make closing a sale easier than is possible in the more competitive environment of a retail outlet where similar and substitute products are displayed. Some advantages of the party plan over cold canvassing and coupon advertising as a means of home selling are (1) less sales resistance is met in the home because the host is sponsoring the product to her friends and the guests know in advance the selling purpose of the party; (2) customer and prospect lists grow faster and each sales call generates a larger sales volume since more than one family attends each party and hears each sales presentation; and (3) its respectability is generally greater in the eyes of the public because of its nonabrasive prospecting and straightforward selling approach. Companies and products that employ the party plan selling method exclusively or in addition to cold canvassing and coupon advertising are:

Cosmetics

Studio Girl, Inc.

Mary Kay, Inc.

Fashion Two Twenty, Inc.

Vanda-Beauty Counselor, Inc.,
a subsidiary of Dart Industries

Vivian Woodward, Inc.,
a subsidiary of General Foods

Apparel

Beeline Fashions, Inc.

Queensway to Fashion, Inc.

Dutchmaid, Inc.

Joya Fashions,
a subsidiary of Jewel Fashions

Lingerie

Claire James, Inc.

Penny Rich, Inc.

Household Products

Tupperware Home Parties

Stanley Home Products

EXHIBIT 1   Summary Information and Terms and Conditions Relative to Proposed Sale by E-I Mutual Association of Its Wholly-Owned Subsidiary, Paint-Pen, Inc.

Paint-Pen, Inc., is located at 82 Main Street, West Orange, New Jersey. It manufactures and distributes, on a nationwide basis, liquid paint dispensed in ball-point tubes. The product is sold under the registered trademarks "Paint-Pen" and "Liquid Embroidery"; and is used primarily for hobby work of a decorative nature. It bears the Good Housekeeping Seal of Approval. In addition, Paint-Pen, Inc., manufactures or subcontracts the manufacture of a line of accessory products, such as sequins, glitter.

The product is distributed chiefly on the so-called party plan basis, with distributors located at various points throughout most of the United States.

The company has operated under its present ownership for the last five years, during which the volume and profit have steadily increased.

Terms and Conditions of Sale

1. Cash bids will be received up to and including April 24, 1997.

2. Bids shall be accompanied by a 5 percent deposit, in the form of a bank check.

3. Bids shall be firm until 5 P.M., May 24, 1997. Acceptance may be made by a fax sent before that date and hour or by letter postmarked prior to that date and hour.

4. Seller reserves the right to reject any or all bids.

5. Closing shall be at Seller's option between June 19 and June 23, 1997, inclusive.

6. Inspection of plant facilities is invited.

7. Bids shall be submitted subject to the understanding that Seller's distributors may not be contacted by, or on behalf of, Bidder and that any violation of this restriction shall result in automatic forfeiture of deposit.

8. Audited financial statements for 1993, 1994, 1995, and 1996 are annexed.

9. All bids shall be submitted to:

   Henry L. Aaron, president
   E-I Mutual Association
   670 Q Street
   West Orange, New Jersey

   Please mark the envelope "Confidential." All inquiries shall also be directed to Mr. Aaron, who may be reached by telephone at (609) 555-1234.

EXHIBIT 2   Copy of Audited Statements: Balance Sheets

	1996	*1995*	*1994*	*1993*
Assets				
Current assets:				
Cash	498,058	878,900	800,440	688,390
Note receivable	623,902	—	—	—
Accounts receivable (Less allowance				
for doubtful collections)	631,070	455,050	357,460	280,910
Inventories	910,790	757,040	590,500	592,610
Prepaid expenses	90,900	61,300	47,000	22,390
Total current assets	2,754,720	2,152,290	1,796,400	1,584,300
Furniture, fixtures, machinery and				
equipment, motor vehicles	226,690	176,040	153,280	151,480
Less accumulated depreciation	139,440	103,230	96,450	64,370
	87,250	72,810	56,830	87,110
Covenant not to compete, foreign license				
agreement, patents, etc.	821,800	1,221,800	1,921,800	1,931,800
Less accumulated amortization	245,660	522,640	519,150	359,630
	576,140	699,160	1,402,650	1,572,170
Goodwill	700,000	700,000	—	—
Total assets	4,118,110	3,624,260	3,254,880	3,243,580
Liabilities				
Current liabilities:				
Note payable		275,000	1,000,000	1,750,000
Accounts payable and				
accrued liabilities	223,970	195,830	117,810	99,930
Federal income tax payable	712,490	609,660	468,890	325,890
Total current liabilities	936,460	1,080,490	1,586,700	2,175,820
Capital stock and surplus:				
Authorized 10,000 shares of				
common, no par value—				
issued and outstanding	2,000	2,000	2,000	2,000
Earned surplus	3,179,650	2,541,770	1,666,180	1,065,760
Total capital stock and surplus	3,181,650	2,543,770	1,668,180	1,067,760
Total liabilities	4,118,110	3,624,260	3,254,880	3,243,580

EXHIBIT 3 **Statement of Income and Surplus**

	1996	1995	1994	1993
Net Sales	$6,883,270	$5,976,030	$4,813,500	$4,665,800
Cost of goods sold	4,319,750	3,599,560	2,891,880	2,895,190
Gross profit	2,563,520	2,376,470	1,931,620	1,770,610
Selling, shipping, general and administrative expenses	873,620	788,930	676,920	647,880
Operating profit	1,689,900	1,587,540	1,254,700	1,122,730
Other income	19,720	16,140	47,060	64,530
Net income	$1,709,620	$1,603,680	$1,301,760	$1,187,260
Other charges:				
Provision for amortization	$ 123,010	$ 128,010	$ 169,520	$ 174,520
Interest	6,240	41,210	62,930	91,850
	1,580,370	1,434,460	1,069,310	920,890
Provision for federal income tax	712,490	609,660	468,890	325,890
Net profit for the year	$ 867,880	$ 824,800	$ 600,420	$ 595,000
Surplus January 1,	$2,541,770	$1,666,180	$1,065,760	$470,760
Add: Partial disallowance by IRS of amortization of foreign license agreement, patents, etc.		124,520		
		$1,790,700		
Deduct: Additional federal income taxes		73,750		
		$1,716,970		
Dividends $23.00 per share	230,000	—	—	—
Earned surplus December 31	$3,179,650	$2,541,770	$1,666,180	$1,065,760

EXHIBIT 4   **Background of the Company (Summarized) as Described by Mr. Aaron**

Paint-Pen was organized in 1967 to exploit the possibilities of the ball-point dispenser. The company was the original manufacturer of ball-point paint dispensers and paint compounds suited to this use. The company originally utilized both manufacturer's agents and direct contacts to sell their products through large retail outlets. By 1976 Paint-Pen sales through the retail outlets had grown to over $1 million.

By 1975, however, the large paint manufacturers were introducing competitive products at a very low price, as they were simply using "over-run" paint from their core business. The company foresaw that additional competition would create a substantial decline in the company's profit margins. This factor, coupled with disagreements within the management group, resulted in the sale of Paint-Pen. Thus, in early 1977, the original owners were approached by E-I Mutual with a purchase offer.

E-I Mutual Association was founded in 1949 by the son of Thomas A. Edison, Mr. Theodore Edison, then president of Edison Electric, as an experiment in labor management relations. It was his thesis that if employees became stockholders in other companies, they would be more sympathetic to the needs of the stockholders and the management of their own company. He set up the association with about $1 million worth of stock in Edison. The original intent was that E-I Mutual should invest these funds in smaller companies, but by 1977 it had sizable investments in AT&T, General Motors, General Electric and other blue chip stocks. An employee of Edison could purchase one share of E-I Mutual $3 dividend stock at $10 a share for each year he worked for the company for a limit of up to 150 shares. If, for any reason, his employment was terminated, the employee had to sell back to the association ten shares of his holdings each year following the separation at the same $10 per share price.

In 1977, Joseph Reimann, as president of E-I Mutual Association, learned of the availability of Paint-Pen and recommended that E-I Mutual purchase 100 percent ownership for some $300,000. The membership voted and approved this recommendation. Subsequently, Mr. Reimann became president of Paint-Pen.

Reimann realized that Paint-Pen's distribution system needed to be revamped, and it was his idea to market the company's products to the consumer market primarily through independent distributors under the home party plan. In developing its distributor organization throughout the United States, Paint-Pen entered into exclusive territorial franchise agreements with its distributors.

Paint-Pen supplied kits consisting of several paint-filled ball-point tubes, various accessories such as embroidery hoops to hold the stamped materials taut, and sample pieces of fabric printed with a design on which the novice could practice. The distributor was free to make his own arrangements with other suppliers to sell, at the same parties, products such as textiles, fabrics, glass, and leather to which the Paint-Pen paints could be applied. The distributors were also free to create and manage their own organization of demonstrators. The growth and selection of the independent distributors for Paint-Pen could be characterized as somewhat haphazard. Vast differences in population, size of territory, and normal trading areas were noticeable between distributors. By 1994, the company had 17 exclusive distributors.

Prior to the end of 1994, several of the company's distributors had indicated an interest in purchasing Paint-Pen if E-I Mutual decided to sell its interest.

In 1973, the Company's products were awarded the Good Housekeeping Seal of Approval by Good Housekeeping magazine.

A quick check of the competitive situation with the Paint-Pen president disclosed that in the specific field of liquid paint dispensed in tubes for use in home decoration, Paint-Pen's sales were larger than any of its six competitors. Of the six competitors, only three distributed their products through the house-party plan. In the more general home hobbycraft and industrial markets, Paint-Pen competed with firms of significantly greater scale and resources.

ALLEN LANE

It was March 1982, and Allen Lane sat at his desk pondering a confusing array of issues relative to his bid for Plas-Tek Industries (PTI). Allen had been trying to buy a company for almost two years. On a number of occasions he had come quite close, only to have one circumstance or another block his way. Would his bid for PTI meet the same fate, or would his search for a business finally be over?

Background

Allen Lane, 45, had had a variety of experiences since his graduation from business school in 1965 (see **Exhibit 1** for résumé). He spent several years with Wagner Electric Co. in Springfield, Massachusetts, eventually filling the role of vice president of operations for this relatively small manufacturer of electronic parts.

Allen left the firm in 1972 to become an independent consultant to industry. He focused primarily on operations-oriented work: inventory control systems, manufacturing methods, material control, etc.

After three years of relative success, Allen disbanded his efforts in order to join James & Co. in New York.

> I enjoyed working for myself and was making a comfortable living. I grew tired, however, of working on the same kind of problems. James offered the opportunity to get involved with more general management issues and strategic problems. I was also excited about working with some people whom I considered to be extremely bright and interesting.

This case was prepared by Michael J. Roberts under the direction of Howard H. Stevenson. Copyright © 1983 by the President and Fellows of Harvard College. Harvard Business School Case 9-384-007.

Allen joined James in January of 1975 and worked with a varied roster of clients and industries. By 1980, however, Allen reached the conclusion that it was time to leave.

> I was becoming frustrated with the cumbersome and generally bureaucratic processes at the very large companies that are the base of James's clientele. James really did expand my horizons and my point of view. My experience there built a lot of general management perspective and honed important general management skills (I thought) that I was eager to use. I wanted to run my own company.

In June 1980, Allen informed James of his intentions to leave. It was important to Allen that James was generous enough to offer the continued resources of the firm, including office space and secretarial services, while he looked for an opportunity. Allen began thinking about how to get into his own business.

Laying the Groundwork

Allen had once before thought about buying a company but had no idea where to begin and did not have any close friends who had tried. His experience at James had given him numerous contacts and some credibility, as well as modest financial resources (i.e., roughly $100,000 in liquid assets that he felt he could afford to invest in a company). He described the thought process behind his plan of action and his progress.

> First, I was sure that I wanted to purchase a going concern rather than start up a business:
>
> - The start-up process is a lot riskier, takes longer to pay out, and requires a more single-minded commitment to the process than does purchasing a going concern.
> - I never felt I had a "better mousetrap" around which to start a business.
> - I enjoy being a fixer, a consultant, more than being a creator.
> - Finally, I had the time and resources to wait until I found a good deal.
>
> Next, I decided that in order to have a shot at finding something you needed to have a *focus:* "If you don't know where you're going, any path will get you there." Even if you change your focus later on, at least people have a sense that you know what you want. I decided to look for an industrial distribution business.
>
> - I specifically excluded high-tech and software-type businesses:
>   — There is a lot of growth, which makes these businesses attractive, but they are "faddish" and as a result there is an incredible amount of competition for deals from large corporations with very deep pockets.
>   — I felt that I had to understand and be able to manage the key aspects of the technology in order to minimize risk and successfully run the business.
>   — I wanted it to be a business where the decisions *I* would make would have a major influence and make the difference—not the research engineer down the hall.

- • I decided to focus on a distribution business:
  - — I had done a lot of work in the industry as a consultant.
  - — Distribution businesses are typically very undermanaged.
  - — One of the key factors for success is excellent systems—a good fit for my skills.
  - — In any given segment (like electronics components distribution) the firms are typically spread over a wide range in terms of their profitability. If you can buy a company in the bottom third of that range, and manage its margin up into the upper third, you can make *a lot* of money. And the skills required to do this are all basic general management skills.
  - — These businesses lend themselves to asset-based financing (i.e., they have heavy current assets).
  - — There are lots of small, owner-managed distributors around, and the competition for deals is less (to a large extent because they are not, historically, favored corporate acquisition targets).

About this time, I started talking with contacts who were in the deal flow, who encouraged me and suggested I look into electronics distribution. They also told me that I wouldn't *really* understand the acquisition process until I actually went through the process of trying to buy a company.

Early that fall (1980), I spoke with another guy, Dan Ray, who was also leaving James, and who had some experience in the electronics distribution business. We decided to work together.

We had just started making contacts in an attempt to look at deals when we heard through an accounting firm that Spectronics might be for sale. We called the president, Bert Spec, and sure enough, it was for real.

We had only been at it for only a short time, and we were ready to chase our first deal.

Spectronics

Spectronics was a $165 million (sales) distributor of electronic components, located in Newark, New Jersey. It was a publicly traded company, but Burt Spec owned a controlling interest of about 55 percent.

> We looked at the numbers and, in the price range he was talking, about $20/share or $15 million, the deal made good economic sense. Spectronics also seemed to offer the potential for improvement in rate of return that we were looking for. (See **Exhibit 2**.) We put together a 200-page business plan that outlined the industry, our credentials, the company, our plans for it—the works. After six or eight weeks, we managed to pull together an $11 million package of financing that included $1 million in equity, $8 million in secured debt, and $2 million of "mezzanine debt" (i.e., a higher risk unsecured loan with a higher return to the lender). We offered $21.50 a share. By now, it was the middle of December, and we had been working on the deal for about three months.
>
> We found out a week later that the company was sold for $2/share *less* than our offer. The other group had offered $19.50 plus a huge "consulting contract" for Bert Spec. We were livid and wanted to sue, but this would have required revealing our equity backer who was anxious to protect his anonymity. So—there went our first deal.

A Reflection

Looking back two years later, it was probably a good thing that we didn't get the first deal that came down the pike. We learned an incredible amount, and it cost us nothing but our time. The valuable lessons included:

- Don't go after a public company unless you have a backer willing to underwrite the process. The lawyers and accounting fees required to put a public deal together are far higher than for a private company. This is a sunk cost, and if the deal falls apart—as they often do—you've lost these fees.

- The acquisition business is a rough-and-tumble one. We were advised not to tell potential investors the name of a company until we absolutely had to. We heard horror stories about guys like us getting squeezed out by the people who had the money and who went around the entrepreneurs and bought the company themselves.

- It is a lucrative business. If you find a deal, *and* hold on to it, you can extract 10 to 20 percent just for finding it and packaging the deal. If you put some money in or are actually going to manage the venture, your share can go up to 50 percent or so with a limited investment in even a large deal.

Back to the Drawing Board

So Dan and I put our heads together to decide where to go. We came to the conclusion that all of our initial thoughts on the industry were correct. Moreover, we knew a lot more about the industry, had some contacts, and we thought we could keep our backers together. So we decided to maintain our focus on the electronics distribution industry.

We called every company—about 60 or so—that met our criteria:

- Northeast corridor location.
- Sales of $5 to $50 million.

We looked for any way in other than a cold call—a lawyer, accountant, friend, anything. We talked to industry observers, customers, suppliers, and banks in an attempt to plug into the grapevine.

We had heard that 5 percent of *all* businesses are "for sale" and that 2 percent are *very actively* for sale. Well, out of our 60 calls, we found 8 that seemed interested enough to warrant a meeting. Of these, we had second meetings with 4, a third meeting with 2, and pursued 1, Ace Electronics, very aggressively.

Ace Electronics

By now it was March of 1981, and we had been looking at the industry for about six months. Ace was a little different—it focused on very low tech and together with current inventories had a large stock of almost obsolete parts. Ace was owned by Abe Fox, who had started the business 25 years ago and was now retiring. He was typically one of the only sources in the *country* for some old condensers, vacuum tubes, and electromechanical parts. You can imagine that his margins were *very* good.

We spent two months haggling and finally shook on a deal. He went away to California for a vacation, and when he came back, he declared that the deal was off.

Another Reflection

Ace really opened my eyes to the world of small business. Most small businesses that we looked at, and of which Ace was the first, have "undervalued inventory." Ace, for instance, had its inventory on the books for $600,000, although the owner claimed (and after some careful checking we concurred) that it was worth at least $4 million. (See **Exhibit 3** for two sets of financial statements.)

This understatement is done because of *taxes.* If you overstate your cost of goods sold, you reduce your stated profit, and hence your taxes. Over time the stated book value of inventory becomes small relative to the actual value.

This is not a problem to the buyer, of course, if you are going to continue this practice. However, I had decided early on that I did not want to play such games.

This can create a problem in a small company acquisition. If you keep the inventory on the books at its understated amount, the IRS is very unlikely to see any potential issue. However, if you mark the inventory up to its "fair market value," the IRS may catch on and can (fairly) claim that the company had been underpaying its taxes all along.

So, then you come up against two issues:

- Sale of stock versus assets: The liabilities of a company always remain attached to the stock. If you buy the assets of a firm, the seller maintains the potential tax liability. However, if you buy the stock, as most sellers prefer, then *you* are stuck with the potential liability.

- Tax on "discovered inventory": Once the inventory is discovered, of course, this item has to be run through the income statement and shows up as profit, which must be taxed. My view, of course, was that Ace should pay this tax since it had been underpaying all along, and that it had, in effect, accrued taxes. Naturally, Ace would think that if I am "stupid enough" to be honest and declare this to the IRS, I should pay the tax.

Perhaps at this point, I should comment on what I perceive as my own style. There is a large gray area between what is ethically right and wrong. There are many opportunities to "play games" in the process of looking for a deal: exaggerating net worth, experience, the numbers on a deal, and so forth. These things may be ethically "wrong," or perhaps they are borderline. Whatever the case, I had decided early on that they just didn't make good business sense for me. One of the critical things I had going for me was my reputation. People "calibrate you" based on the veracity of your total presentation. If they detect that you are being less than totally honest about *anything,* then they discount *everything* that you say—I couldn't afford to let that happen. Thus, I decided that the right style for me was to be very open and straightforward with sellers, financial sources, and others.

Gardenpro

Gardenpro was a distributor of garden products, hardware, and paint, located in New Jersey. I heard about the deal from a business broker who showed me financials (with the name of the company deleted) and I was interested. He set us up to meet Chuck Stamen, Gardenpro's owner/manager.

It was an attractive business in a good location and was a distributor—just the kind of company I was looking for.

I met Chuck, and after the preliminary chat and tour, we started talking price. Pretty soon, Chuck mentioned that "the financials didn't fairly reflect the earning power of the business." Why was that so? Well, it seems that Chuck had a little scheme going where he pulled about $500,000 in cash out of the business—off the books and tax free.

It worked roughly like this: he would take an order for products from one of his "friendly" customers and give the order to his employees to load in the truck. Then Chuck would announce that he had to do some business with the fellow anyway, and he would drive the truck over. His friend would pay about 80 cents on the dollar— in cash—for the goods, and then Chuck would just rip up the order. No one would ever know.

Of course, he wanted me to value this off-the-books amount in making my bid. My position was that I wasn't going to play these games, and further, I was likely to lose these customers altogether, because I wasn't going to accept 80 cents on the dollar for my products if I was selling them.

I did submit a bid and knew that I could obtain financing. By this point, I was familiar with the approximate formula that secured lenders use to calculate the "financibility" of a company.

- 85 percent of the receivables under 90 days old (to solid accounts), plus
- 40 percent to 60 percent of the inventory, depending on its salability, and to some extent on how good the deal is.

In addition, you can usually also borrow one quarter to one third of the appraised value of the plant and equipment; real estate assets can be mortgaged up to 80 percent or 90 percent. This is a very straightforward approach to calculate how much you can borrow on an asset-financed deal.

As you might expect, I lost Gardenpro to someone with a higher bid. But I later found out that the company was never sold.

Hydrapress

A few months later, in October of 1981, I came across Hydrapress, a manufacturer of hydraulic presses for making refractories and special bricks for use in high-temperature processes, such as furnaces for molten metal and glass. I heard about this deal from another business broker. He was hesitant to refer me to Morris Golden, president of Hydrapress, because I did not have the $3 or $4 million in hard cash required to do the deal. But he did set me up with an investment banker who had appraised Hydrapress and who was representing the seller.

We got together, and I learned that it was a fairly typical selling situation. Golden was 68 and had decided it was "time to retire and enjoy life." His wife wanted to go to Florida, and all his friends were telling him to sell the company and tidy up his estate.

The investment banker told me that there were two very serious buyers lined up who clearly had the cash and were interested in purchasing the company as an investment. They would need a management team; perhaps I could work a joint deal with one of them. I did speak with each of these groups, but told them I was also working to raise the capital to make a bid on my own. In any event, under the banker's auspices, I was able to visit Hydrapress and meet with its principals.

After visiting numerous banks, I finally did get an oral commitment for the money from the Fiduciary Bank and wrote my proposal letter. I bid $3.4 million, but lost out by a small margin to a NYSE company.

Six months later, the investment banker called to ask if I was still interested. It seems that when push came to shove, Golden had balked at selling the company. According to the banker, he kept finding little nits with the deal until the buyer got so exasperated that he finally walked away.

By this time, I was chasing Plas-Tek and didn't have the time to get involved. More importantly, I had learned a lesson about buying a company from the founding owner: It's *tough.* No one wants to sell "his or her baby."

A Perspective

Allen commented on a few other aspects of the deal business he had learned about over the past several years.

"Ham and Egging"

One of the real "arts" to the process of trying to buy a company is called *ham and egging.* It refers to the delicate process of trying to get the financing secured before you have the company locked up and trying to get the company committed before you have the financing.

Naturally, potential backers don't want to spend the time evaluating the deal or commit to financing unless they are fairly certain that you have an acceptable deal worked out with the company. The company, on the other hand, feels it is wasting its time talking to you unless you have the money.

I was always very straightforward with companies; I would describe the deal to different financial backers, get an oral commitment of interest, and tell the company that I had this oral commitment. Naturally, I projected the attitude that I was sure that financing would be available.

The process does get much easier as you go along. The first time is always the hardest. On subsequent deals, even if the previous deals have fallen apart, you can talk about having raised money before, and you have a portfolio of backers to deal with. After people know you, and have seen you in action on one deal and have come to trust you, they are far quicker to make a commitment on financing.

A Hierarchy of Buyers

All this leads one to talk about what I call "a hierarchy of buyers." None of the companies would even be talking to me if they could have sold to a NYSE company in an all-cash deal, or a tax-free exchange of stock. From a seller's perspective it appears that there are several classes of buyers doing deals:

- Class A: Another company who views the seller as a business with "strategic fit." They are willing to pay cash, and pay a premium price for the company.

- Class B: Investment bankers representing some company looking for a deal, often a conglomerate. Generally they won't pay the premiums that a strategic buyer will, but in either case, as a seller you don't have to worry about the money being there.

- Class C_1: A leveraged buyout specialist who will in all probability pay even less, but who has done deals before and who has a track record in raising the cash.
- Class C_2: An individual who doesn't have the cash, hasn't done a deal, but knows what he's doing and can probably raise the money. I felt that I was a C_2 given my contacts and experience.
- Class C_3: An individual with nothing but desire; this was me when I started out, before the Spectronics deal.

Plas-Tek

In March of 1982, I ran into Jeff Brewster, an accountant with a Big 8 firm, with whom I had spoken around the time of the Spectronics deal. He thought he might have a few companies I'd be interested in, and we scheduled a lunch for the following week. One of the companies was Plas-Tek.

Background

Harry Elson had founded Plas-Tek, a manufacturer of specialty plastic components, in 1954. When he died in November of 1981, he left an estate that was valued at $7 million or so to a half-dozen well-known charities. Plas-Tek was part of the estate, and the trustee/executor, a big New York bank, had decided to sell it. In fact, PTI was actually two companies: HE Manufacturing and its sister company, Plas-Tek Sales Company. PTI refers to both companies.

The bank had a valuation of the business performed (see **Exhibit 4** for a description of PTI's business and the valuation report) and then contacted customers, suppliers, and competitors to see if any were interested in purchasing Plas-Tek. When none expressed interest, the bank quietly put Plas-Tek on the market.

By the time I heard about the business, it had been on the market for a month or so, and the bank told me that unless I were going to bid $600,000 or more not to bother. They told me that they wanted to close off bidding later that week, but I figured that I could stall them for a little while. When Elson died, all of his estate went into a charitable trust. The bank's trust and estate department had a fiduciary obligation to get the highest price for the business. They would not look good if they refused to let me submit a bid.

So, during the next few days, I raced around trying to put together a deal and submit my bid. I had the valuation and the banks' "... beat $600,000" as a starting point.

Strategy

My strategy was to first *value* the business, and then *price* it. They are two different things. Obviously, I wanted my price to be lower than the business's value but high enough for the bid to get *me* to the bargaining table with the bank.

The Business: Fit with Allen Lane

First, I had to evaluate the business and how it fit with my skills and objectives. Clearly, it wasn't in the distribution area, but they did have some things in common, including the importance of customer service. Further, it was *definitely* going to require a lot of hands-on management. With Elson dead, there was really a management vacuum at Plas-Tek.

The Business Itself

Obviously, a crucial issue was the business itself. I was amazed to see that Plas-Tek had gross margins in excess of 50 percent for a nonproprietary product. Harry was pulling down over half a million a year from a business with a million dollars in sales! Was this a legitimate profit, and, more important, would it continue if I bought the business?

Key Employees

Plas-Tek had the equivalent of eight full-time shop workers as well as a bookkeeper and a customer service/order entry clerk. I spent a day walking around the shop and was convinced that I could learn the manufacturing end of the business. As an engineer, I felt comfortable with the basic molding and machining operations. Still, there were several key employees whose efforts would be crucial to getting off to a good start.

- Bernie, the shop foreman, had been with PTI for 18 years. I talked with him and was convinced of his desire to stay on. He was about 55 and was making almost $50,000 a year, so he seemed to have little incentive to move. Unfortunately, he was in failing health, and if something did happen, we would be in tough shape.
- Sarah, the bookkeeper, knew the financial side of the business as well as Harry's pricing policies.
- Eleanor, the customer service/order entry clerk, knew a little bookkeeping as well as who the key customers were, what they ordered, and how it was priced. She also knew where all of the finished goods inventory was stored.

Harry had been clever in having a lot of part-time people on board, so there were often two people who knew the same job.

A Partner

Since the Spectronics deal, I had looked at doing things both on my own and with a variety of partners. Generally, I am the verbal type and do my best thinking in a teamlike atmosphere. I also wanted someone to mind the store while I was away and vice versa. I didn't want to be tied to the business night and day, every day.

I thought it was important that a partner and I each be able to handle key aspects of the business, but still have a clear enough division of responsibilities that we not get in each other's way. I was also looking for someone with flexibility and a set of values, goals, and expectations that was compatible with mine.

I also knew that if I brought in a partner, I wanted it to be a full 50 percent partner. I had been involved with some less-than-equal partnerships before, and such a partner feels that he is doing more than his share of the work. The individual I chose as a partner was capable of matching my $100,000 equity contribution in order to buy his half of the equity. Dan Ray had joined a semiconductor firm after the Spectronics deal fell through, but we had kept in touch. I knew he was still interested in doing something with me, and I still thought he would make a good partner.

Financing

Because I had the experience of putting together the described deals (and others), I had a portfolio of equity backers, asset-secured financiers, and other lenders to draw on for financing.

I did have about $100,000 in equity, and ideally, I hoped to finance the remainder so that my partner and I could control 100 percent of the equity.

I thought we might be able to get the estate (represented by the bank) to take back a note if we could get a reputable bank to guarantee this debt. I did have excellent relationships with a few banks that I had worked with on other deals, and they seemed eager to work with me.

I also knew that if we borrowed on the business itself, that we would have to personally guarantee at least a portion of the note, and that the interest rate would be about 2 percent over prime (i.e., in the 17 percent to 19 percent range).

A Lawyer

I had worked with a variety of lawyers. Some were good negotiators, others good on tax or securities issues. I had developed a list of criteria to aid in the selection of an attorney (see **Exhibit 5**). We had to pick one and get him up to speed fast.

Stock versus Assets

The purchase of stock versus the purchase of assets was a major issue in the deal structure, and we knew we had to make a decision on this point early on. I would have preferred a simple purchase of assets. In this way, we would not have to assume *any* of the liabilities associated with the old company.

The bank, however, wanted to clean up and settle the estate. They were strongly in favor of a purchase of stock, which would saddle me with all liabilities, including contingent liabilities.

Contingent Liabilities

Contingent liabilities are real or potential liabilities that do not exist on the balance sheet. For instance, if an employee had lost an arm in an industrial accident, but had not sued the company, there was a contingent liability in that he *might* sue later and *might* win some *unknown* amount of money. We thought that the following contingent liabilities might exist for Plas-Tek and checked them out thoroughly:

- Existing lawsuit.
- Potential lawsuit.
- Potential tax liability.

We interviewed employees in an attempt to discover any potential problems (i.e., injuries or customer problems). As best we could determine, there were no existing lawsuits against the company, and we checked the literature to unearth the possibility of potential product liability suits. We made a list of all the major substances the company used and ran computer searches to determine whether any of these was suspected of causing cancer or other diseases. Fortunately, they checked OK.

On the tax issue, however, we were not so lucky. There were two areas of potential liability:

- Unreasonable compensation: Harry had been pulling out *a lot* of money as salary, and hence deducting it on the corporate tax return. If the IRS stepped in, they could declare that some amount of this "salary" was excessive compensation, and reclassify it as a dividend. (See **Exhibit 6** for tax code and explanation.) Then the company would be liable for an income tax on this amount. This issue was complicated by the fact that Harry was operating PTI as two separate companies: HE Manufacturing was a straight corporation, and Plas-Tek Sales was a Sub S. If the IRS questioned the transfer-pricing policies of the company, the potential tax liability could increase to an even greater amount. (See **Exhibit 7** for a full explanation of the potential tax liabilities.)

- Accumulated earnings: HE Manufacturing, the straight corporation, had a substantial amount of interest-earning current assets on its books. (See Exhibit 4 for balance sheet.) The IRS could, on examination, claim that these assets were earnings that Elson had accumulated in HE Manufacturing rather than distributing them as dividends. (Again, see Exhibit 7 for full explanation.)

The Decision

Allen and his partner put a pot of coffee on the stove and prepared themselves for a long evening. They knew that it would not be easy to resolve these issues and value the business, but they had to submit their bid the following morning.

EXHIBIT 1   Résumé of Allen Lane

Allen Lane

Experience

1975 to 1980   NEW YORK, NEW YORK
JAMES & COMPANY, INC.
Engagement Manager. As consultant to top management of large manufacturing and distribution companies, led teams of several consultants and up to 50 client personnel to formulate strategies, and to identify and implement opportunities to increase profitability and improve functional performance.

Served clients in electronics (telecommunications equipment, computers, components), machinery (business equipment), consumer products (sanitary paper, pharmaceuticals) and process (paper, packaging) industries ranging in annual revenues from $150 million to $9 billion.

Developed and presented consultant training in techniques for assisting manufacturers and distributors to reduce costs and improve delivery performance.

1972 to 1975   CAMBRIDGE, MASSACHUSETTS
LANE AND ASSOCIATES
As Principal, designed and implemented management systems to enhance competitive performance and improve profitability of manufacturing and distribution clients. Applications included inventory management, order entry, billing, accounts receivable, sales analysis, purchasing, accounts payable. Industries served included automotive parts and pharmaceuticals.

1965 to 1972   SPRINGFIELD, MASSACHUSETTS
WAGNER ELECTRIC CO.
As Vice President, Operations, for this $30 million manufacturer, responsible for planning and scheduling factory operations and managing inventories (raw material, work in process, finished goods). As Manager, System and Planning, responsible for developing capacity plans to support company's rapid growth. Also developed production planning and scheduling, labor control, budgeting, and other operational and accounting systems.

1958 to 1963   BOSTON, MASSACHUSETTS
ACME STEEL FABRICATORS, INC.
Purchasing Agent and Assistant to Vice President, Manufacturing, for this $5 million manufacturer of steel tanks, pressure vessels, and other weldments.

Education

1965   BOSTON, MASSACHUSETTS
EASTERN BUSINESS SCHOOL
MBA; concentrated in manufacturing and control.

1958   TROY, NEW YORK
RENSSELAER POLYTECHNIC INSTITUTE
Bachelor in Mechanical Engineering; elected member of Tau Beta Pi, Pi Tau Sigma honorary societies.

**EXHIBIT 2   Profitability of 15 Largest Publicly Held Electronic
Components Distributors**

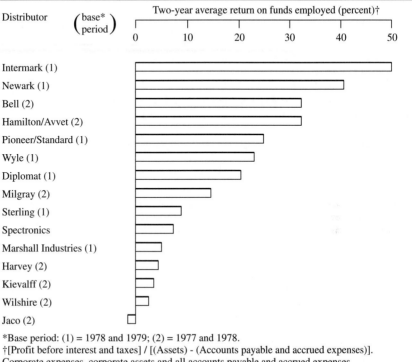

*Base period: (1) = 1978 and 1979; (2) = 1977 and 1978.
†[Profit before interest and taxes] / [(Assets) - (Accounts payable and accrued expenses)].
Corporate expenses, corporate assets and all accounts payable and accrued expenses
have been allocated to electronics distribution business on basis of sales.

Source: Annual Reports (line of business data for electronics distribution).

EXHIBIT 3   Two Sets of Ace Financial Statements, Fiscal 1979 (in thousands of dollars)

	Income Statement #1 (as reported to IRS)	Income Statement #2 (as "estimated" by Fox)
Sales	$4,000	$4,000
Cost of goods sold	3,050	2,250
Gross margin	950	1,750
Expenses	750	750
EBIT	200	1,000
Interest	0	0
Taxes	100	100
Net profit	$ 100	$ 900

	Balance Sheet #1 (as reported to IRS)	Balance Sheet #2 (as "estimated" by Fox)
Assets		
Cash	$ 30	$ 30
Accounts receivable	500	500
Inventory	600	600
Fixed/other	20	20
Additional inventories	—	4,900
Total	$1,150	$6,050
Liabilities and Net Worth		
Accounts payable	$ 250	$ 250
Accrued expenses	50	50
Accrued taxes	25	25
Bank loan	100	100
Net worth	725	725
Additional net worth	—	4,900
Total net worth	725	$5,625
Total	$1,150	$6,050

EXHIBIT 4   Introductory Letter and Valuation Report

March 16, 1982

Dear Mr. Lane:

Enclosed is the evaluation report that we had prepared to guide us in the sale of Plas-Tek, Inc. Based on this report and our own preliminary analysis, we have now set the asking price for the sale of the companies at $750,000, and are so advising all of the parties who have met our preliminary requirements for establishing serious interest in the acquisition.

Please let us know within the next ten (10) days (*a*) if you are willing to pay our asking price, (*b*) the terms of your proposal, and (*c*) if you wish to make a counterproposal.

At this time we will only give serious consideration to offers to purchase at a price in excess of $600,000.

As you were previously advised, we intend to sell the corporation's entire stock (after removal of cash and marketable securities). We will only consider offers on terms if the purchase price is adequately secured by satisfactory collateral security other than the assets of the business itself.

Our plan is to proceed as follows: We will immediately enter into negotiations with qualified buyers in order of the magnitude of their initial offer. We anticipate, based on the interest expressed to date by a number of apparently serious and qualified prospective purchasers, that we can settle within our proposed price range. If we find that we are unable to do so, we intend to broaden the base of prospective purchasers by announcing the availability of the companies to a wide variety of customary sources of prospective purchasers.

We trust that it will be apparent to you that we consider this to be the most expeditious way for us to attain the highest price we can, consistent with our responsibilities as executors of the estate of Harold Elson.

Accordingly, if you wish to be the successful purchaser, it will certainly be in your interest to make the highest offer in response to this request as soon as you can do so, as we intend to complete this transaction as quickly as we can.

Sincerely yours,

Senior Trust Officer
New York Bank

PLAS-TEK INDUSTRIES (PTI)

We have been asked to determine the fair market value of PTI. All of the outstanding common stock of the company is presently held in the estate of Harold Elson. The purpose of this appraisal is to assist the executors of the estate in determining the value of the business in order to sell it.

Conclusion

Based on our analysis of the relevant facts, it is our opinion that the current fair market value, in an all-cash transaction, of the operating assets and business of PTI is $600,000.

Description of Business

The business will be referred to in this report as PTI. HE Manufacturing is a corporation, and Plas-Tek Sales is a Subchapter S company; PTI refers to both companies.

The business was founded some 25 or more years ago by Harold Elson and was operated by Mr. Elson until his death on November 20, 1981, at age 72.

PTI, located in Patterson, New Jersey, is in the business of manufacturing and distributing gaskets, washers, "O" rings, and similar items made of plastic. PTI makes parts out of fluoroplastic resins as well as other materials, including nylon, polyethylene, and acrylic resins.

Products are generally made to industry standards or customer specifications. Approximately 90 percent of sales are made to distributors and original equipment manufacturers (OEM) with the balance sold to end users. PTI's customers come from a variety of industries, the most important being the food and chemical industries.

EXHIBIT 4   *(continued)*

Sales are made primarily in response to requests for quotations and to repeat customers. PTI has no salesmen. Advertising is confined primarily to a small listing in *Thomas' Register.* The company has about 300 active customer accounts. Listed below are the sales figures for the five largest customers, which accounted, in the aggregate, for 35.3 percent of 1981 sales.

	1981 Sales	*Percent of Total Sales*
Customer A	$98,487	10.5%
Customer B	72,377	7.7
Customer C	61,615	6.5
Customer D	51,599	5.5
Customer E	48,362	5.1
		35.3%

Income Statements

Shown following is a summary of income statements of the company for the five-year period ended August 31, 1981.

PTI INCOME STATEMENT (IN THOUSANDS OF DOLLARS)

	Fiscal Years Ended August 31				
	1981	*1980*	*1979*	*1978*	*1977*
Net sales	$942	$1,050	$894	$709	$652
Gross profit	551	640	495	427	369
Operating and overhead expense	97	92	78	76	67
Profit before officer salary, investment income and income taxes	454	548	417	351	302
Investment income*	93	92	65	66	18
Profit before officer salary and income taxes	547	640	482	407	320
Officer salary	480	505	415	360	280
New Jersey sales tax	20	23	18	19	6
Profit before federal income tax	$ 47	$ 12	$ 49	$ 28	$ 34

*Interest and dividends on cash and securities.

Manufacturing

Gaskets and washers are machined principally from cylinders or other shapes molded by PTI itself and also from plastic purchased from outside vendors. The company's facilities occupy a 3,700-square-foot building owned by it in Patterson, New Jersey. Principal items of production equipment include a press, a sintering oven, and a number of lathes and other machine tools. The company has five full-time production employees and four part-time employees. The company is nonunion. Hourly wage rates range from $5 to $9. The office staff consists of a manager and a bookkeeper-secretary-receptionist.

Management

The success of PTI has essentially been based on, and dependent on, the management efforts of Harold Elson. The company built a reputation of fulfilling orders quickly. Mr. Elson put a great deal of personal effort into providing responsive service to his customers, often working on weekends to do so.

EXHIBIT 4   *(continued)*

Approach to Value

The definition of *fair market value* employed in this appraisal is the price at which the property would change hands between a willing buyer and a willing seller when the former is not under any compulsion to buy and the latter is not under any compulsion to sell, both having reasonable knowledge of relevant facts.

In establishing a value for PTI, we have taken into account a variety of factors, including the nature and history of the company, the economic outlook, the book value, financial condition and earnings capacity of the company, its dividend capacity and intangible values, past sales of securities of the company, and comparisons with public companies in the same or similar industry.

It is assumed for the purpose of this valuation that PTI will be purchased exclusive of its excess cash or investment assets. The excess cash and investments would either be removed from the company prior to sale or would be compensated for with an additional dollar-for-dollar payment by the purchaser of the business.

Balance Sheet

Exhibit A shows a combined balance sheet for the business with the excess cash and investments set forth.

It can be seen that, with the excess cash investments removed, the net worth of the operating assets of the business is $200,000. If the land and buildings were carried at their current appraised value of $92,000, the adjusted net worth of the company would be $272,000.

Earnings Capability

In 1981 PTI earned $454,000 before officer salary, investment income, and income tax. Clearly, a buyer would be attracted to the acquisition of PTI for its earnings capability rather than for its asset base. The estimate of fair market value, then, must begin with an analysis of the earnings history and capability of the company.

Set forth below is a summary of the earnings of the company.

Year	Operating Profit* before Officer Salary ($000)
1981	$454
1980	548
1979	417
1978	351
1977	302

*Before investment income and federal and New Jersey income taxes.

Exhibit 4   *(continued)*

A key question is how much of the earnings ability of the company was due to the personal efforts of Mr. Elson and, accordingly, how much of such earnings ability is likely to remain in the future in his absence. The months since his death, in November 1981, have seen a decline in sales as illustrated below. It is the feeling of those presently running the business, however, that a good part of this decline is attributable to softness in the economy in general rather than to the absence of Mr. Elson. Some of the softness had already begun to make itself felt in the months prior to Mr. Elson's death. No customer is known to have ceased doing business with the company because of Mr. Elson's death. We understand that the executors have communicated with all the major customers and these customers have assured the executors of their satisfaction and that they anticipate continuing to do business with PTI.

PTI SALES
(in thousands of dollars)

	3 Months Sept.–Nov. 2		2 Months Dec.–Jan.*		5 Months Sept.–Jan.*	
	Amount	*% Chg from Prev. Yr.*	*Amount*	*% Chg. from Prev. Yr.*	*Amount*	*% Chg. from Prev. Yr.*
1981.............	$214	+ 1.4%	$111	−24.0%	$325	− 9.0%
1980.............	211	− 4.1	146	−17.0	357	− 9.8
1979.............	220	+25.0	176	0.0	396	+12.5
1978.............	176	+10.0	176	+58.6	352	+29.9
1977.............	160	+ 3.2	111	+ 6.7	271	+ 4.6
1976.............	155		104		259	

*Of following year.

We have taken the view that the current decline in sales volume is temporary, being related to the current soft economy and possibly to the uncertainty related to a prospective change in ownership of the company. With new capable ownership in place, there is no reason that the business should not be able to continue at least in the levels of the recent past. Accordingly, we have elected to employ the 1981 levels of profit before taxes and owner compensation as the best available indication of future profitability, and the one on which buyer and seller might be most likely to base a sale price.

Staffing

In view of Mr. Elson's heavy personal involvement in the business and the long hours that he put in, a new owner might well be required to staff the company with more than one person to replace Mr. Elson.

We have assumed that the functions formerly performed by Mr. Elson could be replaced at a cost of $150,000.

Future Earnings Capability

Using this estimate of management cost, and the 1981 level of pretax income before owner compensation, produces the following estimate of the earnings capability of PTI.

EXHIBIT 4   *(continued)*

Pro Forma Earnings (in thousands of dollars)

Profit before owner compensation and increased taxes....................	$454
Management compensation	150
Profit before income taxes...	304
New Jersey income tax (10%)......................................	30
Profit before federal income tax	274
Federal income tax (1982 rates).....................................	106
Net income after taxes...	$168

We have concluded, then, that a party acquiring PTI and staffing it at the annual cost shown above, would be buying a business capable of generating net income after taxes at the annual rate of $168,000.

Capitalization Rate

The capitalized earnings approach to value is based on the premise that a potential investor in a going concern will base the purchase price he is willing to pay on some multiple of the earnings power of the company. The approach consists of applying an appropriate price/earnings multiple (P/E) to the earnings of the company in question. It becomes necessary, then, to determine the appropriate P/E. The most reasonable way to do so is to determine what earnings multiple investors have been willing to pay for stocks of other companies engaged in similar lines of business.

Ideally, in selecting comparable companies, we look for companies not only in the same general line of business, but with a similarity that extends as far as possible into all areas of corporate circumstances, including capital structure, specific services performed, areas and intensity of competition, growth rates, and, if possible, size in terms of assets held, and the volume of sales. Only in the most unusual circumstances, however, will there be available even one publicly traded company that would begin to satisfy these multifarious requirements.

Since PTI is a fabricator of plastic products, we have conducted our search for comparable companies from the industry group of plastic products manufacturers. After examining a large number of companies, we have selected four as comprising a representative group for purposes of this appraisal. Key facts on the companies in this group are set forth in Exhibit B.

Exhibit B shows a range of price/earnings ratios for plastic parts fabricators of from 3.6X to 6.4X with an average of 5.4X. The comparable companies are, of course, considerably larger than PTI. In the case of some of the companies, there is a proprietary element to their product offerings, which is lacking with PTI. They are also possessed of more management depth.

For the above reasons, we have selected a price/earnings ratio of 4.5X for PTI, which is below the average of the group.

Applying the 4.5X multiplier to the previously calculated earnings level of PTI produces a preliminary value for PTI of $750,000.

$$\$168,000 \times 4.5 = \$756,000, \text{ say } \$750,000.$$

This, in effect, represents the hypothetical value at which PTI would trade if it were a public company. It is acknowledged that it is unlikely that a company as small as PTI would trade as a public company. Nonetheless, this approach to value corresponds with that which would be taken by many prospective buyers.

Adjustment for Illiquidity and Control

The valuation procedure above compares PTI to a group of companies whose securities are traded in the public market. The result produced, then, is the hypothetical price at which shares of PTI would trade if it were a public company. Since PTI is not a public company, it is necessary to make an adjustment in the price to reflect the fact that a holder of stock in PTI would not be able to sell his shares without considerable effort or delay. This adjustment is normally made by applying a discount to the price, called a discount for illiquidity.

Exhibit 4   *(continued)*

A further adjustment must be made to reflect the fact that we are valuing PTI as a whole, rather than valuing a minority holding in the company. The market prices that we used to establish value were based upon transactions in minority interests in companies. It is necessary to reflect this difference. This is normally done by applying a premium called a control premium to the price paid on minority transactions.

It is our opinion that in the case of PTI, the appropriate discount for illiquidity and premium for control would approximately cancel each other out, leaving the value, based upon market prices, at what it would be without such adjustment, $750,000.

Dividends

With the exception of Subchapter S distributions, PTI does not have a history of paying dividends to its shareholders. For this reason, the dividend approach to value is not apposite in this case.

Prior Transactions

There are no known prior transactions in the stock of PTI. Therefore, this approach to value is not relevant.

Book Value

As stated earlier, the book value of the operating assets of PTI is $200,000, or $292,000, if the current appraised value of the real estate is taken into account. Since this value is considerably below the value based on earnings, it has little relevance in this case.

Adjustment for Cash Sale

The executors of the estate that owns PTI wish to sell the company in a transaction that will permit a winding up of the estate shortly thereafter. Accordingly, they are not in a position to offer extended payment terms to prospective buyers.

Ordinarily, if a business of this size were sold, particularly to an individual, it would be customary for the seller to permit the payment of a significant portion of the purchase price over time.

Since an extended payment sale is not possible in this case, two effects will be produced, *(i)* the number of willing buyers with means available to consummate a purchase will be reduced, and *(ii)* the remaining buyers, in the absence of the availability of seller financing, will not be willing to pay as much for the company.

Because of these two effects, we have adjusted downward our assessment of the value of PTI by 20 percent, producing a value of $600,000.

Contingent Liabilities

The value determined in this appraisal presumes that a buyer of PTI would, in purchasing the business, assume no liabilities, real or contingent, other than the trade payables and other similar accrued liabilities arising from operations in the ordinary course of business. To the extent that the form of the transaction would require him to become actually or potentially obligated for other liabilities, the appraised value would have to be correspondingly adjusted.

Conclusion

Based on our analysis of the relevant facts, it is our opinion that the current fair market value, in a cash transaction, of the operating assets and business of PTI is $600,000.

EXHIBIT 4   (concluded)

EXHIBIT A
Combined Balance Sheets
(in thousands of dollars)

	HE Manufacturing	Plas-Tek Sales	Eliminations	Combined	Investment Assets and Liabilities	Operating Assets and Liabilities
Assets						
Cash	$170	$133		$ 303	$ 290	
Securities	507	234		741	750	
Accounts receivable	41*	150	$41*	150		$148
Inventory	60			60		60
Loans receivable................	19	20		39	45	
Prepaid expenses	6	—		6		6
Total current assets	803	537	41	1,299	1,085	214
Fixed assets—net						
Equipment	5	6		11		11
Building	10	—		10		10
Land	10	—		10		10
Total assets	$828	$543	$41	$1,330	$1,085	$245
Liabilities and Capital						
Accounts payable	$ 36	$ 50	$41	$ 45		$ 45
Taxes payable	10	7		17	17	
Accrued salary—officers	164	318		482	482	
Accrued expenses..............	10	—		10	10	
Total liabilities	220	375	41	554	509	45
Capital	608	168		776	576	200
Total liabilities and capital	$828	$543	$41	$1,330	$1,085	$245

*All HE accounts receivable are due from Plas-Tek sales.

EXHIBIT B

Earnings per Share
Latest 12 Months

Company (market)	Fiscal Year	Revenues ($millions— 1980 FY)	Amount	Period Ended	Book Value per Share (1980 FY)	Stock Price 2/18/82	Price/Earnings Ratio
Kleer-Vu Industries, Inc. (ASE)	Dec.	$13.5	$1.48	9/81	$5.16	5 1/4	3.5
Liqui-Box Corp. (OTC).....................	Dec.	43.8	1.28	9/81	9.64	8 1/4	6.4
Plymouth Rubber Co. C1.B (ASE)	Nov.	63.8	.38*	11/81	6.75	2	5.3
Star-Glo Industries, Inc. (OTC)..............	Dec.	8.3	.57*	9/81	2.73	3 5/8	6.4
Average							5.4
Range....................................							3.5–6.4

*Excluding extraordinary items.

EXHIBIT 5   Criteria for Selection of Attorney

1. Strong professional orientation—possess strong character, high degree of integrity and honesty, and general business competence.
2. Creative deal maker—ability to spot opportunities for mutual benefit in structuring deal terms.
3. Interest in working with entrepreneurs on a relatively small deal—enthusiasm for working on interesting issues with substantial creativity rather than mega-deal.
4. Caliber of corporate and tax skills—ability to integrate full range of corporate and tax issues into deal structure.
5. Strength as "hands-on" negotiator—ability to achieve goals at the bargaining table; good speaker, fast on feet.
6. Understanding of business issues—ability to craft deal in light of overall business goals, not merely tax and financing considerations.

EXHIBIT 6   Business Expenses—Unreasonable Compensation

TAX CODE SEC. 162. TRADE OR BUSINESS EXPENSES (paragraph a)
(a) In general, business expenses deductible from gross income include the ordinary and necessary expenditures, paid or incurred during the taxable year, directly connected with or pertaining to the taxpayer's trade or business, including
- cost of goods sold, including a proper adjustment for opening and closing inventories,
- a reasonable allowance for salaries or other compensation for personal services actually rendered,
- traveling expenses (including amounts expended for meals and lodging other than amounts which are lavish or extravagant under the circumstances) while away from home in the pursuit of a trade or business; and
- rentals or other payments made as a condition of the use or possession, for purposes of the trade or business, of property to which the taxpayer has not taken or is not taking title or in which he has no equity.

Explanation: Unreasonable Compensation
Compensation deductions are usually questioned by the IRS only in closely held corporations. The usual reason for disallowance is that the compensation paid is "unreasonable." Factors that are generally considered in establishing reasonableness include: the work actually performed by the individuals; their training and experience; the time and effort devoted to the work; the results that have been achieved; the requirement for ability and skill; the inadequacy of compensation in earlier years; and compensation paid for comparable services by similar businesses.
Compensation payments that are based on profits are subject to the same rules as amounts paid as straight salary. Thus, a legitimate bonus arrangement is recognized as an allowable deduction, even though in years of high profits, the amounts paid may be larger than would ordinarily be paid on a straight salary basis.
In all cases, the IRS carefully checks any compensation arrangement that distributes compensation in a way that is proportional to stockholdings. The IRS may reclassify some or all of such compensation payments as dividends.
The wrongful deduction of business expenses, including unreasonable compensation, may be grounds for criminal action.

Exhibit 7   Letter from Accountants on Contingent Liabilities

April 14, 1982

Dear Mr. Lane:

A review has been made of the federal income tax returns and financial statements of HE Manufacturing Corporation and its related company, Plas-Tek Sales Company, for their fiscal years ending in 1979, 1980, and 1981. The purpose of the review was to estimate the magnitude of tax deficiencies from certain adjustments which may result from an examination of their federal returns by the Internal Revenue Service. Our findings were made taking into account certain assumptions regarding reasonable compensation and other matters which were discussed at a meeting last week among ourselves and counsel.

Background

The capital stock of each of the companies was owned entirely by Harold Elson, who died in late 1981. Plas-Tek Sales is a Subchapter S corporation which reports on a fiscal year ended August 31. HE Manufacturing Corporation reports its income on a June 30 fiscal year. The business consists of the manufacture of gaskets, washers, and other plastic products.

Operations over the years have been quite profitable. In each of the three years prior to his death Mr. Elson's salary from both companies amounted to more than $400,000. The balance sheet of HE Manufacturing discloses substantial amounts of cash and investments and relatively small liabilities. For these reasons, concern has been expressed that the Internal Revenue Service could assert an unreasonable compensation and/or accumulated earnings issue if the tax returns of the companies were to be examined.

Since Plas-Tek Sales has a Subchapter S election in effect, the accumulated earnings issue would not result in a tax deficiency unless the company's Subchapter S status could be involuntarily terminated. We believe the prospect of that situation to be extremely remote. While unreasonable compensation is not generally considered in a Subchapter S situation because all earnings are taxed currently to the shareholders, a net deficiency could result if compensation, taxed at a minimum rate of 50 percent, were converted to dividend income taxable (before 1982) at a maximum rate of 70 percent by changing its character to passive income. Since such as assessment would be at the individual level it has not been considered in our review of corporate matters.

Unreasonable Compensation

Based upon our discussions and the valuation appraisal it is believed that compensation of $150,000 per year for PTI could be sustained if the issue were to be challenged by Internal Revenue Service. Using that number as a bench mark, we have calculated the deficiency to HE Manufacturing which would result using three different approaches:

1. Disallow amounts in excess of $75,000 per company.
2. Disallow compensation in excess of $75,000 and allocate the taxable income earned between the companies on an equal basis. This results in allocating income from Plas-Tek Sales to HE Manufacturing.
3. Disallow compensation in excess of $75,000 per company and allow Plas-Tek Sales a return of 5 percent on sales plus its reported expenses. Allocate excess income to HE Manufacturing.

The federal income tax deficiency before interest which would result from adjustments described above, as summarized in Exhibit A, would be as follows:

Alternative 1—$ 86,768
Alternative 2—$196,280
Alternative 3—$369,773

We are not aware that Internal Revenue Service has ever challenged the intercompany pricing of products sold by HE to Plas-Tek. However, considering the structure of the related companies, i.e., HE being taxable but Plas-Tek electing Subchapter S status, the Service could maximize the tax revenue by allocating income back to HE Manufacturing. The fact that the cash ultimately resides in Plas-Tek may be reconciled by the Service by claiming that HE paid a dividend of the excess income to Elson which was then reinvested by him in Plas-Tek, a common position when dealing with related corporations. The result would then be additional income tax to HE with no corresponding reduction of tax at the individual level.

We are not in a position to conclude as to the reasonableness of the profit rate that should be realized by each of the companies, i.e., manufacturing by HE and sales by Plas-Tek. The gross profit reported by Plas-Tek for each of the three years was exactly 40 percent, whereas the gross profit realized by HE ranged from 27 percent to 35 percent. Accordingly, Alternative 2 was predicated upon an equal splitting of the combined net profit between the two companies. It is conceivable, however, that the Service may take the position that Plas-Tek is nothing more than an agency and is entitled only to a reasonable commission on

EXHIBIT 7   *(concluded)*

sales plus its actual selling expenses and officer's compensation of $75,000. If the Service were to take such a position, substantial income would be allocated to HE.

Accumulated Earnings Tax

If it were to be assessed, the accumulated earnings tax would be imposed only upon HE since all of the taxable income of Plas-Tek is taxed currently to its shareholder under the provisions of Subchapter S. The balance sheet of HE at June 30, 1981, included $507,000 of securities on total assets of $828,000 and shows a ratio of current assets to current liabilities after excluding unpaid salary to shareholder of more than 12 to 1. Based upon those statistics, it is reasonable to assume that an accumulated earnings question would be raised upon examination.

If assessed, the accumulated earnings tax is calculated on an annual basis on the "accumulated taxable income" of the corporation. In simplified terms, the tax base is equal to the taxable income for the year less federal income taxes on income and any dividends paid for the year. Because HE paid out substantial salaries to its shareholder, the reported taxable income in the three years in question was relatively modest. Thus, tax for all three years would only amount to approximately $20,000. Of course, the Service could attempt to impose the tax on the income of the corporation after a substantial increase due to disallowed compensation deductions. If that were to happen, however, we believe a successful argument could be made that the excessive compensation should be treated as a constructive dividend to the shareholder, thus reducing the "accumulated income" tax base back to an amount approximately equal to the taxable income reported on the returns. Accordingly, the accumulated earnings tax issue does not appear to be especially troublesome.

Statute of Limitations

It was represented to us that the Internal Revenue Service has examined the returns of PTI through fiscal 1978. While it was stated that the examination resulted in a "no change" report, we have yet to see a copy of the letter. Returns for the three fiscal years since 1978 remain open under the statute of limitations.

While specific representations have not been made, we believe the companies followed the practice of filing returns on or before the original due date, without extension. On that basis, the normal three-year statute of limitations would run as follows:

	Fiscal Year Ending		
	1979	*1980*	*1981*
HE	9/15/82	9/15/83	9/15/84
Plas-Tek	11/15/82	11/15/83	11/15/84

Normally the statute of limitations is not a major consideration to a Subchapter S corporation, unless it has capital gains taxable at the corporate level or loses its qualification, since an adjustment to the corporation's income would be reflected as an assessment to its shareholders. While the matter is somewhat unclear, one case has held that an assessment may be made by reference to the statute as it applies to the shareholders, a point which should be considered in the case of fiscal year corporations.

We will be pleased to provide further services in this area if required.

Sincerely,

DAVID M. DODSON

It was the night of February 5, 1995. David Dodson, President of Falcon Capital Corporation, had just flown into Baltimore for an important meeting with representatives from Rite Aid. Dodson was in the middle of negotiating the acquisition of Auto Palace (ADAP), a subsidiary of Rite Aid. It had been a fast, yet difficult, negotiation process to date and Dodson had many questions about what to do and how to proceed in tomorrow's meeting.

Dodson had been pursuing the acquisition for two months, and although he had been originally told by Rite Aid representatives that the sale would be a "race" among the bidders, lately he had gotten the impression that Rite Aid was trying to hold up his progress. It took a lot of effort to get Rite Aid even to agree to tomorrow's meeting. He knew of at least one other serious bidder and had been told that there were up to two more. He was afraid that if the "race" finished as a tie, he would lose to another bidder because of Rite Aid's persistent concerns about his ability to finance the acquisition.

He had conducted a lot of due diligence, but knew there was more he needed to do. He was also in the middle of negotiations with his investment banker and needed to make a decision as to how to raise the money for the acquisition of ADAP. Finally, he had asked a lawyer to attend the meeting and wondered what roles he, the lawyer, and his investment banker should assume during the negotiations.

This case was prepared by Nick Mansour under the supervision of H. Irving Grousbeck, Consulting Professor of Management, Stanford University Graduate School of Business, as the basis for class discussion rather than to illustrate either effective or ineffective handling of an administrative situation.

This case was made possible by the generous support of Robert Denzil Alexander.

Stanford Business School Case SB185.

Background

David Dodson graduated from Stanford Business School in 1987. He was anxious to get into business for himself, and in order to pursue that interest, he took a job as a casewriter for the Entrepreneurship courses at Stanford. A year later, he left that job and put together a search fund to buy a business.

The search resulted in the $17 million acquisition of Smith Alarm Systems in Dallas, Texas in February of 1990. At the time of the purchase, Smith Alarm had $11 million in sales and 138 employees, ranking 16th in the nation out of 14,000 firms in the industry. The company grew under Dodson's direction, eventually acquiring its largest local competitor. By 1994, Smith had grown to $17 million in revenues and 150 employees. Dodson felt it was time for a change.

> We decided to sell Smith because we had some concerns about the marginal rate of return going forward. The two ways to grow an alarm company would be to either buy other ones or go into some mass market formula where you advertise at low rates and try to get people to subscribe. We didn't like the acquisition route, because the targets were small and required a fair amount of due diligence. There's nothing wrong with the mass market. We just thought there were other people who were established and doing a better job and it would be hard to differentiate ourselves. We had a good story to tell about growth to potential buyers—there were still things left on the table that buyers could get their arms around and say, "Yeah, I can make something out of this company"—and thought the story looked better in 1994 than it might in 1996.
>
> And then, I had some pretty strong career reasons why I wanted to sell the company. There was no challenge at all left in the business for me. Even pursuing one of those growth strategies would have kept me busy for about six months and then I would have been back to a part time job.

In the Spring of 1994, Smith Alarm Systems was sold for $35 million to Tyndall Venture Capital, a subsidiary of a large East coast bank. The investors realized an internal rate of return (IRR) of over 40% on their capital.

Dodson took time off to relax and decide what to do next. Within a few months, he decided to raise a second search fund and buy another company.

> I liked what I was doing. I hadn't maxed out my capabilities and I wanted more challenges to see if I could in fact buy and run a larger company. I wanted to see if it had been luck or if I was O.K. at this. I hadn't reached all my financial targets either.

In late October, he formed Falcon Capital and raised a $350,000 fund from seven investors (including himself). Each investor had the capability to invest at least $1 million later. His search focused on industries with companies that could grow into a big business, industries that were out of favor, and industries where he would be likely to get a deal done. His acquisition target was a company with sales of $50–100 million.

Dodson spent November researching potential industries and decided to focus his initial search on funeral homes, pawn shops, assisted living, electric energy, furniture manufacturing, and retail. On December 5, Dodson read an article in the Wall Street Journal about Rite Aid's failed attempt to sell ADAP, its retail auto parts subsidiary, and was immediately interested (see **Exhibit 1**).

Auto Palace and Rite Aid

Auto Palace was founded in 1976 and focused on the "Do-It-Yourself" (DIY) automotive retail parts market. It finished fiscal 1994 with $108 million in sales, about 1,200 employees, and nearly 100 retail outlets. It was the leading automotive parts retailer in the New England area. All of its stores were located in Massachusetts, Connecticut, Rhode Island, New Hampshire, and New York. Auto Palace was wholly-owned by Rite Aid.

The automotive aftermarket in the United States totaled $148 billion in retail sales in 1994, split almost equally between parts and service. The DIY market was estimated at $30 billion. In 1994, the number of automobiles in operation in the U.S. was at an all time high and the average age of automobiles was the highest it had been since 1948. The market was growing at 6.5% annually, but analysts worried that sales in the DIY market would begin to decline because of the increasing complexity of new automobiles. Public competitors in the DIY market included AutoZone (originally a leveraged buy-out by KKR), Pep Boys, Discount Auto Parts, Hi/Lo Automotive, and O'Reilly Automotive (see **Exhibit 2** for competitor information). Only Pep Boys had any operations in the New England area, with eleven stores in New York, one in Rhode Island, and one in Massachusetts. ADAP had yet to experience any serious competition, but this would likely change as the industry continued to consolidate.

Rite Aid is a large retail drugstore chain. In 1994, it had over $4 billion in revenue and nearly 37,000 employees. The company was led by Alex Grass and his son, Martin. In addition to the retail drugstore business, Rite Aid owned Sera-Tec Biologicals, Encore Books, Concord Custom Cleaners, and Auto Palace. In 1994, Rite Aid decided to sell these subsidiaries in an effort to refocus on its drugstore business.

An investment banking firm was engaged to conduct an auction of these subsidiaries. After contacting several bidders, GL Capital, Inc. offered the winning bid of $75 million for ADAP in the Spring of 1994. GL Capital was owned by Alex and Martin Grass. Alex and Martin Grass had also previously purchased Sera-Tec Biologicals through another investment company. Although the ownership of GL Capital made the sale awkward for Rite Aid, the deal proceeded until late October, 1994. At that point, improprieties in ADAP's operations led to the resignation of ADAP's president and senior vice president of operations. The two managers had been improperly charging personal expenses to ADAP. Subsequently, GL Capital halted its acquisition of ADAP and the subsidiary remained under Rite Aid's ownership and without a president.

Initial Contact

> I saw this Wall Street Journal article and what intrigued me about it was that it was in the automotive aftermarket, which I had some opinions on, and it was retail. Probably more than anything else, it just looked like something wasn't right. The two top guys were gone, Rite Aid was selling to its chairman, and, you know, it just looked intriguing.

Dodson called Mike Hammer, an investment banker who worked for Donaldson, Lufkin, and Jenrette (DLJ), and asked him if he knew anything about the sale of ADAP. Hammer soon discovered that another DLJ investment banker, Peter Bartlett, was representing Rite Aid in the sale. Bartlett was senior to Hammer in the DLJ hierarchy. Hammer contacted Bartlett to get information on the sale of Auto Palace.

Peter Bartlett was skeptical of Dodson as a serious bidder for the company. Hammer learned through numerous conversations with Bartlett that the primary issue was Dodson's ability to raise the amount of capital necessary to finance the deal. Though Dodson had potential equity investors from Falcon, Bartlett thought Dodson was unlikely to raise the $20–25 million that Bartlett estimated would be required. Hammer said:

> When you're auctioning a company, you get lots of calls from flaky people who really aren't credible. It's embarrassing to bring someone without credibility to Rite Aid and have the deal blow up.

Furthermore, Rite Aid was hesitant to enter into negotiations. They were embarrassed by the previous failed deal and wanted to be absolutely certain not to let that happen again. Through the persistence of Hammer and only after a DLJ investigation of Dodson's investors, Bartlett gave Hammer and Dodson a copy of ADAP's "sell book" in late December, 1994 (see **Exhibit 3** for excerpts).

At his parents' house over the holidays, Dodson had a conference call with Bartlett and Hammer to discuss the business and the possibility of an acquisition. Bartlett wanted to determine the seriousness of Dodson's interest before getting Rite Aid involved, and requested a letter from Dodson indicating an initial valuation.

Dodson worked with Hammer on the valuation. They knew the amount of the original deal, but the performance of ADAP had slipped since that time. In addition, a lower valuation meant a better return for Falcon's investors and Dodson himself. They did some financial calculations assuming an 8% IRR for senior debt, 20% for subordinated debt, and 35% for equity. It was also important that Dodson get Rite Aid's attention and prove he was a serious bidder. He also wanted to leave himself "a little wiggle room." He sent a letter to Peter Bartlett on January 2, 1995 indicating a $60–70 million valuation (see **Exhibit 4**).

"The Race"

Within a week of mailing the letter, Dodson talked with Bartlett about the acquisition process. Dodson reflected on the conversation:

> They were not going to do a full auction. They told us that it was a race to the finish
> line. And there was essentially a requested price out there and whoever gets there first
> gets the deal.

Bartlett indicated that there were two or three other bidders. Each bidder would be given a two hour management presentation during the week of January 23 and would be expected to submit a bid within ten days of the presentation. Dodson asked what was expected in terms of the structure and mechanics of a bid.

> Peter Bartlett thought I meant price. He responded by saying they were expecting
> something close to the $70 million. That said to me and Mike Hammer that a bid in
> the high $60s was what they were expecting.

On January 11, Dodson was given access to DLJ's information about ADAP to continue his due diligence. Though he had yet to sign a contract with DLJ, Hammer provided him with an analyst to assist in the due diligence process. The day was spent collecting store-by-store profit and loss statements, a detailed balance sheet, leases, fixed assets, workers' compensation claims, union agreements, pension and health benefit plans, and employee severance agreements. But with almost 100 stores, the volume of material filled seven boxes. Dodson also learned that ADAP used Rite Aid's management information systems (MIS) and that ADAP would need to develop its own system after the company was purchased. He explained this phase of the due diligence process and his reactions:

> The information was reasonably well organized because they had the auction. There
> was just a bunch of files of mostly legalistic due diligence. And there were people representing Rite Aid whom I could question.
>
>   I was very encouraged. The data and discussions indicated an undermanaged situation and some hidden value on the books in terms of land and notes receivable. The
> bad news was that there were few opportunities to close stores and create instant
> EBITDA value. It was also an overwhelming amount of data for me to review.

Mike Hammer very much wanted to represent Dodson. Hammer described the situation:

> David Dodson was trying to do this all by himself. He was trying to negotiate documents with Rite Aid, conduct due diligence on ADAP, and negotiate with his
> equity/subordinated debt partners. We had proposed that DLJ raise senior debt, subordinated debt and equity for fees of 1%, 2.5%, and 5%, respectively, with certain
> minimum fee guarantees. From day one, Dodson said he wouldn't need DLJ's help with
> the equity/subordinated debt money, but would want us to work on the senior debt.

Hammer was also due to be promoted to managing director and bringing in a client for the firm would certainly help get the promotion. Hammer met with Dodson on January 12, to discuss DLJ's involvement in raising the capital. They agreed that the deal would require approximately $30–35 million in senior debt, $10 million in subordinated debt, and $20–25 million in equity. Hammer stated that the equity investors whom DLJ brought into the deal would need one Board seat and one "non-voting 'observer' seat." He also thought that while Peter

Bartlett would ask tough questions about Dodson's financing, in the end Bartlett would be persuaded by Hammer's assurances.

Peter Bartlett called Dodson early the next week to confirm the bidding schedule. Dodson was scheduled to attend the management presentation in one week, on Monday, January 23. Bartlett indicated that there was only one other bidder who would meet the management team later that week. Dodson got the sense that Falcon was the only serious bidder. He pressed Bartlett about the wisdom of submitting a "preemptive bid," but Bartlett felt that was unnecessary. Bartlett also committed to warning Dodson if the other bidders were close to making a proposal.

During the conversation, Dodson asked if Bartlett could send him a "purchase and sale agreement." In prior conversations, Bartlett had told Dodson that Rite Aid would not consider a bid without Dodson's comments about the "purchase and sale agreement." According to Dodson:

> If the selling investment bankers are doing their job right, a lot of times they will write the purchase and sale agreement for the buyers to comment on. They not only have a price, they also have what issues the buyer may or may not have in the contract which could kill the deal. So, I was waiting for that.

DLJ continued to delay sending Dodson the agreement, effectively holding up his progress. Dodson wondered why DLJ should delay sending the purchase and sale agreement if this was really "a race to the finish line." He thought that it might not be a race, or perhaps that Bartlett wanted the other bidder to win the race.

Bartlett also discussed the $42 million in lease obligations that Rite Aid had guaranteed on behalf of ADAP. If ADAP went bankrupt or was unable to fulfill the lease obligations, Rite Aid would still be responsible for this $42 million even after the sale of ADAP. According to Bartlett, this would be a big issue with the Board of Rite Aid, and Dodson would need to assure them that Falcon could meet these obligations.

Dodson knew that Bartlett still had questions about his experience and financing sources. Following their discussion, he wrote Bartlett another letter trying to assure him and Rite Aid of Falcon Capital's capabilities and commitment to the deal (see **Exhibit 5**).

Dodson began to worry about who would accompany him to the management presentation.

> I was just a suit, so I needed to look like I had some "meat" to me. So I called in some favors. I asked Richard Tadler of TA Associates to come to the management presentation and to bring a warm body if he could. So there were a couple of people from TA. I called a banker at Bank of America and asked if he could come and if he could find another person to join him. And then I brought one of my investors.

On January 23, 1995, Dodson and his group met with the management committee for two hours and visited a few Auto Palace stores. Representing Rite Aid and ADAP were the Senior Vice President of Finance, the Vice President of Purchasing, the Director of Store Operations, the Vice President of Distribution, and two junior investment bankers from DLJ. Dodson explained his reactions:

We all arrived at the office. It was just a dog and pony show. I was disappointed that Alex and Martin Grass didn't show up for the presentation as we had been told they would. Not only that, the senior DLJ people from the sell side weren't there. Though it wasn't that important, you would like to see more of a serious commitment from Rite Aid or DLJ. So that concerned me.

On the other hand, I thought ADAP was worth pursuing. So, I wanted to schedule a meeting with the principals at Rite Aid—Alex or Martin Grass—to negotiate a deal.

Getting to the Negotiating Table

After the management presentation, Dodson also learned from Tadler that TA Associates had considered buying ADAP in the first auction. TA ultimately decided not to bid for the company because of ADAP's inflated wage rates, high real estate costs, and poor information systems. Dodson was concerned and knew that he needed to do more due diligence.

Michael Hammer sent Dodson a proposed engagement letter the day after the management committee meeting. The terms covered the senior debt, subordinated debt, and the equity funding and were largely as had been discussed previously. Although he had decided to use DLJ to raise the senior debt, Dodson was uncertain about using DLJ to raise the other money.

Dodson still believed that he would be able to raise the equity and subordinated debt himself. All of Falcon's investors were individuals who could invest at least $1 million in equity to this deal. In addition, TA Associates had been an investor in the Smith Alarm acquisition and Tadler had sat on Smith's board. Dodson hoped he could bring TA Associates and other private equity groups into an acquisition of ADAP. And he hoped he could raise some capital from business associates of the Falcon investors.

Hammer argued that DLJ should help with the equity and subordinated debt financing as insurance. If Dodson was wrong about his ability to raise these funds, the deal would fall through unless DLJ helped. Furthermore, Hammer told Dodson that Rite Aid would be more comfortable with Falcon if DLJ was assisting. The proposal also excluded from DLJ fees "any amounts invested by Falcon Capital Corporation or any of its investors and affiliates."

Another important issue was determining management's equity stake in ADAP after the acquisition. DLJ proposed that 12.5% of the total equity be set aside for management, with 7.5% for Dodson. Dodson thought that 25% should be set aside, with his stake being 15–20%. Hammer thought that these amounts would make the financing difficult. Although investors would want Dodson to have an interest and performance incentives, there was a reasonable range and Dodson's proposal was aggressive. After all, this was a leveraged deal and Dodson was young and had no experience in this industry nor with this size company.

Even more troubling was the disagreement over ADAP's Board of Directors. Hammer thought that the Board would serve a financial oversight function and that the investors should have proportional Board representation. Dodson wanted "operators and business people who could help run the company." He did not care who the members represented. Dodson also believed that DLJ incorrectly viewed the Falcon investors as "Dodson pawns, rather than committed and independent investors."

Dodson was beginning to think that DLJ was really working for the investors it intended to bring into the deal rather than for him. Also, if Dodson engaged DLJ, then they would be representing both the buyer and the seller of ADAP. Dodson saw advantages and disadvantages to this. Rite Aid paid DLJ millions of dollars in fees each year and DLJ might favor Rite Aid over Falcon. On the other hand, DLJ would earn fees from both parties and Dodson might get preferential treatment over the other bidders. Also, Hammer had helped immensely with the negotiations so far and DLJ had assisted in the due diligence process. Dodson felt he owed them.

Later that week, Dodson learned by chance from a business school classmate that the other serious bidder for ADAP was Tyndall Venture Capital (TVC), the group that had purchased Smith Alarm Systems, and that TVC's bid in the first auction for ADAP was $71 million. Since he still served on Smith Alarm Systems' Board, this made the situation awkward for Dodson.

It continued to be difficult to schedule a meeting with Peter Bartlett and Alex or Martin Grass. Dodson was beginning to think that the "race" really wasn't a race, but an auction. He thought:

> Maybe what they are doing is trying to hustle us along. What they want is for three or four to finish at the same time, then they can pick. They really don't want a race. They want to pace the process so that everybody finishes the "race" at the same time.

Dodson was concerned that Falcon Capital would not prevail in such a process. Peter Bartlett would soon be required not only to give Rite Aid an opinion of the bid Falcon Capital offered, but also to give an opinion on the credibility of Falcon Capital. Dodson knew that Bartlett was uncertain about Falcon Capital and that Rite Aid would proceed extremely cautiously into a new deal to sell ADAP. If Falcon finished the race at the same time as the other bidder, Dodson feared that Rite Aid, under Bartlett's advice, would choose the other bidder, even if Falcon's bid was higher. Dodson decided that it was imperative to get Rite Aid to the negotiating table. On January 29, Dodson faxed Bartlett a letter asking to enter substantive negotiations before February 3 (see **Exhibit 6**).

The next day, Hammer and Dodson informed Bartlett that they knew who the other bidder was and what their original offer had been. A series of phone conversations followed. Bartlett was clearly upset that Dodson had that information, and tried to paint a picture of several other bidders. Bartlett also continued to express doubts about Falcon's financial backing. Dodson began to believe that Bartlett was stalling to allow TVC to perfect its offer.

Hammer pressed hard for a negotiating meeting and indicated that Dodson wouldn't proceed any further until one had been scheduled. He also asked that Dodson be given exclusivity on the deal. This would ensure that Falcon would be the only bidder for ADAP, which in turn would help raise the capital from investors. Bartlett insisted that he could not recommend an exclusive arrangement without more information about Falcon.

Finally, Bartlett said that he had sent Dodson's letter to Alex Grass and against his better judgment, had recommended a negotiating meeting. Bartlett also said, "Who knows, if Alex likes this guy he might just sign him up." In order to prepare Alex Grass for the meeting, Bartlett wanted to know what to expect for Falcon's bid. Hammer said it would be in the $60–64 million range. Bartlett wanted to know if Falcon could go to $65 million and recommended that Falcon not offer their best price because Alex Grass wanted to "get something" through the negotiations. Dodson made it clear that this had better be a serious meeting and hung up feeling that a lot would depend on his rapport with Alex Grass.

The meeting was set for February 6. Over the next five days, Dodson, Hammer, and Bartlett had numerous discussions, Bartlett was still concerned about Falcon's ability to finance the deal and asked for assurances. Dodson continued to press Bartlett on the price and learned that it made little difference to Alex Grass if the final price was $63 million or $65 million and that there were in fact three other bidders. Rite Aid continued to refuse Falcon exclusivity on the deal, but agreed not to let any more bidders into the process. Discussions about Dodson's due diligence, particularly about the lease obligations and ADAP's inventory, also occurred.

On advice from a Falcon investor, Dodson contacted Dick Floor and asked him to attend the meeting. Floor was a Boston lawyer with 30 years of experience specializing in securities, finance, mergers and acquisitions, and general business law. His clients included venture capital firms, brokerage firms, mutual fund companies, investment advisers, and small corporations. Although he knew very little about the company or the deal, Floor agreed to attend. He explained the situation:

> I didn't have a lot of time to work with David before the meeting. I think I asked him to send me some background material and I think we chatted a little bit on the plane going from Boston to Baltimore. I knew basically two things: he really wanted to do the deal and he wanted to get it at the best price possible.

February 5, 1996

Dodson, Hammer, and Floor flew to Baltimore on February 5. They were scheduled to meet with Bartlett, Alex Grass, and Rite Aid's lawyer the next day. Bartlett was tired of the deal and looking forward to concluding it. Rite Aid was also anxious to have this troublesome deal closed.

Dodson had several questions in his mind. He felt comfortable with his due diligence to date, but knew more needed to be done. Although Rite Aid continued to insist that ADAP would hit its financial targets, he knew that performance had slipped since the previous spring. Should he be buying a company that Alex Grass had just decided not to buy? ADAP had been operating without a president and senior vice president since October and he wondered who was going to operate ADAP. What did he know about a large retail organization? He knew that inventory and the lease obligations would require adjustments and that the company would need to develop its own MIS system. But he had not read a single lease, knew very little about developing an MIS system, and needed to have his accountants review ADAP's financial records. He had just learned of TA's concerns and wondered if there were other serious problems he had yet to discover. He had only talked with one industry analyst and had done no analysis of competitors. Then there was the issue of the other bidders and their levels of commitment. Should he push to finalize the deal in tomorrow's meeting or wait until he had conducted more due diligence?

He was also concerned about financing the deal. He was certain he could raise the equity and subordinated debt himself, but what if he was wrong? Should he structure an agreement with DLJ involving unrecoverable up-front costs of $100,000–150,000 that would act as "insurance" as Hammer suggested?

There were several ways he could approach the meeting. A lot depended on his rapport with Alex Grass and he had to carefully decide what role he should play. He wondered who should lead his team. Although Floor was experienced, he knew very little about the company and the difficult negotiations to date. Dodson debated whether he should give specific instructions to Floor and Hammer before the meeting.

EXHIBIT 1

> **Agreement Is Terminated On**
> **Sale of Auto Supply Unit**
>
> **Rite Aid Corp.** said a contract for the $75 million sale of its ADAP Inc. unit to **GL Capital Inc.** has been terminated, and it is seeking a new buyer for the automotive supply chain.
>
> GL Capital, an investment company whose owners include Rite Aid Chairman Alex Grass, called off the purchase after ADAP's President and Senior Vice President of Operations resigned in late October.
>
> GL Capital considered the resignations "a material adverse change in the business," Rite Aid said in a statement. The company added, however, that ADAP's current sales and earnings "are in accordance with ADAP's business plan."
>
> Rite Aid, Camp Hill, Pa., is still trying to fill the President's post at ADAP and said it is continuing with its plan to dispose of all non-drugstore businesses.
>
> Rite Aid also said it has completed the sale of its Sera-Tec Biologicals unit for $70 million to AG Capital Inc., an investment company also partly owned by Mr. Grass, who will retire from Rite Aid in March.

Source: *The Wall Street Journal*, December 5, 1994.

EXHIBIT 2

	AutoZone	Discount Auto Parts	Hi/Lo Automotive	O'Reilly Automotive	Pep Boys
Company Profile					
Number of Stores	848	192	150	145	386
Customers	Mainly DIY	100% DIY	65% DIY	50% DIY	90% DIY
SKUs per Store	13–17,000	10–14,000	19–23,000		22,000
Stock Information					
Recent Stock Price ($)	55.75	25.88	12.75	27.25	29.25
Shares Outstanding (000)	74,375	13,957	10,690	8,602	61,891
Market Value ($000)	4,146,406	361,137	136,298	234,405	1,810,312
Last 12 Month Data (000)					
Revenues	1,348,057	198,221	205,235	137,164	1,241,133
Gross Profit	542,562	72,977	78,786	53,062	335,318
EBIT	157,752	24,795	13,378	12,570	120,608
Net Income	96,741	13,651	6,712	8,278	65,512
Valuation Ratios					
Market/Last 4Q Revenue	3.1	1.8	0.7	1.7	1.5
Price/Book	9.2	3.9	1.3	4.1	3.3
Market/EBIT	26.3	14.6	10.2	18.6	15.0
Retail Performance					
Avg. Store Size (Sq. Ft.)	5,764	6,100	7,813	4,500	20,132
Avg. Sales/Store ($000)	1,590	1,032	1,368	946	3,215
Avg. Sales/Store Sq. Ft.	276	169	175	210	160

EXHIBIT 3

I. EXECUTIVE SUMMARY

ADAP, Inc. ("ADAP" or the "Company") is New England's leading specialty retailer of automotive parts and accessories serving the "Do-It-Yourself" ("DIY") customer. In several locations the Company also provides automotive maintenance, repair services and installation of parts. The Company began operation in 1976 and currently operates 96 stores located in six states in the Northeastern United States. The Company's operations are supplied by a single distribution center located in Avon, Massachusetts. Each store contains an extensive product line including (i) hard parts such as new and rebuilt starters, alternators, transmissions, and brake pads; (ii) automotive accessory items such as floor mats, seat covers and windshield wipers; (iii) maintenance items such as antifreeze, oils, batteries, protectants and waxes; and (iv) in its four service center units, a broad selection of tires.

In 1991, the Company improved upon the ADAP concept by converting almost all of its stores to the current Auto Palace format. Such conversion included (i) an increase in its product selection from approximately 10,000 SKUs to 13,000 SKUs; (ii) shifting its pricing strategy from high/low pricing to an everyday low price strategy; and (iii) undertaking a chainwide remodeling program focused on making the stores brighter, arranged more efficiently, and utilizing improved interior and exterior signage. The conversion to the Auto Palace concept was rolled out over the latter part of fiscal 1990 to fiscal 1991, 1992 and 1993 respectively. Over the past year, the Company has further developed the concept by adding service bays in four new units ("Auto Palace Service Center"). The Company believes the addition of service centers satisfies a need for reliable, quality service centers in its markets. In addition, the increased traffic of the service bays has greatly enhanced its retail sales operation by approximately 20%.

ADAP has experienced strong growth as a result of its new store opening program and impressive comparable store increases. Revenue has grown at a compound annual growth rate of 15.2% over the past five years from $61.5 million in fiscal

---
EXHIBIT 3   *(continued)*

1990 to $108.3 million in fiscal 1994. Approximately 38% of this growth is attributed to increases in comparable store sales. In addition, the number of stores increased from 74 in fiscal 1990 to 96 in fiscal 1994. A major component of the Company's growth strategy is to expand its new Auto Palace Service Center concept, in both new and existing markets. The Company expects to open 15 units in fiscal 1995, increasing total store count to 106, net of closings. All but one of such locations are expected to be Auto Palace Service Centers.

ADAP's typical store is 10,000 square feet in size, with 3,000 square feet dedicated to a hard parts counter and inventory. The new Auto Palace Service Centers are approximately 18,000 square feet in size with 10,000 square feet dedicated to retail space and approximately 8,000 square feet dedicated to the automobile repair service center. ADAP stores are designed to have a strong visual impact, utilizing bright, colorful signs to easily direct the customer to a product area. The stores are typically located in areas with high automotive traffic and utilize large, highly visible exterior signs to attract customers. Although the competition varies by individual market, the Company believes that it has a competitive advantage with respect to both its depth and breadth of merchandise and price.

On January 7, 1994 Rite Aid announced a plan of reorganization which included the planned sale of all non-drugstore assets. Such assets include Rite Aid's Retail Division, consisting of ADAP, Concord Custom Cleaner, Encore Books and its Medical Services Division which is comprised solely of Sera-Tec Biologicals.

II. KEY INVESTMENT CONSIDERATIONS

- *Strong Operating Results.* The Company has experienced strong growth over the past five years. From fiscal 1990 to fiscal 1994, revenues have grown by over 76.1% from $61.5 million to $108.3 million. This growth has been attributed 62% to the addition of 22 new stores (net of closures) and 38% to comparable store growth. Over the same period average sales per store has increased from $819,000 to $1,134,000. In addition, EBITDA (defined as earnings before interest, income taxes and depreciation) has grown 183% from $4.1 million to $11.7 million during the same period. The Company currently plans to open 15 stores in fiscal 1995 which should result in strong continued growth in sales and profitability.

- *Dominant Competitor in New England.* The Company's primary competition includes small local operators as well as several regional chains. The Company believes it offers a broader selection of merchandise, and that its everyday low prices are highly competitive. The Company's operating expenses as a percentage of sales have improved over time as the Company has grown its store base without substantial increases in fixed and overhead costs. The resulting increase in revenue has created attractive purchasing opportunities which has allowed the Company to profitably offer prices which are consistently lower than its local competition.

- *Significant Growth Potential.* The Company believes there exist significant growth opportunities to continue expanding its store base in both existing and new markets throughout New England and the Northern Mid-Atlantic Region. Management has successfully expanded the business while maintaining strong profitability. Management has added 22 net new stores since fiscal 1990, growing revenues in excess of 76% (revenues from comparable store sales grew 29%). The Company anticipates expanding primarily with its new Auto Palace Service Center concept. The service center satisfies a need for reliable, quality automotive service centers in its markets as local gas stations and repair centers find it more difficult to afford the required sophisticated equipment of service to today's automobiles. In addition, the increased traffic resulting from the addition of a service center has a significant impact on retail sales. The average total sales per service center unit has been $2.7 million to $3.0 million; of which $1.3 million to $1.4 million are retail sales excluding tire and service sales, versus sales in the ADAP retail concept of $1.1 million. The Company's expansion plan for fiscal 1995 is to open 15 new stores, 14 of which are in the new service center formats.

- *Favorable Industry Trends.*
  Market Growth: The automotive aftermarket industry possesses strong economic fundamentals which are expected to drive its growth in the future. The average age of motor vehicles in operation is currently at an all-time high, averaging 8.4 years in 1993 versus 7.4 years after the last recession in 1983. The total number of vehicles in operation is also at an all-time high, totaling 184 million in 1993 compared to 147 million a decade ago. In addition, Americans are adding an increasingly larger amount of mileage to their cars each year. These factors contribute to the expected growth in demand for after-market auto parts and auto service.
  Competitive Requirements: The recent development in automotive technology and the increased number of car models available has changed the industry's competitive landscape. Automotive technology has become significantly more sophisticated, requiring a significantly greater investment in advanced diagnostic machinery and training by

EXHIBIT 3   *(continued)*

commercial repair outlets. Furthermore, the increase in automobile models in the U.S. market requires greater investment in inventory levels to service the market. These entry barriers benefit large chains, such as ADAP, which can afford such investments in equipment, inventory and technical training at the expense of smaller, independent auto stores and repair shops that will be forced to exit the industry.

- *Excellent Chainwide Store Condition.* Since fiscal 1990, 87 of the Company's 96 stores have either been renovated or are newly opened units. The remodeling program focused on making the stores brighter, more efficiently arranged, and adding new interior and exterior signage.

III. SUMMARY FINANCIAL INFORMATION

ADAP, INC.
(dollars in thousands)

	Fiscal Years Ended			Nine Months Ended		Fiscal Years Ended	
	Feb. 29, 1992	Feb. 27, 1993	Feb. 26, 1994	Nov. 27, 1993	Nov. 26, 1994	Mar. 4, 1995E	Mar. 2, 1996P
Revenues	84,805	96,893	108,610	81,639	97,354	130,131	138,474
Gross Profit	36,520	40,983	45,470	34,175	39,725	53,318	57,862
EBIT	5,657	6,625	7,737	7,259	5,624*	5,969*	8,086*
Net Income	2,108	2,851	3,381	3,316	2,318*	2,447*	3,315*
Comparable Store							
Sales Growth	5.7%	4.9%	5.7%	3.8%	8.0%	7.1%	5.0%
Total Growth	16.6%	14.3%	12.1%	9.3%	19.3%	19.8%	6.4%
Total Stores	89	95	96	95	97	98	98
Capital Expenditures	2,862	6,111	8,288	5,110	7,743	8,483	(1,000)
Balance Sheet Information							
Inventory	34,714	38,739	45,606	42,997	44,297	44,143	42,278
Total Assets	68,055	74,830	85,885	81,065	89,422	88,597	81,127
Accounts Payable	4,098	4,127	6,962	6,032	4,762	6,426	7,721
Working Capital	31,377	35,898	39,723	36,747	40,377	39,139	35,442

*Decrease from historical averages due to write-offs for store closings.

EXHIBIT 3   *(concluded)*

CONSOLIDATED BALANCE SHEETS
($000)

	Fiscal Years Ended			Nine Months Ended
	Feb. 29, 1992	*Feb. 27, 1993*	*Feb. 26, 1994*	*Nov. 26, 1994*
Assets				
Current Assets:				
Cash	423	341	386	445
Accounts Receivable	718	1,216	1,312	1,460
Inventory	34,714	38,739	45,606	44,297
Income Taxes	302	261	137	137
Prepaid Expenses	485	614	510	636
Total Current Assets	36,642	41,171	47,951	46,975
Net PP&E	14,872	18,450	23,476	28,533
Intangibles	14,535	13,700	13,062	12,710
Other Assets	2,006	1,509	1,396	1,204
Total Assets	68,055	74,830	85,885	89,422
Liabilities & Stockholders' Equity				
Current Liabilities:				
Accounts Payable	4,098	4,127	6,962	4,762
Taxes Payable	386	550	560	1,399
Accrued Liabilities	358	255	320	(8)
Total Current Liabilities	4,842	4,932	7,842	6,153
Deferred Taxes	994	937	890	890
Total Liabilities	5,836	5,869	8,732	7,043
Total Stockholders' Equity	62,219	68,961	77,153	82,379
Total Liabilities & Stockholders' Equity	68,055	74,830	85,885	89,422

EXHIBIT 4

January 2, 1995

Mr. Peter Bartlett
Managing Director
Donaldson, Lufkin & Jenrette
2121 Avenue of the Stars
Suite 3000
Los Angeles, CA 90067

Dear Peter:

You had asked that I give you a preliminary indication of our interest in ADAP, Inc. We have reviewed the information contained in the March 1994 information memorandum as well as the supplement. Based on that information, we are estimating an enterprise value between $60 million and $70 million.

In order to narrow that range, we would need to conduct on site due diligence and spend time with the management group. We estimate that we will require approximately two weeks for this process, and during this time we would work toward getting you a firm proposal.

We will likely structure our proposal as a management buy-out with employee participation. What this means to ADAP is that the company will remain intact and the employees of ADAP are likely not only to remain in place, but to participate financially in the success of the venture. Therefore, we are very interested in getting to know the senior managers of the company.

I should note that we have already completed our industry due diligence relating to the automobile aftermarket. This is an industry that we had a strong preexisting interest in, and so our time will be spent reviewing ADAP.

Falcon Capital represents seven private investors who have extensive experience with acquisitions of a similar size and larger. Our equity capabilities exceed those required to adequately finance this transaction, and we foresee no problems financing a well structured proposal.

This letter is an indication of interest, not an offer to purchase. Any offer to purchase ADAP will require approval of our Board of Directors. Thank you for permitting us to review ADAP, and we hope that we can structure a transaction that will be mutually acceptable.

Regards,

David M. Dodson

Exhibit 5

January 19, 1995

Mr. Peter Bartlett
Donaldson, Lufkin & Jenrette
2121 Avenue of the Stars
Suite 3000
Los Angeles, CA 90067

Dear Mr. Bartlett:

Thank you for allowing us to participate in the sale of ADAP; your team has been responsive to our requests and allowed us to proceed very quickly on our due diligence and arrive at the decision to make an offer for the assets of ADAP.

We have approached this process with the understanding that Rite Aid is looking for a qualified buyer who can meet the price expectations they have for the company, as opposed to conducting an auction. We believe we have met those price expectations by making an offer that is at the high end of our original indication of interest.

I hope that you will also find us to be a qualified buyer. In a very short period of time we have conducted extensive due diligence which includes on site review of locations. In addition, our lenders have responded favorably and expeditiously to this transaction knowing full well that Rite Aid is looking for a party that will conclude the transaction quickly. The pace that we have operated under for the past 30 days will continue until we have closed this transaction. 100% of the resources and attention of Falcon Capital will be devoted to this acquisition.

I have attached a list of the principals of Falcon Capital. We are experienced at buying and selling companies and have the financial capability to carry out our intentions. Since each of us has been on the "buy side" and "sell side" of transactions as principals, we know what to expect going forward—you won't be getting any surprises from the way we operate.

Peter, in the past 30 days we worked aggressively on this transaction in an effort to demonstrate to you and your client that we are serious buyers, ones that you can count on to complete this sale. I trust that we have demonstrated that to you, and that our offer will be duly considered.

Regards,

David M. Dodson

EXHIBIT 6

January 29, 1995

Mr. Peter Bartlett
Donaldson, Lufkin & Jenrette
2121 Avenue of the Stars
Suite 3000
Los Angeles, CA 90067

Dear Peter:

Thank you for giving us the chance to review ADAP, Inc. We view it as an attractive opportunity that we wish to pursue.

However, there are other opportunities that we must focus our attention on if the prospects of completing a transaction with ADAP are not high. I'm sure you can understand this position. Therefore we need to enter into substantive negotiations with the sellers no later than February 3, 1995. These negotiations should be in person and with individuals from Rite Aid who are in a position to commit to terms subject only to board approval. We should meet at a mutually convergent location—I recommend the Philadelphia offices of Donaldson, Lufkin & Jenrette.

At that time we will make a purchase proposal in the price range indicated in our initial indication of interest, however not at the high-end of the range. We will also be in a position to answer any questions you or your client might have regarding our financing including the establishment of a timeline for financing commitments. Falcon intends to capitalize the equity portion of this investment with an amount in excess of $20 million. Arrangements could be made for you to discuss this investment with any of the shareholders of Falcon Capital.

If your client views us as a serious buyer of ADAP, and is agreeable to negotiating with us, please contact myself or Mike Hammer by Tuesday January 31, 1995. Otherwise, thank you for allowing us to review ADAP, and I wish you luck in completing a transaction with another buyer.

Regards,

David M. Dodson

PART

IV

MANAGING THE GROWING ENTERPRISE

In this section, we look at what happens after the start-up. Managing a venture in an entrepreneurial manner involves a constant search for new opportunities. Yet growth and wealth often create bureaucracy, specialization, and a desire to protect assets rather than to seek growth. This part provides a good opportunity to review Chapter 1; the ideas therein are useful for existing companies that want to remain entrepreneurial. Chapter 16, "Managing Growth," describes the administrative challenges that growth engenders and how they can be successfully managed.

Sometimes the period after the start-up brings not growth and success, but problems. Chapter 17, "Bankruptcy: A Debtor's Perspective," describes how to deal with the unhappy and final stage in the life of some businesses.

MANAGING GROWTH

The set of changes that smaller, younger firms need to make as they grow is often termed *the transition from entrepreneurial to professional management.* This chapter addresses the issues that firms must deal with in making the transition:

- What is entrepreneurial management and how does it differ from professional management?
- What pressures force the firm to make the transition?
- How can entrepreneurs and their firms make the transition with a greater chance of success?

Entrepreneurial and Professional Management

The terms *entrepreneurial* and *professional management* mean very different things to different people. To some, *entrepreneurial management* suggests creative people and an innovative and successful organization, while *professional management* implies a stifling bureaucracy. To others, entrepreneurs are associated with disorganization, and professional management offers efficiency and effectiveness. For the sake of this chapter, however, *entrepreneurial and professional management* are merely descriptive terms and imply nothing about the creativity, innovation, or success of the organization.

Entrepreneurial Management

Entrepreneurial management is a style of management that is typically used when the firm is young and small. It is characterized by a number of features, including:

This chapter was prepared by Michael J. Roberts.
Copyright © 1986 by the President and Fellows of Harvard College.
Harvard Business School Note 9-387-054.

- *Centralized decision making:* In a small organization, the general manager can usually make most of the decisions required to manage the firm. The business is sufficiently small and simple enough that one person can comprehend all the information required for decision making.
- *Informal control:* The entrepreneurial firm is typically informal. There is little need for formal procedures, systems, and structures because the firm is small enough that activity can be monitored via the personal supervision of the entrepreneur. Moreover, the firm is young and inexperienced and has not yet learned the routines required for success.

The entrepreneur's own ability to collect information, make decisions, and monitor their implementation reduces the need for formal structure, policies, and procedures.

Professional Management

Professional management is characterized by:

- *Delegation of decision-making responsibility:* Larger firms are sufficiently complex that one individual cannot make all of the decisions required to manage the firm. Therefore, the general manager must delegate responsibility to a hierarchy of middle managers. This pattern of delegation both determines and is determined by the firm's structure.
- *Use of formal control systems:* In response to the delegation of decision-making responsibility, formal systems are introduced. Because the general manager does not *personally* make all of the firm's decisions, there is a need for systems to guide and evaluate the performance of those who *are* making those decisions. These systems usually include a mechanism for setting objectives, monitoring performance against those objectives, and rewarding desired performance. In addition, general managers also develop policies and standard procedures to guide the actions of those below.

The "Strategy of Coordination"

Just as the firm has an (explicit or implicit) strategy for its actions in the competitive marketplace, it also has an internal strategy for coordinating its efforts. Essentially, the dimensions of organization that we have been discussing are all elements of the way in which the firm chooses to coordinate its efforts.

There are two key dimensions to the strategy of coordination:

- The delegation of responsibility: whether the general manager makes the day-to-day operating decisions personally or delegates that decision-making responsibility to a hierarchy of middle managers.

- The use of formal control systems: whether the firm uses formal systems to set objectives, monitor performance, and control the activities of organization members.

These two dimensions describe a broad range of approaches to coordinating the firm's efforts. If we simply think in terms of the two-by-two matrix defined by these two dimensions, we can see that there are four archetypical strategies of coordination:

- Entrepreneurial management, which relies on centralized decision making and informal, personal control.
- Professional management, which utilizes the delegation of responsibility and extensive formal controls.
- Laissez-faire management, in which responsibilities are delegated, but control remains informal.
- Bureaucratic management, in which centralized decision making is supplemented with formal control.

		Use of Formal Control Mechanisms	
		Low	*High*
	High	Laissez-faire management	Professional management
Delegation of Responsibility			
	Low	Entrepreneurial management	Bureaucratic management

A *fundamental proposition* that underlies these ideas is that decisions regarding delegation and control have a strong influence on the firm's performance along two critical dimensions:

- Efficiency: the firm's ability to achieve its goals with a minimum of resources.
- Effectiveness: the firm's ability to adapt its goals and innovate to meet the changing needs of its environment.

Moreover, these two performance dimensions—and the decisions regarding delegation and control that underlie them—are fundamentally in *opposition.* Broadly speaking, choices that favor delegation have the potential to increase effectiveness, but simultaneously decrease efficiency; and the use of formal controls increases efficiency while reducing effectiveness. *Thus, the general manager's choices regarding delegation and control determine how these critical trade-offs are made.*

Making the Transition to Professional Management

When properly implemented, professional management offers an approach to coordinating the activities of a larger, more complex organization while avoiding the problems inherent in laissez-faire or bureaucratic management. There are several steps required for a successful transition to professional management.

Recognizing the Need for Change

The first step in the transition process is a recognition of the need for change. This is often extremely difficult because it is a by-product of success. Success reinforces beliefs and behavior that are appropriate to the entrepreneurial mode but that may not fit the needs of a larger, more complex firm.

Frequently, it is a crisis of some sort that highlights the need for change. Fortunately, knowledgeable outsiders can often help the entrepreneur see the need for such change before a crisis. Experienced board members or consultants can spot the early warning signs: lack of follow-up on details, incredible stress on the individual entrepreneur, and a sense of organizational disarray.

Once the entrepreneur has recognized the need for change, it is often difficult to know what to change *to*. Those who have successfully made the transition report that it requires a fundamental change in orientation: The manager must shift from getting personal satisfaction from direct action to a mode where that sense of accomplishment comes from achieving results *through others.*

Developing the Human Resources

Given this change of personal role in the organization, the entrepreneur needs to develop the human resources required to implement that model. Often, individuals who can accept and execute responsibility are not present in the entrepreneurial organization. The entrepreneur's style has made it difficult for aggressive, independent employees to survive. Moreover, many young firms simply lack the resources to attract and hire managerial talent.

In order to develop a competent managerial team, the entrepreneur must overcome personal loyalties that threaten the organization. In virtually every firm, the entrepreneur has a "right-hand person" without whom the business would not have survived in the early years. Unfortunately, many of these employees are unable to develop the more specialized skills needed to grow with the company. Entrepreneurs must overcome their personal loyalties and find more suitable employees for critical positions.

Delegating Responsibility

Once the entrepreneur has perceived the need for change and developed a management team, real delegation of responsibility can begin. The power of professional management lies in placing the responsibility close to the source of information required for sound decision making. Typically, this means delegating responsibility to managers who are close to customers, suppliers, and competitors. In the process of delegating, the general manager must be careful *not* to give up responsibility for key policy issues that require personal perspective. Moreover, delegation does not mean that the entrepreneur loses the opportunity to have *input* into the decision-making process; surely, the benefit of that experience should not be lost.

Developing Formal Controls

A final step in the transition process is the development of formal control mechanisms. Successful entrepreneurs realize that, with the onset of delegation, they can no longer control the behavior of individuals in the organization. It is important that the focus of the control system shifts to performance rather than behavior. In addition, successful firms realize the danger in simply adapting policies and procedures that are used at other firms. Firms that customize policies ensure that the practice makes sense for the organization. The process of devoting time and effort often inspires creative solutions, and builds commitment.

Conclusion

The reason why the transition to professional management is often so difficult is that it requires *far more* than changes in organizational systems and structures. It requires a *fundamental change in the attitudes and behaviors of the entrepreneur.* Merely creating organizational structures and systems accomplishes little if the entrepreneur is unwilling to truly delegate. Control systems are meaningless if the entrepreneur fails to use them. It is this need to fundamentally change the individual general manager's self-concept behavior that makes the transition process so difficult.

BANKRUPTCY: A DEBTOR'S PERSPECTIVE

17

The Bankruptcy Code is a federal statute intended to alter the legal rights and remedies of debtors and creditors to provide a solution to the circumstances which arise when a debtor's financial affairs have reached such a state of disarray that the usual rules no longer work in an orderly and efficient manner. From the perspective of individual debtors, bankruptcy law provides freedom from lawsuits, the discharge of past due obligations, and an opportunity for a fresh start. For business debtors, the Bankruptcy Code provides an opportunity for the debtor to restructure its business, create enhanced value for its creditors (and maybe its stockholders), and provides an opportunity to maintain employment that otherwise would be lost. From the perspective of creditors, bankruptcy provides an orderly and equitable distribution scheme which replaces a race to the courthouse by each creditor seeking to enforce its own rights. Further, in a reorganization, creditors can hope to benefit from the enhanced value of an ongoing enterprise, rather than accepting a pro rata share of a liquidation.

Bankruptcy is by no means the only option in times of financial trouble. There are many types of financial adversity and many solutions other than resorting to bankruptcy proceedings. An individual or a firm which becomes insolvent, without cash to pay the bills, may simply stall creditors until the situation improves. They may also default on loan payments, negotiate reduced schedules, or liquidate inventory to generate funds. Further, options such as trust mortgages to restructure debt, assignments for the benefit of creditors which allow

This chapter was prepared by Professor Howard H. Stevenson and Lecturer Michael J. Roberts, with the assistance of Richard E. Mikels, Esq. (member) and Kevin J. Walsh, Esq. (associate) of Mintz, Levin, Cohn, Ferris, Glovsky and Popeo, P.C., as the basis for class discussion rather than to illustrate either effective or ineffective handling of an administrative situation.

an orderly liquidation in a less formal setting than bankruptcy, and state court receiverships are alternatives to bankruptcy. For a bankruptcy case to be commenced, someone, either debtors or creditors, decides that the individual or firm should not continue in its present financial incarnation. Then, bankruptcy becomes an option under which either the debtors or creditors seek to utilize the bankruptcy law and the courts to resolve the situation.

This chapter will discuss bankruptcy from the point of view of the individual or corporate debtor. First, it will provide a brief overview of existing bankruptcy law. Then, it will examine bankruptcy in general and three forms of bankruptcy in particular: liquidation, reorganization, and the adjustment of debts of an individual with a regular income. Municipal bankruptcies and family farmer bankruptcies will not be covered in detail in this chapter. Finally, it will talk about some of the ways debtors can protect themselves before taking this significant step and discuss what actions are prohibited under bankruptcy law.

Overview

The genesis of our bankruptcy laws can be traced back to the United States Constitution which empowers Congress "to establish . . . uniform laws on the subject of bankruptcies throughout the United States." Until it was repealed by the Bankruptcy Reform Act of 1978, the prevailing law for bankruptcy in the United States was the Bankruptcy Act of 1898. In 1938, through the Chandler Act, Congress amended the Bankruptcy Act to give the debtor the option of rehabilitation. The Bankruptcy Reform Act of 1978 was a total overhaul of the existing bankruptcy system, and its provisions are reflected in the Bankruptcy Code. The Bankruptcy Code has eight substantive chapters. All of the chapters have odd numbers except Chapter 12 which was added in 1986 as an experiment to assist with the adjustment of debts of the family farmer with regular annual income. The first three chapters are administrative provisions which are applicable in all bankruptcy proceedings; the remaining chapters deal with specific types of bankruptcies. The provisions of the operative chapters, Chapters 7, 9, 11, 12, and 13 apply specifically and only to cases filed under those chapters. In other words, the provisions of Chapter 11 do not apply to a bankruptcy case filed under Chapter 13, but the provisions of Chapters 1, 3, and 5 apply to all types of bankruptcy cases. Specifically, the Bankruptcy Code consists of the following chapters:

- Chapter 1 sets forth general definitions and provisions.
- Chapter 3 deals with case administration.
- Chapter 5 deals with creditors, the debtor, and the estate.
- Chapter 7 deals with liquidation.
- Chapter 9 deals with the adjustment of debts of a municipality.
- Chapter 11 deals with reorganization (includes businesses, individuals, and railroads).

- Chapter 12 deals with adjustment of debts of a family farm or with regular annual income.
- Chapter 13 deals with adjustment of debts of an individual with regular income.

The Bankruptcy Code was amended significantly in 1984, 1986, and 1994. The primary purpose of the 1984 amendment was to cure the problem created by the Supreme Court's decision in what is known as the *Marathon* case in which the jurisdictional grant to bankruptcy judges was declared unconstitutional. The 1986 amendments were primarily concerned with establishing Chapter 12 for the rehabilitation of the family farmer. The 1994 amendments were an attempt to address issues concerning case administration and certain substantive issues in commercial, consumer, and municipal bankruptcy cases. The 1994 amendments also established the National Bankruptcy Review Commission which was charged with investigating and evaluating the Bankruptcy Code. The Commission has recently submitted a report to Congress which may lead to significant changes to the Bankruptcy Code.

The Bankruptcy Code is designed to achieve the competing goals of maximizing creditor recovery and providing forgiveness to an honest debtor for its financial failures by providing relief from its debts. Regardless of which chapter a debtor falls under, the filing of any bankruptcy proceedings gives the debtor an initial "breathing spell" through an automatic stay which stops, among other things, all lawsuits against the debtor and all foreclosures of the debtor's assets. A creditor, however, can request that the bankruptcy court lift the automatic stay to allow the creditor to proceed against the debtors assets in which the creditor holds a pre-petition lien. Debtors, particularly in reorganization cases, will often contest such a request by a creditor, particularly when the asset is essential to the proposed reorganization.

It should be noted that not all companies are eligible to file for bankruptcy protection. Under the Bankruptcy Code, banks, savings and loans, insurance companies, and all foreign companies are prohibited from doing so.

Getting into Trouble

For an individual, the path to bankruptcy is often clearly discernible in retrospect; it is easy to see where a person made a bad decision, when they became overextended, how they misjudged their financial situation. There are at least two ways individuals accumulate sufficient unpaid debts to contemplate bankruptcy. The first common experience is painfully simple: They purchase more on credit than they can afford to buy. This happens because they underestimate the amount of money they will have to pay for their accumulated credit purchases or because they overestimate the amount of income they will earn. Thus, the incidence of individual bankruptcies has increased with rises of easy consumer credit and in periods of unemployment, when people may lose their jobs unexpectedly or be unable to find new work if they are laid off. For example, the 1990s has witnessed a tremendous growth in consumer credit card debt, followed by an increase in bankruptcy cases. From 1996 to 1997, consumer bankruptcies rose 20 percent and represented 96 percent of all bankruptcy filings in 1997.[1] It is interesting that during that period, unemployment has been low, unlike typical periods of high bankruptcy filings. However, consumer credit has also reached unprecedented highs. Therefore it appears that an extended period of easy consumer credit coupled with the abundance of confidence arising in response to an economy which can generate extremely high employment levels is a recipe for abnormally high levels of personal bankruptcy filings. This explains why consumer bankruptcies have increased while corporate bankruptcies have significantly diminished in numbers. Over the past few years, however, the market for business debt has evolved from an extremely tight market where loans were often simply unavailable, to a period of easy business credit. The easing of business credit developed later in the economic cycle than did the easing of consumer credit and replaced an environment of far tighter business credit than existed on the consumer side. The question arising from the combination of easy credit and the confidence generated by an economy that can result in stock valuations as high as they presently are, is whether the same factors which have led to such high levels of consumer bankruptcy will also eventually lead to high levels of business bankruptcy.

Another interesting trend is the tendency of consumers to liquidate under Chapter 7 rather than rehabilitate under Chapter 13. In a Chapter 7, an individual will give up all assets except those assets set aside by state or federal law as exempt, but will retain the unfettered use of all future income. In a Chapter 13, the individual debtor will retain his assets but must utilize some future income to pay old debt. This trend for consumers to simply shed their debt is under consideration in Congress and it is possible that amendments to the Bankruptcy Code will require a relatively high earning debtor to utilize some portion of future income to satisfy creditors.

The second common road to individual bankruptcy is more complex. It occurs when an individual's personal finances are in order; but he or she chooses to act as guarantor for a business or for another individual whose situation may not be as fortunate. When an individual agrees to accept the burden of another's debts (either as an individual or a corporation), then that person becomes legally responsible if the first entity defaults on payments. Sometimes, this additional financial requirement is more than the individual's personal budget can accommodate. Bankruptcy then becomes a way of resolving these added debts, leaving the individual free to begin again.

For corporations, the path to bankruptcy is considerably more complicated. Ray Barrickman, in a somewhat dated but nevertheless compelling publication, outlines 20 potential causes of business failure:[2] Excessive competition, the

---

[1] ABI Law Journal, "Bankruptcy Filings Top 1.4 Million in 1997 with 20 Percent Increase in Consumer Filings," (April 1998).

[2] Ray E. Barrickman, *Business Failure, Causes, Remedies, and Cures* (Washington: University Press of America, 1979), p. 28.

general business cycle, changes in public demand, governmental acts, adverse acts of labor, acts of God, poor overall management, unwise promotion, unwise expansion, inefficient selling, overextension of inventories, poor financial management, excessive fixed charges, excessive funded debt, excessive floating debt, overextension of credit, unwise dividend policies, and inadequate maintenance and depreciation.

John Argenti, studying corporate failures in Great Britain, posits a chain of events, beginning with poor management, which usually precipitates a firm's slide into bankruptcy:

> If the management of a company is poor then two things will be neglected: The system of accountancy information will be deficient and the company will not respond to change. (Some companies, even well-managed ones, may be damaged because powerful constraints prevent the managers making the responses they wish to make.) Poor managers will also make at least one of three other mistakes: They will over-trade; or they will launch a big project that goes wrong; or they will allow the company's gearing to rise so that even normal business hazards become constant threats. These are the chief causes, neither fraud nor bad luck deserve more than a passing mention. The following symptoms will appear: Certain financial ratios will deteriorate but, as soon as they do, the managers will start creative accounting which reduces the predictive value of these ratios and so lends greater importance to nonfinancial symptoms. Finally the company enters a characteristic period in its last few months.[3]

These are not all of the root causes of bankruptcy. Each situation contains its own causes and circumstances for financial distress. However, the direct catalyst for bankruptcy proceedings is usually a person or company's inability to pay their debts on time. When this situation occurs, the individual or company may begin voluntary bankruptcy proceedings or their creditors may try to force them into involuntary bankruptcy. With certain exceptions provided in the Bankruptcy Code, any person, partnership, or corporation can file for voluntary relief under the Bankruptcy Code. Even solvent entities can file for bankruptcy (most likely under the reorganization provisions of the Bankruptcy Code) as long as there is no intent to defraud creditors.

For example, Manville Corporation filed for bankruptcy in late 1982, even though the company had a book net worth of nearly $1.2 billion. The asbestos manufacturer was seeking protection from an anticipated 34,000 lawsuits relating to the injury or death of workers who used Manville's asbestos products. Assuming an average settlement of $40,000 per lawsuit, Manville calculated that it could not afford to stay in business and sought bankruptcy relief from these "creditors." Other companies have been forced into Chapter 11 because of potential tort liability. For example, A.H. Robbins Co. filed because of potential liability related to the Dalkon Shield, Dow Corning Corp. filed because of potential liability related to breast implants, and Piper Aircraft filed bankruptcy

---

[3]John Argenti, *Corporate Collapse: The Causes and Symptoms* (London: McGraw-Hill, 1976), p. 108.

because of potential product liability obligations. In fact, because a number of asbestos manufacturers in addition to Manville, like UNR Industries, Inc. and Eagle-Picher Industries, Inc., were forced to file for reorganization, the Bankruptcy Code was amended in 1994 to codify certain of the procedures used in such asbestos cases for dealing with "future claims."

Filing for Bankruptcy

In order to seek relief from their debts, a person or corporation must file in the office of the Clerk of the United States District Court in which the domicile, residence, principal place of business, or principal assets of the entity have been located for the preceding 180 days. The filing fee is $130 for parties commencing a bankruptcy case under Chapter 7 (liquidation) or Chapter 13 (adjustment of debts or an individual with a regular income). The filing fee for debtors seeking relief under Chapter 11 (reorganizations) is $800; railroads must pay a filing fee of $1,000. The filing fee for Chapter 12 (family farm rehabilitation) is $200. Somewhat ironically, there is no *in forma pauperis* in bankruptcy; if the debtor cannot afford the filing fee the debtor cannot file a bankruptcy petition.

In certain instances, creditors can force debtors to go bankrupt. An involuntary bankruptcy case can be commenced by:

- Three or more creditors whose aggregate claims amount to more than $10,775 over the value of any assets securing those claims; or
- One or more such creditors if there are less than 12 claim holders:
- Fewer than all the general partners in a limited partnership; or
- A foreign representative of the estate in a foreign proceeding concerning such person.

Creditors do not have to prove that the debtor has insufficient assets to pay his or her debts; mere failure to generally pay debts on time, regardless of ability to pay, is sufficient grounds for creditors to seek involuntary bankruptcy. However, in an involuntary bankruptcy proceeding, if the creditors cannot meet the burden for even this simple standard, the petition will be dismissed and the creditors will be assessed costs and reasonable attorneys fees. Furthermore, if the creditors are found to have filed the petition in bad faith, the court may award the debtor any damages caused by the proceedings, including punitive damages. In fact, the court may require the petitioners to post a bond to compensate the debtor for costs incurred in defending the involuntary petition. In practice, however, involuntary bankruptcy is uncommon. For example, for the year ending June 30, 1979, only 926 involuntary bankruptcy cases were filed out of a total of 226,476 cases[4] and during 1987, only 260 involuntary Chapter 11 cases were filed out of

---

[4] Table of Bankruptcy Statistics with reference to bankruptcy cases commenced in the United States District Courts during the period July 1, 1978 through June 30, 1979. Administrative Office of the United States Courts.

a total of 18,887 total Chapter 11 cases.[5] It appears that the reasons why there are comparatively few involuntary filings are the possible, but unlikely, significant damages which can be awarded if the debtor successfully defeats an involuntary petition, the lack of available reliable information about the debtor's affairs, and the fact that an aggressive creditor will often pursue remedies designed to benefit itself rather than the entire creditor body. When involuntary cases are filed, it is often to avoid a dissipation of the debtor's assets or to allow for asset recoveries available under the preference and fraudulent conveyance sections of the Bankruptcy Code.

Choosing Your Poison: Which Chapter?

There are five distinct chapters of the bankruptcy code which can shape the outcome of the bankruptcy proceedings: Chapter 7 (liquidation), Chapter 11 (reorganization), Chapter 9 (municipalities),[6] Chapter 12 (family farmer), and Chapter 13 (adjustment of an individual's debts).

In theory, bankruptcy proceedings can be concluded very quickly. In practice, however, they are often long, drawn-out affairs. Corporate reorganizations, in particular, can take many months or even years to reach completion. The average Chapter 11 case in the 1980s lasted just under 18 months.[7]

In a Chapter 7 bankruptcy the assets of the individual or corporation are liquidated and distributed to creditors. By filing for Chapter 11 or Chapter 13 bankruptcy, the debtors typically seek to keep their assets with some arrangement to pay off their debts over time. Since the outcomes of these types of bankruptcies are radically different, affecting the amount of the assets which the debtor keeps as well as the timing and amount of payments which the creditors receive, both groups have some ability to influence the outcome of cases under the prevailing chapters.

When the creditor files for an involuntary bankruptcy case under Chapters 7 or 11, the debtor can convert the case to a bankruptcy under any of the other chapters. When a debtor files for voluntary bankruptcy under any chapter, the creditors can request that the court convert the case to a Chapter 7 or Chapter 11 bankruptcy case. Only a Chapter 13 bankruptcy case cannot be commenced without the debtor's consent. Before choosing a chapter for bankruptcy, debtors should carefully consider whether they would prefer to liquidate their assets or continue their business or personal finances, attempting with reorganization or adjustment to pay off their debts over time.

Chapter 7: Liquidation

Chapter 7 of the Bankruptcy Code provides for either voluntary or involuntary liquidation of the assets of the debtor for distribution to the creditors. When a

---

[5]House Report #686, p. 56.

[6]Given the relatively few number of Chapter 9 and Chapter 12 cases filed, this note will not discuss these chapters in detail.

[7]New Generation Research, The 1992 Bankruptcy Yearbook Almanac (1992).

petition is filed under Chapter 7 it constitutes an Order for Relief. After the entry of the Order for Relief, the debtor has a legal obligation to:

- File a list of creditors, assets and liabilities, and a statement of financial affairs.
- Cooperate with the trustee appointed to the case.
- Give the trustee all property of the estate and all records relating to the property.
- Appear at any hearing dealing with a discharge.
- Attend all official meetings of creditors.

As soon as possible after the entry of the Order for Relief, the Office of the United States Trustee (the branch of the Department of Justice charged with being the watchdog over bankruptcy proceedings) will appoint a disinterested person to serve as the interim Chapter 7 trustee. Creditors holding at least 20 percent of specified unsecured claims may elect a successor Chapter 7 trustee. A Chapter 7 trustee will be elected if the candidate receives a majority of specified unsecured claims. If no trustee is elected in this manner, the interim trustee will continue to serve. The duties of the trustee include:

- Reducing the property of the debtor's estate to cash and closing up the estate as expeditiously as possible.
- Accounting for all property received.
- Investigating the financial affairs of the debtor and examining all claims for validity.
- Providing information about the estate to any interested party, furnishing reports on the debtor's business if it is authorized to be operated, and filing a final report of the disposition of the estate with the court.

Certain of an individual debtor's assets will be exempt from liquidation; that is, they may not be distributed to the creditors, but rather will be retained by the debtor. In many states, the debtor can choose between the federal exemptions provided by the terms of the Bankruptcy Code or the relevant state and federal exemptions which are available to debtors absent bankruptcy. However, states can require their residents to adhere only to the nonbankruptcy exemptions. The following states have enacted legislation prohibiting the election of the bankruptcy exemptions: Alabama, Arizona, California, Colorado, Delaware, Florida, Georgia, Idaho, Illinois, Indiana, Iowa, Kansas, Louisiana, Maine, Maryland, Mississippi, Missouri, Montana, Nebraska, Nevada, New York, North Dakota, North Carolina, Ohio, Oklahoma, Oregon, South Carolina, South Dakota, Tennessee, Utah, Virginia, West Virginia, and Wyoming. In those states, the debtor must rely on the nonbankruptcy exemptions and has no opportunity to choose the exemptions provided by the Bankruptcy Code. As of April 1, 1998, under the current bankruptcy exemptions, a debtor gets to keep:

- The debtor's interest, not to exceed $16,150, in the debtor's (or a dependent's) residence; in a cooperative that owns property used by the debtor (or a dependent) as a residence; and in a burial plot for the debtor or a dependent (so called homestead exemption);
- The debtor's interest, not to exceed $2,575, in a motor vehicle;
- The debtor's interest, not to exceed $425 in value for any particular item or $8,625 in aggregate value, in household furnishings, clothing, appliances, books, animals, crops, or musical instruments, that are kept for the personal, family, or household use for the debtor or a dependent;
- The debtor's interest, not to exceed $1,075, in jewelry held for personal, family, or household use for the debtor or a dependent;
- The debtor's interest in any property, not to exceed $800 (so called wild card exemption) plus up to $8,075 of any unused amount of the homestead exemption;
- The debtor's interest, not to exceed $1,625, in any implements, professional books, or tools of the trade of the debtor or a dependent;
- Any unmatured life insurance contract owned by the debtor, other than a credit lifer insurance contract;
- The debtor's interest, not to exceed $8,625 less any amount transferred to prevent forfeiture of a life insurance contract entered into prior to the bankruptcy case, in any accrued dividends or interest or loan value of any nonmature life insurance contract under which the debtor or a dependent is insured;
- Prescribed health aids for the debtor or a dependent;
- The debtor's right to receive social security benefits, unemployment compensation benefits, local public assistance benefits, veterans' benefits, illness or disability benefits, receive alimony, support, or separate maintenance, a payment under a (subject to certain exceptions) stock bonus, pension, profit sharing annuity, or similar plan on account of illness, disability, death, age, or length of service; and
- The debtor's right to receive an award under a crime victim's reparation law; a payment on account of a wrongful death of an individual of whom the debtor was a dependent; a payment under a life insurance contract that insured the life of an individual of whom the debtor was a dependent; a payment not to exceed $16,150 on account of personal bodily injury, not including pain and suffering or compensation for actual pecuniary loss, of the debtor or an individual of whom the debtor is a dependent; or a payment in compensation of loss of future earnings of the debtor or an individual of whom the debtor is or was a dependent.

In those states where the option exists, the Bankruptcy Code exemptions are available in all cases involving individuals. The 1994 amendments provided for an automatic adjustment of certain dollar amounts found in the Bankruptcy Code, including the exemptions. The adjustments, rounded to the nearest $25, are made every three years (the next adjustment will occur on April 1, 2001) and are tied to the Consumer Price Index for All Urban Consumers.

The rest of the debtor's estate is liquidated by the trustee and distributed first to secured creditors. These secured creditors receive payment up to the amount which can be obtained from the disposition of the asset which constituted the security. Any amount remaining unsatisfied following the disposition of these assets goes into the unsecured creditors pool.

Following the payment of secured creditors with the proceeds from specific assets, the next class of claimants consists of "priority claimants." Priority claims include, in order: administrative expenses and filing fees assessed against the debtor's estate; certain unsecured claims arising from the time of the filing of an involuntary petition and the appointment of a trustee or the entry of an Order for Relief (gap creditors); wages, salaries or commissions, including vacation severance, and sick leave pay to the extent of $4,300 per individual earned within 90 days of the date of filing or the date of cessation of business, whichever occurred first; contributions to employee benefit plans up to $4,300 per employee earned within 180 days; claims of individuals, up to $1,950 each, arising from the deposit of money in connection with purchases of property or services that are not delivered; claims of governmental units for taxes and custom duties.

Next come the general unsecured creditors. In the rare case where the general unsecured claims are satisfied in full, late filed claims may be paid. If funds are still available, fines and penalties and multiple or punitive damages may be paid. Interest may then be paid on the principal amount of the general unsecured claims. Finally, if there is any surplus, it is paid to the debtor. It is rare for distributions to be made beyond distributions to unsecured creditors. If there aren't enough funds to pay a class in full, claims within the class are paid pro rata.

When the debtor is an individual, the court will usually grant a discharge. This means the debtor is discharged from all debts which arose prior to the commencement of the bankruptcy case, except certain debts explicitly excepted from discharge by the Bankruptcy Code, including debts arising from alimony, child support, certain taxes, student loans, drunk driving injuries, willful and malicious torts, or debts that were not listed on the debtor's financial statements when bankruptcy was filed. A debtor who has received a discharge in a case commenced within six years before the date of the filing of a subsequent petition is not eligible to receive a discharge in the subsequent case. A debtor may repay any debt voluntarily, even a debt that has been discharged. A creditor, however, may not enforce any discharged debt.

Chapter 11: Reorganization

The purpose of Chapter 11 of the Bankruptcy Code is to provide a mechanism for reorganizing a firm's finances so it can continue to operate, pay a dividend to its creditors, provide jobs, and hopefully even produce a return to its investors. Usually debtors and creditors will opt for this form of bankruptcy if they think a business has more value as a going concern than would the proceeds of liquidated assets. The objective of the reorganization is to develop a plan which determines how much creditors will be paid and in what form the business will continue. An individual may file a Chapter 11 petition, although Chapter 11 is typically used by businesses. Stockbrokers and commodity brokers are not eligible for Chapter 11 relief. Furthermore, railroads can proceed under Chapter 11, while they are prohibited from seeking liquidation under Chapter 7.

Like Chapter 7, a reorganization case can be either voluntary or involuntary. After the entry of the Order for Relief, the United States Trustee will appoint a committee of general unsecured creditors. This committee is often comprised of those creditors holding the seven largest claims; however, the United States Trustee has great latitude in composing the committee to make it representative of the different kinds of interests in the case. As such the committee may vary in size and may include creditors that are not among the largest, and, maybe more significantly, exclude creditors that are among the largest. The committee, acting as a fiduciary for all like creditors, is primarily responsible for working with the debtor on the administration of the case, investigating the debtor's business and claims against the estate, and negotiating and formulating a plan. The committee may hire professionals which can seek reimbursement for their expenses from the estate. The United States Trustee may appoint, or the bankruptcy court may order the appointment of, additional committees if necessary to assure the adequate representation of other constituencies in the case. For example, if the debtor appears to be solvent, the United States Trustee may consider the appointment of an equity holders committee.

The debtor keeps possession of its assets and may operate its business unless a party in interest can show the debtor is guilty of fraud, dishonesty, incompetence, or gross mismanagement or otherwise proves such an arrangement is not in the interests of the creditors. If the court finds that either of these conditions exist, a trustee will be appointed, although the instances of such appointments are the exception rather than the rule. The duties of a Chapter 11 trustee include being accountable for all of the information and records necessary to formulate the reorganization plan and filing the plan with the court or recommending conversion to a Chapter 7 or a Chapter 13 case, as may be appropriate, or recommending the dismissal of the case altogether.

If a trustee is not appointed, the debtor, as a debtor in possession of its assets, possesses the duties and the powers of a trustee. No court order is necessary for the debtor to continue to run the firm; rather the business is to remain in operation in the ordinary course unless the court orders otherwise. Activities that are not in the ordinary course of the debtor's business must receive prior court approval.

The debtor has a 120-day exclusivity period in which only the debtor may file a reorganization plan and 60 more days to obtain acceptances of the plan, unless the court, for cause, shortens or lengthens these time periods. The exclusivity period terminates automatically upon the appointment of a trustee. After the exclusivity period expires, any creditor or party in interest can file a plan. The debtor's right of exclusivity is of critical importance to the debtor. Once exclusivity is lost, other plans can be filed which could force the debtor to negotiate additional consideration to creditors or could call for the transfer of the debtor's business to a third party at the expense of the debtor's stockholders.

A plan must designate the various classes of creditors and show how they will be treated. Classes will normally include creditors with similar legal rights. Secured creditors (those with lien rights in certain assets of the debtor) are normally separately classified and in typical circumstances, general unsecured creditors will be classified together. The plan can be a liquidating plan. Thus, a business could be liquidated under Chapter 11 rather than Chapter 7. To be confirmed, if the legal rights of the creditors in a class are altered, the class must accept the plan by more than one half in number and at least two-third in amount of these creditors voting on the plan. In the event that a particular class of creditors rejects the plan, the plan proponent may seek to "cramdown" the plan over the objection of that class. The Bankruptcy Code contains extensive criteria establishing when a plan is "fair and equitable" to a dissenting class and may be confirmed over the objection of the class.

Notwithstanding the vote of the creditors, the bankruptcy court may confirm a plan only if the court makes certain findings which are required by the Bankruptcy Code. These findings are required to ensure protection of creditors, the integrity of the bankruptcy system and the policies of the Bankruptcy Code. For example, the court must find that the plan has been proposed in good faith and that if future operations are contemplated by the debtor, they are likely to succeed and will not be followed by a liquidation or further reorganization. Further, with respect to each class that does not accept the plan by a unanimous vote, the plan must provide that each creditor in such class will receive at least as much from the plan as the creditor would have received in a Chapter 7 liquidation. The purpose of this rule (the so-called best interest of creditors test) is to ensure that a minority member of a class is not forced to accept the results of a plan if the majority of the class is motivated by factors other than the amount of the dividend. For example, if most creditors in the class continue to do business with the debtor, they are likely to be more concerned with the debtor's continued existence rather than the amount of the dividend. The rule, therefore, protects the minority claimholder by setting a floor on what may be paid to the class.

If the court confirms a reorganization plan, the individual debtor is discharged from any past debts except as they are handled under the plan. A corporate debtor receives a discharge unless the plan contemplates liquidation. The provisions of the confirmed plan bind the debtor, any entity issuing securities under the plan, any entity acquiring property under the plan, and any creditor, equity security holder, or general partner of the debtor, whether or not they have accepted the plan.

The 1994 amendments to the Bankruptcy Code included provisions designed to streamline "single asset real estate" cases and "small business" Chapter 11 cases. The Bankruptcy Code defines a single asset real estate debtor as one having real property, other than residential property with fewer than 4 residential units, on which the debtor conducts no business other than operating the real estate and from which the debtor generates substantially all of its gross income, where such real estate has secured debt of no more than $4 million. There is a perceived problem that a single asset real estate debtor files for bankruptcy protection only to stall, in bad faith, a foreclosing creditor. To alleviate this problem, the automatic stay was amended to allow a secured creditor relief from the stay 90 days after the commencement of a bankruptcy case, unless the debtor has made a certain level of progress in the case.

A small business is a commercial venture with aggregate secured and unsecured debt not exceeding $2 million. A small business can elect to be treated on an expedited basis, which puts the burden on the debtor to file a plan in a shorter time than allowed in a normal Chapter 11 case. There is little benefit to a small business in making the election and therefore such elections are rare. Congress is presently considering proposals that would alter both the definition of small business and the procedures to be used in their reorganization cases.

Chapter 13: Adjustment of Debts of an Individual with Regular Income

Chapter 13 of the new Bankruptcy Code covers individuals with regular income whose unsecured debts are less than $269,250 and whose secured debts are less than $807,750. This includes individuals who own or operate businesses. It does not include partnerships or corporations. There cannot be involuntary Chapter 13 bankruptcy cases.

The purpose of Chapter 13 is to allow an individual to pay off debts with future earnings while the Bankruptcy Code protects him or her from harassment by creditors and allows the debtor to retain its assets. Furthermore, it allows the debtor to continue to own and operate a business while the Chapter 13 case is pending. A debtor's obligations under a plan pursuant to Chapter 13 is typically payable over three years, with up to a two-year extension allowed for cause. Chapter 13 is popular with debtors who own homes and want to keep them notwithstanding the bankruptcy. Chapter 13 allows a debtor to reinstate a defaulted mortgage, pay it current on a going forward basis, and pay any arrearage in the plan.

In a Chapter 13 case the property of the estate includes property and earnings acquired after the commencement of the case but before it is closed. The standing Chapter 13 trustee administers the case by collecting and disbursing payments made by the debtor under its plan.

Chapter 13 has several major advantages for the debtor:

- Once the case is filed, all of the debtor's property and future income are under the court's jurisdiction. The automatic stay protects the debtor, and any co-debtor on an obligation, against litigation and collection efforts.
- Unlike Chapter 7, the trustee does not take possession of the debtor's property. The debtor can increase the value of his or her estate while in Chapter 13.
- Chapter 13 can help preserve the debtor's credit rating since a Chapter 13 contemplates some effort to repay old debts.
- Only the debtor can file a plan, there are no competing proposals allowed.

The debtor must file a plan within fifteen days after he or she filed the petition. The court will hold a confirmation hearing on the plan and any party in interest may object to confirmation. The court will confirm the plan only after making certain findings. Some of these findings are similar to the findings a court must make before it will confirm a Chapter 11 plan. For example, a Chapter 13 plan must be proposed in good faith and the plan must satisfy the best interest of creditors test.

In addition, unless the holder of each secured claim has accepted the plan, each such holder must either (i) retain the lien securing such claim and receive property of a value not less than the amount of such claim; or (ii) receive the property securing such claims.

If a creditor holding an unsecured claim (or the Chapter 13 trustee) objects to confirmation of the plan, the court cannot approve the plan unless the plan provides either (i) the value of the property to be distributed on account of such claim is not less than the amount of such claim; or (ii) that all of the debtor's projected disposable income to be received over the three-year period commencing on the date of the first payment under the plan is used to fund the plan.

The court will grant the debtor a discharge only after all payments under the plan are completed. A Chapter 13 discharge is broader than the Chapter 7 discharge in that certain debts that would not be discharged under Chapter 7 are discharged under Chapter 13. For example, debts discharged under Chapter 13 include debts for willful and malicious torts and for fines and penalties. In addition, certain tax claims that are nondischargeable in a Chapter 7 case may be discharged in a Chapter 13 case. This explains why some debtors file Chapter 13 cases even though Chapter 7 cases would be fiscally more advantageous.

Powers of a Trustee

In addition to the responsibilities enumerated in Chapter 7 and 11 the trustee in a bankruptcy case has a great deal of power which can determine how assets are allocated and debt restructured. Chapters 3 and 5 of the Bankruptcy Code set forth such powers as the ability to employ professionals to help carry out the duties of trustee; the power to use, sell, or lease property; the power to obtain credits secured by priority claims and new liens; the power to reject or assume contracts and unexpired leases; and the power to avoid preferences and fraudulent transfers, known as the avoiding powers. These powers can change the status of certain classes of creditors, depending on how they are applied. For instance, by rejecting an unexpired lease, the trustee can convert a long-term leaseholder into just another unsecured creditor. If a trustee is not appointed, then the debtor in possession of the estate assumes the trustee's duties and powers.

Negotiations and Settlements

While they may feel persecuted and helpless, debtors actually have a great deal of power to negotiate with their creditors for arrangements that will leave the firm intact, either before or after bankruptcy is declared.[8] This power stems from several sources, including without limitation:

- The incentive for creditors to reach a speedy and workable solution to the debtor's financial problems that could yield earlier payments to creditors;

- The differing interests of various classes of creditors. A creditor for whom speed of settlement is more important than full payment might negotiate with another creditor whose interest lies in full payment rather than a quick solution. In such an instance, both groups of creditors can be satisfied if the first pays the second's claims in order to expedite a settlement. Trade creditors and money creditors might have varying interests, too, with trade creditors preferring a settlement that leaves the firm intact to do business in the future and money creditors preferring a liquidation that provides as much cash as possible. Debtors can use this dichotomy to their advantage, using available cash to pay off money creditors while asking trade creditors to forbear in the hope of putting the firm back on solid financial ground rather than driving it into bankruptcy.

- The automatic stay which can cause substantial delay in a creditor's ability to recover on its debt;

- The debtor's exclusive right to file a plan. As long as the debtor retains this right, the creditors two choices are to accept the plan or accept liquidation value;

- The debtor's threat to cease operations which would impair the value of the assets as a going concern;

- The cost of litigation or extended reorganization proceedings;

- Creditors may be willing to negotiate terms favorable to a debtor if the debtor is an important customer and the continued operations are more valuable to the creditor than an enhanced dividend that is large enough to impair the debtor's operations.

- The debtor's knowledge of its business operations. The debtor will usually have a better grasp of its business and prospects than will the creditors. The debtor, therefore, will have the benefits in negotiations derived from this greater knowledge.

---

[8]For a further discussion of these factors, see Harlan D. Platt, *Principles of Corporate Renewal*, pp. 55–57 (Advance printing, University of Michigan, 1977).

Creditors also have certain leverage in negotiating with debtors. A creditor may derive negotiating strength from the following factors, among others:

- The debtors exclusive right to file a plan is not perpetual. Once exclusivity is terminated, creditors may file competing plans on terms more favorable to the creditors and less favorable to the debtor and its stockholders.
- Some creditors may hold the personal guarantees of the debtor's principals. This significantly enhances the creditor's leverage to influence the operations of the debtor and the terms of the plan.
- Tremendous negotiating leverage can be gained by developing alternatives to the debtor's plan. For example, if a third party buyer for the debtor's business can be located, the debtor may have to increase its price in order to maintain its business.
- If the creditors can discover fraudulent conveyances or preferences between the debtor and its principals, substantial leverage can be gained.

The Bankruptcy Code was designed to provide debtors and creditors motivation for seeking a solution that will maximize the settlement for all parties. While the cases do not always succeed in meeting this objective, and the rights of the debtor or creditors may not be protected to the fullest extent, the Bankruptcy Code does provide a framework whereby the value of the debtor's assets can be enhanced to the benefit of some or all of the parties in interest.

Debtor's Options

While the Bankruptcy Code deals generously with debtors, providing a chance to discharge debts and begin again, no debtor wants to be thrown into bankruptcy proceedings against his will. There are several steps a debtor can take to insure against involuntary bankruptcy. These include being sure that the number of creditors exceeds 12 and that no 3 creditors' claims amount to more than $10,775. Sometimes, this could mean paying off some creditors in full while not paying others all that they are due. If there are more than 12 creditors in a case, 1 or 2 claimants cannot force an individual or a corporation into involuntary bankruptcy.

Further, there are many steps a debtor can take to maximize the amount of exempt assets that can be retained in a bankruptcy case. In contemplating bankruptcy, the debtor should examine exemptions closely, and arrange his affairs in such a way as to give the best possible start following discharge. The legal cases on this point are inconsistent and do not draw a clear line as to when a debtor is simply taking advantage of available exemptions and when a debtor is engaging in fraudulent conveyances by transferring assets that would have otherwise been available for creditors. This uncertainty makes bankruptcy planning extremely difficult. In some cases, a transfer of general assets to exempt assets may be viewed as intelligent planning; in other cases, the same transfer may be viewed by the judge as having civil or criminal implications. There are also many actions debtors cannot take under the law without risking their discharge. For example, hiding assets or liabilities and embezzling from the estate.

One of the most important creditor protections existing under bankruptcy law is the trustee's right to avoid and recover preferential payments made to creditors prior to the bankruptcy case. The trustee has the power to disallow certain payments to a creditor which enables that creditor to receive more than others in the same class. A preferential payment is one made 90 days prior to the bankruptcy filing. If the creditor had an "insider" of the debtor, the 90-day period is extended to one year. The provision ensures the bankruptcy policy of equality of distribution among creditors. Any creditor who manages to receive a larger share than others of the same class during the preference period is forced to return it to the general pot for equitable allocation. The possibility of having to turnover a preference limits the debtor's ability to play one creditor against others in an attempt to avoid bankruptcy, since creditors know such settlements could be disallowed if bankruptcy is declared within three months. There are defenses available to creditors facing a preference lawsuit. For example, payments received by the creditor in the ordinary course of business and payments received at the same time the creditor is providing additional value to the estate cannot be recovered by the trustee.

There are many avenues available for the savvy debtor to pursue, either before filing for bankruptcy or after such proceedings have been initiated. Debtors in financial trouble would be wise to seek competent legal counsel early so as to carve the best path through their predicament.

Bibliography

"A Brief Note on Arrangements, Bankruptcy, and Reorganization in Bankruptcy," Harvard Business School 9–272–148, Rev. 7/75, written by Jasper H. Arnold, Research Assistant, under the supervision of Associate Professor Michael L. Tennican.

"Asbestosis: Manville Seeks Chapter 11," *Fortune,* September 20, 1982.

"A $2.5 Billion Tale of Woe," by Paul Bluestein, *Forbes,* October 30, 1978, p. 51.

"Bankruptcy," Harvard Business School 9–376–221, prepared by Laurence H. Stone, copyright 1976.

Bankruptcy Reform, American Enterprise Institute for Public Policy Research, Washington, D.C., 1978.

Business Failure: Causes, Remedies, and Cures, Ray E. Barrickman, University Press of America, Washington, D.C., 1979.

Corporate Collapse: The Causes and Symptoms, John Argenti, McGraw-Hill: London, 1976.

Corporations in Crisis: Behavioral Observations for Bankruptcy Policy, by Philip B. Nelson, Praeger: New York, 1981.

Current Developments in Bankruptcy and Reorganization: 1980, Arnold M. Quittner, Chairman, Practicing Law Institute, 1980.

"Manville's Costs Could Exceed $5 Billion in Asbestos Suits, Study it Ordered Shows," *Wall Street Journal,* September 15, 1982, p. 7.

Table of Bankruptcy Statistics with reference to bankruptcy cases commenced and terminated in the United States District Courts during the period July 1, 1978 through June 30, 1979, Administrative Office of the United States Courts.

Ibid., July 1, 1976 through June 30, 1977.

The New Bankruptcy Law: A Professional's Handbook, Jeff A. Schnepper (Addison-Wesley Publishing Co., Philippines, 1981).

Bankruptcy Law Letter, Vol. 18, No. 5, p. 2–3 (May 1995).

"Bankruptcy Overview: Issues, Law and Policy," American Bankruptcy Institute (April 1996).

Laurence P. King, et al., Eds., *Collier on Bankruptcy* (3rd ed. 1998).

James F. Queenan, Jr., Philip J. Hendel, and Ingrid M. Hillinger, Editors, *Chapter 11 Theory and Practice: A Guide to Reorganization* (Horsham, Pennsylvania: LRP Publications, 1994).

"Bankruptcy Filings Top 1.4 Million in 1997 with 20 Percent Increase in Consumer Filings," ABI Law Journal 1 (April 1998).

Harlan D. Pratt, *Principles of Corporate Renewal* 55–57 (Advance printing 1997).

4–1

DRAGONFLY CORPORATION

On December 20, 1997, with the close of the Christmas season just a week away, Janet and Michael Thompson received yet another call from their attorney: it was time to make some difficult decisions about their fledgling business. For the past 3 years, the couple had been operating their Dragonfly teenage clothing stores in Seattle, trying to earn a living and keep the business alive despite continuing losses. Now their angry landlord was threatening legal action if Dragonfly did not deliver on its overdue lease payments. The Thompsons' attorney was pushing them for an answer: what did they want to do?

The financial picture was not rosy. Dragonfly had lost money since it opened, with the accumulated deficit from both stores near the end of 1997 reaching over $100,000. (See **Exhibits 1** and **2**.) While the owners believed the business had gone more smoothly over this past year, the numbers were ambiguous. And the Thompsons' best calculations to date still showed Dragonfly losing money (**Exhibit 3**). But the couple believed they were managing the business more wisely and felt they had corrected many of their early operating problems. They weren't sure why their dream child still wasn't profitable. Was it their location? Was there still something wrong with the way they were running the business?

The Thompsons felt they had several possible courses of action. They could try to buy time with the landlord and hope the economy and their business turned around. They could turn to Janet's parents for additional financial help to see them through this crisis. Or they could admit the project wasn't working and begin bankruptcy proceedings.

Martha Gershun, MBA '83, prepared this case under the supervision of Howard H. Stevenson as the basis for class discussion rather than to illustrate either effective or ineffective handling of an administrative situation.

Harvard Business School Case 9-393-118.

The Thompsons felt their decision was complicated by the substantial investment Janet's parents had already made in the business. Could they admit defeat to their family and close up the stores? Even worse, could they ask the family to increase their investment in an endeavor that might fail sooner or later?

There was also the problem of timing. While the Thompsons knew that Christmas was the peak sales season for retail operators, they also knew that January was the peak season for refunds. How should they interpret their recent financial figures in the face of such unevenness? Janet and Michael were inclined to think the entire situation was somehow unfair. Just when they felt the stores were turning around, the issue of the lease payments was raising the specter of bankruptcy and forcing them to make a decision about Dragonfly before all the facts were in.

Background

Janet Hepburn and Michael Thompson met in Seattle as assistant buyers for Bon Marche, a full-line department store chain, and were married in 1985. Three years later, they quit their jobs at Bon Marche—Michael took a job as store manager for the Lerner's chain, and Janet decided to stay at home in anticipation of the birth of their first child. In 1990 the couple moved to Arizona, where Michael took a job working for Kidder Peabody in commercial sales. He hated the environment and found the work boring. He quit in 1991 to return to retailing with a job for a local women's clothing store. Meanwhile, the couple's second child was born. In 1994 the Thompsons returned to Seattle and began looking into franchising a store with the Lady Madonna chain, a successful group of stores offering maternity clothes at the upper end of the pricing scale. Janet was tired of staying home and wanted to get back into the work force. Both the Thompsons liked the lifestyle of retailing. They enjoyed going on buying trips, choosing inventory, and serving customers. With the combined experience in retailing, the couple believed they could make a serious attempt to run their own business.

In the process of investigating the Lady Madonna operation, the Thompsons became intrigued with what they perceived to be an obvious market niche for an upscale store serving Seattle's teenage market. When vigorous research turned up few competitors in the local area, the Thompsons decided to abandon the Lady Madonna franchise idea and pursue opening up their own store instead, selling teenage clothes and accessories at fairly high price points. They developed pro forma cash flows that showed that the business would just break even in the first year of operation (**Exhibit 4**).

Janet and Michael had friends who were successfully operating a chain of T-shirt shops. They liked the idea of opening one store now and using it later to leverage the venture into a thriving chain. Since they believed that most of the expenses involved in running retail stores were fixed on the corporate level, the Thompsons saw the long-term opportunity to generate a sizable income for themselves and a generous profit for their company (see **Exhibit 5**).

Dragonfly

The Thompsons were not particularly worried about financing their new venture. Janet's parents had expressed willingness earlier to finance their entry into the Lady Madonna enterprise, and the couple did not think starting up their own store would take a great deal more capital. They approached Janet's older brother, Charles, who was a corporate attorney in Chicago, and asked him to help them develop a plan to use in approaching the Hepburns for money. Based on Charles's knowledge of business and the Thompsons' retail experience, it was determined that $120,000 would be sufficient to start up the new operation, which by now had been dubbed "Dragonfly."

Janet called her parents to discuss the prospect of underwriting the new store. She asked them for $90,000. The Hepburns offered little resistance to the idea. They were happy to see Janet so excited about the new business and felt that $90,000 was a small investment to help their daughter reach financial independence. Janet's father had recently retired from a successful career in real estate and preferred to give his children money now, rather than having them wait until after his death for an inheritance. He had only two concerns. First, the deal must be structured so that Michael was as responsible as Janet for the financial success of the venture and any obligations to the Hepburns. Second, the Hepburns must receive the tax benefits from any start-up losses.

With those caveats in mind, the family met on June 1, 1994, with Janet and Michael's attorney to set up the Dragonfly Corporation.

The Beginning

The Thompsons thought it seemed like a very informal way to begin such a serious venture. Here they were, serving coffee in their living room to Janet's parents, her older brother, and their attorney, Jeff Lawrence. When the meeting was over and the papers were signed, they would be the owners and managers of the Dragonfly Corporation. The family decided to give the company authorization to issue 50,000 shares of stock with a par value of $1. Initially, 20,000 shares were issued: 15,000 shares to the Hepburns for $15,000 in cash and 5,000 shares to Janet and Michael for their 1990 Volvo, which had a fair market value of $5,000. Jeff Lawrence explained that they would designate Dragonfly as a Subchapter S corporation for income tax purposes and allow the Hepburns to take any tax benefits that might accrue from early losses. Later, when the corporation began to make money, this could be changed so that either Janet and Michael or the company paid any tax liabilities.

The remaining capitalization was undertaken in the form of debt. In order to be sure that Michael was financially tied into the project, the Hepburns loaned the young couple $75,000 at an annual interest rate of 7.75%. The Thompsons, in return, loaned this money to Dragonfly, payable beginning July 1, 1994, in quarterly installments of $1,677.51, including the 7.75% annual interest. Charles felt this capital structure had the additional advantage of giving the couple leverage in any financial adversity, because they would be the store's primary debt holders. The corporation also borrowed $30,000 from Seattle Trust for leasehold improvements, payable in monthly installments of $1,000, with interest at 10% per year. (The debt was guaranteed personally and served by the leasehold improvements.)

Confident that they had enough money to set up shop properly, the Thompsons began looking for a site for their store. They decided to lease a suite at the Crossroads Shopping Center, near the major north/south road in that part of Seattle. Crossroads was in an old, open mall, which had recently been renovated. The Thompsons believed that the emerging character of the shopping center would appeal to their upscale customer base. Also, because the renovation made it a slightly risky location, the rents at Crossroads were roughly half (i.e., $7.50 per foot vs. $15 to $17 per foot) of those in the more fashionable parts of town. Janet and Michael signed a lease on behalf of Dragonfly for 3,000 square feet at $1,875/month or 6% of monthly sales, whichever was greater. The lease was for slightly over 4 years, ending March 1, 1999. They also agreed to pay some portion of common area maintenance costs, averaging about $425/month. (See **Exhibit 6** for sample lease clauses.)

With the signing of the lease, the Thompsons went to work in earnest. Michael supervised the store setup while Janet went off to buy their beginning merchandise. One month later, on August 1, 1994, they were ready to open for business.

Early Results

The results for Dragonfly's first full year in business were not very good. Sales had been lower than expected, and much of the merchandise had been marked down significantly before it was sold. Thus, gross margins were considerably lower than the industry average. In addition, operating expenses were way out of line, bringing the annual loss at December 31, 1995, to $42,253. (**Exhibit 7** gives financial and operating data for the industry. **Exhibit 8** itemizes Dragonfly's expenses.) Faced with cash shortages, the Thompsons fell behind in their rent payments on the store.

The next year brought problems as well. While sales were up slightly, and gross margins were up, Janet had clearly overbought, and inventory levels were up to $80,000. Also, the Thompsons had managed to reduce Dragonfly's expenses but had primarily done so by missing more payments to their Crossroads' landlord and by reducing the amount of money they were taking out of the store. They were forced to borrow $15,000 from Janet's parents to make ends meet at home.

1997: A Tough Year

Thus, the Thompsons began 1997 in a precarious position. Their personal financial situation was very tight (**Exhibit 9**). Janet had cut back on all the extras at home; the family was eating meat only twice a week. Dragonfly was saddled with $80,000 of inventory, and it looked as though only heavy markdowns would move the clothes. To make matters worse, the Crossroads mall was deteriorating rapidly. Already, 10 of the 60 tenants in the new part of the shopping center where Dragonfly was located had begun preparations to move out. It didn't look as though the renovated shopping center was going to make it.

To counter the problems posed by the deterioration of the Crossroads Mall, the Thompsons decided to open a second Dragonfly store in one of the more prosperous sections of Seattle. The new location, in the Bellevue Strip Mall, was 1,450 square feet. The lease, beginning on July 1, 1997, was for two years at $910/month for the first year and $970/month for the second, or 7% of gross sales, whichever was greater. Janet and Michael believed there were a number of reasons for opening a second store, despite their precarious financial condition.

First, they hoped to recycle merchandise between the two stores, selling the clothing faster, and increasing gross margins by avoiding markdowns. Opening a second store provided other merchandising advantages, too. With a larger customer base, Janet felt there was a better chance of approaching a normal curve in the distribution of sizes; she hoped this would lead to greater sales as customers began to rely on Dragonfly to have the sizes they needed. Janet also felt it was a good idea to send sale merchandise to a second location. She knew customers felt badly if they purchased an item at the regular price and then saw it on sale later. Dragonfly also had potential economies of scale in advertising. The Thompsons had developed a large mailing list of existing customers and felt they could spread this advertising cost among the possible revenues from two locations instead of just one. They were also looking for protection in case the situation at Crossroads did not improve. In a worst-case scenario, the Thompsons thought they could fold the first Dragonfly store on March 1, 1999, when the lease was up, and move the merchandise to the Bellevue location. In the four months remaining on the Bellevue lease, they could either try to make the second store successful or use it to liquidate the inventory from both stores. Most important, with many of their significant expenses fixed, the Thompsons saw the second store as a chance to generate excess revenues for the incremental cost of the second set of lease payments. Despite the problems with the Crossroads store, they were pursuing their vision of a profitable multisite operation.

Finally, near the end of 1997, the precarious financial situation forced the Hepburns to reclassify the $30,000 of debt they held as equity.

The Crossroads Situation

In the meantime, faced with increasing cash flow problems, the Thompsons fell further behind on their lease payments for the Crossroads Dragonfly store. In February, they made arrangements with the landlord to begin paying off their previous balance at the rate of $875/month. But this expense left little cash for regular monthly rental payments; these dropped off to $500/month. Thus, the balance owed to Crossroads was still increasing at $925/month.

In late June, the Thompsons talked with the Crossroads landlord again and offered to pay rent of 6% of gross revenues, which at the time was considerably less than the $1,875/month base fee. They would spend the differential in advertising for the store, in the hope of increasing Dragonfly's sales, as well as the shopping center's traffic. In addition, they would still be obligated for the common area maintenance charges of about $425/month. At the same time, the payments on the overdue balance would drop to $650/month (**Exhibit 10**). The landlord agreed, but the Thompsons did not receive any documentation confirming the transaction.

By early October, the Thompsons felt they had spent as much money on advertising as they could reasonably expect to be effective. Michael met with the Crossroads landlord and proposed that Dragonfly begin paying the full $2,300/month towards the rent again, with the payments on the overdue balance remaining at $650/month. He felt that the meeting went well and believed that his proposal had been accepted. Thus, the Thompsons were extremely surprised when Jeff Lawrence called on October 25, 1997, to say that he had received a very inflammatory note from the Crossroads lawyers. The letter (**Exhibit 11**) threatened to pursue further legal action if the Thompsons did not sign a confessed judgment for the entire amount overdue of $21,576.79. Jeff Lawrence responded immediately with another letter explaining the situation as the Thompsons understood it (**Exhibit 12**) and also suggested to the Thompsons that they consider signing the note.

Battening Down the Hatches

Jeff cautioned the Thompsons that this kind of angry response from a creditor often preceded the initiation of bankruptcy proceedings. He told them to be prepared for the worst possibility. Janet was extremely upset by this news. She had known Dragonfly was in trouble, but it did not seem possible that the landlord had suddenly decided to close up their entire operation.

During this time, another distressing piece of news came to light: about six months earlier, one of Janet's vendors had insisted on subordinated credit. Lawrence had gotten the Thompsons to sign a general subordination agreement, which subordinated their debt to that of all trade creditors. While the account had been paid off, this agreement was still in the contract with that vendor. Charles was very anxious that this subordination agreement be terminated before the issue of bankruptcy was discussed further. He did not want this small creditor to destroy the careful chain he had set up, in case bankruptcy was actually triggered. As far as Charles was concerned, this was a further example of incompetence on the part of Jeff Lawrence. He should have known better than to allow Janet to sign such a contract. Thus, Charles proposed that the Thompsons make arrangements with this creditor to change the agreement immediately. As well, he suggested they start to think about the real prospects for Dragonfly and frame their response to the Crossroads landlord in this light. Perhaps there was a way to negotiate their way out of the lease, using bankruptcy as their own threat.

The Decision

By December, the Thompsons still hadn't heard from the Crossroads landlord again. But, Jeff cautioned them that it was unlikely the incident had been dropped. Rather, he suggested, Crossroads might be waiting to see how Dragonfly fared through the Christmas season before determining what action to take. While Crossroads had earlier mentioned bankruptcy as a final recourse, Lawrence now confirmed Charles's earlier opinion that one creditor did not have the power to force involuntary bankruptcy on either a business or an individual. Rather, bankruptcy should be viewed by the Thompsons as a way out, if they decided that the Dragonfly stores were not financially viable.

Now, on December 20, Jeff Lawrence had called again. He felt Crossroads would not wait any longer for an answer about the overdue lease payments. Did Janet and Michael want to stall and hope the after-Christmas season bore out their optimism about Dragonfly's improved performance? Did they want to strike a deal and get out of the lease? Did they want to seek more money from Janet's parents? Or did they want to file for bankruptcy and put the entire disappointing experience behind them?

The Thompsons were very torn. They believed the stores were doing better. Inventory levels were down. Existing merchandise was moving rapidly, with little or no markdowns. Their accounts payable appeared to be good. Just when the situation should be at its brightest, the Crossroads mess was threatening to blow out their light. The Thompsons were resentful and confused: Was it really time to quit?

EXHIBIT 1   Income Statements (unaudited)

	For the Years Ending:	
	December 31, 1995	*December 31, 1996*
Net sales	$246,236	$261,336
COGS	165,358	160,011
Gross margin	80,878	101,375
Operating expenses	117,918	106,951
Interest expense	5,213	4,450
Net loss	(42,253)	(10,076)

EXHIBIT 2 Balance Sheets (unaudited)

ASSETS

	Dec. 31, 1995	Dec. 31, 1996	Dec. 20, 1997
Current Assets:			
Cash	$ 2,560	$ 4,821	$ 4,930
Inventory	61,432	81,846	84,977
Prepaid insurance	408	0	0
Total current assets	64,400	86,667	89,907
Fixed Assets:			
Furniture and fixtures	25,682	26,278	46,429
Office and ship equipment	2,802	2,908	2,805
Leasehold improvements	22,540	22,540	32,321
Less accumulated depreciation	(11,319)	(15,441)	(19,206)
Total fixed assets	39,705	36,285	62,349
Other assets			
Deposits	1,970	1,970	1,970
Organization costs, net of accumulated amortization	2,023	1,463	903
Total other assets	3,993	3,433	2,873
TOTAL ASSETS	**$108,098**	**$126,385**	**$155,129**

LIABILITIES AND STOCKHOLDERS' EQUITY

	Dec. 31, 1995	Dec. 31, 1996	Dec. 20, 1997
Current Liabilities:			
Notes payable—bank	$ 30,116	$ 33,574	$ 33,201
Notes payable—stockholders	4,776	9,901	8,623
Accounts payable—trade	55,514	48,230	90,045[a]
Gift certificates outstanding	284	163	210
Accrued liabilities	7,296	5,520	5,264
Deposits	0	82	0
Long-term debt due within one year	1,053	1,053	1,053
Total current liabilities	99,039	98,523	138,396
Long-term debt due after one year	71,272	70,151	69,098
Debt due Hepburns	—	30,000	—
Stockholders' Equity:			
Common stock, $1 par value— 50,000 shares authorized	20,000	20,000	50,000
Accumulated deficit	(82,213)	(92,289)	(102,365)
TOTAL LIABILITIES AND EQUITY	**$108,098**	**$126,385**	**$155,129**

[a]Includes:

Trade payables	$68,468
Crossroads rent	21,577
	$90,045

Does **not** include remaining balance of lease payments due:

Crossroads, January 1998 through March 1999	$32,200
Bellevue, January 1998 through July, 1999	17,100
	$49,300

EXHIBIT 3   Estimated Financial Condition as of December 20, 1997 (accrual basis)

Sales—gross	$247,000
Sales tax (6.5)	16,066
Sales—net	230,945
COGS	148,506
	82,439
Gross margin expenses:	
Rent[a]	31,360
Payroll[b]	36,000
Advertising	9,000
FICA	8,400
Medical insurance	1,800
Miscellaneous	1,400
Interest	5,320
Net loss	(10,841)

[a]Rent breakdown:

Crossroads	$24,100
Bellevue rent	5,460
Bellevue common area payments	1,800

[b]Does not include $21,000 salary to Thompsons not accrued or paid.

EXHIBIT 4   **Pro Forma Cash Flows, March 1994—February 1995**

	March	April	May	June	July	August	September	October	November	December	January	February	Total
PROJECTED SALES	**20,000**	**18,000**	**18,000**	**20,000**	**25,000**	**27,000**	**20,000**	**16,000**	**20,000**	**30,000**	**16,000**	**17,000**	**247,000**
Cost of merchandise	10,000	9,000	9,000	10,000	12,500	13,500	10,000	8,000	10,000	15,000	8,000	8,500	123,500
Cost of markdowns	1,500	1,500	1,100	1,100	2,500	1,000	1,000	1,000	1,100	1,300	2,000	1,000	16,100
Totals	11,500	10,500	10,100	11,100	15,000	14,500	11,000	9,000	11,100	16,300	10,000	9,500	139,600
GROSS PROFIT	8,500	7,500	7,900	8,900	10,000	12,500	9,000	7,000	8,900	13,700	6,000	7,500	107,400
Selling Expenses:													
Sales salaries	1,700	1,700	1,700	1,800	1,900	2,100	1,800	1,600	1,700	2,200	1,600	1,650	21,450
Advertising	600	500	400	500	600	600	400	400	500	400	600	500	6,000
Buying trips	500					500			500				1,500
Selling supplies	100	1,400	100	100	100	1,400	100	100	200	200	100	100	4,000
Other	50	50	50	50	50	50	50	50	50	50	50	50	600
Totals	2,950	3,650	2,250	2,450	2,650	4,650	2,350	2,150	2,950	2,850	2,350	2,300	33,550
Occupancy Expenses:													
Depreciation	400	400	400	400	400	400	400	400	400	400	400	400	4,800
Insurance	90	90	90	90	90	90	90	90	90	90	90	90	1,080
Maintenance	265	265	265	265	265	265	265	265	265	265	265	265	3,180
Rent	1,875	1,875	1,875	1,875	1,875	1,875	1,875	1,875	1,875	1,875	1,875	1,875	22,500
Other (Merch. Assn.)	150	150	150	150	150	150	150	150	150	150	150	150	1,800
Total	2,780	2,780	2,780	2,780	2,780	2,780	2,780	2,780	2,780	2,780	2,780	2,780	33,360
Administrative:													
Officer's salary	1,200	1,200	1,200	1,200	1,200	1,200	1,200	1,200	1,200	1,200	1,200	1,200	14,400
Bad debt	20	20	20	20	20	20	20	20	20	20	20	20	240
Bank discount	120	110	110	120	150	162	120	100	120	180	100	110	1,502
Dues, etc.	30	30	30	30	30	40	30	30	30	30	30	30	370
Employee benefits	75	75	75	75	75	75	75	75	75	75	75	75	900
Life insurance	50	50	50	50	50	50	50	50	50	50	50	50	600
Loan interest and repayment	253	253	660	660	660	660	660	660	660	660	660	660	7,106
Office supplies	10	20	20	20	20	20	20	20	20	20	20	20	230
Professional services	100	300	100	100	300	100	100	300	100	100	300	100	2,000
Taxes (payroll)	750	730	730	750	780	810	750	705	750	830	705	705	8,995
Taxes (excise)	250	250	250	250	300	325	250	225	250	350	225	225	3,150
Telephone	75	70	70	70	75	75	70	70	70	70	70	70	855
Total	2,933	3,108	3,315	3,345	3,660	3,537	3,345	3,455	3,345	3,585	3,455	3,265	40,348
PROFIT (LOSS)	**(163)**	**(2,038)**	**(445)**	**325**	**910**	**1,533**	**525**	**(1,385)**	**(175)**	**4,485**	**(2,585)**	**(845)**	**142**

EXHIBIT 5   Pro Forma Income Statements for the Years Ending February 28

	1995	1996	1997	1998	1999
Revenues					
Gross sales—Store 1	$247,000	$300,000	$350,000	$350,000	$ 350,000
Gross sales—Store 2	0	0	250,000	350,000	350,000
Gross sales—Store 3	0	0	0	250,000	350,000
Total Gross Sales	$247,000	$300,000	$600,000	$950,000	$1,050,000
Expenses					
Cost of goods sold	$139,600	$165,000	$330,000	$522,500	$ 577,500
Selling expenses	33,550	35,000	40,000	40,000	40,000
Administrative expenses[a]	25,948	30,000	75,000	100,000	100,000
Officers' salary	14,400	20,000	40,000	60,000	60,000
Rent	22,500	22,500	47,000	71,500	73,500
Common area maintenance	3,180	4,000	8,000	12,000	12,000
Other occupancy expenses	7,320	8,000	9,000	10,000	10,000
Total Expenses	$246,498	$284,500	$549,000	$816,000	$ 873,000
PROFIT BEFORE TAXES	$ 502	$ 15,500	$ 51,000	$134,000	$ 177,000

[a]Includes loan repayments and interest; assumes new bank loans to finance opening Store 2 and Store 3.

EXHIBIT 6   Crossroads Shopping Center Lease Index

1. Premises
2. Construction of Premises
3. Lease Term
4. Delayed Possession and Options to Terminate
5. Rent
6. Taxes and Insurance Premiums
7. Utilities
8. Common Areas
9. Common Area and Mall Maintenance
10. Conduct of Business on the Premises
11. Alterations
12. Maintenance and Repair
13. Quiet Enjoyment
14. Assignment or Sublease
15. Indemnification; Liability Insurance
16. Signs and Advertising
17. Entry by Lessor
18. Eminent Domain
19. Fire or Other Casualty
20. Waiver of Subrogation
21. Insolvency
22. Defaults
23. Liens and Encumbrances
24. Advances by Lessor for Lessee
25. Attorneys' Fees
26. Waiver
27. Other Stores
28. Notices
29. Successors or Assigns
30. Lease Consideration
31. Merchants Association
32. Change of Location
33. Subordination; Notice to Mortgagee; Attornment
34. Holding Over
35. Memorandum of Lease
36. Sale of Premises by Lessor

EXHIBIT 6   *(continued)*

SELECTED EXCERPTS FROM LEASE

SECTION 14: ASSIGNMENT OR SUBLEASE

Lessee shall not assign, sublease or transfer this lease or any interest therein or in the premises, nor shall this lease or any interest thereunder be assignable or transferable by operation of law or by any process or proceeding of any court, or otherwise, without first obtaining the written consent of Lessor. No assignment of this lease by Lessee shall relieve Lessee of any of its duties or obligations hereunder. If Lessee is a corporation, then any merger, consolidation or liquidation to which it may be a party or any change in the ownership of or power to vote the majority of its outstanding voting stock shall constitute an assignment or transfer of this lease for the purposes of this section.

SECTION 15: INDEMNIFICATION; LIABILITY INSURANCE

Lessor shall not be liable to Lessee or to any other person, firm or corporation whatsoever for any injury to, or death of any person, or for any loss of, or damages to, property (including property of Lessee) occurring in or about the Shopping Center or the premises from any cause whatsoever. Lessee agrees to indemnify and save Lessor harmless from all loss, damage, liability, suit, claim, or expense (including expense of litigation) arising out of or resulting from any actual or alleged injury to, or death of, any person, or from any actual or alleged loss of, or damage to, property caused by, or resulting from, any occurrence on or about the premises, or caused by, or resulting from, any act or omission, whether negligent or otherwise, of Lessee, or any officer, agent, employee, contractor, guest, invitee, customer or visitor of Lessee, in or about the Shopping Center or the premises. Lessee shall, at its own expense, maintain at all times during the lease term proper liability insurance with a reputable insurance company or companies satisfactory to Lessor in the minimum limit of One Hundred Thousand Dollars ($100,000) (per accident) for property damage, and in the minimum limits of Five Hundred Thousand Dollars ($500,000) (per person) and One Million Dollars ($1,000,000) (per accident or occurrence) for bodily injuries and death, to indemnify both Lessor and Lessee against such claims, demands, losses, damages, liabilities and expense as against which Lessee has herein agreed to indemnify and hold Lessor harmless. Such policy or policies shall name Lessor, its ground lessor and lenders as insureds, be issued by companies noted A+ or better in Best's insurance guide, and shall be noncancellable as to such named insureds except upon at least ten (10) days prior written notice. Lessee shall furnish Lessor with a copy of said policy or policies or other acceptable evidence that said insurance is in effect.

SECTION 21: INSOLVENCY

Lessee agrees that it will not cause or give cause for the institution of legal proceedings seeking to have Lessee adjudicated bankrupt, reorganized or rearranged under the bankruptcy laws of the United States, or for relief under any other law for the relief of debtors, and will not cause or give cause for the appointment of a trustee or receiver for Lessee's assets, and will not cause or give cause for the commencement of proceedings to foreclose any mortgage or any other lien on Lessee's interest in the premises or on any personal property kept or maintained on the premises by Lessee; and Lessee further agrees that it will not make an assignment for the benefit of creditors, or become or be adjudicated insolvent. The allowance of any petition under the bankruptcy law, or the appointment of a trustee or receiver of Lessee's assets, or the entry of judgment of foreclosure in any proceedings to foreclose any such mortgage or other lien, or an adjudication that Lessee is insolvent shall be conclusive evidence that Lessee has violated the provisions of this section if said allowance, appointment, judgment, or adjudication or similar order or ruling remains in force or unstayed for a period of thirty (30) days. Upon the happening of any of such events, Lessor may, if it so elects, elect to terminate this lease and all rights of Lessee hereunder without prior notice to Lessee.

SECTION 22: DEFAULTS

Time is the essence hereof, and if Lessee violates or breaches or fails to keep or perform any covenant, agreement, term or condition of this lease, and if such default or violation shall continue or shall not be remedied within ten (10) days (three (3) days in the case of non-payment of rent or other payments due hereunder) after notice in writing thereof given by Lessor to Lessee specifying the matter claimed to be in default, Lessor, at its option, may immediately declare Lessee's rights under this lease terminated, and reenter the premises, using such force as may be necessary, and repossess itself thereof, as of its former estate, removing all persons and effects therefrom. If upon the reentry of Lessor, there remains any personal property of Lessee or of any other person, firm or corporation upon the premises, Lessor may, but without the obligation to do so, remove said personal property and place the same in a public warehouse or garage, as may be reasonable, at the expense and risk of the owners thereof, and Lessee shall reimburse Lessor for any expense incurred by Lessor in connection with said removal and/or storage.

EXHIBIT 6   *(concluded)*

Notwithstanding any such reentry, the liability of Lessee for the full rent provided for herein shall not be extinguished for the balance of the term of this lease, and Lessee shall make good to Lessor each month during the balance of said term any deficiency arising from a reletting of the premises at a lesser rental than that herein agreed upon as the Minimum Rent, plus the cost of renovating the premises for the new tenant and reletting it.

SECTION 23: LIENS AND ENCUMBRANCES

Lessee shall keep the premises free and clear of any liens and encumbrances arising or growing out of the use and occupancy of the premises by Lessee hereunder. At Lessor's request, Lessee shall furnish Lessor with written proof of payment of any item which would or might constitute the basis for a lien on the premises if not paid.

SECTION 24: ADVANCES BY LESSOR FOR LESSEE

If Lessee fails to do anything required to be done by it under the terms of this lease, except to pay rent, Lessor may, at its sole option, do such act or thing on behalf of Lessee, and upon notification to Lessee of the cost thereof to the Lessor, Lessee shall promptly pay the Lessor the amount of that cost, plus interest at the rate of twelve percent (12%) per annum from the date that the cost was incurred by Lessor to the date of Lessee's payment.

SECTION 25: ATTORNEYS FEES

Lessee agrees to pay, in addition to all other sums due hereunder, such expenses and attorneys fees as Lessor may incur in enforcing all obligations under terms of this lease, including those fees and expenses incurred at trial and on appeal, all of which shall be included in any judgment entered therein. Such covered fees and expenses shall include those incurred in suits instituted by third parties in which Lessor must participate to protect its rights hereunder and those incurred in suits to establish and enforce rights of indemnity hereunder.

SECTION 27: OTHER STORES

Lessee agrees that neither it, nor any subsidiary or affiliate of it, nor any other person, firm or corporation using any store or business name licensed or controlled by Lessee, shall, during the term of this lease, operate a store or business which is the same as or similar to that to be conducted on the premises, or which merchandises or sells the same or similar products, merchandise or services as that to be sold or furnished from the premises, at any location within a radius of four (4) miles from the Shopping Center without the written permission of Lessor. Lessee further agrees that it will not promote or encourage the operation of any such store or business within said radius by any person, firm or corporation. In addition to any and all other remedies otherwise available to Lessor for breach of this covenant, it is agreed that Lessor may at its election either (a) terminate this lease or (b) require that any and all sales made at, in, on or from any such other store be included in the computation of the percentage rent due hereunder with the same force and effect as though such sales had actually been made at, in, on or from the premises.

SECTION 32: CHANGE OF LOCATION

Lessee shall move from the premises at Lessor's written request to any other premises and location in the Shopping Center, in which event such new location and premises shall be substituted for the premises described herein, but all other terms of this lease shall remain the same, with the exception that the Minimum Rent provided for herein shall be abated during the period that Lessee is closed for business as a result of the move to the new location; provided, however, that Lessee shall not be moved to premises of less square footage than those herein leased, and that Lessor shall bear all actual cash expenses incurred by Lessee in so moving. It is further understood and agreed, however, that in the event that Lessee shall move to any other premises and location within the Shopping Center for any reason other than to comply with a request from Lessor, then this paragraph shall be inapplicable and the Lessee shall bear all expenses of moving.

EXHIBIT 7   Industry Operating Results, 1995: Specialty Stores—Sales under $1 Million (% figures unless otherwise noted)

	Average	*Middle Range*
Sales Data:		
Credit sales	20.87	11.70–36.68
Sales per square foot—selling space ($)	114.90	42.61–137.94
Sales per square foot—total space ($)	85.68	37.60–126.00
Returns—% gross sales	1.82	1.00–3.60
Sales per employee ($)	50,643	41,194–68,270
Markdowns	12.15	0.90–15.23
Employee discounts	1.09	0.00–2.12
Shortages	1.90	0.96–2.94
Gross margin	41.47	39.66–43.83
Net Operating Expenses:		
Earnings from operations	3.57	1.59–5.00
Other income	0.62	0.18–1.72
Pretax earnings	4.19	2.52–5.31
Management payroll	8.43	6.57–10.54
Selling payroll	9.13	7.48–9.87
Payroll total	17.56	16.30–20.33
Supplementary fringe benefits	0.73	0.41–0.99
Media costs	3.09	2.21–3.33
Taxes	2.11	1.80–2.23
Supplies	2.99	2.00–3.78
Credit services	0.83	0.43–1.84
Other	1.05	0.81–1.37
Travel	0.85	0.13–1.40
Postage & phone	0.88	0.50–1.20
Insurance	1.29	0.74–1.66
Depreciation	0.97	0.29–1.56
Professional services	0.53	0.18–0.68
Bad debts	0.41	0.09–0.67
Outside maintenance & equipment service	0.26	0.18–0.30
Real property rentals	4.35	3.09–4.97
TOTAL	**37.90**	**36.29–40.60**

Source: Adapted from National Retail Merchants Assn., *Financial and Operating Results of Department and Specialty Stores*, pp. 104–105.

EXHIBIT 8   Statement of Operating Expenses For the Years Ending

---

	December 31, 1995	*December 31, 1996*
Operating Expenses:		
Sales salaries	$22,607	$30,445
Advertising	9,317	10,726
Alteration costs	204	0
Bank card discounts	2,014	2,343
Buying trips	2,648	2,056
Delivery	149	0
Display	330	
Selling supplies	5,559	5,864
Over/Short	45	(629)
	42,873	50,805
Occupancy Expenses:		
Depreciation/amortization	8,964	4,683
Insurance	742	742
Maintenance	542	151
Property taxes	0	542
Rent	20,128	16,942
Utilities	101	95
	30,477	23,155
Administrative Expenses:		
Officer's salary	23,447	13,542
Employee benefits	874	2,169
Bank charges	187	223
Donations	25	40
Dues and subscriptions	101	50
Officer's life insurance	2,231	1,780
Bad debts	367	0
Office expense	1,645	104
Professional services	6,794	5,080
Business taxes	1,216	1,024
Payroll taxes	5,661	5,232
Telephone	854	1,172
Postage	787	712
Temporary help	154	79
Travel and entertainment	225	0
Miscellaneous	0	1,435
	$44,568	$32,642

EXHIBIT 9   Janet and Michael Thompson Personal Balance Sheet—January 1, 1997

Assets

1985 VW	1,000
House	140,000
Marketable securities[a]	20,000
Equity in Dragonfly	5,000
Note receivable—Dragonfly	75,000
Total	241,000

Liabilities

First mortgage on house—bank	47,000
Second mortgage—Hepburns	35,000
Note payable—Hepburns	75,000
Note payable—Hepburns	15,000
Total liabilities	172,000
Net worth	69,000
Total	241,000

[a]While these stocks were in Janet's name, Washington is a community property state.

EXHIBIT 10   History of Lease Obligations and Payments for Crossroads Store

Time Period	Rent Incurred (approxim.)[a]	Rent Paid	Payment on Old Balance	Total Remaining Unpaid Obligation[c]
July–December 1994	$13,800	$13,800	$ 0	$ 0
January–December 1995	27,600	20,128	0	7,472
January–December 1996	27,600	16,942	0	18,130
January 1997	2,300	878	0	19,552
February 1997	2,300	500	875	20,477
March 1997	2,300	500	875	21,402
April 1997	2,300	500	875	22,327
May 1997	2,300	500	875	23,252
June 1997	2,300	500	875	24,177
July 1997[b]	1,425	1,425	650	23,527
August 1997	1,425	1,425	650	22,877
September 1997	1,425	1,425	650	22,227
October 1997	1,425	1,425	650	21,577
November 1997	2,300	2,300	0	21,577
December 1997	2,300	2,300	0	21,577

[a]Including common area maintenance assessments
[b]Thompsons negotiate with landlord to pay rent of 6% of gross sales or $2,300 per month, *whichever is less.*
[c]Does not include future obligations under lease, which runs through March 1999.

EXHIBIT 11

October 25, 1997

Jeff Lawrence, Esq.
Attorney at Law
600 Seattle Trust Building
10655 NE Fourth
Bellevue, WA 98004

        Re: Crossroads Properties
        Janet and Michael Thompson Lease Default

Dear Mr. Lawrence:

    As we have discussed recently by telephone, your clients, Janet and Michael Thompson are currently in substantial default under the terms of their lease with Crossroads Properties. Any prior understanding which may have existed with respect to payment of this default was mutually rescinded by request of your clients on or about June 1, 1997. A subsequent arrangement, which was conditioned upon execution and delivery of an installment note and deed of trust, was proffered to Mr. Thompson on or about July 14, 1997, but he never executed a note and he failed to provide a legal description for his residence so that the deed of trust could be prepared, notwithstanding his repeated assurances that it would be forthcoming. As indicated in our prior correspondence to your clients, that offer has long since lapsed.

    You now indicate that the Thompsons cannot further encumber their residence, that they own no other property on which a deed of trust might be placed, that they have no other security to offer in any form, and that they are even fighting to hold off lien foreclosures on their new store. In spite of all this, you propose that Crossroads Properties should be content without even a promissory note evidencing the indebtedness or the installment terms. You further suggest that no interest should accrue on the lease indebtedness. Moreover, although you acknowledge that the Thompsons' family members are helping them financially, they are reportedly unwilling to provide a guarantee of payment for this debt.

    The fact that the Thompsons desire to avoid signing a note evidencing the terms of payment suggests that they have no intention of paying the lease default. Your suggestion that Crossroads Properties should rely solely on the Thompsons' good faith is completely unrealistic and unacceptable, both as a general business practice and as a result of your clients' past failures to perform as promised. We have enclosed a promissory note, bearing interest at 15% per annum, and requiring payments of $800 per month, which you have indicated are within the Thompsons' means. We have also enclosed a confession of judgment, which is to be entered in the event of default by the Thompsons in their payments due under the note.

    Kindly arrange for Mr. and Mrs. Thompson to sign the note and confession of judgment and return the fully executed documents to us by no later than 5 o'clock p.m., November 5, 1997. If we do not receive them by that date and time, Crossroads Properties reserves all rights to collect the amounts due, without further notice to you.

                        Very truly yours,

                        PELLETT & CRUTT
                        Andrew A. Savage

Enclosures
cc: Crossroads Properties

Exhibit 11 *(continued)*

PROMISSORY NOTE

Seattle, Washington

In the amount of $21,576.79
_____, 1997

FOR VALUE RECEIVED, the undersigned ("Maker") promises to pay to the order of Crossroads Properties, a Washington corporation limited partnership, the principal sum of Twenty-One Thousand Five Hundred Seventy-Six and 79/100 Dollars ($21,576.79), together with interest thereon, all as hereinafter provided and upon the following agreements, terms, and conditions:

Interest All sums which are and which may become owing hereon shall bear interest from the date hereof until paid, at the rate of fifteen percent (15%) per annum.

Payment Maker shall pay principal and interest in consecutive monthly installments of Eight Hundred Dollars ($800.00), or more, commencing on the fifteenth day of November, 1997, and continuing on the fifteenth day of each succeeding calendar month thereafter until the total indebtedness herein is paid in full. Each payment shall be applied first to interest accrued to the installment payment date and then to principal. All payments shall be payable in lawful money of the United States of America which shall be the legal tender for public and private debts at the time of payments. All payments shall be made to the holder hereof at Suite D-9, Crossroads Mall, Bellevue, Washington 98008, or at such other place as the holder hereof may specify in writing from time to time.

Prepayment All or any part of the sums now or hereafter owing hereon may be prepaid at any time or times. Any such prepayment may be made without prior notice to the holder and shall be without premium or discount. All partial prepayments shall be applied first to interest accrued to the date of prepayment and the balance, if any, shall be credited to the last due installments of principal in the inverse order of their maturity without deferral or limitation of the intervening installments of principal or interest.

Late Payment Charge If any installment of principal or interest shall not be paid within five (5) days commencing with the date such installment becomes due, Maker agrees to pay a later charge equal to three percent (3%) of the delinquent installment to cover the extra expense involved in handling delinquent payments. This late payment charge is in addition to and not in lieu of any other rights or remedies the holder may have by virtue of any breach or default hereunder.

Default; Attorneys' Fees and Other Costs and Expenses Upon the occurrence of any Event of Default, at the option of the holder, all sums owing and to become owing hereon shall become immediately due and payable. The occurrence of any of the following shall constitute an "Event of Default": (i) Maker fails to pay any installment or other sum owing hereon when due; (ii) Maker admits in writing its inability to pay its debts, or makes a general assignment for the benefit of creditors; (iii) any proceeding is instituted by or against Maker seeking to adjudicate it as bankrupt or insolvent, or seeking reorganization, arrangement, adjustment, or composition of it or its debts under any law relating to bankruptcy, insolvency or reorganization or relief of debtors, or seeking appointment of a receiver trustee or other similar official for it or for any substantial part of its property; or (iv) any dissolution or liquidation proceeding is instituted by or against Maker, and, if instituted against Maker, is consented to or acquiesced in by Maker or remains for thirty (30) days undismissed or unstayed or remains for thirty (30) days undismissed after such proceeding is no longer stayed. Maker agrees to pay all costs and expenses which the holder may incur by reason of any Event of Default, including without limitation reasonable attorneys' fees with respect to legal services relating to any Event of Default and to a determination of any rights or remedies of the holder under this note, and reasonable attorneys' fees relating to any actions or proceedings which the holder may institute or in which the holder may appear or participate and in any reviews of and appeals therefrom, and all such sums shall be secured hereby. Any judgment recovered by the holder hereon shall bear interest at the rate of eighteen percent (18%) per annum, not to exceed, however, the highest rate then permitted by law on such judgment. The venue of any action hereon may be laid in the Country of King, State of Washington, at the option of the holder.

EXHIBIT 11   *(continued)*

No Waiver The holder's acceptance of partial or delinquent payments or the failure of the holder to exercise any right hereunder shall not waive any obligation of Maker or right of the holder or modify this note, or waive any other similar default.

Liability All persons signing this note as Maker hereby agree that they shall be liable hereon jointly and severally, and they hereby waive demand, presentment for payment, protest, and notice of protest and of nonpayment. Each such person agrees that any modification or extension of the terms of payment made by the holder, with or without notice, at the request of any person liable hereon, or a release of any party liable for this obligation shall not diminish or impair his or their liability for the payment hereof.

Maximum Interest Notwithstanding any other provisions of this note, interest, fees, and charges payable by reason of the indebtedness evidenced hereby shall not exceed the maximum, if any, permitted by governing law.

Applicable Law This note shall be governed by, and construed in accordance with, the laws of the State of Washington.

_____

Michael Thompson

_____

Janet Thompson

_____

DRAGONFLY CORPORATION

By_____

Its_____

EXHIBIT 11   *(continued)*

IN THE SUPERIOR COURT OF THE STATE OF WASHINGTON FOR KING COUNTY

CROSSROAD PROPERTIES, a limited partnership consisting of DICK WILLARD and GEORGE BELL, as general partners, and other persons or entities as limited partners,
 	
                Plaintiff,
   v.
 	
MICHAEL THOMPSON and JANET THOMPSON husband and wife, the marital community thereof, and DRAGONFLY CORPORATION, a Washington corporation,
 	
               Defendants.
	))))))))))))))))	No. _____
		CONFESSION OF JUDGMENT

    Michael Thompson, Janet Thompson, husband and wife, the marital community thereof, and Dragonfly Corporation, defendants, do hereby confess judgment in favor of Crossroads Properties, plaintiff, on the terms and conditions and for the sums set forth below, and do hereby authorize the above Court to enter judgment for said sum and on said terms and conditions against defendants and in favor of plaintiff.

    1. Defendants agree and confess that this confession of judgment and judgment based thereon may be entered immediately herein if, at any time hereafter, an Event of Default occurs, as defined in that certain promissory note (the "Promissory Note") executed by defendants and dated _____, 1997, a copy of which is attached hereto as Exhibit A and incorporated herein by this reference.

EXHIBIT 11   *(continued)*

---

2. In proof of the occurrence of an Event of Default as specified above, it shall be necessary and sufficient proof for plaintiff to present to the Court a writing certified by the then current holder of the Promissory Note that an Event of Default has occurred as defined in the Promissory Note.

3. Judgment may be entered in the principal amount of $21,576.79, together with interest in accordance with the terms of the Promissory Note, save and except the following: (a) any amount paid to plaintiff pursuant to the Promissory Note by defendants shall be deducted from the amount of said principal and interest specified in the Promissory Note; and (b) plaintiff's court costs, disbursements, and attorneys' fees incurred in connection with defendant's default in making payments due under the Promissory Note shall be added thereto.

4. Defendants specifically waive their right to a hearing on the merits of any issues that may arise in connection with the execution or enforcement of, or otherwise relating to, the Promissory Note, and confess and admit that the above-entitled court has full and exclusive jurisdiction over the parties and over the subject matter of any action arising from or relating to the Promissory Note, and defendants, for themselves and for all parties claiming under, by, or through them, hereby waive any and all claims or defenses, whether substantive or procedural, to entry of judgment in accordance with the terms and conditions of this confession of judgment.

5. Defendants state, agree, and admit that this confession of judgment is a completely voluntary and knowing act of defendants. Defendants have been fully advised by their counsel of the effects and scope of the judgment confessed herein.

6. Defendants hereby expressly waive notice of presentation of this confession of judgment to the court. If, notwithstanding defendants' waiver of any notice requirement, plaintiff elects to notify defendants of the time and place for presentation of the judgment, defendants shall have a right to be heard on the following questions only: (a) whether plaintiff has complied with the requirements set forth in paragraph 2 regarding proof that an Event of Default has occurred; and (b) the reasonableness of the attorneys' fees and costs to be included in the judgment.

CONFESSION OF JUDGMENT—2

EXHIBIT 11 *(continued)*

7. Defendants state, admit, and believe that this confession of judgment is for money justly due and owing to plaintiff under the terms of the Promissory Note, which was executed by defendants, as their free and voluntary act, to evidence indebtedness owing by defendants to plaintiff for delinquent lease payments arising under a commercial lease between the parties.

DATED this ___ day of _____, 1997.

_____
Michael Thompson

_____
Janet Thompson

_____
DRAGONFLY CORPORATION

By_____

Its_____

EXHIBIT 11   *(continued)*

STATE OF WASHINGTON   )
)   ss.
COUNTY OF _____   )

MICHAEL THOMPSON, being first duly sworn, states: I am the defendant in the above-entitled action, and I am authorized to make this verification on its behalf. I have read the foregoing Confession of Judgment, know the contents thereof, and that the same is true in all respects; I verify that the Confession of Judgment therein contained has been voluntarily made by Michael Thompson with full knowledge.

_____

SUBSCRIBED AND SWORN TO before me this ___ day of _____,
1997.

                                        _____
                                        NOTARY PUBLIC in and for the
                                        State of Washington, residing at

                                        _____

STATE OF WASHINGTON   )
)   ss.
COUNTY OF _____   )

JANET THOMPSON, being first duly sworn, states that I am a defendant in the above-entitled action, and I am authorized to make this verification. I have read the foregoing Confession of Judgment, know the contents thereof, and that the same is true in all respects; I verify that the Confession of Judgment therein contained has been voluntarily made by Janet Thompson with full knowledge.

_____

SUBSCRIBED AND SWORN TO before me this ___ day of _____,
1997.

                                        _____
                                        NOTARY PUBLIC in and for the
                                        State of Washington, residing at

                                        _____

CONFESSION OF JUDGMENT—4

EXHIBIT 11   *(continued)*

STATE OF WASHINGTON   )
)   ss.
COUNTY OF _____   )

_____, being first duly sworn, states: I am the _____ of
Dragonfly Corporation, the defendant in the above-entitled action, and I am authorized to make this
verification on its behalf. I have read the foregoing Confession of Judgment, know the contents
thereof, and that the same is true in all respects; I verify that the Confession of Judgment therein
contained has been voluntarily made by Dragonfly Corporation with full knowledge.

_____

SUBSCRIBED AND SWORN TO before me this ___ day of _____,
1997.

_____

NOTARY PUBLIC in and for the
State of Washington, residing at

_____

CONFESSION OF JUDGMENT—5

EXHIBIT 11   *(continued)*

STATE OF WASHINGTON   )
)   ss.
COUNTY OF _____   )

On this ___ day _____, 1997, before me, the undersigned, a Notary Public in and for the State of Washington, duly commissioned and sworn, personally appeared MICHAEL THOMPSON known to me to be the party that executed the foregoing Confession of Judgment, and acknowledged the said Confession of Judgment to be his free and voluntary act and deed for the uses and purposes therein mentioned, and on oath stated that he was authorized to execute the said Confession of Judgment.

WITNESSED my hand and official seal hereto affixed the day and year in this certificate first above written.

                                        _____
                                        NOTARY PUBLIC in and for the State of
                                        Washington, residing at _____

STATE OF WASHINGTON   )
)   ss.
COUNTY OF _____   )

On this ___ day _____, 1997, before, me, the undersigned, a Notary Public in and for the State of Washington, duly commissioned and sworn, personally appeared JANET THOMPSON known to me to be the party that executed the foregoing Confession of Judgment, and acknowledged the said Confession of Judgment to be her free and voluntary act and deed for the uses and purposes therein mentioned, and on oath stated that she was authorized to execute the said Confession of Judgment.

WITNESSED my hand and official seal hereto affixed the day and year in this certificate first above written.

                                        _____
                                        NOTARY PUBLIC in and for the State of
                                        Washington, residing at _____

CONFESSION OF JUDGMENT—6

EXHIBIT 11   *(concluded)*

STATE OF WASHINGTON   )
)   ss.
COUNTY OF _____   )

On this ___ day _____, 1997, before me, the undersigned, a Notary Public in and for the State of Washington, duly commissioned and sworn, personally appeared _____, known to me to be the _____ of DRAGONFLY CORPORATION, the corporation that executed the foregoing Confession of Judgment, and acknowledged the said Confession of Judgment to be the free and voluntary act and deed of said corporation, for the uses and purposes therein mentioned, and on oath stated that he was authorized to execute the said Confession of Judgment and that the seal affixed (if any) is the corporate seal of said corporation.

WITNESSED my hand and official seal hereto affixed the day and year in this certificate first above written.

_____

NOTARY PUBLIC in and for the State of
Washington, residing at

_____

EXHIBIT 12

October 27, 1997

Mr. Andrew A. Savage, Esq.
2300 The Bank of California Center
Seattle, WA 98164

RE: DRAGONFLY CORPORATION
   Crossroads Shopping Center

Dear Andrew:

On October 8, 1997, we discussed Michael Thompson's and my meeting with Frank Murdock, Manager of Crossroads properties. On that date, we proposed that the Dragonfly Corporation continue to pay the accrued lease balance in monthly payments of $649.95 with the current lease payments to revert to the pre-percentage rent amount of approximately $2,300 per month.

As you are aware, the Thompsons have paid $875.00 a month on the past-due balance from February through July, at which time it was reduced to the $649.95 monthly installment. Payments were made without a note and without security.

As I informed you, my clients do not have property which they can pledge to secure the unpaid lease amounts accrued and I have advised them that no note should be necessary where all parties are basically going back to their pre-July agreement.

Mr. and Mrs. Thompson have access to additional financial support from their relatives and fully intend to weather the current economic downturn. They have made a great investment in their Dragonfly stores and are excellent managers. They will be around to complete payment of the Crossroads properties lease obligations.

On October 8, 1997, you informed me that you would be consulting with Frank Murdock and return to me with your response to our offer or alternative proposal. Please inform me of Mr. Murdock's response.

Very truly yours,

Jeff Lawrence

4–2

GORDON BIERSCH BREWING COMPANY

It was January 1992. The San Francisco restaurant was three months behind schedule and now was not expected to open until March 1992. As a result, it was consuming most of management's time. The duo had just finished the 1991 fiscal year and had reported revenues of over $5.9 million and net profit of over $570,000. Meanwhile, the two founders of Gordon Biersch Brewing Company, Dan Gordon and Dean Biersch, were determined to expand beyond their three existing restaurants in Palo Alto, San Jose, and San Francisco, and they were in the process of pursuing the funds to finance these plans. The plans had two parts: to engage in retail distribution of their Märzen and Export beers and to open more restaurant/breweries based on the same concept as their established restaurants. To them, these ideas seemed a logical extension of their success. Thus, their most pressing decision was not whether or not to pursue these plans. Instead, they wanted to know from whom they should obtain their financing and whether they had the appropriate organizational structure in place to accomplish their goals successfully.

Gordon and Biersch Meet

Gordon Biersch Brewing Company was the brainchild of two individuals, Dan Gordon and Dean Biersch, each of whom independently developed the concept of a microbrewery/restaurant in response to a 1983 change in California law. The

This case was prepared by L. A. Snedeker under the supervision of H. Irving Grousbeck. All figures have been disguised.

Development of this case was funded by the James G. Shennan (MBA '65) Teaching Fund.
Stanford Business School Case S-SB-130.

511

new law allowed the brewing and serving of beer in the same locale. The previous law had existed to regulate national brewers, as an enforcement of antitrust laws. The "three-tier laws" separated the producer, the distributor, and the retailer, dictating that businesses with liquor licenses could own no more than 10 percent of a brewery. When this changed in 1983, brewpubs started appearing. By 1991, brewpubs accounted for 25 percent of microbrewery production. Many of these microbrewery/restaurants emulated English pubs by serving heavy fried food like french fries and hamburgers, while offering recreation in the form of darts. Both Gordon and Biersch had a different idea.

Dan Gordon, a likable guy with a relaxed outward demeanor that belied his quick mind and acuity, grew up in Los Altos, California. As an economics major at U.C. Berkeley, Gordon spent his junior year as an exchange student in Germany, learning the language and immersing himself in the beer-drinking culture. He graduated the following year, 1982, and worked during the summer as a union laborer for Budweiser. He then returned to Germany to enter the Technical University of Munich. The university's brewing program was rigorous and intense, taught entirely in German and composed of courses in microbiology, chemistry, process engineering, and business. The entire program was five years long, and only 18 percent ultimately graduated. Gordon did, receiving his Dpl. Br. Ing. degree in 1987. This degree was considered the highest technical degree in brewing engineering. Moreover, Gordon was the first American to receive the degree in 30 years. Gordon returned the following summer with plans to open his own German brewery restaurant. He proceeded to write a business plan for a restaurant in Sunnyvale, California, to be known as Gordon's Beer Clinic.

Dean Biersch, a man with high energy and a flair for quality of life, grew up in Southern California. His career was structured around his attraction to food service and his desire to surf and ski. At 15, he began cooking burgers in the evenings to finance his athletic pursuits. After that, he worked as the manager of a liquor store while participating on his high school ski team. At Mammoth Mountain one day, he met a man who promised him a job if he moved up there. He did, but when he got there, he discovered there was in fact no job. Biersch had deferred his college plans, so he decided to stay anyway (since, after all, he could ski every day). Undeterred, he visited an employment agency that got him a job cooking in a little restaurant at night. This left his days free to ski, and he stayed there for a year. Next, at age 20, Biersch went to Portugal for a year to surf with some friends.

He then began college, San Francisco State University, from which he graduated in 1982 (at age 26) with a B.A. in international relations. During summers, between 1979 and 1982, he worked at the Beverly Hills Hilton, first as a server and then eventually as catering manager, maitre d', and office manager. From there, he worked as catering manager and food and beverage manager for Hornblower Yachts, Inc., in San Francisco. This company organized parties on cruises around the San Francisco Bay. While employed there, Biersch established management systems for the "City of San Francisco," a vessel in the Hornblower fleet, and was responsible for all of its food and beverage-related services.

Biersch's idea to combine a fine restaurant with a microbrewery dated back to 1983, when he and a girlfriend wrote a business plan for one in Mendocino, California. Despite his efforts to obtain financing, even attending a microbrewery convention on one occasion, he was unable to do it alone. A family friend, Robert Carrau, a very successful real estate developer, read a business plan from a different brewery/restaurant group and decided to pursue the idea with Biersch. Biersch left Hornblower to work with Carrau, and eight months later, in July of 1987, Biersch and Gordon met. The duo soon decided to enter into a partnership to bring their individual concepts to fruition as a team.

The Plan

That summer, the two budding entrepreneurs spent a week lying around the pool at Gordon's parents' home, discussing their ideas for the venture. They were encouraged to find that their ideas and vision were similar. Biersch's sister loaned them her Macintosh, and they proceeded to combine their two business plans. Gordon's sister's boyfriend, who had his own sophisticated Macintosh equipment, did the page layout. The conception of their partnership was simple: Dean Biersch had the food-service experience and thus would be responsible for conceiving and managing the restaurant half of the business, including running the day-to-day operations. Dan Gordon had the microbrewery experience and thus would be responsible for producing the beer. He also had more business education and thus could handle the financing and accounting issues. As one employee described (although later admitting it was a bit of a simplification), "Dan gets the money and Dean spends it." Each was happy to defer to the strengths of the other, and each half of the business—the restaurant and the beer—was viewed as equally important.

After completing their plan, they initially decided they needed $950,000 to begin the company. After getting some hard numbers, they increased their estimate to $1.1 million. They found that this funding was fairly easy to come by. Gordon's sister, one of the first employees at Silicon Graphics, introduced Dan to several of the founding engineers there. These four people, "beer freaks" by Gordon's description, were immediately interested in investing in the venture. Also interested was a founder of Oracle, a Dutch brewing colleague of Gordon's, a local physician, and Carrau (the largest stockholder). Together, they contributed $720,000 in equity. The ultimate capital needed proved to be about $1.12 million. Fortunately, Gordon and Biersch were able to obtain from Security Pacific a $400,000 line of credit, which Robert Carrau guaranteed. These funds allowed them to start their restaurant, to be known as Gordon Biersch.

The concept they envisioned was "to provide high quality, moderately priced dining and professional service in a lively atmosphere featuring exceptional German-style lagers in on-site breweries." The atmosphere—trendy but upscale—was meant to appeal as much to older generations as young. The distinguishing characteristics were Gordon Biersch's emphasis on fine dining and German beers. The nearest competition, the Tied House in Mountain View, California, was a good 10 miles away and served English ales in a decidedly casual atmosphere. (English ales used a less expensive production process with a different yeast strain and a different fermentation process.) (See **Exhibit 1** for an explanation of the brewing process.)

The brewing received just as much attention as the design of the restaurant. Gordon chose to brew and serve three lager beers. The three beers included the *Export,* a smooth beer light in color but not "light" in alcohol content; *Märzen,* an Oktoberfest style beer; and *Dunkles,* a malty, yeasty Bavarian dark beer. Because of the intricate nature of brewing and the pride Gordon took in his beer, Gordon Biersch espoused a philosophy of offering no other beers in its restaurant. This was a business strategy as well; they would base their identity on their premium, very high quality beers, and it made sense to effect a monopoly. They did, however, offer wine and a number of nonalcoholic beverages.

The Restaurant Realized

The next step for Gordon and Biersch was to locate the appropriate space. Location was crucial in the restaurant business, and they were able to find a good one. The site was two blocks from Palo Alto's University Avenue, a busy street with many restaurants, stores, and movie theaters. The surrounding area, although not as populated with foot traffic, contained a number of retail outfits and office buildings as well. The location in which Gordon Biersch opened had previously been used as a movie theater, the Bijou, and consisted of 5,200 square feet of floor space with 25-foot ceilings. Dean Biersch designed the restaurant to take advantage of the airy feeling within. For example, the dining area, although elevated a few feet above the bar section, was not separated by walls, and the entire space was visible to anyone in it. When the restaurant/brewery was filled with people, the effect was of a huge, boisterous party. Artwork by local artists adorned the walls. The brewery equipment was located in the back but was visible to the guests through glass windows. This was important, in order to establish Gordon Biersch's identity as a microbrewery. The restaurant and bar accommodated 185 people.

To set up his brewery, Gordon used some secondhand equipment that he had bought in his second year of graduate school in 1984 from a friend in Germany; the rest he bought new. The capacity of the brewery was 1,500 barrels per year (or 46,500 gallons per year). He didn't expect to use all of this capacity at first, until he observed the success of the Tied House, which had opened six months earlier. The food Biersch chose to serve was California cuisine, offering elaborate salads, entrees, and decadent desserts. (See **Exhibit 2** for a sample menu.) Meanwhile, delays caused by city hearings consumed four months, as the brewery/restaurant was considered controversial (due to noise and the potential odor). Ultimately, Gordon and Biersch obtained clearance for the project.

The target market was the fairly sophisticated Palo Alto population as well as the Stanford University faculty, staff, and graduate student body. This market appeared open to new concepts. For example, the members of this college town sustained several movie theaters featuring foreign and independent films, a number of health food restaurants, a multitude of coffeehouses, and a variety of frozen yogurt vendors. Certainly, Palo Alto had its share of mainstream eateries too: a Burger King, several Chinese and Japanese restaurants, and several pizza parlors (although many offered "gourmet" selections or a whole wheat crust). Within this market, Gordon Biersch opened in July of 1988.

The Opening

The restaurant was an immediate success. First-year sales were projected at $1.5 million, but actually topped $2.2 million. The following year's sales grew to $2.8 million. Sales stayed at that level during the next year as well, although pretax profit increased from 7 percent to 12 percent. (See **Exhibit 3** for Gordon Biersch Brewing Company financial statements.) The owners paid back their $300,000 loan in six months. The pair learned from their mistakes (they forgot to buy the soup spoons) and slowly began to assimilate this knowledge into a smooth-running operation. As expected, Gordon Biersch derived a larger percentage of its revenues from beverage sales (38 percent) than the restaurant industry average (22 percent). Their income before taxes was double the industry norm (11.3 percent versus 5.6 percent).

However, with a 90 percent failure rate in the industry, this may have been what it took to survive as a restaurant. The industry is very much focused on the moment of service; there is no second chance to "perform" (as Biersch described it). If a guest has a bad experience the first time around, there is little likelihood of return patronage. Thus, a significant expense of the business entails cultivating the appropriate image, in both subtle and overt ways. Upkeep of the physical space, including upgrades, accounts for 2 percent of sales in the industry, although at Gordon Biersch, it accounted for 2.5 percent. This upkeep includes replacing broken or pilfered items (the Gordon Biersch glasses were often stolen), laundering and replacing linens, and repairing and cleaning the physical plant. Employee turnover is another given in the restaurant industry. Servers and bussers tend to quit regularly, thus adding hiring and training costs. Gordon Biersch, however found its turnover quite low, as the restaurant soon came to be considered a desirable place to work.

Gordon Biersch encouraged repeat business by developing a core clientele. Gordon offered his regular guests a beer stein with his or her name on it and a polished wood locker in which to keep it. The duo kept their prices in a moderate range (entrees hovered between $10 and $15) and offered souvenir beer steins and T-shirts for sale. (These items accounted for less than 1 percent of revenue.) They advertised very little, focusing their attention on public relations and customer referrals to attract new business. These public relations efforts included sponsorship of charity events, attendance at local beer festivals, supplying free beer at Stanford parties, and participation in local alcohol safety campaigns. The partners aspired to an image of "gourmet without pretension," and it seemed to work.

They soon began thinking about expansion. Although San Jose was ultimately chosen as the location of the second restaurant, it was not their first choice. Indeed, Gordon later asserted, "If we had had to pay market rates for that location, we would never have built in San Jose." However, another brewery/restaurant in San Jose (Biers Brasserie) went bankrupt within six months, and the landlord, stuck with the facility, approached Gordon and Biersch with an offer to sell the $1.4 million of fixed assets for $400,000. The two decided to do it.

Expansion to San Jose

The location in San Jose was a 10,800-square-foot space. Despite the failure of the previous microbrewery/restaurant, Gordon and Biersch were confident they would succeed. They attributed the failure of Biers Brasserie to its high-priced menu and its decision to serve beers other than those brewed on the premises. This conclusion further reinforced Gordon Biersch's strategy to serve only its own beers and did nothing to discourage the owners from opening their second restaurant on the site. With $600,000 from internal cash flow and a line of credit, plus a landlord note of $350,000, they were able to lease the facility, make the necessary improvements, and open Gordon Biersch San Jose in April of 1990.

In opening a second restaurant, Gordon and Biersch were introduced to several new issues. One of these was city regulations, which vary from town to town; for instance, San Jose was considering a nonsmoking ordinance. San Jose itself was encouraging new business, however, and Gordon Biersch's decision to expand to the city was welcomed. As the *San Jose Mercury News* reported, "Gordon Biersch's arrival was hailed as a healthy sign that the city can attract glitzy restaurants to a downtown that has about 110 mostly low-profile eateries." The building they were in was a designated historical landmark within the city's downtown redevelopment zone. It was close to the Fairmont Hotel and the San Jose Convention Center.

The concept behind the second restaurant was almost identical to the first, with a few minor differences. The menu, although still the same California cuisine style, offered many new items. (See **Exhibit 4** for a sample menu.) The space was much bigger, with a second floor/loft and an outdoor garden area that featured jazz musicians six months a year. (Gordon plays trombone.) The capacity of the brewery was 2,400 barrels per year versus 1,500 per year in Palo Alto. With the establishment of the Tied House and Winchester Brewing Company in San Jose, the challenge of competition had been introduced to the market. However, according to Louis Jemison, the president of Redwood Coast Brewing Company (the Tied House's parent company), "Gordon Biersch is more of a fine dining experience. We are a beer hall and that's what we do." Similarly, Winchester Brewing Company offered simple finger foods and sandwiches.

The type of servers reflected the difference in the market demographics. Whereas patrons in Palo Alto consisted of the Stanford community and an upscale native population, San Jose's consisted of Silicon Valley professionals. Accordingly, the servers were "less pretentious," as one manager described, and more homey than those in Palo Alto. The restaurant also derived more of its revenues from corporate parties (both catered and on site) than in Palo Alto. For example, in the summer of 1991, San Jose Gordon Biersch hosted 60 events versus 30 in Palo Alto. The new facility became an immediate success: sales reached $3.1 million in the first year, more than twice the budgeted level.

Meanwhile, the partnership between Dan Gordon and Dean Biersch proceeded smoothly. Although the two spent little time together outside of the restaurant, their business relationship was a positive one according not only to the duo, but also to their employees. It thrived by nature of their distinct strengths and duties. Each had individual quirks, but because of respect for one another's expertise, tension was uncommon. For example, Gordon recalled, "During our first five months, we were cooped up together in an office the size of a closet, and honestly, we disagreed maybe once." Biersch, obviously, knew little about brewing and Gordon was unfamiliar with restaurant operations, so each stayed clear of the other's area of interest and expertise. The two communicated in weekly management meetings, which also included the general managers from the two restaurants and the director of operations, Mack Tilling. Tilling, a Stanford graduate in his late 20s, had joined Gordon Biersch in its first week as a server and had quickly assumed managerial duties as the restaurant grew. He was considered a crucial member of the senior management team. Decisions were made by all involved in the meetings, as Gordon and Biersch strove for informality, creativity, and decentralized decision making. Even disagreement was usually painless. As Gordon described:

> Sometimes Dean would want to make capital improvements to the restaurants, and I would feel there wasn't enough money to do it. I'd just tell him, "Dean, there's not enough money; we have to wait." And he'd say "OK, we'll wait."

Gordon remembered only a few occasions when miscommunication had caused problems:

> When we first opened, Jaime, our chef, asked me who was going to do the bookkeeping for the previous night's receipts. This took me by surprise; I figured we just made a deposit and that was that. I thought that Dean, with his restaurant experience, would know if we should be doing anything different. He didn't. So, after we figured that one out, we had to go get a bookkeeper in our first week.

Gordon continued:

> The worst it really gets is me saying, "I told you so." For instance, we had trouble getting delivery for some special Mexican tile for our San Francisco restaurant. Finally we got it, after waiting three months. Then, Dean wanted to order more tile from the same place for the area around the pizza oven. I warned him that they had screwed up delivery before, so it wouldn't be a good idea to reorder. But we went ahead, and sure enough now they can't deliver on time. So we have to find new tile before the opening.

The general observation among employees was that while they were two very different people, with individual personality quirks, the combination mixed well. The low rate of turnover attested to the fact that the staff was happy. As one server observed:

> The management will do anything to accommodate our schedules, and they respect our abilities. Our newest bartender has been here for 13 months! Although there's some turnover in the wait staff, it's because of going back to school or something, not because of a better job.

While Dan and Dean possessed the necessary individual skills to create and execute the Gordon Biersch concept, Mack Tilling was viewed as the "glue that held the restaurant together." By 1991, Tilling was responsible for day-to-day management of both restaurants; in fact, the general managers of each of the restaurants reported to him (see **Exhibit 5** for an organization chart). He had devoted himself to the business since the beginning, deferring his graduation with a B.A. from Stanford until 1990, at age 26. Employees found Mack to be very talented, hardworking, and intelligent. According to several, he straddled both the technical requirements of his job (he managed the computer systems) and administrative requirements quite well.

The two founders and Tilling spent most of their time at the Palo Alto restaurant or at their office across the street, with most of their communication with San Jose occurring at the weekly management meetings. Gordon kept on top of the San Jose brewery by means of faxes detailing daily production. This approach was in line with their decentralized philosophy; both Gordon and Biersch wished to encourage personal initiative. Compensation for management even included stock options, an unheard-of-benefit in the restaurant industry. (See **Exhibit 6** for equity distribution.)

By 1991, Gordon Biersch brewery/restaurants ranked as the first (San Jose) and fourth (Palo Alto) largest in the United States. An estimated 45,000 patrons entered Gordon Biersch's two restaurants each month. Furthermore, it was ranked as the best brewery restaurant in *Focus magazine* and one of the top 100 restaurants in California in *California* magazine. Thus, with the concept successfully replicated once, they began planning for the "big time."

San Francisco

San Francisco was considered the ultimate challenge for Gordon Biersch. The potential clientele was much more sophisticated even than Palo Alto and expected both style and exceptional food. With over 3,200 restaurants competing in the city, it would be difficult for a mediocre restaurant to stay in business. As Biersch saw it, "It's like moving from off Broadway to Broadway."

The restaurant was projected to require capital of $3.3 million, including developer contributions of $1.7 million. Gordon and Biersch were pleased with their location, 15,000 square feet on three levels in the Hills Brothers building. The facility was in a redeveloping area near the financial district; it also housed the headquarters of The Gap. Gordon and Biersch expected to get excellent lunchtime traffic in that location.

The competition would be intense, although again, Gordon and Biersch felt there were no other restaurant/microbreweries with quite the same concept as theirs. The most successful of the already-established brewpubs was 20 Tank. 20 Tank was described in the *Guide to the Good Life at Stanford* (a student guide to the Bay Area published in 1991) as follows:

> This newcomer to SoMa [the South of Market area of San Francisco, known for its trendy clubs and funky nighttime inhabitants] has quickly become a hot spot for singles and all variety of trendily garbed San Franciscans (if you're lucky you might see one particularly stylish patron who sports waist-length dreadlocks and a black leather biker's outfit). The interior recalls an ancient beer hall, complete with saw-dusted floor, tin ceiling, and dark, Teutonic tables and chairs. Sandwiches are cheap and excellent, and the handcrafted brews are so enthusiastically appreciated by the crowd that the bartender sometimes runs out of glasses.

Another well-known brewpub was the San Francisco Brewing Company, which featured a menu of very simple fare: hamburgers, fries, and club sandwiches in a pub-like atmosphere; however, it did a low-volume business. Furthermore, Gordon and Biersch felt that their success in the South Bay would produce favorable word-of-mouth publicity.

In order to minimize risk, Gordon and Biersch moved the general manager of the Palo Alto restaurant to San Francisco. Tilling, too, planned to devote his energies to the opening and indeed hoped to move into the city to avoid a 45-minute commute from Palo Alto.

Despite the frenzied activity that preceded the opening (now delayed until March 1992), they were confident of their concept. They planned to replicate it once more by the end of 1993, in Pasadena, California, and again in 1994, in San Diego. The Pasadena site had already been selected, located on Colorado Boulevard in the heart of the city. They planned to build a 180-seat brewery restaurant at a cost of $1.5 million. First full-year revenues were expected to be $3.2 million. Gordon and Biersch intended to expand into several metropolitan areas of the western United States in the coming five years. (See **Exhibit 7** for pro forma income statements.)

The Wheels Keep Spinning

Meanwhile, Gordon and Biersch continued to generate new ideas for expanding their business. One obvious thought was to leverage the local reputation of their beer by bottling it for retail distribution to restaurants, grocery stores, liquor stores, and bars in the San Francisco Bay Area. Outside the northern California market, Gordon and Biersch planned to first establish one or more brewery restaurants, then follow with retail distribution. The brewery restaurants would introduce the consumer to the company's beers, creating brand awareness and spurring retail demand. The retail demand, in turn, would reinforce the consumer's decision to frequent the Gordon Biersch brewery restaurants. They believed this integrated approach would create marketing synergy through strengthening brand awareness and increasing demand for the restaurants and retail beers. Any surplus beer would be used in the brewery restaurants, which sometimes could not keep up with customer demand.

Bottling and retail distribution would present a number of challenges. For one, it would be run entirely by Gordon; Biersch would not be involved managerially. Gordon did not know how much of his time the new brewery would take and whether too much of his attention would be diverted from the restaurants. However, because Gordon and Biersch had espoused a management style of decentralization, lessened involvement might not be a problem. As far as the product itself, the most obvious difference would be the freshness of the beer. Bottled beer would never taste as good as that served fresh from the keg, but Gordon had made provisions to optimize the flavor by imposing on his retailers a maximum shelf life approximately three months.

Perhaps the most exciting challenge was the head-to-head competition (no pun intended) with other microbreweries and other premium beers.[1] Northern California was considered a key geographic market for microbrewed specialty beer, growing 22 percent between 1990 and 1991. (Microbreweries were defined as those with production of less than 35,000 barrels per year.) The total northern California market in 1991 was approximately 181,500 barrels of beer. Three manufacturers comprised the bulk of the market: Anchor Brewing Company, Boston Brewing Co. (Samuel Adams beer), and Sierra Nevada Brewing Co., which together owned 68 percent of the market. (Anchor and Boston Brewing technically brewed more than 35,000 barrels per year, but they competed in the target market.) Pete's Brewing Co., Mendocino Brewing Co. (Redtail Ale), and Redhook Brewing Co. accounted for 22 percent of the total market. Nevertheless, Gordon felt that he would be able to capture 11 percent of the market by 1996. (See **Exhibit 8** for U.S. brewing industry market analysis.)

There were several options for distribution: through a master distributor, direct to the distribution network, direct to retailers, or through a wine/spirits distributor. *Master distributors* provided warehousing, transportation, and sales/distributors management. In particular, the master distributor would manage relationships with the distribution network (approximately 10 distributors, given Gordon Biersch's expected production level of 22,000 barrels). A prime benefit of this arrangement was that Gordon Biersch would not have to worry about receivables; it would simply be issued one check per month. In exchange, the master distributor received a fee of 3 to 5 percent of cost. Additionally, Gordon Biersch would be responsible for creating customer "pull" and providing profit incentives for the master distributors. If Gordon Biersch chose to bypass the master distributor and market directly to the distributors, each one would be required to hold two to three weeks of inventory (as opposed to one to two days). This option,

---

[1]The author is indebted to a project by Peter Cooley, Barry Eggers, Omid Kordestani, and Wini Welch (all Stanford MBA class of 1991) for much of the industry information on retail distribution.

however, would allow Gordon Biersch to maintain more control over sales and distribution, since the brewer would be in direct contact with the people who actually supplied the beer to the retail stores. A third option would be to market beyond the distribution network directly to the *retailers* (bars, liquor stores, restaurants, and grocery stores), but the complexity of dealing with a large number of retailers made it economically infeasible for a microbrewery. The final option would be to go through a *wine/spirits distributor or a major brand network.* These distributors offered excellent retail penetration, but since they carried several brands, their ability to devote attention to Gordon Biersch would be questionable. Furthermore, a wine/spirits distributor might not have the appropriate expertise in beer. With a major brand network (e.g., Budweiser), Gordon Biersch faced the distinct possibility of conflict of interest and a resulting lack of attention.

Gordon planned to market the product as a superpremium microbrewed beer. A six-pack of 12-ounce bottles would retail for about $6.50. This would place Gordon Biersch beer in the same price range as Anchor Steam, Samuel Adams, and Sierra Nevada. A 6-pack retailing at $6.50 assumed that Gordon Biersch would sell it at $3.81 (or $15.26 per case), with a 5 percent markup for the master distributor, 30 percent for the distributor, and a retail markup of approximately 25 percent. Gordon planned to structure his pricing so the final retail price would be competitive in the target market.

In July of 1991, Gordon Biersch had been contacted by Markstein Companies, who offered to act as master distributor. Markstein also distributed Miller beer and several imports (e.g., Corona and EKU). However, Gordon Biersch would be its only microbrewed beer. In return, Markstein would receive a 5 percent fee based on the wholesale price (e.g., $0.76 on a $15.26 case). Gordon had made no decision as of December of 1991.

Meanwhile, Gordon had signed a letter of intent with the property owners for the option to lease 30,000 square feet of production space at the former San Martin Winery facility. Of note, the property owners included the San Jose restaurant's landlord, with whom Gordon and Biersch had a good relationship. Even better, construction costs for the site would be minimized since the facility had previously been used as a winery. For example, the refrigeration warehouse would be ideal for fermentation. Gordon planned a capacity of 100,000 barrels per year, with an expectation of brewing 22,000 barrels in the first year. He would divide this evenly between the Märzen and the Export beers, varying the mix as time went on to satisfy customer demand.

The project would require an investment of $3.75 million: $2.5 million for brewing equipment and $1.25 million for preopening expenses and initial inventory. Gordon hoped to be able to have his brewery in operation by early 1994. (See **Exhibit 9** for pro forma income statements.)

Financing

Gordon and Biersch were seeking $5.5 million (the rest would come from developer contributions) and were considering three alternatives for financing.

(See **Exhibit 10** for pro forma income statements for the entire expansion.) The first was a venture capital firm in the northern California area. Gordon Biersch would benefit from the management experience of the firm, and its proximity would ease communication.

The second alternative was a French investment banking concern. Although it offered an attractive entrance into international distribution (Asahi beer in Japan would handle Japanese distribution, for example), its European location might create communication problems. On the other hand, it might allow Gordon and Biersch to operate more freely.

The final option was to try to finance the expansion entirely from cash flow. This would require the plans to proceed much more slowly, but would allow Gordon Biersch to retain control over both the equity and the expansion plans. Because the San Francisco restaurant had consumed much of management's time, no solid deals had been negotiated. Along with these options, too, Gordon Biersch had "expressions of interest" from friends and associates totaling $500,000.

The expansion would require not only financing, but also hiring a number of new people. Key personnel would include a development director, responsible for site development, and a chief financial officer. In late 1991, Gordon Biersch employed 85 full-time and 95 part-time employees and expected to hire 50 to 70 full-time-equivalent employees as each new restaurant opened. Fifteen people (11 full-time and 4 part-time) would be hired for the brewery. (See **Exhibit 11** for a postexpansion organization chart.)

Conclusion

Gordon Biersch's hope was to increase revenues to over $54 million annually by 1997, with operating earnings before interest and taxes of over $7.8 million. At that point, according to Gordon, they could reach "Phase 3," which would include either going public or selling to a larger brewery or food/restaurant group.

Although they were excited about these prospects, they were consumed with preparations for the San Francisco opening. By mid-1992, they hoped to turn their attention back to the broader expansion plans and carefully consider the financing options available to them. They were confident that they would be successful in these new efforts. Gordon and Biersch had worked hard to ensure that the present restaurants could be operated independently by encouraging decentralized management. This self-sufficiency would be crucial in the coming years, as the founders' attentions became further dispersed.

Certainly, the growth they anticipated would put to the test their organizational theories.

EXHIBIT 1   Brewing Beer

The process of making beer is complicated, involving six exacting processes—milling, mashing, lautering, boiling, fermenting, and filtering—and four ingredients—malted barley, hops, yeast, and water.

Each ingredient serves an important function. Malted barley allows the yeast to metabolize, which in turn ferments the beer by converting the carbohydrates into alcohol. There are hundreds of different yeast strains, each one imparting a different flavor on the finished beer. Hops give beer its slightly bitter flavor, without which beer would taste sweet. Water is used throughout the brewing process and needs to be of drinking quality.

The first step of brewing is *milling* the malted barley to an appropriate degree of fineness. After milling is completed, *mashing* converts the carbohydrates and proteins in the malt to simple sugars and amino acids. Mashing begins when the malt is mixed with warm water. The mixture is then gradually taken to temperature levels that activate specific enzymes. Typically, the brewer will take the mixture to a given temperature level (e.g., 62 degrees Celsius) and hold it there for a specific length of time (e.g., 30 minutes), and then proceed to the next higher temperature level, holding again for a specific period of time. This routine proceeds until the mashing is completed and all enzyme groups have been activated. This usually takes about three hours. From there, the substance is pumped to a lauter tun for *lautering*. Lautering is a two-step process, consisting of the first run-off (*Vorderwürze* in German) and three rounds of sparging (defined below). The lauter tun contains a sieve, through which the mashing liquid is drained into pipes leading to a wort receiver. (This liquid extract is called "wort.") This process of draining is the *Vorderwürze*. When the top of the grain bed is dry, the solid matter is "sparged" with hot water, and the water is allowed to flow through the grain bed and into the wort receiver. This is repeated for a total of three times, with the amount of liquid used for sparging equalling the amount of water used for mashing. The process is not unlike brewing coffee through a filter.

After the liquid from the *Vorderwürze* and the sparging is all collected in the wort receiver, the wort is *boiled*. The hops are added during the process. Hops are of two primary types: bitter and aroma hops. Usually, bitter hops are added at the beginning of the boil, aroma hops at the end. However, Gordon used imported aroma hops at the beginning of the boil, a more expensive process. The boiling process serves several functions, including sterilizing the product, increasing the concentration of the extract to its desired level through evaporation, and coagulating the protein. The wort is boiled for 100 to 120 minutes, depending on the desired final extract concentration.

From there, the hopped wort is pumped into a tank called the whirlpool. In the whirlpool, the sediment from the coagulated protein and the hop particles is allowed to settle at the bottom of the tank. This takes about 25 minutes. The clear hot wort is then fed into the heat exchanger, where the wort is cooled to 6 degrees Celsius. Exiting the heat exchanger, the cold hopped wort is injected with sterile air, which allows the yeast to reproduce. The wort is then pumped into a yeast-lined flotation tank; the turbulence from pumping allows the yeast to blend with the wort.

The beer sits in the flotation tank for 8 to 12 hours, allowing the "cold break" to rise to the top of the tank. This "cold break" is removed, as it leads to an unnatural bitterness and harsh flavor. The beer is then pumped to the fermentation tank. The goal of fermentation is to convert the sugars to ethyl-alcohol and carbon dioxide. Temperature control during fermentation is vital. Lagers ferment best at 9 degrees Celsius. Colder temperatures inhibit the yeast from fermenting; higher temperatures cause the yeast to "sweat," producing undesirable compounds that either affect the taste or result in a higher likelihood of headaches and hangovers. At the end of the primary fermentation, the yeast sinks to the bottom and is removed, although some yeast cells remain suspended in the beer. Next, the fermentation tank is chilled to 4 degrees Celsius. The secondary fermentation, which makes use of these yeast cells, produces carbon dioxide in the beer to absorb or break down chemicals produced during the primary fermentation that adversely affect the flavor of the beer. At least four weeks total is required for proper aging.

Finally, the beer is *filtered* to remove any yeast that hasn't settled during the fermenting process. This is accomplished with sheets of cellulose or metal that are coated with diatomaceous earth. The beer is then ready for packaging and consumption.

EXHIBIT 2   Sample Menu, Palo Alto

LUNCH MENU

APPETIZERS

QUESADILLA OF BBQ CHICKEN AND CHEDDAR CHEESE
WITH AVOCADO SALSA, SOUR CREAM AND ROASTED RED BELL PEPPER 5.95
QUICKLY FRIED CALAMARI TOSSED WITH FRESH GARLIC, LEMON AND PARSLEY 5.75
GRILLED PRAWN SKEWERS WITH SPICY CORAL ISLAND SAUCE 7.95
BAVARIAN PLATE OF ASSORTED SLICED MEATS AND CHEESE 8.50
THAI CHICKEN SKEWERS WITH SPICY PEANUT SAUCE 4.95
MAUI ONION RINGS 3.75
GARLIC FRIES 2.50

SANDWICHES

CHEESE BURGER WITH GARLIC FRIES 6.50
WITH GRILLED ONIONS AND MUSHROOMS ADD .75
PASTRAMI WITH GRILLED ONIONS, MUENSTER CHEESE AND DIJON 6.95
GRILLED CHICKEN BREAST WITH PROSCIUTTO AND PROVOLONE ON SOURDOUGH 6.50
CALIFORNIA RIBEYE CHEESESTEAK WITH RED ONION, GUACAMOLE AND JACK CHEESE 7.50
MESQUITE SMOKED TURKEY CLUB WITH APPLEWOOD BACON ON 9-GRAIN TOAST 6.95
BUFFALO MOZZARELLA, TOMATO, BASIL AND GRILLED EGGPLANT
WITH GAETA OLIVE AIOLI ON SWEET FRENCH BREAD 5.95

SALADS

HOUSE SALAD WITH BALSAMIC VINAIGRETTE 3.75 WITH DANISH BLUE CHEESE 4.50
CHICKEN BREAST WITH BLUE CHEESE, WALNUTS, APPLE AND CREAMY VINAIGRETTE 8.95
SPICY SESAME BEEF SALAD WITH A SESAME-SOY DRESSING, OVER A BED OF MIXED GREENS
TOPPED WITH SHREDDED CUCUMBER, CARROT, RADISH AND GREEN ONIONS 7.95
SOUTHWEST MARINATED CHICKEN WITH BELL PEPPER, RED ONION, TOMATO, CILANTRO,
GUACAMOLE AND SOUR CREAM OVER MIX GREENS WITH TOASTED TORTILLA CHIPS 7.95
POACHED SALMON OVER MIX GREENS WITH TOMATO, RED ONION, GAETA OLIVES
AND LEMON WITH A RASPBERRY-WALNUT VINAIGRETTE 9.50
CAESAR SALAD WITH GARLIC CROUTONS AND PARMESAN CHEESE 7.50

ENTREES

BAKED PASILLA PEPPERS STUFFED WITH CHICKEN, RICE AND
JALAPENO JACK CHEESE SERVED OVER A BED
OF RICE, BLACK BEANS AND CURRY SAUCE AND GARNISHED WITH ROASTED RED PEPPERS 7.95
WARM SPINACH WITH PINEAPPLE, OYSTER MUSHROOMS, RED BELL PEPPERS, RED ONION
AND TOASTED MACADAMIA NUTS IN GINGER-SCALLION DRESSING OVER TOMATO LINGUINE 9.95
SAUTEED GARLIC-FENNEL SAUSAGE WITH BELL PEPPERS AND MUSHROOMS
TOSSED WITH A TOMATO-BASIL PESTO SAUCE OVER LINGUINE 9.95
GRILLED CHICKEN BREAST WITH A FETA CHEESE, ARTICHOKE
HEART, TOMATO AND DILL SAUCE 10.95
PENNE PASTA WITH SAUTEED MUSHROOMS, TOMATOES, BASIL,
GARLIC, OLIVE OIL AND GOAT CHEESE 8.95
CHEESE TORTELLINI WITH PROSCIUTTO, MUSHROOMS AND
BABY SPINACH IN A LEMON BUTTER SAUCE 9.95
FILET MIGNON OVER SPINACH, MUSHROOMS AND
SAUTEED ONIONS WITH GORGONZOLA SAUCE 15.95
SAUTEED BABY SCALLOPS, TIGER PRAWNS, RED PEPPERS, MUSHROOMS AND SCALLIONS
WITH INDONESIAN RED CURRY OVER BLACK FETTUCINE 13.95

DESSERTS

CHOCOLATE PECAN TART WITH FRENCH VANILLA ICE CREAM 4.50
FLORENTINE ICE CREAM SANDWICH WITH JAMOCA ALMOND FUDGE ICE CREAM 4.50
IRISH CREAM TRIFLE WITH LADYFINGERS, FRESH
BERRIES, MASCARPONE, AND CREME ANGLAISE 4.95
FUDGE BROWNIE SUNDAE WITH WHITE CHOCOLATE CHIPS,
MACADAMIA NUTS AND CARAMEL SAUCE 4.50
HAZELNUT CHEESECAKE IN A CHOCOLATE CRUMB CRUST WITH A FRANGELICO SAUCE 4.95

EXHIBIT 3

PALO ALTO AND SAN JOSE
Income Statements
(Year ended November 30)

	1988[a]	1989	1990[b]	1991
Revenues	$719,608	$2,406,770	$4,986,310	$5,926,907
Cost of sales	392,329	1,386,158	3,023,001	3,180,666
Gross profit	327,279	1,020,612	1,963,309	2,746,241
General and administrative expenses	215,297	666,642	1,470,276	1,971,328
Net operating income	111,982	353,970	493,033	774,913
Depreciation	34,982	90,738	110,184	138,503
Interest expense	0	104,541	35,971	50,621
Profit before tax	$ 77,000	$ 158,691	$ 346,878	$ 585,789
Provision for income taxes[c]	15,943	55,500	59,293	12,000
Net income	$ 61,057	$ 103,191	$ 287,585	$ 573,789

[a]Includes five months of operations.
[b]San Jose restaurant opened in April 1990.
[c]Gordon Biersch was incorporated as a C corporation from 1988–1990 and changed to an S corporation in 1991.

EXHIBIT 3   *(continued)*

PALO ALTO AND SAN JOSE
Balance Sheets
(Year ended November 30)

	1988	1989	1990	1991
Assets				
Current assets				
Cash	$ 36,930	$ 0	$ 0	$ 51,106
Accounts receivable	14,759	38,148	41,193	26,354
Inventory	21,777	42,774	104,640	135,109
Prepaid expenses	12,225	14,379	50,342	78,912
Employee receivables	0	4,552	15,109	12,787
Receivable from ltd. partnership	0	0	63,967	0
Total current assets	$ 85,691	$ 99,853	$ 275,251	$ 304,268
Fixed assets				
Leasehold improvements	413,713	479,734	798,509	892,926
Furniture, fixtures, and equipment	226,881	403,909	586,178	634,623
Brewing equipment	233,046	250,863	444,218	462,285
Automobiles	37,661	22,862	24,612	37,930
Total fixed assets	911,301	1,157,368	1,853,517	2,027,764
Less: accumulated depreciation	(35,235)	(124,381)	(239,418)	(409,941)
Net fixed assets	$ 876,066	$1,032,987	$1,614,099	$1,617,823
Other assets				
Start-up costs	172,144	172,144	172,144	172,144
Less: accumulated amortization	(14,345)	(48,774)	(83,203)	(117,632)
Receivables from ltd. partnership	0	0	88,828	550,427
Net other assets	$ 157,799	$ 123,370	$ 177,769	$ 604,939
Total assets	$1,119,556	$1,256,210	$2,067,119	$2,527,030

EXHIBIT 3   *(concluded)*

PALO ALTO AND SAN JOSE
Balance Sheets
(Year ended November 30)

	1988	1989	1990	1991
Liabilities and stockholders' equity				
Current liabilities				
Bank overdraft	$ 0	$ 743	$ 0	$ 0
Accounts payable	1,108	60,525	338,615	256,398
Accrued liabilities	0	0	0	154,173
Interest payable	2,879	109,161	0	0
Payroll and sales tax payable	13,570	24,483	146,145	0
Income taxes payable	11,963	8,800	59,610	10,000
Bank line of credit	303,789	106,326	300,961	100,837
Current portion of notes payable	0	4,891	7,414	121,085
Note payable-stockholder	0	0	116,000	0
Total current liabilities	$ 333,309	$ 314,929	$ 968,745	$ 642,493
Notes payable—less amounts classified as current deferred taxes	0	57,452	52,531	264,905
	3,980	25,571	0	0
Total liabilities	$ 337,289	$ 397,952	$1,021,276	$ 907,398
Stockholders' equity				
Subordinated debentures[a]	720,000	720,000	0	0
Common stock[bcd]	100	100	620,100	620,100
Retained earnings	62,167	138,158	425,743	999,532
Total stockholders' equity	$ 782,267	$ 858,258	$1,045,843	$1,619,632
Total liabilities and stockholders' equity	$1,119,556	$1,256,210	$2,067,119	$2,527,030

[a]Subordinated debentures redeemed for common stock in 1990.

[b]1 for 100 stock split in 1989.

[c]In 1989, 1,000,000 shares of no par value common stock authorized, 90,000 shares issued and outstanding.

[d]In 1990, 1,000,000 shares of no par value common stock authorized, 167,500 shares issued and outstanding.

EXHIBIT 4   Sample Menu, San Jose

APPETIZERS

THAI CHICKEN WITH SPICY PEANUT SAUCE 4.95
GRILLED JERK PRAWNS WITH SPICY HONEY MUSTARD 7.95
QUICKLY FRIED CALAMARI TOSSED WITH FRESH GARLIC, LEMON AND PARSLEY 5.75
HAWAIIAN AHI CARPACCIO WITH TAMARI GLAZE AND EXTRA VIRGIN OLIVE OIL 6.95
BAVARIAN PLATE OF ASSORTED SLICED SAUSAGES, MEATS AND CHEESE 8.50
SMOKED SALMON QUESADILLA WITH CREAM CHEESE,
SAUTEED ONIONS AND BLACK BEAN SALSA 7.50
GARLIC FRIES 2.50

SANDWICHES

CHEESEBURGER WITH GARLIC FRIES 6.50
SPICY BBQ CHICKEN SANDWICH WITH GRUYERE CHEESE ON WHOLE WHEAT 6.95
NEW YORK STEAK SANDWICH WITH CARMELIZED RED ONIONS, HORSERADISH AND SAGE 7.95
MESQUITE SMOKED TURKEY WITH TOMATO, BACON AND GUACAMOLE 6.50

INDIVIDUAL PIZZAS

PROSCIUTTO, GOAT CHEESE, THYME AND OREGANO 7.95
MARINATED ARTICHOKES, GORGONZOLA, JULIENNE VEGETABLES AND MARINARI 7.50
HUNTERS SAUSAGE, LINGUICA, SAUTEED PEPPERS AND SMOKED GOUDA 8.25
CHORIZO, TOMATILLO, MASCARPONE, JALAPENO AND CILANTRO 7.75
FRESH TOMATO, FONTINA, MOZZARELLA, FETA AND BASIL 6.25

SALADS

HOUSE SALAD WITH MUSTARD VINAIGRETTE 4.00 WITH DANISH BLUE CHEESE 4.50
GREEK SALAD WITH FETA, CALAMATA OLIVES, CUCUMBER, TOMATO AND ONIONS 7.95
NICOISE SALAD WITH FRESH TUNA AND A GINGER-TAMARI GLAZE 8.95
SMOKED DUCK OVER MIXED GREENS IN LIGHT SESAME VINAIGRETTE
WITH PAPAYA, BLACK PLUMS, RED ONIONS AND MANDARIN ORANGES 9.95
CAESAR STYLE SALAD WITH FRESH BAY SHRIMP AND CROUTONS 8.95

ENTREES

LOBSTER ENCHILADAS WITH JALAPENO JACK AND FONTINA OVER PAINTED RED BEANS
WITH SALSA FRESCA, TOMATILLO SALSA WITH BASMATI RICE 13.95
TORTELLONI CARBONARA WITH PANCETTA, PEAS, CRACKED BLACK PEPPER AND CREAM 12.95
SINGAPORE STYLE VERMICELLI WITH SHRIMP, PROSCUITTO,
PEPPERS AND BERMUDA ONIONS 13.95
GRILLED CHICKEN BREAST WITH CHIPOTLE, CORN SAUCE,
BLACK BEAN CHILI AND GUACAMOLE 11.95
LEMON BASIL LINGUINE WITH SHITAKE MUSHROOMS, SUN-DRIED AND
YELLOW TOMATOES WITH BALSAMIC VINEGAR AND OLIVE OIL 9.95
BEEF, GINGER, AND ORANGE STIRFRY WITH LEEKS, PEPPERS
AND RED CABBAGE OVER BASMATI RICE 12.95
MEDALLIONS OF FILET MIGNON WITH PRESERVED
MUSHROOM AND PORT SAUCE, TEMPURA EGGPLANT,
AND HERB ROASTED POTATOES 15.95
SEAFOOD AND SAUSAGE ETOUFFEE WITH FLORIDA SCALLOPS, PRAWNS, ONIONS AND PEPPERS,
ENGULFED IN CLAMS AND MUSSELS OVER BASMATI RICE 14.95
CHICKEN BREAST SA-TE WITH PEANUTS, COCONUT MILK, SUGAR
SNAPS AND PEPPERS OVER BASMATI RICE 12.95
MARINATED FLANK STEAK OVER BLACK BEANS WITH ROASTED
TOMATILLO SALSA, SOUR CREAM AND FLOUR TORTILLAS 12.95

DESSERTS

CHOCOLATE DECADENCE WITH RASPBERRY SAUCE 3.95
FLORENTINE ICE CREAM SANDWICH WITH JAMOCA ALMOND FUDGE 4.50
FRUIT CRISP WITH APPLES, PEACHES, PEARS AND FRENCH VANILLA ICE CREAM 4.50
CHOCOLATE, PECAN TORTE WITH FRENCH VANILLA ICE CREAM 4.50
THREE-LAYER MUD PIE WITH OREO COOKIE CRUST 4.95
FRESH FRUIT CHEESECAKE 4.25

Exhibit 5 **Organization Chart (October 1991)**

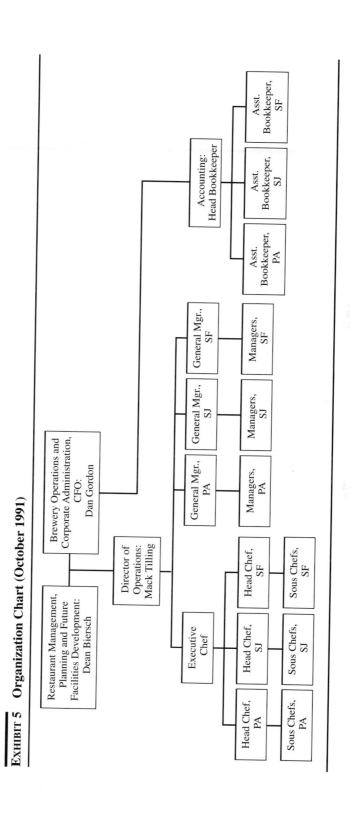

EXHIBIT 6   Equity Distribution

Investor	Shares	Percentage of Shares Issued	Options	Percentage of Fully Diluted Ownership
Dean Biersch	40,500	24.18%	5,000	22.91%
Dan Gordon	40,500	24.18%	5,000	22.91%
Executive chef	0	0.00%	3,524	1.77%
Head chef, San Jose	0	0.00%	2,114	1.06%
Head brewer, San Jose	0	0.00%	1,762	0.89%
General manager, San Jose	0	0.00%	1,762	0.89%
General manager, Palo Alto	0	0.00%	1,762	0.89%
Mack Tilling	0	0.00%	10,180	5.13%
#1	35,714	21.32%	0	17.98%
#2	12,500	7.46%	0	6.29%
#3	12,500	7.46%	0	6.29%
#4	3,518	2.10%	0	1.77%
#5	3,518	2.10%	0	1.77%
#6	3,125	1.87%	0	1.57%
#7	3,125	1.87%	0	1.57%
#8	3,125	1.87%	0	1.57%
#9	3,125	1.87%	0	1.57%
#10	3,125	1.87%	0	1.57%
#11	834	0.50%	0	0.42%
#12	833	0.50%	0	0.42%
#13	833	0.50%	0	0.42%
#14	625	0.37%	0	0.31%
Subtotal	167,500		31,104	
Total shares allocated	198,604			

EXHIBIT 7

NEW RESTAURANT OPERATIONS
Pro Forma Income Statements
(Years ended November 30)

	1993	1994	1995	1996	1997
Revenues	$1,067,000	$4,800,000	$9,600,000	$16,000,000	$24,800,000
Cost of sales	576,180	2,592,000	5,184,000	8,640,000	13,392,000
Gross profit	490,820	2,208,000	4,416,000	7,360,000	11,408,000
General and administrative expenses	317,820	1,321,000	2,550,000	4,176,000	6,385,000
Net operating profit	173,000	887,000	1,866,000	3,184,000	5,023,000
Depreciation	50,000	225,000	450,000	750,000	1,163,000
Interest expense	0	0	0	0	0
Profit before tax	$ 123,000	$ 662,000	$1,416,000	$ 2,434,000	$ 3,860,000
Provision for income taxes	43,050	231,700	495,600	851,900	1,351,000
Net profit	$ 79,950	$ 430,300	$ 920,400	$ 1,582,100	$ 2,509,000

Total number of restaurants (year end)	4	5	7	9	12
Number of operating months—new units	4	18	36	60	93

EXHIBIT 8   U.S. Brewing Industry

Total U.S. beer sales were 188.5 million barrels in 1991. Overall, beer production in the U.S. has increased 1 to 3% annually over the last several years, but declined by about 2% in 1991. The decline is attributed primarily to the increase in federal excise tax enacted in 1991. The U.S. brewing industry is comprised of three types of manufacturers: major national breweries, regional breweries, and microbreweries (defined as breweries with production less than 35,000 barrels per year). The majors account for approximately 94% for all production in the United States. Economies of scale in advertising, production and distribution have benefited the national breweries at the expense of the regional producers, whose output has dropped at rates of 15 to 20% per year. Chapter 11 filings have plagued the regionals, which currently account for 6% of production. Several regional breweries, in order to use excess capacity, also produce specialty brands under contract. Examples of contract brewed brands include Samuel Adams and Pete's Wicked Ale. Microbreweries account for only 0.4% of total production but are the fastest growing segment of the beer industry. During the last four years, microbrewery sales have increased 35 to 40% annually. As the larger microbrewers such as Sierra Nevada and Anchor increase output and geographic distribution, the differences between regional brewers and microbrewers are becoming less distinct. As a result, brewers are better defined by beer styles and price positioning of their brands. Specialty brewers are defined as those marketing high quality, full-bodied ales or lagers priced higher than mass-market brands.

Imports, which enjoyed double-digit growth in the United States during the late 1970s and early 1980s, have more recently faced flat sales growth and saw a 7.6% decline in 1991. Importers attribute the decline to increased excise taxes and competition from U.S. specialty brands. Although imports currently account for only 4% of all beer sold in the United States, they account for nearly 30% of beer consumed in restaurants and bars. Similarly, domestic specialty beer sales account for greater restaurant and bar sales than are represented by total market sales. Fifty-four percent of microbrewery production is sold at bars and restaurants.

The substantial growth in the specialty beer segment has been fueled by an increase in the number of new breweries. Between 1988 and 1991, the number of microbreweries and brewpubs grew from 123 to over 250. Although microbreweries face higher production costs than large brewers, their beers command a premium price. In addition, microbreweries enjoy favorable tax considerations compared to large brewers. Microbrewers pay $7 per barrel for the first 60,000 barrels produced, compared to $18 per barrel paid by large brewers.

Microbreweries are segmented into brewpubs and micros. Brewpubs sell beer for on-premises consumption, typically provide food, and generally produce less than 4,000 barrels per year. Brewpubs, which significantly outnumber micros, account for 25% of microbrewery production. Micros bottle or keg beer primarily for off-premises consumption and produce from 2,000 to 35,000 barrels or more per year. On average, micros keg 54% of their production and bottle the remaining 46%.

EXHIBIT 9

BREWERY PROJECT
Pro Forma Income Statements
(Years ended November 30)

	1993	1994	1995	1996	1997
Revenues	$0	$4,408,477	$8,870,286	$13,772,093	$18,218,733
Cost of sales	0	2,465,628	4,793,488	7,490,036	10,000,119
Gross profit	0	1,942,849	4,076,798	6,282,057	8,218,614
General and administrative expenses	0	1,059,607	1,768,611	2,670,541	3,459,315
Net operating profit	0	883,242	2,308,187	3,611,516	4,759,299
Depreciation	0	310,431	310,431	327,098	343,764
Interest expense	0	0	0	0	0
Profit before tax	0	$ 572,811	$1,997,756	$ 3,284,418	$ 4,415,535
Provision for income taxes	0	200,484	699,215	1,149,546	1,545,437
Net profit	$0	$ 372,327	$1,298,541	$ 2,134,872	$ 2,870,098

EXHIBIT 10

ALL OPERATIONS
Pro Forma Income Statements
(Years ended November 30)

	1992	1993	1994	1995	1996	1997
Revenues	$9,021,000	$11,767,000	$20,176,000	$29,712,000	$41,239,000	$54,715,000
Cost of sales	4,871,340	6,354,180	10,979,808	16,048,168	22,322,216	29,707,959
Gross profit	4,149,660	5,412,820	9,196,192	13,663,832	18,916,784	25,007,041
General and administrative expenses	3,061,660	3,939,820	6,276,192	8,489,832	11,346,784	14,799,041
Net operating profit	1,088,000	1,473,000	2,920,000	5,174,000	7,570,000	10,208,000
Preopening expenses[a]	0	1,129,000	400,000	320,000	480,000	325,000
Depreciation	379,000	593,000	1,035,000	1,260,000	1,602,000	2,032,000
Interest expense	122,000	(10,000)	(80,000)	(60,000)	(35,000)	(90,000)
Profit before tax	$ 587,000	$ (239,000)	$ 1,565,000	$ 3,654,000	$ 5,523,000	$ 7,941,000
Provision for income taxes	0	0	531,000	1,462,000	2,209,000	3,176,000
Net profit	$ 587,000	($ 239,000)	$ 1,034,000	$ 2,192,000	$ 3,314,000	$ 4,765,000

[a]Consists of preopening expenses for new restaurants and $660,000 in 1993 and $250,000 in 1994 for the brewery.

EXHIBIT 11   Proposed Organization Chart after Expansion

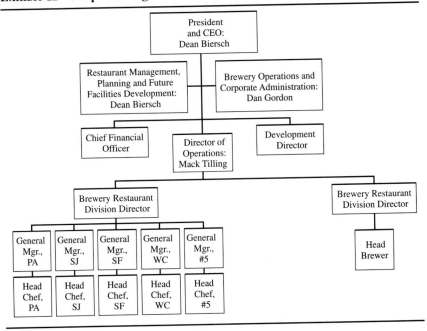

DAN GORDON

Dan Gordon sat at his desk, a blank pad in front of him. It was September 1988, and Dan had finished his first month on the job as chief operating officer of Club Sports International (CSI).

Dan was a 1983 graduate of Harvard Business School who had been hired as chief operating officer to help consolidate the firm's existing operations and to build a base from which the company could grow. As Dan thought back over his experiences at the company so far and reviewed the goals he had been given by the firm's founders and financial backers, he wondered where to begin.

> Initially, I was brought into CSI on a consulting basis, which gave me something of an advantage in that I could position myself as an "objective outsider" who had been hired to help the company. The situation was along the lines of what you'd expect in a small, fast-growing company. There was a high level of energy and enthusiasm but a definite lack of structure and systems; this created a fair amount of flexibility at times, but it also created frustration within the clubs because people felt that they were continually reinventing the wheel, and they were uncertain about what was expected of them.
>
> After a few months, I had helped refine the strategy and developed a more realistic financial plan for the business. I had also developed a good relationship with the founders, Andy and Jay. They asked me to become COO. This would create three managing partners, each with a specific area of responsibility: Andy with construction and industry and investor relations; Jay with new club development; and me with the responsibility for the performance of existing clubs and managing the day-to-day headquarters functions. Essentially, the challenge was to bring some structure and discipline to the operation. This was required to improve the financial performance of

existing clubs and provide us with the funds with which to grow. Moreover, we would need sound operations to both develop the service reputation required to open new clubs and to allow corporate management to focus its efforts on growth, rather than on the day-to-day operating issues.

Background

CSI was founded in 1983 by Andy Bowman and Jay Arthur. Andy had earned an undergraduate degree in business as well as an MBA, and also had some experience as a tennis pro. Andy had come to Denver in 1973 and became a partner in one of the country's first multipurpose athletic clubs, Racquet World. The club had started out as a tennis club, and in 1976 added racquetball, weightlifting equipment, and a basketball court, which was then a unique concept. Jay Arthur joined Andy in the late 1970s as the sales director at Racquet World, and the two built the club into one of the most profitable operations in the country. The concept was later expanded into one of the first new multi-purpose athletic clubs, the 135,000-square-feet Racquet World Inverness, located in southern Denver. When it became apparent that the real estate developer with whom they had worked in Denver was not going to expand beyond the two clubs, the two decided to go out on their own and started Club Sports International.

A key element of the strategy was to avoid the massive investment in real estate and equipment by managing clubs for others, much as Marriott might manage a hotel for an investor group. By 1988 the two had built a company with seven clubs under management, located primarily in Texas. The company had $10 million in total system revenues and 400 employees. As with any new company, creating and managing cash flow was an ongoing challenge, and it became increasingly difficult to continue to both develop the relationships that were needed to build new clubs and at the same time manage the day-to-day operations of the existing clubs. During this period, several of the markets which they had initially pursued, including Dallas, Houston, and San Antonio, suffered the real estate crash of the late 1980s. This made the task of sustaining profitable results at the existing clubs even more important, and some of the company's investors encouraged the founders to look for some help with the operating side of the business.

Dan was looking for a job and doing some consulting in the fitness industry:

I had gone to work for Weight Watchers International (WWI) after graduating from HBS. I knew I was interested in the health and fitness industry, and at Weight Watchers I had the opportunity to be responsible for new business development. My first job there was to start an aerobics business within WWI designed specifically for overweight women. Unfortunately, it was not a success. However, I learned a tremendous amount about field operations and the service business, and the process of starting up and implementing a new business.

Because of my experience in working with the field during the market testing of the aerobics business, I was promoted to General Manager of Operations Support, with responsibility for providing operations, financial, training and organizational development support to the $60 million division of WWI which was company-owned. I was very fortunate in that I was given a lot of freedom and the ability to rebuild a department which had previously been the "company graveyard." I was able to hire new people with excellent experience in service industry management from Hertz, TWA, and a national aerobics company, and I learned a great deal from them about service operations.

After four years, Weight Watchers had grown tremendously and it became more of a big company environment, especially in light of its relationship with its corporate parent, H.J. Heinz. I became increasingly uncomfortable with the planning and reporting requirements which are necessary in a company of that size, and I decided to leave to pursue ownership of a Weight Watchers franchise. A partner and I, also from WWI, raised the $7 million we needed to buy an existing Weight Watchers franchise, but we were unable to complete the transaction when WWI exercised its right to block the sale. The company was pursuing an aggressive strategy to buy back franchises wherever possible and tried to acquire the franchise itself.

I hooked up with CSI through a "friend of a friend of a friend," and I agreed to do some consulting for them, primarily on business strategy and financial issues. Fortunately, I ended up getting along with Andy and Jay, and at the end of the consulting assignment, they asked me to stay on as COO. This was exactly the kind of job I was looking for, and it provided me with the opportunity to earn equity in the company over time. (See **Exhibit 1** for CSI corporate organization chart.)

To outsiders, the athletic club business may not even seem like a "real" business. However, many of the facilities cost between $6 and $12 million to build, and they generate between $2 and $3 million in annual revenues. The club industry is basically fragmented, with lots of individual owners/managers and no major chains at the top end of the market. Many of the employees within the industry have more of an athletic or service background and may not have any of the "classical" business training that is found in other industries.

Andy Bowman offered his perspective on the company's growth, and the rationale for hiring Dan:

> Jay and I were well-suited to the task of starting the business and growing it to six or seven units. But, as we looked at growing the company beyond that point, we realized that we didn't have the disciplined, detail-oriented approach required. We needed someone to add these skills to the team, and take over the day-to-day. That's why we brought Dan on board.

Industry Overview

The health/athletic club business is a $5.5 billion industry (with 16 million members) which remains extremely fragmented. Most clubs are local, owner-managed businesses. Based on his work in the industry, it was Dan's view that there were five principal segments:

- Health club chains: These clubs emphasized the hard-sell, low-priced, multiyear contract, and often positioned themselves as "singles" clubs.

The segment was dominated by Bally under the Holiday, Jack LaLanne, Scandinavian, and Presidents brand names.

- Racquet clubs: These clubs were primarily tennis clubs that may have added racquet ball or other facilities as the market changed. They typically had an annual fee structure with moderate pricing.

- Boutiques: These clubs were small, one-of-a-kind exercise studios that offered special classes or personal training, and charged by the session.

- City dining clubs: The clubs were in downtown locations, emphasized dining and business entertainment, and had a high initiation fee and high monthly dues.

- Full-service athletic clubs: These clubs offered the largest range of athletic and fitness services, including tennis, fitness, aerobics, and swimming. Initiation fees and monthly dues ranged from moderate to high, depending on the service level.

CSI's strategy was to focus on this last segment, at a premium price and service level. The senior management group felt that, in order to compete with single-site "mom & pop" operators with on-site owner managers, CSI needed to develop a standardized, systemized management approach:

> There are advantages to multi-club operations, including the ability to provide training and a career path for management, marketing expertise and purchasing economies. However, we must offer a service level that is competitive with other operators in the market. For customers, this translates into exceptional cleanliness, especially in locker room facilities, up-to-date equipment, and outstanding programs.

CSI's model of the business suggested that there were several important factors that contributed to the success of a club:

> The financial structure of the club makes it easy to identify the critical factors impacting financial performance. The main source of revenues (typically 80% to 90%) is monthly membership dues, which range from $50 to $100 per month depending on club size and type of membership. 5% to 10% comes from the initiation fee a new member pays when joining, which ranges from $75 to $300, depending on club size and type of membership. The remaining 5% to 10% comes from ancillary revenues such as guest fees, locker rentals, massage.
>
> This means that the critical tasks are:
>
> 1. Getting and keeping new members. The upscale athletic club segment is different from some of the chains which emphasize new members, but which place little emphasis on service. Since our "bread and butter" is monthly dues, we need to focus on retention.
>
> 2. Disciplined expense management. The key is not "cost cutting" but "cost efficiency." If we're going to spend a dollar, we should be spending it smart and on something that will directly benefit the members or staff. The main components of expense are salaries, which typically account for at least 50% of what we classify as "controllable" expenses (variable and semi-fixed costs).

Given these main financial "drivers." the focus of the clubs is on 1) getting new members, and 2) keeping members. Expense management should not be a major issue if people are doing their jobs properly.

Membership turnover in the industry is fairly high—4% a month or roughly 50% a year. Even a top performing club will have 3% monthly turnover. Some of the turnover is inevitable, as people relocate or find themselves unable to sustain a fitness program, but we can manage it by providing consistent, good service.

Turnover of members is something that is going to happen, but we can try to manage it by giving good service. This means cleanliness, good athletic programs, quality equipment—all of the things you would think. But it is also something intangible, hard to measure and hard to manage. If the associates at the club know the members' names, greet them when they come into the club, can ask them about their jobs, their spouse, their kids, it all creates an atmosphere that makes people want to stay. Personality is an important factor. If a GM spends half of the day in the office instead of out on the floor talking to members, then the club is going to reflect that personality. These people are hard to find. It is much easier to give a real "people person" some financial skills than it is to turn a finance whiz into a real rah-rah guy.

The same factors that lead to good service also lead to member referrals, which account for 70% of our new members.

When CSI managed a club, the owner provided the capital required and the funding for any operating losses. CSI was responsible for administering all the funds, and billing and collecting all the revenues. As part of the budgeting and planning process, CSI would have to present its requests for capital improvements (new equipment, pool resurfacing, etc.). CSI was compensated with either a fixed management fee or percentage of revenues, and a portion of the profits. Dan explained the effect of this arrangement:

CSI is paid a management fee, and the owner provides the capital for all investments and to cover any operating losses, if required. All of this is negotiated in accordance with a budget prepared by CSI and approved by the owner. However, most management contracts include an incentive fee which is tied to an improvement in operating income, giving us an incentive to manage the clubs as if we owned them. In fact, in many cases, we run the managed (not-owned) facilities more tightly because we feel accountable to the owners and meet with them each month to review our performance.

The Organization

In 1988, CSI operated seven clubs as follows: Dallas (3), San Antonio (1), Denver (1), Indianapolis (1), and San Francisco (1). All of the clubs, with the exception of Denver, were managed rather than owned. Each club was organized along similar lines: four to six department heads reported to a general manager, who in turn reported to Dan through an operations manager. (See **Exhibit 2** for typical club organization chart.) He explained each of the department's functions:

The accounting department is responsible for billing members, cash collections and cash management, as well as financial statement preparation. Their primary task is the timely billing and collection of member dues and charges. The accounting function in a club is relatively simple, the main challenge results from the volume of transactions. A large club may have over 2,000 memberships, sometimes with an average of 1.5 to 3 people per membership (because of family memberships), and there are ongoing member charges in the restaurant, pro shop, and for other services such as tennis lessons, massage, and personal training.

There has been no industry standard for software, so one of the challenges within CSI has been the development of a standardized accounting software system to manage the club.

The athletic department is responsible for much of the service delivery function in the club, including maintaining the exercise equipment, orienting new members, running aerobics, ensuring that there is staff on the floor to help members and answer questions, and organizing leagues and activities such as basketball, racquetball, and volleyball. In this department there are some technically oriented staff who have all the necessary educational qualifications, and at the other end of the spectrum there are "camp counselors" who are friendly, member-oriented individuals. The challenge is to find staff who have the necessary technical knowledge and also have the personality. Surprisingly perhaps, this is often a difficult combination to find.

The sales function in the club is probably the most difficult to manage and the most difficult in terms of recruiting. Clubs succeed or fail on the basis of their sales staff because even a well-performing club will lose over one-third of its members each year due to relocation, financial issues, and a general lack of participation on the part of members. Sales people in the club industry are responsible in most cases for generating their own leads through member referrals, cold calls, and personal direct mail pieces. A sales director is the person who must build the team and keep them motivated. There are not many industries that operate on such a specific monthly cycle, where on the first day of the month there is a whole new scorecard and the cycle must begin again.

The front desk staff are usually the lowest-paid associates in the club, and it is primarily a part-time job for college students or people recently out of school. Yet the front desk, as with many service industry positions, has the most frequent member contact and can make the biggest impression, particularly a negative one. The front desk supervisor is responsible for hiring, training, and scheduling. The job is more difficult than it looks, with front desk associates responsible for checking membership cards upon member entry to the club, handling most member telephone inquiries about schedules and programs, referring prospective member inquiries to the sales department, and maintaining an overall cheerful attitude while standing in place for four to six hours at a time.

The maintenance department is responsible for physical plant maintenance and housekeeping. CSI's clubs are distinguished by the high level of cleanliness, which is again achieved primarily through a part-time staff. Organization, attention to detail, and the ability to motivate an often unmotivated part-time staff are critical elements of success.

At the club level, the financials are basically driven by net adds membership change—the net number of new members, after subtracting members who cancel. This is because most of the expenses are fixed or semi-fixed and any incremental increase falls to the bottom line. Since most of our revenues are from dues, the most important thing is to increase membership. (See **Exhibit 3** for typical club financial statements.)

In terms of the people who fill the General Manager jobs, their experience varies according to the size of the club. Our larger clubs are $3 to $4 million operations, while the small clubs are less than $1 million. The large club GMs ranged in age from 35 to 50, with the majority of their experience being in the small club industry, usually from athletics or operations. Small club GMs are more in the 27–32 age range, typically with experience in sales or athletics. In the small clubs, we are trying more to have a "functional" GM who doubles as a department manager in athletics or sales.

Department managers vary similarly. In large clubs, the department managers are usually 25–35 years old, again with most of their experience in the club industry. Sales staff will be the most likely to have had experience in other industries. Skills most needed and most lacking are budgeting and staff management. Many people are good "do-ers" and need help in becoming managers.

In addition to the club-level organization, certain corporate staff roles were in place, and reported to Dan:

- National Operations Manager: Each of the club's general managers reported to the operations manager. He focused on ensuring that clubs achieved monthly budgets.
- National Sales Director: The sales manager worked closely with the sales director at each of the clubs to help them in training and motivating staff, to develop sales projections and marketing programs and to manage the sales process.
- Controller: The controller worked closely with the accounting managers at each of the clubs on cash management, receivables and payables.

Early Impressions

Dan offered his views based on his first month on the job:

At the strategic level, it is clear that CSI should pursue management contracts rather than club ownership. The financial risk and capital requirements of *owning* the clubs is simply too great. It is also clear that the full service, high-end of the athletic club is the place to be. This in turn, requires a focus on cleanliness, personal service, a "hotel-like" presentation. During the past month, I have gone around and talked to the GMs at each of the clubs. I asked them what they liked about their jobs and what they didn't like. I asked them what they thought the company did well, and what it didn't do so well. (See **Exhibit 4** for excerpts from Dan's notes.)

I know there's a lot to do; the question is where do I start. I can't afford just to "fix" the problems I see. We really need to build a base for growth. The plan calls for having 15 clubs by 1990, and twice that many by 1992.

EXHIBIT 1   Club Sports International Organizational Structure—1988

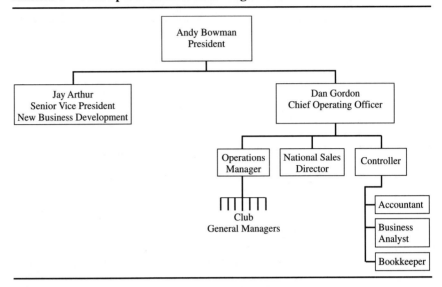

EXHIBIT 2   Typical Club Organization

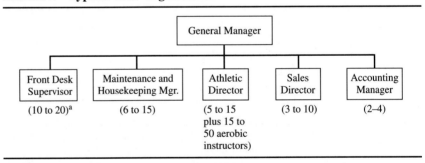

[a]Numbers in parentheses represent number of employees in each function with the lower figure representing the number in a small club, and the higher figure the number in a larger club.

Exhibit 3   Typical Club Financial Statement (for August 1988)

	Actual Current Month	Budget Current Month
Revenue		
Dues	$168,868	$187,000
Initiation fees	20,665	4,375
Other	19,227	18,800
Total revenue	$208,760	$210,175
Controllable expenses		
Salaries	$ 44,351	$ 47,000
Commissions	3,632	1,500
Payroll taxes and benefits	9,000	6,000
Administrative	9,274	8,500
Repairs and maintenance	7,071	8,000
Contract services	1,085	1,500
Professional services	1,330	1,000
Outside advertising	8,012	4,350
In-house promotion	2,606	2,650
Utilities	14,494	14,000
Other miscellaneous	5,334	3,000
Total controllable expenses	$106,190	$ 97,500
Net margin	$102,570	$112,675
Fixed expenses	24,903	24,635
Operating income (loss)	$ 77,667	$ 88,040
Debt service and lease payments	74,686	65,751
Net income (loss)	$ 2,981	$ 22,289
Percentage rent due	$ 0	$ 11,420
Net income after percentage rent	$ 2,981	$ 10,869

EXHIBIT 4   Dan's Notes from Interviews with General Managers

(Note: Items in quotation marks are quotes from the GMs that Dan recorded in his notes. Items without quotation marks are Dan's own impressions.)

- "We are asked to prepare budgets and then Andy revises them based on his experience and knowledge."
- Budgets: Lack of back-up documentation and build-up from assumptions.
- Sales staff compensation (straight commission on new members) is a source of contention. Some in other areas think sales staff paid too much.
- "Marketing programs are responses to short-term sales problems. No real strategy."
- Many club GMs are not "marketing-oriented."
- "We are frequently in the position of reinventing the wheel on sales, accounting, operating issues. There aren't a lot of standardized procedures or approaches, and training from corporate."
- Clubs are well-designed, well-appointed, good equipment.
- "Instead of just telling me what my goals are, I'd like some help in developing plans to help me reach those goals."
- Budgets are all in different formats.
- "We don't know what is really expected of us in the way of operating procedures. I'd also like more regular feedback on how we're doing."
- "CSI is more professional than the average club. More attention to quality and staff."
- "Other than when something goes wrong, you don't really know how you're doing. The budgets often start out pretty unrealistic, so by the time we're into the second quarter, it's hard to use as a yardstick."
- Turnover of low and mid-level club staff is high.
- People are afraid to make a mistake.
- "People at corporate are so busy with new clubs that it is difficult to get someone's attention when you need to."
- "I wish I knew more about what the other clubs were doing so that I could learn from their ideas and their mistakes."
- Much more emphasis on cost control than revenue generation.
- Some resentment that corporate shows up at club without calling.
- Little guidance to clubs on personnel issues—salaries, interviews. Club managers budget own raises.
- Few policies and procedures for club level accounting.
- "Would like budgeting procedures and guidelines."
- "We don't get enough time and attention from corporate. It's hard to get in touch with people because they travel so much."
- "Would like more performance appraisal and skill development."

ARTHROCARE

Dr. Hira Thapliyal rubbed his eyes and looked at the digital clock beside his bed. Was it 2 a.m. or 3 a.m.? Dr. Thapliyal was having a difficult time falling asleep; he couldn't help thinking about the board meeting that would take place later that week, where several important decisions affecting the future direction of his company—ArthroCare—would be made. ArthroCare was a young company in the medical devices arena; the company made small, disposable electrosurgical tools that could be used for cutting and shaping tissue through minute incisions in the body. ArthroCare had gone public in February 1996, at $14/share, raising $32 million for the company, and placing a market capitalization of roughly $120 million on the enterprise. One month later, the stock was as high as $26. Now, Monday, August 12, 1996—six months later—the stock was trading at $13.75, slightly below the offering price. The most immediate cause for the drop in the price of ArthroCare's stock related to issues with the medical device sector overall. As Paul Brown, an equity analyst with Volpe, Welty put it:

> ArthroCare went public at the height of the feeding frenzy. Companies were going public based upon a view of their earnings three or four years out. Now as several other medical device companies have reported sales and earnings figures below expectations, the sector overall has been slammed.[1]

As the first half of 1996 unfolded, ArthroCare had made its first quarter earnings target. Several weeks earlier, on July 25, the company had announced its second

---

[1] Source: Casewriter interview.

Professor Michael J. Roberts prepared this case at the Harvard Business School California Research Center with the assistance of Professor William Sahlman and Professor Jack McDonald of Stanford University Graduate School of Business, as the basis for class discussion rather than to illustrate either effective or ineffective handling of an administrative situation.

Harvard Business School Case 9-898-056.

quarter earnings, which were also in line with analysts' estimates. During the prior week, however, ArthroCare's stock had dropped. On Tuesday, August 6, Phil Nalbone, an analyst at one of ArthroCare's investment banks—Volpe, Welty—had issued a downward revision to their near-term earnings estimates. ArthroCare stock had closed for the week at $13.75.

At the upcoming board meeting, the company would confront several issues that could have a serious impact on its ability to make the future earnings numbers that analysts had forecast during the IPO. Specifically, the company needed to deal with several issues:

- Marketing executives at ArthroCare wanted to drop the price of one of the company's products—the "controller" (see more below)—in order to increase market penetration. This would have a serious impact on the company's near-term margins, making it highly unlikely that the company would be able to meet its near-term earnings estimates.

- ArthoCare was also spending heavily to "extend its technology platform." Thapliyal was an ardent believer in the fundamental electrode technology that underlay ArthroCare's device. He believed that this technology could be extended from its current orthopedic use to other applications, including dermatology, gynecology, cardiology, and ear, nose, and throat surgical procedures. But, the cost of doing this fundamental R&D and getting the devices through the Food and Drug Administration (FDA) approval process had raised ArthroCare's break-even to more than $25 million in sales, roughly double what it would have been had the company pursued a more narrowly focused strategy of simply trying to "get profitable quickly" with its first device, which was targeted towards orthopedic procedures.

Thapliyal explained the difficulty these choices presented:

As we have begun to apply our proprietary technology, we see more and more applications for it. Thus, we face a complicated set of choices about whether to move as quickly as possible to reach profitability, or whether to try to maximize the value of the enterprise by staking out the broadest spectrum of opportunities, getting both the market and technical advantages that we will need to be successful. Similarly, with respect to the pricing of the controller, it is a question of short term profits versus the long-term benefits of increasing our market penetration. People said that being a public company would present us with a host of additional issues to manage. It looks like they were right.

Background

Hira Thapliyal, Ph.D., was 47. He was born in the small village of Thapli in India's Northern Himalayan Mountains, and had come to the United States in 1969 to attend college at Washington State University. He received a masters from the University of Idaho, and a doctorate in Materials Science & Engineering from

Cornell in 1977. Dr. Thapliyal then joined Corning Corporation, in upstate New York, to work on advanced medical device projects. After four years at Corning, he received an offer to join Amdahl Corporation in Silicon Valley as a process engineer. Gene Amdahl, the founder of Amdahl Corporation, had virtually invented disk storage at IBM, and he had then left to form his own business. Soon after Dr. Thapliyal joined Amdahl, however, Gene Amdahl left to start Trilogy, another business aimed at making high-speed computers. Dr. Thapliyal joined Trilogy in its start-up phase and stayed for about a year: "My interest in medical devices had been piqued at Corning, and I wanted to get back to that industry."

In 1982, Dr. Thapliyal joined Oximetrix, a company that made cardiac medical devices. And one and one-half years later, he was offered "the chance of a lifetime":

> Through a mutual friend, I was introduced to Dr. John Simpson, one of the pioneers in the cardiac device field. Simpson had been one of the inventors of balloon angio-plasty. With this technique, a cardiac catheter—a slim tube—is fed through an artery in the leg up to the chambers and blood vessels of the heart. Typically, catheters were used to take readings and measurements for diagnostic purposes. But Simpson had the idea to putting a small balloon at the tip of the catheter, feeding it up to the blood vessels that feed the heart, and then inflating the balloon, to "crack" and compress the plaque—the fatty deposits—that can block the vessel and cause a heart attack.
>
> Anyway, Dr. Simpson was starting a new company—Devices for Vascular Intervention—DVI. Simpson's approach at DVI was actually to remove the plaque with a very small cutting tool on a catheter, rather than compress it with a balloon.

Dr. Thapliyal joined DVI in 1984 as vice president of engineering. He worked not only on perfecting the device design, but also managed the research and clinical trials, quality control, administrative and regulatory functions, including dealing with the FDA. Dr. Thapliyal recalled his work at that time:

> In 1985, we got interested in imaging the interior of blood vessels via ultrasound. It was a seductively defocusing project. Up until then, all of the cardiac catheter imaging devices could only see the inner wall—the lining—of the blood vessel. But, Dr. Yock at Stanford came to us with the idea of imaging the blood vessel in three dimensions by using ultrasonic techniques.
>
> We started work on this project in 1985, and decided to spin out the company—CVIS—in 1986 for the purpose of focusing on this opportunity. I was president of CVIS until 1988. I'd gotten married in 1986 and had my first child in 1988. I decided to take a break and recharge my batteries, and we hired another president to run CVIS. DVI was sold to Eli Lilly in 1989 for about $200 million. CVIS went public in 1992, and was bought in 1995 by Boston Scientific for approximately $100 million.
>
> After a year I was offered the opportunity to run another company—MicroBionics. Between 1989 and 1993, I served as president and CEO of this privately held company that was in the business of continuous monitoring of blood gas levels. Again, it used a catheter technology, this time to measure a vital sign for patients who were critically ill. This was technically a very difficult task, and I was not able to raise sufficient capital to take the idea to a clinical solution.
>
> I left the company in 1993 to pursue another idea that had come to me during my work in the cardiovascular arena. One of the most serious problems in cardiology is a

total occlusion—or blockage—of the blood vessel. Balloon angioplasty is often successful in opening clogged arteries, but—with a total occlusion—there is no space in which the catheter can be worked through. In this case, the patient must have a coronary artery bypass graft (CABG). The CABG is a very common procedure that solves this problem. Yet it is a very debilitating procedure. The entire chest is cracked open at the breastbone, and veins cut from the leg are grafted onto the heart to replace those that are blocked. There are 400,000 CABGs performed every year in the United States.

During my years at Corning, I had worked with a very bright medical device expert who was a consultant in the medical device business—Phil Eggers. I went to Phil with the germ of an idea, and together we developed the concept of taking an electrode and supplying it with an electric current, and basically melting the fatty deposits—like you would melt butter in a frying pan—so that you could then pass a catheter through the occlusion and break it up using traditional angioplasty. We filed an early patent, and in 1992 we founded a company—AngioCare—to pursue this technology.

Together, Thapliyal and Eggers worked on perfecting the electrode devices that could be used for this purpose. While the technique showed promise in cadaver studies, it proved problematic in early tests: "The electricity took the path of least resistance—which was through the blood—and wouldn't travel through the fatty deposits sufficiently to warm and melt them."

Thapliyal and Eggers worked to devise a strategy to overcome this problem:

One day we were at a gas station in Columbus, Ohio and looked around and saw all these cars at all these gas pumps, all these nozzles simultaneously pumping gas to all these cars. And we thought—why not use *multiple* electrodes to deliver current to tissue? In this way, we could activate only those electrodes that were actually touching the fatty deposits, and not give the electricity a chance to avoid the deposits. Phil and I talked, we tried it, and it worked. We quickly sought patent protection for this technology, and moved towards trying to make a business out of it.

In late 1992, as the men were working to perfect the technology, they were also trying to raise money to finance the new company:

I knew several venture capitalists from my prior experiences in the medical device business. But everyone I talked to felt the total occlusion market was too small—only 50,000 cases per year. Finally one of our eventual co-founders—Robert Garvie—said, "Would this technology work in orthopedics?" Garvie's thinking was that there are over two million cases a year of arthroscopic surgery of the knee, shoulder, elbow, wrist, and ankle. In an arthroscopic surgical procedure, a small incision is made near the joint, and a tiny tool and video camera are used to cut and remove tissue.

We didn't know if it would work, but we said we would try. We tested the tool in some animal tissue studies and it worked. It was better than using conventional metal blades that cut tissue because one tool through one incision could be made to do the work of multiple mechanical tools inserted through multiple incisions via the more traditional procedure. And, the electrode approach had the added benefit of cauterizing the blood vessels as it cut, sealing them up and stopping the bleeding of these blood vessels immediately.

Just as the results were starting to come in, I ran into Annette Campbell-White, a VC from Paragon Venture Partners. Annette had been an investor at DVI and CVIS, and when she heard what we were up to, she said to come see her. Phil and I went in to see her in April 1993. One week later, she and her partner, John Lewis, had written us a check for $1 million.

AngioCare was put on "hold," and a new company called ArthroCare was started to pursue the orthopedics opportunity. (For a more complete description of ArthroCare, see **Exhibit 1**, which presents detailed background material from the company's IPO prospectus.) A fourth co-founder, Tony Manlove (a Harvard MBA and past president of Oximetrix), joined Thapliyal, Eggers, and Garvie to co-found ArthroCare and to serve as its CFO. Upon the advice of their lawyers, Thapliyal and Eggers put their patents into a limited partnership, and then licensed the orthopedics applications to ArthroCare. The company raised another $800,000 from wealthy individuals on the same terms as the Paragon investment—a $4 million post-money valuation.

The first $1.8 million of financing was intended to take the company to the point of submitting necessary animal data to the FDA for market approval of the device. (See below for information on the FDA approval process.) By mid-1994, animal tests showed that the device worked well in removing cartilage and other tissues in the joint. The next step in the process required human testing, which the company initiated in France; because of the significant time lag imposed by the FDA regulatory pathway, very few medical device companies performed human testing in the United States.

Meanwhile, in January of 1994, the company raised another round of $4 million, at an $11 million post-money valuation. This was followed by two more rounds prior to the IPO, raising $5.8 million at a $19 million valuation, and $4.1 million at a $37 million valuation (all valuations post-money). All these financings were done in the form of a convertible preferred stock, and the original VC firms of Paragon Ventures Partners, InterWest Partners, institutional Venture Partners, and MedVenture Associates participated. Each firm (except IVP) had a board representative. (See table below for details of financing rounds.)

ArthroCare Financings

Preferred Stock Round	Date Financed	Total Capital Raised	Purchase Price per Share	Preferred Stock Sold— Number of Shares	Conversion Ratio Preferred: Common	Effective Price/ Common Share	Common Shares Outstanding[a]
A	5–12/93	$1,730,816	$0.95	1,856,127	2:1	$1.90	1,176,475
B	1/94	$3,956,159	$1.60	2,500,000	2:1	$3.20	1,186,475
C	5/95	$5,827,777	$2.00	2,922,500	2:1	$4.00	1,792,725
D	10/95	$4,190,251	$3.00	1,399,109	2:1	$6.00	1,792,725

[a]After financing, but excluding the employee stock option pool (see **Exhibit 1** for details).

Dr. Thapliyal described the company's strategy:

> We figured our best strategy was to develop the core technology, sort out the range of possible applications, stake out a broad set of patent claims, get the FDA approvals, and sell the company to one of the established players. That is basically the model that most of these venture-backed medical device companies are based upon, simply because the cost of setting up a proprietary distribution channel is so high. But then we realized, in order to do this "plan A"—and get the highest price, we had to actually do "plan B"—to ramp up and market the product ourselves. Otherwise, we would appear to a prospective buyer as though a sale was our only option, and we'd have a lot less negotiating strength. And, it was also clear that we could command a higher price if we actually started taking sales and margin away from some of the established players. Our device would compete with mechanical shavers made by Bristol-Myers, for instance, so we knew we'd attract their attention if we started affecting their revenue numbers.

As the company's R&D effort proceeded, relationships with the VC's did become contentious over one issue—intellectual property. Another early investor—Bob Momsen, a partner at InterWest Partners—described the tension:

> When Hira first came to us, ArthroCare owned a license on the Eggers/Thapliyal electrode patents for application in orthopedic uses only. The two men had retained the rights to use the technology in other applications in other areas for themselves. I felt strongly that the company in which the VCs were investing should own all the intellectual capital—the rights to apply this technology in all markets. It was clear to us that this technology had broad application. And, I've learned that the business model often changes as you move down the learning curve. Why should we finance this learning, only so it can be applied more profitably in another segment that we wouldn't get to participate in? Dr. Thapliyal and I could not agree on this issue during the first round, so I agreed to invest on his terms, with the understanding that this would be a continuing item of discussion. By the time the third round came up in 1995, I think everyone understood that we were going to have a lot of complicated choices about which markets to pursue on what kind of schedule, and the last thing we wanted was a conflict of interest injected into these discussions as a result of different ownership stakes in different parties' hands.[2]

At the time of the third round of financing, the Eggers and Thapliyal patents were folded into ArthroCare, and the owners received additional cash compensation and stock in exchange for their contribution.

The FDA and Regulations Affecting Medical Devices

Medical devices are subject to stringent FDA regulations and approval processes. The FDA regulates the testing, manufacture, labeling, packaging, marketing, distribution, and record keeping for all classes of medical devices.

---

[2]Source: Casewriter interview.

Most devices require a "premarket" approval from the FDA to ensure their safety and effectiveness. Life-sustaining and life-supporting devices, as well as implantable devices, are subject to Class III restrictions. And any new device which has not been found to be "substantially equivalent" to an existing device is subject to Class III regulation. Approval for this type of device can take from 3 to 5 years.

Class II devices are subject to a lower level of regulation. ArthroCare sought Class II approval to market its device (the ArthroWand) on the basis of its "substantial equivalency," through a process known as a 510(k) premarket notification. ArthroCare had been successful in its applications to the FDA, winning 510(k) clearance for the ArthroWand for the knee, shoulder, elbow, and ankle joint applications prior to its IPO. And in December of 1995, the company submitted 510(k) notifications for urological and gynecological applications; FDA clearance was received for the urological applications in March 1996. In general, it took from 4 to 12 months to obtain the 510(k) clearance from the FDA.

Ramping Up the Business

In March of 1995, the company received a 510(k) clearance from the FDA on its first product—aimed at surgery of the knee. The company had contracted with manufacturers and third-party distributors, and in the summer of 1995, the product was announced.

As this was transpiring, the company was wrestling with the issue of how to finance the next stage of development. The most conservative estimates of the capital that ArthroCare would require were in the $10 to $20 million range. This was for a very minimal strategy of simply proceeding with the knee product and distributing it using a third party. As financing estimates grew to include developing the other applications which Thapliyal and the board believed had merit, as well as building a distribution network for the product, financing requirements grew to the $20 to $40 million range.

As ArthroCare was coming to grips with these figures, the IPO market for medical device companies heated up (see **Exhibit 2** for overall state of equity market and device company IPOs).

The board asked Dr. Thapliyal to initiate discussions with investment banks and to get some sense of the valuation the company might fetch in an IPO. By Fall, the board had selected Robertson Stephens and Volpe, Welty as lead underwriters for an IPO, tentatively scheduled for year-end. The thinking behind the decision was expressed by Dr. Thapliyal:

> We knew we could raise $10 to $15 million in private capital, but that simply was not going to take us where we wanted to go. Public equity is less expensive money, and we knew we could get sufficient capital to fund our aggressive growth strategy.
>
> As far as the selection of Robertson Stephens and Volpe, Welty, we talked to eight different investment banks. Of nine medical device IPOs, Robertson had done four—they knew the pulse of the market. I had known Paul Brown, the head of Volpe,

Welty's research group for 10 years. They had a well-respected analyst following medical device companies. Some of the other investment banks didn't even have analysts covering this industry.

Once we picked these underwriters, we never haggled over valuation or pricing. Since the company had negative earnings, they had to look out to 1999 to get a "normalized" year, and discounted back to get a 1996 value. The board was comfortable with the result.

The rationale for a year-end offering was clear—ArthroCare would have its first quarter of sales history behind it, and the bankers felt that this would allow the company to make more credible projections of future revenues and earnings, and thus, command a higher valuation. In October of 1995, however, the company discovered that it had a problem with the sterile packaging in which the ArthroWands were shipped, and had to undertake a product recall. Dr. Thapliyal recalled the experience:

This was my first experience with an IPO, and I thought that a product recall would present a big problem. We worked like mad, and within a week we had the units recalled, the problem fixed, and the company "closed-out" the issue with the FDA. When I talked with the bankers, I expected bad news about the impact this would have on the IPO. But when they heard how we'd handled it, they said not to worry.

The company submitted a draft of an S-1 registration statement in December, and the SEC approved of the company's offering in January.

The IPO

Dr. Thapliyal went to speak with potential investors on the company's "road show" from January 15 through February 2, 1996. The company went public at $14 on February 5, 1996. The offering raised $32 million for the company, and the $14 share price valued the company at $120 million. As is typical in such cases, "insiders" including officers, directors, and significant shareholders were prohibited from selling their shares during the first 6 months of public trading. By the end of the first day of trading ArthroCare stock was up and closed near $17. Dr. Thapliyal described the experience:

The IPO was very exciting. It was grueling—fifteen cities in two weeks. I gave the same presentation more than fifty times. But, here I was, a fellow from the Himalayas, living the American Dream. It was thrilling to see the stock come across the ticker. We still had a lot of work ahead of us, but it was a very satisfying milestone.

Paul Brown of Volpe, Welty, described the market context in which ArthroCare had gone public:

Like all industry segments, the market for medical device companies goes through cycles. ArthroCare went public near the peak of the cycle that started in the summer of 1995. The cycle prior to that had been stopped dead in its tracks in 1995—the industry was devastated by the Clinton Health Care proposals. By the time analysts determined that the Clinton Plan was not going to pass, they had figured out that managed care was going to force tremendous change. Analysts began to revise their income statement models for these companies, reducing the price of devices, and flowing through the effect to revenues and earnings. And, they were right. By mid-1995, people began to see that some companies had sorted through the managed care model, and that you could make money. The cloud began to lift. This had a follow-on effect in the deal market, as companies that had tried to go public earlier in the year—and failed—now came back up to the plate and were successful. By the end of 1995, it was a feeding frenzy. People were willing to buy stock in companies that hadn't established their sales or earnings model. Institutional investors were willing to play venture capitalists, at least until the waters got choppy again.[3]

Brown, who was involved in ArthroCare's offering, explained how the company had been valued in the IPO:

The only way you could rationalize a valuation for any of the early stage companies that went public during this cycle was off of projected 1999 or year 2000 earnings. So, when we began discussions with ArthroCare about going public, we had to construct a revenue model going out through 2000. We had discussions with Hira about how he saw ArthroCare's strategy playing out. We were impressed with the technology, and did believe that it had broad application. But, the company was already going public relatively early, and we encouraged him to focus on the orthopedic market. We wanted to focus the story around orthopedics, and prove out the business model in this application.

Phil Nalbone—our analyst—came out with a full-blown research report on ArthroCare dated March 4, 1996. This was 30 days after the IPO—pretty much the minimum to live within the SEC's quiet period requirements. This report pretty well captured the argument that Hira had made during the road show. And—while the company is not allowed to share its projections with prospective purchasers of the stock—we as analysts are allowed to present *our* view.[4] (See **Exhibit 3** for excerpts from this report.)

The earnings model upon which these forecasts were based had several assumptions. The first product ArthroCare had introduced (Q4:95) was for the orthopedic application; it included a "controller," which supplied the electric current, and the "wand," which was the disposable tool. First, Volpe, Welty's analyst forecast the average selling price of the wand at $100, and assumed the product had a 68% gross margin at this price. The analyst estimated that the controller would have an average realized selling price of $8,500, and assumed that the unit had a cost to ArthroCare of $2,750. (See **Table 3E** of **Exhibit 3** for the analyst's volume forecasts.) The Volpe, Welty analyst also estimated that, in the base scenario for 1996, at least 75 percent of ArthroCare's R&D spending was associated with the application of technology to the orthopedic application, and less than 25 percent was associated with extending the technology to other markets.

[3]Source: Casewriter interview.
[4]Source: Casewriter interview.

The First Six Months

ArthroCare's stock traded within the $17 to $26 range for the first 4 to 5 months (see **Exhibit 4** for price history and valuation relative to Volpe, Welty medical device index, see **Exhibit 5** for excerpts from follow-on research reports, and see **Exhibit 6** for ArthroCare Institutional shareholdings). In April, ArthroCare announced its first quarter results: "Better than expected Q1 sales of nearly $1.2 million beat our $750,000 projection," was the report from Volpe, Welty (see **Tables 1A** and **1B** of **Exhibit 1** for quarterly financial results). By mid-May, the stock was trading around $25. Then, the price began to drop. According to Paul Brown, this was due to a slide in the market for device companies overall: "A large number of the companies that went public early in the year were having problems meeting the expectations that were set during the IPO. These problems taint the entire sector."

By mid-July, ArthroCare's stock price had briefly dipped below the offering price for the first time. Dr. Thapliyal explained his views: "We looked at 44 medical device IPOs that had been done for the 18 months through mid-1996. Of the 44, 40 were below the offering price." On July 16, an analyst at the investment banking firm DLJ began covering ArthroCare, and rated the stock "outperform." He noted:

> Over the past several weeks, the shares have been particularly weak on little volume. We believe that there could be some investor fall-out from the recent slide in Orthologic (another niche player in the orthopedic segment) shares and general weakness in small capitalization OTC stocks.[5]

In the same report, the analyst for DLJ estimated that ArthroCare was realizing an average price of $3,500 to $4,000 for controller and $100 for the wand. On July 25, the company announced its second quarter results: "Revenues of $1.4 million exceed our estimates of $1.2 million . . . a loss of $0.20 per share in line with forecasts," said Volpe, Welty. The stock was trading at about $16. The Volpe, Welty analyst estimated that ArthroCare had sold the following unit volumes of controllers and wands during the first half of 1996:

Unit Volume	Q1:96	Q2:96
Controllers	140	125
Wands	8,200	10,300

The Company's 10-Q filing for the first quarter indicated that approximately 75 percent of that quarter's sales were attributable to "initial stocking orders" from the 30 dealers/distributors through whom ArthroCare had chosen to sell its product. The Company further indicated that these sales were at or near cost.

---

[5]Source: DLJ research report on ArthroCare dated July 16, 1996.

In its 10-Q for the second quarter, ending June 29, 1996, the Company indicated that it had established an installed base of 300 controllers, and that it had engaged in several promotional programs in which controller prices were discounted in exchange for wand purchase commitments. The company reported that the revenue mix was approximately 33 percent controllers and 67 percent wands for the first 6 months of the year.

Finally, in just the week leading up to August 6, Volpe, Welty had issued its latest research report, in which the analyst revised ArthroCare's sales and earnings forecasts for the first time since the offering (see **Exhibit 5**): the forecast loss for the remainder of the year increased from $0.17 per share to $0.35, largely as a result of an increase in the analysts' estimates of R&D costs associated with moving the technology to additional applications. For FY 1997, 1998, 1999, and 2000, sales and earnings estimates remained unchanged, as the benefits of ArthroCare's investments in the technology platform were seen to pay off.

The Issue

In preparation for the company's August 15 board meeting later that week, ArthroCare's CFO had begun preliminary work on its budget and business plan for the coming year. Dr. Thapliyal described the issues that had arisen:

> First, an immediate issue was the price of the controller. The ArthroCare system depends upon a reliable, steady source of electrical current to deliver the energy to the electrode tip. The source of this electrical current was the "controller." This unit, which had a list price of $12,500, was required in order to power the disposable wand. We had some luck selling these controllers to the very "early adopters," but as we attempted to broaden the penetration of the market, we discovered that it was very difficult to sell these units for anything like the list price. In the old days, the surgeons ruled the roost. If a doctor wanted a new piece of equipment, the hospital would buy it. Today, the managed care environment has shifted a great deal of power to the purchasing manager. It's bad enough for the doctor to say he needs a wand that costs two or three times as much as the old mechanical shaver. But, layer on top of that the need for a $12,500 box, and the purchasing manager is going to give the physician a very hard time. Some doctors may choose to really fight for this, and some of those will win the fight. But many will simply throw up their hands. Conversely if you will *give* the doctor a $12,500 piece of equipment, that is a very compelling argument for the physician to use with the purchasing manager about why the hospital should be willing to stock the wands.

ArthroCare had already discounted the price of the controller unit to help achieve its marketing objectives.

Allan Weinstein, ArthroCare's vice president of marketing, wanted to take further discounts on the price of the controller and simply place the controller units with doctors and hospitals in exchange for an agreement to purchase a minimum number of wands over the coming year. Larry Tannenbaum, ArthroCare's CFO, was worried that this action would cause a further erosion of the company's margins. He was anxious to live up to the expectation that ArthroCare would turn profitable during the second quarter of 1997. He felt that any further reduction in the controller's price would adversely effect the company's ability to achieve this objective.

Dr. Thapliyal found the decision a difficult one:

> We have worked hard to make our numbers. The board has been very supportive in terms of telling me to pay attention to the business and not worry about the stock price. But it is hard. It does affect the way people inside the company think about the business. We have 65 employees, and all have stock options. Lots of our employees are young people who have signed on for the classic start-up: work hard but reap the big rewards. Many people's options are set at the IPO price. When the stock is at $26, they love it. When it's back at $14, or below, it takes its toll on morale. As the stock has been dropping, it has taken more and more of my time to pay attention to this and attempt to manage it.

A second issue which the board would have to take up revolved around ArthroCare's investment in R&D to expand to other product market applications. Dr. Thapliyal explained:

> As we get further down the technology learning curve, we keep finding new and profitable market opportunities: cardiology, dermatology, urology, and gynecology. There are procedures in all of these fields that could be revolutionized by our technology. We spend almost $1 million per quarter on R&D, so it is a large expense for us.
>
> Moreover, some of these other segments offer more margin than the orthopedic segment, even if they are not as large. In the arthroscopy field, we are competing with mechanical shavers that sell for $70 to $90. So, we can price our product somewhat higher than this number because we are delivering a superior result. But, we can't price it at two or three times the price—in the managed care environment, it just won't fly. However, there are certain applications where there is currently no device out there establishing a price point. Take surgery to the head and neck, for example. This is performed today in the "old-fashioned" way—you have to cut to get where you want to be. If our tool enables a surgeon to perform what used to be a $20,000, three-day, in-the-hospital procedure on an outpatient basis, now we are competing against the $20,000 price. There is a lot more room for pricing the wand in this application and getting an outstanding margin. The same kind of argument applies in certain other areas, say cardiovascular applications, where you are competing against a $1,000 device. Again, a lot more pricing flexibility.
>
> We have continued to build our intellectual property base, and have received additional patents since we went public. Still, time is our scarcest resource. When we went public, we indicated to the market that we would be profitable by the second quarter of 1997. We could probably drive the company to profitability by this point if we focus narrowly on this goal. But, we are trying to build long-term value, not simply become profitable.

EXHIBIT 1   Excerpts from ArthroCare's IPO prospectus.

Overview

Since commencing operations in April 1993, ArthroCare Corporation has primarily engaged in the design, development, clinical testing and manufacturing of its Arthroscopic System. ArthroCare Corporation designs, develops, manufactures and markets arthroscopic surgical equipment for use in orthopedics. The Arthroscopic System is designed to replace the multiple surgical tools used in arthroscopic procedures with one multi-purpose, electrosurgery system that ablates (removes) soft tissue while simultaneously achieving homeostasis (sealing small bleeding vessels). This allows the surgeon to remove damaged tissue while reducing the need for the frequent exchange of instruments that is common in arthroscopic procedures. The company received clearance of its 510(k) premarket notification from the FDA in March 1995 to market its Arthroscopic System for use in arthroscopic surgery of the knee, shoulder, elbow and ankle.

The company has experienced significant operating losses since inception and, as of December 31, 1995, had an accumulated deficit of $9.9 million. The company expects to generate substantial additional losses due to increased operating expenditures primarily attributable to the expansion of marketing and sales activities, scale-up of manufacturing capabilities, increased research and development and activities to support regulatory and reimbursement applications.

The company has only sold a small number of units and does not have any experience in manufacturing or selling its Arthroscopic System in commercial quantities. Whether the company can successfully manage the transition to a larger-scale commercial enterprise will depend upon the successful development of its manufacturing capability, the further development of its distribution network, obtaining foreign regulatory approvals for the Arthroscopic System, obtaining domestic and foreign regulatory approvals for potential products and strengthening its financial and management systems, procedures and controls.

Liquidity and Capital Resources

Since inception, the company has financed operations primarily from the sale of Preferred Stock. As of December 31, 1995, the company had raised $15.7 million. As of that date, cash and cash equivalents equaled $4.8 million. The company's cash used in operations increased to $6.6 million for the year ended December 31, 1995 from $2.1 million for the year ended December 31, 1994, reflecting expenditures made primarily to increase research and development, to form a marketing and sales organization, to support administrative infrastructure, to expand to a 22,000 square foot facility, to purchase equipment and to begin building product inventory.

The company believes that the net proceeds from this offering together with interest thereon and the company's existing capital resources, will be sufficient to fund its operations at least through fiscal 1997.

Use of Proceeds

The net proceeds to the company from the sale of the 2,200,000 shares of Common Stock offered by the company hereby are estimated to be approximately $32,140,000 (assuming the Underwriters' over-allotment option is exercised in full), after deducting the underwriting discounts and commissions and estimated offering expenses payable by the company.

The company anticipates using the net proceeds from this offering as follows: approximately $6.0 million to increase manufacturing capacity; approximately $6.0 million to expand its marketing and sales efforts; approximately $5.0 million to fund its research and development efforts; approximately $3.0 million for working capital; and approximately $7.8 million for general corporate purposes.

The ArthroCare Arthroscopic System

The Arthroscopic System is an instrument used to perform surgery upon a site which is visualized with an arthroscope. The company does not manufacture arthroscopes.

The company's Arthroscopic System is comprised of the disposal ArthroWand, a connecting cable and a radio frequency power controller. The controller, approximately 14 inches by 11 inches by five inches, is used to deliver high-frequency power to the ArthroWand. The list price of the controller, including the cable, is $12,500. The voltage level can be changed by the user to ablate different tissues using the keys on the front panel of the controller. The cable, which is approximately 10 feet in length, connects the controller to the ArthroWand. Power is transmitted through the cable to the ArthroWand by depressing the foot pedal, thereby enabling surgeons to utilize the ArthroWand as a conventional probe as well as an instrument that ablates and coagulates. Accordingly, the surgeon using the Arthroscopic System need not remove and insert a variety of instruments to perform different tasks as is required when using conventional arthroscopic instruments. The ArthroWand is approved for sale in tip sizes from 1.5mm to 4.5mm with angles ranging from 0 to 90 degrees. It is currently available in two tip sizes, 2.5mm and 3mm, and each size is available in tip angles of 0, 15, and 90 degrees. These different tip sizes and tip angles enable the surgeon to ablate different volumes of tissue and to access treatment sites not readily accessible by existing mechanical instruments and motorized cutting tools. The list price of the ArthroWand is $120.

The company's patented multi-electrode, bipolar, electrosurgical technology offers a number of benefits that the company believes may provide advantages over competing surgical methods and devices. The principal benefits include:

- Ease of Use. The Arthroscopic System performs many of the functions of mechanical tools, power tools and electrosurgery instruments allowing the surgeon to use a single instrument. The lightweight probe is simple to use and complements the surgeon's existing tactile skills without the need for extensive training.

- Precision. In contrast to conventional tools, the Arthroscopic System permits surgeons to perform precise tissue ablation and sculpting. The company believes this may result in more rapid patient rehabilitation.

- Simultaneous Ablation and Hemostasis. The Arthroscopic System efficiently seals small bleeding vessels during the tissue ablation process. In procedures involving the shoulder, the capability to ablate tissue hemostatically removes the need to introduce coagulating instruments and improves the surgeon's visibility of the operative site.

- Cost Reduction. The Arthroscopic System eliminates the need to introduce multiple instruments to remove and sculpt tissue and seal small bleeding vessels. The company believes this may reduce operating time and thereby produce cost savings for health care providers.

In order to secure these benefits, however, a hospital or surgical center must purchase a specially designed power control unit (controller) which has a list price of $12,500. At hospital sites or surgical centers where several arthroscopic surgery procedures may be performed simultaneously, the purchase of multiple controllers may be required. In addition, motorized and mechanical instruments and electrosurgery systems currently used by hospitals and surgical centers for arthroscopic procedures have a history of success and have become widely accepted by orthopedic surgeons.

ArthroCare Strategy

The company's objective is to utilize its proprietary technology to design, develop, manufacture and sell innovative, clinically superior electrosurgical devices for the arthroscopic surgical treatment of joint injuries and for the surgical treatment of other soft tissue conditions. The key elements of the company's strategy to achieve this objective include:

- Penetrate Existing Arthroscopic Surgical Instrument Market. The company's initial sales efforts are focused on marketing the company's products to orthopedic surgeons performing high volume arthroscopy and to opinion-leaders in orthopedic surgery.

- Expand into New Arthroscopic Surgical Markets. The company intends to encourage surgeons to use its Arthroscopic System to treat joints that have been primarily treated by open surgery, such as the shoulder, elbow, and ankle. Because of the small size, varying shapes and tactile feel of the company's ArthroWand, surgeons will be able to arthroscopically access areas difficult to reach by conventional arthroscopic surgical tools.

- Target Key International Markets. The company intends to market its Arthroscopic System in certain international markets if required regulatory approvals are received. The company is developing a network of independent distributors in Europe and intends to collaborate with one or more marketing partners to assist with regulatory requirements and to market and distribute the Arthroscopic System in Japan.

- Leverage Broadly Applicable Proprietary Technology. The company expects to leverage its proprietary technology by developing additional wands for use in a variety of surgical procedures, including urology (e.g., trans-urethral resection of the prostate), dermatology (e.g., abnormal skin growth and wrinkle removal), gynecology (e.g., endometrial ablation), and periodontics (e.g., gingivectomy).
- Pursue Regulatory Approvals Through 510(k) Applications. The company intends to pursue additional applications of its technology in indications that will require FDA clearance through the shorter, less costly 510(k) regulatory process.

Products Under Development

The company believes that its core technology is applicable to other surgical applications that will utilize the current Arthroscopic System, including the controller. The company is currently developing a urology product designed for use with a conventional resectoscope, a device used to visualize the urethra and bladder during surgical procedures. The company is currently developing a gynecology product designed for use with a conventional hysteroscope, a device used to visualize the uterus during surgical procedures.

Research and Development

The company has undertaken preliminary animal studies and wand development for the use of its ablation technology with its current controller in the following areas: (i) dermatology and plastic surgery for skin resurfacing and for the treatment of epidermal (the outermost layer of skin) and dermal (the deep bed of vascular connective tissue beneath the epidermal layer) disorders; (ii) gynecology for the laparoscopic treatment (a surgical treatment utilizing a miniature video camera and miniature surgical instruments manipulated through small portals in the abdominal wall) of endometriosis (a condition in which tissue growth occurs in the pelvic cavity, accompanied by abdominal pain); (iii) oral surgery for the treatment of gingivitis (inflammation of the gums) and other disorders of mucosal tissue; and (iv) general surgery for use in the dissection, resection and ablation of soft tissue in open surgical procedures and in endoscopically assisted surgery.

Stock Plans

Incentive Stock Plan   A total of 1,536,025 shares of Common Stock has been reserved for issuance under the company's Incentive Stock Plan. Under the Incentive Stock Plan, as of December 31, 1995, options to purchase an aggregate of 493,350 shares were outstanding, 123,750 shares of Common Stock had been purchased pursuant to the exercise of stock purchase rights and 918,925 shares were available for future grant.

Principal Stockholders

Beneficial Owner	Shares Beneficially Owned	Percentage of Shares Beneficially Owned	
		Prior to Offering	*After Offering*
Entities affiliated with InterWest Partners	1,227,695	20.0%	14.7%
Entities affiliated with Institutional Venture Partners	1,212,694	19.8	14.6
Entities affiliated with Paragon Venture Partners	1,088,088	17.7	13.1
Hira V. Thapliyal, Ph.D	628,750	10.3	7.5
Philip E. Eggers	593,750	9.7	7.1
Annette J. Campbell-White	230,467	3.8	2.8
Robert T. Hagen	123,334	2.0	1.5
Al Weinstein	100,000	1.6	1.2
A. Larry Tannenbaum	18,334	*	*
All Directors and executive officers as a group (8 persons)	4,010,418	65.4	48.1

Financial Statements

See **Tables 1A** and **1B** below for ArthroCare's balance sheets and income statements.

TABLE 1A   ArthroCare Corporation Balance Sheets ($000)

	December 31,		1996 YTD[a]	
	1994	*1995*	*Q1*	*Q2*
Assets				
Current assets:				
Cash and cash equivalents	$2,599	$4,774	$33,041	$30,223
Accounts receivable, net	—	212	863	1,176
Inventories	—	315	1,143	1,301
Prepaid expenses and other current assets	31	891	355	334
Total current assets	2,630	6,393	35,402	33,034
Property and equipment, net	275	1,135	1,090	1,477
Related party receivables[b]	—	228	—	1,609
Other	12	49	1,896	329
Total assets	$2,917	$7,800	$38,388	$36,449
Liabilities				
Current liabilities				
Accounts payable:				
Trade	$ 104	$ 732	$ 1,051	$ 439
Related parties	17	35	36	45
Accrued liabilities	35	472	577	922
Capital lease obligations, less current portion	15	34	35	36
Total current liabilities	163	1,274	1,699	1,442
Capital lease obligations, less current portion	15	43	44	35
Deferred rent	12	148	163	163
Total liabilities	190	1,475	1,906	1,640
Stockholders' Equity				
Convertible preferred stock	4	9	—	—
Common stock	1	2	9	9
Additional paid-in capital	5,685	16,869	48,767	48,787
Notes receivable from stockholder	—	(92)	(92)	(92)
Deferred compensation	—	(550)	(509)	(469)
Unrealized loss on investment		—	(37)	(35)
Accumulated deficit	(2,963)	(9,913)	(11,656)	(13,391)
Total Stockholders' Equity	2,727	6,325	36,482	34,809
Total Liabilities and Stockholders' Equity	$2,917	$7,800	$38,388	$36,449

Note: Columns listing 1996 YTD results were *not* included in original prospectus, but *are* included here for ease of comparison.

[a]Unaudited.

[b]Related party receivables consists primarily of several loans made to officers of the company.

TABLE 1B   ArthroCare Statements of Operations

	Period from April 29, 1993 (date of inception) to December 31, 1993	**Year Ended December 31,**		**YTD 1996**[a]	
		1994	*1995*	*Q1*	*Q2*
Net sales	—	—	$ 218	$ 1,159	$ 1,406
Cost of sales	—	—	447	1,065	1,236
Gross margin	—	—	(229)	94	170
Costs and expenses:					
Research and development	750	2,119	4,009	864	950
Sales and marketing	—	—	1,351	658	872
General and administrative	108	128	1,321	576	527
Nonrecurring charge for acquired					
technology	—	—	260	—	—
Total operating expenses	857	2,247	6,940	2,098	2,349
Loss from operations	(857)	(2,247)	(7,169)	(2,004)	(2,179)
Interest and other income	15	126	219	263	444
Net loss	$ (842)	$(2,121)	$(6,950)	$(1,743)	$(1,735)
Pro forma net loss per share	$(0.18)	$ (0.33)	$ (1.00)	$ (0.25)	$ (0.20)
Shares used in computing pro forma					
net loss per share	4,768,466	6,414,664	6,929,202	6,856,086	8,675,055

Note: Columns listing 1996 YTD results were *not* included in original prospectus, but *are* included here for ease of comparison.
[a]Unaudited.

EXHIBIT 2   **Equity Market—Medical Device Companies—at Time of IPO**

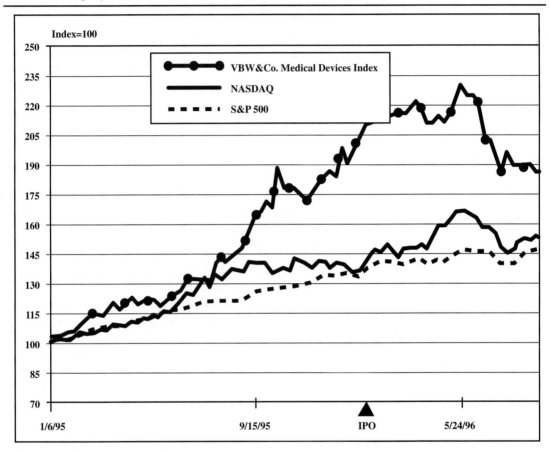

VBW&Co.'s Medical Devices Index includes: ARTC, BSC, BZET, CCVD, CGEN, ESON, GDT, GYNE, IVCR, MDT, OLGC, OPSI, URMD, and VIDA.

Source: Volpe, Welty.

EXHIBIT 3   Excerpts from First Volpe, Welty Research Report dated March 4, 1996

Investment Thesis

ArthroCare Corporation has created a superior product for performing arthroscopic surgery, one of the last great growth markets in the orthopedics industry. We expect significant appreciation in ArthroCare's stock over the next year. We expect this technology to be adapted to several other surgical fields, such as urology, gynecology, dermatology, and periodontics—all of which will add value to the company over time. We are initiating coverage of ArthroCare with a STRONG BUY (1) recommendation and 12-month price target of $30.

Introduction

ArthroCare has developed a core technology platform that simplifies the removal of soft tissue from the body. This technology, which has broad patent protection, has applications in several fields of medicine, including orthopedics, urology, gynecology, dermatology, and periodontics.

ArthroCare's technology entails a razor/razor blades approach. The capital components include a radio-frequency energy power controller and connecting cable, which together sell for approximately $12,500. The disposable component is a bipolar, multielectrode catheter, or wand, which carries a list price of $120.

TABLE 3A   ArthroCare Target Markets

Target Markets	Applications	510(k) Filing	U.S. Launch	U.S. Procedures/Year (Est.)
Orthopedics	Arthroscopy	7/94 (App 3/95)	12/95	2,300,000
Urology	Prostatic soft tissue, bladder tumors	12/95	Expected 2H;97	250,000
Gynecology	Intrauterine soft-tissue resection	12/95	Expected 2H;97	625,000
Dermatology	Wrinkles, discoloration	Expected mid-96	Expected 2H;98	500,000
Periodontics	Gingivectomy	Expected mid-96	Expected 2H:98	1,000,000

Source: ArthroCare Corporation and Volpe, Welty & Co. estimates.

TABLE 3B   ArthroCare Sales by Product Category (US$ in thousands)

	1996E	1997E	1998E	1999E	2000E
Arthroscopy	$7,200	$24,700	$40,200	$49,730	$60,000
Urology		300	4,800	10,800	14,000
Gynecology		600	6,300	12.800	15,500
Dermatology			600	3,220	5,000
Periodontics	—	—	600	3,450	5,500
TOTAL	$7,200	$25,600	$52,500	$80,000	$100,000

Source: Volpe, Welty & Co. estimates.

EXHIBIT 3   *(continued)*

In 1995, we estimate that approximately 2.3 million arthroscopies were performed in the United States. Procedures have grown at a compounded rate of 12 percent over the past couple of years and we are projecting a slight acceleration in this rate of procedure growth to 14 percent over the next several years.

We have surveyed several surgeons who have tested the ArthroCare system. The majority of these surgeons tell us that they believe the ArthroCare system is the most advanced method of performing arthroscopic surgery today. Most say they consider the system a superior tool for arthroscopy: the project simplifies the procedures, makes maneuvering in tight spaces faster and easier and reduces time required to perform the procedure.

Several surgeons have mentioned another advantage of the ArthroCare system: The product fits into the current Medicare reimbursement codes and guidelines for arthroscopic surgery. It is not like a device that requires a completely different surgical technique to be instituted, which often necessitates a new reimbursement code.

ArthroCare has developed a true platform technology that will give it a multitude of opportunities to add to the company's revenue stream over time. We think arthroscopy will be the main driver of the company's growth. In December 1995, the company filed separate 510(k) applications for use of the system in urology and gynecology. In our models, we assume that the product will be cleared for these indications and launched in the U.S. market in late 1997.

Management

ArthroCare has a strong and experienced management team. Directors and executive officers of the company own approximately 48 percent of the company's shares outstanding.

Financial Results and Projections

ArthroCare received net proceeds from its February 5, 1996, initial public offering of $31.8 million which, added to the company's previous balance of cash and equivalents of $4.8 million, gave the company cash and equivalents of approximately $36.6 million. We project that this sum will be more than sufficient to carry ArthroCare through to a cash-flow-positive position in the middle of 1997. We are forecasting cumulative losses of approximately $5.4 million between the first quarter of 1996 and the second quarter of 1997.

For 1996, the company's first full year of sales, we are forecasting that sales will reach $7.2 million—entirely from sales of the Arthroscopic System. Our model assumes that 35 percent of the year's sales, or $2.5 million, will be from sales of the capital component of the product, the controller and connecting cables, and that 65 percent of the total, or $4.7 million, will be derived from sales of the disposable ArthroWand component of the system. We assume that the product will be available in overseas markets in late 1996.

For 1997, we are projecting a jump in sales to $25.6 million, comprised mostly (96.5 percent) of sales of the Arthroscopic System. We project that the company will launch versions of its tissue ablation and coagulation technology for the urology and gynecology market in the second half of the year, and that sales of those products will comprise 1.2 percent and 2.3 percent of total sales for the year, respectively.

For 1998, we forecast that sales will more than double to $52.5 million. Our model assumes that ArthoCare will launch versions of its product for the dermatology and periodontics markets in the second half of that year and that sales into these new markets will add an incremental $1.2 million to sales for the full year (2.3 percent of total sales for the year). Our earnings estimate of the year is $9.4 million, or $1.01 per share ($5.6 million, or $0.63 per share, fully taxed). See **Table 3E** for a build-up of sales and revenues by product.

EXHIBIT 3   *(continued)*

In 1999, with all five currently contemplated versions of the company's technology on the market, we forecast sales growth of nearly 52 percent to $80 million. Of this total, 62.2 percent is expected from the core Arthroscopy System, 13.5 percent from urology applications, 16.0 percent from gynecology, 4.0 percent from dermatology, and 4.3 percent from periodontics. For 1999, we assume a tax rate for the entire year of 38 percent. On this fully taxed basis, we are projecting earnings of $10.2 million, or $1.08 per share.

Valuation

At the current price of $21 3/4, ArthroCare has a market capitalization of approximately $195 million. We think that the stock could carry a valuation of approximately $268 million, or $30 per share, within 12 months. This would represent a gain of 38 percent.

In our valuation models, we are using 1999 as our reference year, since this represents the first full year of "normalized" operations—the first year in which ArthroCare's products for each target-use should be on the market. We are projecting approximately $10.2 million in fully taxed net income for ArthroCare in 1999. We think the stock could trade in late 1998 at a forward multiple of 35 times our projected net income figure, for a market capitalization of approximately $357 million, or nearly $40 per share. That forward multiple would represent a discount to our projected three-year compounded fully taxed earnings growth rate of 85 percent. If we discount this anticipated late 1998 market capitalization back by 25 percent a year to the end of Q1:97, this gives us a one-year target market cap of $268 million, or a $30 per share price target.

TABLE 3C Comparable Company Valuation Analysis of Selected Medical Device Companies

Column groups: *LTM Financial Performance Measures* spans Margins, Gross Margins, Net Margins, LTM ROA[b], LTM ROE[b]. *Ratio Price to* spans Operating Income, LTM EPS, '96 EPS, '97 EPS.

Company	LTM[a] Ended	Margins	Gross Margins	Net Margins	LTM ROA[b]	LTM ROE[b]	MarketCap 3/1/96 ($mil)	Ratio MarketCap to LTM Revenue	Operating Income	LTM EPS	'96 EPS	'97 EPS	Projected 5YR EPS Growth Rate (%)	Ratio '96 PE to 5 YR EPS Growth Rate
Arrow International Inc.	Nov-95	53.5%	25.3%	16.2%	14.6%	21.0%	923	4.2x	16.6x	26.0x	21.5x	18.0x	19.5	110.4x
ArthroCare Corp.	Dec-95	45.5	nm	nm	nm	nm	187	858.0	nm	nm	nm	84.6	50.0	nm
Avecor Cardiovascular	Dec-95	57.4	10.5	9.9	13.5	15.6	99	3.0	28.2	29.9	26.8	19.2	40.0	67.1
Cardiometrics, Inc.	Dec-95	55.1	7.4	2.7	2.4	5.1	55	4.9	nm	nm	nm	nm	nm	nm
Circon Corp.[c]	Dec-95	30.0	nm	nm	nm	nm	161	1.0	13.5	36.6	11.9	9.9	20.0	59.4
EndoSonics Corp.[d]	Dec-95	75.5	31.7	32.9	14.5	15.7	196	11.5	nm	nm	nm	56.3	30.0	nm
ESC Medical Systems Ltd.	Dec-95	5.9	nm	nm	nm	nm	339	40.3	127.1	122.5	90.7	67.2	35.0	259.2
Gynecare Inc.	Dec-95	nm	nm	nm	nm	nm	78	92.4	nm	nm	nm	nm	35.0	nm
MediSense Inc.	Dec-95	66.6	18.8	17.8	33.7	54.2	540	3.2	17.1	18.1	17.3	14.7	18.0	96.2
VidaMed Inc.	Dec-95	nm	nm	nm	nm	nm	87	33.3	nm	nm	nm	25.7	nm	nm
HIGH		75%	31.7%	32.9%	33.7%	54.2%		92.4x	127.1x	122.5x	90.7	67.2x	50	259.2%
LOW		5.9	7.4	2.7	2.4	5.1		1.0	13.5	18.1	11.9	9.9	18	59.4
MARKET WEIGHTED AVERAGE		55.9%	22.5%	17.9%	18.4%	27.0%		72.4X	35.2X	40.8X	31.3X	32.3X	25.1	125.1%
MEDIAN		55.1	14.6	13.8	14.0	15.6		8.2	22.7	33.3	22.1	22.4	27.1	81.6
AVERAGE		48.0	17.1	15.8	16.0	22.6		23.7	46.5	51.8	36.7	32.1	30.5	120.5

Source: Volpe, Welty & Company estimates, First Call, Zack's Investment Research, and I/B/E/S.

[a] LTM = Latest 12 months.

[b] Return on average assets and equity for LTM.

[c] Circon Corporation data exclude nonrecurring charges related to the company's 1995 acquisition of Cabot Medical.

[d] EndoSonics Corporation Q4-95 and FY-95 financial data are preliminary, and were released by the company on January 23, 1996.

TABLE 3D **ArthroCare: Quarterly Results and Volpe, Welty Forecasts ($ in 000)**

	Revenue	COGS	Gross margin	S,G&A	R&D	Operating Income	Operating Margin	Pretax Income	Pretax Margin	Tax Rate	Net Income	Net Margin	EPS
Q1:95a	0	0	NM	395	658	(1,053)	NM	(1,033)	NM	0.0%	(1,033)	NM	(0.15)
Q2:95a	0	0	NM	540	890	(1,430)	NM	(1,365)	NM	0.0	(1,365)	NM	(0.20)
Q3:95a	0	0	NM	730	1,600	(2,330)	NM	(2,265)	NM	0.0	(2,265)	NM	(0.33)
Q4:95a	218	447	NM	1,007	2,121	(2,357)	NM	(2,288)	NM	0.0	(2,288)	NM	(0.33)
FY 95 Total Actual	218	447	NM	2,672	4,269	(7,170)	NM	(6,951)	NM	0.0%	(6,951)	NM	(1.00)
Q1:96e	750	880	NM	1,015	1,140	(2,285)	NM	(2,121)	NM	0.0	(2,121)	NM	(0.27)
Q2:96e	1,200	980	18.3%	1,020	1,150	(1,950)	NM	(1,694)	NM	0.0	(1,694)	NM	(0.20)
Q3:96e	1,840	1,200	34.8	1,030	1,200	(1,590)	NM	(1,260)	NM	0.0	(1,260)	NM	(0.14)
Q4:96e	3,410	1,500	56.0	1,050	1,400	(540)	NM	(290)	NM	0.0	(290)	6.3	(0.03)
FY 96 Total Est.	7,200	4,560	36.7%	4,115	4,959	(6,365)	NM	(5,365)	NM	0.0%	(5,365)	NM	(0.65)
Q1:97e	5,000	2,000	60.0	1,600	1,750	(350)	NM	(120)	NM	0.0	(120)	NM	(0.01)
Q2:97e	5,800	2,300	60.3	1,850	1,780	(130)	NM	70	1.2	0.0	70	1.2	0.01
Q3:97e	6,800	2,500	63.2	1,950	1,790	560	8.2	750	11.0	0.0	750	11.0	0.08
Q4:97e	8,000	2,700	66.3	2,300	1,800	1,200	15.0	1,380	17.3	0.0	1,380	17.3	0.15
FY 97 Total Est.	25,600	9,500	62.9%	7,700	7,120	1,280	5.0%	2,080	8.1%	0.0%	2,080	8.1%	0.23
Q1:98e	10,000	3,300	67.0	3,200	2,000	1,500	15.0	1,700	17.0	0.0	1,700	17.0	0.19
Q2:98e	12,250	4,000	67.3	4,200	2,050	2,000	16.3	2,210	18.0	0.0	2,210	18.0	0.24
Q3:98e	14,000	4,550	67.5	5,000	2,100	2,350	16.8	2,530	18.1	0.0	2,530	18.1	0.27
Q4:98e	16,250	5,280	67.5	5,900	2,270	2,800	17.2	2,930	18.0	0.0	2,930	18.0	0.31
FY 98 Total Est.	52,500	17,130	67.4%	18,300	8,420	8,650	16.5%	9,370	17.8%	0.0%	9,370	17.8%	1.01
FY 99 Total Est.	80,000	25,500	68.1	28,400	10,285	15,815	19.8	16,465	20.6	38.0	10,208	12.8	1.08
FY 00 Total Est.	100,000	30,000	70.0%	35,000	12,500	22,500	22.5%	23,000	23.0%	38.0%	14,260	14.3%	1.50

Note: Amounts may not total due to rounding.

TABLE 3E   ArthroCare Sales Forecast—Units and Revenue ($000)

	1996 Q1	Q2	Q3	Q4	YEAR	1997 Q1	Q2	Q3	Q4	YEAR	1998 Q1	Q2	Q3	Q4	YEAR	1999 Q1	Q2	Q3	Q4	YEAR
SALES-UNITS CONTROLLERS																				
Arthroscopy	48	76	117	217	458	118	130	131	93	472	109	111	108	150	478	191	158	184	146	678
Urology	0	0	0	0	0	0	0	4	8	12	15	22	33	42	113	31	37	41	44	152
Dermatology	0	0	0	0	0	0	0	0	0	0	0	0	5	9	14	8	11	13	14	45
Gynecology	0	0	0	0	0	0	0	8	16	25	19	33	42	54	148	38	42	47	54	181
Peridontics	0	0	0	0	0	0	0	0	0	0	0	0	5	9	14	8	11	13	16	49
Total	48	76	117	217	458	118	130	143	117	509	143	166	188	264	753	268	259	298	274	1105
WANDS																				
Arthroscopy	4,875	7,800	11,960	22,165	46,800	44,444	52,200	56,489	64,533	217,667	79,718	90,047	97,412	109,741	376,918	114,750	123,200	130,500	139,500	507,950
Urology	0	0	0	0	0	0	0	733	1,444	2,167	6,118	8,941	13,176	16,941	45,176	24,200	28,600	31,900	34,100	118,800
Dermatology	0	0	0	0	0	0	0	0	0	0	0	0	1,882	3,765	5,647	6,050	8,250	10,120	11,000	35,420
Gynecology	0	0	0	0	0	0	0	1,444	2,889	4,333	7,529	13,176	16,941	21,647	59,294	29,700	33,000	36,300	41,800	140,800
Peridontics	0	0	0	0	0	0	0	0	0	0	0	0	1,882	3,765	5,647	6,600	8,800	10,450	12,100	37,950
Total	4,875	7,800	11,960	22,165	46,800	44,444	52,200	58,666	68,866	224,167	93,365	112,164	129,411	155,859	492,682	181,300	193,050	219,270	238,500	840,920
SALES—(000$) CONTROLLERS																				
Arthroscopy	263	420	644	1,194	2,520	1,000	1,102	1,116	792	4,010	924	946	920	1,272	4,062	1,620	1,344	1,560	1,240	5,764
Urology	0	0	0	0	0	0	0	35	70	105	130	190	280	360	960	264	312	348	372	1,296
Dermatology	0	0	0	0	0	0	0	0	0	0	0	0	40	80	120	66	90	110	120	386
Gynecology	0	0	0	0	0	0	0	70	140	210	160	280	360	460	1,260	324	360	396	456	1,536
Peridontics	0	0	0	0	0	0	0	0	0	0	0	0	40	80	120	72	96	114	132	414
Total	263	420	644	1,194	2,520	1,000	1,102	1,221	1,002	4,325	1,214	1,416	1,640	2,252	6,522	2,346	2,202	2,528	2,320	9,396
WANDS																				
Arthroscopy	487	480	1,196	2,217	4,700	4,000	4,698	5,084	4,808	19,590	6,776	7,654	8,280	9,328	32,038	9,180	9,856	10,440	11,160	40,636
Urology	0	0	0	0	0	0	0	65	130	195	520	760	1,120	1,440	3,840	1,936	2,288	2,552	2,728	9,504
Dermatology	0	0	0	0	0	0	0	0	0	0	0	0	160	320	480	484	660	810	880	2,834
Gynecology	0	0	0	0	0	0	0	130	260	390	640	1,120	1,440	1,840	5,040	2,376	2,640	2,904	3,344	11,264
Peridontics	0	0	0	0	0	0	0	0	0	0	0	0	160	320	480	528	704	836	968	3,036
Total	487	780	1,196	2,217	4,700	4,000	4,698	5,279	6,198	20,175	7,936	9,534	11,160	13,248	41,878	14,504	16,148	17,542	19,080	67,274
TOTAL SALES (000$)																				
Total Arthroscopy	750	1,200	1,840	3,410	7,200	5,000	5,800	6,200	6,600	23,600	7,700	8,600	9,200	10,600	36,100	10,800	11,200	12,000	12,400	46,400
Total Urology	0	0	0	0	0	0	0	100	200	300	650	950	1,400	1,800	4,800	2,200	2,600	2,900	3,100	10,800
Total Dermatology	0	0	0	0	0	0	0	0	0	0	0	0	200	400	600	550	750	920	1,000	3,220
Total Gynecology	0	0	0	0	0	0	0	2,000	400	2,400	800	1,400	1,800	2,300	6,300	2,700	3,000	3,300	3,800	12,800
Total Periodontics	0	0	0	0	0	0	0	0	0	0	0	0	200	400	600	600	800	950	1,100	3,450
Total $	750	1,200	1,840	3,410	7,200	5,000	5,800	8,300	7,200	26,300	9,150	10,950	12,800	15,500	48,400	16,850	18,350	20,070	21,400	76,670

EXHIBIT 4   ArthroCare Stock Performance Post-IPO

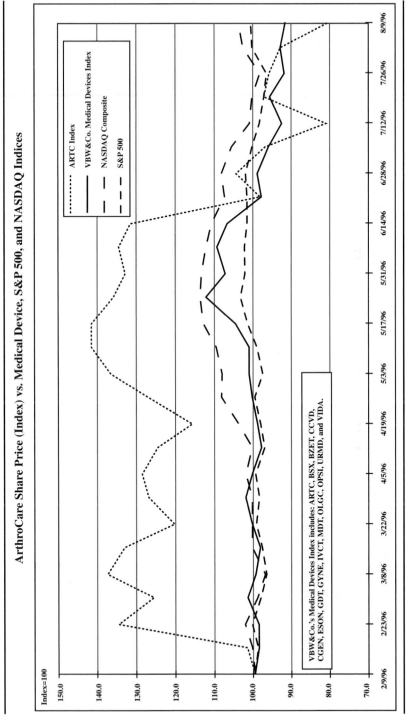

ArthroCare Share Price (Index) vs. Medical Device, S&P 500, and NASDAQ Indices

Source: Volpe, Welty.

EXHIBIT 4 *(concluded)*

ArthroCare Stock: Price and Volume History

COMPOSITE/CLOSE/TRADE		
PRICE		
Last	13¾	on 08/09/96
High	25¾	on 03/11/96
Ave	20.309	
Low	13½	on 08/08/96

Source: Bloomberg.
Note: Volume for days 1 and 2 of trading is excluded.

EXHIBIT 5   Excerpts from Follow-on Volpe, Welty, Research Reports

March 12, 1996
Price $25
Opinion: Strong Buy (1)

ArthroCare Gets 510(k) Clearance for Urology Device—the clearance, which covers ARTC's
bipolar urological loop device, came within 90 days, much sooner than we had expected.

April 26, 1996
Price $22
Opinion: Strong Buy (1)

ArthroCare Reports Better-Than-Expected Q1:96 Sales—Sales for Q1:96 of nearly $1.2 million
beat our $750,000 projection, reflecting not only higher-than-expected sales of demonstration units to
distributors, but also higher sell-through of wands to physicians. The loss of $1.74 million ($0.25 per
share) was slightly better than the estimated $2.1 million ($0.26 per share).

June 6, 1996
Price $23
Opinion: Strong Buy (1)

ArthroCare Gets Second 510(k) Clearance for a Urology Device—the 510(k) clearance, which
was approved in less than 90 days, covers a multielectrode, bipolar device. This complements the
company's previously approved urological loop device. The clearance supports ArthroCare's efforts
to develop its platform technology beyond its initial use in arthroscopy.

July 26, 1996
Price $16 1/2
Opinion: Strong Buy (1)

ArthroCare's Q2:96 revenues of $1.4 million exceeded our estimate of $1.2 million. A reported
loss per share of $0.20 was in line. Product sales were up 21 percent over the previous quarter,
reflecting growing demand for the company's bipolar Arthroscopic system. Ninety controllers were
placed in the second quarter, bringing the total base of installed controllers to roughly 300—
40 percent of those in hospitals where wand usage per controller should be higher. Q2:96 wands
sales were approximately 10,000 units.

Q2:96 gross margins of 12 percent exceeded the 8 percent we had anticipated, and we expect
this margin to continue to improve.

The FDA recently cleared ArthroCare's 510(k) application to market the Arthroscopic system
for use in the wrist and the hip. The wrist indication was approved in 35 days, the hip in 65 days.
The system is now approved for use in all six of the major joints in the body.

We think that upcoming events, including evidence of continued market penetration in
arthroscopy, FDA-clearance of the periodontal and dermatology indications, the signing of a U.S.
marketing partner for the company's urological devices, agreements with international distributors
and the commencement of international sales in early 1997, will help investors recognize the
tremendous potential behind the stock. Our 12-month price target: $30.

August 6, 1996
Price $14 1/2
Strong Buy (1)

We have revised our sales and earnings estimates for ArthroCare Corp. to reflect the following:
We expect higher 2H:96 and FY:97 SG&A expenses associated with aggressive growth plans for

---

EXHIBIT 5   *(concluded)*

U.S. marketing of the company's Arthroscopic System, as well as for the FY:97 launch of devices for the urology and periodontal markets. We have raised our estimate of Q3:96 R&D costs by $50,000 and our estimates of Q4:96 R&D costs by $100,000 to account for development of ArthroCare's technology for the urology and periodontal markets following sooner-than-anticipated 510(k) clearance for these indications. We have also lowered our Q4:96 sales estimates slightly because we now expect ArthroCare to move the launch of its System overseas from late 1996 to the first half of 1997. Accordingly, we have revised our 1997 sales ramp while our FY:97 revenue estimate remains the same. We also expect slightly higher FY:96 and FY:97 interest income.

We think ArthroCare will continue to reap benefits from its 510(k) strategy to gain U.S. marketing clearance for its core technology in several different indications. In orthopedics, the company's Arthroscopic System can now be marketed for use in all major joints in the body, and we expect the company to remain focused on this market in the United States for the rest of 1996. We continue to rate the stock a STRONG BUY (1). Our 12-month price target is $30.

Volpe, Welty Earnings Estimate Change

Period	Estimate	Former	Current	% Change
Q3:96E	Revenues (000)	$1,840	$1,840	0.00%
	Earnings Per Share	($0.14)	($0.20)	NM
Q4:96E	Revenues (000)	$3,410	$3,150	(7.62%)
	Earnings Per Share	($0.03)	($0.15)	NM
FY:96E	Revenues (000)	$7,815	$7,555	(3.33%)
	Earnings Per Share	($0.63)	($0.80)	NM
Q1:97E	Revenues (000)	$5,000	$4,600	(8.00%)
	Earnings Per Share	($0.01)	($0.03)	NM
Q2:97E	Revenues (000)	$5,800	$5,400	(6.90%)
	Earnings Per Share	$0.01	$0.00	NM
Q3:97E	Revenues (000)	$6,800	$7,200	5.88%
	Earnings Per Share	$0.08	$0.10	25.00%
Q4:97E	Revenues (000)	$8,000	$8,400	5.00%
	Earnings Per Share	$0.15	$0.16	6.67%
FY:97E	Revenues (000)	$25,600	$25,600	0.00%
	Earnings Per Share	$0.23	$0.23	0.00%
FY:98E	Revenues (000)	$52,500	$52,500	0.00%
	Earnings Per Share	$1.01	$1.01	0.00%
FY:99E	Revenues (000)	$80,000	$80,000	0.00%
	Earnings Per Share	$1.08	$1.08	0.00%
FY:00E	Revenues (000)	$100,000	$100,000	0.00%
	Earnings Per Share	$1.50	$1.50	0.00%

**EXHIBIT 6   ArthroCare Corporation:
Institutional Shareholdings**

Owner	Holdings 3/30/96	Holdings 6/30/96
Putnam Inv. Mgt.	352,600	505,200
Geocapital Corp.	38,000	363,000
Crown Advisors	35,800	168,800
AIM Mgt. Group	228,400	100,000
BZW Barclays	0	71,500
Columbia Mgt. Co.	11,500	59,000
USAA Inv. Mgt.	40,000	54,000
Sunamer Asset Mgt.	0	31,500
General Motors	21,500	21,500
Strong/Cornelius	11,300	17,900
Calif. Teachers	0	16,100
Bankers Trust	6,400	8,200
Dean Witter Intercapital	0	7,000
Wells Fargo	0	3,350
Merrill Lynch & Co.	0	2,200
Westfield Capital	1,100	1,100
Fred Alger Mgt.	24,000	0
Berkeley Capital Mgt.	120,800	0
Furman Selz	28,000	0
Husic Capital	12,000	0
Jack's National	120,500	0
Nich-Apple Capital	139,400	0
Oppenheimer Mgt.	75,500	0
Piper Capital Mgt.	1,000	0
Frank Russell Co.	81,700	0
Sirach Capital Mgt.	285,500	0
Yale University	0	0
Mellon Bank	0	0
RCM Capital	0	0
Mellon Capital Mgt.	0	0
Travelers, Inc.	0	0
American General	0	0
Bear Sterns	0	0

Note: Ranked based on 6/30/96 ownership.
Source: Carson Group.

HARVESTING VALUE

This final part of the book examines the issue of how to harvest the value that's been created. Of course, this issue needs to be addressed in the very earliest stages of venture planning, as it influences the choice of investors, legal form, and strategy.

Chapter 18, "Securities Law and Public Offerings," examines some of the legal and business issues that surround a public offering of stock in an "IPO." While this represents the entrepreneurial dream for many, it also represents a significant change in the way in which an enterprise is managed. Other paths to liquidity include an outright sale of the business, as well as simply managing the venture to generate cash. And, for some the ultimate reward is not liquidity at all, but the opportunity to pass the enterprise on to the next generation.

SECURITIES LAW AND PUBLIC OFFERINGS

In Chapter 11, "Securities Law and Private Financing," we looked at the process and laws that affected private financings. In this piece, we will look at similar issues as they relate to public offerings.

Why "Go Public"?

For many companies, the decision on whether or not to become a public company is a difficult one. For some, the glamour and prestige of becoming a public company are the deciding factors. For others, the scrutiny and lack of privacy that go along with being publicly held clearly outweigh the advantages.

The Advantages

There are some significant advantages that go along with being a public company. They include:

- A vast continuing source of capital: The public equity markets do represent a vast pool of capital. A healthy, growing firm can often tap this source more cheaply than other private sources of equity. And, as the company continues to grow, the public equity market will be available as long as investors have confidence in the company's prospects.
- Liquidity: A public market for the company's securities makes them far more liquid. The company can give employees stock or options as an

---

This chapter was prepared by Michael J. Roberts, Howard H. Stevenson, and Richard E. Floor, of Goodwin, Procter & Hoar, Boston.

Copyright © 1984 by the President and Fellows of Harvard College.

Harvard Business School Note 9-384-165.

incentive to lure talented individuals. And the principals of the firm can (subject to certain SEC regulations) sell their stock as they desire.

- Wealth creation: Taking a company public establishes its value in the market. In addition, through a "secondary offering" of securities, the principals can often sell a portion of their interest at the time of the initial public offering. This creates wealth for both the founders and the financial backers—such as venture capital firms—who invested in the business.
- Glamour and prestige: For many individuals, "taking their company public" is an important goal. It certainly is one measure of success, as a certain minimum size is generally required in order to take a firm public. Being a public concern may also enhance the company's image with customers, suppliers, and employees.

For some entrepreneurs, these advantages are outweighed by the disadvantages of being a public concern.

The Disadvantages

The disadvantages include:

- Cost: Going public is expensive; estimates run from $100,000 to over $300,000 for an "average" public offering. In addition, there is an underwriters' commission of 7 to 10 percent, which goes to compensate the investment bank for selling the securities. Finally, there is an annual expense associated with the added accounting and record-keeping required for a public company.
- Public scrutiny: A public company must file, and make available to the public, its financial statements, as well as certain information about stockholders, customers, business plans, and officers. A company might prefer that its suppliers, customers, and competitors not know how profitable it is, or be aware of some aspect of its business. Finally, certain business practices, such as officers' salaries and business expenses, also come under public scrutiny.
- Pressures on management: Being a public concern also puts certain pressures on top management. The stock market likes to see constant earnings growth, and the faster the better. There has been a great deal of publicity lately that this "short-term earnings focus" is the cause of serious longer-term competitive problems for many American industries. Finally, management must spend a good deal of time dealing with the financial community, keeping bankers and analysts up to date and interested in the stock.
- Loss of independence: As a sole owner or small group of principals, management could feel securely in control. But public ownership brings with it a larger constituency. Managers must now manage the company for the good of all the shareholders. Previously borderline business expenses may

now be totally inappropriate. In addition, there is always the possibility that some outside group may actually try to take over the company. As a public concern, management is far more vulnerable.

These disadvantages are accentuated by the close relationship that usually exists between ownership and management in the entrepreneurial concern. In large public companies, these disadvantages have been accepted as a way of life by a management team, which typically controls very little of the stock. In entrepreneurial firms, where the founder(s) may still hold a majority of the shares, the distinction between management and ownership may easily blur. This can lead to management that manages for itself rather than the entire group of stockholders. While this can happen in large companies, minority shareholders in small firms have less chance of successfully combating this practice.

The Decision

The decision to go public is an important one and should be made with the counsel of experienced accountants, lawyers, and bankers. Remember, though, that these people have their own stakes: The investment banker stands to gain a good deal on the sale of the company's securities; a local accountant often loses out to a Big Eight firm when a company goes public and seeks an accounting firm with a national reputation.

In general, it does seem that many entrepreneurs overestimate some of the benefits of being a public company. Liquidity, for instance, is often seen as a major advantage. But it is a very difficult task indeed for a president to explain at an analysts meeting why he "dumped" some of his holdings in the market.

Clearly, the need for equity capital must be at the heart of the firm's decision to go public. And, before wandering down this path, the firm would be well advised to consider other options, such as a private placement of debt or equity.

Selecting an Underwriter

Once a company has made a decision to seriously consider going public, it is time to choose an underwriter. Underwriters, or investment bankers, are required both to sell the securities and lead the company through this complex process.

Choosing an Underwriter

The process of selecting an underwriter is not easy. Many investment banks will be anxious to serve the company and will make convincing arguments about why their firms are well suited to execute the company's public offering. When choosing a firm, the following criteria are important.

- Reputation: The underwriter's name will appear at the bottom of the prospectus, often in letters as large as the company's name. The underwriter's reputation will affect its ability to sell the stock both to other investment banks and to institutional and retail customers.
- Distribution: Investment banks have certain strengths and weaknesses in terms of their ability to distribute the stock. Some have a strong institutional network selling to large pension funds and money managers. Others sell primarily to retail accounts—private investors.
- It is often desirable to have a mix of stockholders. Institutions have deep pockets, but can be unfaithful, deserting and selling a stock on the first sign of bad news. Retail accounts tend to be more stable, but are not as big a force in the stock market.
- Aftermarket support: It is important that a bank support a company after the public offering. This support includes:
  - Research—to sustain interest in the stock on the part of investors.
  - Market making—committing capital to buying and selling the stock, to provide investors with liquidity.
  - Financial advice—bankers can provide valuable advice on the subject of dividends, new financing, or mergers and acquisitions.

Recently, underwriters have become more competitive, and investment banking is not the "gentlemanly business" it was considered to be years ago. The entrepreneur would be wise to consider and negotiate with a variety of firms.

What about Stock Price?

Note that we have not mentioned price as one of the criteria. Clearly, you would prefer to sell stock in your company to the underwriters who thought it was worth the most in the market. During the negotiation process, underwriters will often estimate the price at which the stock will be sold in the public offering.

- First, they make projections of the company's earnings per share.
- Then, they attempt to place a price/earnings multiple on this figure to arrive at a per share value.

In theory, this approach should work just fine. But the price/earnings multiple is a very subjective judgment, based on an assessment of what multiples similar companies are trading at.

The night before the offering, after many months of work and after spending a good deal of money, the market will in all likelihood appear quite different than it did at the time of the initial negotiations. The underwriter may suggest an offering price that is substantially different from the price discussed during negotiations. The company has little choice save to cancel the offering entirely.

This fact is *not* lost on the underwriters.

Other Issues

Once a company has decided to go public, and chosen an underwriter, several other important issues remain.

- Listing: The company must decide where its shares will be listed and traded. The New York and American Stock Exchanges, as well as other exchanges, all have certain requirements that must be met in order for the firm to obtain a listing.
- Amount of primary offering: The firm must decide how much money it wishes to raise.
- Amount of secondary offering: In addition to selling its "own shares"— the primary offering—the principals of the firm may sell some of their own stock.

This is called a *secondary offering,* and the owners of the stock, *not* the company, get to keep the money that is raised from sale of secondary stock.

Registered Offerings

All public offerings must be registered with the SEC under the Securities Act of 1933.

The Registration Process

The registration process for a company that is not yet publicly traded involves the preparation by management of a carefully worded and organized disclosure document called a *registration statement.* This includes a prospectus, which will be provided to the potential investor. The registration statement is filed with the appropriate securities agency, which, for federal registrations, is the SEC. The various items of disclosure that must be discussed in a registration statement are fixed by law. In addition, there must be set forth any other material matter that affects or may affect the company.

The SEC staff reviews the disclosure documents and (unless a special "cursory review" procedure is used) makes detailed comments on the disclosure, and the documents are revised as a result of these comments. If the staff is satisfied with the revisions, the SEC enters an order declaring the registration statement "effective," and sale of the offering may commence. The SEC order in no way constitutes an approval by the SEC of the accuracy of the disclosures or the merits of the offering, and any representation to that effect violates the securities laws. At the time of the effectiveness of the registration statement, the underwriters will usually place a "tombstone" advertisement in the financial press announcing the offering. A copy of the final prospectus in an initial public offering must be distributed to persons purchasing company securities of the type sold in the offering for 25 days after the effective date, or until the offering is sold or terminated, whichever occurs last. During this period, if any material event affecting the company occurs, it must be disclosed by a sticker supplement to the prospectus. In general, the disclosure documents become outdated after approximately nine months from the effective date and may not be used thereafter unless updated by posteffective amendment to the registration statement.

Cost

Federal registration is expensive and time consuming. An initial public offering using an underwriter frequently takes four months to accomplish and costs from $150,000 to $300,000, exclusive of underwriting commissions. A typical cost breakdown is as follows: printing, $75,000; legal fees, $100,000; accounting fees, $50,000; and Blue Sky and miscellaneous costs, $25,000. (These figures are rough and may vary considerably from offering to offering.) In view of the amount of the costs involved, federal registration of a first offering using an underwriter is generally not feasible unless in excess of $2 million is involved in the financing.

The cost of a public offering depends as much upon whether or not an underwriter is used as upon whether or not federal registration is required. This is true because the agreement between the company and the underwriter usually requires the company's attorneys and accountants to undertake at the company's expense detailed and costly verification of the disclosures in the prospectus. Underwriting commissions typically run from 7 1/2 percent to 10 percent of the gross amount of the offering in first equity offerings. The underwriter may also require warrants to purchase an amount of stock equal to 10 percent of the shares sold at the offering at a small premium over the offering price as additional compensation. Because placement of a large amount of securities often involves market price stabilization and other sophisticated and highly regulated techniques, an attempt by a company to place a large amount of securities without a professional underwriter or selling agent usually involves an unacceptable amount of risk. Also, it may be extremely difficult for a large amount of securities to be placed without the assistance of a professional underwriter or selling agent with a number of investor customers that rely upon his or her investment advice.

Underwriters

Underwriters essentially agree to sell the company's securities for a fixed percentage of the underwriting. Underwritings are of two types—*firm-commitment underwritings* in which the sale of the entire offering at an established price is guaranteed by the underwriters and *best-efforts underwritings* in which the underwriter uses his best efforts to sell as much as he can of the offering at the offering price. Best-efforts underwritings may also include a provision requiring that either all or a minimum amount of the securities must be sold as a condition of any of the securities being sold. The type of underwriting used is usually determined by the size and strength of the company and of the underwriter.

The first step in an underwritten offering is usually the execution of a non-binding *letter of intent* between the company (or selling stockholder) and the managing underwriter. Although not a legally binding document, the letter of intent is one of the most important documents in the offering, as it establishes the basic terms of the underwriting, usually including the price range—perhaps as a range of multiples of the company's most recent earnings. (If multiples of per share earnings are used, it should be made clear whether the per share figures are to be calculated using the number of outstanding shares before or those after the offering.) After the letter of intent has been signed, the disclosure documents (including the prospectus) are prepared for filing with the SEC.

From the outset of an underwritten offering, the managing underwriter and the company (or selling stockholder) commence subtle negotiation of the price of the offering, which is usually culminated by the setting of the price on the evening before the offering. During the course of the registration, the company incurs substantial offering expenses, which (as both parties well realize) will be to a large extent unrecoverable if the financing is postponed or aborted. In addition to the problems a firm-commitment underwriter has in guaranteeing sale of the entire offering when the price is at a high level, a managing underwriter has an incentive to negotiate a low price for his or her own customers and for those of the members of his or her underwriting and selling syndicate, with which she or he usually has an established business relationship. (A broker with unhappy customers soon has no customers.) She or he often does this by subtly threatening to abandon the deal after the company has expended substantial unrecoverable funds in preparation for the offering and after it has terminated negotiations with competing underwriters. It is thus important for the company, if possible, to require the underwriter to bear his or her own expenses (including attorneys' fees) so that any abandonment will result in some loss (although a lesser one) for the underwriter. This arrangement should be set forth in the letter of intent. On the other hand, the offering price should not be set too high or the price of the securities may suffer in the aftermarket, thereby reducing the value of the remaining securities holdings of the principal owners and diminishing the company's ability to raise capital in the future.

Throughout the period of registration, including the prospectus delivery period following the effective date, the company must carefully monitor the public statements of its management, its public relations advisors, and its advertising program to assure that no optimistic disclosures concerning the company's condition or prospects are disseminated to the investing public. If, for example, an article on the company appears in *Forbes* or *Business Week* during registration, it may be deemed to be part of the company's selling effort (to the extent it is based upon information supplied by management) and thus subject to the rigid standards of the securities laws. Disclosure during the period preceding the initial filing of the registration statement with the SEC (the prefiling period) is particularly sensitive, as such disclosure might be considered to be an attempt to precondition the market ("gun-jumping"). Even the information to be contained in an announcement of the filing of the registration statement is regulated by SEC rule. After the effective date, however, certain types of supplementary selling literature may be used if preceded or accompanied by a final prospectus.

The registration statement as initially filed contains a preliminary prospectus with a "red herring" legend printed in red sideways on the cover page. While the SEC staff is reviewing the registration statement and preparing its comments (the waiting period), the preliminary prospectus will be used by the underwriter in the formation of its underwriting and selling syndicate. Although the various members of the underwriting and selling syndicate often have an established business relationship with the managing underwriter, a new syndicate is formed for each deal. The preliminary prospectus will be used by syndicate members during the waiting period to solicit indications of interest from the investing public. The reception of the investing public to the preliminary prospectus will affect the price of the offering, which, as noted above, is usually established immediately prior to the effective date.

As a result of registration with the SEC, a company becomes subject to the periodic reporting requirements of the SEC. In the case of a first public offering, the company must report the actual use of proceeds to the SEC three months after the offering so the SEC can compare this with the disclosures in the prospectus. If there is a discrepancy, the company can expect SEC inquiry.

Offerings registered with the SEC generally must also be registered with the securities administrators of each of the states in which the offering is to be made. A simplified registration by "coordination" with the federal registration is usually allowed under state law. Many states do exempt from registration offerings of securities that will be listed on the New York or American Stock Exchange. If an underwriter or selling agent that is a member of the NASD is used, the terms of the underwriters' or sales agents' compensation must be reviewed by the NASD.

Form SB-2

In 1992, the SEC adopted a new form to simplify public offerings for smaller companies. The new form replaced Form S-18, which allowed expedited filing procedures and simplified disclosure requirements for companies engaged in small initial public offerings. Under Form SB-2, these advantages are now available to small business issuers, defined as companies with under $25 million in revenues and a public float of under $25 million, making any form of public offering.

The principal features of Form SB-2 are (*a*) the filing is made in the local SEC regional office (nine offices around the country) rather than in Washington; (*b*) an audited balance sheet is required for only the most recent fiscal year, and audited statements of income, cash flows, and changes in stockholders' equity are required for only the two most recent years; (*c*) the general disclosures are significantly simpler and are tailored for smaller and less mature companies. The primary advantage of Form SB-2 is dealing with the lighter workloads and geographical proximity of the regional offices. These, coupled with the reduced disclosure requirements, could be expected to reduce by 25 percent or more both the amount of time and the expenses involved in an offering.

The use of Form SB-2 is limited to offerings by domestic or Canadian issuers that are not investment companies or the subsidiaries of companies that are not small business issuers. If Form SB-2 is used to register an initial public offering, the offering may not be expected to result in a public float of greater than $25 million. The company must also report the use of the proceeds of an initial public offering to the SEC within 10 days after the first three-month period following the effective date of the registration statement, and within 10 days after the application of the offering proceeds of the termination of the offering.

Regulation A Offerings

If the financing involves a public offering on behalf of the company of $5 million or less, and if the company's management, principal equity owners, and other persons whose securities require registration before resale seek to publicly offer not more than $1.5 million as part of that offering, the offering may be made under SEC Regulation A rather than pursuant to full registration. When considering such an offering, an issuer must be aware of several potential obstacles. For example, a company may not issue more than $5 million of its securities under Regulation A during any 12-month period, and, for purposes of calculating that limitation, any offerings made pursuant to an exemption or in violation of the registration requirements are included. Further, insiders and affiliates may sell pursuant to Regulation A only if the company has had profitable operations during one of its last two fiscal years. Finally, the exemption is totally unavailable to issuers that have been *inter alia,* convicted of violating the securities laws or subjected to an SEC refusal or stop order, post office fraud order, or injunction within the previous five years, or whose directors, officers, principal security holders, or underwriters have been convicted of violating the securities laws within the previous 10 years or enjoined from violating the same.

Assuming availability of the exemption, the Regulation A offering procedure is similar to that used with Form SB-2 and is similarly less complex. The primary difference between Form SB-2 and the use of Regulation A is that the latter has no requirement for audited financials. In addition, issuers contemplating a Regulation A offering may "test the waters" before preceding if they file the solicitation materials with the SEC before use and then allow a 20-day cooling-off period before the first sale.

A 90-day prospectus delivery period exists for Regulation A offerings. After each six-month period following the date of the original offering circular and within 30 days following the completion of the offering, the company must report the use of proceeds to the SEC.

Like fully registered offerings, Regulation A offerings must be registered (usually by "coordination") with the securities administrators for the states in which the offering is to be made. Use of an underwriter that is a member of the NASD requires NASD review. In practice, the Regulation A offering is little used.

State-Registered (Intrastate) Offerings (Rule 147)

If a local business seeks local financing exclusively, registration under the federal securities laws is not required. More accurately, if all of the offerees and purchasers in the offering are bona fide residents of the state under the laws of which the company is organized (e.g., the state of incorporation, if the company is a corporation), if the company's business is principally conducted and the company's properties principally located in that state, and if the proceeds of the offering are to be used in the state, the issuer may avail itself of exemption under SEC Rule 147. In such instances, the financing may be made pursuant to a long form ("qualification") registration under the state securities laws.

As a matter of practice, exclusive reliance upon the Rule 147 exemption is a somewhat perilous course. In order to satisfy Rule 147, the issuer must meet various technical requirements as to "residence," some of which are included in Rule 147 and some of which relate to common law standards. At the time of sale, for example, the issuer must obtain from the purchaser a written representation of his residence. Yet there is no provision in the rule that will protect the issuer from a good faith mistake in determining the residence of a purchaser. Moreover, should even a single purchaser resell to a nonresident within nine months of the offering, the exemption will be lost. To prevent this latter problem, certificates evidencing the securities offered under Rule 147 must bear a legend reflecting these transfer restrictions and a "stop transfer" order must be entered.

Rule 147 also provides a means for segregating an intrastate offering from other discrete offerings pursuant to other exemptive provisions of the act. In order to have Rule 147 available, an issuer must not have sold any similar securities to purchasers outside the state in the prior six months and may not make any such sales in the subsequent six months. Rule 147 does not require the filing of any documents.

Because registration-by-qualification requirements vary widely from state to state, it is impossible to estimate the costs of a Rule 147 offering. Such costs are generally somewhat less than are those for Regulation A offerings, however. As in the case of other offerings, NASD review is required if a NASD member serves as underwriter or sales agent.

Acquisitions

Like any other securities, securities issued by a company in the acquisition of another company must be registered under federal and state securities laws unless an exemption from registration applies. Most state securities laws provide registration exemptions for acquisitions by statutory merger or stock for assets. Under federal law, however, full registration is required unless either the intrastate or private offering exemption is available. Thus, regardless of the form of the transaction and the number of separate steps it may involve, the company must consider its overall effect and the identity of ultimate recipients of the securities in determining the availability of an exemption.

Under present law, solicitation of the target company's shareholders requesting the execution of proxies to vote on the acquisition is deemed to constitute an offering of the acquirer's securities. If the private or intrastate offering exemptions are unavailable, the acquirer must therefore register. A registration procedure is available under SEC Form S-4, which requires information about both the acquirer and the target. Form S-4 permits the incorporation by reference of material previously filed under the SEC's annual reporting requirements for companies that are already public. The prospectus under a Form S-4 registration statement is often made up of a proxy statement conforming to SEC rules, to which a cover sheet setting forth the terms of the offering has been added—the combination sometimes being referred to as a "wrap-around" prospectus. As with other offerings, the various state securities laws must also be reviewed.

Securities received by the acquired company's management or principal equity owners as a result of an acquisition are restricted and can be resold only if the resale is registered, exempt, or permitted under Rule 145 (which is similar to Rule 144 but without a holding period or filing requirement). Resales pursuant to a registration statement are particularly hazardous, however, because management may be held personally liable for misstatements in the prospectus concerning the acquiring company as well as any concerning their own company. The risk of liability in this situation is great, as the target company's management rarely has access to information concerning the sometimes unfriendly acquirer.

Acquisitions of equity securities of public companies for either cash or securities is further discussed below in connection with tender offers and takeover bids. See also the section "Investment Companies" for regulation under certain circumstances.

Disclosure of Material Inside Information

In any purchase or sale of a security, whether public or private, if one of the parties has any nonpublic material inside information that relates to the present or future condition of the company's business or its properties, he must disclose it to the person on the opposite side of the transaction or be personally liable under the antifraud provisions of the securities laws for any damages that may result. Similar liability will accrue to any person who aids and abets the misuse of inside information by tipping others or otherwise even if that person does not actually trade. In this regard, both "tippers" and "tippees" are liable under the law.

This simple principle is at the heart of all securities laws and yet is perhaps the most abused. The courts' necessarily amorphous definition of *materiality* is partially responsible for this abuse: Any fact which, under the circumstances, would likely have assumed actual significance to a reasonable investor is deemed material. The liabilities can be enormous in scope, and prudent companies and their management should either disclose significant information or, if such information is particularly sensitive, refrain from trading.

One emerging area of securities law deserves special mention because of the magnitude of the exposure involved and the ease in which violations may occur. If any public pronouncement by a public company (whether by press release, report to stockholders, or otherwise) contains a statement concerning the company's condition or prospects that is erroneous or misleading in a way that is material to an investor, so that the price of the company's securities in the securities markets is affected (either up or down), the company, its management, and its principal owners may be personally liable for any ensuing loss to *all* persons who trade in the company's securities to their disadvantage in the open market, regardless of whether or not management, the company's owners, or the company are concurrently trading in the company's securities in the market. Cases decided in this area so far indicate that management must have some ulterior purpose for the misinformation in order to be held liable; however, this purpose need not include any intention to violate the securities laws.

Manipulation

The securities laws broadly prohibit use of fraudulent or manipulative devices of any type in the purchase or sale of securities, whether in private transactions or in the securities markets. Specifically, market manipulation of securities prices up or down or at any level (except in connection with stabilization in a public offering, as to which special rules apply) or falsely creating the appearance of security trading activity—by the use of fictitious orders, wash sales, or other devices—is prohibited. Again, violation can lead to substantial personal as well as company liability.

Regulation of Public Companies

Companies of significant size that have a larger number of security holders, and companies that are listed on a national securities exchange, are regulated under the Securities Exchange Act of 1934. The filing reporting requirements of this statute attach when the company files a registration statement under the Exchange Act as a result of being listed on a national securities exchange or of having in excess of $5 million in total assets and in excess of 500 holders of a class of its equity securities at the end of one of its fiscal years, or following the effectiveness of a Securities Act Registration statement. (A registration statement under the Securities Exchange Act of 1934 should not be confused with a public offering registration statement under the Securities Act of 1933.) Registration under the Exchange Act submits the company to the periodic reporting, proxy, tender offer, and insider trading provisions of that act. Once registered, the number of equity security holders must drop below 500 and its assets must have been below $5 million for three years before the company may be deregistered.

Periodic Reports

In order to maintain a constant flow of reliable information to the SEC and the financial community, companies registered under the Exchange Act and those that have previously undertaken full registration under the Securities Act are subject to the periodic reporting requirements of the SEC. Under these requirements, the company must file with the SEC annual reports (containing audited financial statements) on Form 10-K, quarterly reports on Form 10-Q, and current reports on Form 8-K. These reports are generally available to the public through the SEC.

Subsequent Offerings

The "continuous disclosure" effect of the periodic reporting requirements has led the SEC to adopt two simplified forms (Form S-2 and Form S-3) for the registration of sales of securities by public companies and their affiliates (secondary offerings). These forms permit the incorporation by reference of material previously filed as periodic reports and may therefore be shorter and simpler. In many cases, the SEC will permit such registrations to become effective immediately without subjecting them to the SEC review and comment process.

Proxy Solicitations

To ensure that security holders of companies registered under the Exchange Act are advised of proposals (including the election of directors) to be acted upon at meetings of security holders, such companies must use proxy or information statements that conform to SEC rules. Such proxy statements are reviewed by the SEC staff prior to distribution to security holders. They must be transmitted at least annually and upon each proxy solicitation to the company's voting security holders. The form of the proxy itself is also regulated.

Tender Offers and Takeover Bids

Tender offers to acquire the securities of a company whose securities registered under the Exchange Act (other than offers by a company to repurchase its own shares, which are regulated separately) must conform to the SEC tender offer rules. These require the filing of certain information with the target company and the SEC not later than the date the tender offer is first made. Securities tendered are recoverable by the tenderer while the offer is open. Acceptance of less than all of the shares in a tender offer must be on a pro rata basis. Of course, if the tender is being made using securities of the acquiring company rather than cash, they must be registered under the Securities Act prior to the offering.

In order to alert the SEC and the management of a target company to an acquisition of securities that could lead to a change of control, any person acquiring any equity security of an Exchange Act–registered company, which results in his owning in excess of 5 percent of the outstanding securities of that class, must file with the SEC within 10 days after the acquisition. He must also transmit to the company certain information concerning the acquiring person, his purpose in making the acquisition, and his method of financing the acquisition. This requirement applies even if the shares were received as a result of an acquisition in which the acquirer exchanged some of its equity securities in return for securities of the acquired company. If two or more persons who together own in excess of 5 percent of a class of equity securities of an Exchange Act–registered company enter into a mutual arrangement, they too must file Form 13 D within 10 days after entering of the arrangement.

If either of the above transactions results in an appointment of a majority of directors for the company other than by vote of security holders, there must be transmitted to all security holders eligible to vote for the election of such directors if elected at a meeting of security holders, at least 10 days prior to the appointment, information equivalent to that contained in a proxy or information statement under the proxy rules.

The securities laws of some states contain tender offer provisions designed to discourage takeover of corporations based in those states or whose principal business and substantial assets are within the state. The federal laws, however, do not purport to discourage tender offers directly but rather seek to ensure full disclosure of information concerning such offers.

Insider Reporting and Trading

Management and 10 percent equity security holders are deemed *insiders* of an Exchange Act–registered company and must report their transactions in the company's equity securities to the SEC on Forms 3 and 4. An annual report on Form 5 is also required to catch up with any transactions during the year that may have been exempt from the monthly filings. The SEC publishes these transactions quarterly.

The insider trading provisions of the Exchange Act contain a section, 16 b(3), which includes an absolute six-month trading rule designed to preclude any incentive for insiders to make use of insider information to gain for themselves short-term profits by trading in the company's securities.

If both a purchase and a sale or a sale and purchase of such securities by an insider falls within any six-month period, any security holder of the company may sue on behalf of the company to recover for the company the "profits" thereby obtained. The word *profits* has a technical meaning in this context and does not necessarily refer to any benefit obtained by the insider—in fact, the insider may have incurred a net overall loss in a series of such transactions and still be liable to the company for substantial sums. The formula used by the courts in measuring the recovery is to match the highest sale with the lowest purchase in any six-month period, then to match the next highest sale with the next lowest purchase, and so on, so that the largest possible amount of profits from any given set of trades is thereby computed. Since theoretical losses incurred are not offset against theoretical profits, the liability to the insider can be substantial even though he sustains an overall loss.

That an insider, in fact, is not trading on inside information is no defense to an insider trading suit. In fact, if an insider purchase and sale have both occurred within six months, there is virtually no defense to a timely and properly prosecuted insider trading suit, and the best course of action is usually to pay the profits to the company as quickly as possible to minimize the ample legal fees that are usually awarded by the courts to plaintiff's counsel in such actions. These suits may be brought by anyone with standing.

Investment Companies

A company whose principal business is investing or trading in securities is subject to regulation under the Investment Company Act of 1940, unless it has not made and is not making a public offering and has fewer than 100 security holders. Although this act is primarily directed toward mutual funds, it also regulates companies that inadvertently fall within the statutory definition of *investment company*. Thus, if a public company sells a major portion of its assets, and, rather than distributing the proceeds to its security holders, holds and invests the proceeds in other than government or commercial paper while exploring alternate business activities, it may be deemed to have become an investment company. "Hedge funds" and investment clubs that rely upon the private offering exemption become investment companies when the exemption is lost and the offering becomes public, or when they have more than 100 participants.

Summary

We have attempted to describe the factors that influence an entrepreneur's decision on whether or not to take a company public. We have also tried to describe the complex process of raising equity through the public markets.

Our placement of this chapter in Part V, "Harvesting Value," bears explaining. We do not mean to imply that going public is a clean exit route for the entrepreneur to take his or her money and move on. While the entrepreneur can often get some money out of the business in a public offering, a large portion of his or her equity will undoubtedly still be tied up in the venture. Rather, we mean to imply that the decision relative to going public is one that is made after the business's start-up. It is a decision about where to obtain capital for growth.

TELESWITCH (A)

It was February 14, 1997—Valentines Day. Bob Goodman and the management team from U.S. Teleswitch, Inc. (Teleswitch) stepped into the elevator on the 36th floor of a New York office building and began a trip that would take them back to Memphis, Teleswitch's headquarters. Teleswitch was a young company with an innovative approach to producing switching equipment for the wireless communications (cellular telephone) market.

The trip was a familiar one. The same team had been in Boston in mid-November, 1996, for the same reason—to choose an investment bank to take Teleswitch public. Goodman recalled the excitement and enthusiasm that had punctuated the prior trip. Based on the mid-November presentations they had selected Wellstone & Co., a prominent west coast underwriter, to lead their IPO.

Now, three months later, there was a sense of déjá vu as they had spent the morning listening to two more investment banks present their views of Teleswitch's prospects. Goodman and Teleswitch's team was revisiting their earlier decision, and contemplating changing underwriters. Goodman described the sense of frustration he and the team were experiencing: "We are back where we were in November, and we are burning cash at the rate of over $1 million per month."

Background

Bob Goodman graduated in 1982 from Brown University with a degree in Latin American Studies. During his time at Brown, he had been friends with Sarah

Professor Michael J. Roberts prepared this case as the basis for class discussion rather than to illustrate either effective or ineffective handling of an administrative situation. The names of certain individuals and institutions have been disguised. This case is a rewrite of an earlier HBS case.

Flanagan, the daughter of Bob Flanagan, the Chief Executive of Western Union. He became friendly with Bob Flanagan, and after graduation Flanagan asked him to work on a consulting project for the company. Goodman performed well, and the two became even better friends. Flanagan left Western Union, and based upon his relationships and expertise, put together a deal to acquire the license for operating a cellular system in the British Virgin Islands. Because of the large number of charter boats and cruise ships that plied these waters, the system did well, but it was clear the business would have greater value if it was combined with cellular systems in the rest of the Caribbean. Goodman and Flanagan struck a deal with Cable & Wireless (C&W), a very large British firm with a host of cellular operations in the Caribbean. Goodman and Flanagan's business was combined with C&W's to form BoatPhone. The two men and a third partner held 49 percent of BoatPhone, the cellular system in the Caribbean. Ultimately, they sold their share back to Cable & Wireless at a profit, and held on to the piece of the business that dealt with cruise ships—CruisePhone.

While looking to hire a chief engineer for CruisePhone, Goodman happened to meet Tony Fletcher, one of the founders of a well-known company in the cellular switching business—Plexsys. Fletcher had developed a new technology that allowed "microcellular systems" (covering a very small area) to operate within buildings, and offer essentially free "wireless" service to occupants of the building. Fletcher was working on the technology with two other founders, and the three wanted Goodman to back them. Goodman agreed to invest $40,000 to determine if the technology had a market application, and the men flew around the country talking to prospective customers. Goodman developed some interest among potential customers at Southwestern Bell to buy this "wireless PBX" product. A PBX was a "private branch exchange"—essentially the switchboard used by many companies to route phone calls within the organization. A wireless PBX allowed users to roam from office to office with a cordless phone. Based upon their interest, Goodman capitalized Teleswitch with $500,000. The three technical founders each kept 10% of the stock as their "founders' share." And Goodman, who put up more than half of the $500,000, ended up with about 50%, including his 10% "founder's share." Twelve months later the company needed another $500,000. He explained how the second financing worked:

> I pulled $500,000 together and used it to buy a CD, which was then pledged to the bank as collateral for a $500,000 loan to Teleswitch. I just knew that—if we needed more capital—investors down the road wouldn't want us to take our original investment out of the company. But, if we had to pay back a bank loan, that would be another story.

Teleswitch—Early Strategy

The key technology behind Teleswitch's product was a "low power" cellular (or "wireless") switch. This was the technology that one of Teleswitch's founders had developed after leaving Plexsys. Cellular switches were—in themselves—nothing new. Many of the world's leading telecommunications companies had entered the cellular market with the advent of this wireless technology in the early 1980s; Northern Telecom, Ericson, and AT&T all sold cellular switches. These switches were largely based on the technology that these companies used in their "land line" switches (the wired phone network that ran to most homes and businesses) and as such they were quite expensive. A basic cellular switch—which could service 100,000 subscribers—could easily cost several million dollars.

The key to Teleswitch's product was that the founders had come up with a way to make a small switch much less expensively. This made it more economical to serve a smaller number of users. At the same time, these cellular systems used lower powerful radio waves, so that they covered a much smaller area, and consequently interfered less with other systems.

As Teleswitch was developing and selling the "microcellular system" it was also developing a new product based on the same technology—the "GlobalHub." Goodman explained the GlobalHub system:

> With GlobalHub, we developed an intelligent hub which connected to phones made by Motorola and others. The combination of the hub and the phones allowed you to have one phone number. You used your basic cellular phone when you were in the car, or traveling. Then, when you came home, you used the same phone, but it ran off of a low power base—and you didn't have to pay any "airtime" fee—it was like a cordless phone. When you were at home, calls to your cellular number were automatically directed to your home number.

By the fall of 1993, the Company's original financing was largely exhausted. Goodman arranged a deal with one of Teleswitch's customers, Archer Telecom Group, which provided another year or so of financing. Goodman described the deal: "Archer loved our product. We got them to sign a deal to buy $1.6 million of our product, which had a 75 percent gross margin to us. And, they prepaid. This funded us through the fall of 1994."

In the summer of 1994, Goodman began talking with venture capital firms to try to raise several million dollars to fund Teleswitch's development efforts. By this time, it was becoming clearer that the two product segments in which Teleswitch was participating were not going to develop into sufficiently attractive markets. Goodman was aware, however, that there was a demand for a small switch that could be used with a new digital technology that had been developed in Europe—"GSM." GSM stood for "Groupe Special Mobile," the French name for the European working group that promulgated this technical standard.

The first cellular systems that were developed utilized analog technology—radio waves that captured voices and simply broadcast them over radio waves, until they were picked up by the systems' antennas, amplified, and put back over the wired phone network. The U.S. system was called AMPS for American Mobile Phone System. In Europe, each of the national phone companies developed an analog mobile phone system that worked on slightly different frequencies and according to different technological specifications. Thus, a consumer from England could not expect to use their cellular phone in France or Germany.

As with many electronic devices, it was soon discovered that digital technology could create a superior service. As U.S. companies raced to develop a technical standard for use in the United States, the European Commission began developing a common digital standard for all of Europe called GSM. Not only would this allow consumers to take their phones from one country to another, but it would also allow producers to manufacture to a single design specification, and therefore, presumably enjoy higher volumes and lower production costs. In turn, it was expected that this would lead to lower costs for consumers.

By the mid-1990s, many other countries had adopted the GSM standard; Teleswitch estimated that by the year 2000, 48 percent of the world's cellular use would be on GSM systems, compared with 28% for the two standards that were in use in the United States. However, it was still true that most of the equipment was designed for large markets, where phone companies wanted to install a switch that could handle 100,000 subscribers or more. From his days at BoatPhone, Goodman was aware that there were a large number of markets where there would never be a lot of users, and where a smaller switch would allow a more economical system to be implemented:

> There are lots of markets in the developing world where the teledensity [number of phones per 100 of population] is very low. In the United States, it is 60 lines per 100 of population, but it is less than 20 in Hungary, Russia, Poland and Argentina. And it is close to zero in many parts of Africa and India. The economics of large phone systems just don't work where people can't afford service, or where the density of population is just too low to justify the investment. But, if you can make a small system economical, you can serve just the people who can afford it. We knew how to make small switches, and we decided that there would be a big market for a small GSM switch. Not only could you use it to provide mobile phone service to some markets, but you could provide the only phone service to lots of developing countries where you couldn't afford to run copper wire to everyone's home and business.

The GSM Strategy

In late 1994 and early 1995, Teleswitch raised $6 million from three venture capital firms at a $26 million post-money valuation. The VC firms included Williams, Jones & Associates, Charles River Partners, based in Boston, and Bessemer Venture Partners, also based in Boston.

This $6 million was to be used to fund the development of a small GSM switch and to build out the sales and marketing team for the AMPS product. While Teleswitch had the basic technology, it would take an immense amount of software programming to develop a product for the GSM market. Goodman knew Teleswitch would really have to begin to focus its development efforts on the GSM product: "I knew we needed someone to help us grow to the next level, to focus our efforts. We hired Tom Berger as president in March of 1995." Berger had a background in the cellular business, having worked for Motorola for 20 years. Berger described the challenges at Teleswitch at that time:

> Developing a GSM switch was a huge undertaking. We talked to one of the companies that had developed a GSM switch, and they said they had 500 person-years invested in software development. We knew we could never afford that, so we went out and learned about the latest "object-oriented" programming tools. We had to accomplish this development task fast and inexpensively.

Berger described the environment at Teleswitch when he joined:

> There were 40 people here, but the Company didn't have the organization it needed to grow. There were no systems, no process. They had a solid development team, but no infrastructure. But the magnitude of the GSM challenge was huge. We grew to 100 in 8 months.

As the development effort progressed, Goodman and Berger saw that it would require more than the $6 million originally raised; Berger explained:

> Not only did we need to develop a switch, but we needed to sell an entire system. The purchasers of this equipment don't want to buy the pieces from three or four different suppliers and integrate them—and they often don't have the expertise to do this. They want to sign a deal with you and know that they have someone to hold accountable. So, the development task expanded to include building a whole system. Many of these pieces were available off the shelf, but it still took some work to put them all together.

Goodman realized it would take more financing to accomplish their goals. He described how Teleswitch raised its next round of capital:

> I saw a private placement memo for a company that looked just like ours—they raised $30 million at a $160 million post-money valuation. Morgan Stanley and Stuart & Co. had gotten this deal done with no problem. So, I called them and said we wanted to do something similar. Morgan thought we were too small, but Stuart jumped all over it. We had three meetings, wrote the prospectus, and they raised $18 million at a $108 million post-money valuation. The deal closed October 31, 1996.

In the private placement financing, Teleswitch had projected 1996 revenues of $36 million, principally from the AMPS and GlobalHub businesses. But the business wasn't materializing. By the spring of 1996, Goodman knew Teleswitch would require yet another round of financing to get into the GSM business:

> By this time we were far enough along in our plans to see that a key issue would be selling and supporting customers around the world with the GSM product. But, we were a little company in Memphis. It was clear we needed a strategic partner. Our VP of sales had done a lot of international work for Motorola, including lining up financing for their Iridium project. We sat down to talk about who might make a good strategic partner for us, and he had some excellent contacts in Thailand, especially at a company called Ucom. We went to Bangkok in early summer of 1996, and Ucom loved us. They wanted to buy 20 percent of the company for $32 million. The VCs didn't want to give up that much of the company, so we settled for 10 percent—we raised $16 million.

The deal closed in late summer of 1996. At the company's fall board meeting, the board decided that because of the Company's stage of development, as well as its projected financial needs, it was a good time to think about going public. (See **Exhibit 1** for Teleswitch financials.) The company would need more money for the commercial rollout of the GSM product, as well as have a pool of money available to provide financing to customers, a common practice in the industry. Goodman described what transpired:

> We knew from day one that we would need to go public to get our investors liquid. And, I had been doing the conferences for a couple of years, telling the Teleswitch story and getting to know bankers and analysts so that when the time came, they would be aware of our story. We spoke with quite a few bankers to see what they thought of our prospects for an IPO. We got a book from Volpe, Welty, but the analyst at Volpe had just left that firm to go to H&Q to follow Internet companies. We talked to Morgan Keegan and JC Bradford, because they were Tennessee firms, but we never considered them to lead the deal. We liked Deutsche Morgan Grenfell, but they looked at our numbers and said it was really a 3Q '97 deal. I had a long-standing relationship with a banker at Alex. Brown, who I liked a lot. We talked, and he said their analyst was really stretched thin, and they were looking to divide up the territory he covered, hire a new analyst, and only then would he feel comfortable with making a commitment to me to get a deal done. The fact that he had been so straight-forward with me made me want Alex. Brown even more. In fact, we had liked the analyst at another regional bank a lot, and I called this analyst and told him he should go work at Alex. Brown. At the end of the day, the firms we had in the "bake off" were the four who had been foaming at the mouth at the prospect of a 1Q '97 deal. Based on our own sense and our VC's experience, we narrowed the selection down to 4 firms, and invited them to the "bake-off" in Boston on November 18. We made it clear that we were looking to raise about $50 million, and that we hoped to get $10 to $12 per share. (See **Exhibit 2,** letter from Teleswitch's CFO Joe Gonzalez, inviting banks to present on November 18.)

In order to aid the banks in their analyses, Teleswitch also provided their internal financial projections to the underwriters. Because of the company's stage of development, sales and earnings projections were necessarily speculative. For 1996, Teleswitch had earned $2,756,000 in revenues for the first three quarters, and was projecting $3.1 million in sales for the fourth quarter. The reason the company anticipated a strong fourth quarter was explained by Goodman: "We had a $4 million contract signed to deliver a system to Indonesia. And, we were in the middle of negotiations for another system."

For 1997, the company was projecting $24 million (low case) to $48 million (high case) in sales, and earnings of −$5.1 million (low case) to $3.3 million (high case). Finally, for 1998, Teleswitch was projecting $76 million in sales and $8.7 million of earnings. (For detailed forecast, see **Appendix A,** page 601, in which Wellstone has reproduced the Company's financial projections.)

The "Bake-Off"

The investment banking firms of Wellstone; Peterson & Co.; and, Banc Europe Industriale (BEI) presented to Goodman, Berger, Gonzalez and Felda Hardymon of Bessemer Ventures in Boston on November 18. See **Appendices A, B,** and **C** for excerpts from each bank's presentation.

Based on these meetings, Goodman and the team had tentatively decided to go with Wellstone as the lead investment bank. However, they were also impressed with BEI's European strength, and felt that this was particularly important, given the markets into which they were trying to sell their product, and the fact that GSM was fundamentally a European technology. Finally, they felt that Peterson would round out the team with a New York retail strength. Goodman described the initial attempts at putting this structure in place:

> Felda really pushed for Wellstone, arguing that they had the "muscle" to get a deal done. Felda thought that this trading capability was a lot more important than a good analyst. And, Wellstone was really the only firm that had indicated it could get a deal done in the first quarter.
>
> We didn't really announce a decision after the bake-off. I told Wellstone that they were the leading contender, and I told BEI that we liked them a lot, and wanted to work out a deal where they could play a major role in Europe. And, I kind of nodded to Peterson and told them it looked like we would ask them to be part of the team. One of the reasons that we didn't simply issue a decision was that I wanted to hold on to some negotiating leverage to push Wellstone to let BEI be a European lead manager, and have Wellstone handle only the United States. I had heard some horror stories how BEI put together a great book of business in Europe, and then the book running lead manager never gave them any stock. I didn't want that to happen. The other reason was that I just wasn't thrilled with Wellstone. Felda liked them because he thought that they could "power out a deal," but I was just underwhelmed. So, I kept talking to people, kept thinking that there was a better deal out there.

Initial Progress

In late 1996, Goodman worked to get Wellstone's assent to allow BEI to manage a European tranche of 20 percent to 25 percent of the deal. Wellstone never agreed to this, but ultimately did agree to give BEI some voice in allocating the shares for sale, effectively committing a portion of the stock for sale in Europe. At the same time, Goodman and Hardymon wanted more of a firm commitment from Wellstone that they could get a deal done in the first quarter of 1997. Goodman recalled:

> Felda and I flew out to the west coast to meet with the three top investment bankers at Wellstone, trying to determine if they were really behind the deal. They said all the right things, and we left thinking that it was probably going to happen. We started getting down to the nitty gritty, talking about the economics of the deal. One question was whether we would use "jump ball" economics or a fixed split. In the end, everyone was OK with a 40–30–30 split [among the three lead underwriters] and fixed economics.
>
> But, I still had some reservations. In the couple of months after we'd tentatively decided on Wellstone, I kept hearing horror stories about people who were in our situation who hadn't made it out. People were surprised that we weren't using Vail, Jackson & Stowe (VJS)—they said they were just the right firm given what we were trying to do.

Another issue that was affecting the progress of the prospective offering was Teleswitch's own development. While the firm had projected a $3.2 million (revenue) fourth quarter for 1996, the actual figure had come in at slightly under $1 million; losses had run at $4.6 million, rather than the $1.9 million forecast. And, in order to meet even the $4.4 million revenue figure that was the first quarter portion of the forecast that rolled up to the "low" 1997 revenue projection of $24 million, Teleswitch would have to beat its fourth quarter 1996 performance by a wide margin. Goodman explained the underlying issues that were causing the revenue ramp to be lower than anticipated:

> The Indonesian order that we were counting on made it to the freight forwarder, but there were problems with the letter of credit. We decided not to ship because these issues were not resolved. We just didn't want to take the risk. Nonetheless, we were optimistic that this system would ship in the first quarter.

Revisiting the Decision

Early in 1997, Goodman was still feeling uncomfortable with where Teleswitch stood. These issues came to a head when Goodman received another piece of news:

> I was feeling pretty torn when the head of research at Wellstone called and said their analyst had just left to go to a hedge fund. He did the right thing and called immediately, and said that they were working hard to get someone, and thought they'd have an analyst in place in 30 to 45 days. But, I felt like the whole thing was wide open again.
>
> We decided to reevaluate our decision and ask VJS to make a pitch (see excerpts from VJS's pitch in **Appendix D**). Felda knew a very senior banker at VJS—Greg Lamont—and they made a pitch to us. At the same time, Felda thought that if we did end up with VJS, we didn't need Peterson for a New York presence, and would be better off with Springer, Mathis, a firm he knew well and liked a lot from the Midwest (see excerpts from Springer, Mathis' pitch in **Appendix E**).

EXHIBIT 1   Teleswitch Financial Statements

Statement of Operations	1994	1995	September 30, 1996	December 31, 1996
Net revenues	$ 2,166,050	$ 4,907,855	$ 2,756,000	$ 3,680,032
Cost of revenues	709,404	1,762,013	918,000	1,350,854
Gross profit	1,456,646	3,145,842	1,838,000	2,329,178
Operating expenses:				
Research and development	1,033,315	3,261,607	4,765,000	6,700,300
Sales and marketing	546,974	2,104,720	2,883,000	4,207,391
General and administrative	595,571	2,288,190	4,560,000	6,560,377
	2,175,860	7,654,517	12,208,000	17,468,068
Operating loss	(719,214)	(4,508,675)	(10,370,000)	(15,138,890)
Other income, net	5,098	235,576	341,000	507,451
Net loss	$ (714,116)	$ (4,273,099)	$(10,029,000)	$(14,631,439)
Net loss per common share	$ (0.07)	$ (0.27)	$ (0.56)	$ (0.81)
Weighted average common shares outstanding	10,000,000	16,038,045	18,042,272	18,042,272

Selected Balance Sheet Data ($000)	December 31, 1994	December 31, 1995	September 30, 1996	December 31, 1996
Cash and equivalents	$2,315	$14,468	$19,785	$12,056
Working capital	2,271	16,558	21,244	15,304
Total assets	3,313	20,910	27,287	22,827
Short- and long-term debt	—	—	912	829
Convertible redeemable preferred stock	3,163	23,189	39,146	39,293
Shareholders' equity (deficit)	(507)	(4,951)	(15,108)	(19,768)

**TELESWITCH FINANCIAL STATEMENTS—TELESWITCH CAPITALIZATION
AS OF DECEMBER 31, 1996**

		Closing Dates	Gross Proceeds	Number of Common Equivalent Shares	Total Percentage of Ownership
Common stock	Founders	Nov-94		5,500,000	26.14%
Series A preferred stock	Seed capital	Nov-94		4,500,000	21.38
Series B preferred stock	Venture	Feb-95	$ 6,000,000	3,000,000	14.26
Series C preferred stock	Institutional	Nov-95	18,228,274	3,038,045	14.44
Series D preferred stock	UCOM	Sep-96	16,033,816	2,004,227	9.52
1996 Option plan					
Granted (489,750 vested)				2,342,875	11.13
Reserved				615,625	2.93
Exercised				41,500	0.20
				21,042,272	100.00%

EXHIBIT 2   Excerpts from Teleswitch Memo to Prospective Investment Bankers

---

Assumptions

1. A $50 million offering.

2. Proposed timetable:

   Organizational meeting November 25, 1996
   Filing with 9/30 unaudited numbers by December 20, 1996
   Roadshow week of February 17, 1997
   Pricing week of February 24, 1997

3. The proceeds will be used for the following purposes:

   - Accelerate the rollout of the GSM systems
   - General corporate purposes
   - Working capital

4. The following assumptions should be used in your valuation analysis:

   - $50 million primary share offering
   - 21,042,272 shares outstanding (as of December 31) on a fully-diluted basis
   - IPO net proceeds invested at 5 3/4% pre-tax
   - Closing date February 28, 1997

5. We expect to include Asian and European locations in the roadshow.

6. The book running manager is to provide us with regular access to the book and syndicate manager. We expect to receive daily updates while we are on the roadshow, and to be kept fully informed of any matters that may materially affect the pricing.

7. We expect to have the right to allocate 5 to 10% of the IPO shares to employees, existing shareholders, friends, and customers. A discussion will take place regarding the Series C shareholders.

8. We reserve the right to restrict the syndicate to firms approved by us.

9. We expect that the underwriter's spread and the split between managers will be fixed in total at the time of banker selection.

10. We expect to be invited to speak at any technology conference sponsored by the bankers selected.

11. We expect the underwriter's counsel to be an Atlanta firm and that drafting sessions will take place in Atlanta, using a local printer of our choosing.

12. We expect the managers to provide margin loans and a cashless exercise of options to officers and key employees. We expect the managers to provide ongoing rights for employees who exercise options to sell the stock without fees. We also expect managers to provide ongoing support to officers and key employees who wish to trade the stock.

13. We expect the Green Shoe to be no more than 15% of the offering.

14. We expect that the lock-up period will not exceed 180 days and that it may be reduced if circumstances warrant.

Questions

Please respond to the following questions in your presentation:

1. Why should your firm be selected to lead Teleswitch's IPO?

2. How would you sell the "Concept" and how confident are you that when we go to the market it will be understood? Exactly how will you position Teleswitch?

3. You should present details regarding recent concept deals that you managed, including stock performance to date and support provided by your firm.

4. What will you do to avoid the pitfall of having major investors asking for shares at less than $10 per share?

5. How will you value Teleswitch and why?

Exhibit 2   (*continued*)

Please present the information contained in the following table. You should provide information for four of your most recently managed IPOs in the wireless or related industry.

	Teleswitch	*IPO 1*	*IPO 2*	*IPO 3*	*IPO 4*
An offer price:					
Valuation ($m)—post-money					
Valuation ($m)—pre-money					
P/E multiple—current year					
P/E multiple—next year					
Multiple of projected revenues					
Fully distributed trading valuation					
Immediately post deal ($m)					
Price per share:					
Proposed at banker selection*					
Filing range					
Actual pricing					
Closing price on offering date					
Price one week after closing					
Current price					

*Presented at a similar meeting.

Valuation Changes
What are the factors that may cause a lower valuation at the time of filing and at the final pricing compared to your current valuation?

Aftermarket Support
Research
1. Who will cover Teleswitch on a day-to-day basis and who will actually write the research reports?
2. How often can Teleswitch expect a major report to be written? And when will the first report be issued?
3. Please provide details on the frequency that reports were written on the companies listed in the valuation schedule above and other recent relevant IPO companies.
4. If you have dropped coverage on any company that you have taken public in the last three years, please provide the circumstances.

Trading
Please present the information contained in the following table.

EXHIBIT 2   (*concluded*)

	IPO Date	IPO Date Plus							
		Q1	*Q2*	*Q3*	*Q4*	*Q5*	*Q6*	*Q7*	*Q8*
Company									
% Trading volume									
Book managed IPO									
IPO 1									
IPO 2									
Co-managed IPOs									
IPO 1									
Market maker rank:									
Book managed IPO									
IPO 1									
IPO 2									
Co-managed IPOs									
IPO 1									

Percent of trading volume is the percentage of total trading volume that your firm represents of the entire volume. Market maker ranking should be expressed as 1, 2, 3, etc.

A P P E N D I X A

Excerpts from Wellstone Presentation

Wellstone Offers

- Bulge Bracket Capabilities
  - –Institutional and retail brokerage
  - –Established international and domestic presence
  - –Small and large cap client base

- Focus
  - –Technology
  - –Senior Management involvement
  - –M & A Capability

Overall Initial Public Offerings, YTD 1996

YTD 1996 Ranked by Transactions

Rank	Manager	# of Issues
1.	*Wellstone Securities*	*86*
2.	Alex. Brown & Sons	85
3.	Morgan Stanley	65
4.	Smith Barney Inc.	64
5.	Donaldson, Lufkin & Jenrette	62
6.	Hambrecht & Quist	62
7.	Goldman, Sachs, Inc.	59
8.	Merrill Lynch & Co.	58
9.	Robertson Stephens	56
10.	Lehman Brothers	50
11.	Salomon Brothers	42
12.	Cowen & Co.	40
13.	Oppenheimer	38
14.	Bear, Stearns	35
15.	CS First Boston	34
	Top 15 Total	836

Recent Wellstone Wireless and Related IPOs ($ in millions, except per share data)

	Teleswitch[2]	Lightbridge	Orckit	Omnipoint	Westell
Ticker	TBD	LTBG	ORCTF	OMPT	WSTL
Date of offering	TBD	9/27/96	9/27/96	1/25/96	11/30/95
Shares outstanding after the offering	23.1	14.5	14.1	43.8	17.2
Primary shares offered	4.5	3.0	3.3	7.0	7.8
Shares outstanding before the offering	18.5	11.5	10.8	36.8	9.5
Post-money valuation	$254	$145	$226	$702	$224
Amount raised	$50	$30	$53	$112	$101
Pre-money valuation	$204	$115	$173	$590	$123
Offer price per share	$11.00	$10.00	$16.00	$16.00	$13.00
P/E Multiple current calendar year[1]	NM	113x	NM	NM	90x
P/E Multiple next calendar year[1]	24x	32x	NM	NM	17x
P/R Multiple next calendar year[1]	4x	3x	3x	NA	1x
Fully distributed trading valuation:					
One week following offering	NA	$189	$249	$1,074	$203
One month following offering	NA	$124	$203	$1,030	$217
Price per share:					
Filing range	$10 to $12	$8 to $10	$12 to $14	$13 to $15	$10 to $12
Actual pricing	TBD	$10.00	$16.00	$16.00	$13.00
Closing price on offering date	NA	$11.88	$19.88	$21.00	$11.63
Price one week after closing	NA	$13.00	$17.63	$24.50	$11.78
Price one month after closing	NA	$8.50	$14.38	$23.50	$12.56
Current price	NA	$9.88	$12.75	$28.25	$26.38

[1]P/E and P/R multiples based on EPS and Revenue estimates current as of first research report issued by Wellstone Securities. Teleswitch current and next calendar year P/E Multiples are for 1997 and 1998 respectively; all P/R Multiples on CY97E.

[2]Teleswitch data reflects midpoint of Wellstone's preliminary filing range; shares outstanding include vested options only which are estimated at 500,000.

1995–2000 Compound Annual Growth Rates

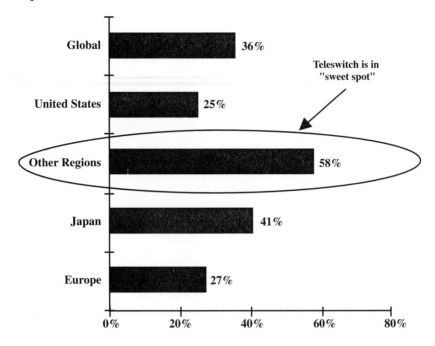

Balancing Per-Capita GDP for Ubiquitous Basic Service

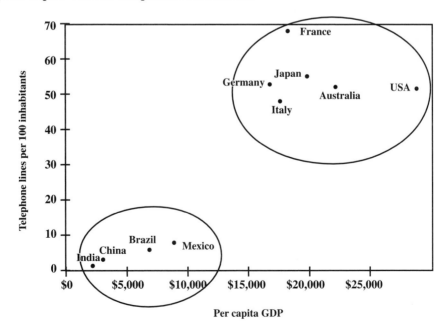

Source: European Mobile Communications, Kagan, Schostek, Dataquest, MS, company data.

Key Factors Influencing Valuation

- Teleswitch's business and financial performance
- Financial market performance of comparable companies
- State of the communications equity market: receptivity to concept stories –1998 P/E Multiples; 1997 Revenue Multiples
- State of public equity markets generally and the technology sector specifically
- Significant events in Teleswitch's competitive environment
- Strategic or distribution relationships

Structuring Considerations

Managers
- Two or three managing underwriters; *fixed* economics

Syndicate:
- Mix of national, regional, specialty and international securities firms ensures balanced placement of shares
- Special allocations of stock to increase aftermarket coverage and support
- Highly visible and ranked securities analysts with specific focus on sector
- Use of the syndicate to gain incremental coverage
- Proven track record in underwriting technology deals; strong distribution capabilities

Proposed Distribution:
- Placement of 85 percent with institutional investors, with the remaining 15 percent to retail investors
- Placement of 75 percent to 85 percent with domestic investors, with a minimum of 15 percent to 25 percent placed internationally
- Possibility of a separate international traunche

Lock-up Provisions:
- 180 days (waiver rights available through managing underwriters)

Structure

Transaction Summary and Assumptions:	
	$254 million Post-Money valuation at filing mid-point
	18.5 million shares outstanding before the offering
	4.5 million primary shares offered at $11 per share

Proceeds (MM)	Shares (MM)	Percentage	
$50.0	4.5	100%	primary offering before overallotment option
$ 0.0	0.0	0	secondary offering before overallotment option
$50.0	4.5	100	total offering before overallotment option
$ 7.5	0.7	15	overallotment option
$57.5	5.2	115	total offering assuming exercise of overallotment option
	23.1		total shares outstanding after the offering (excluding overallotment option)
		20	percent of Company sold to public in primary offering (excluding overallotment option)
		22	percent of total shares sold to public, including overallotment option

Summary IPO Valuation ($ in millions; except per share data)[1]

Teleswitch, Inc. Financial Information

	Filing		Trading								
Post-Money Valuation	$231	$254	$277	$ 289	$ 300	$ 312	$ 323	$ 335	$ 346	$ 358	$ 369
Primary Proceeds	$ 45	$ 50	$ 55	$ 50	$ 50	$ 50	$ 50	$ 50	$ 50	$ 50	$ 50
Pre-Money Valuation	$185	$204	$223	$ 239	$ 250	$ 262	$ 273	$ 285	$ 296	$ 308	$ 319
Price Per Share	$ 10	$ 11	$ 12	$12.50	$13.00	$13.50	$14.00	$14.50	$15.00	$15.50	$16.00

CY98E Net Income $ 9 — Post-Money Val./CY98E Net Inc.	27x	29x	32x	33x	35x	36x	37x	39x	40x	41x	43x
CY97E Revenue (High) $49 — Pre-Money Val./CY97E Rev.	3.8x	4.2x	4.6x	4.9x	5.2x	5.4x	5.6x	5.9x	6.1x	6.3x	6.6x
CY97E Revenue (Low) $24 — Pre-Money Val./CY97E Rev.	7.7x	8.5x	9.3x	9.9x	10.4x	10.9x	11.4x	11.9x	12.3x	12.8x	13.3x

Market Information / Operating Statistics

	P/E CY97	P/E CY98	P/E CY97E to Secular Gr. Rate	Adj. Mkt. Value/ CY96 Rev	Adj. Mkt. Value/ CY97 Rev	Adj. Market Value [2]	Secular Growth Rate	CY97/ CY96 Revenue Gr. Rate	CY96 Rev	CY97 Rev	LTM Operating Margin
Mean Multiple Analysis											
Wireless Growth Comparables	32x	24x	84%	5.9x	4.1x	$766	37%	51%	$223	$386	17%
Wireless Cyclical Comparables	22x	18x	101%	2.7x	2.2x	$8,831	23%	24%	$4,702	$5,373	17%
Concept Communications Comparables	7.3x	51x	204%	153.3x	8.5x	$821	40%	78%	$77	$120	18%
Networking Comparables	51x	34x	112%	9.9x	6.3x	$9,863	44%	56%	$1,372	$2,037	24%
Overall Mean	43x	30x	113%	8.4x	5.3x	$5,345	37%	53%	$1,431	$1,836	20%
Teleswitch, Inc. pricing at $11.00 per share	NM	29x	NA	34.5x	4.2x	$204	NA	721%	$6	$49	NA
Teleswitch, Inc. trading at $13.50 per share	NM	36x	NA	44.3x	5.4x	$262	NA	721%	$6	$49	NA

[1]Estimates normalized for calendar year end. All estimates are from Wellstone, First Call, Investext or Street; when necessary, 1998 P/E multiples derived using est. secular growth rate applied to CY 1997E EPS.

[2]Adjusted market value defined as equity market value plus total debt less cash and cash equivalents.

[3]NM = Not Meaningful; NA = Not Applicable/Not Available.

IPO Valuation and Comparable Company Analysis[1] ($ in millions, except per share data)

		Market Information						Operating Statistics				
	Stock Price 11/15/96	P/E CY 97	P/E CY98	P/E CY97E to Secular Gr. Rate	Adj. Mkt. Value/ CY96 Rev	Adj. Mkt. Value/ CY97 Rev	Adj. Market Value[2]	Secular Growth Rate	CY97/ CY96 Revenue Gr. Rate	CY96 Rev	CY97 Rev	LTM Operating Margin
Wireless Growth Comparables												
AML Communications, Inc.	$16.38	34x	26x	113%	6.8x	5.2x	$90	30%	30%	$13	$17	27%
DSP Communications, Inc.	$37.38	27x	18x	67%	8.0x	5.6x	$703	40%	42%	$88	$125	24%
P-COM, Inc.	$24.50	31x	25x	NA	5.2x	3.1x	$421	NA	66%	$81	$135	12%
Proxim, Inc.	$20.38	27x	19x	68%	3.6x	2.3x	$150	40%	57%	$41	$65	11%
QUALCOMM Incorporated	$43.75	31x	24x	89%	2.5x	1.4x	$2,631	35%	80%	$1,050	$1,889	NM
Sawtek Inc.	$31.63	40x	28x	NA	9.3x	7.1x	$604	40%	31%	$65	$85	10%
Mean		32x	24x	84%	5.9x	4.1x	$766	37%	51%	$223	$386	17%
Wireless Cyclical Comparables												
Allen Group Inc.	$19.63	18x	15x	88%	1.6x	1.3x	$570	20%	21%	$367	$445	14%
Andrew Corporation	$57.75	31x	26x	153%	4.5x	3.8x	$3,511	20%	18%	$779	$921	19%
Glenayre Technologies, Inc.	$25.13	17x	13x	59%	3.2x	2.2X	$1,356	28%	44%	$429	$620	25%
LM Ericsson Telephone Company	$30.75	23X	19X	102%	1.7X	1.5X	$29,888	23%	13%	$17,231	$19,507	8%
Mean		22x	18x	101%	2.7x	2.2x	$8,831	23%	24%	$4,702	$5,373	17%
Concept Communications Comparables												
Aware, Inc.	$9.50	79x	53x	158%	24.6x	13.2x	$172	50%	86%	$7	$13	6%
Orckit Communications, Ltd.	$12.75	NM	NA	NM	16.7x	8.1x	$185	35%	107%	$11	$23	NM
PairGain Technologies, Inc.	$66.50	55x	37x	NA	10.5x	7.4x	$2,029	NA	42%	$193	$275	30%
Westell Technologies, Inc.	$26.38	85x	63x	243%	9.4x	5.4x	$899	35%	76%	$95	$168	NM
Mean		73x	51x	201%	15.3x	8.5x	$821	40%	78%	$77	$120	18%
Networking Comparables												
Ascend Communications, Inc.	$70.00	561x	36x	114%	14.6x	8.6x	$7,639	45%	70%	$522	$888	35%
Cascade Communications Corp.	$76.38	73x	46x	147%	20.1x	12.7x	$6,705	50%	59%	$334	$530	32%
Cisco Systems, Inc.	$64.75	27x	20x	78%	7.1X	4.7x	$36,322	35%	51%	$5,100	$7,700	36%
FORE Systems, Inc.	$42.75	61x	42x	136%	10.2x	7.1x	$3,563	45%	44%	$349	$502	17%
Shiva Corporation	$50.13	49x	33x	98%	8.1x	5.0x	$1,329	50%	62%	$165	$267	14%
Xylan Corporation	$43.13	63x	36x	115%	4.9x	2.9x	$1,668	55%	69%	$338	$572	4%
3Com Corporation	$72.25	29x	22x	96%	4.2x	3.1x	$11,814	30%	36%	$2,800	$3,800	28%
Mean		51x	34x	112%	9.9x	6.3x	$9,863	44%	56%	$1,372	$2,037	24%
Overall Mean		43x	30x	113%	8.4x	5.3x	$5,345	37%	53%	$1,431	$1,836	20%
Teleswitch, Inc. pricing at $11.00 per share	NM	29x	NA	34.5x	4.2x	$204	NA	721%	$6	$49	NA	
Teleswitch, Inc. trading at $13.50 per share	NM	36x	NA	44.3x	5.4x	$262	NA	721%	$6	$49	NA	

[1]Estimates normalized for calendar year end. All estimates are from Montgomery, First Call, Investext or Street; when necessary, 1998 P/E multiples derived using est. secular growth rate applied to CY 1997E EPS.

[2]Adjusted market value defined as equity market value plus total debt less cash and cash equivalents.

[3]NM = Not Meaningful; NA = Not Applicable/Not Available.

607

Financial Model ($ in millions, except per share data)

Fiscal Year Ending December 31,	CY1996E					CY1997E(4)					CY1998E				
	Q1-MarA	Q2-JunA	Q3-SepA	Q4-Dec	TOTAL	Q1-Mar	Q2-Jun	Q3-Sep	Q4-Dec	TOTAL	Q1-Mar	Q2-Jun	Q3-Sep	Q4-Dec	TOTAL
Revenues	$1,566	$207	$983	$3,153	$5,909	$5,472	$7,464	$11,029	$12,306	$36,270	$15,573	$18,334	$19,684	$22,160	$75,756
Cost of revenues	446	81	391	1,302	2,220	2,312	3,035	4,396	5,044	14,787	5,518	6,707	6,969	8,036	27,230
Gross profit	1,120	126	592	1,851	3,689	3,160	4,429	6,633	7,262	21,483	10,055	11,627	12,715	14,124	48,521
Research and development	1,391	1,677	1,697	1,705	6,470	1,835	1,760	1,817	1,945	7,356	2,668	2,488	2,493	2,490	10,139
Sales and marketing	711	1,000	1,172	1,225	4,108	2,161	2,279	2,314	2,651	9,404	3,940	3,877	4,282	4,339	16,438
General and administrative	1,312	1,331	1,917	1,920	6,480	2,004	2,077	2,273	2,247	8,601	2,557	2,744	2,843	2,917	11,091
Total operating expenses	3,414	4,008	4,786	4,850	17,058	6,000	6,116	6,403	6,842	25,360	9,165	9,109	9,618	9,776	37,668
Operating income (loss)	(2,294)	(3,882)	(4,194)	(3,000)	(13,370)	(2,841)	(1,687)	230	420	(3,878)	890	2,518	3,097	4,348	10,853
Interest income from net proceeds(1)	0	0	0	0	0	218	654	654	654	2,180	654	654	654	654	2,616
Other income (expense), net	159	92	90	100	441	109	58	46	62	275	(18)	(65)	(43)	22	(101)
Income (loss) before income taxes	(2,135)	(3,790)	(4,104)	(2,900)	(12,929)	(2,513)	(975)	930	1,136	(1,423)	1,526	3,107	3,708	5,024	13,365
Income tax provision (benefit)(2)	(747)	(1,327)	(1,436)	(1,015)	(4,525)	(880)	(341)	326	397	(498)	534	1,087	1,298	1,758	4,678
Net income (loss)	($1,388)	($2,464)	($2,668)	($1,885)	($8,404)	($1,634)	($634)	$605	$738	($925)	$992	$2,020	$2,410	$3,266	$8,687
Earnings (loss) per share	($0.07)	($0.13)	($0.14)	($0.10)	($0.45)	($0.09)	($0.03)	$0.03	$0.03	($0.04)	$0.04	$0.09	$0.10	$0.14	$0.38
Wtd. avg. shares outstanding(3)	18,542	18,542	18,542	18,542	18,542	18,542	23,088	23,088	23,088	21,951	23,088	23,088	23,088	23,088	23,088
Revenue Growth Rate															
Growth rate—Quarterly year over year						249%	3506%	1022%	290%	514%	185%	146%	78%	80%	109%
Growth rate—Consecutive qtr. to qtr.		-87%	375%	221%	NM	74%	36%	48%	12%		27%	18%	7%	13%	
Margins															
Gross margin	72%	61%	60%	59%	62%	58%	59%	60%	59%	59%	65%	63%	65%	64%	64%
Research and development	89%	810%	173%	54%	110%	34%	24%	16%	16%	20%	17%	14%	13%	11%	13%
Sales and marketing	45%	483%	119%	39%	70%	39%	31%	21%	22%	26%	25%	21%	22%	20%	22%
General and administrative	84%	643%	195%	61%	110%	37%	28%	21%	18%	24%	16%	15%	14%	13%	15%
Operating margin	**NM**	**NM**	**NM**	**NM**	**NM**	**NM**	**NM**	**2%**	**3%**	**NM**	**6%**	**14%**	**16%**	**20%**	**14%**
Effective tax rate	35%	35%	35%	35%	35%	35%	35%	35%	35%	35%	35%	35%	35%	35%	35%

Notes:

(1) Assumes offering of $50 million with net proceeds of $45.5 million reinvested at 5-3/4% interest rate beginning March 1, 1997.

(2) Assumes 35% tax rate; does not reflect any benefit from net operating loss carryforwards as they are deemed to be extraordinary and not a true indication of the underlying earnings power of the business.

(3) Assumes 18.5 million shares outstanding before the offering which assumes the inclusion of 500,000 vested options out of the 2 million total options outstanding associated with the 1995 Option Plan.

(4) FY1997 income statement data derived by taking the midpoint of the low and high case scenarios provided by the company for that period.

The 1997 projections represent the midpoint of the company's low and high estimates.

Preliminary Initial Public Offering Timetable

Nov-96

S	M	T	W	T	F	S
					1	2
3	4	5	6	7	8	9
10	11	12	13	14	15	16
17	18	19	20	21	22	23
24	25	26	27	28	29	30

Dec-96

S	M	T	W	T	F	S
1	2	3	4	5	6	7
8	9	10	11	12	13	14
15	16	17	18	19	20	21
22	23	24	25	26	27	28
29	30	31				

Jan-97

S	M	T	W	T	F	S
			1	2	3	4
5	6	7	8	9	10	11
12	13	14	15	16	17	18
19	20	21	22	23	24	25
26	27	28	29	30	31	

Feb-97

S	M	T	W	T	F	S
						1
2	3	4	5	6	7	8
9	10	11	12	13	14	15
16	17	18	19	20	21	22
23	24	25	26	27	28	

Timing	Activity	Participants
November 25th	• IPO Organizational Meeting	All
	• Due Diligence	All
Weeks of December 2nd, 9th and 16th	• Drafting of S-1	All
Week of December 16th	• File Registration Statement with SEC	CC
	• Prepare Roadshow Presentation	Company, U
Weeks of December 23rd through January 20th	• Receive SEC Comments	CC, U
Week of January 27th	• Respond to the SEC	A, CC
	• Print and Distribute Preliminary Prospectus	Company A
	• Drop in year-end financials	
Week of February 3rd	• Presentations to Underwriters' Sales Forces	Company, U
Weeks of February 10th, 17th and 24th	• Roadshow Presentations/Meetings — Europe and Asia — Domestic	Company, U
Week of February 24th	• Pricing (Closing—3 days later)	Company, U

CC = Company Counsel   U = Underwriters   A = Accountants

609

APPENDIX B

Excerpts from BEI Presentation

Why Hire BEI as a Lead Manager?

- Superior equity research coverage
  - Paul Frankel has a strong understanding of Teleswitch's business and industry
  - The leading voice in wireless technology
  - High credibility with domestic and international institutional investors

- Benefits of a technology boutique with the resources of a full-service investment bank
  - *Full-Service Firm:* capital strength, global presence, full range of investment banking services
  - *Boutique:* dedicated, experienced technology bankers and analysts who understand Teleswitch and know how to position it
  - *Full-Service Firm:* BEI's international network and global resources will be at Teleswitch's disposal during and after the IPO
  - *Boutique:* technology is one of only six vertical industry groups at BEI Securities

- Powerful, value-added international distribution capability
  - Uniquely positioned to create broad-based international investor support for Teleswitch's offering
  - Will significantly heighten Teleswitch's international profile in the investment and corporate communities
  - Strong and deep relationships with major investors around the world, including the #2 institutional penetration in Europe
  - Top equity management ranking and highly experienced U.S. and European equity capital markets and sales teams

Wireless Technology League Table
BEI has become the leading underwriter of wireless technology deals

Company	Deals
BEI Securities	$304.2
Montgomery Securities	299.5
Alex. Brown	247.5
Hambrecht & Quist	238.7
Prudential Securities	237.4
Merrill Lynch	203.7
Oppenheimer	104.0

Deals completed and filed in the twelve months ending November 1996. Full credit to all managers.
Deals include: Coral Systems, DSP Communications, Geoworks, Lightbridge, MDSI Mobile Solutions, P-COM, Powerwave, Proxim, Saville Systems, SpectraLink, and TCSI.

BEI's International Equity Distribution Capabilities
Global Equity Distribution Capability

- 350+ International Equity Sales Professionals

USA	Europe	Japan	Far East
• San Francisco 4 Salespeople	**• London** 144 Salespeople, 87 Traders	**• Tokyo** 27 Salespeople, 23 Traders	**• Hong Kong,** **Singapore** **and Far East** 45 Salespeople, 24 Traders
• New York 48 Salespeople, 35 Traders	**• Paris** 5 Salespeople, 3 Traders **• Zurich** 66 Salespeople, 89 Traders **• Geneva** 2 Salespeople, 2 Traders **• Luxembourg** 5 Salespeople, 3 Traders **• Frankfurt** 10 Salespeople, 9 Traders		

- Covering over 1,700+ Institutions
  - 450 U.S. institutions
  - 450 U.K. institutions
  - 225 Swiss institutions
  - 370 European and Middle East institutions
  - 200 Far Eastern
  - 70 accounts based in Japan

Valuation Analysis

Overview

- BEI believes the market will value Teleswitch by examining three groups of companies: *Wireless Systems Companies, xDSL Companies* and *Selected Other Communications Infrastructure Companies*
- The *Wireless Systems Companies* will serve as a floor to Teleswitch's valuation. These companies have lower expected growth rates than Teleswitch and are further down the value chain than Teleswitch in that they primarily provide sub-systems as opposed to total solutions. These companies are, however, selling proven technologies into existing markets.
- The *xDSL Companies,* while not focused on the wireless marketplace, are selling communications technology into new markets, which makes them

good comparables for Teleswitch. Additionally, the strong expected growth rates for these companies parallel that of Teleswitch.

- The *Selected Other Communications Infrastructure Companies,* with their strong growth rates, will serve as additional benchmarks for institutional investors in valuing Teleswitch.

Factors Teleswitch Valuation Influencing

- Given Teleswitch's desire to conduct a public offering in early 1997, institutional investors will primarily focus on multiples on 1997 revenue and multiples of 1998 earnings for Teleswitch's comparable companies.

- Teleswitch's 1997 revenues are virtually all from the Company's existing product portfolio. These revenues are "lower risk" and could receive revenue multiples similar to those for the *xDSL* and *Selected Other Communication Infrastructure Companies.*

- In 1998, two-thirds of Teleswitch's revenues are expected to come from sales of the Company's GSM product. As this is projected to be the first full year of profitability, investors will examine multiples of 1998 earnings. Since, however, these earnings are "higher risk" as a result of deriving from the GSM product, multiples will be more in line with those for *Wireless Systems Companies.*

Annual Projected Income Statement (in thousands)

	Year Ending December 31,		
	1996	*1997*	*1998*
Revenues	5,909	24,024	75,751
Growth Yr-Yr	*NA*	*307%*	*215%*
Gross profit	3,689	13,375	48,521
Gross margin	*62%*	*56%*	*64%*
Operating expenses:			
Research and development	6,470	7,121	10,139
% of sales	*110%*	*30%*	*13%*
Sales and marketing	4,108	8,632	16,438
% of sales	*70%*	*36%*	*22%*
General and administrative	6,480	7,910	11,091
% of sales	*110%*	*33%*	*15%*
Income (loss) from operations	(13,370)	(10,288)	10,853
Operating margin	*(226)%*	*(43)%*	*14%*
Other income and (expense), net	441	238	(104)
Income (loss) before taxes	(12,929)	(10,050)	10,749
Pretax margin	*(219)%*	*(42)%*	*14%*
Net income (loss)[1]	(12,929)	(10,050)	6,987
Net margin	*(219)%*	*(42)%*	*9%*

[1]Assumes 35% tax rate in 1988.

Financing Alternatives for Teleswitch

- Assuming Teleswitch can defer a public offering from the beginning of 1997 to mid-year 1997, the Company could achieve a substantially higher valuation.
- By mid-year 1997, the GSM product will have successfully completed beta.
- While commercial GSM product shipments are not expected to begin until September 1997, Teleswitch will likely begin receiving orders.
- With backlog beginning to build and with better visibility to 1998 revenues, Teleswitch could achieve a fully distributed trading multiple of 35x–40x 1998 earnings. This means that the Company could file a public offering in the 30x–35x 1998 earnings range, which translates to $10–$12 per share.

Concluding Thoughts for Teleswitch

BEI wants very much to lead manage Teleswitch's IPO and believes it offers several important differentiating qualities

- **Significant Experience**
  - BEI has lead managed $10.7 billion in equity offerings in the past three years
  - BEI is the leader in managing equity offerings for wireless technology companies, having received 7 mandates in the past year
- **Leading Research**
  - Paul Frankel knows and understands Teleswitch and is very excited about the Company's future prospects
  - He is the leading voice in wireless technology and has high credibility with institutional investors
  - He is skilled in positioning high-growth, high quality infrastructure companies
- **Global Distribution**
  - BEI has an unparalleled global sales infrastructure which will be used to create broad-based support for Teleswitch's offering
  - Will significantly heighten Teleswitch's international profile in the investment and corporate communities
- **Responsiveness**
  - Teleswitch is very important to the team at BEI
  - BEI as an institution is committed to going the extra mile for Teleswitch
  - The banking, sales and trading, and research teams are anxious to begin working with Teleswitch
  - Our commitment will continue long after the IPO has been completed

BEI Valuation Analysis ($ in millions)

Valuation Parameters	Teleswitch Amount	Comparable Multiple	Pre-Money Valuation	Offering Size	Post-Money Valuation
1997 Revenue	$24.0	5.0x–7.0x	$120–$168	$50	$170–$218
1998 Earnings	7.0	18x–24x	126– 168	50	176– 218

BEI Summary Offering Terms

Proposed market capitalization[1]	$180 MM–$220 MM
Proposed 1997 revenue multiple	5.5x–7.3x
Proposed 1998 earnings multiple[2]	21x–25x
Proposed share price[3]	$6.00–$8.00

[1]Assumes $50 million offering.

[2]Assumes net proceeds invested at 5.75% and a 35% tax rate.

[3]Assumes 21.0 million shares outstanding pre-offering.

A P P E N D I X   C

Excerpts from Peterson & Co. Presentation

Unique Positioning

Unique Blend of Resources, Focus and Experience:

Bulge Bracket Like Capabilities:
- Deep and broad domestic institutional presence
- Major international presence
- Large infrastructure and stature
- Large market exposure for offering
- Experience in structuring and lead managing offerings
- Experience in domestic and foreign issues
- Experienced corporate finance and capital market professionals
- Aftermarket support of large sales and trading organization

Boutique Focus and Commitment to Technology
- Technology commands the largest share of the firm's resources
  - 18 bankers, 14 research analysts in New York and San Francisco
  - Strong emphasis on Technology results in high level of knowledge throughout organization
- Industry knowledge for expert advice in positioning
- Excellent Technology track record results in strong institutional credibility
  - 70+ deals since 1993 raising approximately $4.6 billion

Trading Performance

#1 or #2 trader in wireless company underwritings

Issuer Rank	1994 Rank	1995 Rank	1996 TYD*
DSP Communications, Inc.	—	1	2
California Microwave, Inc.	1	1	2
Glenayre Technologies, Inc.	2	2	1
Gilat Satellite Networks, Ltd.	—	1	1
Vitesse Semiconductor	—	—	1

*As of October 1996

Preliminary IPO Analysis (in thousands, except per share amounts)

Adjusted Net Income

	31-Dec.-97
Projected revenues (a)	$75,751
Projected net income (a)	6,450
Incremental income on net proceeds (b)	1,513
Post-offering net income	$ 7,963
Average shares outstanding @ $10/share	26,042
Projected EPS	$ 0.31

Filing Range Valuation

	$8.00	$9,00	$10.00	$11.00	$12.00
Proposed filing range	$8.00	$9,00	$10.00	$11.00	$12.00
Projected EPS	$0.29	$0.30	$0.31	$0.31	$0.32
Filing multiple	27.4x	30.1x	32.7x	35.3x	38.0x
Fully-distributed trading multiple	31.5	34.6x	37.6x	40.6x	43.7x
Fully diluted outstanding—Post offering (c)	27,292	26,598	26,042	25,588	25,209
Implied market value—Filing post-money	$218,292	$239,380	$260,423	$281,465	$302,507
Implied market value—Filing pre-money	$168,338	$189,380	$210,423	$231,465	$252,507

Summary of Proposed Shares Offered and pro Forma Shares Outstanding

	27.4x	30.1x	32.7x	35.3x	38.0x
Filing multiple range	27.4x	30.1x	32.7x	35.3x	38.0x
Primary proceeds	$50,000	$50,000	$50,000	$50,000	$50,000
Secondary proceeds	0	0	0	0	0
Over-allotment	0	0	0	0	0
Total offering proceeds	$50,000	$50,000	$50,000	$50,000	$50,000
Primary shares offered:					
Filed shares	6,250	5,556	5,000	4,545	4,167
Over-allotment shares	0	0	0	0	0
Total (c)	6,250	5,556	5,000	4,545	4,167
Secondary shares offered:					
Filed shares	0	0	0	0	0
Over-allotment shares	0	0	0	0	0
Total	0	0	0	0	0
Total shares offered:					
Filed shares	6,250	5,556	5,000	4,545	4,167
Over-allotment shares	0	0	0	0	0
Total	6,250	5,556	5,000	4,545	4,167
Pre-IPO fully diluted shares outstanding	21,042	21,042	21,042	21,042	21,042
Total primary shares offered	6,250	5,556	5,000	4,545	4,167
Post-IPO fully diluted shares outstanding	27,292	26,598	26,042	25,588	25,209
Percent of company sold to public	22.9%	20.9%	19.2%	17.8%	16.5%

[a]Represent projections provided by Teleswitch's management. Assumes a closing date of February 28, 1997 for the offering and a 40% tax rate.

[b]Assumes incremental interest income from proceeds, earning 5.5% and taxed at a 40% tax rate. Also assumes 7% gross spread and $650,000 of offering expenses. Net proceeds based upon midpoint of filing range.

[c]Adjusted for $50,000 divided by different share prices.

Teleswitch vs. Comparables

Company	Fully-Diluted E.P.S.				Price/Earnings Ratio		Agg. Value/ CY1997E Rev.	Agg. Value/ CY1998E Rev.
	FY1995	CY1996E	CY1997E	CY1998E	CY1997E	CY1998E		
Teleswitch, Inc. (Post-Offering)	NA	($0.61)	($0.34)	$0.31	NMx	32.7x	10.8x	3.4x
Capacity-Increasing Technologies								
Amati Communications Corp.	$0.16	($0.16)	($0.29)	$0.02	NMx	NMx	NAx	NAx
Aware Inc.	(0.17)	0.03	0.12	0.30	79.2	31.7	12.3	4.1
Orckit Communications Ltd.	(0.19)	(0.27)	(0.07)	0.48	NM	26.5	8.4	2.9
Qualcomm Inc.	0.52	0.34	1.28	1.70	34.2	25.7	NA	NA
					56.7x	28.0x	10.4x	3.5x
Network Access								
Cascade Communications Corp.	$0.56	$0.68	$1.07	NA	71.4x	NAx	12.5x	NAx
Premisys Communications Inc.	0.18	0.76	NA	NA	NA	NA	NA	NA
Verilink Corp.	0.04	0.31	0.61	NA	56.2	NA	5.5	NA
Xylan Corp.	(0.45)	0.28	0.72	NA	59.8	NA	7.7	NA
					72/4x	NAx	8.5x	NAx
Communications Infrastructures								
ADC Telecommunications Inc.	$0.51	$0.66	$0.77	NA	48.2x	NAx	4.6x	NAx
Adtran Inc.	0.75	0.97	1.28	NA	33.8	NA	5.3	NA
Advanced Fibre Com., Inc.	0.09	0.35	0.68	$1.26	86.7	45.7	11.0	6.3
Cellnet Data Systems Inc.	(1.22)	(1.76)	(2.27)	NA	NM	NA	NA	NA
Glenayre Technologies, Inc.	1.22	0.94	1.37	NA	18.3	NA	3.0	NA
Pairgain Technologies Inc.	0.16	0.90	1.24	1.75	53.6	38.0	6.6	NA
Westell Technologies Inc.	(0.00)	(0.02)	0.29	0.87	90.0	30.3	4.8	2.6
Teledata Com. Ltd.	(0.12)	0.40	0.57	NA	38.5	NA	3.0	NA
					52.7x	38.3x	5.5x	4.5x
Overall Average					55.8x	33.1x	7.1x	4.0x

Preliminary Term Sheet

Type of Issue:	Initial Public Offering
Issuer:	Teleswitch, Inc.
Proposed Price Range:	$9–$11
Shares sold by Company:	5 million shares (excludes 15% over-allotment option)
Gross Proceeds to Company:	$50 million (excludes 15% over-allotment option)
Number of Fully-Diluted Shares Outstanding:	
Pre-Offering	21.0 million
Post-Offering	26.0 million (excludes 15% over-allotment option)
Fully-Diluted Market Capitalization:	
Pre-Offering	$210 million
Post-Offering	$260 million (excludes 15% over-allotment option)
Financials:	Audited three years ended December 31, 1995 and unaudited nine months ended September 30, 1996
Over-Allotment Option:	The Company will grant the underwriters an option to purchase an additional 15% of the common stock offered in connection with the initial public offering for a period of 30 days subsequent to the closing of the offering for the purposes of covering over-allotments.
Anticipated Gross Spread:	The gross underwriting discounts and commission will approximate 7.0%, the exact amount to be based on market conditions at the time of the offering.
Lock-Up Agreements:	Peterson & Co. requests all selling shareholders, officers, directors, employees and significant shareholders to lock-up for a period of 180 days following the date of the offering.

APPENDIX D

Excerpts from Vail, Jackson & Stowe (VJS) Presentation, February 14, 1997

A. TELESWITCH POSITIONING

SERVED MARKET RAPIDLY EXPANDING DUE TO:

- Falling Equipment and Service Cost
- Improving Quality
- Increasing Customer Acceptance
- Expanding Minutes of Use
- International Efforts to Increase Teledensity

ANALOG TO DIGITAL CONVERSION CREATING OPPORTUNITY

- Digital Lowers Infrastructure Costs Thereby Stimulating Demand
- Entry Point for New Supplier
  — New Equipment Purchases
  — New Licensees
- Switching Not Hurt By A to D Conversion

TELESWITCH HAS THE RIGHT PRODUCTS

- Cost Effective and Scaleable Architecture
- Low Entry and Lifetime Cost
- Based on Industry Standard Components & Platforms
- Starting With Analog & GSM Worldwide Standards, But Basically Standards Independent

TELESWITCH IS WELL-POSITIONED FOR A SUCCESSFUL IPO

- Teleswitch is Providing a Rapidly Growing Market That Provides a Fertile Medium for Innovative Small Companies to Realize Substantial Success.
- Teleswitch Possesses the Core Competencies in Vision, Technology and Management to Exploit the Market Opportunities.
- Teleswitch is Unique in That Both the Market Opportunity and the Technology Exist Today. While the Revenue and Profit Ramp is Still Some Time Away, No Leap of Faith is Necessary to Appreciate the Potential.

CONCLUSION

VJS advises valuing the Company on the basis of other smaller telecommunications equipment suppliers that have already executed on this model and discounting farther out rather than relying on other concept companies that still have substantial market and technology risks.

B. PRELIMINARY VALUATION ANALYSIS

Comparable Companies to Teleswitch, Inc.

Company	Ticker	Business Description
ADC Telecommunications	ADCT	Develops, manufactures and markets a variety of transmission and networking systems for voice, data and video networks.
Advanced Fibre Communications, Inc.	AFCI	Designs, manufactures, markets and supports telecommunications delivery systems
DSC Communications Corp.	DIGI	Produces, services and sells digital switching, transmission, test and control systems that are used in public and private communication networks.
Pairgain Technologies, Inc.	PAIR	Designs, manufactures, markets and supports products that allow telecommunications carriers with private networks to more efficiently provide high speed digital service over standard copper wires.
Tellabs, Inc.	TLAB	Designs, manufactures, markets and services voice and data transport and network access systems.

COMPARABLE COMPANY MARKET MULTIPLE SUMMARY
($ in millions, except per share data)

	Share Price 02/12/97	Market Cap.	TEV[1]	TEV/LTM			EPS[1]		P/E Ratio	
				Revenue	EBITDA	Ebit	CY 1997	CY 1998	CY 1997	CY 1998
ADC Telecommunications Inc.	$35.38	$4,615.8	$4,439.5	5.4x	26.6x	33.3x	$0.99	$1.48	35.7x	24.0x
Advanced Fibre Comm Inc.	44.38	1,449.1	1,340.7	10.3	62.1	64.9	0.63	1.30	70.4	34.1
DSC Communications Corp	23.13	2,711.3	2,566.8	1.9	19.3	67.7	0.90	1.38	25.7	16.8
Pairgain Technologies Inc	38.88	2,463.5	2,372.4	13.4	50.2	55.5	0.74	0.95	52.5	40.9
Tellabs Inc.	41.75	7,484.6	6,845.1	8.8	28.7	32.9	1.19	1.56	35.1	26.8
Average (excludes high and low).				8.2x	35.2x	51.2x			41.1x	28.3x

[1]Total enterprise value.

Preliminary Valuation Matrix
($ in millions, except per share data)

IPO Price Per Share	$8.00	$9.00	$10.00	$11.00	$12.00
Existing Shares Outstanding (in millions)	21.0	21.0	21.0	21.0	21.0
Pre-Money Equity Valuation	$168.0	$189.0	$210.0	$231.0	$252.0
IPO Offering Size	50.0	50.0	50.0	50.0	50.0
Post-Money Valuation	$218.0	$239.0	$260.0	$281.0	$302.0
% of Company Sold	22.9%	20.9%	19.2%	17.8%	16.6%
Pro Forma 1998 Net Income	$8.0	$8.0	$8.0	$8.0	$8.0
Effective 1998 P/E Multiple	27.3x	29.9x	32.5x	35.1x	37.8x
1998 P/E Multiple of Comparable Companies	28.3x	28.3x	28.3x	28.3x	28.3x
% Premium (Discount) to Comparable Multiple	(3.7)%	5.6%	14.8%	24.1%	33.4%

KEY VALUATION ISSUES

- Initiation of One GSM Beta Site
- Meet or Exceed March Projections
- Projections at or above Current Model
- Strength of Equity and New Issue Markets

C. IPO TIMING

SAMPLE TIMETABLE BASED ON MARCH FINANCIALS

File and Print "Red Herrings" with Audited 1996 Results and Unaudited 1997 IQ Results

Date	Activity
March 10	Organizational Meeting and Due Diligence
Weeks of March 10 & 17	Drafting Sessions and Due Diligence
Week of March 24	Drafting Sessions at Printer File Registration Statement
Week of April 7	Commence Preparation of Roadshow
Week of April 14	File Amendment Incorporating SEC Comments
Week of April 28	Receive SEC Comments on Registration Statements Print and Distribute "Red Herrings" Management Sales Force Presentations
Weeks of May 5 and 12	Roadshow Meetings in Selected International and Domestic Cities
Week of May 19	Complete Roadshow; Price Offering; Closing

D. MARKETING STRATEGY: VJS's APPROACH

- Define Investment Thesis
  - —Work with Teleswitch's management to develop investment "hooks"
  - —Highlight competitive advantages and specific growth prospects
- Structure Marketing Materials
  - —Preliminary prospectus
  - —Internal selling memorandum
  - —Equity research investment themes
  - —Targeted investor list
- File offering with an Initial Price Range Based on a Set of Projections which are Realistic and Attainable
- Develop Road Show Presentation
  - —Focused on concise 25 minute presentation based on investor thesis
  - —Dress rehearsal with senior VJS marketing professionals
  - —Anticipate questions to be encountered
- Introduce Company and Transaction to Marketplace
  - —Kick off with presentation to VJS sales force
  - —Hold multiple research analyst conference calls
  - —Generate interest from institutional accounts to attend Company presentations
- Focus Marketing Efforts on Selected Institutional Accounts
- Road Show: Will Reach 10 or more Domestic and International Cities
  - —One-on-one meetings
  - —Group meetings
- A VJS Sales Professional Will Accompany Management to Substantially All One-On-One Meetings (Bankers Will Attend Every Session)
- Research and Sales Follow-up To Institutional Meetings
- Sales Force Closes Orders
- Sales and Marketing Management and Capital Markets Group Refine Institutional Order Book

A P P E N D I X   E

Excerpts from Springer, Mathis & Co. Presentation, February 14, 1997

SPRINGER, MATHIS OVERVIEW

- Founded in 1986
- Focus on Research in defined segments within Technology & Communications, Healthcare and Consumer.
- Founding Principles
  — "Narrow and deep research coverage"
  — Research drives Sales and Trading
  — Research drives Investment Banking
- Springer, Mathis & Company Today
  — Approximately 130 people in St. Louis, Chicago and Denver
  — Technology constitutes three quarters of our business
  — Over 57 transactions in 1995 and 1996, raising over $3.6 billion in capital and executing 19 merger and acquisition advisory assignments with aggregate transaction values exceeding $2.9 billion

TELESWITCH POSITIONING

- Teleswitch is a leading developer and manufacturer of distributed switching systems, base stations, network management systems and intelligent network platforms for the worldwide wireless telecommunications market
- The Company's GlobalSystems portfolio supports the development of affordable and scaleable cellular, micro-cellular, wireless local loop, AMPS, GSM and PCS systems. Its technology supports the transition from traditional switch-centric networks to cost effective, flexible architectures, offering international service providers and businesses economical alternatives for new systems deployment in low traffic density markets (rural, suburban and small urban areas) developed and developing countries.
- Because its systems are software intensive, service providers gain added flexibility in network deployment with the ability to expand coverage in the existing markets or enter into new markets to meet growing demand. Additionally, software upgrades enable advanced features that allow operators to differentiate service offerings.
- Teleswitch is the first company to fully integrate the MSC, BSC, VLR and HLR functions, minimizing equipment needs. Teleswitch's intelligent network platforms support one phone, one number services whether at home, work, or on the road.

IPO Summary

Company Data:

Fiscal Year End:	31-Dec
Last Quarter Pre-Offering:	3/31/97
Proposed Nasdaq Symbol:	CLCR
Closing Date:	6/7/97
Projected Tax Rate:	37.0%

Filing Data:

Midpoint of Filing Range/Price per Share:	$12.00	
Preliminary Filing Range:	$11.00	$13.00

Shares Offered (000's)(1):

Suggested Primary Shares Offered:	4,000	$48,000	100%
Potential Secondary Shares Offered:	0	$0	0%
Suggested Total Shares Offered:	4,000	$48,000	100%

Post-Offering Valuation:

% of Pre-Offering Shares Sold to Public:	29%
% of Post-Offering Shares Sold to Public:	22%

	CLCR	COMPS	%
1997 P/E Ratios:	NM	34.4x	NM
1998 P/E Ratios:	22.6x	26.4x	(15%)
Market Cap / 1997 Revenues:	11.0x	3.2x	246%
Market Cap / 1998 Revenues:	2.8x	2.5x	14%

Fully-Diluted Pre-Split Shares (000's):	21,042
Fully-Diluted Pre-Split Shares:	

Stock Split Ratio   2   For   3

	# of Shares
Fully-Diluted Post-Split Shares (000's):	
Common Share Equivalents:	14,028
Total Post-split Fully Diluted Shares:	14,028
New Primary Shares Offered:	4,000
Fully-Diluted Post-Split Shares	18,028

Market Capitalization Summary:

Pre-Offering Valuation:	$168,338,184
Post-Offering Valuation:	$216,338,184

Proceeds from Offering (000's):

	Amount	%
Total Offering Size:	$48,000	100.00%
Gross Proceeds to the Company:	48,000	100.00%
Gross Spread of Company Proceeds:	3,360	7.00%
Estimated Offering Expenses:	750	1.56%
Net Proceeds to the Company:	$43,890	91.44%

Use of Proceeds from Offering (000's):

	Amount	%
Cash Reinvested @ 5.75%:	$43,890	5.75%
Closing Date/% of Year Remaining:	56.7%	
Annual Interest Income from Net Proceeds:	$2,524	
Actual Cal 1997 Interest Income:	$1,431	
Quarterly Interest Income:	$631	

(1)Certain selling shareholders can be accommodated in the Offering.

Projections

	Calendar Year 1997 (E) quarters ended				Calendar Year 1998 (E) quarters ended				Calendar Years ended	
	3/31/97	6/30/97	9/30/97	12/31/97	3/31/98	6/30/98	9/30/98	12/31/98	1997 (E)	1998 (E)
Total sales	$2,468	$5,448	$5,621	$6,182	$13,612	$17,572	$19,057	$25,986	$19,719	$76,227
Cost of sales	1,206	3,742	3,687	3,323	5,647	7,021	7,588	10,535	11,958	30,791
Gross profit	1,262	1,706	1,934	2,859	7,965	10,551	11,469	15,451	7,761	45,436
Operating expenses:										
Sales and marketing	1,780	1,908	1,765	1,977	3,168	3,232	3,579	3,609	7,430	13,588
Research & development	1,766	1,727	1,829	1,835	2,260	2,217	2,179	2,228	7,157	8,884
General and administrative	1,788	1,800	2,156	2,033	2,299	2,451	2,542	2,637	7,777	9,929
Total operating expenses	5,334	5,435	5,750	5,845	7,727	7,900	8,300	8,474	22,364	32,401
Operating income	(4,072)	(3,729)	(3,816)	(2,986)	238	2,651	3,169	6,977	(14,603)	13,035
Other income (expense)	92	32	(19)	(60)	(93)	(114)	(90)	(40)	45	(337)
Income before taxes	(3,980)	(3,697)	(3,835)	(3,046)	145	2,537	3,079	6,937	(14,558)	12,698
Income taxes (1)	(1,473)	(1,368)	(1,419)	(1,127)	54	939	1,139	2,567	(5,386)	4,698
Net income	($2,507)	($2,329)	($2,416)	($1,919)	$91	$1,598	$1,940	$4,370	($9,172)	$8,000
Weighted average shares	14,028	14,028	14,028	14,028	14,028	14,028	14,028	14,028	14,028	14,028
EPS	($0.18)	($0.17)	($0.17)	($0.14)	$0.01	$0.11	$0.14	$0.31	($0.65)	$0.57
As a % of revenue										
Cost of sales	48.9%	68.7%	65.6%	53.8%	41.5%	40.0%	39.8%	40.5%	60.6%	40.4%
Gross profit	51.1%	31.3%	34.4%	46.2%	58.5%	60.0%	60.2%	59.5%	39.4%	59.6%
Sales and marketing	72.1%	35.0%	31.4%	32.0%	23.3%	18.4%	18.8%	13.9%	37.7%	17.8%
Research & development	71.6%	31.7%	32.5%	29.7%	16.6%	12.6%	11.4%	8.6%	36.3%	11.7%
General and administrative	72.4%	33.0%	38.4%	32.9%	16.9%	13.9%	13.3%	10.1%	39.4%	13.0%
Operating margin	NM	NM	NM	NM	1.7%	15.1%	16.6%	26.8%	NM	17.1%
Income before taxes	NM	NM	NM	NM	1.1%	14.4%	16.2%	26.7%	NM	16.7%
Net income	NM	NM	NM	NM	0.7%	9.1%	10.2%	16.8%	NM	10.5%
Normalized tax rate	37.0%	37.0%	37.0%	37.0%	37.0%	37.0%	37.0%	37.0%	37.0%	37.0%

*All projected financial statements are derived from information provided by Teleswitch, Inc.
(1) Assumes a 37.0% normalized tax rate.

625

Pro Forma Operations

	Calendar Year 1997 (E) quarters ended				Calendar Year 1998 (E) quarters ended				Calendar Years ended	
	3/31/97	6/30/97	9/30/97	12/31/97	3/31/98	6/30/98	9/30/98	12/31/98	1997 (E)	1998 (E)
Total sales	$2,468	$5,448	$5,621	$6,182	$13,612	$17,572	$19,057	$25,986	$19,719	$76,227
Cost of sales	1,206	3,742	3,687	3,323	5,647	7,021	7,588	10,535	11,958	30,791
Gross profit	1,262	1,706	1,934	2,859	7,965	10,551	11,469	15,451	7,761	45,436
Operating expenses:										
Sales and marketing	1,780	1,908	1,765	1,977	3,168	3,232	3,579	3,609	7,430	13,588
Research & development	1,766	1,727	1,829	1,835	2,260	2,217	2,179	2,228	7,157	8,884
General and administrative	1,788	1,800	2,156	2,033	2,299	2,451	2,542	2,637	7,777	9,929
Total operating expenses	5,334	5,435	5,750	5,845	7,727	7,900	8,300	8,474	22,364	32,401
Operating income	(4,072)	(3,729)	(3,816)	(2,986)	238	2,651	3,169	6,977	(14,603)	13,035
Other income (expense)	92	193	612	571	538	517	541	591	1,468	2,187
Income before taxes	(3,980)	(3,536)	(3,204)	(2,415)	776	3,168	3,710	7,568	(13,135)	15,222
Income taxes (1)	(1,473)	(1,308)	(1,186)	(894)	287	1,172	1,373	2,800	(4,860)	5,632
Net income	($2,507)	($2,228)	($2,019)	($1,522)	$489	$1,996	$2,337	$4,768	($8,275)	$9,590
Weighted average shares	14,028	15,050	18,028	18,028	18,028	18,028	18,028	18,028	16,284	18,028
EPS	($0.18)	($0.15)	($0.11)	($0.08)	$0.03	$0.11	$0.13	$0.26	($0.51)	$0.53
As a % of revenue										
Cost of sales	48.9%	68.7%	65.6%	53.8%	41.5%	40.0%	39.8%	40.5%	60.6%	40.4%
Gross profit	51.1%	31.3%	34.4%	46.2%	58.5%	60.0%	60.2%	59.5%	39.4%	59.6%
Sales and marketing	72.1%	35.0%	31.4%	32.0%	23.3%	18.4%	18.8%	13.9%	37.7%	17.8%
Research & development	71.6%	31.7%	32.5%	29.7%	16.6%	12.6%	11.4%	8.6%	36.3%	11.7%
General and administrative	72.4%	33.0%	38.4%	32.9%	16.9%	13.9%	13.3%	10.1%	39.4%	13.0%
Operating margin	NM	NM	NM	NM	1.7%	15.1%	16.6%	26.8%	NM	17.1%
Income before taxes	NM	NM	NM	NM	5.7%	18.0%	19.5%	29.1%	NM	20.0%
Net income	NM	NM	NM	NM	3.6%	11.4%	12.3%	18.3%	NM	12.6%
Normalized tax rate	37.0%	37.0%	37.0%	37.0%	37.0%	37.0%	37.0%	37.0%	37.0%	37.0%

*All projected financial statements are derived from information provided by Teleswitch, Inc.
(1)Assumes a 37.0% normalized tax rate.

626

Valuation Summary

	Fully-diluted Shares Outstanding		
	Pre-Offering	*Primary*	*Post-Offering*
Mid-point Share Price of Proposed Filing Range: Teleswitch	14,028,182	4,000,000	28,028,182
Mid-point Share Price of Proposed Filing Range:		$12.00	
Pre-money Valuation: Post-money Valuation:		$168,338,184 $216,338,184	

Comparable Company Summary (2)

	P/E Multiple					
			Market Cap. to Revenue			*1998 P/E to Growth Rate*
	Calendar 1997 P/E	*Calendar 1998 P/E*	*1997*	*1998*	*3 Yr. EPS Growth*	
Teleswitch	NM	22.6x	11.0x	2.8x	30%	75%
Comparable Universe:	34.4x	26.4x	2.3x	2.5x	28%	97%
Premium/(Discount) to Selected Comparable Universe:	NM	(15%)	246%	14%	9%	

[1]See initial Public Offering Summary for detailed analysis of the offering.
[2]See Comparable Company Analysis for a detailed description of current market multiples.

Preliminary Initial Public Offering Time Schedule

Week(s) of	Activity
March 11th	Organizational Meeting/Initial Due Diligence Session
March 18th–April 8th	Due Diligence and Drafting Sessions
April 15th	First Quarter Financials Available Final Drafting Session and Review Draft at Printer Registration Statement Form S-1 Filed with SEC Print Preliminary Prospectuses
May 13th	Receive Comments from SEC File Amendment #1 to S-1 Registration Statement Commence International Roadshow
May 20th	Commence Domestic Roadshow
May 27th	Continue Domestic Roadshow Price
June 3rd	Close

Springer, Mathis Research Productivity, 1996

Rank	Firm Name	Number of Reports	Number of Companies Covered	Reports per Company
1	Springer, Mathis & Co.	1,708	161	10.61
2	Rodman & Renshaw/ABACO	1,600	168	9.52
3	Needham & Company	1,588	209	7.60
4	Merrill Lynch & Co.	5,937	1,165	5.10
5	Raymond James & Assoc.	1,029	238	4.32
6	Hambrecht & Quist	1,526	372	4.10
7	ABN AMRO Chicago Corp.	1,043	74	3.81
8	Robert W. Baird & Co., Inc.	1,153	323	3.57
9	Dean Witter Reynolds	2,158	635	3.40
10	Morgan Stanley & Company	3,269	1,003	3.26

GRAND JUNCTION

It was September 16, 1995. As Howard Charney caucused with his investment bankers, he continued to debate the last offer he had just made to Cisco Systems. The past two months had been filled with meetings and negotiations with his senior management team, his investment bankers, and representatives of Cisco to discuss whether his company, Grand Junction, should be acquired by Cisco or issue stock in an initial public offering (IPO). He hoped the meeting today would decide that question once and for all.

The negotiations with Cisco had happened very rapidly. Until sixty days ago, Charney had not really given any thought to being acquired. Grand Junction was on a fast growth curve, the IPO market was hot, and he and the other founders had planned from the beginning to take the company public. Yet Cisco was very interested, and although it had required a lot of work to get them to a reasonable price, it was possible that the two companies would reach an agreement that day.

Charney was torn between the two options. There were so many issues to consider. He wondered which was more attractive financially. He knew his life would be very different under the two scenarios, but was uncertain how different. And then there were his employees. How would they feel about being acquired? Was going public really that important?

This case was prepared by Nick Mansour under the supervision of H. Irving Grousbeck, Consulting Professor of Management, Stanford University Graduate School of Business, as the basis for class discussion rather than to illustrate either effective or ineffective handling of an administrative situation.

Stanford Business School Case SB186.

Background

Grand Junction was founded in 1992 by Howard Charney, Jack Moses, and Larry Birenbaum. The three originally met when they worked together at 3Com, a successful networking equipment manufacturer. Charney was one of five founders and the Vice President of Manufacturing at 3Com. Moses and Birnbaum were also high level executives at 3Com. At Grand Junction, Charney was President and CEO, Moses was the Vice President of Marketing, and Birnbaum was the Vice President of Engineering. The company raised capital from a number of venture capital firms, including TVI and Merrill Pickard.

Grand Junction originally aimed to take advantage of an emerging networking technology known as "fast ethernet." When the market for fast ethernet products did not develop as quickly as they had anticipated, the team decided to change the focus of the company. They saw an opportunity in the ethernet local area network (LAN) switching market.

At the time of the decision, ethernet LAN switching was a two-tiered market consisting of backbone switches and workgroup switches. Backbone switches were higher capacity switches and carried the bulk of the network communications traffic throughout a LAN. Workgroup switches only carried traffic between specific user groups. Prices in the LAN switching industry were measured on a "cost per port" basis. Backbone switches cost approximately $500 per port and workgroup switches cost about $300 per port. Both of these switches served multiple computers or multiple groups of computers. But as networking software applications became more complex, there was a growing demand for a relatively inexpensive ethernet switch dedicated to a single computer. The prices of the existing ethernet switches made them inappropriate for the "desktop switching market," as the demand came to be known.

Applying some of the fast ethernet technology to differentiate itself in the emerging ethernet desktop switching market, Grand Junction was able to produce a very competitive product which cost $150 per port. The company focused on selling to specific industries that needed the capacity that the desktop switch was able to provide. In less than a year, sales grew from nothing to a projected $8 million per quarter by the third quarter of 1995. Over half of the revenue came from the ethernet desktop switch, and the remainder came from fast ethernet and other network equipment. Grand Junction had also grown to eighty-five employees. The company was projecting revenues of over $65 million in 1996 (see **Exhibit 1**).

In 1995, the backbone and workgroup ethernet switching markets were dominated by 3Com, Cisco, and Bay Networks (see **Exhibit 2** for competitor information). Only 3Com, however, had a desktop switch product, and 3Com and Grand Junction each had a fifty percent share of that market. Though the ethernet desktop switching and fast ethernet markets were small, they were projected to grow to $650 million and $1.5 billion in annual revenues, respectively, by 1997.[1]

---

[1]"Cisco's Grand Idea," *LAN Times*, October 23, 1995, p. 37.

Cisco Systems

Cisco was founded in 1987 by a married couple who worked in the Stanford Graduate School of Business computer center. The company was extremely successful and had a market capitalization of nearly $19 billion by September, 1995. It was a recognized leader in the production of networking equipment and maintained a dominating position in the router market, a market it had pioneered.

Based on the strength of its router position and with the financial resources its success had generated, Cisco had acquired several network equipment manufacturers since 1993. In September, 1993, Cisco entered the ethernet backbone switching market with the acquisition of Crescendo Communications for $80 million in Cisco stock. A year later, in October, 1994, Cisco paid $200 million for Kalpana and in the process, became a leading provider of ethernet workgroup switches. 3Com and Bay Networks had also been acquiring a number of network equipment manufacturers (see **Exhibits 3** and **4**).

Go Public or Be Acquired?

At the same time that Grand Junction was experiencing tremendous growth, the market for initial public offerings was very attractive. Network-related companies were doing particularly well. Fore Systems and Alantec were two network equipment manufacturers that had recently gone public (see **Exhibit 5**). "Switching is the hot word in the LAN area," said venture capitalist Geoffrey Yang of Institutional Venture Partners. "Any IPO that's related to the internet is hotter than a pistol."[2] Industry analysts were particularly interested in Grand Junction. In the Summer of 1995, Grand Junction retained the investment banking firm of Goldman, Sachs, and began preparing for an initial public offering, to occur before the end of 1995.

In late July, 1995, Goldman, Sachs approached Charlie Giancarlo, Vice President of Business Development of Cisco, about a possible acquisition. Giancarlo explained:

> That seems to be something that investment bankers have done more and more over the last couple of years. It was just a check to see whether or not there was a corporate buyer interested in the company. We decided to take a look. We were led to believe that an acquisition would be in the $200 million range.

Giancarlo went with Mario Mazzola to see Grand Junction. Mazzola was a founder of Crescendo Communications and was now the Vice President for Cisco's switching products. Mazzola had known Charney and his senior management team and was already interested in Grand Junction.

Cisco quickly decided that Grand Junction was worth pursuing. Cisco recognized the huge potential of the ethernet desktop switching market. Furthermore,

---

[2]"The New Sultans of Cyberspace," *Business Week*, June 26, 1995, p. 114.

Grand Junction had a very talented management team and several interesting new products it was about to release.

Strategic reasons for Cisco to acquire Grand Junction were even more important. Only 3Com, Cisco's largest competitor, offered products in ethernet backbone, workgroup, and desktop switching. Cisco believed that 3Com could use the low-end desktop switching product to attract customers in the more profitable workgroup and backbone markets. It might eventually be possible for 3Com, which at the time had a poor position in the router market, to use its full line of ethernet switching products to threaten Cisco's lucrative router business. Cisco also worried that an acquisition of Grand Junction by Bay Networks could breathe new life into Bay Networks. At the time, Bay Networks was Cisco's second biggest competitor, and Cisco believed that Bay Networks was beginning to show signs of financial difficulty. Like Cisco, Bay Networks had no ethernet desktop switching product. Bay Networks could also use the Grand Junction desktop switch to gain a competitive advantage in the more profitable markets. Moreover, Bay Network's router market share was better than 3Com's. Acquiring Grand Junction would be a good way both for Cisco to "push back" this threat from 3Com and keep Bay Networks from gaining an advantage.

Cisco made an initial offer in the low $200 million range in early August. Grand Junction and Goldman, Sachs countered that the offer would have to be over $300 million. Throughout August, there were a number of meetings involving Charney, Grand Junction's investment banker, Giancarlo, and John Chambers (CEO of Cisco). The main focus of the meetings was price. Goldman, Sachs and Charney believed that Grand Junction would be going public at an initial valuation in the $300 million range. In addition, IPO stock prices are generally set so that the price increases, or "bounces," on the first day of the offering. Typically the company and investment bankers expect that increase to be 15%. Charney argued that Cisco should be prepared to pay for the "bounce" as well. Finally, Grand Junction representatives argued that Grand Junction should be worth at least as much as Kalpana in terms of the shares of Cisco stock involved. Since the Kalpana acquisition was at seven million shares of Cisco stock, a Grand Junction acquisition would require at least that. Cisco's stock price had increased from $28 per share at the time of the Kalpana acquisition to $54.25 per share in early August, 1995.

Chambers and Giancarlo argued that Cisco should get a "liquidity preference" price benefit. If Grand Junction was acquired, Charney and the other shareholders of Grand Junction could sell their Cisco stock immediately. On the other hand, if Grand Junction went public, Charney and the other officers of Grand Junction would not be able to sell their stock until at least six months after the IPO. In those six months, due to the risk of a new stock, Grand Junction stock could lose any "bounce" it had gained. Also if Grand Junction chose to go public, it would be very difficult for Charney or any other members of the senior management team to sell any stock, because investors would read this as a bad sign and drive the stock price down. Finally, Chambers and Giancarlo pointed out the historic strength of Cisco stock and that it was very likely that the price would continue to rise (see **Exhibit 6**).

While price negotiations were the primary focus of discussion with Cisco, Charney was also discussing a number of other issues with his management team. Of primary concern was the future of Grand Junction after the IPO. Above all else, the management team wanted to win—to make their product and their technology pervasive in the market. Grand Junction certainly had a strong position in the desktop switching market, but the management team wondered what Grand Junction's position would be in three years, or even in one year. Though neither Bay Networks nor Cisco had a competitive product offering, they both had the financial and technological capability to enter the market quickly. Once they entered, Charney and his team thought the big customers would definitely buy from Cisco, Bay Networks, and 3Com and doubted that Grand Junction would be able to sustain its growth. Grand Junction had been able to compete with these larger firms through superior technology, but the management team wondered if Grand Junction would be able to attract top engineering talent after the IPO without the equity incentives of a start-up. If winning in the market was the main objective, Cisco was an attractive mechanism through which their technology could be accepted.

The management team also considered the prestige of taking a company public. Important members of the senior management team and some members of the Board wanted to go public. Charney and several managers had also led certain recently-hired key employees to believe that an IPO was an important goal. This was the reason that many employees, especially several engineers, had joined Grand Junction. The senior managers had never mentioned that being acquired was an option. Of the eighty-five total employees, half were considered key employees, and all owned common stock or held stock options. Charney wondered how the employees would react.

Personally, at 3Com, Charney had already taken a company public. He knew the glamorous side of an IPO, but he also knew the dark side. As an officer, he could be subject to lawsuits. As CEO, he would be accountable to the stock market for Grand Junction's stock price. This could be a large distraction, particularly in a small company like Grand Junction where missing quarterly targets by a small margin can have a large effect on stock price. Charney was not sure that he wanted to be the CEO of a public company.

The management team really did not know Cisco's culture very well. Charney and his management team knew Mazzola and were comfortable with his working style. Mazzola assured them that the cultures were similar, but they believed that several employees would leave if Cisco acquired Grand Junction. Many of the employees did not want to work for a large company. Some had actually come to Grand Junction from Cisco. It would be awkward for them to return, and a few would definitely not be welcomed back by Cisco.

Also, Charney and the management team would be demoted if Grand Junction was acquired. Most of them were in their mid to late forties. Instead of being senior management of a small company, they would be middle managers of a large company. In fact, they had all been vice presidents at 3Com and although Cisco was roughly the same size as 3Com, they would be working at an even lower level at Cisco than they did at 3Com. They knew this would mean less authority and autonomy. Were they ready to go back to a situation where they would be reporting to others?

On the other hand, there were advantages to the lifestyle at Cisco as well. Building Grand Junction had been a rewarding experience. But it had also been a very demanding three years. Life at Grand Junction would not change much after an IPO. The lifestyle at Cisco was likely to be more relaxed, or at least require fewer hours at work.

Final Offer

In late August, in the hopes of getting a deal completed, John Chambers offered 5 million shares of Cisco stock for Grand Junction. It was an offer worth just over $325 million dollars. Charney and Goldman, Sachs still thought the offer was too low.

Bay Networks and two large computer manufacturers had also begun to show an interest in Grand Junction. Grand Junction informed Cisco that there were other interested parties.

In early September, the parties had still not reached an agreement. Charney was beginning to think that they would not be able to agree. He also did not want to miss the window of opportunity for an IPO. On September 11, 1995, Grand Junction filed an S-1 form, notifying the SEC of Grand Junction's intentions to go public (see **Exhibit 7** for excerpts). Charney hoped that this would quickly close the negotiations with Cisco one way or another. Grand Junction would issue three million new shares in the IPO, and would have twenty-one million shares outstanding upon completion of the transaction. Although the S-1 stated a range of $12 to $14 per share, Goldman, Sachs was recommending that the company issue stock at $16 per share.

On September 16, Grand Junction and Cisco representatives engaged in a series of negotiating meetings. Cisco was still hoping to acquire Grand Junction for approximately $325 million. Since the price of Cisco stock had risen to $69.25 per share, this was less than the five million shares of Cisco stock Chambers had last offered. Charney said he was now willing to take the five million shares of Cisco stock which was then worth $346 million. The two parties broke into caucuses to debate this final offer.

EXHIBIT 1

	($ in millions)										
	1994	**1995**					**1996**				
	Q4A	Q1A	Q2A	Q3E	Q4E	Total	Q1E	Q2E	Q3E	Q4E	Total
Revenues	3.2	5.1	6.3	8.0	10.6	30.0	12.4	14.7	17.5	20.9	65.5
Cost of Sales	1.3	1.9	2.5	3.3	4.3	12.0	4.7	5.5	6.3	7.5	24.0
Gross Profit	1.9	3.2	3.8	4.7	6.3	18.0	7.7	9.2	11.2	13.4	41.5
Operating Expenses											
R&D	1.0	1.2	1.2	1.4	1.5	5.3	1.7	2.1	2.5	2.9	9.2
Marketing	1.5	1.4	1.6	1.9	2.0	6.9	2.3	2.8	3.3	4.0	12.4
General & Admin	0.2	0.3	0.3	0.4	0.4	1.4	0.5	0.6	0.7	0.8	2.6
Total	2.7	2.9	3.1	3.7	3.9	13.6	4.5	5.5	6.5	7.7	24.2
EBIT*	(0.8)	0.3	0.7	1.0	2.4	4.4	3.2	3.7	4.7	5.7	17.3
Net Income**	(0.9)	0.2	0.4	0.7	1.6	2.9	2.0	2.5	3.1	3.6	11.2

*EBIT and EBITDA are essentially equal as depreciation and amortization expenses are very low for the networking industry and are included in general and administrative expenses for accounting purposes.
**Net income is after-tax income.

EXHIBIT 2

	Cisco	Bay Networks	3Com
Stock Information***			
Stock Price ($)	69.25	51.63	43.50
Shares Outstanding	272,246,000	114,915,000	138,462,000
Market Value ($MM)	18,853	5,933	6,024
Last Twelve Months Financial Results ($000)			
Revenue	1,978,916	1,342,293	1,479,385
Gross Profit	1,334,764	742,747	792,578
EBIT*	642,939	199,540	305,486
Net Income**	421,008	130,999	188,632

*EBIT and EBITDA are essentially equal as depreciation and amortization expenses are very low for the networking industry and are included in general and administrative expenses for accounting purposes.
**Net income is after-tax income.
***As of September 15, 1995.

EXHIBIT 3   Transactions Involving Network Switching Companies

Acquiree	Acquiror	Date of Acquisition	Last 12 Months Revenue ($MM)	Acquisition Value ($MM)
Crescendo Communications	Cisco	09/21/93	9.0	81.9
Synernetics	3Com	12/17/93	27.0	107.3
NiceCom	3Com	09/20/94	0.7	58.5
Kalpana	Cisco	09/20/94	30.0	198.9
Lightstream	Cisco	12/08/94	NA	120.0
Centillion	Bay Networks	05/10/95	NA	140.0
Chipcom	3Com	07/27/95	39.0	720.6

EXHIBIT 4   Cisco's Acquisitions

Acquiree	Business Description	Date of Acquisition	Last 12 Months Revenue ($MM)	Acquisition Value ($MM)
Crescendo Communications	Backbone switches	09/21/93	9.0	81.9
Newport Systems Solutions	Routers	07/12/94	5.4	82.9
Kalpana	Segmentation switches	09/20/94	30.0	198.9
Lightstream	ATM switching technology	12/08/94	NA	120.0
Combinet	Remote-access products	08/10/95	NA	111.5
Internet Junction	Internet gateway software	09/06/95	NA	5.5

EXHIBIT 5

	Fore Systems	*Alantec*
Date of Initial Public Offering	May 24, 1994	February 2, 1994
S-1 Filing Price Range ($)	11–13	8–10
Millions of Shares Issued	3.1	2.5
Total Shares Outstanding (Millions)	13.0*	8.3
IPO Price ($)	16.00	13.00
Stock Price at Close of IPO Date ($)	23.75	14.88
Stock Price on September 16, 1995 ($)	33.00*	37.25
Last Twelve Months Financial Results ($000)		
Revenue	95,510	37,583
Gross Profit	51,105	25,527
EBIT**	13,843	7,381
Net Income***	7,934	7,303

*Adjusted for stock split.

**EBIT and EBITDA are essentially equal as depreciation and amortization expenses are very low for the networking industry and are included in general and administrative expenses for accounting purposes.

***Net income is after-tax income.

EXHIBIT 6   Cisco Systems Adjusted Stock Price ($)

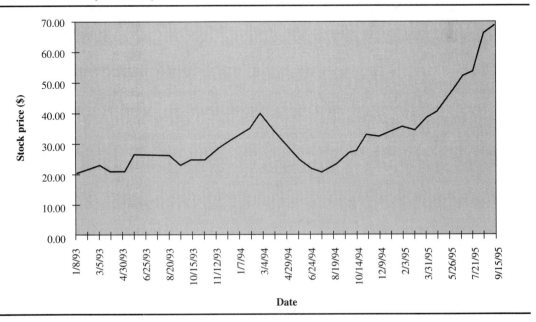

EXHIBIT 7

SECURITIES AND EXCHANGE COMMISSION
Washington, D.C. 20549
Form S-1
REGISTRATION STATEMENT
Under
THE SECURITIES ACT OF 1933
GRAND JUNCTION NETWORKS, INC.
(Exact name of Registrant as specified in its charter)

DELAWARE	3577	77-0300115
(State of other jurisdiction of incorporation or organization)	(Primary Standard Industrial Code Classification Number)	(I.R.S. Employer Identification No.)

47281 Bayside Parkway
Fremont, California 94538
(510) 252-0726
(Address, including zip code, and telephone number, including area code, of Registrant's principal executive offices)

Howard S. Charney
President and Chief Executive Officer
GRAND JUNCTION NETWORKS, INC.
47281 Bayside Parkway
Fremont, California 94538
(510) 252-0726
(Name, address, including zip code, and telephone number, including area code, of agent or service)

Copies to:

JAMES M. KOSHLAND, ESQ.	LARRY W. SONSINI, ESQ.
CARLA S. NEWELL, ESQ.	JOHN V. ROOS, ESQ.
REBECCA K. SCHMITT, ESQ.	PAGE MAILLIARD, ESQ.
Gray Cary Ware & Freidenrich,	Wilson, Sonsini, Goodrich & Rosati
A Professional Corporation	Professional Corporation
400 Hamilton Avenue	650 Page Mill Road
Palo Alto, California 94301	Palo Alto, California 94304

Approximate date of commencement of proposed sale to the public: As soon as practicable after this Registration Statement becomes effective.

If any of the securities being registered on the Form are to be offered on a delayed or continuous basis pursuant to Rule 415 under the Securities Act of 1933, check the following box. ☐

If this form is filed to register additional securities for an offering pursuant to Rule 462(b) under the Securities Act, please check the following box and list the Securities Act registration statement number of the earlier effective registration statement for the same offering. ☐

If this Form is a post-effective amendment filed pursuant to Rule 462(c) under the Securities Act, check the following box and list the Securities Act registration statement number of the earlier effective registration statement for the same offering. ☐

If delivery of the prospectus is expected pursuant to Rule 434, please check the following box. ☐

CALCULATION OF REGISTRATION FEE

Title of Each Class of Securities to be Registered	Amount to be Registered (1)	Proposed Maximum Offering Price Per Share (2)	Proposed Maximum Aggregate Offering Price (2)	Amount of Registration Fee
Common Stock ($.001 par value)	3,450,000 shares	$14.00	$48,300,000	$16,656

(1) Includes 450,000 shares issuable upon exercise of an option granted by the Company to the Underwriters to cover over-allotments, if any.

(2) Estimated solely for the purpose of computing the registration fee.

EXHIBIT 7   *(continued)*

The Registrant hereby amends this Registration Statement on such date or dates as may be necessary to delay its effective date until the Registrant shall file a further amendment which specifically states that this Registration Statement shall thereafter become effective in accordance with Section 8(a) of the Securities Act of 1933 or until the Registration Statement shall become effective on such date as the Commission, acting pursuant to said Section 8(a), may determine.

PROSPECTUS SUMMARY

The following summary is qualified in its entirety by the more detailed information and the Financial Statements and notes thereto appearing elsewhere in this Prospectus. Except as otherwise noted, all information in this Prospectus (i) gives effect to the reincorporation of the Company in Delaware prior to the effectiveness of the offering and the associated exchange of three shares of the Delaware corporation for every two shares of the California predecessor corporation, (ii) reflects the conversion of all outstanding shares of Preferred Stock into shares of Common Stock effective automatically upon the closing of the offering, (iii) reflects the issuance of 54,636 shares of Common Stock pursuant to the exercise of outstanding warrants of the Company which terminate upon the closing of the offering and (iv) assumes no exercise of the Underwriters' over-allotment option. See "Description of Capital Stock" and "Underwriting." See "Glossary" on page 56 for definitions of various acronyms and technical terms used in this Prospectus.

The Company

Grand Junction Networks, Inc. ("Grand Junction" or the "Company") is a leader in providing high performance, cost-effective solutions for desktop connectivity. The Company's FastLink product line reduces network congestion by providing Ethernet network workgroup through switching and higher data transmission speeds through the use of Fast Ethernet. Grand Junction's products provide the large installed base of Ethernet users with an Ethernet-based solution for high speed desktop connectivity. International Data Corporation projects the installed base of Ethernet NIC connections will reach 66 million by the end of 1995.

Grand Junction's FastLink product family is comprised of the FastSwitch series of desktop and workgroup switches and the FastHub series of Fast Ethernet repeaters. Grand Junction's FastSwitch product series enables organizations to economically dedicate 10 Mbps of bandwidth to a single desktop to enhance performance, manageability and security. In addition, FastSwitch products operate with existing desktop Ethernet hardware, software and cabling, preserving customer LAN investments. In August 1995, Grand Junction began commercial shipments of the FastSwitch 2000, a new series of workgroup switches intended to ease the migration of organizations from shared to switched 10Base-T networks. The FastHub line of 100 Mbps Ethernet repeaters increases bandwidth tenfold from 10 to 100 Mbps, allowing network managers to increase the number of users per network segment without creating network congestion.

Grand Junction employs the following five key strategies to achieve leadership in the market for high performance, cost-effective solutions for desktop connectivity: (i) focus on Ethernet connections with feature sets optimized for desktops; (ii) enhance technology leadership by being first to market with cost-effective, reliable products through the use of custom ASICs and innovative architectures; (iii) provide products that interoperate with a range of existing and emerging backbone technologies; (iv) market to users of targeted applications where congestion is particularly severe such as digital color pre-press, CAD, CAE and software development; and (v) utilize diverse sales channels to reach a broad range of customers.

Grand Junction's products are sold directly to large corporate customers in the U.S. The Company uses a select group of VARs and two-tier distributors to complement its direct sales efforts. The Company reaches its international customers through country-specific distributors. Representative end user customers include: Intel Corporation, Motorola, Inc., US WEST, Inc. and Sun Microsystems, Inc.

EXHIBIT 7   *(continued)*

THE OFFERING

Common Stock offered hereby	3,000,000 shares
Common Stock to be outstanding after the offering	21,348,919 shares (1)
Use of proceeds	For working capital and other general corporate purposes
Proposed Nasdaq National Market symbol	GJNI

SUMMARY FINANCIAL INFORMATION
(in thousands, except per share data)

	Year Ended December 31,			6 Months Ended June 30,	
	1992	*1993*	*1994*	*1994*	*1995*
Statement of Operations Data:					
Net Revenues	—	321	6,180	1,275	11,382
EBIT	(1,806)	(6,050)	(4,833)	(3,133)	1,017
Net income	(1,723)	(6,022)	(4,864)	(3,156)	895
Pro forma net income per share			(0.28)		0.05
Pro forma shares used in per share calculations			17,530		19,397

	June 30, 1995	
	Actual	*Adjusted (2)*
Balance Sheet Data:		
Cash and cash equivalents	3,507	39,131
Working capital	3,948	39,572
Total Assets	9,825	45,449
Long-term obligations, less current portion	618	618
Total stockholders' equity	5,106	40,730

(1) Excludes (i) 1,592,714 shares of Common Stock issuable upon exercise of options outstanding as of September 1, 1995 with a weighted average exercise price of $0.66 per share, (ii) 3,884,752 shares of Common Stock reserved for issuance upon exercise of options that may be granted in the future under the Company's 1992 Stock Plan, (iii) 375,000 shares of Common Stock reserved for issuance upon exercise of options that may be granted in the future under the Company's 1995 Outside Directors Stock Option Plan, (iv) 600,000 shares of Common Stock reserved for issuance under the Company's 1995 Employee Stock Purchase Plan and (v) 137,749 shares of Common Stock issuable upon exercise of outstanding warrants which do not terminate upon the closing of the offering.

(2) Gives effect to the sale of the 3,000,000 shares of Common Stock offered hereby at an assumed initial public offering price of $13.00 per share (after deduction of the estimated underwriting discounts and estimated expenses of the offering).

EXHIBIT 7   *(continued)*

RISK FACTORS

In addition to the other information in this Prospectus, the following factors should be carefully considered in evaluating the Company and its business before purchasing the Common Stock offered by this Prospectus.

Changes in Technology and New Product Risk

The market for the Company's products is characterized by rapidly changing technology, evolving industry standards and frequent new product introductions. The introduction of products embodying new technologies or the emergence of new industry standards can render existing products obsolete or unmarketable. The Company's success will depend upon its ability to enhance its existing products and to develop and introduce, on a timely and cost-effective basis, new products that keep pace with technological developments and emerging industry standards and address increasingly sophisticated customer requirements. There can be no assurance that the Company will be successful in identifying, developing, manufacturing and marketing product enhancements or new products that respond to technological change or evolving industry standards, that the Company will not experience difficulties that could delay or prevent the successful development, introduction and marketing of these products, or that its product enhancements and new products will adequately meet the requirements of the marketplace and achieve market acceptance. The Company's business, operating results and financial condition would be materially and adversely affected if the Company were to incur delays in developing product enhancements or new products or if such enhancements or products did not gain market acceptance.

The Company's introduction of product enhancements or new products with reliability, quality or interoperability problems could result in reduced orders, manufacturing rework costs, delays in collecting accounts receivable, increased service and warranty costs and a decline in the Company's competitive position, which in turn could have a material adverse effect on the Company's business, operating results and financial condition. In addition, significant delays can occur between a product's introduction and commencement of volume production. The Company began commercial shipments of its FastSwitch 2000 product line in August 1995. Despite testing by the Company and its customers, there can be no assurance that the FastSwitch 2000 product line will not experience some or all of the problems described above, which could have a material adverse effect on the Company's business, operating results and financial condition. Product enhancements and new product introductions could also contribute to quarterly fluctuations in operating results as orders for enhanced or new products commence and orders for existing products decline.

Market Acceptance of Competitive Technologies

The Company is focused on Fast Ethernet and Ethernet switching technologies for high performance connections for desktops rather than on Fiber Distributed Data Interface ("FDDI"), Asynchronous Transfer Mode ("ATM"), 100VG-AnyLAN or other alternative technologies. If Fast Ethernet fails to become widely accepted, or if any alternative technology were to become widely accepted for desktop applications, the Company's business, operating results and financial condition would be adversely affected.

Competition

The networking industry is intensely competitive. The Company competes directly with a number of established and emerging computer, communications and networking device companies. The Company's competitors include 3Com Corporation, Cisco Systems Inc., Bay Networks, Inc., Cabletron Systems, Inc., Digital Equipment Corporation, FORE Systems, Inc., Hewlett-Packard Company and International Business Machines Corporation. Many of the Company's competitors have significantly greater financial, technical, marketing, distribution and other resources and larger installed customer bases than the Company. Several of these competitors have recently introduced or announced their intentions to introduce new competitive products. Many of the larger companies with which the Company competes offer customers a broader product line which provides a more comprehensive networking solution than the Company's products. The ability to act as a single source vendor and provide a customer with an enterprise-wide networking solution has increasingly become an important competitive factor. In addition, there are a number of early stage companies which are developing alternative Fast Ethernet and Ethernet switching solutions and such solutions, if developed successfully, could be higher in performance or more cost-effective than the Company's products. As the Company broadens its product offerings, it may also face competition from new competitors. Moreover, companies in related data communications markets could offer products with functionality similar or superior to that offered by the Company's products. The Company also expects that competitive pricing pressures could result in price declines for the Company's and its competitors' products. Such increased competition could result in reduced margins and loss of market share which would materially and adversely affect the Company's business, operating results and financial condition.

Exhibit 7   *(continued)*

The networking industry has become increasingly concentrated in recent years as a result of consolidations. These consolidations are likely to permit the Company's competitors to devote significantly greater resources to the development and marketing of new competitive products and the marketing of existing competitive products to their larger installed bases. The Company expects that competition will increase substantially as a result of these and other industry consolidations and alliance, as well as the emergence of new competitors. There can be no assurance that the Company will be able to compete successfully with its existing or new competitors or that competitive pressures faced by the Company will not materially and adversely affect its business, operating results and financial condition.

Fluctuations in Quarterly Operating Results

The Company generally ships products as orders are received and as a result typically has little or no backlog. Quarterly revenues and operating results therefore depend on the volume and timing of orders received during the quarter, which are difficult to forecast. Operating results may also fluctuate due to factors such as, among others, new product introductions or technological advances by the Company and its competitors, market acceptance of enhanced or new versions of the Company's products including FastSwitch 2000 product line, price reductions by the Company or its competitors, mix of distribution channels through which the Company's products are sold, addition or loss of significant customers, mix of products sold, accuracy of resellers' forecasts of end user demand, ability of the Company to obtain sufficient supplies of sole or limited source components for the Company's products and general economic conditions. In addition, changes in the mix of products sold and distribution channels through which the Company's products are sold, including an increase in the Company's expense levels, are based, in part, on its expectations as to future revenues and, as a result, net income may be disproportionately affected by a reduction in revenues. The absence of significant Company experience with the FastSwitch 2000 product line limits the Company's ability to plan for the production, market demand and sales of those products and may adversely affect the Company's operating results.

The growth in revenues and operating income experienced by the Company in recent quarters is not necessarily indicative of future results. In addition, in view of the significant growth of the Company's operations in the past two years, the Company believes that period-to-period comparisons of its financial results should not be relied upon as an indication of future performance. The Company has not experienced seasonal trends to date but the Company's business, operating results and financial condition may be affected by such trends in the future. Fluctuations in operating may result in volatility in the price of the Company's Common Stock.

Dependence on Key Personnel

The Company's success depends to a significant extent upon a number of key technical and management employees. The loss of the services of any of the Company's key employees, none of whom is bound by an employment agreement, could have a material adverse effect on the Company. The Company does not maintain life insurance policies on such employees. The Company's success also depends upon its ability to attract and retain highly skilled technical, managerial, sales and marketing personnel. Competition for such personnel is intense. There can be no assurance that the Company will be successful in retaining its existing key personnel and in attracting and retaining the personnel it requires.

No Prior Market; Possible Volatility of Stock Price

Prior to the offering there has been no public market for the Common Stock of the Company. The initial public offering price will be determined by negotiations among the Company and the representatives of the Underwriters. There can be no assurance that an active public market will develop or be sustained after the offering or that the market price of the Common Stock will not decline below the public offering price. In addition, numerous factors including but not limited to future announcements concerning the Company or its competitors, quarterly variations in operating results, announcements of technological innovations, the introduction of new products or changes in product pricing by the Company or its competitors, proprietary rights or product liability litigation or changes in earnings estimates by analysts could cause the market price of the Common Stock to fluctuate substantially. In the event that the Company's operating results for some future quarter fall below the expectations of securities analysts and investors, the market price of the Company's Common Stock could be materially and adversely affected. In addition, stock prices for many technology companies fluctuate widely for reasons which may be unrelated to operating results. These fluctuations, as well as general economic, political and market conditions such as recessions or international instabilities, may materially and adversely affect the market price of the Common Stock.

EXHIBIT 7   *(concluded)*

PRINCIPAL STOCKHOLDERS

The following table sets forth certain information regarding the beneficial ownership of the Company's Common Stock as of September 1, 1995, and as adjusted to reflect the sale of the shares offered by this Prospectus, (i) by each of the Company's directors and each of the Named Executive Officers and (ii) by each person who is known by the Company to own beneficially more than 5% of the Company's Common Stock.

Name	Number of Shares Beneficially Owned	Percentage of Shares Owned	
		Before Offering	*After Offering*
Merrill, Pickard, Anderson & Eyre V, L.P.	3,579,917	19.5	16.8
Technology Venture Investors IV	3,579,917	19.5	16.8
Matrix Partners III, L.P.	1,981,406	10.8	9.3
Associated Venture Investors II	1,576,041	8.6	7.4
Howard S. Charney, President and CEO	1,350,000	7.4	6.3
Lazar Birenbaum, V.P. of Engineering	802,500	4.4	3.8
Jack T. Moses, V.P. of Marketing	502,500	2.7	2.3
John Celli, Jr., V.P. of Sales	375,000	2.0	1.8
Anthony J. Banta, V.P. of Manufacturing	247,500	1.3	1.2
V. Orville Wright, Director	67,500	0.4	0.3

ELLER MEDIA

I think Karl Eller should be in the entrepreneurs' hall of fame.

Jack Bunce, Partner, Hellman & Friedman

It was January 21, 1997. The Board of Eller Media Corporation (EMC), an outdoor advertising company, met to decide whether to proceed with an initial public offering or sell the business to Clear Channel, a publicly-held radio and television company. Less than eighteen months earlier, Warren Hellman, Jack Bunce, and Joe Niehaus, three partners at Hellman & Friedman (HF), had teamed up with Karl Eller, EMC's Chief Executive Officer (CEO), to buy the company. Since the acquisition, Eller Media had far exceeded their original projections, and at the same time, public stock values in the billboard industry had exploded. By all accounts, the investment was a home run.

In the fall of 1996, HF and the executive management team decided to hold an initial public offering (IPO) of the company's stock in order to establish a path to liquidity and take advantage of the high valuations being offered for outdoor advertising companies at that time. Their investment bankers anticipated a market capitalization for the stock of more than $1 billion. Shortly thereafter, Clear Channel offered to acquire the company outright for approximately the same price in a combination of stock and cash. Karl, Warren, Jack, and Joe were uncertain how to proceed.

This case was prepared by Nick Mansour under the supervision of Lawrence G. Mohr Jr., Lecturer in Business, Stanford University Graduate School of Business, and H. Irving Grousbeck, Consulting Professor of Management, Stanford University Graduate School of Business, as the basis for class discussion rather than to illustrate either effective or ineffective handling of an administrative situation.

This case was made possible by the generous support of Frank P. Quattrone.

Stanford Business School Case S-SB-191.

Hellman & Friedman

Hellman & Friedman is a private equity firm in San Francisco, founded in 1984 by Warren Hellman and Tully Friedman. It was initially devoted to providing financial advisory services for large corporations. The firm quickly established an impressive reputation, attracting clients such as Levi Strauss, Clorox, and Hewlett-Packard.

In 1987, Hellman & Friedman raised its first investment fund, a $325 million limited partnership. The intent was to apply the funds to leveraged buy-outs. Gradually the firm concentrated more resources on the investment business; and in the early 1990s, it withdrew from advisory work altogether. A second fund of $875 million was raised in 1991. And then, in 1995, Hellman & Friedman raised a third fund of $1.5 billion (see **Exhibit 1** for Hellman & Friedman's summary of the investment opportunity).

In these investment partnerships, the limited partners contributed the vast majority of the equity to be invested. In the latest fund, the limiteds were corporate pension plans, private university endowment funds, foundations, and public employee retirement systems (see **Exhibit 2** for a selected list of limited partners). As the general partners, HF made the investment decisions. In return, the firm received an annual management fee of 1.25% of the funds raised and 20% of the net gains from investments. Joe Niehaus explained the investment philosophy of the firm:

> We tell our limited partners that we are going to earn superior risk-adjusted returns. When we look at a new investment, we are very analytical about determining the appropriate rate of return. We look at industry risk and expected unlevered equity returns by utilizing the capital asset pricing model and information from comparable companies in the same industry. And we look at financial risk, adjusting the unlevered equity return for the amount of debt our specific investment will have.
>
> We do not have a target return, as such. However, there is a minimum threshold below which we will not invest, because our limited partners compare our returns to the market. After deducting our management fees and portion of the gains, the returns to the limiteds would need to be at least 15%. So we probably would not invest in a deal which we projected would have less than a 20% internal rate of return (IRR), even if it had very little risk.
>
> The partnership is structured so that the limiteds have committed funds to us for five years. We call the capital as needed, and committed capital we do not invest at the end of five years is effectively returned to the limited partners. Then, we have another five years to realize a return on the capital deployed. This period can be extended for another year or two if needed. Generally, we expect to hold our investments for five to six years, but if we invest early in the life of the partnership, we can hold an investment for ten or eleven years.

Outdoor Advertising

With the funds raised, Jack Bunce and Joe Niehaus, partners with prior experience in the media industry, were interested in pursuing opportunities in outdoor advertising. The industry was started in the early 1900s, and enjoyed a period of tremendous growth in the 1940s and 1950s. Soon, billboards were being constructed throughout the country. In response to the growing public outcry against this rapid development, federal, state, and local governments passed laws to regulate the industry. In general, the legislation severely restricted billboard construction in commercial and residential areas.

The partners were primarily attracted by the "quality of the cash flow" of the industry. Jack and Joe believed that the strong regulatory barrier to new entrants produced "one of the most defensible" businesses. As a result of the low unit growth in the industry, outdoor advertising companies had the ability to increase prices fairly easily, which produced very high profit margins.

It was also a very simple business. And, unlike other high cash flow industries, very little capital was required to maintain the billboards. This provided owners with a fair amount of discretionary income that could be used to pay debt, distribute dividends, or make acquisitions.

Outdoor advertising was also a fragmented industry. In 1995, Gannett, Patrick Media Group (PMG), and 3M had the largest inventories of billboards, collectively owning 20% of the over $3.0 billion market. There were also seven medium-sized, regional companies named Lamar Advertising, Outdoor Systems, Universal, Whiteco, Ackerley, TDI, and Martin Media. They held another 16% market share. The rest of the market consisted of 1,000 small businesses. In addition, outdoor advertising sales were largely made to small, local companies. Therefore, market share within a metropolitan area, for example, was more important than national market share.

Finally, Bunce and Niehaus believed revenues were likely to increase in the near future, as companies began to spend more on advertising after the economic recession of the early 1990s. Furthermore, they saw the industry as a "play on traffic jams," and thought the value of billboard companies would rise as traffic congestion would surely increase in the future. In 1995, industry revenue had grown 8%.

Hellman & Friedman had looked at a number of opportunities in the industry over the years, but had never found one which would warrant an investment of the size the firm wanted to make. In the spring of 1995, the management of Patrick Media Group approached HF about the possibility of providing capital for a management buy-out.

Patrick Media Group

Patrick Media Group was one of the oldest companies in the industry. Started in the early 1900s under the name Foster & Kleiser, the company had recently fallen into financial hardship. It had been bought as part of a leveraged buy-out in the late 1980s, using debt provided by General Electric Capital (GECC). In 1991, GECC assumed ownership after PMG defaulted on its debt payments, and installed GECC management on a temporary basis.

In early 1995, GECC decided to sell PMG. The management learned of this and hired Chase Manhattan Bank to find an equity partner. Chase led them to Hellman & Friedman. Despite its recent troubles, HF felt that PMG was an outstanding business. Bunce and Niehaus believed that the oldest companies tended to have the best locations for their billboard plant, and PMG's locations were superb. It was the market leader in all of its major markets. Hellman & Friedman offered General Electric $480 million for the company, but GECC decided to hold an auction. Bunce explained HF's reaction:

> We were disappointed. We rarely buy companies out of auctions because the price gets bid up too high. But we kept thinking how attractive the business was. So we tried to get an edge in the auction. We concluded that finding an excellent management team was our only hope. The team at PMG was decent, but not great, and had only been in the industry four years. We called Richard Reiss, a friend in New York who knows the media industry well, and he recommended Karl Eller.

Karl Eller

Karl Eller graduated with a business degree from the University of Arizona in 1952, and immediately joined Foster & Kleiser as a billboard salesman. He was promoted often during his career at the company, and became head of the Chicago office in 1957. That same year, John Kluge of Metromedia bought the business, and began looking for a new president. Eller confidently asked Kluge for the job. When Kluge declined, Karl left.

Seeking exposure to advertising in other media, Eller worked as an account supervisor for an advertising agency for the next five years. In 1962, Kluge offered to sell Foster & Kleiser's Phoenix billboards to Karl for $5 million, and gave Eller thirty days to raise the money. The deal was closed on March 17, 1962, and the Eller Outdoor Advertising Company was born.

Eller built the business in the ensuing years, merging it with KTAR Television in 1968 to form Combined Communications, the first multimedia company. Combined Communications went public later that year. Over the next decade, the company acquired a number of outdoor advertising businesses, fourteen radio stations, seven television operations, two newspapers, and a few magazine companies. It eventually became one of the largest billboard companies in the industry. In 1980, Combined merged with Gannett, a newspaper company. Karl recalled his tenure at Gannett and his relationship with Allen Neuharth, Gannett's Chairman:

> I lasted six months. I argued with Allen about whether we should start *USA Today* or buy ABC. We just didn't get along and I decided to leave. Neuharth later wrote an autobiography. I've got two chapters in his book—nothing good.

After leaving Gannett, Eller worked as the President of Columbia Pictures, which he helped sell to Coca Cola in 1982. As a result of his success with Combined Communications, Karl had become wealthy, and in the early 1980s was the most prominent business executive in Arizona.

In 1983, Karl joined the Board of Circle K Corporation at the behest of the company's Chairman. A few months later, Eller accepted the position of CEO. He also invested a large portion of his wealth in the company, and in the process became one of Circle K's largest shareholders. Karl believed the convenience store industry in general and his company in particular had a high potential for rapid growth. He set a goal of building the company from 800 stores to 5,000 outlets by the end of the decade. Eller described the experience with Circle K:

> We grew very fast. By 1990, we had 4,500 stores. We were selling gasoline and planned to sell the business to an oil company. I spent 1989 looking for a buyer, but no one was interested.
>
> Then the convenience store industry fell on rough times. The banks thought the companies had too much leverage, and were asking for certain restrictive covenants and thinking about withdrawing lines of credit. We had over $1 billion in debt. Financing was just too damn cheap during the 1980s. But we were meeting our payments, unlike 7-11, Magic, and our other competitors which had declared bankruptcy.
>
> So I tried to do a leveraged buy-out, but one of the largest shareholders was against it. That put me against the Board, so I left after the LBO attempt. Four days later, the company declared bankruptcy. Maybe I expanded too fast and didn't realize where the market was going. I probably thought I was invincible. I take the blame for it, but they really shouldn't have gone bankrupt.

Now personally in debt with a negative net worth, Karl returned to the outdoor advertising business in August 1992, when he bought Gannett's Phoenix billboard plant using borrowed money. He reasoned:

> I wanted to get back into the outdoor advertising business, because I knew it best. I had worked in the industry for twenty-eight years and I always thought I was the best outdoor guy in the country. Gannett's Phoenix operations were very poorly run. I was persistent and finally talked them into selling.

Karl's son, Scott Eller, joined him in the business as Executive Vice President and Chief Operating Officer. Scott reported to Karl and had responsibility for operations, accounting and finance, legal issues, public affairs, and real estate. Karl focused his efforts on marketing, sales, and acquisitions. Over the next three years, Karl bought billboard operations in El Paso and Atlanta. The El Paso company had been owned since 1987 by the venture capital firm where Scott Eller was a partner prior to joining Karl. In June 1995, Karl decided to try to acquire PMG. In search of an equity partner, he also called his friend, Richard Reiss, who told him to contact Hellman & Friedman.

Eller Media Corporation

Over the next few weeks, Karl Eller met with Warren Hellman, Jack Bunce, and Joe Niehaus several times. Each group checked references on the other. Joe commented:

> Allen Neuharth gave a very candid reference. He said that Karl was one of the best managers of outdoor assets he had ever seen. In his experience, Karl was someone we

would more likely have to rein in versus kick in the pants to get going. If we kept Karl focused, we had a gem.

Warren talked with Carl Lindner, who had backed Eller in Combined. Lindner was also going to give Karl Eller the equity to do the LBO of Circle K, and was one of Circle K's large shareholders at the time. Lindner said Eller was trustworthy, honest, and an expert in outdoor. But he warned us to keep control of the balance sheet and the leverage deployed.

Jack summarized HF's findings:

His integrity was obvious, and he never compromised it, even during his hardships. Despite all his personal financial troubles, he never declared bankruptcy. His work ethic was superb. He would call me at my house at 6:30 a.m. to talk about business. During our discussions, he gave us an excellent analysis of the strengths and weaknesses of the competitors in the industry. It was clear he was an expert. In addition, when he did not know something, he admitted it right away.

Karl's best credential was the fact that he had already built two successful outdoor advertising businesses. The company he was running at the time had some of the highest margins in the industry. It was a real testament to his ability to operate.

Circle K concerned us, but we concluded the mistakes were financial, not operational. And we add value on the financial side of the business. We were confident in our ability to structure a sound balance sheet, and in Karl's ability to operate the company.

Karl was impressed with Hellman & Friedman as well:

I talked with a lot of people about them and they came out smelling like a rose. Their reputation was impeccable. Everyone stressed their ethics and integrity. And they were not going to charge any fees to do the deal, which said a lot to me.

Karl Eller and Hellman & Friedman decided to work together to buy PMG. They bid $520 million for Patrick Media. Despite the existence of two slightly higher bids, their team was chosen because their financing was more certain. PMG and Eller's company, which HF valued at $29 million in equity, were merged. Hellman & Friedman and a few small co-investors contributed an additional $163 million in equity. $414 million of debt was provided by a group led by Chase Manhattan to assume Eller's company's liabilities, pay $10 million in transaction fees, and cover the remainder of the financing. The deal closed in August 1995 (see **Exhibit 3** for equity ownership distribution).

The new entity, Eller Media Corporation, was the largest company in the industry with over 50,000 billboards. Jack Bunce recalled the expectations at the time of the acquisition:

We agreed to a set of projections produced by Karl that showed modest growth. We made sure that he knew we were not going to take on too much debt. The company needed a CFO, whom Karl would propose but over whom we had veto rights. We were looking to be in the investment for five to seven years. In fact, at the time, we felt we might want to hold this investment for an even longer period if we could provide our limited partners with some liquidity along the way. On behalf of HF's general partners, we thought we might be able to recapitalize the business, pay off our limited partners, and continue owning the company ourselves. It was clear that Karl wanted to re-establish himself. It was probably his dream to have his son take over the business, but he was never too vocal about that.

Karl described his needs:

> I had invested my entire net worth, so the financial aspects were important. Also, I wanted to re-establish my reputation, and wanted my name to be on the company. But mostly, I expected to do the best job I could for the next five years.

Based on the projections, Hellman & Friedman estimated their annual returns would be 24–30% over the next five to six years (see **Exhibit 4** for selected financial projections).

Eller Media was HF's largest investment to date, and the firm wanted to give it appropriate attention. As a result, Warren Hellman, Jack Bunce, and Joe Niehaus all sat on the Board. In addition, Hellman & Friedman asked Art Kern, Irv Grousbeck, Pat Pineda, and Richard Reiss to be Directors, each of whom invested in the deal. Kern had been backed by Hellman & Friedman previously, and the HF partners respected his operating ability in the radio industry. Grousbeck had served on other boards with the partners, had good judgment, and also had relevant media experience. Warren Hellman worked with Pineda on Levi's Board, and valued her general business perspective as well as her legal background. Finally, Reiss was invited onto the Board for his professional investor viewpoint.

Karl Eller was also a Director, and named his long-time friend and sometime business partner Bruce Halle to the Board (see **Exhibit 5** for backgrounds of each Director). In addition, although they were not on the Board, EMC's executive team actively participated in all Board meetings. This included Scott Eller; Paul Meyer, Vice President of Legal Affairs; and Tim Donmoyer, Chief Financial Officer.

Karl made an immediate impact on the company's margins, primarily by increasing revenues. He believed that the outdoor advertising sector needed to create interest in the billboard medium from industries that had not traditionally used their space. EMC hired a creative staff to develop unsolicited ad campaigns that Eller Media could sell to these new buyers. Though this department cost 2% of revenues, Karl believed it allowed the company to achieve better advertising rates. Furthermore, although outdoor companies published advertising rates, generally billboard space was sold at a discount to the published rates. Unlike the competition, which discounted rates in order to have 100% of the billboard space sold, Eller focused on "rate attainment" which was the product of the percent of published rate charged and the percent of billboard occupancy. For example, whereas the competition might have 100% occupancy at 50% of the published rate, Karl would prefer to have only 80% occupancy at 70% of the published rate. EMC easily surpassed its projections for 1995.

While the company continued to improve its margins, Karl focused on acquisitions in 1996. He worked hard on a deal to buy Gannett's billboards, but was ultimately outbid by Outdoor Systems. Four smaller competitors were acquired by

EMC in 1996, totaling 1,500 billboards and $37 million of additional debt. At the end of 1996, 3M announced its intention to sell its business. With 25,000 billboards and poorly run operations, Karl and HF saw the opportunity to buy a significant amount of inventory at a cheap price. Bunce explained:

> 3M got into the business in the 1940s as a way to market a reflective material they had developed for use in traffic signing. They have billboards all over the country, so in that sense, it is the most valuable plant in the country. But they don't run it like a media company. Their rates are lower than the norms of the industry and they have a lot of unoccupied signs. We thought it would be a great buy, and that Karl could quickly improve the margins. We offered $780 million based on $65 million in annual EBITDA, expecting to double the cash flow in two years.

3M turned down the proposal and hired Goldman Sachs to hold an auction.

Harvesting the Deal

The industry changed drastically in 1996. Outdoor Systems, Lamar, and Universal all held initial public offerings (IPOs), and their stocks were trading at very high valuations (see **Exhibit 6**). They were the first public companies with operations in the billboard industry only. Since their IPOs, these companies acquired sixteen competitors totaling $1.4 billion of acquisitions. There were still over 1000 outdoor advertising companies, and the ten largest owned approximately 54% of the $3.6 billion US market.

For 1996, EMC once again performed better than expected (see **Exhibit 7**). Attracted by the high valuations and the prospect of taking some money off the table, Hellman & Friedman decided to take the company public in the fall of 1996. Alex. Brown & Sons; Bear, Stearns & Company; and Donaldson, Lufkin & Jenrette were the investment banks selected to represent Eller Media. The company began to prepare for a $225 million offering at an initial price that would value the company at $1.2 billion including the capital raised through the IPO. However, the bankers expected the stock price to increase 10–15% from this offering price during the first day of trading. EMC planned to offer $50 million of primary stock and the rest would be a secondary offering to sell the stock of existing shareholders. Hellman & Friedman hoped to sell $156.6 million of their shares which would equal their original investment and reduce their equity stake to 49.5%.

In September 1996, Clear Channel, a radio and television broadcasting company, approached Hellman & Friedman about the possibility of acquiring Eller Media. In October, they offered $1 billion for EMC. Clear Channel would assume EMC's debt and a large majority of the remainder of the offer would be funded with the company's stock. Concerned about the price and wanting more cash rather than stock, HF rejected the offer in November. In December 1996, Eller Media filed its S-1 form with the Securities Exchange Commission, announcing its intention to go public. The company anticipated holding the IPO in February or March of 1997.

Early in January, Clear Channel offered $1.15 billion for Eller Media. The price would consist of the assumption of $425 million of debt, $325 million in cash, and $400 million in Clear Channel stock. $250 million of this stock would be registered and sold by Clear Channel at the time of the closing, but the remaining $150 million would have to be held for at least six months by EMC's shareholders.

There were several other potential buyers of Eller Media. Westinghouse, MGM, Disney, News Corporation, Viacom, another radio broadcasting company, and a billboard competitor had expressed interest in EMC. None had made offers, however, and HF believed they would not do so for at least another two or three months.

The Board needed to consider several issues in making its decision. First, although Clear Channel stock would offer diversification into radio and television broadcasting, the shares were currently trading at even higher multiples of cash flow than the outdoor advertising industry (see **Exhibit 8** for financial information). HF was impressed with Clear Channel's management team and their ability to integrate acquisitions. Therefore, the stock looked interesting, but Jack Bunce wondered if the company's high market valuation would be sustainable.

Eller Media would constitute roughly a third of the combined entity. The owners and managers of Clear Channel had indicated that EMC would be run as a separate, fairly autonomous subsidiary. Karl would be a Director of Clear Channel and report to the CEO. The sale would also relieve him of the hassles associated with being a CEO of a public company.

It also appeared that EMC would have a better chance to buy 3M's outdoor assets if it was acquired by Clear Channel. The Board knew the price for the billboards would be very steep in an auction situation. Because Clear Channel's stock was trading at a generous multiple, it would be able to pay a higher price.

Finally, there was the potential for synergies between the two companies. Radio advertising, like billboards, is dominated by local advertisers. Of Eller Media's fifteen major metropolitan markets, Clear Channel and its affiliates operated in eleven. The combined operation might be able to offer unique marketing programs that its competitors could not match.

On the other hand, the Board liked the prospects of EMC after an IPO. The recent consolidation was transforming the industry into an oligopoly. This had very positive implications for future margins. Furthermore, Hellman & Friedman believed outdoor advertising would become more valuable as a mass medium relative to broadcast media which were increasingly targeting smaller audiences due to the proliferation of radio formats and television channels.

Eller Media also had an excellent executive team. Jack Bunce reviewed HF's experience with Karl and his key managers:

> Working with Karl has been great. He's probably the best operator with whom we have been associated in terms of his work ethic, values, and what he instills in the company. Just last week, he discovered that the sales were looking slow in Los Angeles for this month. The morning he learned of this, he flew to the local office and started making sales calls. He solves problems immediately, and does not wait for someone else to explain things.

> The top management group also works well together. They put in long hours, have complementary skills, and do not have big egos. It is a great team.

The quality of the management and the changes in the industry had resulted in an extraordinary return on investment so far. However, when they looked ahead, HF was not certain that the high multiples paid for outdoor advertising stocks would last much longer. They estimated annual appreciation of 10–20% at best, if they continued to hold EMC (see **Exhibit 9**).

There were other complicating factors. The history of Eller Media was strikingly similar to a $100 million HF investment in a paging company called MobileMedia (MM). At the time of MM's IPO a year and a half earlier, the investment had been a huge success as HF had nearly tripled its initial investment; then the company made a large acquisition and fell on hard times as a result of a poorly executed integration of that acquisition. It now looked like MobileMedia would declare bankruptcy and the partnership would lose all of its money in the deal. While an IPO would enable Hellman & Friedman to pull out its initial investment in EMC, a sale to Clear Channel would allow the firm to realize almost all of its returns immediately. Niehaus said:

> It would be nice to lock in a win on Eller, since we were probably going to lose our money on MobileMedia. But MobleMedia was an investment made by our second fund, not the third fund which invested in Eller Media. So the returns from Eller would not have directly offset the losses on MobileMedia.

Unlike Eller Media, however, MM never had a good management team.

Jack Bunce also thought that Karl's desires might be another dilemma for the Board:

> Karl made it clear that his preference was to go public in order to stay independent. He met the people who owned and ran Clear Channel. He was impressed by them and felt he could work with them. But selling to another company was never his first choice.
> He was also sixty-eight years old, and wanted to work only two more years.

After a Board meeting in late 1996, Irv Grousbeck commented to some of the other Directors. "In my opinion, Karl is grooming his son, Scott, to be CEO. This makes Karl even more inclined toward an IPO." On January 21, 1997, the Board met to decide whether to sell Eller Media to Clear Channel or proceed with an IPO.

Exhibit 1   Hellman & Friedman Capital Partners III, L.P.: The Investment Opportunity

---

Since its formation, Hellman & Friedman has made a variety of equity investments both domestically and internationally including restructurings, friendly investments in public and private companies, leveraged buyouts, and investments in undervalued special situations. Hellman & Friedman's focus is to invest with strong management partners in companies with attractive business franchises, characterized by high free cash flow returns on capital and attractive growth prospects, which have included businesses in the media/communications and financial service industries and infrastructure providers in developing countries. The partners of Hellman & Friedman, as the principals of the General Partner (the "Principals"), seek to augment the capital available for investment in order to further strengthen their position as a leading source of equity capital for the large investment opportunities which the Principals generate. The Principals seek total commitments available to Hellman & Friedman Capital Partners III, L.P. ("HFCP III") of $1.5 billion, although the Partnership may be established with a minimum of $1.0 billion. The Principals reserve the right to accept additional commitments.

HFCP III offers investors the opportunity to participate in a special situation equity partnership with a number of attractions:

- *Demonstrated Investment Performance*
  The Principals have established reputations and records as **disciplined, long term investors.** Through Hellman & Friedman Capital Partners II, L.P. ("HFCP II") and previous investment activities, they have made and structured sensible investments through numerous business cycles and in varying economic climates. The investments of HFCP II that are more than twelve months old, while still relatively immature, indicate an IRR **in excess of 60%** to date. The combined IRR on the investments of Hellman & Friedman Capital Partners, L.P. ("HFCP") and HFCP II is estimated to be **in excess of 40%.** These returns are especially attractive on a risk-adjusted basis since they have been achieved while generally avoiding situations involving high levels of financial leverage. (Of the eleven investments of HFCP II, four investments are in companies with virtually no leverage and three other investments are in companies with a debt to equity ratio of less than 1:1; the remaining investments are in companies with less leverage than the average company in their industries.)

- *Deal Flow*
  The Principals have demonstrated the ability to generate large and attractive investment opportunities. The average investment in HFCP is $18 million and the average investment in HFCP II is $56 million. HFCP II made four investments in 1993 totaling $313 million with an average size of $78 million (including the exercise of options). The Principals believe that with additional capital HFCP II would have made larger investments in several transactions and believe they can continue to generate investment opportunities as large or larger than those available to HFCP II. HFCP II and HFCP were formed to capitalize on the increasingly large investment opportunities generated by the Principals; HFCP III continues this trend.

- *Investment Structuring Expertise*
  The Principals have demonstrated the ability to make a variety of opportunistic, special situation investments. These transactions have been structured to address the risks and rewards in specific situations and to respond to varying economic conditions. Often these investments are made in the context of a complicated situation where the Principals' financial, analytical and structuring skills add substantial value. HFCP III is structured to continue to permit the Principals the flexibility to utilize a wide variety of investment structures.

- *Demonstrated International Investment Capability*
  HFCP II has invested or committed to invest over $225 million in companies located in Argentina, Australia, Hong Kong and Mexico. (A significant portion of HFCP II's 1991 investment in Australia, John Fairfax Holdings Limited, has been realized.) These investments were motivated by the opportunity to earn attractive returns (adjusted for political and foreign exchange risks) due to the attractive growth prospects and relative scarcity of private equity capital in these countries. Hellman & Friedman Asia, Limited, an affiliate of the General Partner, was formed in 1992 to pursue investment opportunities in Asia and operates an office in Hong Kong. Hellman & Friedman also maintains a representative office in Sydney. HFCP III will continue this foreign investment activity and will benefit from the Principals' international investment experience.

- *Continuity of Investment Team*
  Hellman & Friedman was founded 10 years ago; its five senior partners have been with the firm for an average of almost 9 years. While Hellman & Friedman relied historically on the relationships of its managing partners to generate virtually all of its investment opportunities, for the past few years investment opportunities have also been the result of incremental relationships developed by Hellman & Friedman's younger partners as well as the institutionalization of the firm.

- *Significant Financial Commitment of the General Partner*
  General Partner will commit to purchase $50 million of partnership interests in HFCP III.

Exhibit 2   Selected Limited Partners of Hellman & Friedman Capital Partners III, L.P.

Corporate Retirement Plans
Aluminum Company of America
Atlantic Richfield Company
American Telephone & Telegraph Company
Dow Chemical Company
General Motors Corporation
IBM Retirement Plan Trust
NYNEX Corporation

Public Employee Retirement Systems
California Public Employees' Retirement System
Commonwealth of Pennsylvania Employees' Retirement System
Iowa Public Employees' Retirement System
Minnesota State Board of Investments
New York State Common Retirement Fund
New York State Teachers' Retirement System
San Francisco City and County Employees' Retirement System
Virginia Retirement System

Endowments and Foundations
Duke University
Ford Foundation
Massachusetts Institute of Technology
Metropolitan Museum of Art
Princeton University
Stanford University
University of Notre Dame
Yale University

EXHIBIT 3   Distribution of Equity Ownership of Eller Media

Shareholder	Shares	Options	Fully-Diluted Ownership (%)
Hellman and Friedman	1566.1	0.0	73.2
EM Holdings, LLC*	284.4	0.0	13.3
Karl Eller, CEO	0.0	155.7	7.3
Irving Grousbeck	50.0	1.0	2.4
Art Kern	10.0	1.0	0.5
Richard Reiss	2.5	12.2	0.7
Timothy Donmoyer, CFO	1.0	31.1	1.5
Paul Meyer, General Counsel	0.0	20.5	1.0
Others	3.0	1.5	0.1
Total	1917.0	222.0	100.0

*EM Holdings, LLC is a limited liability corporation 76.0% owned by Scott Eller and 24.0% owned by five other private investors.

EXHIBIT 4

ELLER MEDIA
Pro Forma Leverage and Performance Metrics
as of September 21, 1995

($MM)	LTM* 8/31/95	Projected December 31					
		1995	1996	1997	1998	1999	2000
Net Debt	414	409	380	339	285	228	168
Net Revenue**	216	213	227	241	225	268	281
EBITDA***	73	75	82	89	96	103	110

*Estimated last twelve month data.
**Total revenues less agency commissions.
***Earnings before interest, taxes, depreciation, and amortization.

EXHIBIT 5   Biographies of the Board of Directors

Karl Eller, Chairman

Jack Bunce, Director

Mr. Bunce is a General Partner of Hellman & Friedman, a private investment firm. Prior to joining the firm in 1988, Mr. Bunce was a Vice President with the venture capital firm of TA Associates. Previously, he was employed in the Mergers & Acquisitions and Corporate Finance Departments of Lehman Brothers Kuhn Loeb. Mr. Bunce graduated from Stanford University in 1980 and the Harvard Business School in 1984. Mr. Bunce is a director of Western Wireless Corporation, MobileMedia Corporation and numerous private companies. He is 38 years old.

Irv Grousbeck, Director

Mr. Grousbeck is a Consulting Professor of Management at Stanford Business School, where he began teaching in 1985. From 1981 to 1985, Mr. Grousbeck was a Lecturer at Harvard University, Graduate School of Business Administration. Mr. Grousbeck was a co-founder of Continental Cablevision, Inc. where he served as President from 1964 to 1980 and Chairman of the Board of Directors from 1980 to 1985. Mr. Grousbeck is currently a director of numerous private companies. He is 62 years old.

Bruce Halle, Director

Mr. Halle has been the Chairman and CEO of Discount Tire Company since he founded the company in 1960. Discount Tire is the largest independent retail tire chain in the United States with $700 million in revenue and 334 stores in thirteen states. Mr. Halle graduated from Eastern Michigan University in 1956. He is 67 years old.

Warren Hellman, Director

Mr. Hellman is a General Partner of Hellman & Friedman. Previously Mr. Hellman was a General Partner of Hellman, Ferri Investment Associates; Matrix Management Company; Matrix II Management Company; and Lehman Brothers. At Lehman Brothers, he served as President and Director of the firm, as well as head of the Investment Banking Division, and Chairman of Lehman Corporation (a closed-end investment company). Mr. Hellman graduated from the University of California at Berkeley in 1955 and the Harvard Business School in 1959. Mr. Hellman is a director of Williams-Sonoma, Inc., Levi Strauss Associates, Inc., Franklin Resources, Inc., APL Limited, MobileMedia Corporation and numerous private companies. He is 62 years old.

Art Kern, Director

Mr. Kern is Chairman and CEO of American Media, a company he started in 1981 which owns and operates commercial radio stations. Mr. Kern is a director of Yahoo! Inc. and Total Entertainment Network, a new on-line game company. He is 50 years old.

Joe Niehaus, Director

Mr. Niehaus is a General Partner of Hellman & Friedman. Prior to joining the Firm in 1989, Mr. Niehaus was employed in the Merchant Banking and Mergers & Acquisitions Departments of Morgan Stanley & Co. Mr. Niehaus graduated from Dartmouth College in 1985 and the Harvard Business School in 1989. Mr. Niehaus is a director of Hoyts Cinemas Limited, Hoyts Cinemas America Limited and numerous private companies. He is 33 years old.

Pat Pineda, Director

Ms. Pineda has been a practicing attorney for nineteen years. Ms. Pineda is presently the Vice President and Corporate Secretary of New United Motor Manufacturing, Inc. (NUMMI) with primary responsibility for the Legal, Environmental and Government Relations Departments. Ms. Pineda has been with NUMMI since its inception in 1984. Ms. Pineda also serves as director of Levi Strauss Associates, Inc., Trustee of RAND and director of The James Irvine Foundation. She is 44 years old.

Richard Reiss, Director

Mr. Reiss has been a Managing Partner of Cumberland Associates, a private investment firm, since 1982. Mr. Reiss has over twenty-five years of investment experience in the media and communications industries. Mr. Reiss is currently a director of O'Charley's, the Lazard Funds, Inc. and Page One Communications, Ltd. He is 52 years old.

EXHIBIT 6   Selected Information for Outdoor Advertising Companies

	Lamar Advertising	Universal	Outdoor Systems
December 31, 1996 Last Twelve Months Financial Information ($MM)			
EBITDA*	68.4	88.4	137.0
Total Long-Term Debt	132.0	349.1	606.4
Common Stock Information			
Shares Outstanding (millions)	28.8	24.0	40.2
Adjusted Stock Price ($)			
At Initial Public Offering	16.00	14.50	10.00
As of January 15, 1997	24.50	23.50	30.13

*Earnings before interest, taxes, depreciation, and amortization adjusted for recent acquisitions.

EXHIBIT 7

ELLER MEDIA
Consolidated Statement of Operations

	Year Ended December 31,	
($000)	*1995*	*1996*
Gross Revenues	249,400	270,413
Agency Commissions	31,388	33,381
Net Revenues	218,012	237,032
Operating Expenses		
Cost of Sales	89,006	91,615
Selling, General, & Administrative	39,977	43,924
Corporate Overhead	12,783	10,204
EBITDA*	76,246	91,289
Depreciation & Amortization	39,385	40,269
EBIT**	36,861	51,020
Interest Expense	44,485	35,626
Loss on Sales of Fixed Assets	8,354	6,721
Income Before Taxes	(15,978)	8,673
Income Tax (Benefit)	(3,858)	5,514
Income After Taxes	(12,120)	3,159

*Earnings before interest, taxes, depreciation, and amortization.
**Earnings before interest and taxes.

EXHIBIT 7   *(concluded)*

ELLER MEDIA
Consolidated Balance Sheets

	Year Ended December 31,	
	1995	*1996*
Assets		
Current Assets		
Cash & Cash Equivalents	2,453	873
Accounts Receivable, Net	30,510	35,627
Current Portion of Prepaid Leases	10,077	10,774
Total Current Assets	43,040	47,274
Prepaid Lease, Net of Current Portion	4,593	8,378
Property and Equipment	448,345	460,066
Other	17,704	13,282
Goodwill, Net	130,164	131,678
Total	643,846	660,678
Liabilities & Stockholders' Equity		
Current Liabilities		
Accounts Payable	5,930	4,638
Accrued Liabilities	25,652	32,667
Current Portion of Long-Term Debt	10,176	12,320
Other	5,268	4,438
Total Current Liabilities	47,026	54,063
Long-Term Debt, Net of Current Portion	394,336	399,403
Other Liabilities	13,358	14,829
Total Liabilities	454,720	468,295
Stockholders' Equity		
Common Stock	1	1
Additional Paid-In Capital	191,659	213,297
Deferred Compensation	0	(15,240)
Accumulated Deficit	(2,534)	625
Total Stockholders' Equity	189,126	198,683
Total	643,846	666,978

EXHIBIT 8   **Selected Information for Clear Channel**

	Clear Channel
December 31, 1996 Last Twelve	
Months Financial Information ($MM)	
EBITDA*	177.9
Total Long-Term Debt	726.6
Common Stock Information	
Shares Outstanding (millions)	76.0
Jan. 15, 1996 Stock Price ($)	36.13

*Earnings before interest, taxes, depreciation, and amortization
adjusted for recent acquisitions.

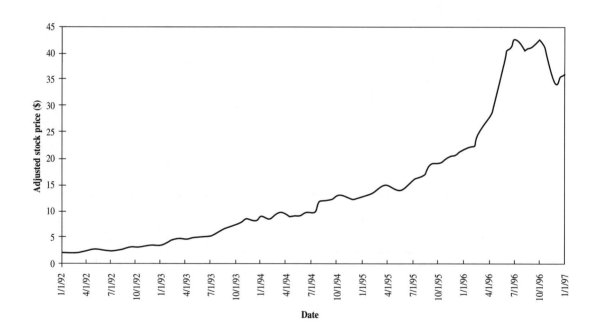

EXHIBIT 9   Hellman & Friedman Sensitivity Analysis of Holding Eller Media

($MM)	Projected Calendar Years				
	1997	*1998*	*1999*	*2000*	*2001*
Revenues	263	276	290	304	320
EBITDA*	109	117	125	131	137
Net Debt**	330	268	199	122	39
H&F Equity Ownership***	49.5%	49.5%	49.5%	49.5%	49.5%

*Earnings before interest, taxes, depreciation, and amortization.
**Net debt equals total liabilities less total current assets.
***Fully diluted ownership after an IPO through which H&F sells $156.6 million of stock.

Trailing EBITDA Multiple	Hellman & Friedman Future Equity Value				
	1997	*1998*	*1999*	*2000*	*2001*
8.0X	268.2	330.6	396.6	458.3	523.4
10.0X	376.1	446.4	520.3	588.0	659.0
12.0X	484.0	562.3	644.1	717.7	794.7

Trailing EBITDA Multiple	Hellman & Friedman Projected Three Year Returns*				
	1997	*1998*	*1999*	*2000*	*2001*
8.0X	(29.0)%	(6.4)%	1.6%	5.0%	6.7%
10.0X	(0.4)%	8.7%	11.3%	11.7%	11.8%
12.0X	28.1%	22.0%	19.5%	17.4%	16.0%

*Table should be read as follows: if Hellman & Friedman does not sell Eller Media to Clear Channel and sells Eller Media for 10.0 times EBITDA in 1999, then Hellman & Friedman would realize a 11.3% future annual return on equity (assumes the current cost to hold the equity is $377.8 million which is the difference between the H&F equity value of $534.4 million if the company is sold to Clear Channel and the IPO proceeds of $156.6 million).

SUGGESTED READINGS

Finance Textbooks

Brealey, Richard and Myers, Stewart C. *Principles of Corporate Finance* (Fifth Edition). New York: McGraw Hill, 1994. [Best book on the theory of finance.]

Copeland, Tom, Koller, Tim and Murrin, Jack. *Valuation: Measuring and Managing the Value of Companies.* New York, NY: John Wiley & Sons, 1990. [An excellent guide to modern valuation theory written by some consultants at McKinsey & Co.]

Levin, Dick. *Buy Low, Sell High, Collect Early and Pay Late: The Manager's Guide to Financial Survival.* Englewood Cliffs, NJ: Prentice-Hall, Inc. 1983. [Tongue-in-cheek view of key concepts—Out of print, but in Baker Library.]

Rappaport, Alfred. *Creating Shareholder Value: The New Standard for Business Performance.* New York, NY: The Free Press, 1986. [The leading proponent of using discounted free cash flow as a metric for making business decisions.]

Steward, G. Bennett III. *The Quest for Value: EVA Management Guide.* New York: Harper Business, 1991. [Addresses valuation issues, includes rationale for using EVA as well as practical implementation guidelines.]

Entrepreneurship

Allen, Sheila and Truman, Carole (editors).*Women in Business: Perspectives on Women Entrepreneurs.* New York: Routledge, 1993. [Profiles of successful female entrepreneurs.]

Amabile, Teresa M. *Motivational Synergy: Toward New Conceptualizations of Intrinsic and Extrinsic Motivation in the Workplace.* Human Resources Management Review, Issue 3, 1993. [Article on intrinsic and extrinsic motivations towards work and relation toward creativity.]

Research Associate Andrew S. Janower prepared this bibliography under the supervision of Professor William A. Sahlman.

Harvard Business School Note 9-396-040.

Birch, David. *Job Creation in America: How Our Smallest Companies Put the Most People to Work.* New York, NY: The Free Press, 1987. [Research on job formation in the U.S.]

Bygrave, William D. *The Portable MBA in Entrepreneurship.* New York: John Wiley & Sons, 1994. [Great, hands-on overview on entire entrepreneurial process.]

Clifford, Donald K. and Cavanagh, Richard E. *The Winning Performance: How America's High-Growth Midsize Companies Succeed.* New York, NY: Bantam, 1988. [A very insightful study of successful mid-size companies.]

Collins, James C. and Lazier, William C. *Beyond Entrepreneurship: Turning Your Business into an Enduring Great Company.* Englewood Cliffs, NJ: Prentice Hall, 1992. [Discussion of roles of leadership, vision and creativity in growing, entrepreneurial ventures.]

Drucker, Peter. *Innovation and Entrepreneurship: Practice and Principles.* New York, NY: Harper, 1993. [A "process" definition of entrepreneurship.]

Ford, C. M. and Gioia, D. A. (editors). *Creativity in Organizations.* Newbury Park, CA: Sage Publications, 1995. [See chapter by Amabile, T. A. entitled "Discovering the unknowable, managing the unmanageable" for perspectives on role of creativity in management and entrepreneurship.]

Godfrey, Joline. *Our Wildest Dreams: Women Entrepreneurs Making Money, Having Fun, Doing Good.* New York: HarperBusiness, 1992. [Profiles of successful female entrepreneurs.]

Kao, John J. *Entrepreneurship, Creativity, & Organization.* Englewood Cliffs, NJ: Prentice Hall, 1989. [Focuses on the human side of entrepreneurship—used as a textbook at HBS.]

Stevenson, Howard H. and Sahlman, William A. *The Entrepreneurial Venture: Selected Readings.* Boston: Harvard Business School Press, 1991. [Overview of course notes and other interesting readings on entrepreneurship.]

Timmons, Jeffry A. *Entrepreneurial mind: Winning Strategies for Starting, Renewing and Harvesting.* Andover, MA: Brick House Publishing Company, 1994. [Excellent overview of the entrepreneur.]

Timmons, Jeffry A. *The New Business Opportunities: Getting to the Right Place at the Right Time.* Andover, MA: Brick House Publishing Company, 1990. [Focuses on identifying and pursuing opportunities.]

Biographies of successful entrepreneurs often offer a good, hands-on perspective of what it takes to start, grow and manage your own business. Several recent books on Bill Gates and Sam Walton are worthwhile, as well as historical biographies on Andrew Carnegie, Henry Ford, etc. See also:

Bhide, Amar (editor). *Tales of Successful Entrepreneurs.* Boston: HBS Press, 1995. [Contains over fifty profiles of entrepreneurs. Written by past HBS Entrepreneurial Management students.]

Joyner-Kersee, Jackie and Johnson, Lindsey. *A Woman's Place is Everywhere: Inspirational Profiles of Female Leaders Who Are Shaping and Expanding the Role of Women in American Society Today.* New York: Mastermedia, 1994. [Profiles of high profile female executives in a range of undertakings including business, government, non-profit and academia. Co-authored by a 1995 HBS graduate.]

Longsworth, Elizabeth K. (editor). *Anatomy of a Start-Up: 27 Real-Life Case Studies.* Boston: Inc. Publishing, 1991. [Inc. Magazine case studies on start-ups in a range of industries.]

Venture Capital

Bartlett, Joseph W. *Venture Capital Law, Business Strategies and Investment Planning.* New York, NY: John Wiley & Sons, 1988. See also Cumulative Supplement, 1993. [Excellent overview of the legal issues in venture capital.]

Burrill, G. Steven and Norback, Craig T. *The Arthur Young Guide to Raising Venture Capital.* Blue Ridge Summit, PA: Tab Books, Inc., 1988. [Good basic overview.]

Bygrave, William and Timmons, Jeffry. *Venture Capital at the Crossroads.* Boston: Harvard Business School Press, 1992. [Recent profile of history of and current developments in the venture capital industry.]

Gladstone, David. *Venture Capital Handbook.* New Jersey: Prentice Hall, 1988. [Solid description of the venture capital process, and how private investors evaluate and structure deals.]

Lipper, Arthur with Ryan, George. *Venture's Guide to Investing in Private Companies.* Homewood, IL: Dow Jones-Irwin, Inc., 1984. [A good overview of some of the key issues—Out of print, but in Baker Library.]

Pratt, Stanley E. and Morris, Jane K. (editors). *Pratt's Guide to Venture Capital Sources* (New edition published each year). Needham, MA: Venture Economics. [The first section contains very useful articles on venture capital: also included is a list of venture capital firms.]

Silver, David. *Venture Capital Sourcebook.* Danvers, Mass: Probus, 1994. [Listings of venture capital firms including recent investment activity, portfolio investments, and short resumes for fund partners.]

Wilson, John W. *The New Venturers: Inside the High-Stakes World of Venture Capital.* Reading, MA: Addison-Wesley Publishing Company, 1985. [A fun book about some of the legendary venture capitalists—Out of print, but in Baker Library.]

Entrepreneurship and Innovation in Large Companies

Brandt, Steven C. *Entrepreneurship in Established Companies.* Homewood, IL: Dow Jones-Irwin, Inc., 1986. [An excellent overview—Out of print, but in Baker Library.]

Kanter, Rosabeth Moss. *The Change Masters: Innovation and Entrepreneurship in the American Corporation.* New York, NY: Simon & Schuster (Touchstone Division), 1985. [An excellent, well-researched overview of the process within large companies.]

Kanter, Rosabeth Moss. *When Giants Learn to Dance: Mastering the Challenges of Strategy, Management and Careers in the 1990's.* New York, NY: Simon & Schuster, 1989. [A good overview of entrepreneurial management within large companies.]

Block, Zenas and MacMillan, Ian. *Corporate Venturing: Creating New Businesses Within the Firm.* Boston: Harvard Business School Press, 1993. [A new look at entrepreneurial management within large companies.]

General Texts on Starting Businesses, Raising Money and Leveraged Buyouts

Blackman, Irving. *Valuing Your Privately Held Business.* New York: Irwin, 1995. [Practical guide to valuation and deal related issues in selling private companies.]

Chimerine, Lawrence, Cushman, Robert F., and Ross, Howard D. (editors). *Handbook for Raising Capital: Financing Alternatives for Emerging and Growing Businesses.* Homewood, IL: Dow-Jones Irwin, 1986. [This book has chapters on most of the key issues in financing.]

Diamond, Stephen C. (ed.). *Leveraged Buyouts.* Homewood, IL: Richard D. Irwin, Inc., 1985. [The best text on the subject—pre new tax law—Out of print, but in Baker Library.]

Gumpert, David. *How to Really Start Your Own Business.* Boston: Inc. Publishing, 1994. [Hand's on step by step description of thought process behind starting a business.]

Gumpert, David. *How to Really Create a Successful Business Plan.* Boston: Inc. Publishing, 1994. [Hand's on step by step description of thought process behind putting together a business plan.]

Henderson, James W. *Obtaining Venture Financing: Principles and Practices.* Lexington, MA: Lexington Books, 1991. [Good overview of financing issues.]

Merrill, Ronald and Sedgwick, Henry. *New Venture Handbook.* New York: American Management Association, 1993. [Guide to starting and financing new ventures.]

Michel, Allen and Shaked, Israel. *The Complete Guide to a Successful Leveraged Buyout.* Homewood, IL: Dow-Jones Irwin, 1987. [An excellent overview of LBOs in the post-1986 period.]

Owen, Robert R., Garner, Daniel R., and Bunder, Dennis S. *The Arthur Young Guide to Financing for Growth: Ten Alternatives for Raising Capital.* New York, NY: John Wiley & Sons, 1986. [An introductory description of the sources of finance—Out of print, but in Baker Library.]

Purvin, Robert Jr. *The Franchise Fraud.* New York: John Wiley & Sons, 1994. [Good overview of common issues encountered in franchise businesses.]

Rich, Stanley R. and Gumpert, David E. *Business Plans that Win $$.* New York: Harper & Row, 1987. [The best book on business plans.]

Siegel, Eric, Schultz, Loren, Ford, Brian, and Carney, David. *The Arthur Young Business Plan Guide.* New York, NY: John Wiley & Sons, 1987. [Good basic overview.]

Timmons, Jeffry A. *Planning and Financing the New Venture.* Andover, MA: Brick House Publishing Company, 1990. [Great book on business plans and financing strategies.]

Timmons, Jeffry A. *New Venture Creation: Entrepreneurship in the 1990s* (Fourth Edition). Homewood, IL: Richard D. Irwin, Inc., 1994. [An excellent overview of the process at the implementation stage.]

Negotiations and Deals

Dixit, Avinash and Nalebuff, Barry. *Thinking Strategically: The Competitive Edge in Business, Politics, and Everyday Life.* New York: Norton, 1991. [An excellent book on logic and game theory—very applicable to thinking about how to structure deals, and how to approach negotiations.]

Fisher, Roger and Ury, William. *Getting to Yes: Negotiating Agreement without Giving In.* (Revised Edition). New York: Viking Penguin, 1991. [This book presents a useful set of principles to follow when negotiating. Used in HBS first year negotiations course.]

Fisher, Roger. *Getting Together: Building a Relationship that Gets to Yes.* Boston: Houghton Mifflin, 1988. [Concentrates on interpersonal relations aspect of negotiations.]

Lax, David and Sebenius, James. *Manager as Negotiator: Bargaining for Cooperation and Competitive Gain.* New York: Free Press, 1987 [An excellent book on the subject. Used in HBS first year negotiations course.]

Schelling, Thomas C. *Strategy of Conflict.* Oxford University Press, 1983. [This is a great book on strategy and negotiations.]

Ury, William. *Getting Past No: Negotiating with Difficult People.* New York: Bantam Books, 1991. [Useful ideas for breaking negotiation log jams. Used in HBS first year negotiations course.]

Selling and Salesmanship

Boress, Allan S. *The "I Hate Selling" Book.* New York: American Management Association, 1995. [Concentrates on selling in professional service settings (e.g. investment banking, consulting, venture capital, etc.)]

Girard, Joe. *How to Close Every Sale.* New York: Warner Books, 1989. [Dime store paperback chock full of practical sales techniques.]

Girard, Joe. *How to Sell Anything to Anybody.* New York: Warner Books, 1977. [Dime store paperback chock full of practical sales techniques.]

Rackham, Neil. *SPIN Selling.* New York: McGraw Hill, 1988. [More technical view of sales process—also laden with practical tips and techniques.]

Rose, Richard. *How to Make a Buck and Still Be a Decent Human Being: Sales and Marketing Strategies that Catapulted Dataflex into the Top 100 Best Small Companies in America.* Boston: Goldhirsh Group, 1992. [Good anecdotes]

Ziglar, Zig. *Ziglar on Selling.* Nashville: Oliver-Nelson, 1991. [Comprehensive book of sale tactics and techniques.]

Peering Intelligently into the Future

Davis, Stanley M. *Future Perfect.* New York: Addison-Wesley Publishing, 1987. [Considers implications of shift from Industrial Age to a new technology and information based marketplace.]

Davidson, Bill and Davis, Stanley M. *20:20 Vision: Transform Your Business Today to Succeed in Tomorrow's Economy.* New York: Simon & Schuster, 1991. [Futuristic view of what it takes to develop and maintain competitive advantage in light of rapid technological change.]

Handy, Charles. *The Age of Paradox.* Boston: Harvard Business School Press, 1994. [Perspectives on how individuals and organizations can deal with the intended and unintended consequences of change.]

Handy, Charles. *The Age of Unreason.* Boston: Harvard Business School Press, 1989. [Perspectives on how developments in technology, global economics and the pursuit of efficiency impact organizations, careers and lifestyles.]

Reference Books

Accounting Desk Book: The Accountant's Everyday Instant Answer Book (Ninth Edition). Englewood Cliffs, NJ: Prentice Hall, 1989. [Clear and comprehensive summary of key accounting concepts and techniques, written in plain English.]

Lawyer's Desk Book (Ninth Edition). Englewood Cliffs, NJ: Prentice Hall, 1989. [Clear and comprehensive summary of key legal concepts and holdings, written in plain English.]

Additionally, the Big 6 accounting firms periodically publish booklets with good overviews on key accounting, legal and small business related areas including securities law, intellectual property, regional business customs and practices, etc.

Selected Periodicals

Babson College Frontiers of Entrepreneurship Research (Babson College in Wellesley, MA) [An annual collection of research articles in entrepreneurship.]

Black Enterprise. [Has articles on Black entrepreneurship.]

Entrepreneur. [Focuses on new business opportunities.]

Entrepreneurial Woman. [A new magazine focused on women and entrepreneurship.]

Going Public: The IPO Reporter (Howard Publishing in Philadelphia) [Provides useful data on IPO market trends.]

Inc. [A great magazine. Inc. also publishes various guides and videos that highlight information from the magazine.]

Journal of Business Venturing (Elsevier/North Holland) [Comprised of academic articles in the field.]

Private Equity Analyst. [Newsletter serving investors in and managers of alternative assets such as LBO and venture capital funds.]

Red Herring. [New magazine covering technology, strategy, finance and investment. Widely read by entrepreneurs, CEOs and venture capitalists.]

Success. [A magazine comprised of short stories of entrepreneurial opportunities.]

Upside. [Similar to *Red Herring.*]

Venture Capital Journal (Venture Economics in Needham, MA.) [The best overview of trends in the industry. Note also that Venture Economics publishes a number of in-depth studies of the venture capital industry each year.]

Wired. [Irreverent magazine covering developments in technology and multi-media.]

Useful Software for Entrepreneurs

@ Risk. Palisade Corporation—(607) 277-8000. [Excel add-in to run Monte Carlo simulations.]

BizPlan Builder. Jian Software—(415) 941-9191. [Design and write a business plan.]

Cashé. Business Matters—(617) 899-8700. [Design and run complex financial projections / proformas. Easier to structure than Excel, strong graphics capability.]

Crystal Ball. Market Engineering Corporation—(303) 449-5177. [Run Monte Carlo simulations.]

D&B MarketPlace. MarketPlace Information Corporation—(617) 894-1661. [Utilizes subset of D&B credit report database. Great for developing prospect lists and doing quick and easy market research on companies and industries.]

Decision Analysis. TreeAge Software—(617) 536-2128. [Run complex decision tree analysis.]

The Digital MBA (Book with CD-Rom—IBM only). New York: Osborne McGraw Hill, 1995. [Contains wide range of business management programs covering: managing people and projects, strategic planning, financial forecasting, and business process modeling.]

Select Phone. Pro CD, Inc.—(617) 631-9200. [Business and residential phone numbers and addresses in the U.S. and Canada.]

Internet Related Books

Janal, Daniel. *On-line Marketing Handbook.* New York: Van Nostrand Reinhold, 1995. [Chock full of ideas and examples for marketing on the internet.]

Wolff, Michael. *Net Money: Your Guide to the Personal Finance Revolution on the Information Highway.* New York: Random House, 1995. [Reasonably comprehensive directory of finance related world wide web sites.]

EXHIBIT 1   Useful Internet Addresses

Site Name	Address*	Description
NEWS / INFORMATION SERVICES		
Electronic Newsstand Homepage	www.enews.com/	Index of magazines offered on-line
Financial Times	www/usa.ft.com	Daily recap of leading stories from the *Financial Times,* with international market recaps and index reports
Harvard Business School Publishing	www.hbsp.harvard.edu/	Online catalog of HBSP products and publications
Hot Wired	www.hotwired.com	*Wired* magazine on-line
Inc.	virtumall.com/newsstand/Inc/	On-line version of magazine
Interactive Age	techweb.cmp.com:80/techweb/ia/current/	Internet-related magazine
MecklerWeb Home Page	www.mecklerweb.com/	Publisher focused on Internet and WWW-related topics
New York Times	nytimesfax.com	Digest of the *New York Times* presenting highlights of front page articles, top foreign and national news, sports, editorials and commentary
Newspage	www.newspage.com/NEWSPAGE/newspagehome.html	Subscription news service with over 500 data sources. Articles classified into detailed industry sub-groupings
Pathfinder	www.pathfinder.com	Time Warner home page. Links to all TW publications on-line
Red Herring	www.herring.com/	On-line version of magazine—most functions under development
San Jose Mercury News	www.sjmercury.com/today.htm	Local newspaper serving the Silicon Valley
Upside	www.upside.com/	On-line version of the magazine
Wall Street Journal Front Page	update.wsj.com/update/edit/front.html	WSJ front page, updated daily
SMALL BUSINESS / ENTREPRENEURSHIP		
Bio Online	www.bio.com/	Comprehensive site for biotechnology-related information
Business Resource Center	www.kciLInk.com/brc/	Formerly called Small Business Help Center. Offers useful information on starting and growing small businesses.
Entrepreneur's Law Center	www.axxs.com//lawctr/lawctr.html	Legal resources relating to capital formation and business enterprise
Entrepreneurs on the Web	sashimi.wwa.com/~notime/eotw/EOTW.html	Index of entrepreneurs on the web

EXHIBIT 1   (*continued*)

Site Name	Address*	Description
Ewing M. Kauffman Foundation	www.emkf.org	Wealth of information on this organization's programs and lots of research on entrepreneurship
Franchise Network	www.frannet.com/	Everything you ever wanted to know about franchising, including what to look for and lists of franchise opportunities
International Bureau of Chambers of Commerce	www1.usa1.com/~ibnet/ibcchp.html	World forum of Chambers of Commerce. Links to other interesting international sites, and listings of international business opportunities
Jet Propulsion Laboratory (NASA)	www.jpl.nasa.gov/	Active in technology transfer and licensing
Market Link	nwlink.com/marketlink/	Designed to facilitate the formation of international business partnerships. Great links to other international business sites
Master-McNeil	www.naming.com/naming.html	Product and corporate naming service
NetMarquee: Information and Guidance for Executives	199.232.60.143/default2.htm	Information and guidance for executives in emerging and family-owned businesses
Seamless Website	seamless.com/	Covers topics relating to law, homepages of law firms, and pointers to other interesting law-related sites
Small Business Resource Center	www.webcom.com/~seaquest/welcome.html	On line reports and other resources for small business owners
Technology Registry	www.techreg.com/techreg/	Employment service for technology-related industries
Trade Compass	tradecompass.com/	Provides a daily summary of the days events, access to newsletters, trade journals, and links to news sources around the world
WWW Multimedia Law	www.batnet.com/oikoumene/index.html	Useful overview of legal and business issues surrounding multi-media development and distribution

FINANCE / VENTURE CAPITAL

Site Name	Address*	Description
IBC: Venture Capital Firms on the Net	tig.com/IBC/NetStats/Names.html	Listing of VC firms with servers on the net
M&A On-line	www.maol.com/maol/	Comprehensive listing of companies for sale, equity and debt sources, as well as advisors and intermediaries
Price Waterhouse National Venture Capital Survey	www.sjmercury.com/features/venture/menu.htm	Quarterly survey of venture capital investments categorized by company, industry, amount, and venture capital investors involved

---

EXHIBIT 1   *(concluded)*

Site Name	Address*	Description
Wall Street Net	www.netresource.com/wsn	Index of public deals in registration and completed deals
GOVERNMENT		
Census Bureau	www.census.gov/	Mother lode of demographic information
Commonwealth of Massachusetts—MAGNet	www.magnet.state.ma.us/home.htm	Index of state resources available through the web
Department of Commerce	www.doc.gov/services/doc.services.html	Index to DOC-related on-line information services
Department of the Treasury	www.ustreas.gov/	Index of Treasury resources available through the web
EBB	gopher://una.hh.lib.umich.edu/11/ebb	Index of government statistics and reports, including economic indicators, Dept. of Commerce Data, etc.
Federal Reserve Reports	gopher://town.hall.org/1/other/fed	Federal Reserve data and reports
FedWorld Beta Home Page	www.fedworld.gov/	Index of Federal Government resources on the web
Internal Revenue Service	www.ustreas.gov:80/treasury/bureaus/irs/irs.html	IRS home page, including down-loadable tax forms and instructions
Penn World Tables	cansim.epas.utoronto.ca:5680/pwt/pwt.html	Easy-to-use source for international economic data
Regional Economic Information System	ptolemy.gis.virginia.edu:1080/reis1.html	Source for regional, state, and local economic and employment data
Search SEC EDGAR Archives	town.hall.org/cgi-bin/srch-edgar	Public company SEC filings available on-line
Search U.S. Patent and Trademark Office Archives	town.hall.org/cgi-bin/srch-patent	Patent and trademark databases
SEC Filing Retrieval Tools	edgar.stern.nyu.edu/docs/general.html	A useful glossary with definitions of the various different SEC filings
Small Business Administration	www.sbaonline.sba.gov/	SBA resources and information
Thomas	thomas.loc.gov/	Legislative information; full text bills and Congressional Record
U.S. Tax Code On-Line	www.fourmilab.ch/ustax/ustax.html	It's all there—happy reading!!

---

*Notes and disclaimers: All addresses begin with "http://" (except those which start with "gopher://" as marked).

Given the rapid pace of change and sheer volume of information on the world wide web, it is difficult to monitor content quality and to compile a comprehensive listing of interesting web sites. By definition this list will be at least partially obsolete by the time the ink dries. Periodic searches on entrepreneurship, small business, venture capital, corporate finance, etc. via Yahoo and other internet search engines are likely to be fruitful in revealing new and interesting sites.

CASE INDEX

INDEX